XPLORATION AND IXED GAS DIVING ENCYCLOPEDIA

Friends of Oceanic Ventures,

Thank You for supporting IANTD

THE TAO OF VAL UNDERWATER

MOUNT, DITURI ET AL

Foreword

School of life's knowledge for technical diving never takes a vacation.

The era of the pioneer diver extends many decades beyond the alluded golden years' reputation. As a pioneer diver, I remember we were learning on every dive. We were no different than the Wright Brothers at Kitty Hawk with the grand plan, per chance, to fly from America to Europe. We grasped and gasped with odd pieces of gear we put together while making discoveries in the fresh age of diving underwater. Regulations were simple: Never hold your breath. Surface slowly.

Diving history has always been fascinating to me. My compass of erudition came from reading the typed paperbound editions of the ***Bureau Of Ships Diving Manual*** and ***The Experimental Diving Unit,*** U.S. Naval Gun Factory, Washington, D.C. issues. Other captivating books included the works of John 'J.B.S.' Haldane; his son, Jack S. Haldane; Sir Robert H. Davis; Christian J. Lambertsen, M.D. (who, by the way, coined the acronym "scuba" in 1954); Albert R. Behnke, M.D.; E. R. Cross; Colonel John D. Craig; Parry E. Bivens, M.D.; Edward H. Lanphier, M.D.; Peter B. Bennett, Ph.D.; many more. Add a diet of the teachings of Aldous Huxley (Haldane's friend, too), Oscar Janiger, M.D., Joseph Campbell, Deepak Chopra, to spice my spiritual might. Each one was ahead of the curve when it came to designing equipment, splaying the medical and the spiritual countenance with their support of research to keep the diver safe from diving accidents. More than half of these gurus I had met personally.

If you are like most divers today, you have probably never given a second thought to any one of the various important topics presented in this book. Skin and scuba diving have become common activities offered at sport clubs, resorts, on cruise ships everywhere. Perhaps you were certified in your very own neighborhood dive store classes. You may have learned a little or a lot for the purpose you took the instruction. There is more to diving than meets the eye.

Detailed treatments of various aspects, whichever best fits your purpose of particular search, are specialized and more advanced in this encyclopedia. The value of the articles of technical diving information for mind, body, and soul are presented in an educational form to increase the appreciation of your lessons for your life, your safety, your secured fun in the sport of diving.

Authors, whose expert knowledge, competence, and material, were chosen for this book's completion. Their chapters prove they are a hunk of the underwater community's genius.

You hold in your hands a dive tech guide to acquaint yourself with the progress of where diving is today. Enjoy this specialized encyclopedia for diving. Imagine a recipe for a healthy life for mind, body and soul with ingredients glad-wrapped to keep you safe in all you do in one of your favorite experiences called sport diving.

It is my pleasure with honor to present to you the intelligent details for safe tech diving written by doctors, scientists, and educators. May the wisdom you find in the ***Exploration and Mixed Gas Diving Encyclopedia - The Tao of Survival Underwater*** enhance your joy while keeping you unharmed in your diving journeys. Let's begin...

~ Zale Parry

Photo by CourtneyPlatt.com

Introduction

Anyone who knows me will wonder why I have been audacious enough to write an introduction to a subject about which I know nothing! The closest I have come to underwater exploration is snorkeling in the Bahamas, admiring the remarkable beauty of this paradise hidden from our ordinary eyes. I have seen videos of the wonders deeper in the ocean but have not even had an urge to explore this mysterious realm. On the other hand I know a great deal about heroes and warriors and the psychology of exploration of new frontiers. Therein lies the fascination that the authors of *Exploration and Mixed Gas Diving Encyclopedia - The Tao of Underwater Survival* are presenting for us ordinary mortals who marvel at their technology and their bravado.

Warriors defend us from aggression. It certainly takes at least a strong warrior instinct to tackle both oceanic depth but also the threats that seem larger than life. Heroes go forth to help others, with no primary egotistical agenda. The hero's journey is often lonely and must include a variety of experiences. The journey begins with a call to adventure, sometimes refused at first but ultimately accepted. Acceptance leads to trials that are the warrior's delight, threatening and intimidating but energizing, often accomplished with supernatural help. Success requires initiation into a higher state of cosmic consciousness. And with victory, there is return and rebirth into the new awareness of unity with the spiritual whole.

It is easy to see these patterns in the call to explore the underworld of the oceans. There are clearly adventures and many potential benefits of undersea exploration for all humanity. The perils require a psychology of mental health that few have inherently. And the struggles often lead to psychological stress that long outlast the adventure itself. Medical science requires exploration of new frontiers, sometimes as risky as diving. Madame Curie and Ignaz Phillip Semmelweis are perfect examples of the traumas of exploration; but their contributions to society are unexcelled.

Thus, I encourage you, the reader, to enter this wonderful exploration of another frontier. It is as exciting as any great saga, filled with beauty, excitement, wonder and appreciation for those who explore for us and return to provide us with the wealth they have discovered.

C. Norman Shealy M.D., Ph.D.

President, Holos University Graduate Seminary

www.holosuniversity.org

Producer of Medical Renaissance - The Secret Code

Acknowledgements

Project Management	Joseph Dituri, M.S.
	Tom Mount, D.Sc., Ph.D., N.D.
Cover Design	Jeff Gourley
Layout & Design	Patti Mount, M.A., Design & Art Director
	Eric Keibler
Technical Editors	Patti Mount, M.A., Editor-in-Chief
	Peri Blum, Psy.D.
	Joseph Dituri, M.S.
	Thomas Huff
	Eric Keibler
	Tom Mount, D.Sc., Ph.D., N.D.
	David Snyder

Photographers

The photographs in this book were gratiously supplied by IANTD divers from around the world.

We appreciate their letting us bring some of their work to you.

Jim Akroyd
Fabio Amaral
Matti Anttila
Eric Bancroft
Leigh Bishop
Jean Marc Blache
Curt Bowen
Mel Briscoe
Mel Clark
Amy Dituri
Joseph Dituri
Dive Rite
DiveTech, Grand Cayman
Michael Dudas
Jay Easterbrook
Robert Foster
Rick Freshee
Bob Friedman
Steven Frink
Georges Gawinowski
Lucie Gawinowski
John Gavin
Kevin Gurr
Jill Heinerth
Paul Heinerth
Robert Hew
Ann Keibler
Eric Keibler
Jim Kozmik
Simon Mitchell
Patti Mount
Tom Mount
Oceaneering International
Oliver Paoli
Courtney Platt
Richard Pyle
Martin Robson
James Rozzi
Saraya Seas
Don Shirley
R. Todd Smith
Andrew Trent
Jerry Whatley
Greg Wolkfill

Table Of Contents

Page

Table Of Contents

Section One
Physiological Aspects of Exploration & Mixed Gas Diving

Photo by Tom & Patti Mount

Always remain in life itself, and not on the problems that exist along the path.

~ Tom Mount

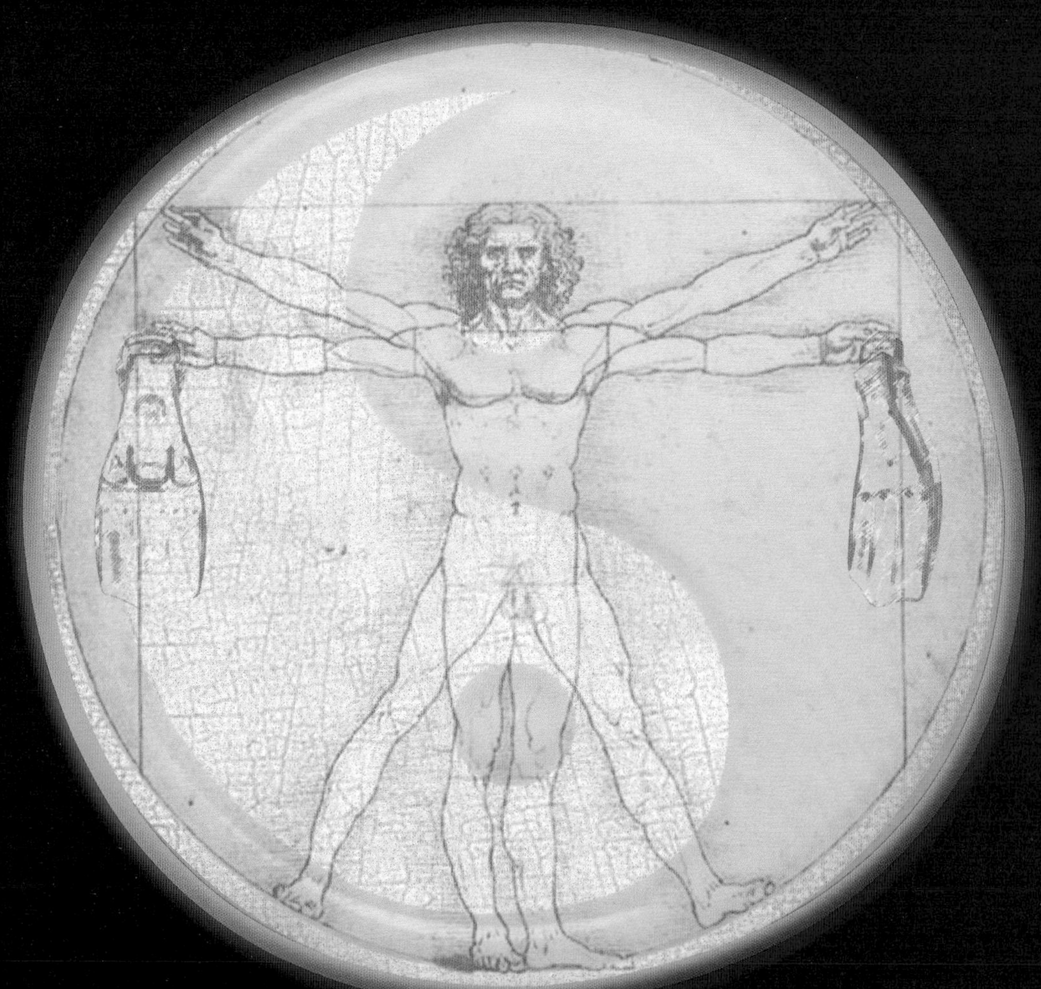

Chapter One
The Basics Of Physiology For Technical Divers

Tom Mount D.Sc., Ph.D., N.D.

Introduction

We expose ourselves as divers to numerous environmental, physiological, and operational events that affect our well being and safety. Ideally, a technical diver will seek out more information and thereby develop a comprehensive understanding of anatomy, physiology, and behavior mechanics. Given the space allotted for this chapter, we cannot provide as much in-depth knowledge in these areas as we wish. However, we can provide the technical diver with a foundation in these areas. We are also able to encourage technical divers to engage in their own research as to how our physiology and anatomy functions on a day-to-day basis, as well as how diving affects our bodies. It is difficult to avoid activities that may predispose us to injury without an understanding as to how the body works. A prudent diver will use this chapter to structure their own quest for knowledge.

Technical diving not only exposes us to various diving maladies, it also presents opportunities for physical injury and strain due to the weight bearing nature of the sport. Due to the physical stresses of diving, one should also maintain a level of fitness beyond that of the average person in order to avoid injury. The following discussion concerns the circulatory, neurological, and respiratory systems, and combines with an overview of PH balance. This chapter also includes a section on exercise, which emphasizes exercise as applicable to divers. We feel this is only the minimum a technical diver should explore, as in technical diving all of our anatomical and physiological systems are at risk. To reduce the threat please stay informed. Understanding physiology is the first step toward becoming a survivor.

The Circulatory System

The circulatory system is a closed-loop system consisting of the heart, arteries, veins, tissue capillaries, and lung capillaries. The circulatory system provides a steady source of blood to the body and a continuous supply of oxygen to the tissues. The circulatory system also removes carbon dioxide from the tissues. Nutrients are also delivered to the body's cells through the circulatory pathway. Along with carbon dioxide, the circulatory system removes the body's metabolic wastes. The complete circuit goes from one side of the heart to the other side of the heart.

The heart is the pump that propels blood through the circulatory system. The heart's contractions produce blood pressure, propelling blood, which carries gasses and nutrients to the arteries. In order to maintain an adequate flow of blood to all parts of the body, it is necessary that the body's physiology sustain a certain level of blood pressure. The force and amount of blood pumped and the size and flexibility of the arteries determine blood pressure. Since the heart adjusts its blood pressure to meet the body's needs, blood pressure changes constantly. Your blood pressure depends on your activity level, temperature, diet, emotional state, posture, physical state, and medication use. The carotid sinuses, which are a type of artery found in the neck, are pressure-sensing nerves that are highly sensitive to fluctuations in the blood's

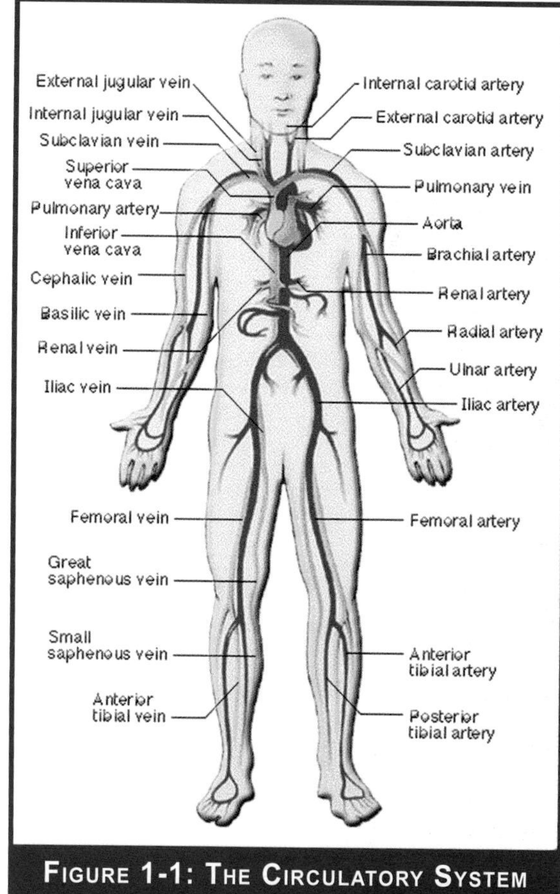

Figure 1-1: The Circulatory System
Courtesy the American Medical Assoc.
www.ama-assn.org

pressure throughout the body. The carotid sinuses aid in regulating overall blood pressure by informing the brain, via impulses, about any changes in blood pressure.

Oxygen, which is critical to life, binds with an iron-rich protein found in red blood called hemoglobin. Arteries and capillaries transport oxygenated hemoglobin to the body's cells. The body's tissues absorb the oxygen, use it, and give off carbon dioxide (***CO_2***). CO_2 then combines with the de-oxygenated hemoglobin and returns to the lungs via the veins. Correct breathing technique insures that the hemoglobin maximizes its capacity to transport oxygen efficiently. Improper breathing such s shallow or erratic breathing results in the "clumping" of oxygenated red blood cells (***RBC***), whereas proper breathing results in a smooth distribution of oxygenated RBC. See Figure 1-1 for a diagram of the circulatory system.

It is notable that the circulatory system functions as one system containing two separate subsystems, the pulmonary system and the systemic system. The pulmonary system supports the circulation dedicated to the lungs, while the systemic system services the body tissues. Nerve impulses,which transfer information regarding the body's physiological state to and from the brain control these systems. By studying the diagram of the circulatory system below, it is apparent that the circulatory system functions as a transport mechanism for gas to travel to and from the tissues.

The overall health of a person depends on the body's ability to maintain a healthy circulatory system. Any alteration to the circulatory system will have a corresponding effect on gas transport. These alterations can include blood vessel injuries, fat concentration, blood vessel disease, or even the effects of prescription or common across-the counter drugs.

Blood Transport & the Circulatory System

To improve one's understanding of the circulatory system and the role blood transport, pressure, and flow has in maintaining life, please refer to the ***Cardiovascular System*** section on the website of ***Anatomy and Physiology***, which details the role of veins and arteries in blood transport (***Please Note: Diagram placement was altered for formatting purposes.***) **To quote:**

Blood Vessels

Blood vessels are the channels or conduits that distribute blood to body tissues. The vessels make up two closed systems of tubes that begin and end at the heart. One system, the pulmonary vessels, transports blood from the right ventricle to the lungs and back to the left atrium. The other system, the systemic vessels, carries blood from the left ventricle to the tissues in all parts of the body and then returns the blood to the right atrium. Based on their structure and function, blood vessels are classified as arteries, capillaries, or veins.

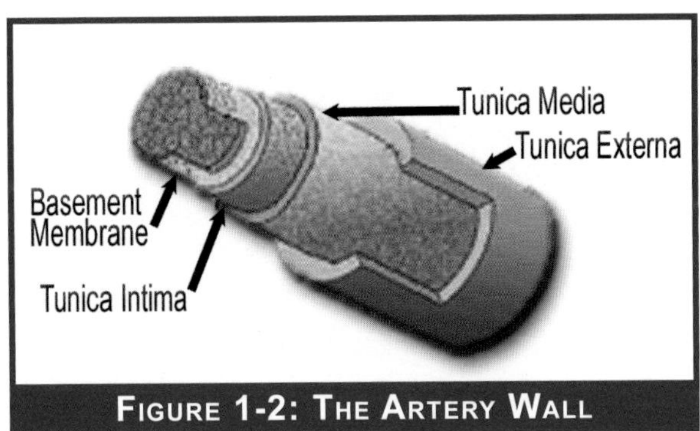

Figure 1-2: The Artery Wall

Arteries

Arteries carry blood away from the heart. Pulmonary arteries transport blood with low oxygen content from the right ventricle to the lungs. On the other hand, systemic arteries transport newly-oxygenated blood from the left ventricle to the body tissues. Blood pumps from the ventricles into large elastic arteries that branch repeatedly into smaller and smaller arteries until the branching results in microscopic arteries called arterioles. The arterioles play a key role in regulating blood flow into the tissue capillaries.... The wall of an artery consists of three layers....The middle layer... is usually the thickest layer. It not only provides support for the vessel but also changes vessel diameter to regulate blood flow and blood pressure....

Veins

Veins carry blood toward the heart. After blood passes through the capillaries, it enters the smallest veins, called venules. From the venules, blood flows into progressively larger and larger veins until it reaches the heart. In the

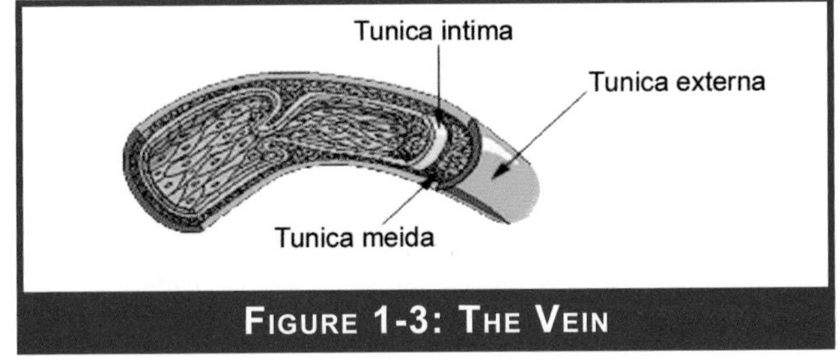

Figure 1-3: The Vein

pulmonary circuit, the pulmonary veins transport blood from the lungs to the left atrium of the heart. This blood has high oxygen content as it recently passed through the lungs. Systemic veins transport blood from the body tissue to the right atrium of the heart. This blood has reduced oxygen content, as oxygen depletes during metabolic activities in the tissue cells.... Almost 70% of the total blood volume is in the veins at any given time.... Medium and large veins have venous valves.... Venous valves are especially important in the arms and legs, where they prevent the backflow of blood in response to the pull of gravity.

Capillaries

Capillaries, the smallest and most numerous of the blood vessels, form the connection between the vessels that carry blood away from the heart (***arteries***) and the vessels that return blood to the heart (***veins)***. The primary function of capillaries is the exchange of materials between the blood and tissue cells. Capillary distribution varies with the metabolic activity of body tissues. Tissues such as skeletal muscle, liver, and kidney have extensive capillary networks because they are metabolically active and require an abundant supply of oxygen and nutrients. Other tissues, such as connective tissue, have a less abundant supply of capillaries.... About 5% of the total blood volume is in the systemic capillaries at any given time... In addition to forming the connection between the arteries and veins, capillaries have a vital role in the exchange of gases, nutrients, and metabolic waste products between the blood and the tissue cells...

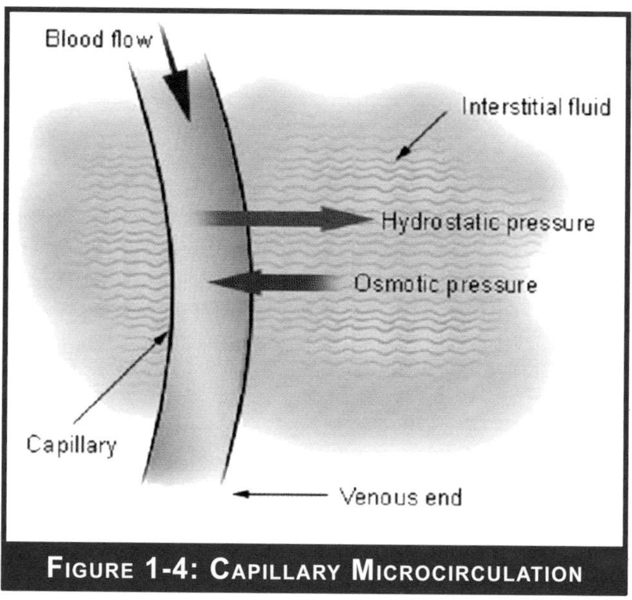

Figure 1-4: Capillary Microcirculation

The rate, or velocity, of blood flow varies inversely with the total cross-sectional area of the blood vessels. As the total cross-sectional area of the vessels increases, the velocity of flow decreases. Blood flow is slowest in the capillaries, which allows time for exchange of gases and nutrients. In blood vessels, most of the resistance is due to vessel diameter. As vessel diameter decreases, the resistance increases and blood flow decreases. Very little pressure remains by the time blood leaves the capillaries and enters the venules. Blood flow through the veins depends on skeletal muscle action, respiratory movements, and constriction of smooth muscle in venous walls.

Pulse refers to the rhythmic expansion of an artery that caused by ejection of blood from the ventricle. The pulse is felt where an artery is close to the surface and rests on something firm. In common usage, the term blood pressure refers to arterial blood pressure, the pressure in the aorta and its branches. Systolic pressure is due to ventricular contraction. Diastolic pressure occurs during cardiac relaxation. Pulse pressure is the difference between systolic pressure and diastolic pressure.

Blood: Plasma & Serum

Blood plasma and blood serum are important components in blood, which, among other uses, measures overall blood volume and hydration level. When dehydrated, blood volume reduces; therefore maintaining proper levels of hydration assures adequate gas exchange on dives. **Moreover, dehydrated divers may be more prone to decompression illnesses, oxygen toxicity, and other diving maladies. According to the the online encyclopedia, Wikipedia, in conjunction with online blood bank clearing house, Blood Plasma Donation Center:**

> Blood plasma is the liquid component of blood.... Plasma is the largest single component of blood, making up about 55% of total blood volume.... Blood plasma contains many vital proteins including fibrinogen, globulins and human serum albumin.... "***Serum***" refers to blood plasma in which clotting factors (such as ***fibrin***) have been removed.... Plasma resembles whey in appearance (transparent with a faint straw color). It is mainly composed of water, blood proteins, and inorganic electrolytes. It serves as a transport medium for glocose, lipids, amino acids, hormones, metabolic end products, Carbon Dioxide and Oxygen (O_2). The oxygen transport capacity and oxygen content of plasma is much lower than that

of the hemoglobin in red blood cells; the CO_2 will, however, increase under hyperbaric conditions...

A simpler explanation of blood plasma and serum, is provided by Professor John Waters of Penn State University's Biology Department; he says: ***If you take a sample of whole blood, and remove all of the formed elements, the liquid that remains is call blood plasma. Blood plasma is comprised of clotting proteins that help blood clot to seal broken blood vessels, osmotic proteins that help keep the blood isotonic to the extracellular fluid, and blood serum.***

Blood serum is comprised of:

- Dissolved nutrients such as glucose, amino acids, and fats
- Dissolved wastes, mostly urea
- Dissolved gasses, such as oxygen, carbon dioxide, and nitrogen, and
- Dissolved electrolytes such as sodium, potassium, and chloride.

Blood: Clotting Mechanisms

The human body does not handle excessive blood loss well. Therefore, the body has ways of protecting itself. If, for some unexpected reason, sudden blood loss occurs, the blood platelets kick into action. Platelets and fibrinogen are important clotting mechanisms in blood. They are essential for healing injuries. Their sticky surface lets them, along with other substances, form clots to stop bleeding. When a wound occurs, the platelets gather at the site and attempt to block the blood flow. The mineral calcium, Vitamin K, and a protein called ***fibrinogen***, help the platelets form a clot.

A clot begins to form when blood meets air. The platelets sense the presence of air and begin to break apart. They react with the fibrinogen to begin forming fibrin, which resembles tiny threads. The fibrin threads then begin to form a web-like mesh that traps the blood cells within it. This mesh of blood cells hardens as it dries, forming a clot, or "***scab***." Calcium and vitamin K must be present in blood to support the formation of clots. A healthy diet provides most people with enough vitamins and minerals, but vitamin supplements are sometimes necessary.

A scab is an external blood clot that we can easily see, but there are also internal blood clots. A bruise, or black-and-blue mark, is the result of a blood clot. Both scabs and bruises are clots that lead to healing. However, some clots can be extremely dangerous. A blood clot that forms inside of a blood vessel can be deadly because it blocks the flow of blood, cutting off the supply of oxygen. A stroke is the result of a clot in an artery of the brain; without a steady supply of oxygen, the brain cannot function normally. If the oxygen flow is broken, paralysis, brain damage, loss of sensory perceptions, or even death may occur. Moreover, when bubbles form in the bloodstream while diving under pressure, the clotting process can contribute to bubble massing. **Janis O. Flores, a well known medical author, elaborates on the clotting process in a Gale Group article; she says:**

Fibrinogen plays two essential roles in the body: it is a protein called an acute-phase reactant that becomes elevated with tissue inflammation or tissue destruction, and it is also a vital part of the "***common pathway***" of the coagulation process. In order for blood to clot, fibrinogen must be converted to fibrin by the action of an enzyme called thrombin. Fibrin molecules clump together to form long filaments, which trap blood cells to form a solid clot.

The conversion of fibrinogen to fibrin is the last step of the "***coagulation cascade***," a series of reactions in the blood triggered by tissue injury and platelet activation. With each step in the cascade, a coagulation factor in the blood is converted from an inactive to an active form. The active form of the factor then activates several molecules of the next factor in the series, and so on, until the final step, when fibrinogen is converted into fibrin.

When fibrinogen acts as an "***acute-phase reactant***," it rises sharply during tissue inflammation or injury. When this occurs, high fibrinogen levels may be a predictor for an increased risk of heart or circulatory disease. Other conditions in which fibrinogen is elevated are cancers of the stomach, breast, or kidney, and inflammatory disorders like rheumatoid arthritis...

Oxygen & the Circulatory System

The transport of oxygen, which is vital to metabolism, is among the circulatory system's most important functions, see Figure 1-5. If the oxygen tension and concentration within the circulation varies outside of a known limit, it will produce adverse effects to the organism. Virtually every cell in our bodies requires oxygen, nutrition, and waste removal in order to survive. Diseases such as hardening of the arteries reduce the supply of both oxygen and nutrients to every cell, including the brain. Our memory,

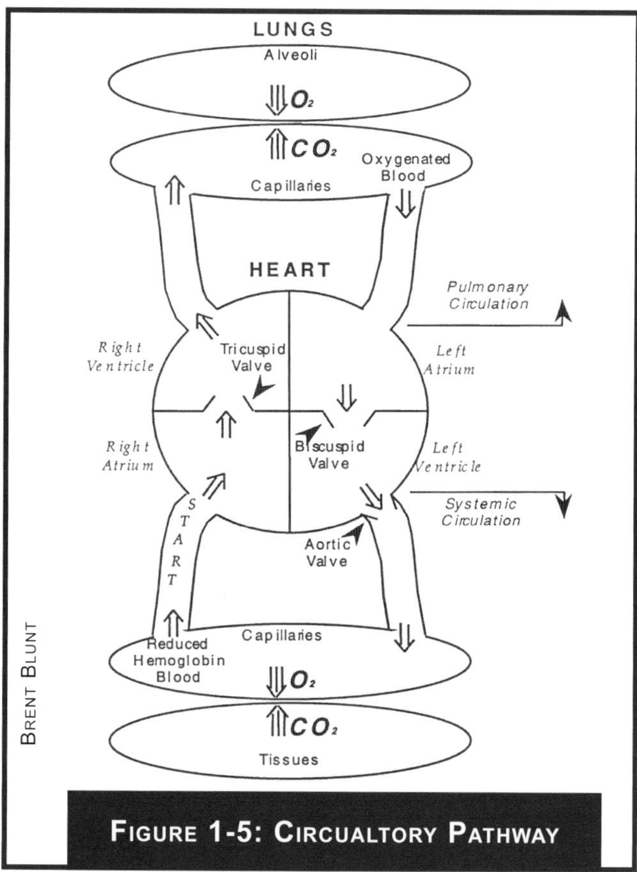

FIGURE 1-5: CIRCUALTORY PATHWAY

learning skills, and virtually all our mental cognitive skills depend on a steady supply of oxygen and nutrients. For a more in-depth understanding of blood chemistry, please refer to the material presented online by the Linus Pauling Institute at Oregon State University.

Maintaining Circulatory Health Through Diet & Exercise

Diet is a vital aspect of overall health; we actually are what we eat. A fitness program that disregards the importance of diet provides minimal results. Our diets should feature a balance in five essential areas: water, grains, fruits, proteins, and vegetables. Ideally, each of these is included in every meal. Maintaining the correct amount of protein, carbohydrates, and fat is extremely important for our long-term health. The USDA recommends that the normal diet for human beings be composed of 14% protein, 25% fats, and 60% carbohydrates.

It is interesting that the USDA recommends almost the exact same diet for fattening hogs. Thus, one may want to consider using different diet guidelines. When selecting fats to be included in a diet, emphasize the Omega 3 group and avoid as many Omega 6 fats as possible. The fat in the daily diet should not exceed 30% of the total calories and should represent at least 10% of our daily intake. (I recommend 20 to 25% of good fats.) Protein should be between 20 to 40%, while the total of fat and protein should be 60 to 70% of the daily diet.

Carbohydrates provide our natural sugars and are essential for energy. Carbohydrates may range between 15 to 40% of our total calories. One's activity level and individual physiology will dictate the exact distribution of calories. Processed sugars should be minimal and completely avoided if possible. Too much sugar has adverse effects on our circulatory system and our bodies in general. Moderation is the essential word in maintaining a healthy diet. Attempt to fill sugar needs and cravings from natural substances such as fruits and vegetables.

Most adults in the USA have some degree of circulatory disease due to poor dietary and exercise habits. However, this is a reversible situation by altering certain factors, such as improving eating habits, supplementing the diet with nutrients and vitamins, and implementing a cardiovascular exercise program.

One of the most common diseases of the circulatory system is arteriosclerosis. Plaque buildup in the blood vessels leads to this condition. As the plaque accumulates, the vessel clogs and its effective diameter reduces. Arteriosclerosis results in less circulatory efficiency, which causes the heart to work harder and reduced circulation means less oxygen to tissues. The three areas of the body that are hypersensitive to decreased oxygenation are the heart, the legs, and the brain.

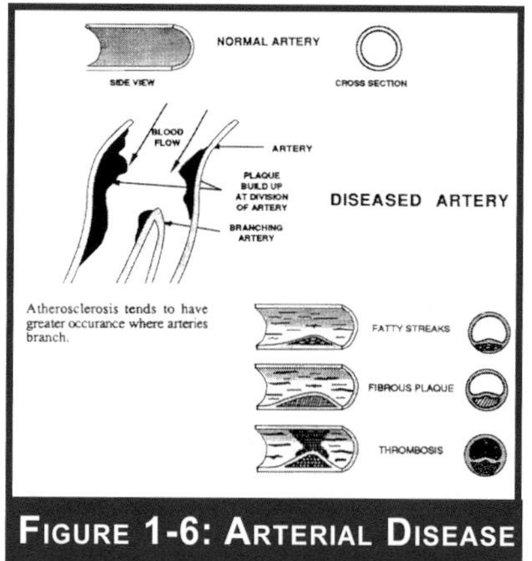

FIGURE 1-6: ARTERIAL DISEASE

Free Radicals

Free radicals are implicated in the development of arteriosclerosis, among other illnesses. Free radicals are volatile, short-lived chemicals that are a byproduct of specific types of diet, poor exercise habits, and certain metabolic processes. Free radicals, such

as the superoxide radical, have one missing electron with a single covalent bond. These radicals attack any double bond within the system, such as fatty acids and intracellular membranes.

Once the free radicals produce an injury site, plaque forms and, eventually, cholesterol attaches to it, producing circulatory system disease. The following foods produce free radicals in the human organism: fried foods, cooked fats, cooked cholesterol, alcohol, and tobacco smoke. Divers who consume a high fat diet which is similar to the Standard American Diet (***SAD***) and contains 40% fat, are at serious risk of increased free radical development and low-density cholesterol. This combination leads to circulatory problems and illnesses.

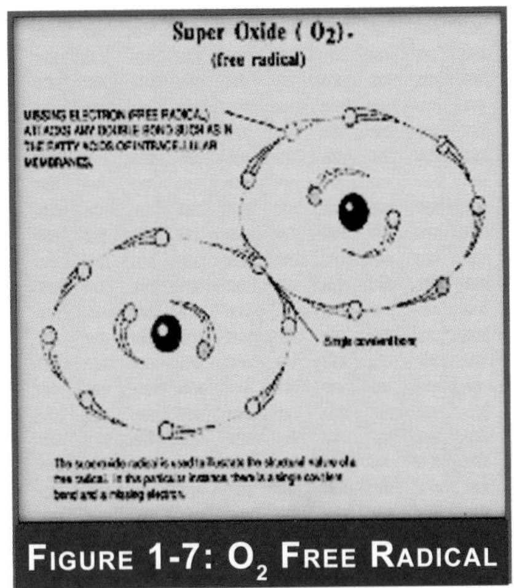

FIGURE 1-7: O_2 FREE RADICAL

FATS

When fat and cholesterol combine, especially if the cholesterol is exposed to air and heat such as when cooking red meat, ***cholesterol oxide*** forms. Cholesterol oxide, which acts as a free radical, damages the lining of the arteries. A fatty meal produces immediate changes in the circulatory system. Within an hour of completing a fatty meal, the red blood cells begin to stick together and form clumps. As this process continues, circulation slows down, which creates a phenomenon described as ***sludging***. About six hours following the meal, the sludging is severe enough that circulation in the smallest of blood vessels almost halts. This has several effects on the body, including reduced O_2 to the tissues and a lessened ability to remove CO_2 and waste from the system. Figure 1-8, shows the time release effects of fatty food intake and sludging.

In diving, we are concerned with the transport of inert gas as well as metabolic gases. Circulatory diseases, circulatory inefficiencies, and the physiological changes associated with fat ingestion will all interfere with the elimination of inert gases while diving.

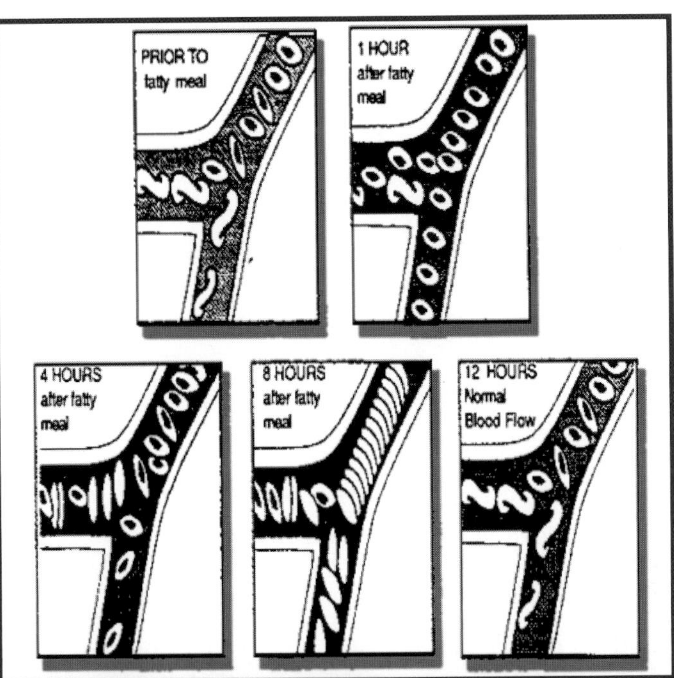

FIG. 1-8: EFFECTS OF FATTY MEALS ON BLOOD FLOW

In the case of circulatory disease and the corresponding decrease in the diameter of the blood vessel, it is easy to see that gas transport will not be effective. Sludging, which decreases gas transport efficiency throughout the cardiovascular system, is associated in the literature with decompression sickness (***DCS***).

Further, if sludging occurs and a bubble of inert gas forms, the bubble is more likely to lodge in the blood vessels. This outcome increases the chance bubbles will remain in the vascular system rather than filter out through the lungs. Such a bubble has a greater likelihood of growing and creating DCS-related problems. Moreover, the changes in blood gas given sludging contributes to a host of other issues, including an increased susceptibility to oxygen toxicity, inert gas narcosis, helium tremors, carbon dioxide retention, and changes in the blood's PH balance.

However, keep in mind that not all fats are "bad," and so we need to mention "good or "cis" fats as well. Good fat produces High Density Cholesterol (***HDL***) which is thought to pick up cholesterol from body tissues and return it to the liver for reprocessing or excretion. Although this type of fat is good for us, we must be aware of the quantity we consume; the old adage, "*... **too much of a good thing***..." should be kept in mind, as obesity can strike those on an overly-high HDL diet. Foods that are high

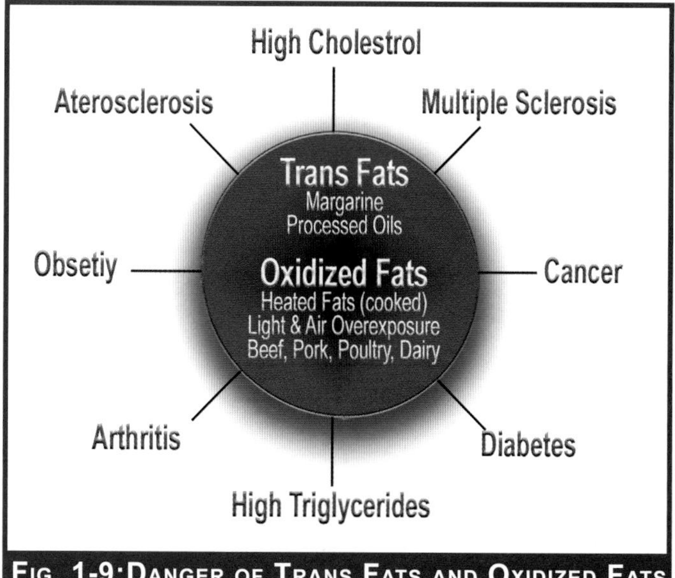

Fig. 1-9: Danger of Trans Fats and Oxidized Fats

in HDLs include certain fish and dark green vegetables, whole grains, certain fruits, and oils such as olive, flaxseed, and canola oil. Fats group into two types: ***Omega 3***, which is "***good***" fat, and ***Omega 6***, which is "***bad***" fat. In general, one should avoid the Omega 6 fats and insure some Omega 3 fats are in the diet.

Figure 1-9, the ***Trans Fats and Oxidized Fats*** chart, shows the type of fats and their effects. Much of the trans fats in the American diet come from hydrogenated vegetable oils. Other sources include red meats and margarine. Trans fats cause the mitochondria to swell. Since metabolism occurs in the mitochondria, trans fatty acids interfere with metabolism and increase blood cholesterol up to 15% and triglycerides by 47%. In contrast to trans fats, cis fats such as butter are necessary for vision, nerve function, coordination, memory, and the vital functions of life itself.

In addition, cis fats may reverse the effects of trans fats. Oils such as olive, fish, krill, flax, corn, and sesame all represent forms of cis fats and are beneficial to cells.

Antioxidants & Fiber

Antioxidants such as Vitamin E do much to reverse the development of free radicals in the body. Vitamin E elevates HDL levels and provides numerous health effects. Other antioxidants include Vitamin C, Beta-carotene, Co-enzyme Q-10 (***CoQ-10***) and Melatonin. These substances, when combined with nutrients and vitamins, especially the B-vitamins, are effective in promoting a healthier body and circulatory system. In addition to antioxidants, a healthy circulatory system needs fiber; therefore, fiber helps reduce diving-related injuries.

Figure 1-19, ***Fats/Oils and Their Prostaglandins*** shows some interesting effects of fiber on cholesterol levels in the blood.

Sugar

The body needs sugar for energy expenditure and prolonged endurance. A warm muscle will burn fat and use the sugars gained from the carbohydrates we eat. Explosive action by muscles not properly warmed up tends to burn only sugar. Thus, prior to exercise or a dive, it is wise to take a few moments to stretch and warm up the muscles before placing a demand on them. However, too much sugar, especially processed sugars, is harmful. Excess sugar forces the pancreas to secrete additional insulin, which increases the liver's efforts at storing and releasing glucose.

Aortas examined by Howard A. Neuman, Ph.D. disclosed that in areas where the sugar intake is low, people have high chromium levels and a lower incidence of arteriosclerosis. In the USA, where sugar uptake is high, chromium levels are lower, and there is an higher incidence of arteriosclerosis. This finding is associated with the pancreas' inability to

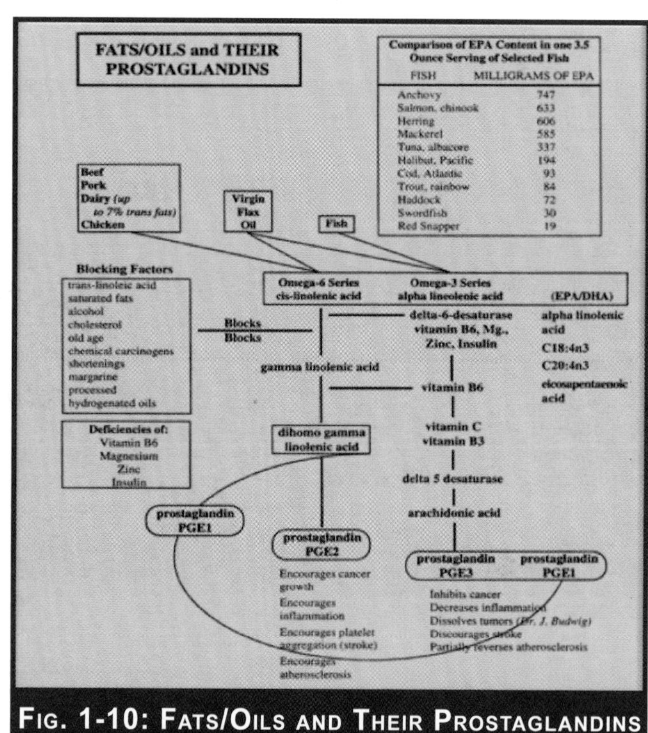

Fig. 1-10: Fats/Oils and Their Prostaglandins

meet insulin demands, which in turn raises the amount of blood fats in the circulatory system.

Increased sugar also has the side effect of weakening the immune system's ability to fight off bacteria. In one test, individuals given sucrose and fructose experienced a depression of white blood cells that lasted for up to five hours. If you are becoming ill, avoid all sweets.

High levels of sugar are also bad for the heart. By now, you should realize that a combination of excessive sugar and fats could be very damaging to the circulatory system. Certain supplements may be helpful in enhancing the heart and circulatory system's performance. In contrast, particular prescription drugs and specific supplements react in a way that is harmful to our physiology. Therefore, if you are taking prescription medications consult with your health care provider to ensure there are no drug interactions.

Supplements & Herbs for Increased Health & Well-Being

A possible effect of heart supplements that is of special interest to divers is that such supplements lower cholesterol levels in the blood vessels. Therefore, these supplements may reduce the possibility of micro bubbles that many feel contribute to decompression issues. Those who experience irregular heart beat (***arrhythmias***) should consider the supplement Taurine to assist in prevention of cavitation effect in the heart valves as this could also contribute to bubble formation. Most people would benefit from taking 30 to 60 mgs a day of CoQ-10 to strengthen the heart and act as a strong antioxidant. Anyone who has a form of heart disease should consider 150 to 300 mgs a day of CoQ-10. However, such individuals should consult with their healthcare provider about an appropriate healing strategy.

There is no need to take all of the supplements listed in this chapter. Choose one to three from each list at most, and add them, in moderation, to your diet.

The following is a list of supplements to consider for improved heart and circulation:

- **Beta 1.3 Glucan** is a polysaccharide. It helps maintain safe cholesterol levels. Beta 1.3 Glucan tends to raise the HDL and lower triglycerides, and works as an overall immune system enhancer. It also is effective in killing tumor cells and increases bone marrow production. Additionally, Beta 1.3 Glucan is effective in healing sores and ulcers in women who have underwent a mastectomy. The suggested dose is 2.5 milligrams (***mgs***) per day.
- If you suspect you may have clotting problems, consider using **Bromelain**, which aids in preventing blood clots and reducing inflammation. For divers, this may be a better option than aspirin, which some divers insist on taking. The suggested dose is 500 mgs per day.
- **CoQ-10** should be on everyone's "must take" supplement list. 60 mgs per day is appropriate for normal maintenance, and up to 300 mgs per day may be used as part of a cardiac recuperation regimen. CoQ-10 strengthens the heart, fights allergies, develops energy, stimulate the immune system, increase tissue oxygenation and may be a valuable anti-aging supplement. One six-year study at the university of Texas found that people being treated for congestive heart failure taking CoQ-10 in addition to conventional medicine had a 75% chance of survival after three years, as opposed to a 25% survival rate for those using conventional therapy only. Several studies here and in Japan reflect the CoQ-10 is effective in lowering blood pressure without using conventional medication. CoQ-10 has also been widely used in treating neurological abnormalities such as schizophrenia and Alzheimer's disease. CoQ-10 is also frequently used to fight obesity, candidiasis, multiple sclerosis, and diabetes. This supplement appears to have universal benefits. It should be used by all, and especially by those who are older, given its positive effects on the cardiac and cognitive processes. CoQ-10 is available in capsules; however, the liquid or oil form is preferable. Recent research reviewed in the magazine *Life Extension* February/ March 2008 edition provides in depth coverage of CoQ-10 and its affect on our physiology. It also points out our natural loss with age and loss due to statin and other drugs. This is necessary read fro all interested in ultimate health. It is especially important to aging divers, and those who may have heart issues or those being treated for cancer. The article also

states the only way higher levels in people with heart conditions are obtained are with ***ubiquinol*** and are not with the traditionally used ubliqinone. According to research cited in this publication, CoQ-10 from ubiquinol_absorbs into the blood stream eight times better than CoQ-10 from ubliqinone. This paper goes on to explain patients in the studies quoted who uses CoQ-10 from ubiquinol, who follow up with echocardiograms experience a recovery of up to 88%. It points out an even more insidious reason why more cardiac patients are dying is due to the prescribing of statin drugs without sufficient CoQ-10 intake.

- **Flax Seed Oil** is good for the heart, as it is rich in Omega 3 acids, magnesium, potassium, and fiber. Findings indicate that Flax Seed Oil lowers blood cholesterol and triglyceride levels, and reduces cholesterol's hardening effects on cell membranes.
- **Ginkgo Biloba** enhances blood circulation and increases the availability of oxygen to the heart, brain and other body parts. Ginko biloba also improves memory, reduces muscle pains, and acts as an antioxidant. Moreover, Ginko biloba has anti aging properties, reduces blood pressure, inhibits blood clotting, and is helpful for tinnitus, vertigo, hearing loss, and Reynaud's disease.
- **Hemp Oil** helps prevent heart disease, is good for pain, and works as a skin refresher. The suggested dose is 1000 mgs per day.
- **L-Carnitine** is involved in carbohydrate and protein metabolism, as well as in fat transportation to the mitochondria. Studies reflect the L-Carnitine reduces damage to the heart associated with cardiac surgery, helps the heart and legs use oxygen, and assists in prevention of memory loss.
- **Olive Leaf Extract** protects the heart and increases the immune system's capabilities. The standard dose is 500 mgs, 1 to 3 times per day.
- **Taurine** strengthens the heart, as it has an effect similar to digitalis. In Japan, it is used to treat heart disease. Since Taurine helps regulate the heart, it is an effective treatment for cardiac arrhythmias. In addition, Taurine lowers blood pressure and cholesterol levels, restores heart muscle. Taurine reduces fat deposit levels, increases vitamin C levels. Taurine is also used to treat anemia, and is believed to be effective in preventing Alzheimer's disease. Do not take Taurine in conjunction with heart medication in the form of drugs unless advised by your health care physician. In particular, do not take Taurine with Digoxin. However, under the guidance of a health care provider, Taurine is an excellent replacement for Digoxin. The standard dose is 500 mgs, 1 to 3 times per day.

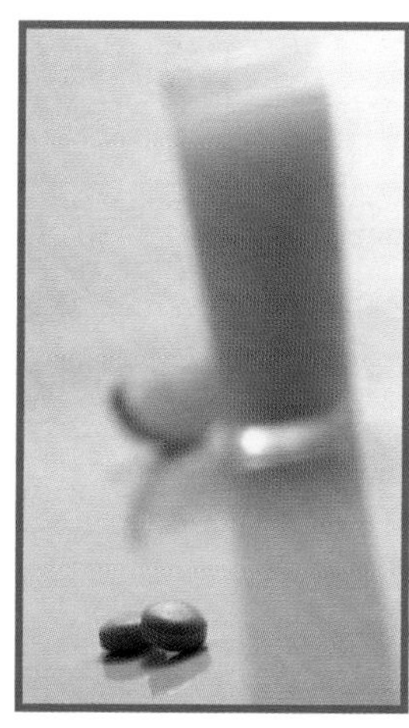

- **Trimathylglycine** (*TMG*) lowers Homocystein levels, which reduces the risk of heart disease, as high levels of Homocystein increase the risk of heart disease to three times that of the normal population. Trimathyglycine is also thought effective in preventing Alzheimer's disease. The standard dose is 100 mgs, 1 to 3 times per day.
- **Polifcosanol** appears to slow down the synthesis of cholesterol in the liver, while increasing the liver's absorption of LDL and HDL. Polifcosanol works well when combined with L-Arginine (such as in Polifusia) or taken with CoQ-10.
- **Magnesium** is known to increase cardiovascular health. One of the leading contributors to heart disease is low blood magnesium levels. Most adults in the United States of America (*USA*) have low blood magnesium. Magnesium can be taken orally, or massaged into the skin.
- **Calcium** should be taken in conjunction with Magnesium and Vitamin C, as magnesium and Vitamin C help the body to absorb calcium. A good combination supplement is Cal-Max, which is a blend of 400 mgs of Calcium, 200 mgs of magnesium, and 500 mgs of Vitamin C.
- **Vitamins C and E** also have beneficial effects on the heart.
- **Choleslo, Chitosan or Chelation therapy** may help lower blood cholesterol levels.
- **Medium Chain Triglycerides** (*MCT*), which derive from coconut oil, are some of the saturated fats that benefit the body. Moreover, since MCTs provide an energy boost, assist in weight loss, and improve endurance by lowering blood cholesterol,

they may also have a positive effect on cardiac health.

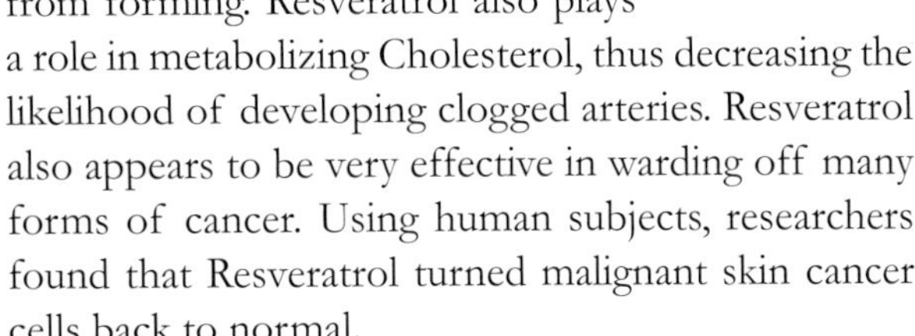

- **Resveratrol** may assist in preventing heart disease by inhibiting blood clots from forming. Resveratrol also plays a role in metabolizing Cholesterol, thus decreasing the likelihood of developing clogged arteries. Resveratrol also appears to be very effective in warding off many forms of cancer. Using human subjects, researchers found that Resveratrol turned malignant skin cancer cells back to normal.

This list concerns herbs for heart support:

- **Artichoke** promotes heart health by reducing cholesterol. It also enhances liver function. The standard dosage is 500 mgs up to four times per day.
- **Butchers Broom** improves circulation and reduces swelling in the hands and feet. The standard dosage is up to 3 capsules a day or 20 drops of extract added to juice or water.
- **Celery** is proported to lower blood pressure.
- **Garlic** helps prevent heart disease by reducing blood pressure and blood lipids. The standard dosage is 1 to 3 capsules a day. For ear aches, put warm garlic drops in the ear.
- **Ginko Biloba** improves circulation throughout the body. The standard dosage is 60 mgs, 2 to 3 times per day.
- **Green Tea** helps prevent heart disease; drink as many cups a day as desired.
- **Pine Bark Extract** protects against heart disease and stroke, and keeps the immune system strong
- **Red Yeast Rice** is excellent for the heart. However, it should only be taken under the guidance of a health care provider.

This list concerns supplements that support muscle building, muscle toning, or fat burning. In addition, some of these supplements relieve spasm and cramps:

- **Beta-hydroxy beta methylbutyrate (*HMB*)**: 1000 mgs has been shown to increase athletic ability and for those who workout to increase muscle mass while reducing fat. Many hail HMB as a safe alternative to anabolic steroids which also builds muscle but has serious side effects that may be life threatening. As a natural supplement HMB has no side effects other than assisting muscle growth for those who workout and reducing fat. It works even better if combined with Creatin. The recommended dose is 3 grams per day.
- **Hydro Citric Acid (*HCA*)**: Ideal for weight management, this supplement suppresses hunger, and prevents the body from turning carbohydrates into fat by inhibiting the action of an enzyme called ATP-citrate lyase. HCA enhances the ability of the muscles and liver to store glycogen therefore reducing fat production. It also prevents the brain from stimulating our appetites. HCA is believed to be an effective supplement to prevent heart disease by lowering blood triglyceride levels. Take up to 1500 mgs per day (total) one half hour before meals. HCA may provide additional energy for strenuous workouts.
- **L-Carnitine** is good for increasing the heart's ability to use oxygen. The dose is up to 1500 mgs per day. The increased capability to use oxygen results in being able to do more intense workouts and thus contribute to muscle or endurance development. (See a more complete description under heart supplements.)
- Amino acid complexes result in a balance of muscle support and the ability to recover from workouts. Some blends such as **L-Arginine** (which should not be taken independently by those who have herpes simplex) and **L-Ornthine** are felt to stimulate the production of growth hormone.
- **MCT** may assist in weight loss, stimulate the production of more energy, which increases athletic endurance, aids in muscle recovery, lowers cholesterol, and improves athletic performance.
- **Pyruvate** burns fat increased cardiovascular health increases energy levels.
- **Vanadyl Sulfate** is effective in normalizing blood sugar levels and is used with diabetics. It also has become popular as a supplement among athletes due to improving nutrient support. This results in increased energy and it stimulates muscle growth. The typical dose is 10 mgs one half hour before workout.
- **Cordyceps** is known to improve endurance. This is believed to be due to opening up breathing passages,

thus enabling the body to use more oxygen. The increased use of oxygen contributes to strength as well as endurance. The standard dose is 2 capsules of 525 mgs each per day with meals.

- **Creatin Monohydrate** reenergizes tired muscle cells, allowing for longer intense workouts. One study reported that people who take creatin with exercise gain more muscle and lose more fat than control groups working out but not taking creatin. Creatin is most useful for development of large muscles and not as effective for endurance sports where speed counts, as mass may interfere with speed. Creatin was found, in a study at the Cooper Clinic and Texas Women's University, to lower both cholesterol and Triglycerides with a recommended daily dosage of 5000 mgs per day.

Exercise

The second prime need for a healthy circulatory system is cardiovascular exercise. Exercise benefits the respiratory system by producing healthier lungs. Healthy lungs in turn provide better ventilation. The in-shape diver's ***VO_2 max***, which measures the body's ability to utilize oxygen efficiently, is higher than that of a non-fit diver. The increased VO_2 max allows the conditioned diver to work harder without a dramatic increase in RMV. In life threatening situations, this respiratory efficiency may prove to be the dividing line between survival and non-survival.

Another advantage of regular exercise is that it places demands on every organ in the body. The liver responds to exercise by producing glycogen more efficiently. Insulin and glucose regulation is fine-tuned by the pancreas as a reaction to exercise. The heart and lungs deliver more oxygen, and the circulatory system builds more capillaries. LDL cholesterol drops while the level of good cholesterol and HDL elevate. The mitochondria enlarge and produce additional adenosine triphosphate (***ATP***), thus providing us with more energy. As an added benefit, the body's ability to burn fat increases. The more intense the aerobic program, the better the VO_2 development. Tour-de-France cyclists have among the highest VO_2 max of all athletes. It is this high pulmonary efficiency that allows them to perform well on a long-endurance race. A diver in good physical condition is able to swim farther, successfully assist another diver, and get out of bad situations more often and with better results than an out-of-shape diver.

Progressively Accelerated Cardiopulmonary Exertion (*PACE®*) & Exercise

Divers should also take into account the need for short-duration, high energy output. This type of training is useful for diver rescue, and many researchers are currently in agreement that a regimen incorporating this form of cardiovascular and muscular development significantly increases overall fitness, as well as improving the heart's ability to withstand stressors. Please keep in mind that this exercise technique differs from cardio and long-distance endurance training. Dr. Albert Sears, who developed the PACE® program outlined below, is an excellent reference source for additional information. Dr. Sears publishes on the internet.

In an overview, the program consists of:

1. A warm up
2. A short high-intensity exercise period that can be either distance or time derived
3. A low intensity exercise segment following the high-intensity workout phase which acts as a recovery period. This process repeats in sets.

An example of this method that I might use in one of my Martial Arts classes is:

1. **Warm up**
2. **Set One:** Full out attack on heavy bag. Maximum power and maximum speed for one minute followed by two minutes low intensity exercise while heart and breathing rates recover
3. **Set Two:** Full out attack on heavy bag. Maximum power and maximum speed for 45 seconds followed by two minutes low intensity exercise while heart and breathing rates recover
4. **Set Three:** Full out attack on heavy bag. Maximum power and maximum speed for 30 seconds followed by two minutes low intensity exercise while heart and breathing rates recover
5. **Set Four:** Full out attack on heavy bag. Maximum power and maximum speed for 15 seconds followed by two minutes low intensity exercise while heart and breathing rates recover

This approach may adjust to running, cycling, swimming, stair masters, tread mills, elliptical machines or any other

exercise where high intensity, cardio-strength training is possible. An ideal work out of this nature is approximately a 10 to 20 minute routine. This type of program combines two issues that are often at odds: Cardio/strength conditioning and time consideration. Although my regimen includes separate weight, cardio, and strength/agility training in order to stay fir for Martial Arts and diving, I include this program into my overall routine and that of my martial arts students. Since we added the PACE® approach to our regimen, both my students and I have experienced noticeable, and in some cases dramatic, improvement in fitness levels.

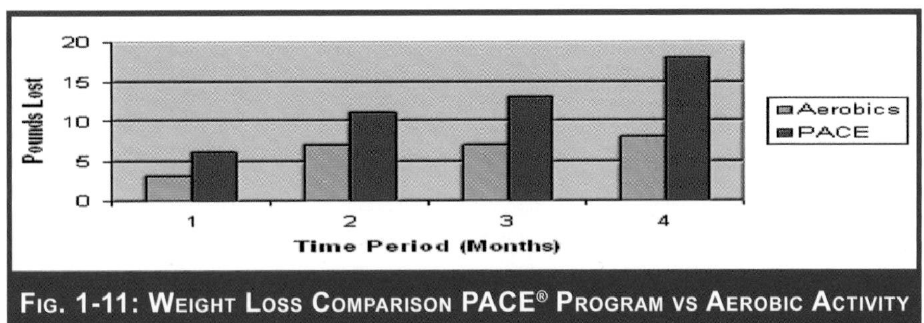

Fig. 1-11: Weight Loss Comparison PACE® Program vs Aerobic Activity

Whether you choose to incorporate the program into a current routine or use it as a stand-alone system, I personally assure you it will provide you with increased energy, endurance, and the ability to sustain an explosive use of energy. It may be the best form of cardio conditioning for those in fields such as firefighting, where there is a need for a quick and strong cardiac output without risking overstressing the heart.

Although Dr. Sears does not emphasize the benefit his program offers endurance athletes, I firmly believe that his program potentiates, when combined with a cardio regimen, thereby significantly increasing overall conditioning.

Dr Al Sears, in one of his newsletters, gives additional insight into the PACE® program and expounds on its usefulness as a weight management program as well. According to Dr. Sears:

"Researchers at George Washington University looked closely at how well diet, aerobic exercise, and dieting combined with aerobics work to help you lose weight… the researchers analyzed 25 years worth of study results to see what is most effective for weight loss…"

People using diet alone to lose weight lost an average of 10.7 pounds. A person using both together lost an average of 11.1 pounds… adding aerobic exercise to a weight loss diet makes hardly any difference at all. It's no wonder aerobics leave you feeling disappointed and frustrated. It's just a poor weight loss tool.

Now contrast this to the results of my PACE® program from my "twin" study. Over 4 months, the "***PACE®***" twin lost over 18 pounds of fat. The "***aerobics***" twin lost just 7 pounds. And the "aerobics" twin also lost 2 pounds of critical muscle mass. What's more, the PACE® twin's workouts lasted less than 15 minutes. Her "aerobic" sister sweated for hours….What works when it comes to weight loss is a different kind of activity.

Researchers from Laval University in Quebec compared long duration cardio exercise with short duration high intensity workouts. For 20 weeks, half the participants did five 45-minute workouts a week at moderate intensity. The other half did 19 high intensity interval workouts… over the course of 15 weeks.

Although the second group spent less time exercising, and only did half the work as the first group, they increased their aerobic capacity by 30 percent. What's more, the second group lost nine times as much body fat as the first group 2. That's right... they lost ***nine times more fat.***

So what is PACE®? Well first of all, it's simple, fun, and it's easy to stick with. ***PACE®*** stands for ***P***rogressively ***A***ccelerated ***C***ardiopulmonary ***E***xertion. It's a type of workout that uses short duration bursts that slowly get stronger as you get more fit.

Exertion periods are always followed by recovery periods. Together, they make an exercise set. So let's use this 10-minute program to get a better idea of how it works.

Look at the program chart in Figure 1-12, above. After an easy warm-up, your first minute is an exertion period. For the next sixty seconds, you're going to exercise at a pace that gives your heart and lungs a challenge.

If you're new to exercise, or feel out-of-shape, take it easy for the first two weeks. The speed and intensity of your exertion period should be fast enough for you to break a sweat, but not so intense that you can't finish the 10-minute program.

Let's say you're in the gym and you decide to try the stationary bike. First, make sure you're comfortable. Adjust the seat and choose a level of resistance that will give you a slight challenge. On a stationary bike, the resistance will make it harder to pedal.

Begin to pedal and make note of the time. Your first exertion period is just 60 seconds so time yourself accordingly. After your first exertion period, begin your first recovery period. During your recovery period, slow down to an easy pace - as if you're walking. If you need to stop, you can. Otherwise, simply slow down and go at a slow, easy speed. This gives your body a chance to rest and recover.

Your recovery periods are crucial. They're more than just empty spaces between the repetition intervals. Recovery is the flip side of exertion. Training your body to recover is one of the keys to your success. During your recovery periods, focus on your breath and feel your heart rate starting to slow down. Feel your heart and breath returning to a resting level before you move on.

Now that you have a feel for it, repeat the process. Start your next exertion period and follow it with a recovery period. You'll soon get into the groove of exercising in short bursts followed by periods of rest."

Getting your feet wet with the basics will help you get started right away. What's more, it will prepare you for a deeper level of your PACE® program, which adds other dimensions like acceleration, intensity, and duration.

The combination of exercise and prudent diet habits will produce a healthier body, reverse circulatory problems that may already exist, and act as a preventative step for most diving-related illnesses. In short, it is not logical to eat a fatty diet, be a couch potato, and participate in a strenuous form of diving or in other activities. In numerous studies, regular exercise has been shown to lower the incidence of heart disease. It is effective both in lowering blood cholesterol levels and in conditioning the heart. Exercise stimulates collateral circulation. If blood vessels leading to the heart are clogged, collateral vessels can take over the job of supplying the tissues with circulation. Exercise increases the amount of collateral circulation, and thus reduces instances of sudden death from heart attack.

However, before starting any exercise have a complete physical exam, and ask your healthcare provider to arrange

	Warm Up	Exertion	Recovery
Warm-up	2 Minutes		
Set 1		1 Minute	1 Minute
Set 2		1 Minute	1 Minute
Set 3		1 Minute	1 Minute
Set 4		1 Minute	1 Minute

Figure 1-12: Sample PACE® Style Workout

ether a stress test or VO_2 max test to ensure that you are healthy enough to increase your fitness level. As a indicator of what is going on in your body, once a base line stress test has been accomplished, follow up every other year with an additional stress test. Another advantage of the stress test and its associated echocardiograms is they can detect problematic areas that a complete physical would not reveal. These areas may be either due to disease or genetically driven. My personal example of the importance of a stress test is reflected below. Note in my case that I have exercised and maintained good physical condition since I was nine years old (1948), except for one year (1981) that I only dived. The following events occurred in 2006.

A Personal Account

I always told mysely that someday I had needed to have a stress test so I could have a base line from which to work. In November of 2006, I went to Physician who is both a Doctor of Osteopathy (***D.O.***) and a Doctor of Pharmacology (***Pharm. D.***) I had her do my complete physical, plus every form of blood work, including intracellular nutrient use. I went off supplements for 3 months prior to the blood work. This enabled me to see what my body produces and uses on its' own. (This is something I would also recommend to everyone.)

Essentially all my blood work came back excellent. The only negative I had was higher heavy metal toxins than expected. To correct this I started Zinc supplements. We then made a custom vitamin & nutrient program. My Cholesterol was fine, as my HDL was high, with a low LDL. According to the blood work I was in excellent condition; I passed the physical with "flying colors."

I requested a stress test as at age 68 (03-21-07) it was about time to do so. In the past, I have completed two VO_2 max tests but not a stress test. Dr. Diaz arranged for me to go

Some benefits of having a high rate of O_2 uptake due to an increased VO_2 max from excercise include:

- ◊ Lower Blood Pressure
- ◊ Better Heart Regualation
- ◊ Stronger Tendons and Ligaments
- ◊ Thicker Cartilage
- ◊ Larger Muscles
- ◊ Greater Blood Volume
- ◊ More Hemoglobin
- ◊ Less Body Fat
- ◊ Denser Bone
- ◊ More Effiecient Lungs
- ◊ Heart Pumps More Blood w/Each Stroke
- ◊ More Oxygen Extracted from Blood
- ◊ More Capillaries
- ◊ Lower Heart Rate

to a Dr. Sende at Mount Sinai Medical Center in Miami Beach Florida in early February 2007. The scan, stress test, post-scan, and echocardiogram were completed at that time. Although I "maxed" the stress test, the post-scan and the echocardiogram picked up some cardiac abnormalities. After reading the post scan and echocardiogram findings, Dr. Sende scheduled me for a procedure known as cardiac catheterization. The outcome of the "cardiac cath" is as follows: My aorta was 7 centimeters (***cm***) wide, whereas it should be around 3 cm wide. The enlarged aorta was causing blood to regurgitate back into my heart (essentially an aneurysm), leading to dilation of the left ventricle.

Based on aortic size, I had a 32% probability of a sudden death heart attack at any moment, as the aorta could rupture. The doctors were shocked that I was ***asymptomatic*** given my arduous exercise levels. They were even shocked I was still alive!

I was sent to Dr. Williams, a cardiac surgeon believed to be one of, if not ***the***, best in South Florida. Dr. Williams recommended a mechanical valve, but once I researched mechanical valves, I discovered such valves require that the patient remain on blood thinners for the rest of their life. Blood thinners increase the risk of severe bleeding if a cut or deep bruise occurs. Bruises are a given in contact martial arts, and both bruises and cuts are common with wreck and cave diving. In addition, one has to have the discipline to take a medication every day of their life.

I elected to have the surgeon implant a tissue valve instead of a mechanical valve. Post surgery, the cardiologist and surgical resident agreed that with my lifestyle the tissue valve, which does not require any continued medication use, was the best choice for me.

Pre-surgery, members of the cardiac team performed an ultra-sound on my blood vessels (with an accent on my carotid artery) and the technician told Patti (Mount) and I that I have the circulation of a 15 year old and should live "forever." The surgery was a success. Later I discovered the aortic valve dilation was a genetic issue that my mother had and it is believed my uncle also had, as he died of a sudden death heart attack. It is suspected that my grandfather may have had the same problem, as he was in perfect health until age 77 at which time he had a stroke that left him paralyzed until his death a few months later.

Open heart surgery is tough on the body. Post surgery I had problems trying to stay warm, my endurance was totally whacked, and I lost a lot of muscle, even though I immediately became active. In my case, I lost over 20 pounds, which I feel was all muscle loss. My waist remained the same size before and after surgery so it was only arms, chest, and legs that became smaller. My chest was very tender, as they literally cut everything in the middle of the chest cavity to do the surgery. My hemoglobin count dropped to about 11 from 16, thus I was unable to utilize as much oxygen as before surgery. For the first time in my life, my blood pressure was high. Moreover, the heart has to undergo a remodeling process during the healing phase; therefore, I had to use medication to ensure proper cardiac functioning.

According to my surgeon and cardiologist, I was to take a large quantity of the aforementioned drugs, gradually build up to a one quarter mile walk and not to lift more than 10 pounds for three months in order to allow the chest, bones, muscle attachments, etc. to heal. I was told not to do any weight lifting, jogging, or martial arts for at least three months and after three months gradually ease back into diving. They did reassure me I could do everything, and most likely better than, I had before, once healed.

However, during the first week home I started with a one and one half mile walk. At the second week, I started weight lifting with 10 to 20 pounds, and 3 pounds for shoulders and curls. Each week I added weight and by week 6 was using 80 pounds for benches, laterals, triceps, and biceps, with 20 pounds for lateral and shoulder work

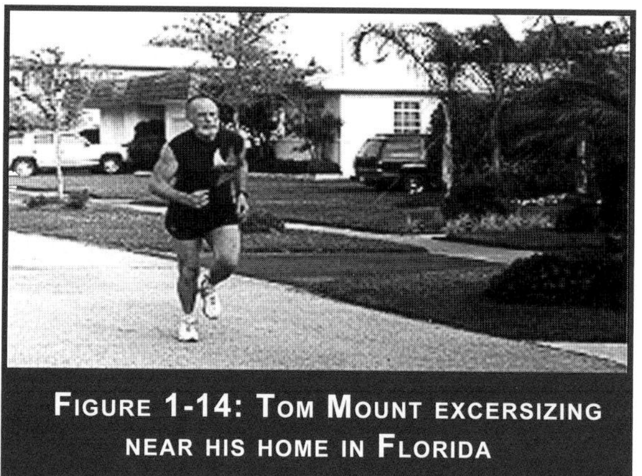
Figure 1-14: Tom Mount excersizing near his home in Florida

and 200 pounds on the leg press. I increased my walk to three and one quarter mile, and by the third week, my best pace was 65 minutes.

On the fourth week, I added in jog-walking for the same distance. At first, I could only jog about the width of a house. My endurance, as measured by my jogging, was slow to return. By week 9, I started taking one of my dogs on the walk jog routine; at this time I had the times down to 36 minutes and change. Within two weeks, or week eleven, I had the walk jog routine down to 35 minutes and two seconds. Competing with oneself is always a form of survival training. At the beginning of week 16, I had the time down to 31 minutes and 35 seconds. It was at this time, I knew I would soon be back to normal with the distances being in a full jog mode and times in the 8 to 9 minute a mile range. I plan to reduce the days of jogging to 2 days (from experience know my knees do better with this plan) and cycle 2 days so I can take advantage of cross training more effectively.

I started back diving at week nine, and made my first 200 fsw (60 msw) dive post surgery at week ten. I had also returned to light martial arts by week three, and by week twelve, I was back to full workouts, with the exception of sparring. I also started back to doing four sets of 100 pushups; two sets on my knuckles and two sets on my palms. I held off on sparring and ***take downs*** until week sixteen. Both my cardiologist and doctor said they certainly did not recommend what I did/do but it works for me - therefore ***keep it up and see you at the next 3 month appointment***. When I started back into diving (week nine) I threw all my medications away, after having reduced the dosages slowly to a fraction of what was prescribed. I replaced them with natural substances to accomplish the same goals.

Exercise, Naturopathy, Homeopathy & Conditioning

As a Naturopathic Doctor (***ND***) I self-prescribed, and also used the homeopathic remedies my wife, Patti, recommended, as she is a homeopath. If you are to go this route, be sure to consult with a health care provider before removing yourself from medications and starting supplements and herbs. Do not combine supplements with medications unless you have your physician's permission due to possible interactions. Exercise has also been shown to be a release of good HDL, therefore improving its' chance of reducing LDL cholesterol. The preferred type of exercise for circulatory conditioning is an aerobic or PACE® program. To accomplish an aerobic level of exercise, you must work at an elevated heart rate that is safe, yet high enough to effect physical change.

To determine a maximum safe heart rate, subtract your age from 220. During aerobic exercise, your target heart rate should be 80% of your safe heart rate. For example, if your age is 60, subtract 220 - 60 = 160 ***x*** 0.80 = 132. If your age is 30, subtract 220 - 30 = 190 ***x*** 0.80= 152. It is apparent that aging reduces the target aerobic rate. The aerobic workout is performed at least two times a week with a minimum time of 20 minutes per session. Ideally, one hour per day, 5 to 6 days a week will be devoted to some form of physical training.

Seek out a training program with which you will be happy. There are many machines on the market that tone both the upper and lower body and some even double as strength exercises. General swimming, swimming with fins on to duplicate diving activities, cycling, jogging, rollerblading and so forth are all excellent for cardio-vascular conditioning. For added benefit, and to prevent boredom, incorporate cross training by doing more than one form of exercise. One day you can cycle and the next day row or swim.

If you are limited on time include interval training or utilize the PACE® program. In this do maximum output for seconds to a couple of minutes then allow your body to recover and repeat. This type of exercise will let you crowd in a 15 minute routine rather than an hour. My personal philosophy is to use both interval (due its increased intensity) and endurance training, as one's life may depend on endurance in extreme environments. Numerous research programs indicate short intense interval training may even be better for cardio than our established theories of longer times.

On the web page ***Heart Matters***, author Jeremy Likeness, a specialist in performance nutrition discusses recent findings regarding exercise capacity. **He writes:**

> "Heart rate can still be a useful tool for training, but you must learn to use your body as the tool, not the equation. For example, if you want to understand what your anaerobic zone is, instead of plugging away at a formula, why not perform anaerobic work? I can guarantee that you will be using your ATP-CP system (a completely anaerobic system) when you perform a one-rep max. So instead of taking 90% of 220 minus your age, just strap on a heart rate monitor the next time you perform a maximum lift. Then, instead of relying on statistics, your body will tell you what your "anaerobic" zone is.
>
> Once you have this useful information, you can apply it to your training. If you are performing high intensity interval training, and would rather have your heart dictate the intervals than your perception, let your body be the guide. Start by walking on an incline for several minutes. This is your low intensity zone. Now go outside and perform an all-out sprint. This will be your high intensity zone. Now you simply build intervals between those two heart rates for your training…
>
> As a final note, heart rate can apply to resistance training as well… Pick a target rate for your training. Your "75% effort" (somewhere between your sprinting and incline walking) could be the bottom line. Simply rest until your heart rate drops to that level, and then perform the next set. This will ensure your heart rate is always elevated to a minimal level while allowing sufficient recovery to move on. When you are training for strength or heavy lifts, how long should you rest... Again, why not let your body decide? Rest until you fall to the fat-burning zone or even less, then start the next set… The key is that your body is telling you when sufficient recovery has taken place to perform the next set…
>
> When you are training, don't forget the most important muscle: your heart. Not only is it an indicator of health, it is a tool that can help to improve your health… You can use your heart as an interactive gauge to tailor your workouts to your own unique body. Learn that the heart matters and use the powerful information it provides to build your peak physique."

Shorter intervals maximize your exercise potential and prevent boredom. You may even do cross training within an individual workout. Ideally, develop a program and keep your commitment to that program. Make this an integral part of your normal daily habits. Place its priority above all other items during the time you select as a daily exercise time. Most people are more prone to maintain an exercise regime if they do it in the morning before becoming involved in daily activities.

To gain more insite into heart rates and exercise capacity refer to following web pages:

www.bodybuilding.com/fun/moser9.htm
www.wikihow.com/Calculate-You-Target-Heart-Rate
www.heartmonitors.com/zone_calc.htm
www.freewebtown.com/provenbrands/data/aerobics-cardio/35374.html

Another area that may be of interest to those involved in fitness training is determining their VO_2 max, which is usually determined in a clinical setting. As we are aware, The circulatory system is vital to our overall health. However, there are programs that can help you approximate your VO_2 max at home. The following list of web pages is a guide to practical VO_2 max computations; however, please remember that there is greater room for error in a non-clinical, rather than a clinical, setting. Of the three web pages offered below, the third may be the simplest to use.

www.rajeun.net/vo2max.html
www.nismat.org/physcor/max_2.htmlformulafitness/vo2max.htm#impatient

If the recommendations discussed in this chapter are adhered to, circulatory problems will most likely be reduced and gas transport will improve. This in turn will help protect the body from decompression illness and other diving disorders. If you are going to be a serious diver, be prepared to take serious actions, including lifestyle change, to insure your safety.

The Nervous System

The Central Nervous System (***CNS***) controls the actions of all the other systems that make up our bodies. However, before starting our discussion, let's review some terms:

- **Central Nervous System:** The brain and the spinal cord

- **Nerves:** One or more bundles of fibers that transmits electrical signals, or impulses, to and from the CNS
- **Neurons:** Electrically excitable cells in the nervous system that process and transmit information. Neurons are composed of a cell body, or soma, a dendritic tree made of branching dendrites, and an axon. Neurons are the main component of the central nervous system
- **Axons:** Long, slender nerve fibers that carry the nerve's outgoing impulses
- **Dendrites:** Branched projections of a neuron that conduct the electrical signals received from the axon of other neural cells to the cell body
- **Afferent Neurons:** A type of neuron that carries nerve impulses from the receptor site to the CNS. In other words, this type of neuron transmits the body's messages to the brain for processing.
- **Efferent Neurons:** Are neurons involved in muscular control that convey central nervous system signals to muscles, glands, and other physiological structures
- **Peripheral Nervous System (*PNS*):** The part of the nervous system that resides outside of the CNS and serves the limbs and organs. The PNS consists of two parts: the autonomic and the somatic nervous systems.
- **Autonomic Nervous System (*ANS*):** The nervous system that regulates involuntary and glandular activity through two separate nervous systems: the **Sympathetic** and **Parasympathetic System**.
- **Somatic Nervous System:** This part of the CNS processes sensory information and controls voluntary muscular systems within the body.

A brief and simple explanation of the nervous system may be found published at the website "***The Autonomic Nervous System***."

Overview

"The nervous system therefore has a tremendous part to play in enabling us to survive in the world. It can be thought of as the telecommunications system of the body. Sending information from various sources to a vast computer network (the brain) which analyses and solves the problems presented to it and then passes the appropriate information out to the field workers (muscles, glands, etc.) enabling the appropriate actions to take place in a coordinated and logical fashion, The nervous system works in close conjunction with another body system known as the endocrine system. This has effects on the body's function by producing organic chemical substances known as hormones, Taking the analogy above and relating this to the endocrine system, it can be likened to a road & rail network communication system transporting bulk items (***hormones***) around the body to enable essential works to be carried out.

...The CNS may be thought of as the Master Computer it ultimately controls all functions based on the feedback from its "feedback" systems. Like computers, it makes decisions based on the information fed to it and then processed. It can receive good or bad information based on environmental conditions, the consciousness of the person and the learned traits that have become habitual within the ANS. Its influence on health is also dependent on the nutrition of the brain."

The staff at the Buckinghamshire School of Nursing, London, gives us additional insight on the CNS and PNS; they write:

> "The cranial nerves run from the head and neck to the brain by passing through openings in the skull, or cranium. Spinal nerves are the nerves associated with the spinal cord and pass through openings in the vertebral column. Both cranial and spinal nerves consist of large numbers of processes that convey impulses to the central nervous system and also carry messages outward... Afferent impulses are referred to as sensory; efferent impulses are referred to as either somatic or visceral motor, according to what part of the body they reach. Most nerves are mixed nerves made up of both sensory and motor elements."

Within the PNS there are 12 pairs of cranial nerves (which link directly to the brain) and 31 pairs of spinal nerves (which link to the spinal cord and then to the brain.) Cranial nerves are distributed to the head and neck regions of the body, with one conspicuous exception: the tenth cranial nerve, called the Vagus.

In addition to supplying structures in the neck, the Vagus nerve is distributed to structures located in the chest and abdomen. Vision, auditory and vestibular sensation, and taste are mediated by the second, eighth, and seventh

cranial nerves, respectively. Cranial nerves also mediate motor functions of the head, the eyes, the face, the tongue, and the larynx, as well as the muscles that function in chewing and swallowing.

The Nervous System

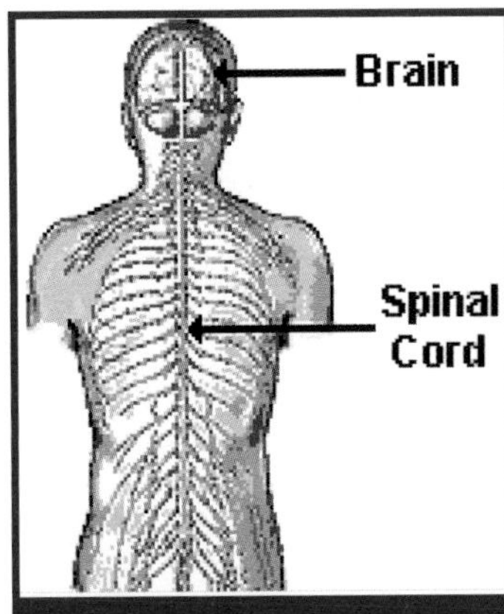

Fig. 1-16: Spinal Cord

The **Autonomic Nervous System** ***(ANS)*** regulates functions such as secretion, salivation, lung control, heartbeat, emotions, and temperature regulation. By assuming control over some functions of the ANS, breathing can be controlled and, thus, our internal environment. The **ANS** is divided into the **Sympathetic** ***(SyNS)*** and **Parasympathetic** ***(PaNS)*** **Systems**. The sympathetic system is composed of two vertical rows of ganglia, nerve cell clusters, on either side of the spinal column. These branch out to glands and viscera in the thorax and abdomen, forming integrated plexuses, or energy centers, with nerves ending in the parasympathetic system.

The sympathetic and parasympathetic nervous systems insure body/nerve functioning and reaction to stimuli. The parasympathetic system tends to slow the heart, while the sympathetic system speeds the heart up. Therefore, the sympathetic nervous system may play a role in our innate "***fight or flight***" reactions to stress or trauma.

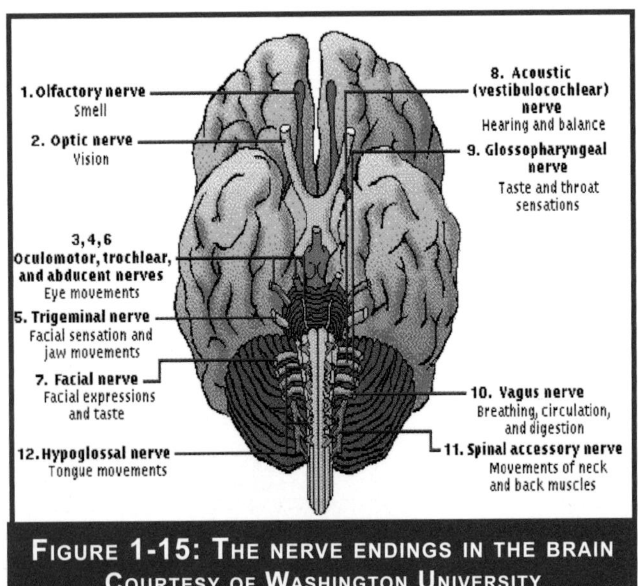

Figure 1-15: The nerve endings in the brain
Courtesy of Washington University

The parasympathetic and sympathetic systems regulate heart activity, and keep our bodies in balance. Although the ANS is responsible for maintaining so-called "automatic functions," the ANS can be affected by our habits. Thus, we may change how the ANS works and modify it to our advantage in both stressful situations and everyday life.

"The Autonomic Nervous System" continues:

"The ANS is part of the peripheral nervous system PaNS. It has an important function in maintaining the internal environment of the human body in a steady state. This role is vital in returning the body to a homeostatic state after trauma. As various changes occur within the environment, both internal and external, the ANS reacts by regulating such things as the Blood Pressure, Heart Rate, and Concentration of salts in the Blood Stream… If the body becomes dehydrated… the SyNS will pick up sensory information on the depletion of body fluid and the ANS will activate the mechanisms that conserve and replenish body fluids.

The ANS is also involved in many other body activities such as, waste disposal, response to stress, and sexual response. The functions of the ANS underlie the physiological aspects of coping during stress and forms a major link between the nervous system and the endocrine system during these times. The system generally works automatically without voluntary control… We do not consciously direct the rate of our heart beating nor are we normally aware of the diameter of our blood vessels or the need to stimulate our salivary glands to produce saliva. However, the effects of the ANS do impinge upon our consciousness, especially at times of heightened emotion. For example, most of us have experienced fear, either real or imagined, at some time in our lives and have been aware of our hearts beating faster. The increased heart rate is due to the effects of the ANS.

Once physiologists believed the system was wholly independent of the CNS. However, we now realize that this is not quite the picture and that there is some CNS component involved. This includes the spinal cord, the brain stem, and the hypothalamus. The hypothalamus is probably the most important area of the brain involved with the ANS but other areas such as the medulla oblongata and parts of the limbic system of the cerebral cortex have an important part to play…"

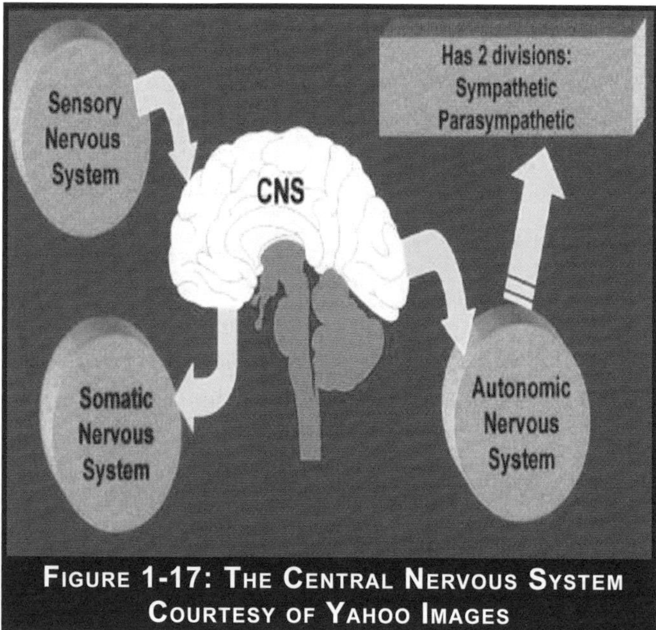

Figure 1-17: The Central Nervous System Courtesy of Yahoo Images

Studies of people practicing Transcendental Meditation claim that it is possible to gain conscious control over autonomic activities... Heart beat, metabolic rate and blood pressure decrease and alpha-waves are shown to increase when brain activity is monitored by electroencephalogram (***EEC***). The studies have also suggested that the body's response to noradrenaline (sometimes known as ***norepinephrine***) is lowered. As we shall see later, noradrenaline is a hormone important in autonomic response.

In recent years, "***biofeedback***" techniques have been developed in order to teach people to relax by controlling their brain wave patterns. These techniques provide the individual with some recognizable indication of the status of their autonomic functioning. By using biofeedback readouts as a guide, subjects learn to exert some conscious control over certain aspects of the ANS such as blood pressure, blood sugar levels, and abnormal heart rhythms. People also learn to prevent or reduce pain from problems such as headaches and panic responses.

It is quite easy to understand how the ANS influences all of our actions, and given its' effect on all our bodily and mental functions, it becomes clear as to how our reactions form. Moreover, it is evident that habit influences ANS functioning. As we train or are trained in certain actions such as adopting incorrect breathing patterns, the ANS transforms these learned responses into automatic reactions. Therefore, in order for internal change to occur, we must review the habits driven into ANS memory. We can then alter these habits by practicing the correct methods; essentially, we are retraining the ANS. Meditation and affirmations are two ways in which the ANS memory may be changed. Keep in mind that ingrained habits, when converted to automatic responses, will determine how we react to stress and trauma.

We should also be aware that in a diving environment many environmental features contribute to ANS effects. The partial pressures of gases at depth can, like drugs, modify our reactions due to their influence on the nervous system. CO_2 retention is known to create confusion, and may lead to panic. Imagine then the combined effects of drugs and the increased partial pressures of nitrogen, carbon dioxide or oxygen. To increase their chance of survival in life threatening situations, divers should have a thorough understanding of the ANS. With such knowledge, divers can increase their control over their own physiological response system. Such knowledge and control could, in some situations, be the difference in living and dying.

Moreover, by studying our physiology, habits and automatic responses, as well as developing breath control techniques, we increase our mastery of the self, improve our ability to heal, and increase our resistance to diseases. In addition, with correct breathing, one develops the ability to control the right side of the brain, which improves the ability to control the mind. It is thought that many diseases are due to an imbalance in energy, which is tied to improper breathing, stress, and negative mental states.

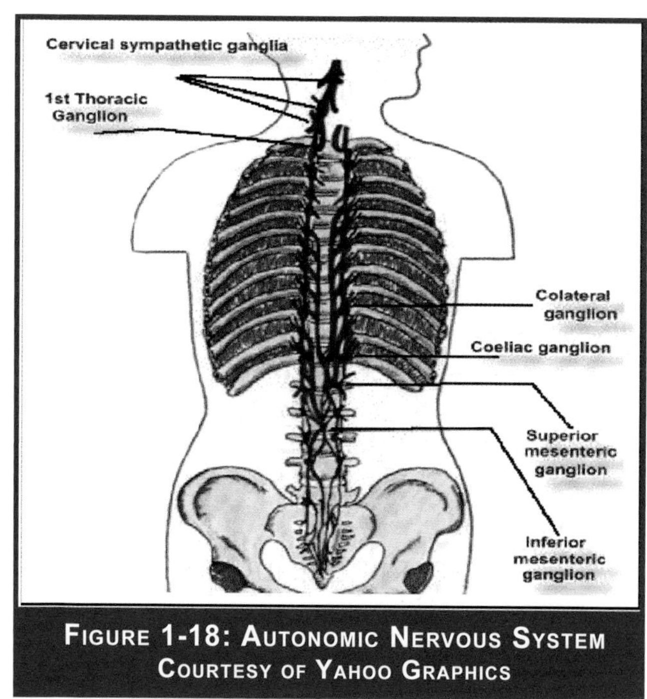

Figure 1-18: Autonomic Nervous System Courtesy of Yahoo Graphics

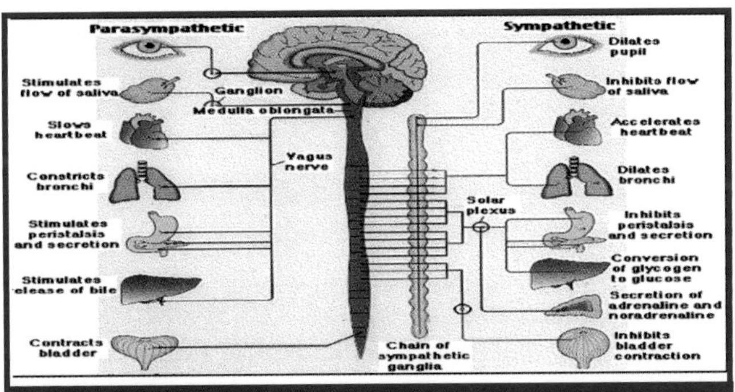

FIGURE 1-19: THE AUTONOMIC NERVOUS SYSTEM

If you search your past, you may remember that at times when a great deal of stress existed in your life, there was probably a corresponding lowering of your immune system and an increase in your susceptibility to colds and other disease. We suggest that you regularly practice good breathing techniques, meditation, and some form of physical toning, not only to lower your stress levels but also to improve your diving controls. In doing so, you may experience less mental fatigue and, perhaps, a healthier body.

As explained, there are two ways we can gain control over the involuntary nervous system (*ANS*). The first, and easiest to accomplish, is the control of respiration. This can be accomplished through the practice of breathing exercises, which will not only make us better divers, but can also be incorporated into our everyday lives. Breath control regulates heart function by bringing the right vagus nerve under control. This action allows access to the involuntary nervous system, or ANS, and its conscious direction. The second means of controlling the ANS is by developing a stronger will. What we mean is, through meditation, we can sharply focus mental energy, thus gaining access to our minds. To maximize our self-control, we need to incorporate both correct breathing and meditation.

Supplements for the nervous system that may improve functioning include:

- **Vitamin E and C** are foundation vitamins that everyone should take. Vitamin C should be at least 500 mgs per day and Vitamin E should be 400 IUs per day. Do not overdose Vitamin E; if one takes this vitamin in larger doses do so under the guidance of a health care provider
- **Taurine** is the building block of all the other amino acids, as well as one of the key components of bile, which is necessary for the digestion of fats, the absorption of fat-soluble vitamins, and the control of serum cholesterol levels. Taurine provides a protective mechanism for the brain, especially under the strain of dehydration. It is also used in treating anxiety, epilepsy, hyperactivity, poor brain function, and seizures
- **Calcium** and **Magnesium** combined (see heart supplements)
- **Valerian** is used as a relaxant as it acts as a sedative, therefore reducing anxiety levels. It also reduces cramps and spasms. It is often used to treat pain, blood pressure irregularities, insomnia, irritable bowel syndrome (***IBS***), and ulcers
- **St. John's Wort** is good for depression and nerve pain. It aids in the control of stress and some studies suggest it protects bone marrow and intestinal mucosa from X-ray damage
- **DMG** boosts mental activity, and enhances the immune system. It also reduces elevated cholesterol levels. It improves oxygen utilization by the body and brain
- **GABA** is an amino acid that acts as a CNS neuronal transmitter, and is essential for brain metabolism. Its function is to regulate neuronal activity, thereby inhibiting nerve cells from firing excessively. When combined with niacin and inositol, GABA may prevent anxiety- and stress-related messages from reaching certain areas of the brain. However, excess GABA produces increased anxiety, shortness of breath and numbness around the mouth. Therefore this supplement should be used sparingly. Although youthful, healthy divers most likely do not need GABA, older divers may benefit from it in moderation, taken on a cycle of three days on and one day off
- **Garlic** is a viable healing herb, as it helps eradicate heavy metal toxins, oxidants, and free radicals from the body. Aged garlic protects against DNA, liver, and vessicular damage. Garlic also prevents blood clots, is an immune system stimulant, and is a natural antibiotic. Garlic is also a strong memory-enhancing herb. Ideally, it should be part of everyone's daily diet
- **L-Asparagine** helps maintain emotional balance by keeping anxiety and euphoria levels within tolerable limits. L-Asparagine also releases energy that the brain and nervous system use for metabolism

- **L-Phenylatanine** is able to cross the blood-brain barrier, and as a result has a direct effect on brain chemistry. This amino acid, like others, converts to various forms and thus plays a role in alertness, elevate mood, decrease pain, aid in memory and learning capability, It has been used to treat depression, migraines, Parkinson's disease, and schizophrenia

- **L-Tryosine** is important to our overall metabolism. It is a precursor of adrenaline and the neurotransmitters norepinepthrine and dopamine. As such, it stimulates mood. A shortage of L-Tryosine in the nervous system contributes to depression, and low blood levels are associated with hypothyroidism. However, those who use MAO inhibitors should consult a physician before adding L-Tryosine supplements to their diet or eating foods rich in L-Tyrosine

- **TMG** reduces unusually high levels of homocysteine, and helps prevent Alzheimer's disease, improves memory, assists in preventing depression, lowers the risk of birth defects, and reduces the risk of heart disease and some forms of cancer

- **CoQ-10** (also see heart supplements) is a "must" supplement as it supports all systems in the body

- **L-Glutamine** is critical for normal brain and immune function. It helps build muscle, aids in the production of **Human Growth Hormone (*HGH*)**, and is effective as a part of bone marrow transplant therapy for cancer victims.

- **Zinc** aids in the detoxification of heavy metals stored in the body

- **NADH** protects the brain and improves memory. It is also an effective adjunctant treatment for Alzheimer's disease, and works as a preventative against Alzheimer's. NADH taken daily improves cognitive function and memory. Do not exceed two 5 mgs doses per day unless under the direction of a health care provider

- **Ginkgo Biloba** increases the nervous system's ability to transmit information. It also increases the capacity to problem solve by enhancing higher-order thinking

- **Magnesium** is essential for nerve cell regulation and plays a role in controlling the response of neurons. Magnesium is another "must take" supplement for the whole body health

- **Pregnenolone** boosts learning skills; it is thought by many researchers to be the most potent memory enhancing agent known to date

- **Phosphatidylserine** is exceptionally beneficial in treating memory impairment (***forgetfulness***)

- **Acetyl-L-Carnitine (*ALC*)** is considered one of, if not the best, supplement for memory disorders, especially Alzheimer's dementia. It enhances brain metabolism, slows down memory deterioration and reduces the production of free radicals

- **S-Adenosylmenthionine (*SAMe*)** lowers unusually elevated homocysteine levels. It is felt to be of value in treatment of Alzheimer's or other memory-related disorders. Do not take this supplement if you have a manic-depressive disorder or are on prescription anti-depressants

The Respiratory System

Respiration is a major body function. Breathing is the source of all life-sustaining energy. Breathing dictates emotional stability, health and happiness. A stressed person produces even more stress by breathing incorrectly. This type of individual will tend to breathe shallow and rapidly. This pitfall can be avoided by concentrating on slow, deep breathing to release stress and tension.

The respiratory system functions in conjunction with the circulatory system, as it provides hemoglobin with an appropriate environment for gas exchange. When the body is at rest, the body's breathing cycle starts. First, the nervous system detects an increase in carbon dioxide, which alters blood PH levels, is the primary stimulus for initiating breathing. The increase in CO_2 combine with the decrease in blood O_2 levels to stimulate afferent nerve impulses, which relay this information to the brain. The brain, in turn, fires efferent nerves in the lungs, which initiate inspiration of breathing gasses.

Stress and increased exercise levels also affect breathing rhythms. As our CO_2 level increases, a signal is sent to the "***inhalation***," or inspiratory, center in the medulla oblongata, which is located at the base of the brain, and controls autonomic functions by relaying nerve signals between the brain and spinal cord. In this case, the medulla oblongata transmits a signal telling the respiratory muscles to contract. When this happens, the diaphragm contracts, causing the lungs to expand. The lungs are composed of billions of alveoli which are coated with a surfactant-type protein substance. The alveoli are the final branchings of

the respiratory tree and act as the primary gas exchange units of the lung. This surfactant reduces surface tension. Surface tension maintains the shape of the alveoli as well as the lungs themselves.

Turbulent Versus Smooth Gas Flow

In order for inhalation to occur, the contraction of the respiratory muscles must overcome this surface tension. Upon relaxation of the muscles, the surface tension draws the lungs back to a "normal" shape and the chest and diaphragm follow this action. Inhalation and exhalation at rest is caused by the contraction and relaxation of respiratory muscles combined with alveolar surface tension.

The human respiratory system is a complex arrangement of tissue groups beginning with the nasal and oral cavities and extending to the diaphragm. When air is drawn down the trachea, or the airway that allows air to move from the throat to the lungs, the air is divided between the bronchi that serve the two lungs. The bronchi transport the air from the trachea to the lungs. The bronchi resemble branches of a tree, becoming smaller until they terminate into bronchioles which end in a series of tiny air sacs, or alveoli. Once initiated, inhalation continues until the stretch sensors within the lungs sense an adequate degree of expansion and the cycle is completed.

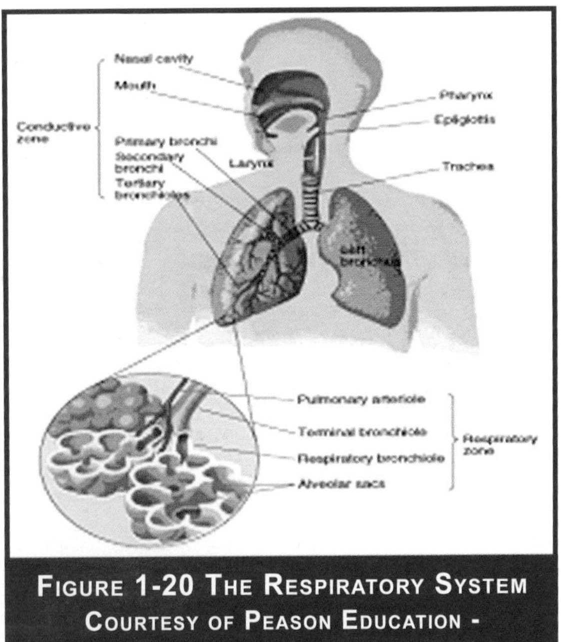

Figure 1-20 The Respiratory System
Courtesy of Peason Education - A Global Leader in Educational Publishing

During inhalation, gas traveling through an airway may meet frictional resistance caused by gas molecules bouncing off the trachea's walls. These molecules oppose the flow of additional gas, which results in a turbulent flow. Turbulent breathing patterns are inefficient and may lead to hyperventilation. Inadequate ventilation generates a sensation of gas starvation. If the autonomic nervous system reacts to this sensation, it will stimulate an increased breathing rate. In divers, turbulent breathing results in "gulping" gas. This pattern, if left unchecked, precipitates improper ventilation, producing stress, and, most certainly, ending in panic caused by the perception of a gas failure.

To avoid this reaction, it is important that divers be trained to inhale and exhale slowly. The volume should be deep and evenly paced. In other words, the respiratory rate and **Respiratory Minute Volume (*RMV*)** should be slow and deep. An RMV of this nature avoids turbulence, maintains Laminar flow, or the smooth flow of gas from the trachea through the lungs. Laminar flow assures the diver of proper ventilation. Deep, slow breathing causes a greater fraction of the tidal volume to enter the alveoli. Shallow breathing causes a smaller fraction of the tidal volume, or the amount of air breathed in or out during normal respiration, to enter the alveoli. Gas exchange does not begin until inhaled gas reaches the alveoli. A complex network of capillaries surround the alveoli, allowing O_2 from the lungs to enter the circulatory system. At the same time, CO_2 is transferred from the bloodstream and exhaled.

Blood & Breathing

Blood is a complex, multi-faceted liquid tissue that evolved to meet the complex demands placed on the circulatory system. Among its many functions are the supply of oxygen and nutritional materials to the body's cells, the removal of waste and waste gases, and the activation of the body's immune system.

The quantity of blood in the lungs is not evenly distributed, and it is gravity-dependent. When we are upright, more blood is in the lower portion of our lungs than in the middle and upper parts. Conversely, the flow of gases is at its peak in the upper portions of the lungs. Thus, gas transfer is not as efficient as one would assume. To provide gas to the lower third of the lungs and to their rich vascular network, slow, deep diaphragmatic breathing is essential. If the alveoli are injured due to a physical accident, they become inefficient.

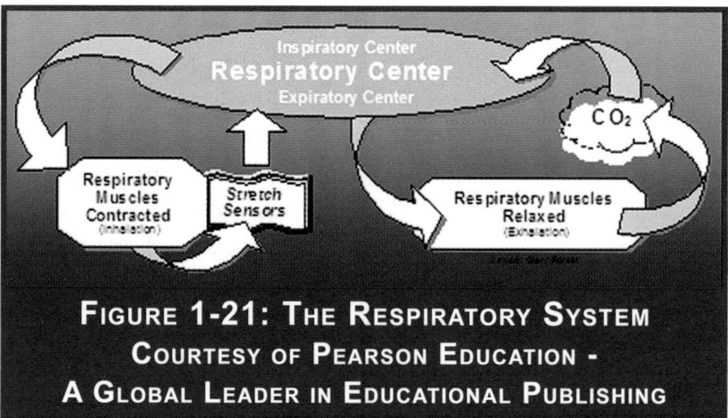

Figure 1-21: The Respiratory System Courtesy of Pearson Education - A Global Leader in Educational Publishing

Tobacco smokers (or smokers of other substances) will eventually lose pulmonary efficiency. This loss is called emphysema. Smoke produces a breakdown in the lining of the lungs, resulting in a "***visible hole.***" This hole reduces the amount of surface area available for oxygen to come into contact with blood across the alveoli. This decreases the amount of gas exchanged across the alveoli. To simplify, there is a significant difference between the lungs of a non-smoker and those of a smoker.

The diffusion of gases across the alveoli results from a difference in hydrostatic pressures. Upon inhalation, the gas in our lungs has a higher oxygen level than does the blood in the alveoli, causing a pressure difference that is equalized through gas exchange. Once in the alveoli, oxygen diffuses into the pulmonary capillaries. At this point, we have high oxygen pressure. Upon exhaling, the blood in our capillaries contains a reduced volume of oxygen. Moreover, the carbon dioxide (***PCO_2***) bonded to our hemoglobin is high. The pressure created by the increase in carbon dioxide forces the gas into our blood. The carbon dioxide buildup in our blood then enters the alveoli, where it is exhaled.

Red blood cells (erythrocytes) carry the majority of the oxygen required by the body's tissues. Red blood cells transport oxygen via hemoglobin, a molecule capable of easily bonding and unbonding with oxygen.

Once oxygen has been diffused into the pulmonary system, it is transported by two mechanisms. Some oxygen will remain in simple solution or blood plasma. However, most of the oxygen will bond to hemoglobin. Hemoglobin is composed of four protein chains attached to one atom of iron. It is the iron in hemoglobin that attracts oxygen. This enables the circulatory system to transport oxygen.

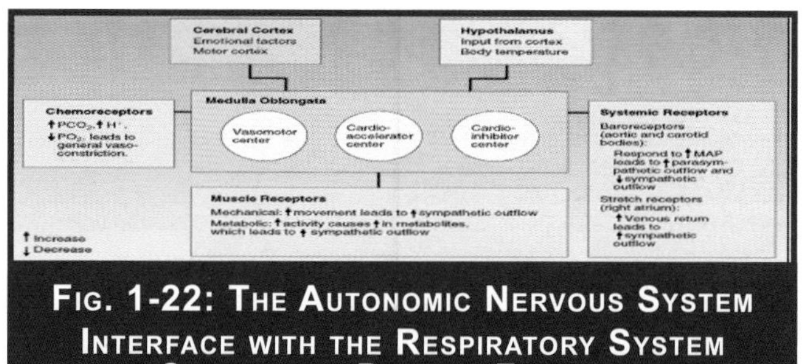

Fig. 1-22: The Autonomic Nervous System Interface with the Respiratory System Courtesy of Pearson Education

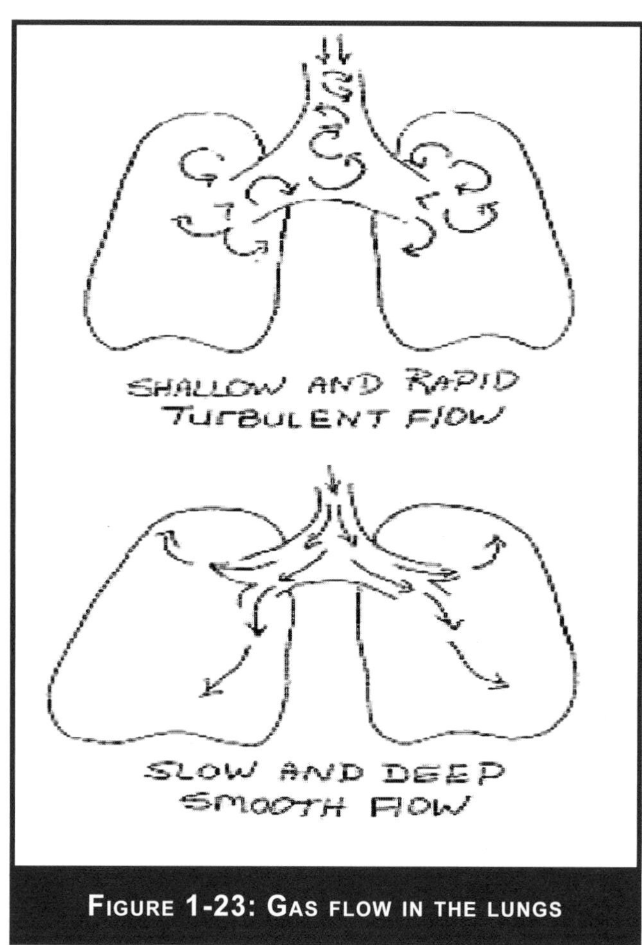

Figure 1-23: Gas flow in the lungs

Blood turns bright red when hemoglobin becomes oxygenated. People who have low hemoglobin levels are called anemic. People who suffer from severe anemia should be very cautious when diving. They should be especially careful when making deep dives, as the increased partial pressures of oxygen and carbon dioxide may complicate the anemic condition. Hemoglobin also transports carbon dioxide from the body's cells. This CO_2-enriched hemoglobin turns the blood a bluish color.

With proper gas supplies, the only gases that will combine with hemoglobin are oxygen and CO_2. However, if the gas supply contains carbon monoxide (***CO***), it will combine with hemoglobin 250 times more readily than O_2. In diving, CO poisoning generally originates from a contaminated air supply. It is colorless, odorless, and tasteless.

Carbon monoxide will not support life and renders one anemic and hypoxic quite rapidly. If unchecked, high levels of CO may lead to unconsciousness and possible death. Smokers can have 5% to 15% of their hemoglobin combined with CO. As depth increases, so does the partial pressures of all gases in the breathing medium. This compounds the effects of CO.

Respiration: Breathing

As inhaled gas diffuses across the alveoli, it travels from the capillaries in the lungs and enters the heart via the pulmonary veins. The heart pumps this oxygen-enriched blood via the arteries, where it then enters the capillaries and nourishes all the cells in the body. The body eliminates CO_2 by transporting it back to the lungs where it diffuses across the alveoli and is exhaled.

In addition to oxygen, blood transports nourishment absorbed from the body's digestive system. When the body's cells receive the oxygen and nourishment, a chemical reaction occurs, creating a type of "fuel." The fuel comes from the carbohydrates and fats we consume. Oxygen "burns" the fuel, producing energy. This reaction, which is known as metabolism, takes place within the cells in an area known collectively as mitochondria. Mitochondria contain specialized protein molecules, or enzymes. The particular type of enzyme that produces the fuel we are referring to is cytochrome oxidase. These enzymes take energy released from the oxidation of food (fuel) and transfer it to an energy storage molecule called adenosine triphosphate (***ATP***). ATP stores energy within our cells.

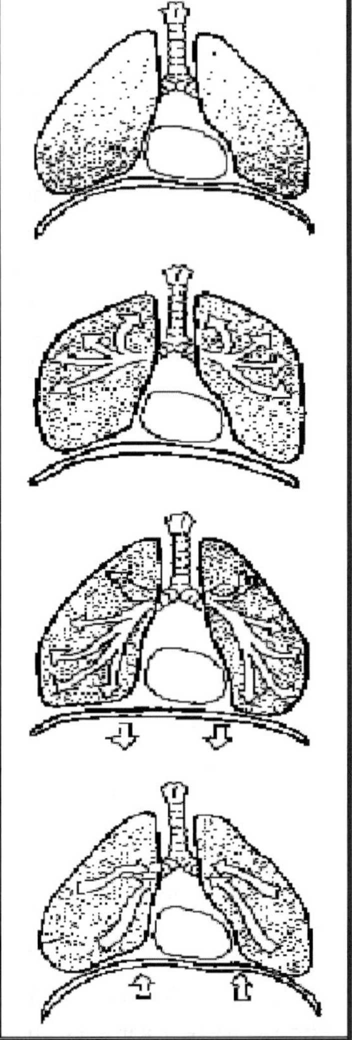

BLOOD DISTRIBUTION
The darker the area, the greater the concentration of blood available for gas exchange.
CHEST BREATHING
(INCORRECT)
Chest wall expands, pulling outward, creating a partial vacuum.
DIAPHRAGMATIC BREATHING
(CORRECT)
Diaphragm contracts pulling down (flat) creating a more complete vacuum that pulls air down into lowest lobes.
EXHALATION
Diaphragm relaxes flexing back into a dome-shape forcing air out of the lungs.

Fig. 1-24: The Interaction of Blood & Breathing

As energy is produced, wastes are generated and carbon dioxide, which is also considered a metabolic waste,is produced. Carbon comes from the food "burned" at the cell level in an oxygen-rich environment. The result is carbon dioxide. The pressure of CO_2 rises as a result of oxidation, which forces CO_2 into the venous capillaries. Larger and larger veins then transport the CO_2 until it is returned to the heart and the cycle begins again. If the body retains CO_2 or has a reduced capacity to eliminate it, it has an adverse physiological effect on the body.

Respiration at Depth

Divers must compensate for gas density as they dive deeper. The typical ANS response to increasing gas density is to breathe faster, which is a reaction that increases turbulence in the airways. This in turn leads to reduced breathing efficiency. As the water depth or workload increases, it becomes important for the diver to discipline him-or her-self to maintain slow, deep breathing. There are some techniques that may help improve breathing habits. While swimming, experiment with a swim pace that balances pace with the ability to maintain a slow, deep breathing pattern. Swimming faster than this is inefficient, as it alters one's breathing pattern, which could cause increased turbulence in one's airway, possibly leading to an inadequate gas supply to the alveoli.

Frequently, divers will accelerate their swim pace under stress. This may lead to a loss of breathing control. Conversely, divers in an air-sharing situation will drastically slow their pace. This could leave them with insufficient gas to reach the surface. Therefore, the aware diver's conscious reaction to a gas sharing situation should be to maintain a normal pace that allows a balanced swimming pace in harmony with safe breathing patterns.

Surface breathing is usually done through the nose. It takes up to 150% more effort to pull gas through the nose than the mouth. Nasal breathing filters, moisturizes, directs gas flow, warms and conditions the gas, produces the sense of smell, brings in oxygen, creates mucus, provides drainage for the sinuses and affects the nervous system. However, the diver must be equally capable of mouth breathing as nasal breathing. If breathing through the mouth leads to a sense of discomfort, stress will enhance that feeling, which could lead to situations where the diver, in a state of high anxiety, dispenses with his or her regulator in order to return to the more natural nasal breathing. Spitting out regulators when tanks are full is not uncommon among panicked divers.

Supplements for the Respiratory System

- **Astragalus** is excellent for bronchial irritation and the treatment of chronic bronchitis. It is a long-term immune tonic, so it is ideal for boosting the immune system when the body is under duress It is effective in preventing colds, allergies, upper respiratory infections. It also works well with people who are subject to asthma, and is beneficial in treating edema. Its ability to activate immune cells such as macrophages, or natural "killer" cells known to destroy cancer cells has made it popular among those who have cancer
- **Bee Pollen** is excellent for hay fever. Many people find it to be their first choice when a hay fever attack starts. It is useful for treating allergies, depression, and for increasing energy and endurance. A few people are allergic to Bee Pollen, so if used, make a gradual introduction; should any negative reaction occur, discontinue use.
- **Elderberry Defense** is effective against the flu and upper respiratory infections
- **Echinacea** boosts the efficacy of our immune systems. It is ideal for use with colds, as it speeds recovery, minimizes symptoms, and fights mild infections
- **Golden Seal** has numerous uses that attributed to its antibiotic, anti-inflammatory, and astringent properties. It soothes irritated mucus membranes, aiding the eyes, ears, nose, and throat. Take at the first signs of respiratory problems, colds, or flu
- **Herbal Teas**, such as Elderflower, relieves cold symptoms and sinus problems

The Role of Potential Hydrogen Imbalance on PH; Health & Safety Underwater

Rebreather use, and the possible flooding of absorbent canisters possibly leading to a "***caustic cocktail***," which occurs when a mixture of water and soda lime enters the rebreather diver's "breathing loop," breathing mixed gases, and switching gases, may have localized or systemic effects on the body's PH level. Therefore, the diver of today must understand what changes PH and how a change in PH may affect the diver underwater and on the surface.

Our blood PH has a great influence on health. Moreover, our reactivity to changes in systemic or local PH levels is on a continuum from nil to catastrophic. Divers expose themselves to numerous environmental elements that may affect local or systemic PH levels. Changes in PH levels can be life threatening. Severe metabolic alkalosis, defined as a blood PH >7.55, is a serious medical problem. Researchers

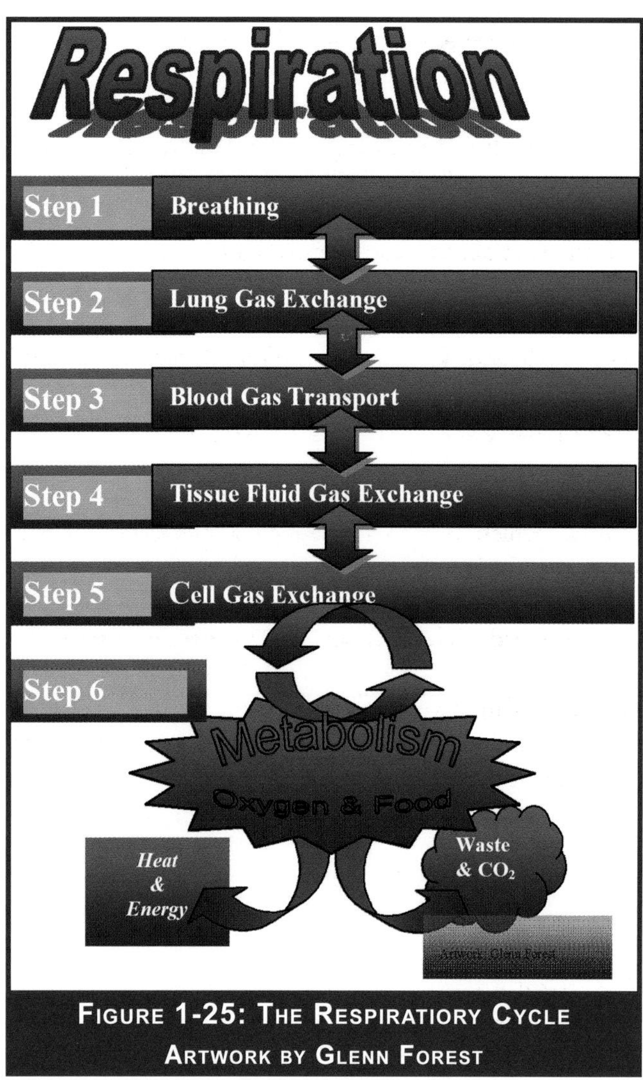

Figure 1-25: The Respiratiory Cycle
Artwork by Glenn Forest

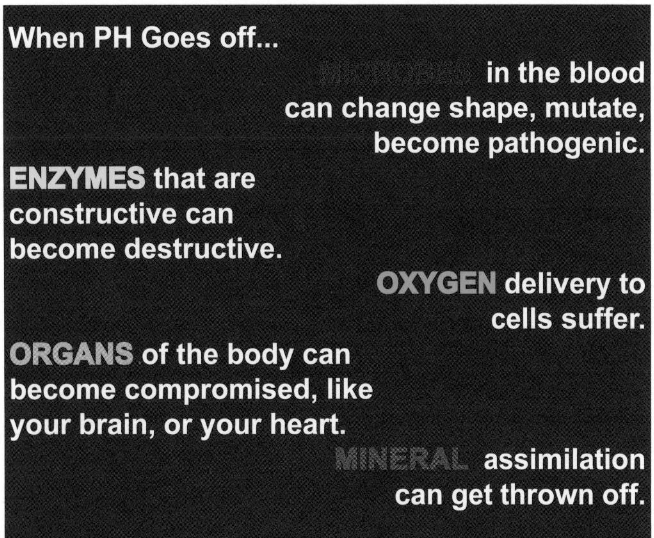

When PH Goes off...

MICROBES in the blood can change shape, mutate, become pathogenic.

ENZYMES that are constructive can become destructive.

OXYGEN delivery to cells suffer.

ORGANS of the body can become compromised, like your brain, or your heart.

MINERAL assimilation can get thrown off.

Figure 1-26: The effects of PH on the body

report mortality rates as high as 45% in patients with an arterial blood PH of 7.55, and such rates jump to the 80% range when blood PH is greater than 7.65. On a scale of 0-14, an extremely severe caustic cocktail could raise metabolic alkaline levels to between 7 and 13.

Metabolic alkalosis is almost always associated with hypokalemia, or low calcium levels, which can cause neuromuscular weakness and arrhythmias, and, by increasing ammonia production, it can precipitate hepatic encephalopathy, or kidney failure, in susceptible individuals. Alkalosis also suppresses coronary blood flow, thereby lowering the threshold for anginal symptoms and again increasing the chance of cardiac arrhythmias. Moreover, alkalosis decreases cerebral blood flow, which may lead to delirium, seizures, and decreased mental status. In addition, metabolic alkalosis causes hypoventilation, which may lead to hypoxemia, or deficiency in the concentration of oxygen in arterial blood. High alkaline levels are also associated with headaches, lethargy, and neuromuscular excitability.

With high PH values, our immune system becomes less efficient. While the immune system assists us in warding off normal disease it also determines our resistance to diving related "***illnesses***." If our acid content is too great, we may be predisposed to oxygen toxicity. Moreover, as PH effects respiration and gas transport, PH may play a role in all diving maladies, including decompression illness and inert gas narcosis. A wise diver will try to maintain a diet an exercise program to ensure PH remains in the 7 to 7.4 range. A simple manner to track ones PH is to use PH strips and do test periodically. PH strips may be found from a variety of sources on the internet and at many health food stores.

Moreover, mild, yet chronic PH imbalances relate to various disease states. Steven Charles, Director of Biomedx, an online resource for bioengineering and biotechnology students, has a very informative article available on the Biomedx website regarding PH regulation and its effect on human physiology. **According to him:**

The PH Regulatory System of the Body

"PH... is the degree of concentration of hydrogen ions in a substance or solution. It is measured on a logarithmic scale from 0 to 14. Higher numbers mean a substance is more alkaline in nature and there is a greater potential for absorbing more hydrogen ions. Lower numbers indicate more acidity with less potential for absorbing hydrogen ions... PH controls the speed of our body's biochemical reactions ... by controlling the speed of enzyme activity as well as the speed that electricity moves through our body."

The Disease Paradigm Shift

"...most disease is caused by some imbalance in the body. The imbalance occurs in some nutritional, electrical, structural, toxicological, or biological equation... The human body strives to maintain the PH of the blood at around 7.3. Above or below this level, the colloids in your blood merge into forms... One contention is that these forms constitute pathogenic microbes... that affect immune function.

...According to many health researchers, total healing of chronic illness takes place only when and if the blood is restored to a normal, slightly alkaline PH... The magnitude of meaning behind this research is of incredible importance to someone who is fighting a disease, overcoming an illness, or just desiring to feel better... When PH goes off, microbial forms in the blood can change shape, mutate, mirror pathogenicity, and grow ... enzymes that are constructive can become destructive... and oxygen delivery to cells suffers. More and more research is showing that low oxygen delivery to cells is a major factor in most if not all degenerative conditions. Nobel laureate, Dr. Otto Warburg of Germany, won his Nobel Prize for his discovery of oxygen deficiency in the cancer growth process... Cancer thrives under an acid tissue PH/

oxygen deficient environment.

As the PH of the blood goes more acid, fatty acids, which are normally electro-magnetically charged on the negative side switch to positive and automatically are attracted to and begin to stick to the walls of arteries, which are electro-magnetically charged on the negative side… When the body has an excess of acid it can't get rid of, the acid gets stored for later removal in the interstitial spaces, or the spaces around the cells. If the body has an acid overload, it stores the acid in the tissues… and the blood compensates and becomes alkaline.

Minerals on the lower end of the atomic scale can be assimilated in a wider PH range, and minerals higher up on the scale require a narrower PH range in order to be assimilated by the body. For example, sodium and magnesium have wide PH assimilation ranges. It narrows somewhat for calcium and potassium, and more for iodine… Iodine is one of the most important minerals for proper functioning of the thyroid. Malfunctioning thyroids are connected to arthritis, heart attacks, diabetes, cancer, depression, overweight, fatigue and more.

With rising alkalinity, blood can increase its oxygen uptake; therefore, the blood cells can hold more oxygen… The Bohr effect states that with rising blood alkalinity, the red blood cells can saturate themselves with ever more oxygen. The problem is, they can't let go of it! If the blood cells can't let go of oxygen, then the oxygen isn't getting down to the other cells of the body… This state could be termed an anaerobic or overly anabolic condition. The opposite state… would see blood shifting to the acid side... This leads to an anaerobic or overly catabolic condition."

Smoking & Respiratory Health

The lungs, which consist of alveoli, are divided into five lobes. The right lung contains three lobes and the left lung has two lobes. If all the alveoli that compose the lungs were laid out on land, they would cover more than half of a tennis court. The airways connecting the lungs to the nasal passage and mouth are lined with thin, membranous cells called "***ciliated epithelial***" cells. The cilia, which are small or microscopic hairs, prevent pollutants and dirt laden particles from entering the lungs.

When a person smokes, there is an immediate effect on the nervous, circulatory and respiratory systems. One early effect is to paralyze the cilia's actions. A single cigarette will stop cilia action for 20 minutes. Smoking also causes an immediate increase in mucus production and interferes with oxygen uptake. Moreover, smoking creates a faster respiratory rate. This increased respiratory rate combined with density at depth leads to turbulent airflow, which increases the work of breathing and, as stated before, causes carbon monoxide (***CO***) to bind with the blood. Moreover, the CO released into the lungs by lighting a cigarette displaces the oxygen in hemoglobin. CO combines with hemoglobin 210 times more readily than oxygen.

Further, smoking causes the heart to work harder, thereby producing a higher pulse rate and increasing blood pressure. At the same time, blood flow decreases, due to the constriction of blood vessels reacting to tobacco smoke. This eventually predisposes one to heart disease, but more immediately, increases a diver's susceptibility to decompression sickness, as it reduces circulatory efficiency. Smoking also creates a reaction that causes a drop in body temperature.

One additional risk that divers who smoke face is the possibility of mucus plugs trapping gas and behaving as if it were a gas bubble. In addition, these plugs form a base for bubble attachment and may prevent the lungs from filtering bubbles. Given the smoker's characteristic lung congestion combined with damaged alveoli, there is a marked probability of gas trapping and a higher risk of pulmonary barotrauma.

A Prescription for Diving Health

As stated at the outset, this chapter contains information

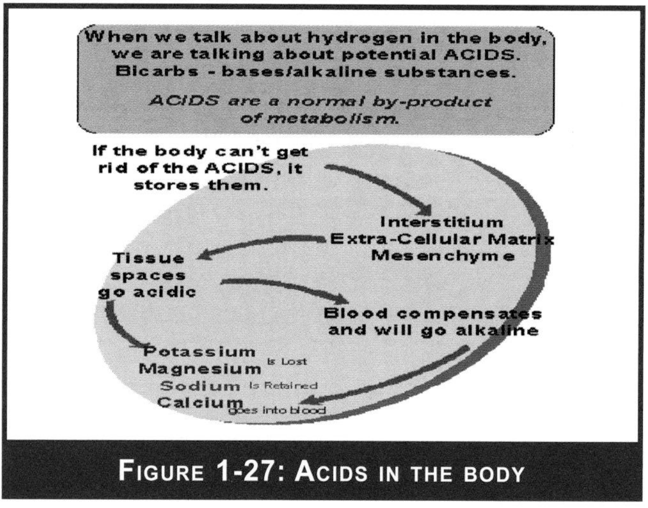

FIGURE 1-27: ACIDS IN THE BODY

!Tom Mount's note: "*Anaerobic*" is a technical term for '"without air;" "*anabolic*" refers to cell growth and differentiation, and "*catabolic*" is the metabolic process that breaks molecules down into smaller units.

from two worlds: Western science and Eastern metaphysical doctrines. Keeping an open mind, digesting all that is essential to your personal needs, learning how to breathe correctly, and continuing to practice correct breathing techniques will help you become a better diver and quite possibly improve your health. We're certain you'll be amazed at the overall results.

If we eat correctly, avoid smoking cigarettes and other substances, keep alcohol consumption to no more than one to two ounces a day, and exercise daily, we will enjoy both a safer dive and better overall health. Many common diseases derive from a failure to take the basic preventative steps necessary to ensure good health. Although it is our choice to be fit or unfit, the more fit we are, the safer our dives will be. Choose to smoke a cigarette, eat a donut, and drown the donut with a six-pack of beer or a couple shots of whiskey, and you will eventually discover the ills such behaviors bring to your body. Conversely, you can be moderate in your habits, avoid cigarettes, exercise regularly, limit alcohol intake and enjoy a healthier lifestyle. It isn't just the benefit of feeling good day to day; the increased resistance to diving related injuries that a fit and smoke free lifestyle will reward you is more than worth the effort.

Other Supplements of Interest to Divers

As a health guard, supplements may prove a valuable resource for divers. Most supplements and the majority of herbs do not have adverse side effects. However, many of both do have negative interactions with certain drugs. For those who are taking prescription medication, a consult with a health practitioner, such as a medical doctor, naturopathic doctor, osteopathic physician, energy practitioner, homeopath, or herbologist. In this chapter, we have included numerous supplements and herbs that benefit various systems within the body, some of which may provide additional buffering from dive related injuries such as DCI. From a decompression-diving viewpoint, the supplements that promote healthy blood vessels are ideal. Below are additional supplements divers in particular may find beneficial.

- **Silymarin** protects the liver and may be helpful in treating cirrhosis and other forms of liver damage. Studies reflect that patients taking Silymarin live longer than those who did not. These patients also enjoyed better health in addition to longevity
- **Phosphatidylcholine (*PC*)** supports liver functions and, according to numerous studies, reverses and heals liver damage
- **Cynarin** lowers blood lipids and also enhances liver function. It is related to Milk thistle
- **Milk Thistle** is an excellent liver tonic. It is widely used by those who have liver damage, as it stimulates liver repair and cleansing
- **Saw Palmetto** is a supplement all men over 40 should take as an aid to keep the prostate healthy
- **Lycopine** reduces the risk of prostate cancer
- **SAMe** is an excellent antidepressant which also reduces joint pain
- **Organic Lithium** calms and provides a relaxing mood. This supplement is useful for depression and other psychological disorders

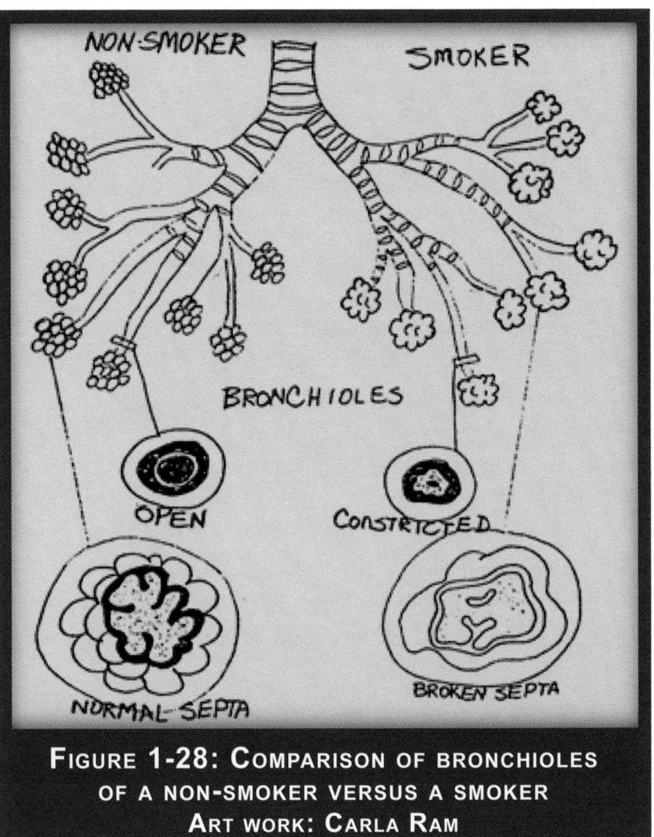

Figure 1-28: Comparison of bronchioles of a non-smoker versus a smoker
Art work: Carla Ram

- **5 HTP** may replace Prozac, as it works as an antidepressant with adjunctive appetite suppressant effects. Moreover, 5 HTP promotes sleep. However, take this supplement on an empty stomach
- **Rutin** is good for bruises
- **Arnica** is tremendous for reducing the swelling and pain caused by muscle injuries and strains (my martial arts students and one of my editors and divers, who tends to fall off her trail bike, "live" on this)
- **N-Acetyl Cysteine (*NAC*)** increases glutathione and assists in preventing ear and lung infections. It also speeds up recovery from exercise
- **Monolaurin** fights viral infections
- **Lacteferrin** is a natural antibiotic
- **Hudroxyapatite** is good for burns
- **Malic Acid** is useful for the treating fibromyalgia, a chronic condition noted for widespread pain
- **DeglycerrhizinetedLicorice**isananti-inflammatory agent
- **Lycine** is good for keeping skin tone, may prevent herpes, and helps control herpes reoccurrences. The standard dosage is 500 to 1000 mgs per day
- **Lutien** is good for the eyes; most people would benefit from its use
- **Alpha Lipoic Acid** reduces free radicals, protects diabetics from free radical damage, enhances workouts, and is a treatment for strokes, which can be caused by clots interrupting blood flow to the brain, brain bleeds, or a sudden, transient loss of the blood supply to the brain
- **Grape Seed Extract** is useful for toe and finger fungus and also fights yeast infections
- **EMU Oil** helps heal bruises and cuts when rubbed onto the injured surface
- **Eldeberry Extract** is good for influenza attacks and head-colds
- **DHEA** is necessary only if blood work indicates a need for this supplement

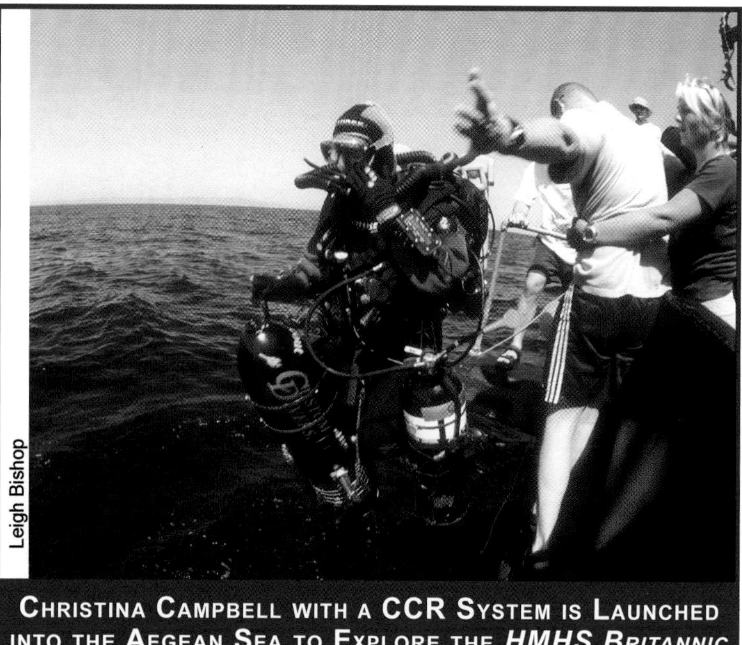
Leigh Bishop

CHRISTINA CAMPBELL WITH A CCR SYSTEM IS LAUNCHED INTO THE AEGEAN SEA TO EXPLORE THE ***HMHS BRITANNIC***

- **DHA** is a strong immune enhancer, but should not be taken if someone has prostate or breast cancer
- **Maca Herb** improves energy; and is nature's version of Viagra. It is also known as "***Peruvian Ginseng***." Maca is also used for anemia, tuberculosis, menstrual disorders, menopause symptoms, stomach cancer, and sterility. Maca also stimulates the immune system, and enhances memory. Moreover, it can stabilize blood pressure, boost immunity, and increase the body's overall vitality

A Word to the Wise

It is highly recommended that prior to undertaking a complete supplement regimen a comprehensive set of blood work with ultra cellular testing, a PH check, and urine samples is completed in order to note which supplements will be of the greatest benefit. As a rule, taking inadequate or inappropriate types and or amounts of supplements may not harm, but could be a waste of effort and money. For general usage consider a multi vitamin combined with Vitamin C at 500 mgs per day, a calcium-magnesium supplement, CoQ-10 at 60 mgs per day, and Vitamin E at 400 IUs per day. The most effective method for determining which supplements one needs is to visit your health care provider for a full work-up of blood, urine, and PH levels.

References

- Barry Sears Ph.D., Enter The Zone, Harper and Collins 10 East 53rd St., NY, NY 10022
- Bach A. Phyllis CNC, Prescription for Nutritional Healing 4th Edition, 2006, Penguin Group, NY, NY
- Comroe, Forster, Briscoe, Carlsen, The Lung, 1964, Year Book Medical Publishers Inc., Chicago, IL
- Drs. Eades Power Protein Plan, The, Colorado Center for Metabolic Medicine, 7490 Clubhouse Rd., CO
- Dr. Duarte's Health Alternatives, Alex Duarte, O.D. Ph.D., 10175 Joerschke Drive #335, Grass Valley, CA 95945
- Health Rider
- Giese, Cell Physiology, 1962, W.B. Saunders Co., Philadelphia, PA
- Mindell Earl, Supplement Bible, 1998, Fireside, NY, NY
- Null Gary Ph.D., The Complete Encyclopedia of Natural Healing • Updated & Revised, 2005, Bottom Line Books, Stamford, CT
- Peskin, Peamk, Performance Radiant Health Moving Beyond The Zone, 2001, Noble Publishing, Houston, TX
- Nuernberger Phil Ph.D., Freedom From Stress, Himalayan International Institute of Yoga RD 1 Box 88, Honesdale, PA 18431
- Stengler N.D., Proven Remedies That Medical Doctors Don't Know - The Natural Physicans Healing Therapies, 2001, Prentice Hall, NY, NY
- Swami Rama, Rudolph Ballentine MD, and Alan Hymes MD, Science of Breath: International Institute of Yoga, RD 1 Box 88 Honesdale, PA 18431
- Tom Mount, Practical Diving, 1973 University of Miami Press - out of print
- Tom Mount, The New Practical Diving, 1976, University of Miami Press - out of print
- Tom Mount et al, Mixed Gas Diving, 1994, Watersports Publishing - out of print
- Tom Mount, The Technical Diver Encyclopedia, 1998, IANTD Miami, FL - out of print
- Life Extension Magazine February/March 2008, Ft. Lauderale, FL 32008

E-References ~ Anatomy & Physiology

- http://training.seer.cancer.gov/module_anatomy/anatomy_physiology_home.html
- http://images.search.yahoo.com/search/images/view?back=http%3A%2F%2Fsearch.yahoo.com%2Fsearch%3Fp%3Dpicture%2Bof%2Bthe%2Bcentral%2Bnervous%2Bsystem%26toggle%3D1%26cop%3Dmss%26ei%3DUTF-8&h=239&w=319&imgcurl=
- http://training.seer.cancer.gov/module_anatomy/anatomy_physiology_home.html
- www.drstandley.com%2Fbodysystems_centralnervous.shtml&rurl=http%3A%2F%2F
- www.healthatoz.com/healthatoz/Atoz/common/standard/transform.jsp?requestURI=/healthatoz/Atoz/ency/fibrinogen_test.jsp
- www.freewebtown.com/provenbrands/data/aerobics-cardio/35374.html
- www.drstandley.com%2Fimages%2Fbrain4.bmp&size=75.7kB&name=brain4.bmp&rcurl=http%3A%2F%2F
- www.bodybuilding.com/fun/moser9.htm
- www.wikihow.com/Calculate-Your-Target-Heart-Rate
- www.heartmonitors.com/zone_calc.htm
- www.rajeun.net/vo2max.html
- www.nismat.org/physcor/max_o2.html
- http://formulafitness.ca/vo2max.htm#impatient
- http://greenfield.fortunecity.com/rattler/46/autonomic.htm
- www.jdaross.cwc.net/nervousframe.htm
- http://faculty.washington.edu/chudler/introb.html
- www.drstandley.com%2Fimages%2Fbrain4.bmp&imgurl=
- www.drstandley.com%2Fbodysystems_centralnervous
- www.ama-assn.org/ama/pub/category/7152.html
- http://en.wikipedia.org/wiki/Blood_plasma

Chapter Two
Inert Gas Narcosis

David J. Doolette Ph.D.

DIVERS PREPARING FOR A WRECK DIVE OFF THE COAST OF MIAMI - L TO R, DIRECTOR IANTD KOREA: JANG-HWA HONG, ERIC COOPER & IT GEORGES GAWINOWSKI

Introduction

The narcotic effects of breathing compressed air at depths greater than 100 fsw (30 msw)[1] are probably familiar to most divers. The collection of neurological effects from breathing air at high pressure, including intoxication, slowing of mental processes and reduced manual dexterity are generally referred to as ***nitrogen narcosis***. Such effects can be produced by breathing many other inert gases[2] in addition to nitrogen, so the condition is more generally known as inert gas narcosis. After describing the signs and symptoms of inert gas narcosis, this chapter will show that such narcosis can be interpreted as the effects of anesthesia prior to unconsciousness. Although the underlying mechanisms of narcosis and anesthesia are not completely understood, a number of features of both theoretical and practical interest will be presented, including features other than inert gas partial pressure which modify narcosis.

Historical Descriptions

Intoxication of caisson workers and divers was noted by the middle of the 19th century when engineering advances allowed work at sufficiently elevated pressure. The seminal work describes the narcotic effect of deep air diving dates from the 1930s. Narcosis was encountered during the first Royal Navy deep air diving trials to 300 fsw (91 msw) and was appropriately described as a "slowing of cerebration" or "as if ... under an anesthetic," but was at that time attributed to "mental instability" in some deep diving candidates (Hill and Phillips, 1932). The role of raised inspired partial pressure of nitrogen in producing narcosis was suspected by 1935, and the use of an alternative breathing gas mixture to eliminate narcosis was proposed[3] (Behnke et al., 1935). Since then, the threshold pressure for air diving that consistently produces a decrement in diver performance has been considered to be 4 ATA [100 fsw (30 msw)]. Confirmation of the role of nitrogen in narcosis came with the report of Max Nohl's 410 ffw (128 mfw) fresh water dive using a Heliox Rebreather of his own design (End, 1938).

Signs and Symptoms of Inert Gas Narcosis & Behavioral Modification

Classification of Signs & Symptoms

Inert gas narcosis is an alteration of function of the nervous system that produces behavioral modifications that may impair a diver's ability to work effectively or even survive. In order to recognize all the potential performance impairments resulting from inert gas narcosis and to help understand the causes of narcosis, it is useful to classify the various effects. Behnke originally divided the effects of narcosis into three categories: emotional reactions, impairment of higher mental processes and impairment of neuromuscular control (Behnke et al., 1935). A similar classification is used here: subjective sensations, impaired cognitive function, slowed mental activity and impaired neuromuscular coordination.

The effects of inert gas narcosis on cognitive function includes:

- **Difficulty assimilating facts**
- **Slowed and inaccurate thought processes**
- **Memory loss**

In the laboratory, inert gas narcosis is measured by tests for impaired cognitive function including:

- **Conceptual reasoning**
- **Sentence comprehension**
- **Mental arithmetic ability**
- **Short-term memory**

Subjective Sensations

Subjective sensations are the sensations that any diver would associate with inert gas narcosis. These include euphoria, intoxication hyper-confidence, recklessness and various altered states of consciousness and attention. Subjective sensations of inert gas narcosis can be assessed using questionnaires asking for a global estimate of the magnitude of narcosis and responses to adjectives, checklists describing work capability (for instance, ability to work, alertness, concentration) and body/mental sensations (for instance, intoxicated, reckless, dreamy, uninhibited) (Hamilton et al., 1992; Hamilton et al., 1995).

Slowed Mental Activity

In addition to increased errors in cognitive function tests, narcosis significantly reduces the speed at which such problems are solved. Apparently information processing in the central nervous system is slowed, and this can be measured in two ways: the rate at which test problems are attempted, or by testing reaction time. Reaction time measures the time between receiving a sensory signal and reacting with the appropriate response and represents the speed of higher mental processes, particularly decision making. Inert gas narcosis slows the reaction time. In a typical laboratory reaction time test one of a series of LEDs is illuminated and the time until it is extinguished by pushing its matched microswitch is measured.

Reduced Neuromuscular Coordination

Neuromuscular coordination (***manual dexterity***)[4] is impaired by inert gas narcosis, but usually only at greater depths than the intellectual impairments described above. Neuromuscular coordination is often assessed by peg board and screw board tests that involve assembly and disassembly of patterns of nuts, bolts and pegs.

Inert Gas Narcosis at Extreme Depth on Air

Air breathing at depths greater than 300 fsw (91 msw) produces altered states of consciousness including manic or depressive states, hallucinations, time disorganization and lapses of consciousness[5].

Thermoregulation

In addition to the obvious actions of narcosis on brain activity, other body activities are affected as a result of changes in the nervous system. Of particular importance

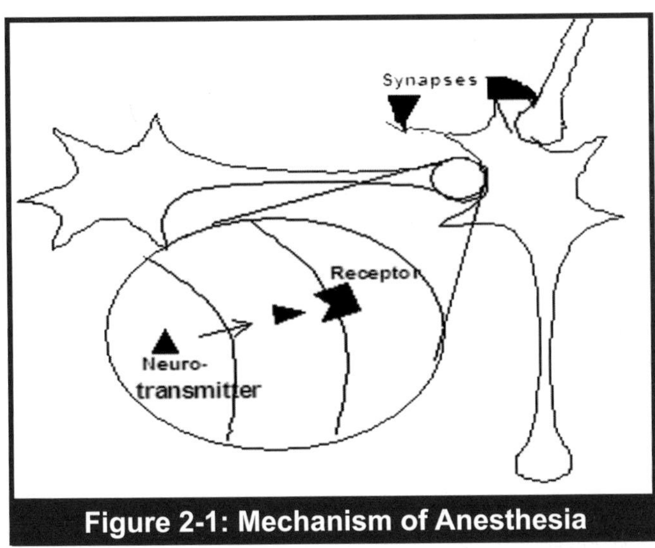

Figure 2-1: Mechanism of Anesthesia

to divers, but less widely known, is the distortion caused by inert gas narcosis of the physiological and behavioral control of body core temperature (***thermoregulation***). Narcosis reduces shivering and therefore the production of body heat (***shivering thermogenesis***), the main defense against body cooling. As a result, narcosis allows a more rapid drop in body core temperature than expected during cold water (Mekjavic et al., 1995). Additionally, despite body core cooling, perceived thermal comfort is greater with narcosis than otherwise expected. (Mekjavic et al., 1994). As a result, the diver may neglect to take action to reduce heat loss (***behavioral thermoregulation)***.

Mechanism of Inert Gas Narcosis Anesthesia

It is apparent that the signs and symptoms of inert gas narcosis result from an alteration of the function of the nervous system. It was noted prior that breathing air at depths greater than 300 fsw (91 msw) produces lapses of consciousness. At much greater depths, air will cause complete unconsciousness (***anesthesia***)[6]. Indeed, many of the inert gases will produce anesthesia, each such gas having a characteristic anesthetic potency. For instance, the approximate inspired partial pressure required to produce anesthesia for nitrogen is 33 ATA, for argon is 15 ATA, for nitrous oxide is 1.5 ATA and for halothane[7] is 0.008 ATA. (Smith, 1986). Some inert gases, notably helium and neon, have no practical anesthetic potency. Owing to its similarity with anesthesia, inert gas narcosis is now generally accepted to be a manifestation of the effects of anesthetic gases at sub-anesthetic doses (***incipient anesthesia)***. The severity of narcosis increases as the inspired partial pressure of the inert gas approaches the anesthetic level.

Different Inert Gases & Anesthetics Produce Identical Narcosis

The narcotic effects of the inert gases and other anesthetics are identical. In specific test of narcosis in either monkeys or humans, argon, nitrogen, nitrous oxide and other general anesthetics have identical effects (although at different partial pressures). Nitrous oxide, which is sufficiently potent to produce narcosis at the surface, has been used extensively in laboratory tests to simulate nitrogen narcosis.

Mechanism of Anesthesia

The mechanism by which any anesthetics, including the inert gases, produce anesthesia is not entirely understood. However, it is widely accepted that the site of anesthesia and narcosis are the synapses in the central nervous system[8]. The majority of drugs which act on the nervous system work by modifying chemical synaptic transmission (see Figure 2-1). Anesthetics enhance the action of a variety of the inhibitory neurotransmitters (particularly ***GABA***) at their specific post-synaptic receptors[9], resulting in a reduced frequency of action potentials. Such depression of central nervous system activity ultimately produces anesthesia. Synapses (enlarged in Figure 2-1) between neurons. Signals in the brain are carried along neurons in the form of an electrical potential called an action potential.Signals are transmitted across the synapse between neurons by chemicals called neurotransmitters, released in response to an action potential. Neurotransmitters combine with specific receptor proteins on the post-synaptic (***target***) neuron. Some neurons release inhibitory neurotransmitters which make the target neuron less likely to fire an action potential while other neurons release excitatory transmitter which make the target neurons more likely to fire an action potential.

Meyer-Overton Correlation & the Critical Volume Hypothesis

Early hypotheses of anesthetic mechanisms pre-date the discovery of chemical synaptic transmission. The most famous of these is the Meyer-Overton correlation, which originated at the turn of this century. Meyer (1899) and later Overton (1902) noticed that there exists a remarkably strong correlation between an anesthetic's potency and its solubility in olive oil. The Meyer-Overton hypothesis states that anesthesia occurs with certain molar concentration of a compound in the lipid (***fat***) of a cell[10]. An elaboration of this hypothesis was proposed by Mullins[11] (1954), and states that narcosis occurs as the volume of some hydrophobic site[12] (probably lipid) expands due to uptake of inert substance (Smith, 1986). It is implied in both these hypotheses that the lipid site is the neuronal cell membrane and that anesthetics work by dissolving in the cell membrane and disrupting the voltage-gated ion channels which allow the neuron to conduct electrical impulses[13].

It is no longer widely believed that the membrane voltage-gated ion channels are the site of anesthesia because evidence has accumulated that any effects of anesthetics on neuronal membranes are physiologically insignificant. Anesthetics may act by occupying hydrophobic pockets inside the neurotransmitter receptor proteins[14] and it is not altogether surprising that a strong correlation exists between anesthetic potency and hydrophobicity. Also, the receptors are embedded in the cell membrane and lipophilic compounds will diffuse rapidly through the membrane and reach high concentration surrounding the receptors. Additionally, lipid soluble compounds readily cross the blood-brain-barrier. So, rather than explaining anesthesia, the Meyer-Overton hypothesis is a useful, incidental relationship. Indeed, it was the low lipid solubility of helium that originally suggested it be tested as a non-narcotic breathing gas diluent (Behnke, et al., 1935).

Narcosis Produces Slowed Mental Processing

Many of the actions of narcosis can be attributed to slowed information processing in the central nervous system. The slowed processing model is a useful tool to understand and investigate narcosis (Fowler et al., 1985). The slowed processing model suggests that decreased arousal due to the anesthetic properties of inert gases slows the processing of information in the central nervous system and results in the some of the behavioral modifications typical of inert gas narcosis. In order to understand this model one must consider the underlying model of information processing and then how it is affected by narcosis.

Information Processing Model

Information processing occurs in a series of stages. For instance, a simple information processing task such as a reaction time involves a perceptual and evaluation stage, a decision making stage and an effector stage. An example of a reaction time is the delay between seeing a red stop light while driving and applying the brakes. Recognizing a red stop light amongst the thousands of other stimuli occurs in the

perceptual and evaluation stage. The decision whether or not to brake, involving calculating speed, distance and chance of a collision, occurs in the decision making stage. Activating the neuromotor programs to operate the leg muscles occurs in the effector stage. There are three aspects of such a system that could be influenced by narcosis. Firstly, is the structure of the system. Each information processing stage occurs in a different brain area and narcosis could disturb those areas. Secondly, the functional aspect of this model is the overall performance of the system due to the speed of information processing at each stage. Within limits, decreasing the speed of information handling at any stage impairs performance. Thirdly, the strategy for information handling includes distribution of attention, decision criteria, rehearsal strategies, and speed-accuracy trade-offs.

Functional Component

Slowed processing of information due to inert gas narcosis is evident in laboratory tests of cognitive function where the number of problems attempted is reduced (Hesser, et al., 1978; Fothergill, et al., 1991) and in increased reaction time (Hamilton, et al., 1995; Fowler, et al., 1986; Fowler et al., 1993). Considerable experimental data indicates that narcosis produces a general functional deficit rather than distorting the structural components[15] (Fowler, et al., 1986; Fowler, et al., 1985). This functional deficit can be explained as slowed processing at any of the stages owing to decreased arousal (decreased general level of brain activity) or reduced activation (reduced readiness for activity). It is now thought that narcosis may influence multiple processing stages. Reaction time tests in combination with recording of brain electrical events indicate that slowed processing by narcosis seems to involve both slowing of the perceptual evaluation stage and also reduction of motor readiness at a later effector stage (Fowler, et al., 1993). The notion of narcosis resulting from slowed processing is supported by the effects of amphetamine which increase arousal and reduce the effects of narcosis and by the effects of alcohol which reduce arousal and increase the effects of narcosis. (Hamilton, et al., 1989; Fowler, et al., 1986).

Strategic Component

Decreased accuracy on cognitive function tests with narcosis (Moeller, et al., 1981; Hesser, et al., 1978; Fothergill, et al., 1991) may be due to strategic changes in information handling attempting to compensate for slowed processing. One strategic variable is the speed-accuracy trade-off and a shift in this variable can mean that accuracy is sacrificed in an attempt to maintain the speed of responses (Fowler, et al., 1985; Hesser, et al., 1978). Curiously, such a rapid guessing technique has been found to be typical of one population of occupational divers at the surface (Williamson, et al., 1987).

Modification Dive Profile

Since inert gas narcosis is dependent on the partial pressure of the narcotic gas, it is depth dependent. As already noted some effects are more apparent at shallower depths, with other effects becoming evident deeper. The onset of narcosis upon breathing a narcotic partial pressure of gas is rapid but not instantaneous. The time to onset of narcosis should represent the time for a narcotic tension of inert gas to be achieved in the brain, and thus can be characterized by the half-time of the brain[16] and on the depth of the dive. For typical descent rates, narcosis will onset during compression past 100 fsw (30 msw) or soon after arriving at depths. Rapid compression can temporarily raise alveolar carbon dioxide levels that can exacerbate narcosis causing a temporary higher peak level of narcosis.

Oxygen

Theoretical and experimental evidence suggests that oxygen is also narcotic, producing performance deficits similar to inert gases. Although central nervous system oxygen toxicity prevents pure oxygen breathing at sufficiently high partial pressure to cause subjective sensations of narcosis, it can produce cognitive function impairment alone or in gas mixtures containing another narcotic gas. Lipid solubility predicts oxygen could be two times as narcotic as nitrogen and cognitive function tests indicate oxygen may be three to four times as narcotic as nitrogen (Hesser, et al., 1978). It is therefore prudent to include oxygen in any calculations of equinarcotic depths in mixed gas dive planning.

Carbon Dioxide

Carbon dioxide (CO_2) produces a form of narcosis that is somewhat different to inert gas narcosis, and probably involves a different mechanism (Hesser, et al., 1978; Fothergill, et al., 1991). Whereas inert gas narcosis decreases both speed and accuracy in cognitive function tests, carbon dioxide tends to decrease the speed only without influencing accuracy. CO_2 is relatively more potent than inert gases at reducing neuromuscular coordination. CO_2 is narcotic at extremely small alveolar partial pressure and can be debilitating alone or can act additively with inert gas narcosis. An increase in alveolar CO_2 from its normal level of 5.6-6.1 kPa to 7-8 kPa causes significant narcosis. Alveolar carbon dioxide can easily rise to this level due to respiratory resistance from poor equipment or the high breathing gas density of nitrogen mixtures at depth, breathing equipment dead space or inadequate pulmonary ventilation. For instance, a diver swimming at a fast sustainable pace breathing less than 15 litres per minute (*BTPS*) may be at risk of alveolar CO_2 reaching narcotic levels due to inadequate alveolar ventilation.

Anxiety

Anecdotal evidence suggests that anxiety can enhance narcosis. There is some experimental evidence, mostly arising from greater test score decrements under open-sea conditions suggested to produce anxiety in comparison to chamber tests. In one study describing the effects of narcosis in a cold open-water test at 100 fsw (30 msw), urine adrenaline and noradrenaline was elevated (a sign of stress) in those subjects showing the worst narcosis on cognitive function and dexterity tests (Davis, et al., 1972).

Arousal: Fatigue, Drugs & Alcohol

According to the slowed processing model of inert gas narcosis, any condition that influences the level of arousal will modify narcosis. Fatigue would be expected to enhance narcosis and this is in fact the case. As previously described for amphetamine and alcohol, any drugs which produce increased or decreased arousal are likely to interact with narcosis.

Tolerance or Adaptation

Tolerance

Drug tolerance is the phenomena of reduced effect of a drug due to repeated exposure. In the context of narcosis, development of tolerance would imply a reduced narcotic potency of inert gas with repeated diving exposure, but this is apparently not the case since repeated diving exposure does not reduce the objective behavioral measures of inert gas narcosis. Five successive daily chamber air dives to 7 ATA each produce the same deterioration compared to 1.3 ATA in cognitive tests, reaction time and dexterity tests (Moeller et al., 1981). Body sway (a measure of intoxication) is similarly increased by narcosis at 5.5 ATA compared to 1.3 ATA over 12 successive daily air dives (Rogers and Moeller, 1989). Clearly, tolerance to the narcotic actions of inert gases does not develop; repetitive diving exposures do not reduce the anesthetic potency of inert gases.

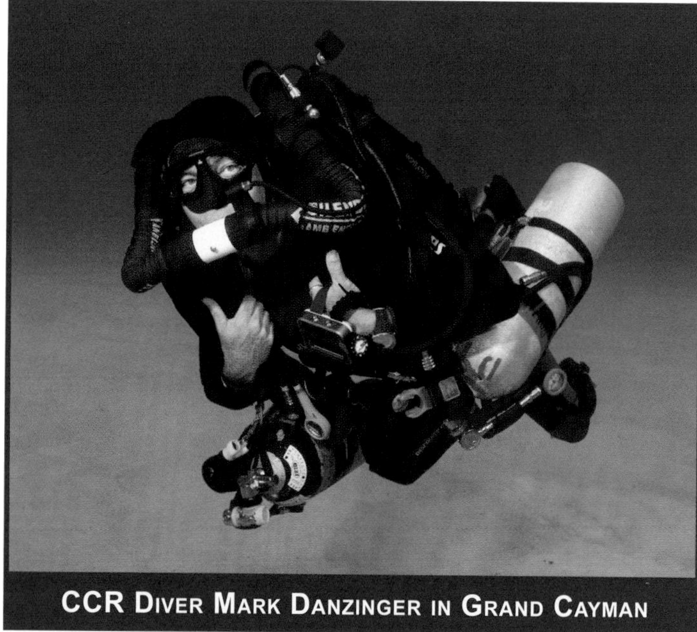

CCR Diver Mark Danzinger in Grand Cayman

Subjective Adaptation

Adaptation is the adjustment by an organism to its environment; in the case of narcosis, adaptation would be a rearrangement of behavior that allows a performance enhancement[17]. Repeated diving produces a dissociation of behavioral and subjective components of narcosis. It is unclear whether this represents a true tolerance[18] or an adaptation. During five consecutive daily dives to 6.46 ATA on air, reaction time does not improve relative to 1 ATA, but subjective evaluation of narcosis does change. Global estimates of the magnitude of narcosis begin to decline by the third daily dive as does identification of body/ mental sensations associated with intoxication; however, subjects continue to describe their ability to work as being equally impaired (Hamilton, et al., 1995). It is evident that it is inappropriate to use the intensity of sensations of intoxication sensation as a gauge for underwater efficiency.

Specific Adaptation & Individual Variability

It is deeply entrenched in the diving community that some individuals can work effectively at depth and that diving experience improves performance during deep dives. Indeed, as with any biological phenomena, there is some individual variability in susceptibility to narcosis, but whether adaptation specific to the narcotic situation occurs with repeated exposures is speculative. For instance, reduction in subjective sensations of intoxication may allow better focus of the task at hand. Also, some individuals may adopt more appropriate adaptive strategies to cope with narcosis and experience may also help identify such

strategies. For instance, it is possible to control accuracy on tests for narcosis, allowing only speed to decline (Fowler, et al., 1993), so a potential strategic adaptation could be to choose an appropriate speed-accuracy trade-off. Indeed, one of the earliest observations of narcosis is that using deliberately slow movements can lessen neuromuscular impairment (Behnke, et al., 1935).

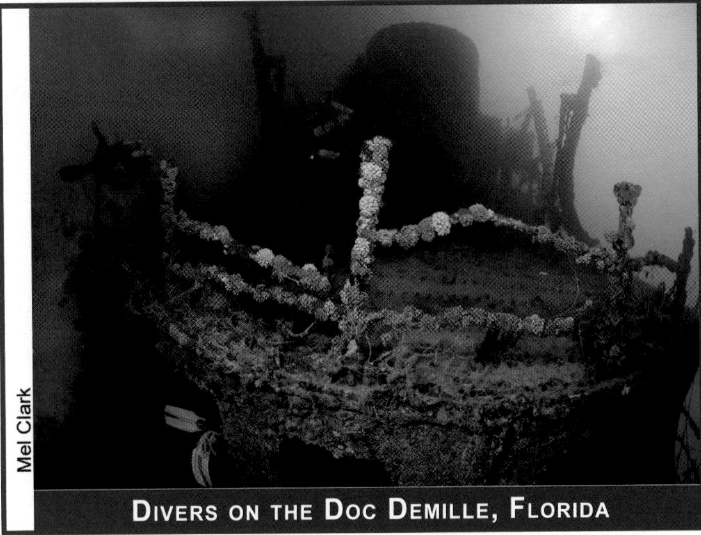

Mel Clark

DIVERS ON THE DOC DEMILLE, FLORIDA

SUMMARY & PRACTICAL STRATEGIES

Some inert gases possess anesthetic properties, narcosis results from breathing these gases at sub-anesthetic doses and is an unavoidable consequence of air diving beyond 100 fsw (30 msw). A possible explanation of the effects of narcosis on behavior is a slowing of information processing in the central nervous system, often combined with a shift in the speed-accuracy trade-off making the diver more prone to errors. The subjective sensations of inert gas narcosis include intoxication and repeated diving may reduce these sensations. Objective laboratory tests of narcosis show slow and inaccurate cognitive function, slowed reaction time, and decreased neuromuscular coordination. Performance on such objective tests does not improve with repeated dives. A less well appreciated action of inert gas narcosis is impaired thermoregulation which can result in greater heat loss during water immersion. Since narcosis is enhanced by factors such as carbon dioxide retention, anxiety and fatigue, narcosis can increase during a dive without further change in depth.

Strategies to enhance performance while under the influence of narcosis might exist. Although the nature of such strategies is unknown, some issues are worthy of consideration. First, it is important to recognize that narcosis will reduce overall efficiency during air dives deeper than 100 fsw (30 msw). Also, owing to subjective adaptation, it is inappropriate to use the intensity of intoxication as a gauge for underwater safety and efficiency. Secondly, over-learned skills are less likely to be influenced by impaired information processing. Furthermore, subjective adaptation may be of some value particularly for performing over-learned tasks. On the other hand, subjective adaptation will be of no value to novel situations or situations that require cognitive information processing or memory (for instance, gas management or decompression calculations). Thirdly, if some of the performance decrement is due to an inappropriate shift in speed-accuracy trade-off, training may allow more appropriate information processing strategies to be implemented. Finally, it must be recognized that such strategies may improve performance with moderate levels of narcosis but are unlikely to protect against the debilitating effects of extreme narcosis.

By far the best choice is to avoid narcosis where feasible and in particular where safety may be reduced. The level of narcosis is primarily influenced by inspired partial pressures of nitrogen and oxygen and therefore the depth of a dive and the breathing gas mixture. The use of helium as a partial or complete replacement for nitrogen as a breathing gas diluent reduces or eliminates inert gas narcosis and owing to lower breathing gas density reduces the level of narcosis due to CO_2 build-up.

Notes

1 Depths quoted as meters sea water gauge (***MSWG***) imply the information results from open-water dives whereas pressures quoted as atmospheres absolute (***ATA***) imply chamber tests. Approximate conversions to feet sea water gauge (***FSWG***) are included.

2 Inert gases exert biological effects without change in their own chemical structure. In terms of respiration, inert gases exclude oxygen, carbon dioxide and water vapor.

3 Helium had been proposed as a breathing gas diluent that might accelerate decompression but the cost of helium required for standard dress had prevented human dives.

4 Neuromuscular coordination, also called manual dexterity, is a consequence of not only muscle contraction, but the nervous system control of muscle contraction and the neuromotor (movement) programs in the central nervous system.

5 Reports by divers of lapses of consciousness might actually be memory lapses.

6 Anesthesia can be defined as an unconscious state that eliminates response to surgical pain.

7 Halothane is used for clinical anesthesia.

8 Neurons are the cells that carry the electrical signals in the nervous system, synapses are a type of junction between neurons.

9 Many drugs alter synaptic transmission owing to a chemical similarity with particular neurotransmitters; however, anesthetics do not resemble neurotransmitters. How such a variety of chemically different anesthetics exert similar effects on the nervous system is an area of ongoing research. Some evidence suggests that the mechanism by which inert gases produce their anesthetic actions may be slightly different to other general anesthetics.

10 According to Henry's Law, molar concentration = partial pressure ***x*** solubility. According to the Meyer-Overton correlation the potency of an anesthetic should be determined by its solubility in lipid.

11 Miller (1971) later expounded Mullins idea in the form of the critical volume hypothesis to explain the opposing actions of narcosis and high pressure nervous syndrome.

12 Solubility in water and lipid are often inversely related. Non-polar compounds typically have a low solubility in water (***hydrophobic***) and a high solubility in lipid (***lipophilic***).

13 There is an electrical potential difference across a neuronal cell membrane (***inside negative***) that is maintained by an unequal distribution of small charged particles called ions. There are channels in the membrane through which ions can flow, but these are closed in the resting state. Opening of these channels causes a brief, localized reversal of the membrane potential called an action potential. These channels open in response to small voltage changes (***voltage-gated ion channels***) and thus are triggered by electrical activity in an adjacent area of the membrane, propagating the action potential. Neurotransmitter receptors produce smaller, decaying electrical potentials by opening different ion channels (***receptor-gated ion channels***).

14 In support of a protein site for anesthesia is another strong correlation, that between anesthetic potency in mammals and luciferase (***firefly light emitting protein***) activity depression over 100,000 range of potency.

15 Using the additive factor method where stimulus intensity is varied under control and narcotic conditions, a parallel shift, rather than a change in slope, of the stimulus intensity/response relationship indicates that narcosis produces a general functional deficit rather than interfering with structural stages.

16 Unpublished experiments in my laboratory indicate that the half-time of the brain after a step change in arterial nitrogen partial pressure should be approximately 1 minute.

17 Adaptation also has a meaning similar to tolerance but is a reduced nervous system response to continual stimulation, this is not implied here.

18 Development of tolerance would imply that narcosis produces these subjective effects by a different mechanism to the other behavioral effects that are not altered by repeated exposures.

Footnotes

1 Depths quoted as meters sea water gauge (mswg) imply the information results from open-water dives whereas pressures quoted as atmospheres absolute (ata) imply chamber tests. Approximate conversions to feet sea water gauge (fswg) are included.

2 Inert gases exert biological effects without change in their own chemical structure. In terms of respiration, inert gases exclude oxygen, carbon dioxide and water vapor.

3 Helium had been proposed as a breathing gas diluent that might accelerate decompression but the cost of helium required for standard dress had prevented human dives.

4 Neuromuscular coordination, also called manual dexterity, is a consequence of not only muscle contraction, but the nervous system control of muscle contraction and the neuromotor (movement) programs in the central nervous system.

5 Reports by divers of lapses of consciousness might actually be memory lapses.

6 Anesthesia can be defined as an unconscious state that eliminates response to surgical pain.

7 Halothane is used for clinical anesthesia.

8 Neurons are the cells that carry the electrical signals in the nervous system, synapses are a type of junction between neurons.

9 Many drugs alter synaptic transmission owing to a chemical similarity with particular neurotransmitters; however, anesthetics do not resemble neurotransmitters. How such a variety of chemically different anesthetics exert similar effects on the nervous system is an area of ongoing research. Some evidence suggests that the mechanism by which inert gases produce their anesthetic actions may be slightly different to other general anesthetics.

10 According to Henry's Law, molar concentration = partial pressure ***x*** solubility. According to the Meyer-Overton correlation the potency of an anesthetic should be determined by its solubility in lipid.

11 Miller (1971) later expounded Mullins idea in the form of the critical volume hypothesis to explain the opposing actions of narcosis and high pressure nervous syndrome.

12 Solubility in water and lipid are often inversely related. Non-polar compounds typically have a low solubility in water (hydrophobic) and a high solubility in lipid (lipophilic).

13 There is an electrical potential difference across a neuronal cell membrane (inside negative) that is maintained by an unequal distribution of small charged particles called ions. There are channels in the membrane through which ions can flow, but these are closed in the resting state. Opening

of these channels causes a brief, localized reversal of the membrane potential called an action potential. These channels open in response to small voltage changes (voltage-gated ion channels) and thus are triggered by electrical activity in an adjacent area of the membrane, propagating the action potential. Neurotransmitter receptors produce smaller, decaying electrical potentials by opening different ion channels (receptor-gated ion channels).

14 In support of a protein site for anesthesia is another strong correlation, that between anesthetic potency in mammals and luciferase (firefly light emitting protein) activity depression over 100,000 range of potency.

15 Using the additive factor method where stimulus intensity is varied under control and narcotic conditions, a parallel shift, rather than a change in slope, of the stimulus intensity/response relationship indicates that narcosis produces a general functional deficit rather than interfering with structural stages.

16 Unpublished experiments in my laboratory indicate that the half-time of the brain after a step change in arterial nitrogen partial pressure should be approximately 1 minute.

17 Adaptation also has a meaning similar to tolerance but is a reduced nervous system response to continual stimulation, this is not implied here.

18 Development of tolerance would imply that narcosis produces these subjective effects by a different mechanism to the other behavioral effects that are not altered by repeated exposures.

References

- Behnke A.R., Thomson R.M., Motley E.P. (1935). The psychological effects from breathing at 4 atmospheres pressure. American Journal of Physiology; 112:554-558.
- Cheung S.S., Mekjavic I.B. (1995). Human temperature regulation during subanesthetic levels of nitrous oxide-induced narcosis. Journal of Applied Physiology; 78:2301-2308.
- Davis F.M., Osborne J.P., Baddeley A.D., Graham I.M.F. (1972). Diver performance: nitrogen narcosis and anxiety. Aerospace Medicine; 43:1079-1082.
- End E. (1938) The use of new equipment and helium gas in a world record dive. J. Ind. Hyg. Toxicol.; 20:511-520
- Fothergill D.M., Hedges D., Morrison J.B. (1991). Effects of CO_2 and N_2 partial pressures on cognitive and psychomotor performance. Undersea Biomedical Research; 18:1-19.
- Fowler B., Ackles K.N., Portlier G. (1985). Effects of inert gas narcosis on behavior - a critical review. Undersea Biomedical Research; 12:369-402.
- Fowler B., Hamilton K., Portlier G. (1986). Effects of ethanol and amphetamine on inert gas narcosis in humans. Undersea Biomedical Research; 13:345-354.
- Fowler B., Hamel R., Lindeis A.E. (1993). Relationship between the event-related brain potential P300 and inert gas narcosis. Undersea Hyperbaric Medicine; 20:49-62.
- Hamilton K., Fowler B., Porlier G. (1989). The effects of hyperbaric air in combination with ethyl alcohol and dextroamphetamine on serial choice-reaction time. Ergonomics 32:409-422.
- Hamilton K., LaLiberté M.F., Heslegrave M.A. (1992) Subjective and behavioural effects associated with repeated exposure to narcosis. Aviation Space Environmental Medicine; 63:865-869.
- Hamilton K., Laliberte M.F., Fowler B. (1995). Dissociation of the behavioral and subjective components of nitrogen narcosis and diver adaptation. Undersea Hyperbaric Medicine; 22:41-49.
- Hesser C.M., Fagraeus L., Adolfson J. (1978). Roles of nitrogen, oxygen, and carbon dioxide in compressed-air narcosis. Undersea Biomedical Research; 5:391-400.
- Hill L., Phillips A.E. (1932). Deep Sea Diving. Journal of the Royal Naval Medical Service; 18:157-183.
- Mekjavic I.B., Passias T., Sundberg C.J. and Eiken O. (1994). Perception of thermal comfort during narcosis. Undersea Hyperbaric Medicine; 21:9-19.
- Mekjavic I.B., Savic S.A., Eiken O. (1995). Nitrogen narcosis attenuates shivering thermogenesis. Journal of Applied Physiology; 78:2241-2244.
- Moeller G., Chattin C., Rogers W., Laxar K., Ryack B. (1981). Performance effects with repeated exposure to the diving environment. Journal of Applied Physiology; 66:502-510.
- Rogers W.H., Moeller G. (1989). Effect of brief, repeated hyperbaric exposures on susceptibility to nitrogen narcosis. Undersea Biomedical Research; 16:227-232.
- Smith E.B. (1986). On the science of deep-sea diving-observations on the respiration of different kinds of air. Undersea Biomedical Research; 14:347-369.
- Williamson A.M., Clarke B., Edmonds C. (1987). Neurobehavioural effects of professional abalone diving. Br. J. Ind. Med. 44:459-466.

Chapter Three
Oxygen & Its Affect On The Diver

David Sawatzky M.D.

Introduction

Oxygen (***O_2***) is a vital necessity for life, and a frequent cause of death in divers. In open circuit diving, divers frequently die from hyperoxia (too much O_2) and occasionally from hypoxia (too little O_2). In CCR diving, hyperoxia and hypoxia are two of the major problems and frequent causes of death (hypercarbia, too much CO_2, is the third). The physiology of O_2 and O_2 toxicity is fairly complex, but it is worth learning as much as possible so that you can dive in a safer fashion. In this chapter we are going to look at the physiology of O_2, acute hypoxia, O_2 toxicity, acute hyperoxia, and some of the potential longer-term effects of hyperoxia.

Physiology of O_2 Transport at the Surface

Oxygen has atomic number 8, which means the nucleus is composed of 8 protons and 8 neutrons. It is a colourless, odorless, tasteless gas and by volume, air is composed of 21% O_2. Therefore, the partial pressure of O_2 on the surface is 0.21 ATA, or approximately 160 mm Hg (1 ATA is 760 mm Hg ***x*** 21% = 160 mm Hg). Oxygen normally exists as a molecule made up of two oxygen atoms.

When we take a breath, the air we inhale is mixed with the air that remained in the mouth, airways and lungs at the end of the last breath. This air contains approximately 17% O_2 and 4% CO_2. In addition, water vapor is added to the inspired air until it is 100% saturated at body temperature (water vapor pressure of 47 mm Hg at 37°C). The net effect is that the gas in the alveoli has a partial pressure of O_2 (***PO_2***) of around 105 mm Hg.

It takes a small difference in PO_2 to drive the O_2 across the alveolar walls into the blood, and some blood passes through the lungs without completely equilibrating with the air in the alveoli so that the arterial blood leaving the lungs and being pumped by the heart to the tissues of the body has a PO_2 of around 100 mm Hg in a normal, healthy person.

However, PO_2 is only part of the story. What we really care about is the ***amount*** of O_2 the blood is carrying to the tissues. At a PO_2 of 100 mm Hg, approximately 0.3 ml of O_2 will dissolve in every 100 ml of blood. This is a trivial amount of O_2 and not nearly enough to sustain life. The secret of life is hemoglobin (***Hb***). Hemoglobin is a complex protein that is designed to carry 4 molecules of O_2. It is contained inside Red Blood Cells (***RBC***) and gives blood its' red colour. The amount of Hb in blood varies from approximately 12 to 18 grams per 100 ml with 15 gms being a normal value in males (slightly lower in females). One gram of Hb can carry 1.36 ml of O_2 and at sea level in a normal healthy person, Hb is approximately 97% saturated with O_2 when it leaves the lung.

Mel Clark

Gordy Hendrickson on the stern of the *Gordy Kamloops, Isle Royale*

Therefore, the Hb in every 100 ml of blood can carry 15 ***x*** 1.36 ***x*** 0.97 = 19.8 ml of O_2. When we add the 0.3 ml of O_2 dissolved in the plasma, each 100 ml of blood can carry roughly 20 ml of O_2. How much O_2 is off loaded in the tissues depends primarily on blood flow and how much O_2 the tissues are using. In most tissues, the blood leaving the tissues has a PO_2 of 40 mm Hg. When the O_2 requirement of a tissue increases (a muscle starts to work), the tissue has some capacity to off load more O_2 from the blood but the primary mechanism used to deliver more O_2 to a working tissue is to increase the amount of blood going to the tissue. For example, a muscle working at maximum capacity will have a blood flow approximately 100 times greater than the same muscle at rest.

It is also important to understand that tissues cannot "store" a significant amount of O_2. Muscle contains a small amount of myoglobin. Myoglobin is a protein like Hb, but it can only bind one molecule of O_2. The rest of the O_2 in tissues is dissolved in the fluid, and we have already seen that very little O_2 dissolves in body fluids. Finally, O_2 is used in the cells to generate Adenosine Triphosphate (***ATP***). ATP is the molecule that actually "makes things happen," like causing muscles to contract. A small amount of energy is also stored as creatine phosphate (***CP***) but the combined energy stores of ATP and CP will only supply enough energy for a hard working muscle for a few seconds. The bottom line is that tissues need a continuous supply of O_2 to continue functioning.

Table of approximate O_2 stores in a person breathing air at sea level:

450 ml O_2 in the lungs
850 ml O_2 in the blood
50 ml O_2 in dissolved in body fluids
200 ml O_2 bound to myoglobin

When asleep (totally at rest), a 150 pound (70 kg) person requires about 250 ml of O_2 per minute. When that same person is exercising at their maximum capacity, they will require up to 4000 ml of O_2 per minute (if they are a highly trained athlete). An average, reasonably fit technical diver will require 3000 to 3500 ml of O_2 per minute at maximum exercise.

The reason I went through the above explanation is that it is critical for a technical diver, and especially a CCR diver to fully understand what happens in the normal person on the surface so that they can understand what happens when we breathe gases other than air, and when we breathe those gases under increased pressure.

Physiology of O_2 Transport & Absorption When Diving

Does breathing Nitrox deliver more O_2 to the cells? When we are breathing Nitrox 40 on the surface (PO_2 of 0.4 ATA), the PO_2 in the alveoli will be approximately 200 ml Hg, or about twice what it is when we are breathing air. Therefore, the blood leaving the lungs will have about 0.6 ml of O_2 dissolved in every 100 ml of blood, and 19.8 ml of O_2 attached to Hb in every 100 ml of blood. The total amount of O_2 carried by the blood will have increased only 0.3 ml for every 100 ml of blood, even though we have doubled the inspired PO_2! This point is VERY important. Breathing O_2 at elevated pressures does not significantly increase the amount of O_2 being carried by the blood. What happens in the tissues? The amount of O_2 in the tissues does not change significantly, but the PO_2 will increase. The important point about using Nitrox is not that we are breathing more O_2, but that we are breathing less nitrogen.

Extending this discussion to CCR diving, we know that PO_2 is kept constant by the rebreather. If we use a set point of 1.3 ATA, we will have a PO_2 in arterial blood roughly 6.5 times higher than breathing air on the surface. Therefore, we will have 6.5 ***x*** 0.3 = 1.95 or 2 ml of O_2 dissolved in the plasma of every 100 ml of blood. This is still a very small amount compared to the 20 ml of O_2 carried by the Hb in the same 100 ml of blood. Even though we are breathing the equivalent of 130% O_2 on the surface, the amount of O_2 being delivered to the cells is not significantly changed.

As with Nitrox, the primary reason we dive with an elevated PO_2 when diving rebreathers is to reduce the amount of inert gas we are breathing and thereby absorbing during the dive. A lot of technical divers "push" the PO_2 during the bottom phase of a dive. Does this make any sense? Let's look at an example. We are going to do a dive to 300 ft (90 m). At this depth, the total pressure will be 10 ATA (9 ATA water pressure plus 1 ATA for the atmosphere). If we use a PO_2 of 1.6 ATA, we will be breathing 8.4 ATA of inert gas (84%). If we use a set point of 1.3 ATA, we will be breathing 8.7 ATA of inert gas (87%). The risk of having an O_2 convulsion with a PO_2 of 1.6 ATA is far higher than with a PO_2 of 1.3 ATA. It makes no sense to dramatically increase the risk of an O_2 convulsion to reduce the inert gas percentage by only 3%, as this will have a very small effect on the required decompression time.

Another vital factor is O_2 absorption and use when diving. We mentioned above that the average person will use between 500 ml and 3000 ml of O_2 per minute, depending on their activity level. A vital fact to understand when CCR diving is that the amount of O_2 used by the body does NOT CHANGE WITH DEPTH! This is critical. When you are working while diving, the muscles require the same number of molecules of O_2 to make ATP as they do on the surface. Depth is not a factor.

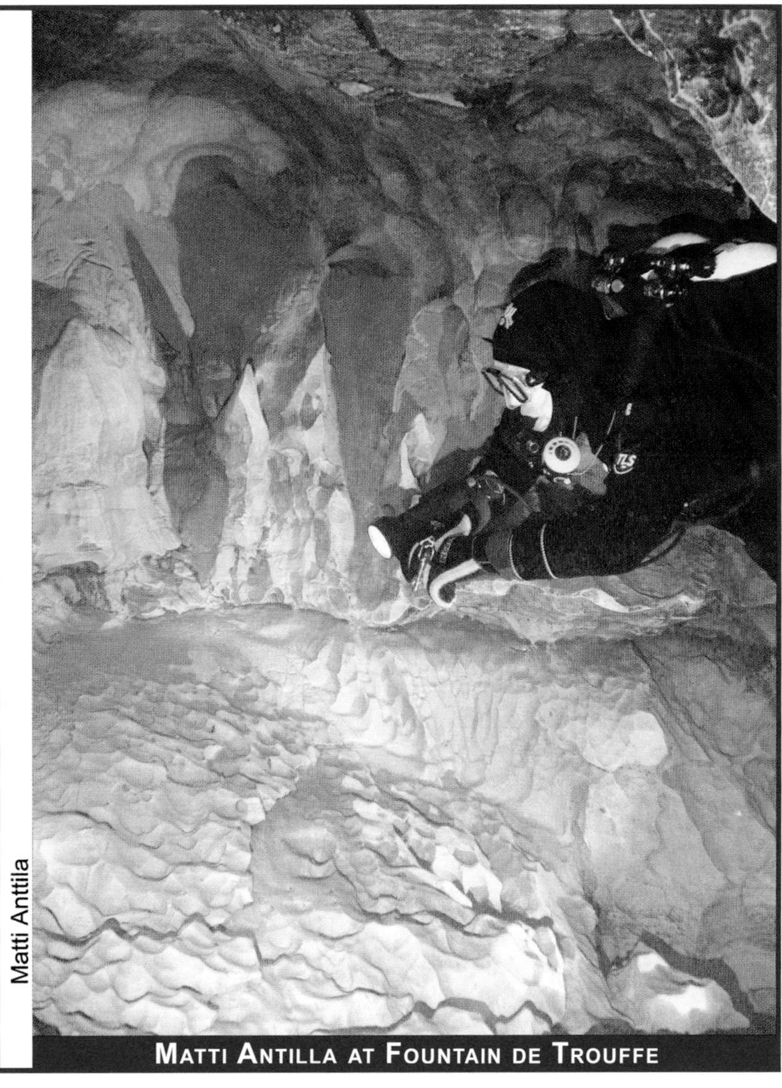
Matti Anttila

MATTI ANTILLA AT FOUNTAIN DE TROUFFE

When you increase the PO_2 of the inspired gas, slightly more O_2 will dissolve in the blood, but there is no significant change in the amount of O_2 delivered to the cells and no change in the amount of O_2 used by the body. So who cares? CCR diving is unique in that only the O_2 your body uses is added to the loop (ignoring O_2 lost in bubbles, but there shouldn't be any at constant depth).

So what happens when we are sitting breathing on the surface? There are approximately 6 liters of gas in your lungs at full inspiration, and very roughly 4 liters of gas in the scrubber and loop for a total of 10 liters of gas. If we use a set point of 0.7 ATA, how long will the O_2 in the system sustain us at light work (1.0 liter of O_2 per minute)? We have 10 liters of gas at 1.0 ATA, 70% is O_2 so we have 7.0 liters of O_2 that we are using at 1.0 liter per minute, so the O_2 will last 7 minutes. (In reality we would loose consciousness after about 6 minutes as the PO_2 drops towards 0.1 ATA.) Of course we will have to add diluent to maintain the breathing volume as the O_2 is absorbed, but that will add more O_2 and make the gas last even longer.

Now, what happens at depth? If we take the same situation at a depth of 300 ft (90 m) where the total pressure will be 10 times surface pressure, the gas will be 10 times as dense. Therefore the 10 liters of gas in the loop and our lungs will contain 10 times as many molecules. A common mistake (unfortunately one I have made in print) is that there will be 10 times as many O_2 molecules and therefore the gas should last 10 times longer. This would be true if we were breathing 70% O_2 ATA depth. However, if the CCR set point is maintained at 0.7 ATA, we will be breathing the surface equivalent of 7% O_2 at depth and this means there will be exactly the same number of O_2 molecules in the loop as at the surface. Therefore, at the same work level it will last the same length of time. In reality the set point will almost always be elevated to around 1.3 ATA at depth and therefore the gas will contain almost twice as many molecules of O_2, and will last almost twice as long.

Acute Hypoxia

We will examine the fairly complex situation in CCR diving and then review what happens with hypoxia while open circuit diving.

When diving CCR, one of the primary concerns is having enough O_2 in the breathing mix. There are several ways the concentration of O_2 in the breathing mixture can decline, including solenoid failure closed, O_2 tank turned off, O_2 tank empty, O_2 tank containing something other than O_2, electronic failure, etc. Our purpose here is not to review these failure modes, but to examine the physiology of what is happening when they occur.

For discussion purposes, let's look at what happens to the CCR diver who leaves the O_2 tank turned off and does not check their gauges. They get dressed and start breathing on the rebreather. The gas in the rebreather is most likely a fairly high percentage Nitrox if they have celebrated their O_2 sensors. As they continue to breathe, the CCR will remove the CO_2 they produce and the PO_2 will slowly fall. If the diver continues to breathe the loop on the surface, they will loose consciousness after several minutes as explained above.

Usually the diver will enter the water and start to descend before this happens. As they descend, the gas in the loop will be compressed and they will add diluent (air or Nitrox) to maintain a breathable volume of gas. This fresh gas adds O_2 to the breathing loop. In addition, as the diver descends the increasing pressure will increase the PO_2 in the breathing loop (therefore the diver will have lots of O_2). Once the diver reaches the bottom, the PO_2 in the loop will very slowly fall. Eventually, they will become hypoxic, but this might not happen until 10 minutes or more into the dive! Factors that determine how long this takes include the initial PO_2 in the loop, the initial volume of the loop, the rate at which the diver descends, the rate at which the diver uses O_2, the PO_2 of the diluent, the amount of diluent that is added, etc.

As we reduce the PO_2 in the inspired gas, the PO_2 in the alveoli and therefore the arterial blood starts to fall. The body is very well designed however and Hb is very effective in savaging O_2 from the gas in the lungs, even when the PO_2 is less than normal. The Hb/O_2 dissociation curve shows that if the PO_2 in the blood falls from 100 mm Hg (normal) to 60 mm Hg, the Hb saturation will fall from 97% to approximately 85%. In this part of the curve a relatively large fall in PO_2 causes a small fall in Hb saturation. Therefore, a virtually normal amount of O_2 is being delivered to the tissues by the blood even though the inspired PO_2 is significantly less than normal.

If the PO_2 in the blood continues to decline, say from 60 mm Hg to 20 mm Hg, the Hb saturation will fall from 85% to approximately 25%. In this part of the curve a small change in PO_2 results in a large change in Hb saturation. This feature is critically important to the normal functioning of the body and results in large amounts of O_2 being off loaded in the tissues. Unfortunately, in the situation of hypoxia this means that a slowly falling PO_2 in the blood will result in no symptoms initially and then fairly rapidly cause loss of consciousness.

The brain is a tissue that is totally dependant on O_2 to function. Most of the other tissues in the body have alternative biochemical pathways that do not involve $O_2$to generate small amounts of energy. These pathways are very inefficient, and they generate waste products that build up and ultimately limit the ability of the cells to function, but they do allow muscles to work for a few minutes at a level greater than can be supported by the amount of O_2 being delivered to the muscle by the blood. The brain does not have this capability and it also does not have the O_2 stores that muscle contains (no myoglobin and very little CP). The end result is that the brain is very sensitive to inadequate O_2 supplies and it is the cause of most of the signs and symptoms of hypoxia.

In open circuit diving hypoxia is usually the result of breathing from the wrong tank, filling the tank with the wrong gas, or having the O_2 consumed by oxidation in the tank before the dive (water in a steel tank that has sat for a long time). The seriousness of the hypoxia will be determined by the percentage O_2 in the tank and the resulting PO_2 as determined by the depth of the diver. In general we have no signs or symptoms of hypoxia even at maximum exercise until the PO_2 is less than 0.16 ATA. At rest we are usually asymptomatic until the PO_2 is less than 0.12 ATA. Therefore, an open circuit diver should not breathe a mixture of less than 16% O_2 on the surface. This is one of the reasons a travel gas is required on a deep Trimix dive.

A special situation exists when the diver breathes a pure

inert gas. Many tech divers use argon for suit inflation and some rebreathers use pure inert gas as the diluent. Unfortunately, many divers have ended up breathing pure inert gas by mistake. If a person breathes a pure inert gas the PO_2 in the lungs becomes extremely low after a couple of breaths. The blood returning from the body to the lungs normally has a PO_2 of around 40 mm Hg and contains almost 60% of the O_2 it started with. This O_2 moves from the blood into the lungs and when the Hb returns to the tissues it REMOVES O_2 from the tissues. What happens is that the person looses consciousness after only a few breaths of a pure inert gas and after a minute or two they become virtually impossible to revive and they die. For this reason many people (including the author) believe that pure inert gases should NEVER be used in diving. (Argon provides only a trivial reduction in heat loss by the body so purchase better drysuit underwear.)

Signs & Symptoms of Hypoxia

Loss of consciousness is often the first sign of hypoxia, especially if the fall in PO_2 is rapid. Other signs include poor performance and in-coordination. Symptoms of hypoxia include euphoria, over confidence, apathy, fatigue, headache, and blurred vision. Hyperventilation is usually not present if the PCO_2 is normal. Defective memory and impaired judgment are common. These often cause the diver to respond inappropriately to an emergency, and to ignore other signs and symptoms of hypoxia. Therefore, loss of consciousness is very common in hypoxic divers.

A further problem is that many of the signs and symptoms of hypoxia are the same as those of narcosis, O_2 toxicity, and elevated PCO_2. In addition, these problems are additive. For example, if the PCO_2 is slightly elevated (scrubber starting to break through or the diver is working) and the PN_2 a little high (diving a bit deep on Nitrox), the resulting mental impairment will be far worse than expected from either one alone. If the PO_2 is also slightly high or low, the diver will be in serious trouble. This is why the first response to any perceived problem while diving CCR should be to go OC on a safe gas until you have determined exactly what the problem is and have resolved it. It is also why most CCR units have alarms that go off when the PO_2 drops below 0.5 ATA, hopefully the diver will be able to recognize and correct the problem before the level of hypoxia impairs their thinking processes.

Hypoxia of Ascent

When we descend while diving CCR, we must add diluent to the loop to maintain a breathable volume of gas. At the same time, the gas in the loop is being compressed and the PO_2 is climbing. For example, if we used no O_2, added no diluent, and left the surface with a PO_2 of 0.7 ATA, when we arrived at 100 ft (30 m) the PO_2 would be 4 * 0.7 = 2.8 ATA. If we balance our rate of descent, work rate, and addition of diluent, it is often possible to leave the surface with a PO_2 of 0.7 ATA and arrive on the bottom with a PO_2 of 1.3 ATA, without changing the set point from 0.7 ATA, or injecting any pure O_2.

When we ascend, the gas in the loop is expanding and we must vent gas. At the same time the PO_2 is dropping. For example, if we leave the bottom at 100 ft (30 m) with a PO_2 in the loop of 1.3 ATA, used no O_2 and added no O_2, the PO_2 would be 1.3 ATA / 4 = 0.325 ATA when we arrived on the surface. Of course we use O_2 during ascent so the real PO_2 would be even less. A trick while CCR diving is to make sure you are at minimum loop volume when you start your ascent, and to vent frequently during ascent to maintain minimum loop volumes so that the unit will have to inject less O_2 to maintain the PO_2 as you ascend.

Oxygen Toxicity

In Open Circuit technical diving, O_2 toxicity is a relatively common cause of death (breathe a deco gas while deep by mistake). In CCR diving, O_2 toxicity is also a major cause for concern. To have a reasonable understanding of the danger of excessive O_2, we have to understand the physiology of O_2 toxicity.

The first and most basic point is that MOLECULAR OXYGEN IS NOT TOXIC! The problem is that whenever molecular O_2 exists, it forms other substances known as "oxygen radicals." Oxygen radicals are highly reactive molecules, formed from oxygen, which contain at least one extra electron. These molecules are formed from collisions between oxygen and other molecules, and as a result of metabolic processes in the cells. Examples include superoxide anions, hydrogen peroxide, hydroperoxy and hydroxyl radicals, and singlet oxygen. Oxygen radicals will bind to and react with the next molecule they come in contact with, often damaging or changing that molecule. Therefore, whenever you have O_2, you will have O_2

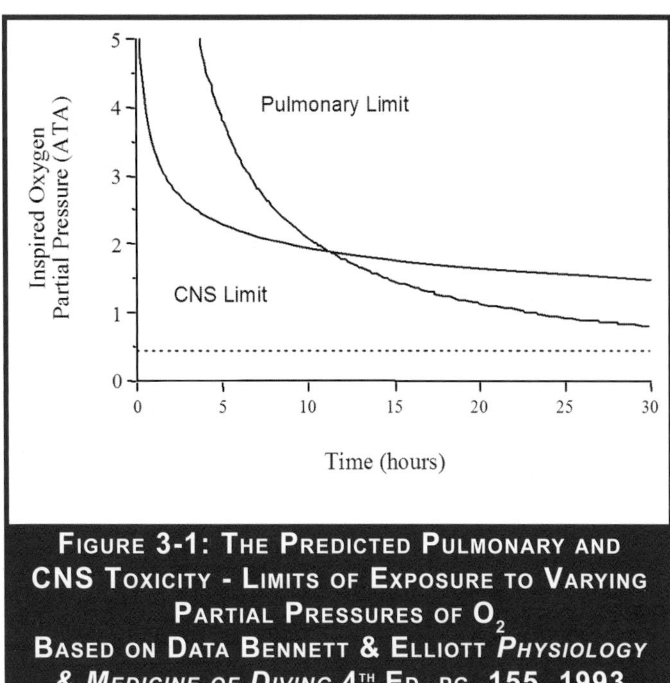

Figure 3-1: The Predicted Pulmonary and CNS Toxicity - Limits of Exposure to Varying Partial Pressures of O_2 Based on Data Bennett & Elliott *Physiology & Medicine of Diving* 4th Ed. pg. 155. 1993

radicals. The number of O_2 radicals is proportional to the partial pressure of O_2.

There are hundreds of specific chemical reactions that oxygen radicals can be involved in that damage the cell but in general terms there are three ways that they cause damage. The first is through inactivation of enzymes. Enzymes are proteins that work as catalysts, causing reactions to occur that would not normally occur at body temperature. They do this by holding the two molecules that are to react in exactly the right orientation to each other so that they join. The resulting molecule is released and the enzyme starts again, repeating the process thousands of times. If the shape of the enzyme is changed, the molecules will not be held in the right orientation and the reaction will not occur. Oxygen radicals cause cross-linking of sulphydryl groups, thereby changing the shape of the enzyme and inactivating it. They also cause changes in the shape of proteins responsible for transport of ions in and out of the cells across the cell membrane, stopping them from functioning. Finally, oxygen radicals cause peroxidation of the various lipids in the cells.

All cells in oxygen breathing animals have ways to inactivate oxygen radicals and to repair some of the damage done by them. The two main defenses are superoxide dysmutase and catalase. Both of these enzymes help maintain a good supply of reduced glutathione. Reduced glutathione has many sulphydryl groups and oxygen radicals will bind to them, and thus be unavailable to cause damage to the cell. Vitamins E and C are also antioxidants.

Oxygen radicals are not only important in diving, but are becoming very important in medicine. One of the methods white blood cells use to kill bacteria is to enclose the bacteria in a membrane and then to inject oxygen radicals into the vacuole. (The white blood cells makes the O_2 radicals.) The oxygen radicals actually kill the bacteria. In addition we now know that O_2 radicals are the final method of damage in many diseases. Oxygen radicals are therefore both "***good***" and "***bad***."

It would seem reasonable to conclude that if O_2 radicals cause cellular damage, taking ***antioxidants*** should help reduce the damage. So far, the results of many well-designed studies have failed to show any benefit from taking antioxidant supplements. Some benefit has been shown when increased amounts of anti-oxidants are consumed by eating foods high in anti-oxidants. This suggests that something else in the food is required to get the beneficial effect of the antioxidants that is not available in the supplements.

The bottom line is that anytime O_2 exists, O_2 radicals will be formed. The number of O_2 radicals is proportional to the PO_2. All of our cells have defenses against the damage caused by O_2 radicals. At normal PO_2s, our cells are more than capable of repairing the damage being caused by the O_2 radicals. As the PO_2, and the number of O_2 radicals is increased, a point is reached where the cells cannot repair the O_2 radical damage as quickly as it is occurring. Therefore, the damage will accumulate until the function of the cell is impaired or the cell dies.

Signs & Symptoms of Oxygen Toxicity

Given the above explanation, it should be obvious that the toxicity of O_2 will depend on the PO_2 and the time of exposure. The other factor is that we are all biologically different and some individuals will have more defenses against O_2 radicals than others. To further complicate the issue, our defenses against O_2 radicals also change greatly from day to day. Therefore, we have marked differences in sensitivity to O_2 radical damage in different people and on different days in the same person.

In general, the susceptibility of a cell to oxygen toxicity

is related to its rate of metabolism in that a resting cell is relatively resistant. This makes sense in that O_2 radicals interfere with cell processes and the slower these processes are occurring; the longer it will take for the damage to matter. We also know that things that stimulate the cells, like caffeine, increase the risk of O_2 toxicity while things that slow down the cells have some protective effect.

Every cell in the body will eventually die if it is exposed to enough O_2 radicals. But in the intact person the lungs and the brain will suffer serious damage before the other tissues. The eyes can also suffer damage at relatively modest exposures.

The human body is able to tolerate increased levels of oxygen, up to about 0.45 ATA, without problem. At PO_2s of between 0.45 ATA and 1.6 ATA, the toxic effects are mainly on the lungs and take many hours or days to develop. At pressures over 1.6 ATA, the toxic effects are mainly on the brain (CNS) and may develop in a few minutes.

The majority of recreational divers will not have to worry about oxygen toxicity because the PO_2 will never be high enough, for long enough, to cause problems. However, the rapidly rising use of Nitrox makes O_2 toxicity a problem that all divers should understand. As technical divers, and even more as CCR divers, a thorough understanding of O_2 toxicity is critical.

Dr. J. Lorrain Smith first described the toxic effect of oxygen on the lungs in 1899. He noted that the severity of the effect increased with increasing PO_2 and that the effects where largely reversible.

The earliest sign of pulmonary (***lung***) oxygen toxicity is a mild irritation in the trachea (***throat***) that is made worse with deep inspiration. A mild cough develops next, followed by more severe irritation and cough until inspiration becomes quite painful and the cough becomes uncontrollable. If exposure to oxygen is continued, the person will notice chest tightness, difficulty breathing, shortness of breath, and if exposure is continued long enough, the person will die, from lack of oxygen! The progressive damage to the lungs eventually makes it impossible for the oxygen to get to the blood as it passes through the lungs.

The time to onset of symptoms is highly variable but most individuals can tolerate 12-16 hours of oxygen at 1.0 ATA, 8-14 hours at 1.5 ATA, and 3-6 hours at 2.0 ATA before developing mild symptoms. There are several ways to track developing pulmonary oxygen toxicity but the most sensitive and accurate is the development of symptoms. A second technique is to monitor the vital capacity. Vital capacity (the amount of air that can be moved in one large breath) decreases with increasing pulmonary toxicity. A reduction of approximately 2% in vital capacity correlates with mild symptoms while a reduction of 10% correlates symptoms so severe that most individuals will not voluntarily continue breathing oxygen. These mild effects are completely reversible and no permanent lung damage occurs. However, the damage will take 2 to 4 weeks to heal. The pathology of pulmonary oxygen toxicity is understood but beyond the scope of this discussion.

			Air ($21\%\ O_2$ $79\%\ N_2$)		Nitrox ($40\%\ O_2$ $60\%\ N_2$)	
Depth (fsw)	**Depth (msw)**	**Pressure (ATA)**	**PO_2 (ATA)**	**PN_2 (ATA)**	**PO_2 (ATA)**	**PN_2 (ATA)**
Surface	**Surface**	1.0	0.21	0.79	0.4	0.6
33	10	2.0	0.42	1.58	0.8	1.2
66	20	3.0	0.63	2.37	1.2	1.8
99	30	4.0	0.84	3.16	**1.6**	2.4
132	40	5.0	1.05	3.95	**2.0**	3.0
218	66	7.61	**1.6**	6.01	**3.0**	4.6
297	90	10.0	**2.10**	7.90	**4.0**	6.0

Figure 3-2: PO_2 and PN_2 of Air and EAN 40 at Various Depths

A third way to keep track, in rough terms, of pulmonary oxygen toxicity is to keep track of the oxygen exposure. This technique is called calculating the Unit Pulmonary Toxic Dose (***UPTD***) and one UPTD is equivalent to

CONVULSIONS	**Grand Mal Siezure, usually without warning**
VISION	**Tunnel Vision or any other visual change**
EARS	**Ringing in the Ears or other hearing changes**
NAUSEA	**Mild to Severe, continuous or intermitent**
TWITCHING	**Usually facial muscles, most frequent symptoms**
IRRITABILITY	**Behaviour or Personality Changes**
DIZZINESS	**Vertigo, Disorientation**

FIGURE 3-3: SYMPTOMS OF CNS OXYGEN TOXICITY

breathing 100% oxygen, for one minute, at 1.0 ATA. As a guide, 615 UPTDs in one day will cause a 2% reduction in vital capacity and 1,425 units will cause a 10% reduction. There are several different ways to calculate the UPTD (some try to correct for increasing toxic effects with increasing dose, in addition to the simple PO_2) and there is quite wide variation in individual tolerance so that symptoms are still the best guide. The situation where UPTDs are most useful is in planning a large number of dives, in a few days, all involving a large amount of oxygen decompression or CCR diving. Even then, the dive plan may have to be altered if the diver develops symptoms of pulmonary toxicity.

The first and most important method to prevent pulmonary oxygen toxicity is to limit exposure to the lowest possible PO_2 for the shortest period of time. If you dive only air and limit your depth to a maximum of 130 fsw (40 msw), pulmonary oxygen toxicity is unlikely to be a problem. The second method to prevent pulmonary oxygen toxicity is to provide air breaks. The damage to the cells is cumulative and if for every 25 minutes of oxygen exposure you provide the cells with a five-minute period where the diver breathes air, the diver can tolerate twice as much oxygen before toxic symptoms develop when air breaks are given compared to breathing oxygen continuously. Basically what happens is that during the air breaks the cells are repairing the damage due to O_2 radicals much faster than damage is occurring so they "catch up" on some of the damage. Therefore, it will take much longer for a given level of damage to accumulate.

Oxygen toxicity in the brain (CNS) is a problem of higher PO_2s for shorter periods of time. While breathing air, a PO_2 of 1.6 ATA is not reached until a depth of 218 fsw (67 msw). Therefore, CNS oxygen toxicity is not a problem for standard recreational diving. However, more and more divers are using Nitrox and if you dive breathing a 40% oxygen mixture, the PO_2 will be 1.6 ATA at a depth of only 99 fsw (30 msw) and if you decompress on 100% oxygen, the PO_2 will be 1.6 ATA at a depth of 20 fsw (6 msw)! Therefore, CNS oxygen toxicity is a serious problem for some recreational divers and a major problem for technical and commercial divers.

The first and most serious sign of CNS oxygen toxicity is often a grand-mal type convulsion. There are many other signs and symptoms of oxygen toxicity but there is no consistent warning that a seizure is about to occur. Even the EEG is completely normal until the convulsion starts. The convulsion due to oxygen toxicity is not believed to cause any permanent problems in and of itself because the body starts the convulsion with a surplus of oxygen on board and thus the hypoxia seen with normal seizures is not a problem. However, the diver who convulses while in the water may drown or, if they ascend while the glottis is closed, may suffer pulmonary barotrauma.

There is huge variation in the amount of oxygen individuals can tolerate before they show signs of CNS oxygen toxicity and of even more concern, a huge variation in the same person on different days. A diver may do many dives in which they are exposed to high PO_2s with no difficulties and falsely conclude that they are resistant to oxygen toxicity. Then, for no apparent reason, they may suffer a CNS hit on a dive where they are exposed to a lower PO_2. In general, people can tolerate more oxygen in a dry chamber than in the water. In fact, most divers can tolerate two hours of oxygen at 3.0 ATA (66 fsw or 20 msw) in a chamber with few difficulties. While exercising in the water however, several divers have had convulsions at PO_2s as low as 1.6 ATA. To make matters worse, in the chamber divers often have one of the less serious signs of oxygen toxicity such as tunnel vision, ringing in the ears or twitching, whereas in the water the first sign is often a seizure. The seizure starts with an immediate loss of consciousness and a period of about 30 seconds when the muscles are relaxed. All of the muscles of the body then contract violently for about one minute. The diver then begins to breathe rapidly and is very confused for several minutes afterwards. As you can well imagine,

if this happens during a dive, the diver usually dies. The table gives a short list of the signs and symptoms of CNS oxygen toxicity but almost anything is possible.

There are some factors that are known to increase the risk of CNS oxygen toxicity. I have already mentioned two, submersion in water and working hard. The risk with working hard is that the PCO_2 in the body is increased and this increases the blood flow to the brain. Other causes of increased PCO_2 are skip breathing and increased carbon dioxide in the breathing gas. For the CCR diver, the primary cause of elevated CO_2 is scrubber failure. Increased stress on the diver and increased levels of adrenaline, atropine, aspirin, amphetamine and other stimulants (caffeine and some decongestants) all seem to increase the risk of CNS oxygen toxicity.

There are no drugs that can be used to prevent CNS oxygen toxicity. In animal experiments, the seizures could be prevented but the CNS cellular damage found after prolonged seizures still occurred. The only effective methods to prevent CNS oxygen toxicity are to limit the PO_2, the time of exposure, and to give air breaks during oxygen breathing.

As general guidelines, the PO_2 during decompression while at rest should never exceed 2.0 ATA and most divers use 100% oxygen at a maximum depth of 20 fsw (6 msw), 1.6 ATA. During the active part of the dive, the PO_2 should never exceed 1.6 ATA and many divers are using 1.5, 1.4, or even 1.3 as the maximum PO_2. NOAA, the US Navy, the Royal Navy, the Canadian Forces, and many other organizations have guidelines for acceptable PO_2s and the maximum time that may be spent at each.

Hyperoxic Induced Myopia

We have been discussing the effects of O_2 toxicity on the brain and the lungs and until fairly recently, that would have been the end of the discussion on O_2 toxicity in diving. However, with the rapid increase in popularity of diving rebreathers, and with the phenomenal bottom times possible when diving CCR, another problem has started to appear.

It has been known for years that if you do daily hyperbaric oxygen treatments in a chamber, over several weeks some people gradually develop progressive myopia (***near-sighted***). The rate of onset is approximately one diopter per month and the rate of recovery after the treatments are stopped is approximately the same. In most people their vision returns pretty much to its' pre-treatment level.

Several CCR divers have noted a similar problem after a series of prolonged CCR dives. One 47 year old CCR diver developed the problem after doing 47 dives in 12 days with a PO_2 of 1.3 ATA. The near-sightedness developed near the end of the trip and completely recovered over the next 2 months. He then did 16 dives over 11 days and the problem returned. Again, he recovered over about 2 months. Based on these and other case histories, it seemed that you needed to do at least 45 hours of diving in 12 days or less, and in general the problem did not occur before age 40.

In 2003, one of my students developed the problem after approximately 30 hours of dive time in 11 days with a PO_2 of 1.3 ATA. She was in her early 40s and fully recovered in a few weeks. Her problem was very mild but it developed with far less exposure than previously noted. A few divers have noted a hyperopic change (***far-sighted)***.

Not much is known about this problem. It seems to involve a stiffening of the lens and there is definitely a difference between people in their susceptibility to this problem. It does not seem to cause any permanent damage, but once you have experienced the problem, you seem to be more likely to have the problem in the future, with less provocation. The only treatment is to avoid elevated PO_2, and the only way to prevent the problem is to also avoid elevated PO_2s.

So what does this mean for the tech diver? First, it is yet another reason to be conservative with your O_2 exposures. If you are going to be doing a "lot" of diving in a short period of time, it makes sense to reduce the set point on your rebreather to a PO_2 of 1.2, 1.1 or even 1.0 ATA. You will need to do a bit more decompression, but the risk of O_2 toxicity will be greatly reduced. For open circuit divers, don't push the PO_2 during your dive or during decompression. Finally, if you notice your vision has degraded near the end of an intense tech dive trip, and if it recovers over the next several weeks of not diving, you most likely have experienced the problem and you will need to reduce you PO_2s for future diving.

MIKE FOWLER SWIMS WITH MANTA RAY - PHOTOGRAPH COURTESY OF STEVEN FRINK

Chapter Four
Carbon Dioxide Retention

Simon J. Mitchell M.B. Ch.B., DipHOM.

Introduction

Carbon dioxide (***CO_2***) is a "by-product" of metabolism and is removed from the body by breathing. Failure to match the rate of CO_2 elimination with the rate of its production will result in increasing CO_2 levels. This, in turn, will result in "***CO_2 toxicity***" symptoms such as headache, shortness of breath and mental impairment. If levels become very high there will be loss of consciousness. The interesting thing about diving is that there are reasons why CO_2 production may be increased and elimination impaired, thus making divers particularly vulnerable to CO_2 toxicity. These issues will be explored in this chapter.

How Is Carbon Dioxide Produced?

Oxygen is metabolized in cells to produce the high energy molecules required to fuel all bodily functions. Virtually all tissues have some requirement for oxygen, and therefore produce some CO_2, but some tissues produce more than others. At rest, the heart muscle and brain are important contributors, and during exercise, skeletal muscle becomes important as you might expect.

There is nothing unusual about diving in this regard. That is, work performed in diving is no different to work performed at the surface. Oxygen will be consumed and CO_2 will be produced in the same quantities for the same amount of work. However, there is one important distinction that should be mentioned; the fact that the work involved in breathing can be much greater during diving. Indeed, it is important for divers to understand that breathing requires physical work. It is fairly obvious that if the lung is elastic, then work must be done during inspiration to overcome that elasticity and stretch the lung. Similarly, there is work involved in moving the "weight" of the chest wall and other soft tissues during inspirations. Less obvious is the work that must be performed to overcome resistance to gas flow through the airway passages in the lung. Like any other work, the work of breathing results in the consumption of oxygen and production of CO_2.

We don't notice work of breathing under normal circumstances because we are well adapted to the normal demands. However, it is important in diving because as will be discussed, it can be increased by immersion, the use of underwater breathing equipment, and by increases in gas density. Though perhaps stating the obvious, the diver's ability to respond to increases in work of breathing is not unlimited. The corollary is that respiratory muscle exhaustion or failure to respond to increased work demand for any reason will result in inadequate ventilation (***hypoventilation***) and an increase in arterial CO_2 as is described below.

How Is Carbon Dioxide Eliminated?

As described above, CO_2 is produced in the body tissues. Because the partial pressure of CO_2 (***PCO_2***) is lower in the arterial blood than in the tissues, some CO_2 diffuses from the tissues into the blood and is carried away in the venous system to the lungs. Once again, because the PCO_2 in the lung alveoli is kept lower than in the venous blood by breathing (see below), some CO_2 diffuses from the blood into the alveoli from where it is removed when we breathe, see Figure 4-1.

The most useful way to conceptualize this process is to consider the circulatory system depicted in Figure 4-1 as being like a clockwise conveyor belt in continuous operation. The conveyor has some objects on it that are

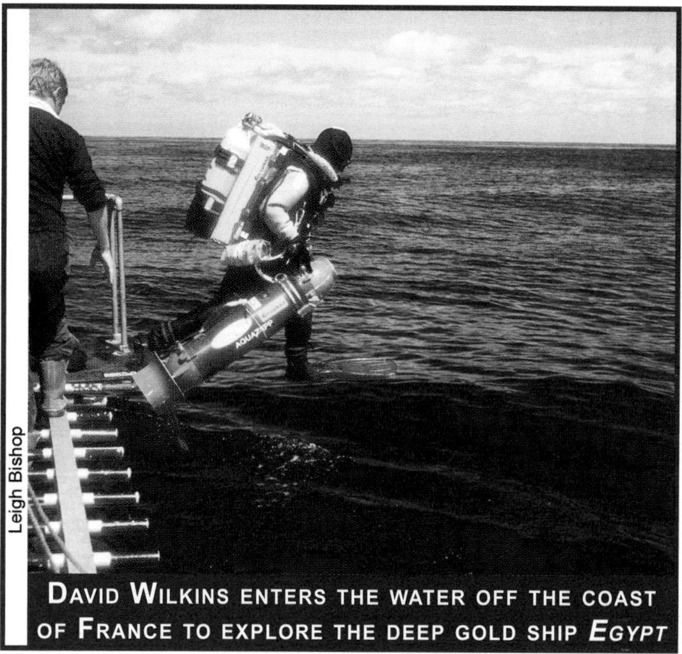

David Wilkins enters the water off the coast of France to explore the deep gold ship *Egypt*

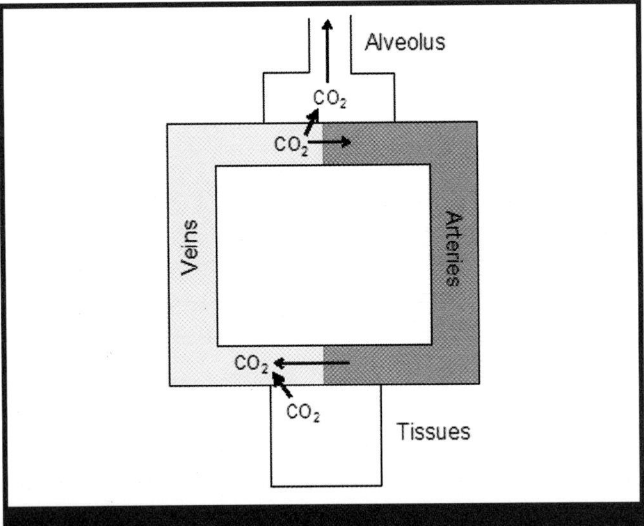

Figure 4-1: Simple functional depicition of CO_2 procuction by the tissues and its removal by the cardiovascular and respiratory systems

constantly circulating around. In addition, there is a worker on one side of the conveyor putting more of these objects on, and another on the other side taking the objects off. As long as these workers continue to work (that is, put objects on and take them off respectively) at the same rate, then the number of objects on the conveyor will not change. However, any imbalance in the activity of the two workers will cause the number of objects on the conveyor to change. For example, if the worker taking objects off slows down in comparison to the worker putting them on, then objects will accumulate on the conveyor belt. Obviously, in this analogy, the objects represent CO_2 molecules, the worker putting objects on the conveyor represents CO_2 production by the tissues, and the worker removing objects represents the removal of CO_2 from the blood into the alveoli.

CO_2 production by the tissues (and therefore the process of "putting objects on the conveyor") is a simple function of tissue metabolism and oxygen consumption. The harder a tissue is working, the more oxygen will be consumed and the more CO_2 will be produced. Carbon dioxide removal by the alveoli (and therefore the process of "***taking objects off the conveyor***") is dependent on maintaining a partial pressure gradient for CO_2 diffusion between blood and the alveoli. This is achieved by flushing CO_2 out of the alveoli during breathing. The more air moved in and out of the alveoli during breathing, the more CO_2 is flushed out, and the greater the pressure gradient between the venous blood and alveolar gas that encourages CO_2 to leave the blood. To reinforce this further, if there is ***hypo***ventilation of the lungs relative to CO_2 production , then blood CO_2 will increase because more objects are being put on the conveyor than removed. Maintenance of the correct CO_2 levels is therefore critically dependent on adequate lung ventilation. This simple statement is probably the single most important point in this chapter because there are multiple aspects of diving that can interfere with adequate ventilation of the lungs as will be discussed later.

For reasons that will not be discussed here, maintenance of adequate oxygen levels in the blood is not as dependent on lung ventilation as maintenance of correct CO_2 levels, especially in technical diving when high fractions or oxygen, or high PO_2s are often breathed. It is therefore not surprising that changes in arterial CO_2 appear to be more important than the arterial blood PO_2 in the control of lung ventilation.

Control of lung ventilation (or ***respiration*** as it is commonly referred to) arises from the brainstem. There is a centre which acts as a respiratory "rhythm generator"; instigating periodic inspirations and maintaining a basic respiratory rhythm without any conscious input from us. This centre receives modifying input from a variety of other centers in the brain and brainstem. Perhaps the most important of these comes from specialized nerve cells or "receptors" that lie nearby, also in the brainstem. These receptors are very sensitive to the hydrogen ion concentration (which we measure using the PH scale) of their surrounding tissue fluids. Carbon dioxide is free to diffuse from the arterial blood into these tissues and the nearby cerebro-spinal fluid. Here, it rapidly reacts with water to form bicarbonate and hydrogen ion, and the consequent increase in the concentration of hydrogen ions is sensed by the receptors. This is a potent breathing stimulus. Simply put, when CO_2 rises, respiration will be stimulated, and when CO_2 falls, respiratory drive will be reduced. When you think about the critical dependence of CO_2 levels on lung ventilation, it makes sense that respiration would be controlled in this way.

For completeness, it should be pointed out that the body does monitor the arterial PO_2; primarily by using receptors in the carotid arteries whch have links to the respiratory control centre in the brainstem. A slightly lowered PO_2 appears to sensitize the response to increasing CO_2, rather than to stimulate breathing directly. However, if the PO_2 falls sufficiently, then there will be direct stimulation of breathing.

There are several variable characteristics of this control system that are relevant to diving. First, there are differences between individuals in respect to their respiratory response to CO_2.[1] Specifically, in some individuals, the CO_2 has to rise more before increased ventilation is stimulated. These differences may be innate or acquired, and in respect to the latter, there is some evidence that diving may somehow ***reduce*** sensitivity to CO_2. Second, it seems that if maintenance of CO_2 requires more work than is involved in normal air breathing, the respiratory control centre may be "content" to allow the CO_2 to rise somewhat, rather than perform the work (i.e., breathing) required to lower it again.[2] This is relevant because diving does increase the "work" involved in breathing as will be discussed later. Once again, there appears to be a degree of individual variability in this characteristic. Third, just as low PO_2 increases the brainstem's sensitivity to CO_2, high PO_2 and high PN_2 (as often encountered in diving) may decrease sensitivity.[3] Finally, divers are to some extent able to consciously overrule the "automatic" breathing control system, even if CO_2 levels are rising a little. This is sometimes seen in divers who try to conserve gas by "skip breathing" or some other method to consciously reduce ventilation. All of these factors potentially contribute to an increase in arterial CO_2 during diving.

How Diving Affects Lung Ventilation

So far we have established that blood CO_2 levels are critically dependent on the amount of gas being shifted in and out of the lungs (***lung ventilation***), and that there is an automatic system to control ventilation so that CO_2 levels are maintained correctly. We have also established that this control system is variable between individuals, and can be affected by diving in ways that favor an increase in CO_2. Now we move on to discuss how diving affects our ability to ventilate the lungs, irrespective of whether the control system is responding appropriately. As you will see, diving can limit our ability to ventilate the lungs so that it may be inadequate to maintain normal CO_2 levels, even if the control system is working perfectly; indeed, even if we consciously try to ventilate more. There are a number of factors that contribute to this limitation and they are described below.

Immersion

Immersion, even in shallow water, causes a number of important physiological changes which impact on respiratory system function.

Redistribution of Blood Volume

Irrespective of a diver's orientation in the water, there is a centralization of blood volume because of peripheral vasoconstriction and the loss of the gravitational effect that usually results in pooling of blood in the dependent veins (especially in the legs). This blood volume shift results in a relative (though tolerable) "congestion" of the distensible pulmonary circulation with blood. This makes the lungs a little "stiffer" which may marginally increase the work required to maintain the same ventilation. As an aside, this blood volume shift is also responsible for the highly annoying (especially if you are a dry suit diver) increase in urine production that occurs in diving. The body's blood volume control mechanism incorrectly interprets the "central hypervolemia" as an indication of fluid overload, and signals the kidneys to make more urine.

Static Lung Load (*SLL*)

When immersed, the body is exposed to a vertical pressure gradient in the water column. Simply put, and as every diver knows, pressure increases with depth. This sets up an important interaction between diver and breathing apparatus.

Consider a rebreather diver with a front mounted counter-lung lying horizontally in the water. Notwithstanding the presence of one way check valves in the loop, the diver's airways are in continuity with the counter-lung which lies slightly deeper and therefore at higher pressure than the lungs. This means that the lung airways are subject to a positive pressure equal to the vertical height of the water column between counter-lung and the lung itself. We refer to this as a "positive static lung load," see Figure 4-2. The diver will notice that inhalation seems assisted, whereas exhalation requires extra effort. The reverse would be true

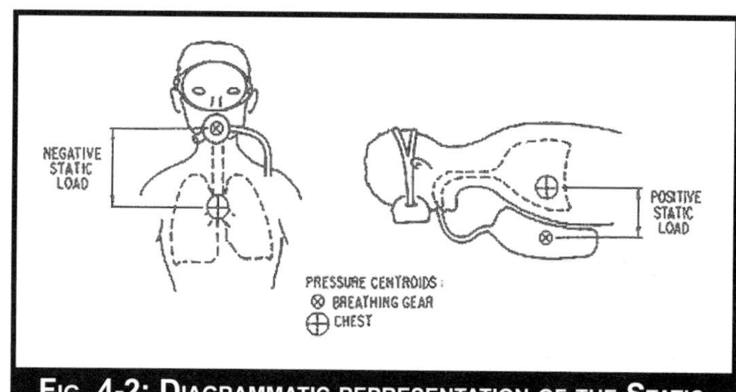

Fig. 4-2: Diagrammatic representation of the Static Lung Load Diagram from Warkander et al. 1989[4]

for a horizontal diver wearing a back mounted counter-lung. The resulting "negative static lung load" would make inhalation seem harder and exhalation seem easier. These effects are not limited to rebreather divers. The same phenomenon arises when there is a vertical differential between an open circuit demand valve (which supplies gas at ambient pressure) and the lungs, see Figure 4-2. Because the demand valve is higher than the lungs, the gas is supplied at a slightly lower pressure than that to which the lungs are exposed, thus constituting a negative static lung load.

It would seem natural to assume that the opposite effects of a SLL on the effort of inspiration and expiration would somehow "balance each other out," and that overall it would be of negligible importance. Unfortunately, this does not seem to be the case. In fact, the physiological significance of a SLL is actually quite complex, and we discuss it here at only a superficial level.

The negative SLL is arguably the most relevant to the majority of diving situations since it applies to upright (or slightly head up) open circuit divers and at least some rebreather diving scenarios. A negative SLL further enhances the redistribution of blood into the very distensible blood vessels of the lungs (described above in relation to immersion). This redistribution is simply in response to pressure gradients. It is the same as going below the water-line of a ship, drilling a hole in the side, and somehow sealing a balloon over the hole. The balloon would fill with water until its elasticity overcame the pressure tending to force the water inward. In the case of the lung in the upright diver, the "water" is the blood in the circulatory system which is exposed to the surrounding water pressure, and the "balloon" is the distensible lung blood vessels.

This increased congestion of the lung circulation with blood causes further "stiffening" of the lung tissue, and the volume of gas left in the lungs at the end of a normal expiration falls. This means that at the start of an inspiration the lungs are at a lower volume and the airways are narrower, thus increasing the resistance to gas flow (see later). Not surprisingly, there are data that demonstrate both an increase in the work of breathing and an increase in the subjective sense of breathlessness when a negative SLL is imposed.[5] Positive SLLs are less commonly encountered, but can also be disadvantageous at extremes. Nevertheless, there is some data to suggest that divers are most comfortable and work is best facilitated at a slightly positive SLL.[6]

There has been much discussion on how to compensate for SLL during diving, but there are significant practical obstacles and virtually all diving is undertaken with uncompensated equipment. In this regard, it is important to maintain some perspective on the problem represented by SLLs. This phenomenon is part of everyday diving and most dives do not result in overt respiratory discomfort let alone accidents resulting from respiratory failure. It follows that under normal circumstances the physiological challenge of a modest SLL can be met and managed without problems. However, the issue is worthy of note as one of several potential contributors to respiratory difficulties (other examples being hard work, high equipment breathing resistance, and denser gas) that, should they become relevant simultaneously, might result in difficulty maintaining adequate ventilation.

Diving Equipment

The use of diving equipment will almost invariably impose an extra resistance to breathing that would not be present if the diver was simply breathing from their own airway. This is another potential contributor to increased work of breathing and respiratory failure (inadequate ventilation), and it is universally agreed that minimization of equipment-related breathing resistance is desirable. At the same time, it is acknowledged that some resistance is inevitable. For example, the CO_2 scrubber canister in a rebreather will always cause some resistance to gas flow.

Since the order of components in a rebreather can be varied, there has been investigation of where their associated resistance might be best tolerated. Warkander et al.[7] separated equipment-related breathing resistance into its inspiratory and expiratory components, and showed that divers react to an imposed resistance by prolonging the phase (inspiration or expiration) that is loaded. More importantly, they showed that expiratory resistance seems better tolerated in terms of both the divers' subjective impressions of discomfort and objective respiratory parameters. This suggests, for example, that rebreather CO_2 scrubbers should be placed on the expiratory side of the counter-lung, and not the inspiratory side.

Increasing Gas Density

The density of any given breathing gas increases linearly

GREG WOLKFILL

MEL CLARK ON HELICOPTER DECK AT CAPE BRETON, NANAIMO, BC, CANADA

with depth. Technical divers substitute helium for nitrogen in gas mixes for deeper diving, which substantially reduces density. Nevertheless, at the depth targets being set by some extreme exponents, gas density still increases significantly despite the use of helium. For example, in one widely reported fatal dive, the use of Trimix 4 82 at 872 ffw (264 mfw) equated approximately to air at 233 ft (70 m) (8 ATA) in terms of gas density.[8]

Dense gas impacts significantly on respiratory function primarily by ***increasing resistance to flow*** through airways and thereby limiting ventilatory performance. Indeed, if you ask a subject to ventilate as hard as they can whilst breathing air at the modest pressure of 4 ATA (equivalent to 100 ft (30 m) depth), the maximum volume they can shift over a minute ***is only half of that at 1ATA.***[9] In part, this is just a function of the increased effort required to move denser gas through the airways and is analogous to showing that someone can only run half as fast up a hill as they can on the flat.

In addition, there is evidence that at high gas densities a phenomenon known as "effort independent exhalation" may arise at quite low rates of gas flow through the airways. This is a complicated physiological phenomenon that largely defies succinct description! However, it occurs because the pressure inside the airway drops as gas passes outwards from the alveoli along the airways during an

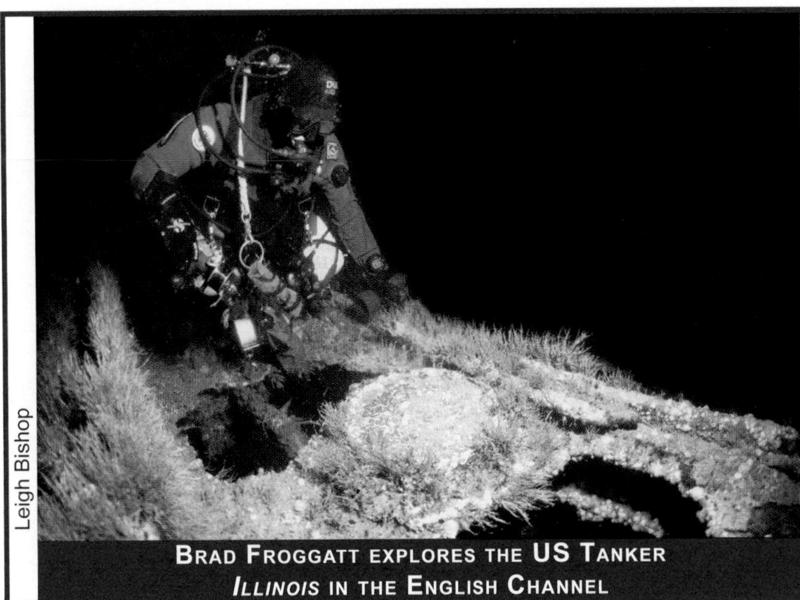

BRAD FROGGATT EXPLORES THE US TANKER *ILLINOIS* IN THE ENGLISH CHANNEL

exhalation. This pressure drop will occur more quickly when the gas density is increased because there is more resistance to flow. The diver trying to exhale rapidly will be contracting the chest wall muscles hard, increasing the pressure inside the chest to force the gas out. However, this pressure not only pushes on the alveoli, but also on the ***outside*** of the airways. When the pressure *inside* the airways is falling rapidly because the gas density is high, a situation can arise in which the pressure on the outside of the airway is greater than the inside, and the airway collapses thus restricting gas flow. Once this occurs, straining harder to exhale does not achieve any more gas flow (hence the reason it is called "effort independent"). Indeed, all it does is cause the diver to perform more work.

If this occurs, it is not difficult to imagine that it creates a very dangerous situation. The diver's capacity to ventilate the lungs (and therefore to eliminate CO_2) is restricted. In addition, the work undertaken in fruitless attempts to increase ventilation simply produces more CO_2. A vicious circle is created because the resulting increased levels of arterial CO_2 then stimulate or "drive" the diver to make even more respiratory effort, which just produces more CO_2 and so on. This scenario was predicted by Wood and Bryan in 1969,[10] and may well have been demonstrated in a practical sense by one recent and widely discussed diving fatality[8] and other accidents caused by hypercapnia.

Interestingly, effort independent exhalation is a normal physiological phenomenon that occurs during very rapid exhalations when air breathing at 1 ATA. However, it does not matter in this context because the flow through the airways which can be generated before it occurs is so great that very hard exercise can be undertaken and sustained without CO_2 increasing. The problem in diving is that effort independent exhalation will occur at much lower flow rates when a denser gas is breathed, because the pressure drop along the airway is much greater. Wood and Bryan (1969) demonstrated that effort independent exhalation was almost encountered during breathing ***at rest*** when breathing air at 10 ATA.[10] Put in more practical terms, if a diver breathing air at 10 ATA tried to do much more than normal quiet breathing, they may have difficulty increasing their ventilation much no matter how hard they tried. While air at 10 ATA seems far fetched, it is not difficult to imagine gas mixes of equivalent density being used at extreme depth given the rate at which technical diving is progressing.

How Does CO_2 Toxicity or Hypercapnia Occur?

Hypercapnia is a potentially dangerous state of excessive arterial PCO_2. Most of the mechanisms that might contribute to its occurrence have been mentioned in the previous sections of this chapter, but it is such an important subject that it justifies an integrated summary here.

In its early stages hypercapnia may produce a headache and mild shortness of breath. At more severe levels it can produce debilitating shortness of breath, disorientation, impaired cognition, and ultimately unconsciousness. Hypercapnia also enhances the effect of nitrogen narcosis, and increases the risk of oxygen toxicity.

As implied earlier, in the absence of CO_2 rebreathing (see later), hypercapnia is due to inadequate lung ventilation relative to CO_2 production. Indeed, the determination of alveolar (and arterial) CO_2 can be expressed by the simple equation:

$$P_ACO_2 = VCO_2 \div VA$$

Where: P_ACO_2 = the alveolar PCO_2
VCO_2 = CO_2 production
VA = alveolar ventilation

Thus, anything that ***increases CO_2 production***, or ***reduces alveolar ventilation*** will favor an increase in alveolar and arterial CO_2. Potential contributors are listed below.

Causes of Inadequate Ventilation

1. Reduced sensitivity to the drive to breathe caused by CO_2

Several mechanisms which by the brain stem respiratory controller (see earlier) may become less sensitive to rising CO_2 have been mentioned in this chapter.

a. Individual variability: Some individuals appear to be less sensitive to CO_2. That is, arterial CO_2 can rise further before a significant drive to breathe harder is developed. The term "CO_2 retainer" is sometimes used in relation to such individuals. There is some evidence that this desensitization to CO_2 can be acquired as a result of diving.[1] A consequent small increase in arterial CO_2 which does not produce any symptoms is, of itself, not necessarily harmful. However, the main concern is that such individuals may be at higher risk of oxygen toxicity and more susceptible to the effects of nitrogen narcosis

b. Increases in work of breathing. As previously mentioned there is a tendency for the respiratory controller to reduce its sensitivity to CO_2 (and therefore not respond to rising levels by increasing ventilation) if work of breathing increases.[2] Put another way, the respiratory controller will tolerate higher levels of CO_2 if an increase in work would be required to eliminate it. Although there may also be some individual variation in this tendency, this is relevant to all divers because, as previously discussed, the work of breathing virtually always increases during diving

c. Higher pressures of oxygen and nitrogen. There is some suggestion that the sensitivity of the respiratory controller to CO_2 falls in the presence of hyperoxia or when high pressures of nitrogen are breathed[3]

2. Conscious overriding of the drive to breathe

To a point, divers are able to consciously override the urge to increase ventilation. This is sometimes invoked as a strategy to conserve gas and has in the past been referred to as "skip breathing." This will result in CO_2 retention and is a dangerous practice that should be discouraged

3. Adoption of a disadvantageous breathing pattern

There is about 150 ml of dead space in the respiratory tree and this is inevitably increased by the addition of underwater breathing apparatus, though good equipment is designed to minimize this. For arguments sake, let's assume that a diver has about 200 ml of dead space accounting for both the anatomical and equipment dead spaces. Dead space gas is "last out and first in". Thus, it is gas from the alveoli that occupies the dead space at the end of an exhalation, and it is the first gas to be drawn back into the alveoli during an inhalation. Dead space gas is oxygen-depleted, and CO_2-rich when compared to fresh gas, and its re-inhalation with each new breath represents wasted ventilation

Under normal circumstances, this should not matter much. The normal tidal volume is about 10 ml/kg, so for a 70 kg adult it is approximately 700 ml. Assuming 200 ml of dead space for a diver this means that 500 ml of each breath is fresh gas. However, problems can arise if a diver adopts a rapid breathing pattern with low tidal volumes. If the tidal volume were to drop to 400 ml, then dead space gas represents half of each breath. It is for this reason that divers are encouraged to adopt a pattern of slower deep breaths in preference to a pattern of fast shallow breaths

4. Respiratory Failure

This term implies that ventilation is inadequate despite a strong drive to breathe. The main contributors to this scenario in diving are the breathing of a dense gas and the physiological consequences of this (such as effort independent exhalation), the extra breathing resistance imposed by underwater breathing apparatus, and potentially, respiratory muscle exhaustion as a terminal event. These concepts have been discussed in detail earlier and so will not be amplified here

Causes of Increased CO_2 Production

Fundamentally, the only cause of increased CO_2 production is increased work. Thus, exercise results in production of more CO_2 whereas rest should reduce it. The only point that requires emphasis in regard to diving is that breathing itself requires work, and results in production of CO_2. When a diver breathes dense gas, and/or if the underwater breathing apparatus imposes significant degrees of resistance, then the work of breathing can be a significant contributor to CO_2 production and in some

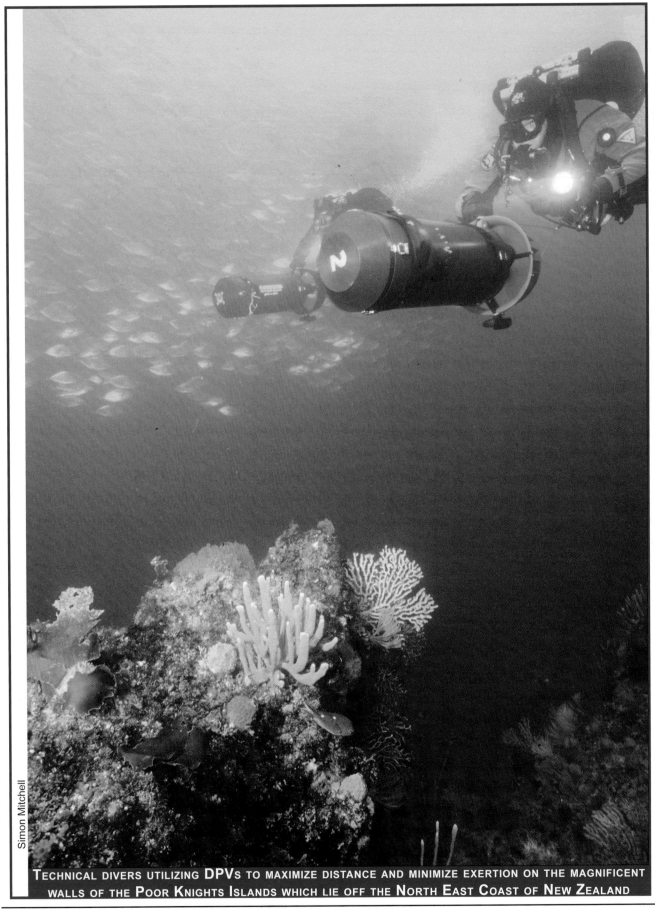

Simon Mitchell

TECHNICAL DIVERS UTILIZING DPVS TO MAXIMIZE DISTANCE AND MINIMIZE EXERTION ON THE MAGNIFICENT WALLS OF THE POOR KNIGHTS ISLANDS WHICH LIE OFF THE NORTH EAST COAST OF NEW ZEALAND

scenarios (such as a very deep dive with a dense gas and/or high resistance breathing equipment) may be virtually all that the diver is capable of doing.

CO_2 Rebreathing

Rebreather divers should note that this extensive discussion of mechanisms of hypercapnia has taken place to this point in the absence of any mention of CO_2 scrubber failure. Yet the potential causes of hypercapnia that have been discussed here are often ignored in the analysis of hypercapnia events during rebreather diving, where most commentators immediately assume that scrubber failure is the culprit.

This is not to suggest that scrubber failure is unimportant, for it certainly is another potential cause of hypercapnia in rebreather diving. In the presence of inspired CO_2, as occurs during scrubber failure, the relationship described by the equation $PACO_2 = VCO_2 \div VA$ is no longer strictly true. Indeed, depending on the amount of CO_2 in the inspired gas, the $PACO_2$ may continue to rise no matter what the level of alveolar ventilation. The technical aspects of CO_2 scrubber failure are beyond the scope of this chapter.

Preventing & Treating Hypercapnia

A relatively simple list of strategies for the avoidance of hypercapnia during diving can be constructed from perusing the list of its causes. Thus, one might aim to:

1. Ensure that the underwater breathing apparatus used is optimally maintained and configured to reduce breathing resistance. In rebreather diving one might choose a larger mesh scrubber material to reduce flow resistance for very deep diving
2. Choose a bottom mix gas with low density, and make this a priority over other considerations for very deep dives where significant exercise is anticipated
3. Avoid significant exercise if possible on any deep dive. The use of DPVs in this context is a significant safety advantage
4. Adopt a breathing pattern that is slow and deep rather than fast and shallow
5. Never intentionally resist the urge to breathe, or "skip breathe"
6. Stay physically fit, which might help avoid respiratory muscle exhaustion
7. Discard scrubber material well before its predicted "end of life" and always pack and install the scrubber meticulously

One controversial issue relating to prevention of hypercapnia that is frequently debated on internet forums is the possibility of identifying those individuals who are not sensitive to rising CO_2 and who therefore are more likely to get into trouble. One potential means of doing this is to have the subject breathing from a closed system in which the CO_2 can be both measured and increased, and in which the amount of air the diver is breathing in and out per minute can be measured. In theory, those divers who allow the CO_2 in the inspired and expired gas to rise without mounting an early and adequate respiratory response would be defined as ***CO_2 retainers.*** However, problems arise when you try to define an ***early and adequate response***, and the level of CO_2 at which this should occur. Attempts to do this have demonstrated considerable variability in the population, and it is not clear where lines should be drawn. Most diving physicians have put this in the ***too hard*** basket, even in occupational and military settings.

In terms of treating hypercapnia, the time-honored "PADI advice" for an out-of-breath diver to ***"stop, breathe deeply, and rest"*** remains valid, but should be appended with ***"... as soon as you feel symptoms of hypercapnia"*** because it is often not followed until it is too late by highly motivated technical divers. John Chatterton uses the excellent expression ***staying ahead of the wave*** to describe this advice. The period of rest should be used to review options to favorably modify the situation. A quick review of the breathing equipment may be rewarding. For example, hypercapnia may be caused by the added breathing resistance of partially closed cylinder or rebreather mouthpiece shutoff valves. Consideration can be given to lowering the density of the breathing gas by changing to a different mix (often not possible) or by decreasing the depth.

Rebreather divers are taught various strategies that may be invoked if symptoms of hypercapnia are recognized. These include flushing the loop with fresh gas, reverting to a semi-closed circuit mode, or "bailing out" to an open circuit gas supply. All of these strategies are designed to be effective if the problem is caused by failure of the CO_2 scrubber. They are all valid strategies for that scenario (particularly bailing out in the opinion of this author) but several cautionary points arise. First, if the problem is caused by respiratory failure rather than scrubber failure,

then none of these strategies are likely to help unless the work of breathing is actually lowered in some way, for example, by changing to a low resistance open circuit regulator. Indeed, if the regulator were poorly tuned it could make the problem worse. Second, many rebreather divers have reported extreme difficulty in removing their rebreather mouthpiece to facilitate a change to open circuit whilst affected by CO_2-induced breathlessness. This illustrates the advantage of a ***bailout valve*** which allows access to open circuit gas without removing the rebreather mouthpiece. Finally, the gas consumption will be extremely high when a breathless rebreather diver changes to open circuit, especially if the change occurs in deep water. Small open-circuit supplies will not last very long.

Key Points

1. CO_2 is a product of oxygen metabolism whose removal from the body is entirely dependent on lung ventilation. If ventilation is decreased, removal is decreased and vice versa. For this reason, the respiratory controller in the brain monitors CO_2 levels in the blood and adjusts lung ventilation accordingly
2. Diving tends to reduce the sensitivity of the respiratory controller to CO_2
3. The physical capacity to ventilate the lungs is reduced in most diving situations
4. Scrubber failure in a rebreather may result in rebreathing of CO_2
5. Because of points 2, 3, 4, divers are vulnerable to hypercapnia
6. Hypercapnia potentiates narcosis, predisposes to oxygen toxicity, and can cause symptoms ranging from shortness of breath to unconsciousness
7. Prevention of hypercapnia involves optimizing performance of underwater breathing equipment, adopting an optimal pattern of deep breathing, minimizing gas density at depth, and minimizing underwater work
8. Shortness of breath underwater should prompt *immediate* rest and evaluation of options to modify the situation

References

1. Lanphier EH. Nitrogen-oxygen mixture physiology, phases 1 and 2 (Technical Report). Washington DC: US Navy Experimental Diving Unit; 1955.
2. Poon CS. Effects of inspiratory resistive load on respiratory control in hypercapnia and exercise. J Appl Physiol 1989; 66:2391-9.
3. Linnarsson D, Hesser CM. Dissociated ventilatory and central respiratory responses to CO_2 at raised N_2 pressure. J Appl Physiol 1978; 45:756-61.
4. Warkander DE, Nagasawa GK, Lundgren CEG. Criteria for manned testing of underwater breathing apparatus. In: Lundgren CEG, Warkander DE (eds). Physiological and Human Engineering Aspects of Underwater Breathing Apparatus. Proceedings of the Fortieth Undersea and Hyperbaric Medical Society Workshop. Bethesda MD, 1989. UHMS:77-86.
5. Taylor NAS, Morrison JB. Lung centroid pressure and its influence on respiratory and physical work during immersion. In: Lundgren CEG, Warkander DE (eds). Physiological and Human Engineering Aspects of Underwater Breathing Apparatus. Proceedings of the Fortieth Undersea and Hyperbaric Medical Society Workshop. Bethesda MD, 1989. UHMS:33-42.
6. Lanphier EH. Immersion effects and apparatus design: The view from Wisconsin. In: Lundgren CEG, Warkander DE (eds). Physiological and Human Engineering Aspects of Underwater Breathing Apparatus. Proceedings of the Fortieth Undersea and Hyperbaric Medical Society Workshop. Bethesda MD, 1989. UHMS:45-56.
7. Warkander DE, Nagasawa GK, Lundgren CEG. Effects of inspiratory and expiratory resistance in divers' breathing apparatus. Undersea Hyperb Med 2001; 28:63-73.
8. Mitchell SJ, Cronje FJ, Meintjes WAJ, Britz HC. Fatal respiratory failure during a "technical" rebreather dive at extreme pressure. Aviat Space Environ Med 2007; 78:81-6.
9. Camporesi EM, Bosco G. Ventilation, gas exchange, and exercise under pressure. In: Brubakk AO, Neuman TS (eds). Bennett and Elliott's Physiology and Medicine of Diving (5th ed). Edinburgh 2003, Saunders Publishers: 100-1.
10. Wood LDH, Bryan AC. Effect of increased ambient pressure on flow-volume curve of the lung. J Appl Physiol 1969; 27:4-8.

Chapter Five High Pressure Nervous Syndrome

John Zumrick M.D.

History of HPNS & Deep Diving Research

The late 1960's and early 1970's saw a major expansion in the search for oil into deeper waters in the Gulf of Mexico and elsewhere. Fueled by this enterprise, investigations in the use of helium gas mixtures (***Heliox***) for diving in deeper water expanded greatly. These experiments led to the description of the signs and symptoms of High Pressure Nervous Syndrome (***HPNS***).

In 1965, Bennett first described the presence of tremors in divers during experiments conducted at the Royal Naval Physiologic Laboratory (***RNPL***) using rapid compression to 600 to 800 fsw (183.5 to 244.6 msw). Divers experienced dizziness, nausea, and vomiting in addition to tremors. In 1968 during experiments as deep as 1189 fsw (363.3 msw), Brauer noted periods of somnolence termed microsleep and changes in the brains electrical activity as recorded on the electroencephalogram (***EEG***). By comparing these EEG changes together with the appearance of tremors, and a correlative similar change in animals, he predicted the appearance of seizures at a depth of about 1200 fsw (367 msw). Later, he coined the term HPNS to describe the combination of tremor, dizziness, nausea, vomiting, microsleep and EEG changes.

In 1970, using compression rates significantly lower than those used in the above experiments, Comex, a French diving firm, successfully exceeded the proposed 1200 fsw (367 msw) barrier. Divers in this study experienced the effects of HPNS with prominent tremors and EEG changes, but were able to function depth although at a lower level of performance.

In 1974 Duke University and Tarreytown Labs conducted the first experiments using Trimix - the combination of oxygen, helium, and nitrogen - in an attempt to reduce the effects of HPNS and permit more rapid decompression rates. These experiments led to divers successfully reaching 2250 fsw (688.1 msw) (1981; Duke University). Although these dives allowed divers to reach record depths using faster compression rates than when using Heliox, high gas density led to shortness of breath and limited exercise tolerance.

Manifestations of HPNS

Syndromes such as HPNS are defined as the occurrence of certain signs and symptoms together, often associated with some external event such as a deep dive. For HPNS

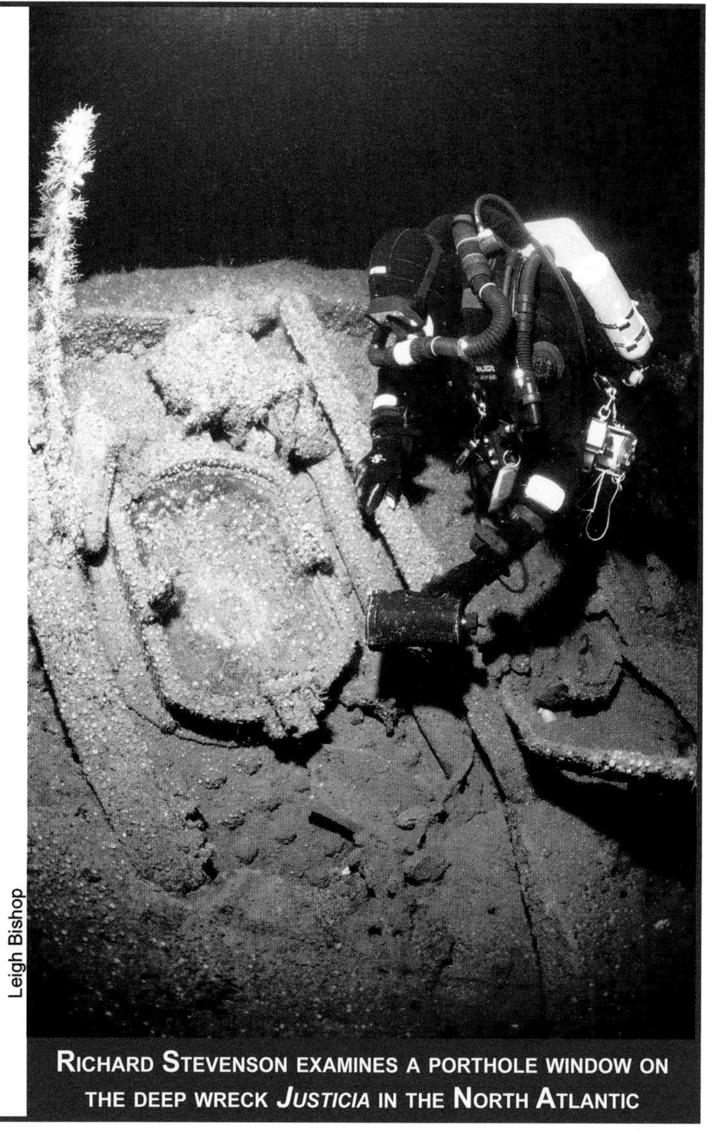
Leigh Bishop

RICHARD STEVENSON EXAMINES A PORTHOLE WINDOW ON THE DEEP WRECK *JUSTICIA* IN THE NORTH ATLANTIC

these include dizziness, nausea, or a sense of disorientation. External signs can appear as tremors, vomiting, tonic-clonic muscle jerks, microsleep, EEG changes, and chances in performance tests. Based on the above, HPNS can be described as the syndrome of dizziness, vertigo, nausea, vomiting, tremor, microsleep and EEG changes associated with deep diving. Investigators observe these signs in divers and attempt to quantitate them in an effort to objectively evaluate the effects on certain dive procedures on the diver. EEG testing, performance tests and tremor are generally used to evaluate the severity of HPNS.

EEG Changes

The electroencephalogram (EEG) was the first apparatus to be used in an attempt to quantify the HPNS. EEG is the recording of the brains electrical activity by means of electrodes applied to the divers scalp. Recordings taken at depth are compared with those taken on the surface to evaluate the changes introduced by depth and to follow their changes throughout the dive.

EEG recordings taken during dives reveal an increase of theta waves, a slow wave component of the EEG (4 to 7 per second), and an associated decrease in alpha waves (8 to 13 per second), a faster wave component of the EEG. These changes are often associated with focal spikes in the EEG. These changes provide an objective measurement of the changes produced by depth and changes in compression rate, as well as recovery from HPNS.

EEG changes begin to appear at about 1000 fsw (305.8 msw), when slow compressions are used and to appear at progressively shallower depth as compression rate increases. Thus, while a compression to 1189 fsw (363.6 msw) for over 2 hours - such as those conducted by Comex in 1968 - resulted in severe EEG changes and severe HPNS resulted in the dive being aborted. The US Navy Experimental Diving Unit in 1969 during a deep dive conducted at Duke University noted no such changes. This dive used a much slower compression rate of 77 hours to reach 1000 feet (305.8 m). Rapid compression at the rate of 100 feet (30.58 m) per minute can be expected to result in severe changes that develop as shallow as 600 fsw (183.5 msw) when breathing Heliox. EEG changes seem to persist and even worse for a period of about 6 hours after reaching maximum depth. Rapid excursions deeper, after reaching depth, dramatically worsen these changes.

Microsleep

During dives below 1000 fsw (305.8 msw) researchers commonly noted increasing signs of somnolence (sleepiness) in divers. When divers were un-stimulated they readily appeared to fall asleep. However, once stimulated - usually with only a word or light touch they would instantly wake-up. The transition between sleep and wakefulness was almost imperceptible.

This author experienced microsleep during a dive to 1500 fsw (458.7 msw). I was asked as a part of the experimental studies to memorize from a list as many words and associated two digit numbers as I could during a one minute period. Later, I was asked to reconstruct this list from a rearranged list of words and numbers. During the one minute memorization period, I noted my vision blurring and had to stimulate myself to continue memorizing the list. This happened at least three times during the one minute memorization period. This is best classified as mild microsleep. Experiences at even shallower depth, but with more rapid compression have resulted in serious microsleep where divers were experiencing microsleep at least 50% of the time at depth.

The appearance of microsleep is different from normal sleep and can be detected by noting associated changes on EEG. Normal sleep consists of two phases: rapid eye movement (***REM***) sleep, and non-rapid eye movement (***NREM***) sleep. Microsleep associated with HPNS is associated with a NREM sleep pattern. This EGG pattern did not progress to a REM sleep pattern as would have occurred during normal sleep.

Performance Testing

Knowledge on the effects on diver performance of deep diving procedures is central to safe diving practice. Tests such as placing small pegs in holes using pickups, and solving math problems are practiced at the surface until peak proficiency is obtained to eliminate the effects of learning from disturbing test results. These results are then compared to those taken at depth.

Tests such as moving small pegs or ball bearings with pickups are useful in testing manual dexterity. Similarly, tests of mathematical ability evaluate decision making and are useful in evaluating cognitive function. In general, HPNS tests evaluating manual dexterity and alertness showed deterioration, while those evaluating cognitive function showed less affectation. However, as we shall see later, this was not the case while breathing Trimix where tremors were decreased, but cognitive function also decreased.

Although these tests are useful in determining the effects of a certain dive on diver performance, they provide little if any information in defining the cause of this decreased performance. Thus, for example, if the nausea of HPNS were relieved by medication would performance improve, or is the decrease in performance due to altered function in other areas of the brain, or both? Moreover, there is no general agreement on how these tests might be used to determine when a diver is not fit to dive.

Tremor is the most prominently noted sign of HPNS. If severe it can greatly affect ones ability to perform fine motor tasks. It can be measured in a variety of ways including tests of dexterity such as lifting and placing a ball bearing with tweezers, but is better quantified by placing an accelerometer on a person's finger and noting the frequency and amplitude of the tremor using power spectral analysis.

Tremor is normally present in all individuals. It is classified as either normal rest tremor, normal postural tremor or normal intention tremor, depending on whether the measurements were to taken during a resting posture, while holding the finger outstretched or performing some motion. Normal rest, postural and intention tremors have a prominent frequency component of 8-12 cycles per second which sets it apart from abnormal tremors which have a slower frequency component between 3 and 8 cycles per second.

Tremors associated with HPNS occur in a frequency range of 5-8 cycles per second and tend to be continuous and rhythmic, and predominantly demonstrated in the arms, hands, upper torso and head. Overall, this tremor is similar to that seen in Parkinson's disease. Symptoms of tremor were reported as shallow at 429 fsw (128.72 msw) during rapid compression. The amplitude of HPNS tremor seems dependent on compression rates being much worse with faster compressions.

Other Signs & Symptoms of HPNS

Symptoms reported by divers consistent with HPNS include dizziness, vertigo, nausea, visual distortions, and altered sleep. Although it is difficult to quantify these, clearly they have effects on diver performance. Taken together with the other previously discussed signs these often result in a divers inability to perform certain essential tasks during the dive. The challenge for researchers is to define dive procedures that minimized the effects of HPNS while allowing as rapid as possible rate of compression to depth.

HPNS is a syndrome primarily of neurologic dysfunction. Its diverse signs and symptoms suggest that its causes are complex. While originally termed helium tremors, it is now clear that hydrostatic pressure rather than helium is the cause of HPNS.

Causes of HPNS

The current theory on the cause of HPNS stems from the work of anesthesiologists. They were investigating the phenomenon of pressure reversal of anesthesia. They noticed that increased pressure tended to reverse the effects of narcotic anesthetics. It holds that the narcotic potency of anesthetics and certain other gases relates to their solubility in lipid-rich membranes such as those in the central nervous system. Such distortions in membrane structure could disrupt sodium and calcium channels and various receptor sites where neurotransmitters that regulate normal function act. The application of pressure has been found to reverse these narcotic properties presumably due to the direct effects of pressure that tend to offset the increased lipid volume. Helium is very poorly lipid soluble and appears to be inadequate to cause lipid volume increase to offset the increased pressure. Thus, helium itself appears to be related to HPNS only in its ability to help prevent it.

The membrane effects appear to result in biochemical alterations within cells. The precise biochemical alterations that occur with HPNS have not been well defined. Observations in man as well as animal studies suggest that reductions in gamma amino butyric acid (*GABA*), a neurotransmitter that has an inhibitory effect on the central nervous system (thereby reducing excitability), may play a role in HPNS. Similarly it has been suggested that increases in excitatory neurotransmitters may occur and may also contribute to HPNS symptoms.

However, drugs given in an attempt to alter these agents have not convincingly proven their usefulness. When four drugs known to have GABA enhancing effects were tested in animals only one, sodium valproate (***VPA***), was shown to have a broad range of effects on HPNS. VPA also reduces the level of aspartic acid, another neurotransmitter that has excitatory effects. Studies have shown a reduction in aspartic acid also reduces the symptoms of HPNS. Thus, GABA alone does not appear to play an exclusive role in the manifestations of HPNS. It is likely that a reduction of HPNS is dependent on both an enhancement of GABA production and an associated decrease in excitatory neurotransmitters such as aspartic acid.

The actual structures affected by HPNS have been studied in animals. These electrophysiological experiments compared with observations in man indicate that the brain cortex, lower brain centers, the spinal cord and peripheral nervous system all may play a role in the expression of the signs and symptoms of HPNS.

Limitations of HPNS Research

The interpretation of the current literature on HPNS, as an attempt to define safe diving practice, is complicated by a number of variables. Most dive profiles were designed at least in part with the intention of satisfying the interests of program sponsors. Often this was a navy or commercial diving firm seeking some competitive advantage. As a consequence much of what we know about factors essential in planning very deep dives are empirical in nature. Based on such a limited understanding of HPNS, new and different dive profiles, which differ from those already in use, must be carefully tested to ensure their safety.

This empirically driven research often led to an experimental design where compression rates were varied in an attempt to achieve the optimum profile; often conflicting with the desire to systematically explore those important factors that affect HPNS severity. Other limiting factors include the limited number of divers as the test group (due to chamber size), thus limiting the amount of data that could be collected. Often, the amount of testing and the type of quantifiable tests for HPNS varied greatly between studies carried out at the various research centers. Finally, the compression rates and dive profiles differed greatly, complicating any attempt to clearly isolate and quantitate the effects of variables such as absolute depth, rate of compression, and diver variability on the manifestations of HPNS.

Four factors that affect the depth and onset of HPNS are the:

1. **Absolute hydrostatic pressure (depth)**
2. **Individual diver susceptibility**
3. **Rate of compression**
4. **Composition of the breathing gas**

Nonetheless, we have learned much about factors that affect the onset and severity of HPNS. Knowledge of these factors has led to the level of deep diving practice used by various navies and commercial diving companies throughout the world. Unfortunately, our understanding of these effects is still not sufficient to allow the development of new diving procedures without their careful testing – first under rigidly controlled conditions prior to use in the open sea.

Factors Affecting the Onset of HPNS

The studies done at different research centers all using differing compression rates, hydrostatic pressure, gas compositions and divers, often in a non-systematic fashion. This has often resulted in conflicting results in tests conducted at the various research centers.

Individual Susceptibility is a 5 to 1 Effect

One important emerging concept about HPNS is that individuals vary in their susceptibility to it. This inter-individual variability can be large. If EEG changes alone were compared, then the difference can be as great as 5 to 1 between divers. The effects of severe HPNS and its differing effect on divers is illustrated in US Navy experience during a dive 1800 fsw (550.5 msw) using Heliox. Of six divers, two were severely affected by HPNS and unable to perform usual work. They were essentially confined to their bunks. The second two divers could function only marginally – passing tools, etc. and only for brief periods. The remaining two divers who showed the least effects of HPNS, could function, but only at reduced ability. For example, these two divers were asked to replace a breathing gas heater. This task consisted of removing three threaded hoses, two gas hoses and the hot water supply hose. This

took approximately 30 minutes to accomplish, and it was discovered they had inadvertedly reattached the heater they were supposed to remove. All divers showed sleep alterations, no appetite, and lost significant weight during 4.5 days at 1800 fsw (550.5 msw).

Comex conducted a series of experiments in an effort to define a means to select the most HPNS resistant divers to use in their very deep dives. These studies consisted of measuring both EEG changes and a battery of performance tests at 590 fsw (180.4 msw) breathing 10% nitrogen in Trimix, and again using the same divers at 1500 fsw (458.7 msw). Compression rates were 40 ft per min (12.2 m per min) to 590 fsw (177 msw) and compression to 1500 fsw (458.7 msw) was in stages taking 38 hours in overall. All divers were ranked as to magnitude of EEG changes noted as well as toperformance test results. They found that as a group EEG changes and performance test results decreased with depth. When individuals were compared there was no such correlation. While EEG changes and performance correlated, meaning that those divers most affected shallow were also the most affected deep, the same could not be said for the performance test results. Deeper, some divers actually did better on performance tests than others who had better performance scores at shallower depths.

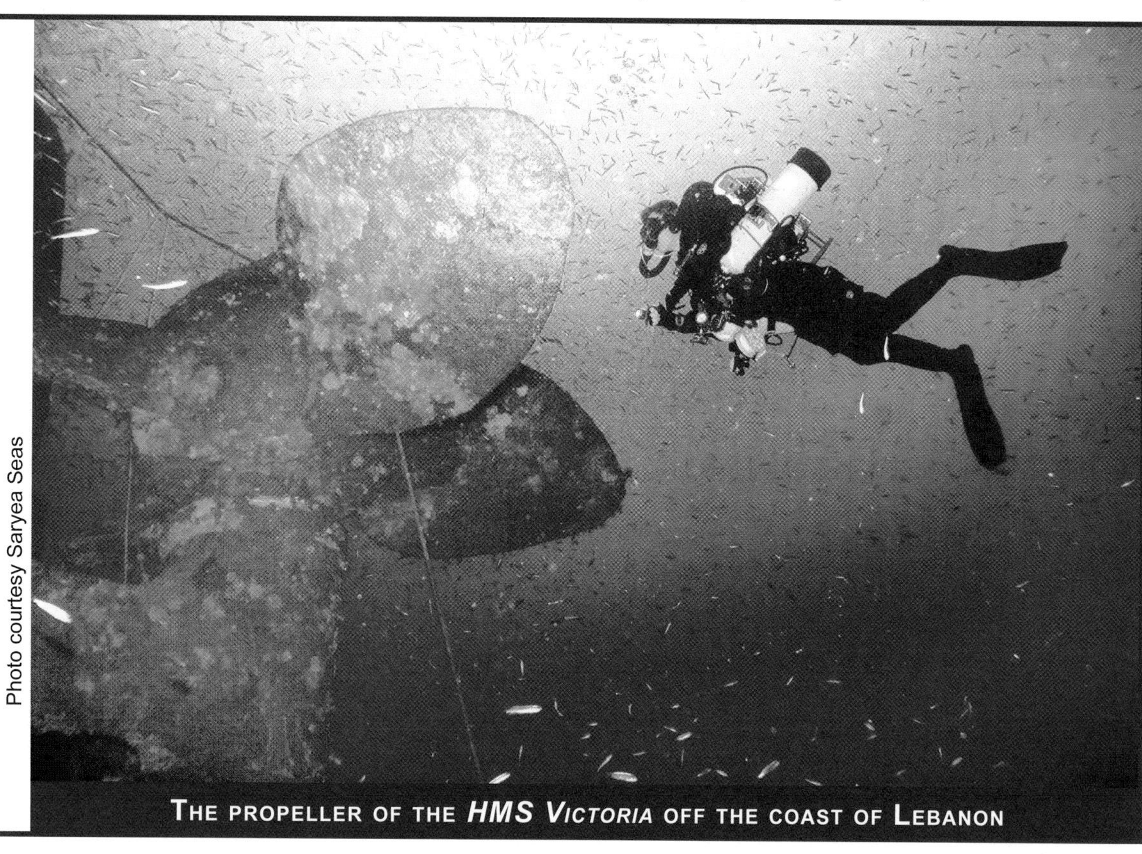

Photo courtesy Saryea Seas

THE PROPELLER OF THE ***HMS VICTORIA*** OFF THE COAST OF LEBANON

Thus, one is forced to conclude that there is no easy test to evaluate susceptibility to HPNS. One might be tempted to evaluate deep performance based on performance test results, but because of the relationship of EEG changes to seizures, using performance tests alone as a measure of performance at depth is dangerous. These same investigators also noted a latency of between 30 and 60 minutes in the onset of symptoms; with symptoms appearing sooner in some divers than others did.

Rate of Compression

The depth at which HPNS appears and its severity is influenced by the rate of compression. In early studies of HPNS using Heliox mixtures compression rates as fast as 100 fsw per min (30.6 m per min) were used. These tests uniformly documented severe tremors, along with performance deterioration and EEG changes before reaching 1000 fsw (305.8 msw). For example Bennett documented test decrements of approximately 25% in arithmetic and manual dexterity at 600 fsw (183.5 msw). These changes doubled at 800 fsw (244.6 msw). In addition the divers reported severe nausea, dizziness, and increased tremors. Comex found that tremors appeared well before 1000 fsw (305.8 msw) resulted in complete incapacitation of the divers requiring immediate termination of the dive. Based upon these studies rapid compression deeper than

600 fsw (183.5 msw) was largely abandoned using Heliox measures.

Absolute Pressure - Heliox

If divers were to successfully dive at or beyond 1000 fsw (305.8 msw), slower rates of compression would have to be used. Focus of research efforts turned to defining the optimum compression profile, or at least those were divers can be expected to be productive soon after reaching working depth.

Further studies in diving to and beyond 1000 fsw (305.8 msw) focused on using slower compression rates and with holds at various intermediate depths. Experiments by numerous labs indicated that compression to 1000 fsw (305.8 msw) with minor changes in diver performance could be conducted only if compression was less than 3 fsw per min (0.9 msw per min). Often these were exponential compressions with faster rates being used shallow, gradually slowing as depth increased, but resulting in a rate less than 3 fsw per min (0.9 msw per min).

If more rapid compression rates were used diver performance would not be guaranteed. The following examples illustrate the combined effects of compression rate and diver variability on the manifestations of HPNS. Comex found that a compression rate of 10 fsw per min (3 msw per min) resulted in severe tremors and gross motor difficulty in their divers. On the other hand three divers were able to perform tasks after a compression of 16.7 fsw per min (5 msw per min) to 1000 fsw (305.8 msw) for Bühlmann. Using a linear compression rate of 3.3 fsw per min (1 msw per min) investigators at the Admiralty Marine Technology Establishment, Physiological Laboratory (AMTE per PL) noted severe nausea and impending unconsciousness at 820 fsw (250 fsw).

Using these and even slower overall rates of compression dives below 1000 fsw (305.8 msw) were attempted. Often compression was stopped at intermediate depths prior to reaching the maximum depth. This had the overall effect of reducing overall compression rate as well as allowing recovery of the divers from the increasing effects of HPNS. Past 1000 fsw (305.8 msw) the question is not: was the diver affected by HPNS, rather how much the diver is affected?

In general depth increases as do the symptoms of HPNS. In shallower dives HPNS was found to have a latency of onset, mentioned previously, along with gradual increase in symptoms over a period of 4 to 6 hours once maximum depth had been reached. Afterwards, symptoms tend to decline, and performance testing results to improve, but with residual EEG changes. As dives progressed deeper toward 1600 fsw (489.3 msw) performance decrements increased and no longer showed improvement with time at depth.

It was clear that beyond 1600 fsw (489.3 msw) using very slow compression so as to eliminate any compression rate effect on symptoms, high hydrostatic pressure itself induces severe and incapacitating HPNS. The deepest dive accomplished using Heliox mixture was to 2001 fsw (610 msw) by Comex in 1972. Bottom time was limited to 80 minutes due to severe HPNS.

Helium, Oxygen, & Nitrogen (Trimix) Research

The above studies using Heliox mixtures clearly demonstrate that by using very slow and largely impractical compression rates divers could function as deep as 1500 fsw (458.7 msw), but that something else must be done to allow faster compression and/or allow deeper dives without severe HPNS. In 1973 Bennett began conducting initial investigations on the use of nitrogen to offset the effects of HPNS. He noted that nitrogen had the opposite effects on a phospolid monolayer such as those comprising nerve cell membranes, causing them to expand while increased hydrostatic pressure caused them to contract. He concluded that the narcotic potency of nitrogen may be sufficient to offset the pressure changes. Helium, on the other hand, seemed to have little effect on the monolayer. He reasoned that this might provide protection from HPNS by offsetting the pressure effects on the nerve cell membranes and allow deeper dives and/or faster compression rates.

Bennett compressed divers to 720 fsw (220.2 msw) using Trimix with 25% nitrogen at a rate of 26 fsw per min (7.95 msw per min). The same divers also performed dives to 1000 fsw (305.8 msw) using Trimix and Heliox mixtures with a compression rate of 33 fsw per min (10 msw per min) and an air dive to 200 fsw (61.2 msw). Except for the Heliox dive, all three exposures had an equivalent partial pressure of nitrogen of 5.6 atmospheres absolute or an equivalent air depth of 200 fsw (61.2 msw). In the studies,

Trimix suppressed symptoms of HPNS, but also reduced the intellectual performance of the divers. Subjectively, two divers who were more sensitive to HPNS preferred the Trimix while two other less sensitive divers preferred the Heliox mixture because of reduced euphoria and other symptoms of nitrogen narcosis. These studies showed that nitrogen and other more lipid soluble inert gases than helium might be useful in reducing HPNS.

Based on these experiments, researchers developed a model based on the physiochemical properties of inert gases dissolved in lipids. This model predicted 10% nitrogen, 0.5% nitrous oxide, or 16% hydrogen as the optimum concentrations for these narcotic gases to offset the effects of HPNS. A series of subsequent dives to 1000 fsw (305.8 msw) using compression rates from 33 fsw per min (10 msw per min) to 100 fsw per min (30.6 msw per min) confirmed the ability to offset the effects of HPNS. Although the nitrogen markedly reduced the tremors and other symptoms of HPNS, it also produced euphoria and shortness of breath in the divers.

Comex conducted a dive series to 1000 fsw (305.8 msw) comparing the efficiency of using 4.5%, and 9% Trimix and compared these results to a similar Heliox exposure. This dive series differed from the previous ones in that a slower average compression rate of 4 fsw per min (1.2 msw per min) was used. They concluded that efficiency was better with 4.5% nitrogen after such compression than with Heliox to 1300 fsw (397.6 msw) and slow compression, and the efficiency was much worse than with 9% Trimix. Divers demonstrated euphoria and behavioral problems, and were unable to work for at least 4 hours after arrival at depth.

These studies demonstrated two problems with the use of Trimix. First, nitrogen seems to produce narcosis effects that adversely affect diver performance. Second, higher concentrations of nitrogen seem necessary to allow more rapid compressions. While on the one hand, one would want to use higher concentrations of nitrogen to allow rapid compression; such dives invariably produce undesirable narcosis. It would appear that the trick would be to the optimum dosing of helium to allow rapid compression with minimal narcosis.

In England, a dive series was performed comparing Heliox, Trimix and Nitrox dives where the nitrogen partial pressure and compression rate was the same as the Trimix dive. During the Trimix dive, divers reported symptoms of narcosis, including euphoria, inability to concentrate, amnesia and inability to perform complex tasks. No such effects were seen on either the Heliox or the Nitrox dives. This observation would suggest that the divers were affected by HPNS symptoms unreversed by nitrogen, and narcotic effects unreversed by pressure. The combination of these two effects proved worse than can be explained by nitrogen alone. This makes it difficult to establish an appropriate dose for nitrogen based upon equivalent air depth, since clearly other factors than the direct narcotic effects of nitrogen are affecting diver performance. Without knowledge of these effects, it is impossible to plan a compression rate and nitrogen concentration that would provide optimum results without individual testing.

For dives to 1000 fsw (305.8 msw), current studies would suggest that for compression at a rate of 30 fsw per min (9.2 msw per min), 10% nitrogen concentrations are best, but that divers can be expected to demonstrate significant narcosis effects. For faster compression rates the optimum Trimix is unknown. Slowing compression to 3-4 fsw per min (0.9-1.2 msw per min) will permit the use of 5% nitrogen with little narcosis effect. As dives progress deeper to 1500 fsw (458.7 msw), 5% is effective, but with slower compression rates on the order of 38 hours to 1500 fsw (458.7 msw). More rapid compression, or the use of higher concentrations of nitrogen has produced undesirable effects to cause some investigators to prefer slow compression with Heliox over Trimix for dives to 1500 fsw (458.7 msw).

Deeper than 1500 fsw (458.7 msw), 5% nitrogen is insufficient to reduce the effects of HPNS. The results of studies using 10% nitrogen are mixed. At Duke University, divers on two dives were successfully compressed to 2250 fsw (688.1 msw) using 10% nitrogen over an approximate 7 day compression period. On these dives, divers reported feeling well, and were able to perform complex tasks. However, in a similar dive to 2250 fsw (688.1 msw) also using 10% nitrogen conducted at AMTE/PL, divers reported feeling good on arrival at depth, but within 4 hours subjects developed nausea and vomiting, fatigue, shortness of breath and became semi-conscious. In this case, the compression rate was over 3 days and 6 hours, roughly twice as fast as in the Duke dives. These mixed results, combined with a similar Norwegian experience where divers actually performed better on Heliox than Trimix at 1650 fsw (504.6 msw), suggests that further

research is needed. During a Norwegian dive, Trimix was changed to Heliox with rapid reduction in narcotic symptoms in divers, but increased tremors.

Hydrox (Hydrogen-Oxygen or Hydrogen-Helium-Oxygen)

A series of experiments were conducted by Comex that investigated the use of Hydrogen-Oxygen mixtures and Hydrogen-Helium-Oxygen mixtures (Hydrox) as a means to facilitate deep diving. Since hydrogen is more soluble in lipid membranes than helium, it follows that hydrogen in the proper proportion would function like nitrogen in reducing HPNS. Although hydrogen reacts violently with Oxygen to produce water, when the proportion of either oxygen or hydrogen is sufficiently low this mixture is stable. Hydrogen has the advantage of being lowest density gas available and thereby lowering the work of breathing and, hopefully eliminating the dyspnea (shortness of breath) seen when breathing Trimix at very deep depths.

Initial experiments were conducted with divers breathing a hydrogen oxygen mixture at various depths to 1000 fsw (305.8 msw), however, severe narcosis bothered the divers below 700 fsw (214.1 msw). To minimize the narcosis further experiments were conducted using 50% hydrogen in Helium-Oxygen. These studies conducted as deep as 1500 fsw (458.7 msw) showed EEG changes similar to those seen with Heliox, and performance decrements consistent with narcosis. Furthermore, three divers were noted to paradoxically develop tremors during the dive and have a psychotic episode similar to that seen on one very deep dive with Trimix. Although an open sea dive with Hydrox has been successfully conducted most research using it has ceased.

Other High Pressure Physiologic Effects

Two other physiologic phenomenon related to deep diving deserve mention: Hyperbaric arthralgia and paradoxically induced diver dyspnea. Associated with the first descriptions of HPNS, divers reported stiffness and pain in the joints. Most commonly affected in decreasing order were the shoulders, knees, wrists, hips and backs. Divers described this as "no joint juice," or a gritty sensation in the joint. These symptoms may begin as shallow as 300 fsw (91.8 msw) and increase in intensity as depth increases. Once a bottom depth is reached these symptoms tend to decrease with time. Most often these symptoms are uncomfortable, but not incapacitating to the diver.

I have coined the term "paradoxically induced diver dyspnea" to describe an observation made by Bennet. He noted on a rapid compression Trimix dive that the divers complained of dyspnea worsened on switching to Heliox even though it had a less dense gas it should of eased these symptoms. This paradoxical dyspnea is probably an uninvestigated subtle effect of HPNS. Perhaps HPNS can affect the divers respiratory control center in the brain that controls the rate of breathing. A side effect could be to increase the divers gas consumption rate. This could explain the larger than expected gas usage in a recent deep dive by Jim Bowden past 900 fsw (275.3 msw) at Zacaton in Mexico.

How HPNS Might Affect Diver Safety?

The table included in this chapter was adapted from Bennett in ***The Physiology of Medicine and Diving, 4th Edition***. It lists those dives which best illustrates the principles discussed previously. Most of the experiments referred to in the table and in the proceeding discussion were conducted in dry hyperbaric chambers most often without the diver immersed in water. How might one relate these various tests of diver performance under experimental conditions to actual diving operations? How much a decrement in performance seen in these dry experiments should be allowed before a diving procedure or guideline is considered unsatisfactory for actual diving operations? There are no easy answers to these questions.

However, one must consider that while diving in open ocean conditions the lack of light, extreme cold and presence of currents is likely to add to the performance deficits one can expect. Furthermore, the amount of time pressure is imposed, especially when conducting dives using open circuit scuba apparatus, should further confound the diver attempting a complex technical dive.

Open Sea Diving to 600 fsw (183.5 msw)

Current information suggests the rapid compression of up to 100 fsw per min (30.6 msw per min) to a depth of about 600 fsw (183.5 msw) on Heliox can be conducted without severe HPNS. There would not appear to be any advantage using Trimix in this range because HPNS should not be a major problem except for reduced cost and possibly reduced compression time for short bounce dives. On the other hand, using Heliox has the advantage of avoiding the potential narcosis problems associated

Gas Consumption Rate in CFM (FLPM)	Bottom Time (Minutes) 10	12	14
0.6 (16.99)	362 (10,252)	446 (12,631)	526 (14,896)
0.7 (19.82)	423 (11,979)	518 (14,670)	613 (17,360)
0.8 (22.66)	483 (13,679)	592 (16,765)	701 (19,852)

FIGURE 5-1: GAS REQUIRED TO REACH THE 350 FSW (107 MSW) STAGE BOTTLE

with Trimix, and offers lower work of breathing because it is less dense than Trimix.

Dives to 600 fsw (183.5 msw) are commonly done in the commercial diving industry with the aid of a chamber and mate-able diving bell. With the divers at surface pressure the bell is lowered into working depth. Once the divers are geared up the pressure inside the ball is increased to the ambient pressure of the work site, the hatch is opened, and the diver exits to complete the task. A tender usually remains inside the bell to end to the diver who is supplied with the umbilical, communications, and a hot water supply to the hot water suit. Once the task is completed the diver re-enters the bell, the hatch is closed maintaining bottom pressure, the bell is raised to the surface, and mated to the surface decompression chamber. While raising and mating the bell to the decompression chamber, the surface diving supervisor begins diver decompression, and decompression is completed in the surface decompression chamber.

In such a diving operation, the various tasks necessary to conduct such a dive are shared among team members. The divers need only concern themselves with the bottom tasks they need to perform. The divers need not concern themselves with the bottom time, decent or ascent rate, or even the gas mix they are breathing since these tasks are handled by others on the surface. Gas supply is from large surfaced mounted banks being essentially unlimited given the planned course of the dive. The divers have a plentiful and temperature regulated hot water supply to heat the diver and breathing gases if needed. Contrast this situation to deep technical diving using open-circuit scuba techniques. In this situation, the diver alone must handle all these tasks, and with considerably less backup support. In this type of diving scenario with a high degree of task loading, should we tolerate more performance decrement than might be tolerated by the commercial diver?

OPEN SEA DIVING IN THE 600 TO 1000 FSW (183.5 TO 305.8 MSW) RANGE

Most open sea diving in the 600 to 1000 fsw (183.5 to 305.8 msw) range is done on Heliox using saturation diving techniques with a surface chamber and a mate-able diving bell. In this method of diving the divers are compressed to bottom depth in the surface chamber. Upon reaching bottom and being declared fit to dive, the divers move the diving bell, and are lowered to bottom depth and exit the bell to conduct their work. Often divers work 6 hour shifts diving, and are replaced with a second diving crew. This dive, rest, dive procedure is continued for up to 30 days before decompression to the surface is conducted. This approach is very efficient in accomplishing a construction task such as constructing an undersea oil pipeline. After 24 hours on the bottom decompression becomes fixed at about 1 day per each 100 fsw (30.6 msw) depth plus an additional 24 hours. Thus, for a dive to 1000 fsw (305.8 msw), decompression is about 11 days regardless of bottom line. When diving in this manner, slower compression rates are feasible compared with bounce diving techniques.

Bell diving using bounce techniques from the surface such as that described for 600 fsw (183.5 msw), are less commonly used. Such a procedure requires a fast compression rate that can be expected to cause severe HPNS in nearly all divers especially near 1000 fsw (305.8 msw), decompression is about 11 days regardless of bottom time. As a consequence, Trimix must be used to prevent expected severe HPNS. However, such short interventional dives were not a major part of commercial deep diving practice. This, together with the increased use of remotely operated vehicles (***ROV***) and one atmosphere diving suits (i.e., the ***NEWT*** suit), means that the necessary empirical research defining a safe, rapid compression profile and optimum nitrogen dose has not been established. Thus, any planned profile cannot be guaranteed to allow a diver to function adequately in most dives.

Recently several divers have begun conducting dives with the goal of reaching 1000 fsw (305.8 msw) using open-circuit scuba. In addition to the problem of preventing HPNS and narcosis, consider for a minute the additional issues of gas planning, the use of equipment designed primarily for recreational use and in the darkness. Together, these problems represent a major risk that cannot be adequately and reliably controlled at our present state of knowledge.

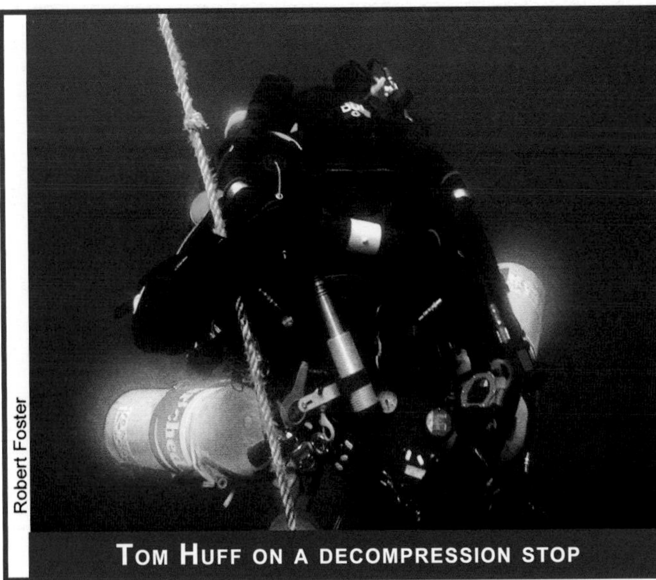
Robert Foster

TOM HUFF ON A DECOMPRESSION STOP

The discussion below is based upon an actual planned scenario for a dive to 1000 fsw (305.8 msw).

Gas Planning: The volume of gas used per minute increases proportionately with depth. At 1000 fsw (305.8 msw) (31.3 ATA) the diver will use 31.3 times the amount of gas than will be used at the surface. Moreover, the amount of gas available from each cylinder will be proportionately reduced due to the high ambient pressure. At 1000 fsw (305.8 msw) the ambient pressure is 460 psig (31.3 ATA). Thus when tank pressure falls to 460 psig (31.3 ATA) no additional gas will be available. Since regulators are set for an intermediate pressure of 125 psig (8.5 ATA) or greater depending on model, a cylinder is effectively empty at about 600 psig (40.8 ATA). If a diver consumes gas at 1 cubic foot (28.32 free liters) per minute, one can expect an 80 cu ft (2.8 free liter) cylinder to last 2.0 minutes at 1000 fsw (305.8 msw).

Assume, for planning purposes, a gas consumption rate of 0.6 cu ft (16.99 free liters) per minute throughout the dive, and that a diver used dual 120 cu ft (19 L), and two 80 cu ft (10 L) stage bottles. The diver would be carrying either 522 cu ft (14,783 free liters) of Trimix in the doubles pumped to 3600 psig (244.9 bar), or 559 cu ft (15,830 free liters) if doubles were pumped to 4000 psig (272.1 bar). This corresponds to an available gas volume of 475 or 513 cu ft (13,452 or 14,528 free liters) of gas respectively with the diver at 350 fsw (107 msw), the location of the first decompression bottle. Figure 5-2 shows the expected gas requirement to reach 350 fsw (107 msw) at gas consumption rates of 0.6, 0.7, and 0.8 cu ft (16.99, 19.82, and 22.66 free liters) per minute. This table in Figure 5-2 also indicates the volume of Trimix needed to support the various bottom times including decent from 350 fsw (107 msw) to 1000 fsw (305.8 msw), and ascent including decompression stop to the first decompression bottle. The diver would have had sufficient gas to support the 10 minute bottom time throughout planned decompression on Trimix, but insufficient gas to reach the 350 fsw (107 msw) stage using the 14 minute schedule. If gas consumption increased to 0.7 cfm (19.82 flpm) then the diver would have had insufficient gas to reach the fsw (107 msw) bottle.

The chart calculations assume that no gas was used to inflate the buoyancy compensator. However, a portion of his bottom mix would have been used to maintain buoyancy during descent. The buoyancy compensator used has an internal volume of at least 1 cu ft (28.32 free liters) that would require 31 cu ft (877.6 free liters) to fill at 1000 fsw (305.8 msw). If only 20 lbs. of lift was needed then only 10 cu ft (283.2 free liters) of gas would be needed.

As can be seen from this discussion, even minor delays in descent, or ascent will increase the gas needed during the dive. This is the compounded by the that minor difficulties that might be encountered during the dive can easily increase the rate of gas consumption above 0.6 cfm (16.99 flpm) that is a very slow swimming gas faster than at a shallower depth. There clearly is ***no*** margin for error during such a dive.

Equipment Function: Most diving equipment used by technical divers was never intended for use at these depths. This can present major problems if the component is unable to function adequately at depth. The regulator is the most critical component in this regard.

Sheck Exley, a practitioner of deep diving, had reported to me that he felt considerable inhalation effort during his deep Mante Dives at 800 fsw (244.6 msw). This could have been dyspnea secondary to pressure, or regulator resistance due to breathing very dense gas. At, 1000 fsw (305.8 msw) the gas density on bottom mix (6% oxygen, 22% nitrogen, 72% helium) would be 15.5 grams per liter. The density of air at 200 fsw (61.0 msw) is 9.1 grams per liter. The density of the bottom mix was equivalent to the density of air at 364 fsw (111.3 msw). These are gas densities well beyond the limit in which conventional regulators are designed to function. High breathing resistance due to the regulator, in addition to the increased work of breathing dense gas,

Investigator	Dive Gas	Depth fsw (msw)	Compression Rate fpm (mpm) Overall	Notes
Duke University	Trimix 18%	1,000 (305.8)	37 (11.3) continuous	Narcosis, euphoria, decreased tremors
Tarrytown Labs	Trimix 13%	1,000 (305.8)	100 (30.5) continuous	Mild tremors, dyspnea, 15% performance deficit
Duke University	Trimix 10%	1,000 (305.8)	37 (11.3) exponential slowing	No changes noted
Comex Coraz 1	Trimix 9%	1,000 (305.8)	4 (1.2) exponential slowing with holds	No tremor, euphoria, EEG changes, 15% performance deficit
Comex Coraz 2	Trimix 4.5%	1,000 (305.8)	4 (1.2) same as Coraz 1	Slight tremor, less euphoria than Coraz 1, EEG changes, 5% performance deficit
Comex Coraz 3	Trimix 4.5%	1,000 (305.8)	4 (1.2) same as Coraz 1	Diver fatigue. Others same as Coraz 2
Comex Coraz 4	Heliox	1,000 (305.8)	4 (1.2) same as Coraz 1	EEG changes, marked tremor, 20% performance deficit
Duke University & AMTE/PL	Trimix 6%	1,312 (401.2)	13.2 (4) exponential slowing with short holds	Greater than 25% performance deficit, marked tremor, dizziness, lightheaded, confusion, moderate HPNS
Duke University & AMTE/PL	Trimix 5%	1,512 (462.3)	8.6 (0.24) to 1312 (401.2) 6.3 (1.9) to 1512	Fewer effects at 1,312 (401.2) than above dive 1,512 (462.3), unable to keep eyes open, severe HPNS, aborted dive
AMTE/PL	Heliox	1,000 (305.8)	2.8 (0.86)	60% decrease in performance test, marked tremor, nausea, vertigo
Comex Janus 4A	Trimix 4%	1,312 (401.2)	0.9 (0.28)	Exponential slowing with holds, light tremor, major EEG changes
Comex Janus 48	Trimix 4%	1,508 (461.2)	0.8 (0.24) 6 day hold at 1500 fsw (485.7 msw)	Underwater pipe connection made. Used selected divers
AMTE/PL	Heliox	1,000 (305.8)	3.3 (1.0)	Light headed, imbalance at 686.7 (210), 30-50% decrease in performance tests
AMTE/PL	Heliox	1,377 (421.1)	0.11 (0.03)	Decreasing rate with holds. No serious symptoms, intention tremor, decreased appetite
AMTE/PL	Heliox	1,377 (421.1)	0.14 (0.04) decreasing rate with holds	Marked intention tremor. No appetite
Duke University Atlantis 1	Trimix 5%	1,510 (461.8)	2 (0.61) decreasing rate with 1 hour holds	Dyspnea worse on Heliox, no postural tremor, mild intention tremor, performance decreased, dizziness
AMTE/PL	Heliox	1,770 (541.3)	0.4 (0.12) decreasing rate with holds	Severe tremor, no appetite, dizziness
DRET	Trimix 4.8%	1,476 (451.4)	0.65 (0.2) decreasing rate	10% performance decrease, no tremors
Duke University Atlantis 2	Trimix 10% (1,510) Trimix 7% (2,132)	2,132 (652)	1.8 (0.55) to 1510 (461.8) 0.19 (0.06) to 2132 (652)	Performance better than Atlantis 1
AMTE/PL	Trimix 10%	2,164 (661.8)	0.5 (0.15) exponential slowing with holds	No signs HPNS on arrival later tremor, breathing difficulty, semi-consciousness
Duke University Atlantis 3	Trimix 10%	2,250 (688.1)	0.21 (0.06) exponential slowing with holds	Subjects well. 15% performance deficit
Duke University Atlantis 4	Trimix 5%	2,132 (652)	0.21 (0.06) exponential slowing with holds	Two divers well & one diver hyper manic, mild tremors, good performance
GISMER	Trimix 4.8%	1,476 (451.4)	0.65 (0.2) exponential slowing with holds	Diver drowsiness, no tremor, 10% performance deficit
NUTEC DEEP EX80	Trimix 10% (1,510) Trimix 7% (2,132) Heliox	1,000 (305.9)	3.5 (1.1) exponential slowing	Heliox divers severe HPNS, 20% performance deficit. Trimix divers less tremor, 15% performance deficit, euphoria
NUTEC DEEP EX81	Trimix 10% Heliox	1,640 (501.5)	Heliox 1 (0.31)	Both groups ill. Trimix associated with deficit in cognitive performance that cleared on Heliox
GISMER Entex 9	Heliox	2,000 (611.6)	0.35 (0.11) exponential slowing with holds	20% performance deficit, microsleep, tremor

Figure 5-2: Summary of HPNS Research

may easily result in carbon dioxide retention that would further hamper diver performance. Recognizing these problems, a special second stage regulator commonly used by commercial diving services was designed with performance characteristics compatible with this increased gas density. Even if such a regulator were used with Scuba, flow limitations due to the tank valve port size or the first stage regulator may limit available flow over that delivered to an umbilical supplied diver.

Flow limitations secondary to increased gas density may also limit the speed with which a diver can adjust buoyancy. This may mean that the diver becomes overly heavy and may not be able to arrest descent where planned.

Finally, one must consider the effects of environmental factors such as cold and darkness. Imagine a diver descending rapidly to 1000 fsw (305.8 msw), feeling dizzy and nauseous from HPNS, while rapidly descending a single line without any visual reference points. One would easily expect the feeling of dizziness and nausea to be heightened when no stable reference points aid in maintaining orientation. At Bushmangat, a deep underwater cavern located at a 5000 ft (1529.1 m) elevation in South Africa, Sheck Exley attained a depth of 860 fsw (263 msw) on his depth recorder. Upon reaching 700 fsw (214.1 msw) following a rapid 100 fsw (30.1 msw) per minute descent, Sheck first experienced the effects of HPNS even though he breathed a 22% nitrogen Trimix. In his dive log Scheck reports, "Itching and tingling in the skin (Argon in the suit)," and "Regular spaced sparkles in vision, slight blurring," and, "Deeper got uncontrolled shivering." He therefore slowed his descent rate to approximately 30 fsw (9.2 msw) per minute eventually attaining the bottom at 860 msw (263 msw) after a 12 to 13 minute descent. His vision continued to deteriorate on the bottom and the uncontrolled shaking also worsened. Sheck reported that the symptoms disappeared upon reaching 400 fsw (122.3 msw) during the ascent. Had Sheck remained on the bottom longer, one would have expected the symptoms to continue to intensify as this is common during dives of rapid descent.

Time pressure due to gas consumption could be reduced if one used closed-circuit units whose duration theoretically is independent of depth. However, the time pressure if mounting decompression obligation still remains. Additionally, these rigs present unique planning problems of their own, the details of which could occupy a chapter of their own. Suffice it to say that such a diving is ill- advised without the availability of a diving bell with mate-able diving chamber, an umbilical support diver, and a good surface support team.

Conclusion

Less than 600 fsw (183.5 msw) HPNS is not a significant problem while using Heliox. Since the use of Trimix involves an element of nitrogen narcosis that may be worse than predicted by an equivalent air depth computation, there seems no valid reason to prefer it to Heliox. HPNS is a significant problem when diving Heliox below 600 fsw (183.5 msw). Its effects are greatest after rapid compression and in certain susceptible divers. Utilizing Trimix can reduce the effects of HPNS. While Trimix decreases the tremor and other effects of HPNS, it also includes narcosis in the diver. Trimix can be helpful on dives from 1000 fsw (305.8 msw) to 1500 fsw (458.7 msw), and is essential for dives deeper than 1500 fsw (458.7 msw). Optimum concentrations of nitrogen in Trimix have been established by empirical testing for certain compression rates and depths. However, our knowledge is still insufficient to establish the necessary nitrogen concentration for other compression rates.

In open-sea diving the negative effects of HPNS on diver performance and safety can be increased by environmental factors. Commercial diving companies have developed procedures using diving bells, and a team approach to diving that minimizes these negative effects on the diver and allows open-sea operations to be conducted with reasonable safety. However, without such extensive equipment and personnel support, deep technical dives, especially those beyond 600 fsw (183.5 msw), must be considered highly hazardous and beyond the scope of the technical scuba diver.

References

Most of the above material was drawn from The Physiology and Medicine of Diving and Compressed Air Work by Bennett and Elliot 4th Edition, available from Best Publishing Company from the Proceedings of the Fifth through Eighth Symposia on Underwater Physiology available through the Undersea and Hyperbaric Medical Society.

Chapter Six
Counter Diffusion

Joseph Dituri M.S.

Iso, meaning singular or alone and ***baric,*** referring to pressure, the isobaric issues in diving tend toward those involving breathing different gasses while remaining at a singular pressure. This chapter will discuss Isobaric (***inert gas***) Counter Diffusion (***ICD***) as well as Isobaric Otological Barotrauma (***IOB***). Since these topics are inadequately understood, neither this paper, nor any other reference, represents the complete knowledge of the subject. Great care must be taken when performing dives outside what is widely accepted as the boundary of technical diving.

History & Background

In 1975, Lambertsen & Idicula first hypothesized that when different tissue types were exposed to two different gasses with different solubility and diffusion coefficients, a ***super-saturation*** of these tissues could occur. The initial identification came during neon-oxygen mixtures while divers were surrounded by helium. The super-saturation effect would occur at the interfaces because this effect could ***violate*** Dalton's law. The whole of the partial pressures of the gasses would be greater than the sum of its parts given ambient pressure at the interface. This super-saturation would lead to bubble formation without a pressure change. The bubbles could consequently lead to these rare forms of DCS observed as gas lesions in man as well as embolization in animals[1]. The assumption respective to DCS is based on the premise that bubbles have something to do with DCS. This premise remains to be proved and the discussion is beyond the scope of this paper, but worth mentioning in this advanced diving literature. Additional authors have described gas filled blisters after sequential exposures to different gasses at constant ambient pressures.[2] As a means of achieving a visual reference for the advanced diver, the amount of inert gas (molecular nitrogen and helium) absorbed into the body's tissues on a deep and long Trimix dive would physically fit into a tablespoon.

Isobaric Otological Barotrauma

Isobaric Otological Barotrauma (***IOB***) is the partial or complete loss of complex functioning in divers exposed to a different gas than that which they are breathing. Symptoms include vertigo, nausea and/or nystagmus (***involuntary eye movement***). Recently some divers pushing beyond the depths of even the most experienced technical divers, up to and in excess of 500 fsw (152 msw), may have experienced these symptoms. We may never know the exact reasoning or cause of this affliction because a controlled study was not performed and a limited amount of divers expose themselves to these pressures. Also relatively few incidences of this affliction have occurred (5 total reported). Some divers have experienced a complete loss of vestibular processes, and have regurgitated repeatedly, with seemingly no reason or rhyme. It is noteworthy that some of the divers were breathing a different breathing media than the one surrounding them. Because of this, IOB is most likely not a concern for divers performing deep mixed gas dives.

One of the postulated etiologies of IOB is that the sudden addition of a second (dissimilar) gas at a deep depth (under conditions of high partial pressure of dissolved helium in tissue fluids) causes the rate of increase in the concentration of the dissolved second gas in perilymph and endolymph, which is different because of the varience in osmotic pressure between these two spaces. This differential produces the subsequent flux of water between the perilymphatic and endolymphatic spaces and distortion of the vestibular membraneous labyrinth. The more likely explanation involves the isobaric counter diffusion principles detailed above.[3]

Isobaric (Inert Gas) Counter Diffusion

ICD is a malady that is generally considered probable

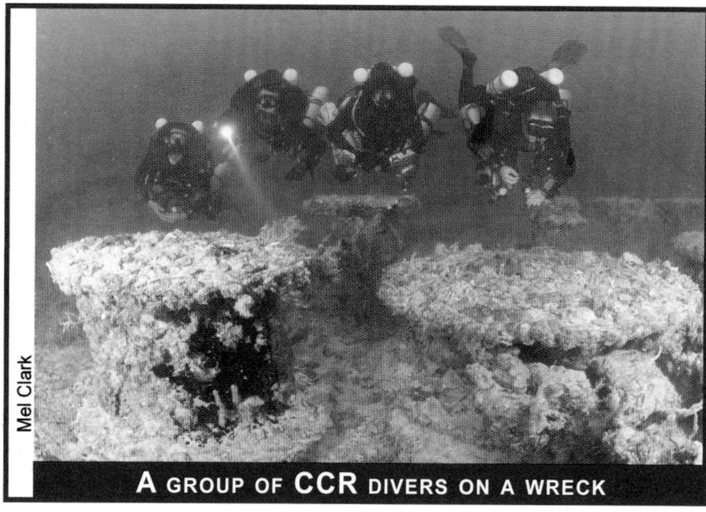

A group of CCR divers on a wreck

PATRICK WIGET DIVING ON THE KT12 NEAR SARDINA

when performing very deep dives and switching inert gasses from one that is high solubility to one that is less soluble with decompression stops in excess of 100 fsw (33 msw). The reasoning for the consideration of max depth is the assumption that the dives are planned to the point of saturation (longer stay times) which indicates a decompression ceiling limited by the slower tissue groups. Generally speaking, the diver would require a hypoxic Trimix as a bottom gas. ICD seems to be a very fast reaction in the fast tissues immediately following a significant inert gas shift.

The solubility of nitrogen is 0.067 and the solubility of helium is 0.015. Nitrogen is 4.46667 times more soluble than helium. Another important number is the speed of diffusivity or speed the gas goes into and out of solution. Helium diffuses 2.67 times faster than nitrogen.

Initial Gas Switch on Ascent

If the diver is at a critical level of solubility with a Trimix at 5 ATA that contains 30% helium, 50% nitrogen and 20% oxygen, a switch to EAN 32 would deliver a rapid spike of nitrogen (+18%) and a marked decrease in helium content (-50%). ICD occurs every time a diver makes this kind of a significant switch from a helium rich mixture to nitrogen rich mixture or any time a diver has a marked increase in Equivalent Narcotic Depth (***END***). Most often these switches will be asymptomatic, but the severity of the incident will most probably correlate to the tissue that is controlling the ascent. As a matter of exactness, every time a diver takes an air break from oxygen decompression there is a significant change in END and therefore an ICD occurs. Most often, this example of shallow water ICD is uneventful because by this depth the limiting tissues are the slower ones. Slower tissues are less sensitive to a spike in END. Additionally, the final gas switch from OC or rebreather loop to surface air is a change in END and may yield symptoms. This is another reason divers should not make haste to get out of the water following a deep dive.

Breaks on Gases other than Air

Another time an ICD can occur is when a diver takes a break from diving mixtures high in oxygen content to avoid the Paul Bert (***CNS Oxygen Toxicity***) and the Lorraine Smith effect (***Pulmonary Oxygen Toxicity***). Technical divers are very familiar with CNS oxygen toxicity. Pulmonary oxygen toxicity (less common) is a direct time/dose relationship on the lungs caused by the effect of oxygen on the lungs, blockage of airways, increased carbon dioxide as well as pulmonary surfactant changes. The most common treatment is prevention and removal of high oxygen media at the first signs of toxicity.

As a growing trend, divers are taking ***air breaks*** on their bottom gas. The reasoning is two-fold. Back-gas is a handy, easy-to-breathe gas (containing helium) with a low content of oxygen. Secondly, because oxygen is a vaso-constrictor the lower the content of oxygen on these breaks, the more open the body will be to receiving oxygen when transferring back to the high oxygen breathing mixture. In hyperbaric treatments, it is found that hyperoxia interspaced with small periods of hypoxia have a profound improvement on oxygen transport. Breathing the hypoxic back-gas is a loose association of this principle.

The Issue

This ICD issue comes from the generally high helium content of the back-gas. The helium rushes into the tissues faster than the nitrogen has time to escape. The overall tissue gas super-saturation increases and can exceed the critical limit. This is termed ***Deep Tissue ICD***. Generally, this type of switch is done at very shallow depths and it is not considered a problem.

Divers that experience ICD often have problems with vestibulo-cochlear apparatus or Inner Ear DCS (***IEDCS***). The further technical divers expand the boundary of deep

diving, the more we can expect to see this and other rare or previously undiscovered maladies. Currently, approximately 26% of patients suffering "***serious***" or "***neurological***" DCS exhibit evidence of inner ear involvement. These numbers are confounding since residual deficits in balance and in hearing are common despite recompression treatment, and the window of opportunity for treatment is relatively short[4]. As seems evident, the differential diagnosis of ICD from an issue with a perforated eardrum or the most common form of barotraumas (middle ear) is required.

Most of the studies and trials observing ICD and IOB are conducted in dry chambers that simulate depth of seawater with increased pressure. Those body spaces that are exposed to dry environments as opposed to wet environments may on gas at different rates given the different environments. Diffusion across the tympanic membrane accounts for most of the inert gas entering the middle ear from ambient and respiratory environments containing the inert gas.[5] Given this information, perhaps the literature involving testing for ICD and IOB in dry environments is incorrect or in need of rework.

Finally, the gas uptake models are mostly predicated upon the absorption of inert gas from the blood. The ear is a slow tissue group that on/off gasses from both the blood as well as through the round window. There may be a time during the gas shift where there is a high partial pressure of helium in the middle ear. This indicates the helium partial pressure may not be able to fall because the helium is being replaced at the same time (***and perhaps rate***) as it diffuses out into the blood. Normal tissue compartment saturation rates are difficult to calculate but the inner ear is especially difficult because of the multiple on/off gas methods in the ear.

Avoidance Techniques

The difference in solubility of the two most common inert gasses and a desire to remain within more "well-known" parameters of diving would lead to the conclusion that a decrease in helium content should NEVER exceed the 4.46667 times increase in solubility from nitrogen to helium. The assumption here in is the overall change in inert gas levels should be linked to the solubility of the gasses. Some suggestions for managing ICD state a rule of thumb ensuring that a 5:1 ratio (4.46667:1 presumed rounded for easy math) of inert gas change limitation should be used to avoid ICD DCS[6]. Please be mindful that these discussions have no basis in fact, nor have clinical trials been performed as is the case with most widely accepted dive tables. The math seems to work at this point, but as we well know even the best mathematical algorithm for preventing DCS is not 100% effective. Individual susceptibilities may vary. To modify a quote from Dr. Bill Hamilton, "What works… works, but may not for everyone." The 5:1 ratio indicates that a diver should not switch to a gas that has a helium drop of 5% (actual percent by volume) for every 1% (actual percent by volume) increase in nitrogen content. For instance, if the diver has completed a dive that has the first decompression ceiling at 150 fsw (45 msw) and decides to switch from Trimix (Helium 30%, Nitrogen 50% and Oxygen 20%) the maximum EANx to which the diver should switch is 56%. A switch larger than this could lead to an ICD.

As the growing trend is to dive and decompress on helium rich mixtures all the way to the surface, I believe ICD will be less and less of a problem. It is noteworthy that the same calculations could be (***and are***) practiced using different inert gasses if the diver intends on switching between helium-rich and neon-rich mixes or neon-rich and nitrogen-rich.

Another ICD avoidance technique is detailed in Sheck Exley's book ***Caverns Measureless To Man***. The main premise of this technique was to make the switch as "gradually as possible." The supposition is 1-2-2-1 for a phase-in. For example, take a single breath from a Nitrox tank and then back to Trimix for two breaths and then

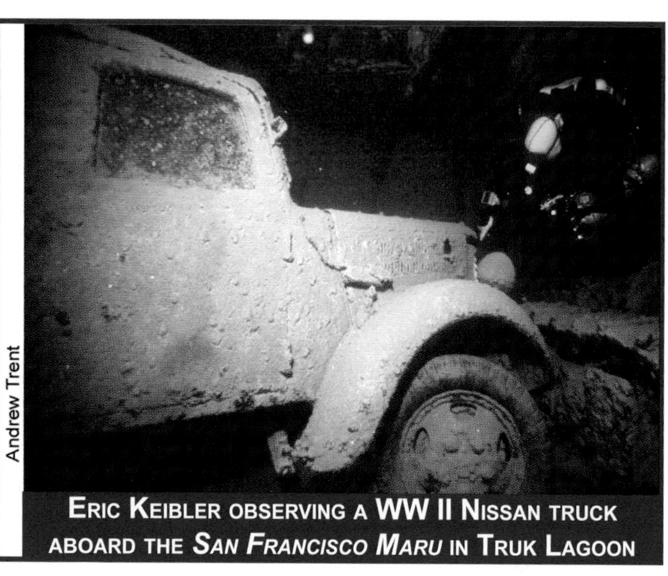

Andrew Trent

Eric Keibler observing a WW II Nissan truck aboard the *San Francisco Maru* in Truk Lagoon

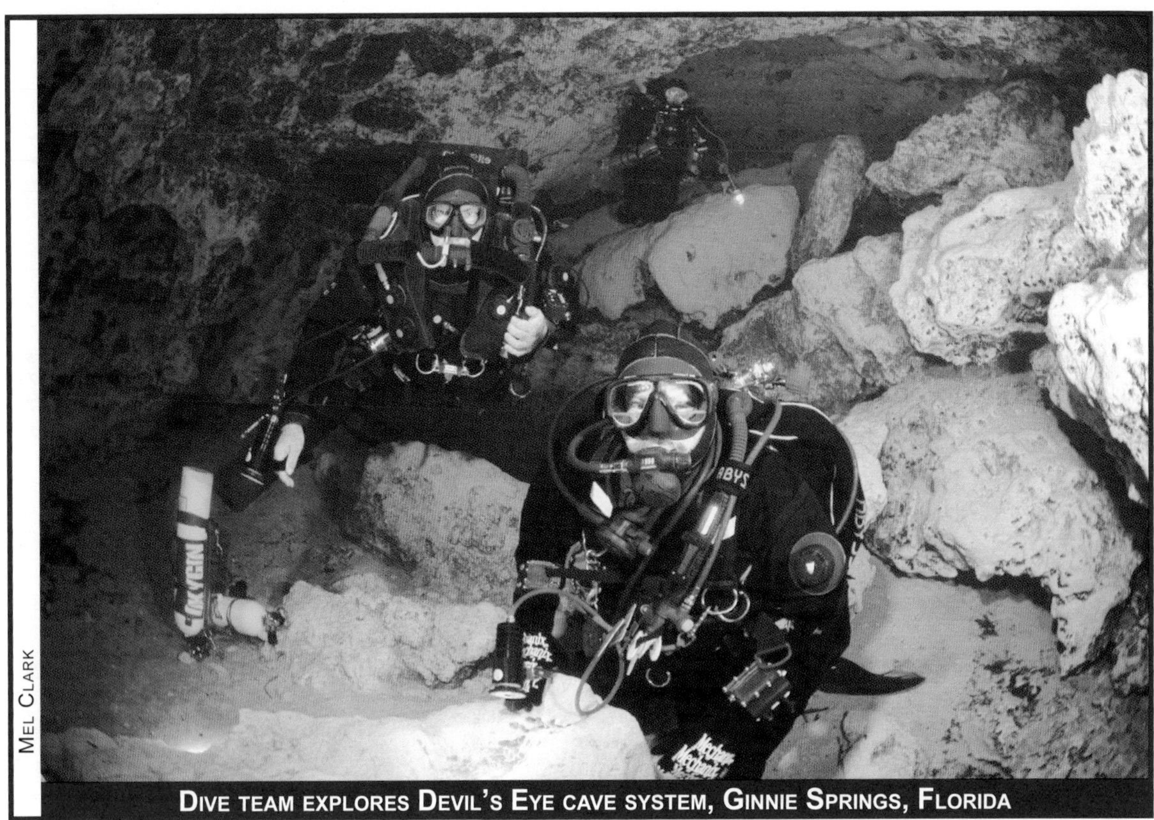

MEL CLARK

DIVE TEAM EXPLORES DEVIL'S EYE CAVE SYSTEM, GINNIE SPRINGS, FLORIDA

switch back to Nitrox for two breaths then back to Trimix for one breath and finally back to Nitrox for the balance of the dive. This allows the fast tissues an opportunity to phase-in the off-gassing. This is a complex maneuver and at this time in diving, significantly higher PPN_2's were more prevalent. In Sheck's case, this also seemed to limit the amount of narcosis he experienced although we no longer recommend switching to a nitrogen based mixture deeper than 100 fsw (30 msw).

Conclusion

Expedition diving is just that. The voyage to erudition about present day expedition diving should be filled with trepidation. Those who pave the way should be prepared to deal with new and poorly understood issues. The threat is real and independent of the malady or method isobaric issues can be avoided with a reasonable expectation of success. To avoid IOB, evade breathing a different (less soluble) gas than that used to complete volumetric make up in your dry suit. Also, there are at least two different methods to avoid or reduce the likelihood of ICD. Maintaining a 5:1 ratio of helium to nitrogen appears successful as well as the phase in methodology detailed by Sheck Exley. Regardless of the avoidance technique, take great care when performing this type diving as there are many unknown un-knowns that remain as we expand the boundaries along with our knowledge. The informed and educated diver is the one with the greatest chance of survival.

Notes

1. Karreman and Lambertsen, Kinetics of Isobaric Counter Diffusion, Bulletin of Mathematical Biology, pg 588, Volume 39, 1977

2. Bennett and Elliott, The Physiology of Medicine and Diving, 4th edition, W.B. Saunders Company Ltd.

3. Bennett and Elliott, The Physiology of Medicine and Diving, 4th edition, W.B. Saunders Company Ltd.

4. A biophysical basis for inner ear decompression sickness, Doolette, Mitchell, Journal of Applied Physiology, JAP-01090-2002-R1 pg 2 2003

5. Middle Ear Gas Exchange in Isobaric Counter Diffusion, Dueker, Lambertsen, Rosowski and Sanders, Journal of Applied Physiology Vol 47 Issue 6, 1239-1244, 1979.

6. Steve Burton, http://www.scubaengineer.com/isobaric_counter_diffusion.html, February, 6th, 2007

Chapter Seven
Decompression Injuries & Emergency Treatment

Joseph Dituri M.S.

Decompression Illness (DCI)

What's in a name? Decompression Illness (*DCI*) is commonly known as Decompression Sickness (*DCS*). However, DCI includes Arterial Gas Embolism (*AGE*) where DCS is only decompression-related. Also, this cluster of afflictions can be prevented. If a patient is suspected of having a DCI and a positive determination cannot be made, have the patient consult a Diving Medical Physician. DCI is broken down into three major categories: DCS Type I, DCS Type II and Pulmonary Over-Inflation Syndromes (*POIS*).

DCS: There is no clear source for DCS although there does seem to be a correlation between inert gas bubbles in the blood and patients who suffer from DCS. It is for this reason that the following theory of DCS is discussed in detail.

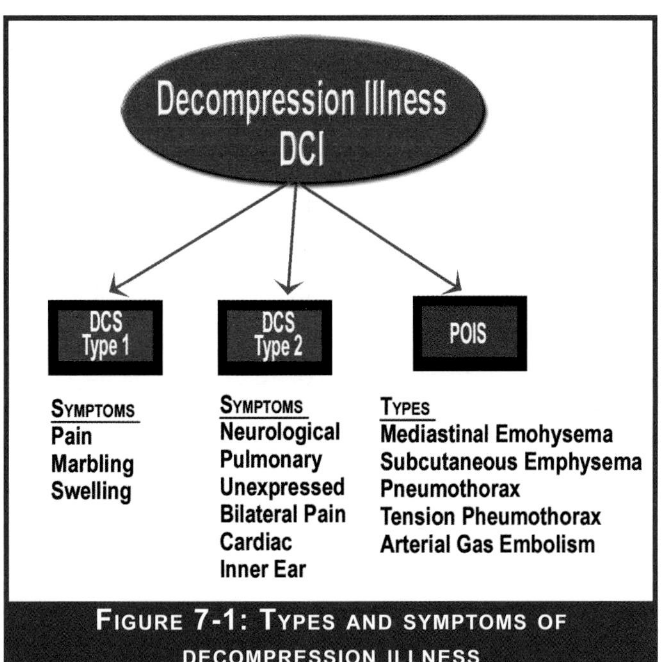

Figure 7-1: Types and symptoms of decompression illness

Alexander Sotiriou and Jim Holt during a deco stop at Four Sharks Blue Hole, S.Andros Isle, Bahamas

Henry's Law governs DCS in divers. The amount of gas capable of absorption into a liquid at a given temperature is invariably proportional to the Partial Pressure of the gas (***PPgas)***. Only inert gases are of concern to divers with respect to DCS since oxygen will be metabolized prior to absorption. (Concern for high Partial Pressure of O_2 exists, but not when dealing with DCS.) DCS is believed to be a result of inert gas being absorbed into the tissues on compression and while at depth during the dive. They in turn do not have sufficient time to escape during the ascent to the surface. At surface pressure, body tissues are saturated with the inert gas being breathed. As pressure is increased with depth, the partial pressure of the gas inhaled increases. Simultaneously, due to the increased pressure, the body's tissues are capable of absorbing a proportional amount more of the inert gas being breathed. While maintaining a constant increased pressure (at depth), the tissues can absorb an amount of inert gas consistent to the pressure.

As the external pressure is reduced at a decreased depth, tissues begin the process of off-gassing. The tissues are attempting to return to equilibrium equivalent with external pressure by releasing the previously absorbed gas into the blood stream where it is carried to the lungs for filtering. The amount of blood filling the capillary bed at any one time is about 5% of the entire body's blood volume. The capillary bed is the area where the exchange of O_2 and other nutrients with CO_2 and wastes takes place. The exchange can only take place at the capillary bed because

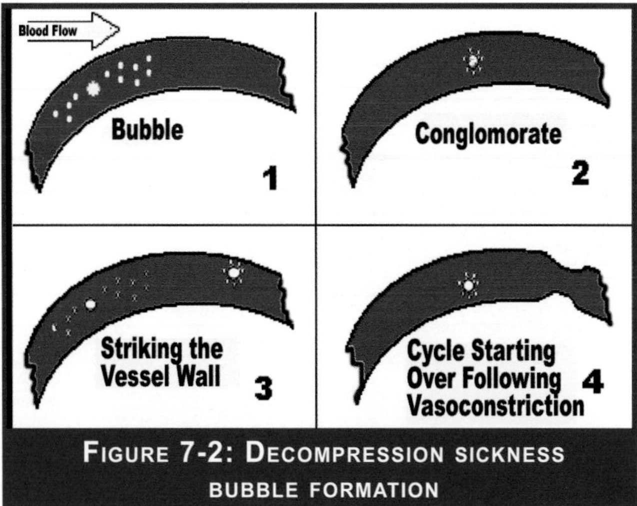

FIGURE 7-2: DECOMPRESSION SICKNESS BUBBLE FORMATION

they are lined with one thin layer of porous endothelial cells capable of allowing solutes smaller than proteins to diffuse between blood and tissue. The endothelial cells are surrounded by a basement membrane which does not interfere with diffusion but serves to hold the capillary together.

When the inert gas solubility capability is exceeded such that the gas is forced out of solution, a bubble is formed to transport the gas out of the system. Upon realizing the presence of the gas bubble, the body immediately sends antibodies to inspect this new foreign body. When it is discovered to be a foreign element to the body, the immune system dispatches phagocytes and leukocytes to attack and remove the bubble by attaching themselves onto the bubble. Another problem associated with the gas bubble trapped in the bloodstream is the surface of the gas bubble tends to attract other particles found in the blood stream such as fat. The result is a large mass consisting of the gas bubble, fat and phagocytes/leukocytes making its way through the blood stream.

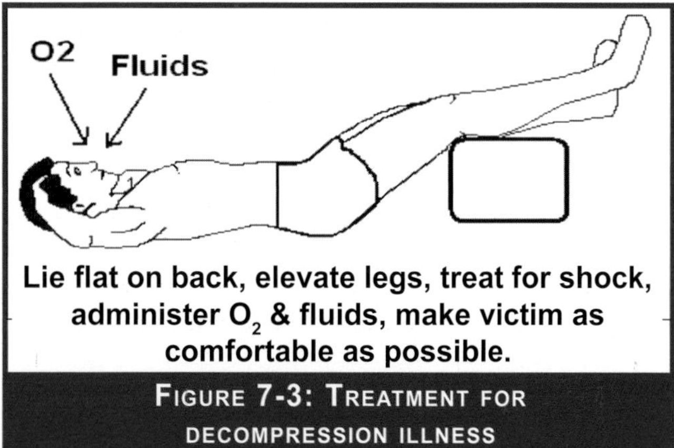

O2
Fluids
Lie flat on back, elevate legs, treat for shock, administer O_2 & fluids, make victim as comfortable as possible.

FIGURE 7-3: TREATMENT FOR DECOMPRESSION ILLNESS

A common misunderstanding is that the bubbles lodge in the veins and block blood flow. While this may be true in the worst case scenarios, it is not the standard manifestation. Usually this conglomerate easily fits through all vessels. The problems arise when the conglomerate moves through the blood stream and ***bounces off the walls***.

When the endothelial cells on the blood vessel walls are damaged in any form by striking or grazing, the body reacts to ensure there is minimal loss of blood. These responses potentially worsen the DCI. The first response is the adhesion of the blood platelets to the exposed collagen fibers (in the wall of the injured vessel), which causes the release of serotonin from platelets resulting in strong vasoconstriction. This process of vasoconstriction and platelet aggregation instigates a vicious cycle which could eclude the vein after a series of conglomerates does its damage.

Categories of DCS: The first significant symptom of DCS is psychological, not physical; ***denial***. Divers believe that, "***This could never happen to me***," which often worsens the more concrete effects of DCS, which are categorized in the list below.

1. **Type I:** This is the less severe of the two types. Even though the symptoms are not very severe, they cannot be ignored. Common symptoms are pain, marbling and swelling

   a. **Pain:** Dull or aching type pain, usually in a joint. Pain origin is non-descript and can normally not be pinpointed, similar to a sprain. It may/may not get worse during movement, but is usually present at rest. It is generally confined to a specific area and is not attributable to another injury

   b. **Marbling:** Skin bends (***Cutis Marmorata***) Condition starts with intense itching and yields way to a bluish gray bruise like discoloration.

POINTS TO REMEMBER

DCS Type 1 Decompression Sickness

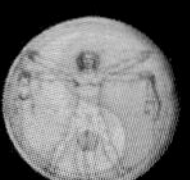

- Simple joint pain
- Marbling of the skin
- Swelling of the lymph nodes
- Denial is common

Skin will look marbled or mottled. Symptoms may get progressively worse. Symptoms which start as itching may not lead to marbling; itching alone is not DCS Type I

c. **Swelling of the Lymph Nodes:** Significant lymph node pain and swelling

2. **Type II:** Unlike Type I, Type II may not be readily apparent. A diver may feel "funny" or over-tired. Normally these symptoms would not be problematic. However, post dive they pose a significant health risk. Type I symptoms may/may not accompany these symptoms. Many of the symptoms of DCS Type II mirror those of an arterial gas embolism (*AGE*)

a. **Unexpressed:** These are symptoms such as over tired and weakness. They may become more severe as time progresses. If treatment is not provided, these "minor symptoms" could progress to a severe neurological deficit

b. **Neurological:** These are any symptoms which may be seen or discovered as a result of a comprehensive neurological assessment. Symptoms include, but are not limited to: numbness, tingling, increased or decreased sensation in an area, muscle weakness

c. **Pulmonary:** Commonly referred to as ***chokes***. A great deal of inert gas bubbles inundate the vascular area in the lungs. This is intravascular bubbling (***cavitation***). Substernal pain which is aggravated by inspiration along with an irritating possibly productive cough. This is generally accompanied by an increase in breathing rate and may progress to circulatory collapse, unconsciousness and death

d. **Inner Ear:** Sometimes called ***Staggers***. Tinnitus (ringing in the ears), hearing loss, vertigo, dizziness, nausea, and vomiting are some of the symptoms. Inner Ear DCS is associated with mixed gas diving and during decompression when the diver switched from breathing helium to air. Even though the symptoms are similar, Inner Ear DCS must be differentiated from ear barotrauma. The symptoms of the "***staggers***" may be due to neurological decompression sickness where symptoms of barotrauma may be due to a ruptured TM. A quick check of both ears by a medically trained individual will help to differentiate these problems

e. **Cardiac:** Very rare. One report of 1st degree AV block which responded to recompression. Symptoms are similar to heart attack or stroke

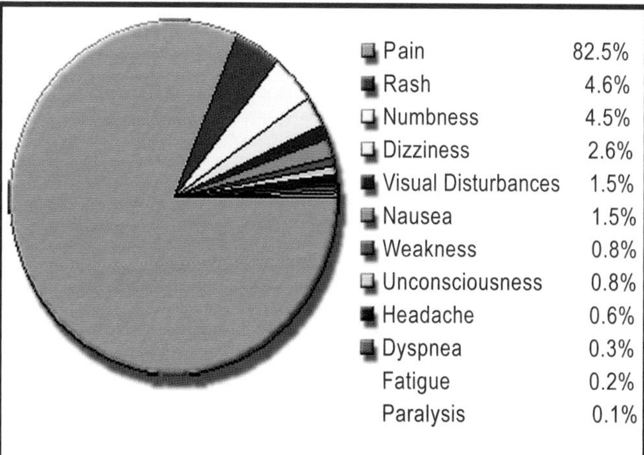

Figure 7-4: Decompression Sickness & the Distribution of Typical Symptoms

Points to Remember

DCS Type II Decompression Sickness

- **Any symptom following a dive that is not Type I DCS**
- **Similar symptoms to an AGE**
- **Watch for unexpressed symptoms**

Pulmonary Over-Inflation Syndrome (POIS) & Extra Alveolar Air (EAA)

All POISs/EAAs are caused by an over-inflation or a rupture of the alveoli lining which leads to Pulmonary Interstitial Emphysema. It is caused by excessive positive pressure within the lung or some kind of blockage which does not allow the expanding air in the alveoli to escape during a decrease in external pressure. It could manifest itself by a permanently or temporarily congested or blocked brachial tubes, a diver failing to breathe continuously during ascent, or a diver who performs the Valsalva Maneuver on ascent. The route which the escaping gas takes determines the type of POIS and ultimately the treatment.

1. **Mediastinal Emphysema:** A mediastinal emphysema occurs when the bubble of gas which

escaped from the rupture leaks into the mediastinal tissues in the middle of the chest. It is characterized by substernal pain which may be mild to moderate and is often described as a dull ache or a feeling of tightness across the chest. The pain may become worse with deep inspiration or coughing and may radiate to the shoulder, back or neck

2. **Subcutaneous Emphysema:** A subcutaneous emphysema is a mediastinal emphysema which has leaked upward into the subcutaneous tissues in the neck and lower face. It is characterized by a voice change, crepitating or the feeling/appearance of fullness in the neck, shoulder or collarbone area

3. **Pneumothorax and 4. Tension Pneumothorax:** In a pneumothorax the gas which has escaped, leaks into the space between the chest wall and the lining of the lung. This leak causes a pocket of gas which may cause respiratory distress. If the leak is an isolated incident, the gas will normally be reabsorbed with time. If the leak continues, the pressure within the cavity could force the whole lung or a lobe to collapse. This situation is severe. Indications of a pnuemothorax include a sudden sharp flank pain in the chest followed by breathing difficulty. A tension pneumothorax occurs when the lung collapses completely and presses on the heart. The collapsed lung pushes the heart and its blood vessels to the other side of the chest, and the heart cannot pump normally

5. **Arterial Gas Embolism (*AGE*):** An AGE is caused by entry of gas bubbles into the arterial circulation which then could act as blood vessel obstructions or similarly to any inert gas bubble such as those which come from decompression sickness. These emboli are frequently the result of pulmonary barotrauma caused by the expansion of gas taken into the lungs while breathing gas under pressure and held in the lungs during ascent. The gas might have been retained in the lungs by choice or accident. The organs that are especially susceptible to arterial gas embolism and that are responsible for the life threatening symptoms are the central nervous system (*CNS*) and the heart. In all cases of arterial gas embolism, associated pneumothorax is possible and should NOT be overlooked

Points to Remember

Pulminary Over-Inflation Syndrome

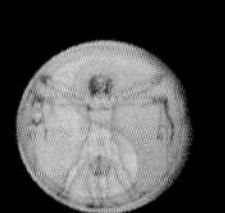

- Mediastinal Emphysema
- Subcutaneous Emphysema
- Pneumothorax
- Tension Pneumothorax
- Arterial Gas Embolism (*AGE*)

Initial first aid is a must. If a person is suspected of having a DCI, ***IMMEDIATELY*** administer fluids, oxygen and transport in supine position (***lying on the spine***) to the nearest hyperbaric facility. A POIS indicates a hole in the alveoli. For this reason, recompression is NOT normally recommended because of the risk of introducing more gas into the blood via the existing hole. AGE's are an exception to that rule because the result of the introduction of additional gas into the blood via the hole in the lung is overshadowed by the severity of the symptoms.

Risk Factors that May Hasten the Onset of DCS

Patent Foramen Ovale (*PFO*)

All fetuses have a hole between the chambers of the heart; the lungs are non-functional in the fetus so the hole allows blood to bypass the lungs. Technically, the hole is called a foramen ovale that is patent (***open***). Normally, this hole seals within 24 hours of birth. Adults have the advantage that blood is transported across the lung capillary bed which is insensitive to bubbles. The fetus does not have this advantage. The fetus does absorb nitrogen across the placenta, but any bubbles that may be formed in the fetus would end up in the fetus's circulation, or possibly in the placenta. This is why woman who think they are pregnant should not dive.

The PFO, or opening in the wall of the heart, is necessary to transfer oxygenated blood via the umbilical cord. However, a PFO can create a myriad of problems if it is found intact or only semi-closed more than 24 hours after birth. This patency can cause a shunt of blood from right to left, but more often there is a movement of blood from the left side of the heart (***high pressure***) to the right side of the heart (***low pressure***). People with shunt lesions are less likely to develop syncope or hypotension with diving than are obstructive valve lesions, but are more likely to develop pulmonary congestion and severe shortness of breath from the effects of combined exercise and water immersion.

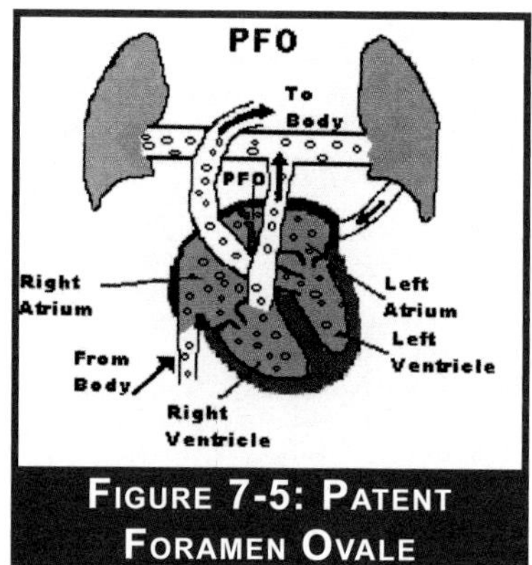

Figure 7-5: Patent Foramen Ovale

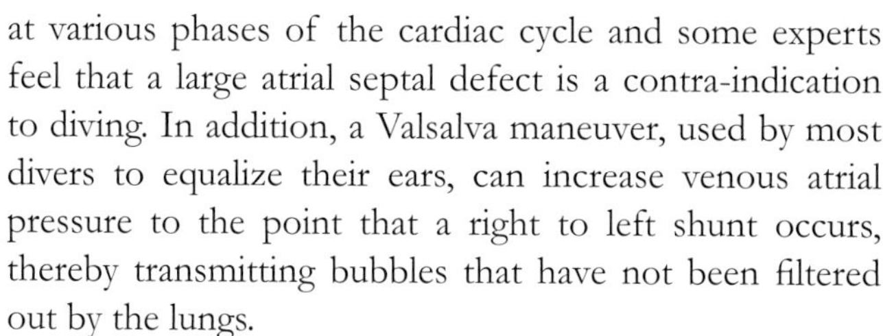

Ordinarily, the left to right shunt will cause no problem; the right to left shunt, if large enough, will cause low arterial O_2 tension and severely limited exercise capacity. In divers there is the risk of paradoxical embolism of gas bubbles which occur in the venous circulation during decompression. Intra-atrial shunts can be bi-directional at various phases of the cardiac cycle and some experts feel that a large atrial septal defect is a contra-indication to diving. In addition, a Valsalva maneuver, used by most divers to equalize their ears, can increase venous atrial pressure to the point that a right to left shunt occurs, thereby transmitting bubbles that have not been filtered out by the lungs.

If a diver is concerned or is having some of the symptoms noted above he or she should seek medical attention. Normally a diver who already has dove to in excess of 100 fsw (930 msw) would have had problems before if a significant PFO was present.

Previous DCS or Problematic Areas

People who have been previously exposed to DCS are more likely to have DCS in the same area. The area where the former insult or previous injury was has probably developed scarring. The increase of scarred tissue over the area makes it less wide. When a bubble tries to pass, it may come in contact with the already scarred tissue faster than would have if there was no scar tissue present.

Age

More applicable than the specific numerical age is the fact that the body changes as people age. Increased body fat, degenerative joint disease, alterations in pulmonary function and cardiac disease are among those changes that increase the risk of DCS with age. This may or may not be the driving ideology, however we know that the U.S. Navy dive tables were established using Navy divers. These individuals are 18-25 years old and in top physical condition. Diving within the limits of the Navy dive tables may be ill-advised practice for an older person.

Body Fat

Fat has high nitrogen solubility. High nitrogen solubility increases nitrogen absorption and bubble growth. We also know that the U.S. Navy dive tables were established using Navy divers who are 18-25 years old and in top physical condition. Diving within the limits of the Navy dive tables may be ill-advised practice for a heavier person or someone who is less physically fit.

Post-Dive Exercise

Doppler scores and the likelihood of DCS increase with post dive exercise. The probable reason is the increase of circulation post dive pushes the decompression progress too far. Your body may attempt to off-gas too quickly causing bubbles to form. These bubbles decrease the tissue and arterial inert gas tensions which reduce the elimination rate.

Body Temperature

Cold decreases your body's ability to off-gas. The problem here is most divers start off relatively warm and as the dive progresses become increasing cold. At the point in the dive where the diver ascends to begin decompression they are cold.

Workload at Depth

Presumably this increase of risk is due to an increase in circulation allowing more inert gas to be absorbed.

Hydration Level

This is the largest contributing factor of DCS. Divers are dehydrated due to immersion diuresis as well as sun exposure and decreased fluid intake. This combination reduces circulation and the rate of off-gassing.

In-Water Recompression

No established course exists to certify anyone to perform in-water recompression. This procedure should not even be attempted if the patient is unconscious or vomiting. If

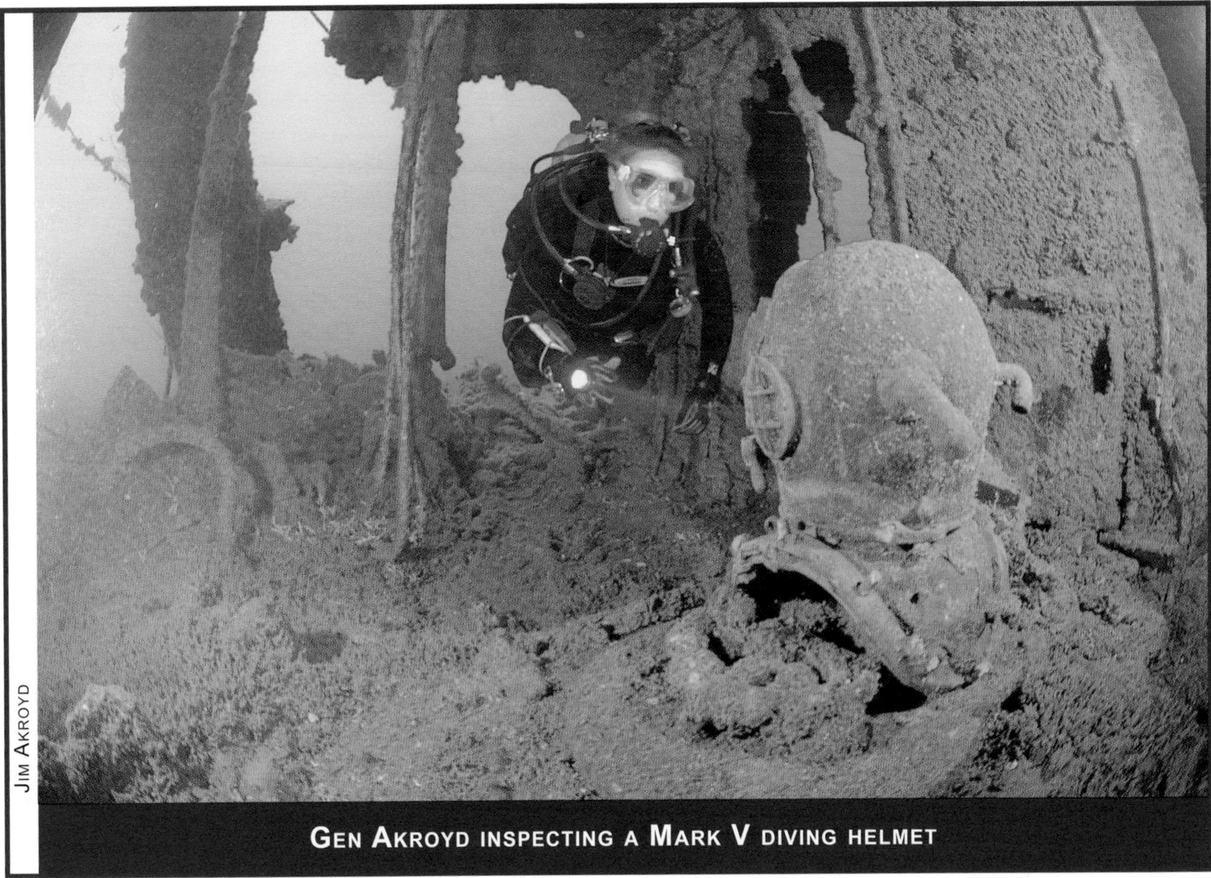

Jim Akroyd

Gen Akroyd inspecting a Mark V diving helmet

it must be attempted, a diver should always accompany the patient and observe his or her condition very closely as the incidents of CNS oxygen toxicity increase when the patient is in the water. The patient should use a full-face mask to decrease the problems associated with an oxygen convulsion. The volume of oxygen required to complete this treatment in water is about 300 cu ft. Using a rebreathing apparatus would reduce consumption to about 300 liters, but the patient must be trained in the use of a rebreather. As water removes heat 25 times faster than air, a patient should also have adequate exposure protection. Hypothermia is a major concern.

If there is no recompression chamber in a reasonable proximity, a stricken diver could be placed on 100% oxygen and brought to not greater than 30 fsw (9 msw). There should be some means of ensuring the patient is not able to descend deeper than 30 fsw (9 msw). A flat bottom is best for this purpose, however surge may be a factor if swells are high enough. The patient should stay a minimum of 60 minutes and a maximum of 90 minutes. The patient should ascend to 20 fsw (6 msw) and stay for 60 minutes. Repeat the 60 minute stop at 10 fsw (3 msw). Patients should continue to breathe 100% oxygen en route to the nearest hospital or hyperbaric facility.

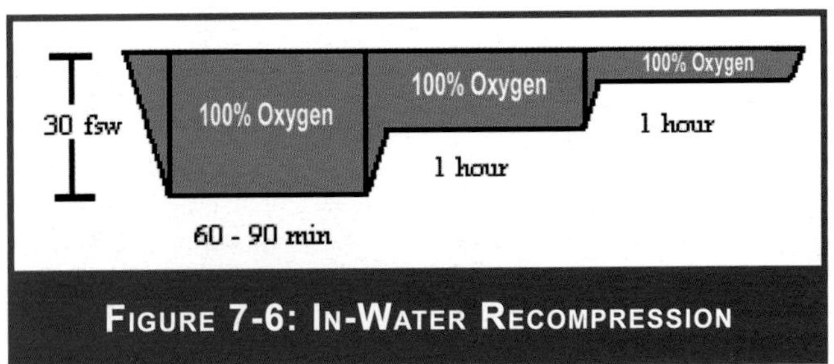

Figure 7-6: In-Water Recompression

The Effect of Cold on DCS

As most divers learned in the open water class, water conducts heat away from the body 25 times faster than air. However, heat escapes from the body several ways when in the water. Convection, conduction and evaporation are the methods of heat transfer although respiration is also applicable. Heat loss by convection occurs when warm air surrounding the body is pushed away by moving cool air. While this is not directly applicable to diving, indirectly, divers whose body parts come out of the water for periods of time (such as the head when surfacing) would be susceptible to convection.

A diver can get colder much more quickly when diving than he or she would in the same air temperature. This is due to conduction or the transfer of heat via direct contact. A diver can easily become chilled and then hypothermic in water whose temperature is less than 98.6°F (37°C) because the body is in direct contact with the water.

COURTNEY PLATT & DIVETECH

ROBERT HEW DECOMPRESSING WITH SQUID FAMILY AT COBALT COAST, GRAND CAYMAN

Heat loss through evaporation is needed to regulate your body temperature in hot weather or when a diver is working hard. In cold conditions, evaporation can quickly suck away warmth, especially if you've been active and then are stationary, like when you are on the bottom working and then while hanging on decompression. Evaporation removes heat (***energy***) from the body as water is converted from liquid to gas. For this reason it is very important for deep divers to wear appropriate thermal protection to include (if wearing a dry suit) underwear that wicks water from the skin.

A primary indication of mild hypothermia in divers is uncontrollable shivering. Other indications include blue color and numbness. More severe signs include lack of coordination, weakness, weak pulse, confusion and death. Prior to a diver becoming cold enough to shiver uncontrollably, they should discontinue diving. Appropriate exposure protection should be used with consideration to water temperature, thermoclines and duration of dive.

Divers that are planning long exposures, such as those found in technical diving, should be adequately protected from the cold. This is particularly important when decompression diving. During a deep dive, the inert gas is absorbed while at depth when the diver is relatively warm because they just started the dive and they are working. The diver consequently becomes cold during decompression because of the reduced work with respect to being on the bottom and the duration of time in the water. When a diver is very cold, the body's protection system will shunt the blood to the extremities and heat the core. Because of the body's natural ability to protect the core, the diver will not have the same circulation to the extremities and there fore will not decompress efficiently which could lead to DCS. Wearing a hood on decompression dives is an excellent method for stopping heat reduction. Rebreather divers maintain a significant advantage with respect to cold temperatures because they are breathing a warm and moist media. Breathing media such as this promotes heat retention.

Conclusion

Since we do not know what the true cause of DCI is, it is difficult to prevent. Some people who have made seemingly innocuous dives have suffered from this malady, albeit others who have "earned" hits by skipping stops have gotten away without being bent. The bottom line with any

Points to Remember

Risk Factors

- **PFO**
- **Previous DCS or areas with previous problems**
- **Age**
- **Body fat**
- **Post dive exercise**
- **Body temperature**
- **Workload at depth**
- **Hydration level (*Largest Contributor*)**

MATTI ANTTILA

WINTER DIVING IN THE ICE & SNOW HAS IT'S OWN SPECIALIZED DECO NEEDS

DCI is that the symptoms should be treated. The cause is not relevant to treatment. The suggestions herein are merely suggestions. Your local Diver's Alert Network or hospital should be consulted to ensure you are affecting the correct type of treatment. None of these treatments should be performed without proper training. Divers should err on the side of safety when it comes to deep decompression and become as learned on the current theories as possible in order to make the best decisions in a bad situation.

MATTI ANTTILA

Chapter Eight Hypothermia & Hyperthermia

Roberto Trindade M.S.

The origin of the word hypothermia comes from the Greek words hypo, meaning under or deficient, and therme, meaning heat or warmth. This term indicates a condition where loss of body temperature, caused by an undue exposure to a cold environment, takes place. Humans become hypothermic when the combined body heat produced and retained is less than the predisposing factors that cause one to be cold.

Hypothermia is defined as a body core temperature less than 95°F (35°C). Core temperature is the temperature of the heart, lungs, brain, and internal organs.

Every year, thousands of divers experience immersion hypothermia. This happens all over the world. Although hypothermia is more common in cold waters, it can also be developed in mild temperatures. Actually, it's not a rare condition in places with a gentle climate and warm waters. This happens because water conducts heat 25 times faster than the air does, making it an excellent heat conductor. Conduction is the heat transfer derived from direct contact, under a temperature gradient, from the warm body into the cold environment.

Homeostasis Physiology

The human being is homeothermic and is adapted into a stable temperature range, where its enzymatic reactions come about adequately. The human body contains a mechanism, called thermoregulation, to help gain and maintain heat against heat loss. This mechanism is controlled by the hypothalamus and includes the brains and spinal cord's nervous and chemical connections, and special thermoreceptors. The core temperature is rigorously maintained between 97.7°F (36.5°C) and 99.5°F (37.5°C). Below this temperature range several signs and symptoms will develop.

Physiopathology & Clinical Aspects

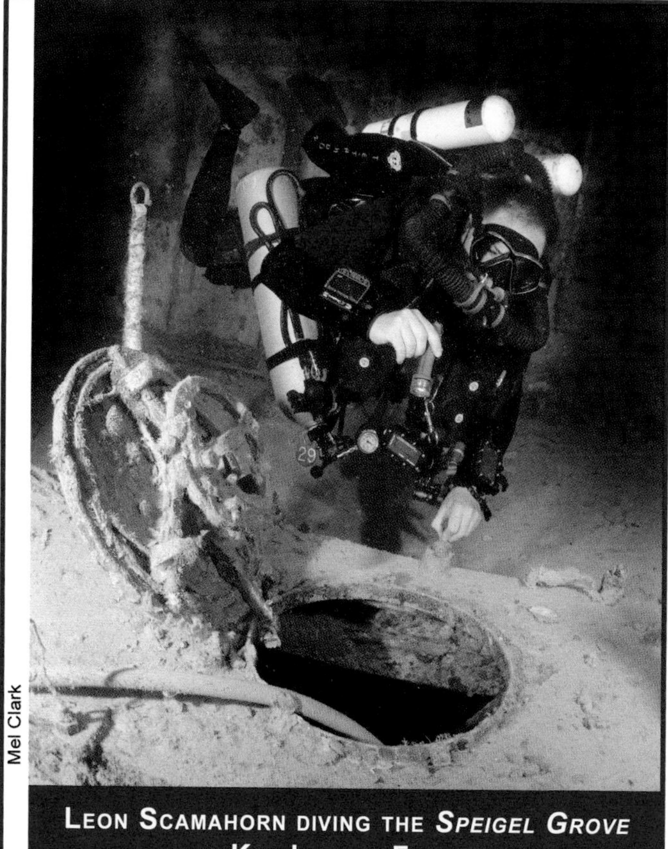

Mel Clark

Leon Scamahorn diving the *Speigel Grove* in Key Largo, Florida

Temperatures between 89.6°F (32°C) and 95°F (35°C) characterize light or mild hypothermia. There is a subjective feeling of being cold, shivering, peripheral vasoconstriction (***lumen narrowing***) of blood vessels, especially in the skin, in the attempt to reduce body heat loss. In that temperature gradient, the diver is kept at an exhilaration level where heat retention and production is maintained by physiological adjustments. When vasoconstriction can't keep up with the heat loss, involuntary muscle contractions (***shivering***) occur. There is also a loss of motor activity and muscle spasms. The skin becomes cold; body extremities (***finger tips, ears, nose and lips***) become cyanotic. The diver shows signs of mental confusion.

Body temperatures below 89.6°F (32°C) face moderate hypothermia. Long exposures to cold may reduce or halt shivering, leading to mental alterations and into a progressive drop in motor function. The diver becomes prostrate, lethargic, and almost unconscious. Humor changes into a state of irritability, aggressiveness and depression. Sometimes euphoria and loss of self-critique may occur. The diver has memory and speech alterations, disorientation, and becomes hypertonic. Pulse rate slows down or become irregular.

Extreme hypothermia, which is defined as body temperatures below 86°F (30°C), renders the diver unconscious. Thermoregulation will eventually collapse and, in severe cases, vasodilatation takes place in the skin, causing even more heat loss to the environment. Pupils expand, while pulse rate and respiration become imperceptible. Mobilization and transport of a victim suffering from extreme hypothermia should be very careful as cardiac arrhythmia might develop. Extreme hypothermia is a life threatening situation if not controlled.

Water Tempature °F (°C)	Survival Time in Hours
> 70° F (21.1° C)	Indeterminate
> 70 - 60°F (21.1 - 15.5° C)	< 12
60 - 50° F (15.5 - 10° C)	< 6
50 - 40° F (10 - 4.4° C)	< 3
40 - 35° F (4.4 - 1.6° C)	< 1.5
< 35° F (1.6° C)	< .25

Figure 8-1: Survival time rate without exposure protection in cold water

Immersion Hypothermia Etiology

Immersion hypothermia can develop quite fast. Exposure to water can cause hypothermia even to healthy individuals; the effects vary for each individual. **There are five factors that influence the development of hypothermia:**

1. **Water Temperature:** The colder the water, the larger the heat loss. Hypothermia is a problem associated with regions of big latitudes but, this is a problem not exclusive of polar or sub-tropical waters.
2. **Time of Exposure:** Hypothermia develops once the body loses more heat to the environment than it can produce. The core temperature diminishes gradually with time of exposure.
3. **Physical Attributes:** Some people believe that the energy reserve found in individuals with large bodies might help prevent hypothermia, this is not the case. In fact, body fat impairs blood flow and increases oxygen consumption. The obese individual needs more energy than a fit individual to complete a certain task. The increased energy consumption yields a more rapidly state of hypothermia. Being better prepared to face cold water means being physically fit. The amount of energy spent in cold water is inversely proportional to the physical condition of the diver, better fit means less waste of energy. An individual who follows a well-balanced diet and is in a good fitness condition is less susceptible to hypothermia.
4. **Diving Behavior:** Every time a diver moves he looses heat, movement accelerates heat loss. A person in cold water has the tendency to move or exercise vigorously in the attempt to warm up, this is a wrong attitude. By moving, a person wastes the body's last heat reserves, diminishing the chance of survival. Someone in the water waiting for rescue should keep calm and make no unnecessary movements. If alone, adopt the Heat Escape Lessening Position (*HELP*) by keeping head and neck out of the water, crossing one's ankles, elevating knees, placing arms close to the body or hugging the legs, and/or placing hands in the arm pits. The idea is to reduce heat loss. If another diver is present, assume a huddle position.
5. **Body Area Exposure:** Concerning the physics of heat transfer process, the area of the surfaces with touch contact is directly proportional to the amount of heat transferred.

Points to Remember

If you are alone in a hypothermic situation, assume the HELP position; keep your head and neck out of the water, cross your ankles, elevate your knees with your hands placed near your body or hug yourself with your hands in your armpits.

Neoprene wet suits are efficient isolators for most recreational diving situations in water temperatures of 69.8°F (21°C) and above. Dry suits are recommended for long term exposures and colder water. An inadequate choice of body exposure protection and long exposures favors the onset of hypothermia.

Prevention

- Maintain body warmth before the dive. Don't unnecessarily lose body heat

- Use an adequate body exposure suit for the water temperature of your dive
- When using wet suits, move slowly and carefully during the dive. Prevent water circulation inside the suit
- Use a hood to protect your head and neck
- Deeper dives will have a crushing effect on neoprene suits and, consequently, the suit will provide less insulation
- While at the surface, protect from the wind as it accelerates heat loss
- Do not consume alcoholic beverages before or after the dive. The false feeling of warmth it provides will produce peripheral vasodilatation, favoring heat loss and the onset of DCS
- Maintain a balanced diet, especially on diving days; your body will have enough energy to dive comfortably.

Dealing With Hypothermia

If you feel cold on a particular dive, increase your insulation for the next dive. Use a thicker suit, hood, gloves or boots. If the cold feeling persists, try a semi-dry or dry suit. When using dry suits, try using different undergarments. You can always leave the water if you feel cold, if not doing a decompression dive. Remove the wet suit, dry your skin, and put on dry and warm clothes as soon as you can. Warm beverages will help; just avoid alcohol or caffeinated drinks.

Hyperthermia

Under special circumstances the human being can survive an extreme loss of body heat. On the other hand, a body temperature over 107.6°F (42°C) could be fatal.

For divers, heat related problems can develop at the surface, while donning the gear, or when one waits to get in the water. It's important to remember that exposure protection suits are designed to work while underwater but can create problems before and after a dive. It is very unlikely that hyperthermia develops while underwater, but it can happen in warm, tropical waters especially during decompression.

Points to Remember

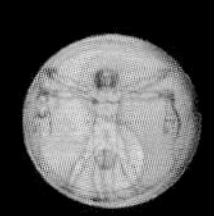

If you feel cold on a particular dive, warm-up between dives and increase the insulation factor of your dive suit for the next dive.

Points to Remember

Treating a Hypothermic Diver

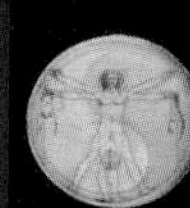

Remove diver from the water if possible. Remove all wet items to prevent evaporative cooling. Replace with warm dry clothing. Administer warm clear liquids but refrain from giving beverages that contain caffeine. If possible place diver out of the direct wind, but in the sun. For more severe hypothermia heating of the groin, neck, and armpits is indicated. Prevent further heat loss and transport to a hospital. A physician should treat hypothermia.

~ Joe Dituri

Thermoregulation Mechanism

As we mentioned before, the human body contains a complex temperature control mechanism called thermoregulation. This mechanism includes the brains and spinal cord's nervous and chemical connections, special thermoreceptors, glands, blood vessels and the spinal cord. This mechanism is controlled by the hypothalamus, located in the brain.

The body core temperature should be maintained between 97.7°F (36.5°C) and 99.5°F (37.5°C). Above this temperature range, organic dysfunctions can develop, sometimes with tragic consequences.

Under normal conditions, the blood carries most of the body heat to the skin, where it will be dissipated into the environment by:

- Conduction (direct contact with the air or cloth)

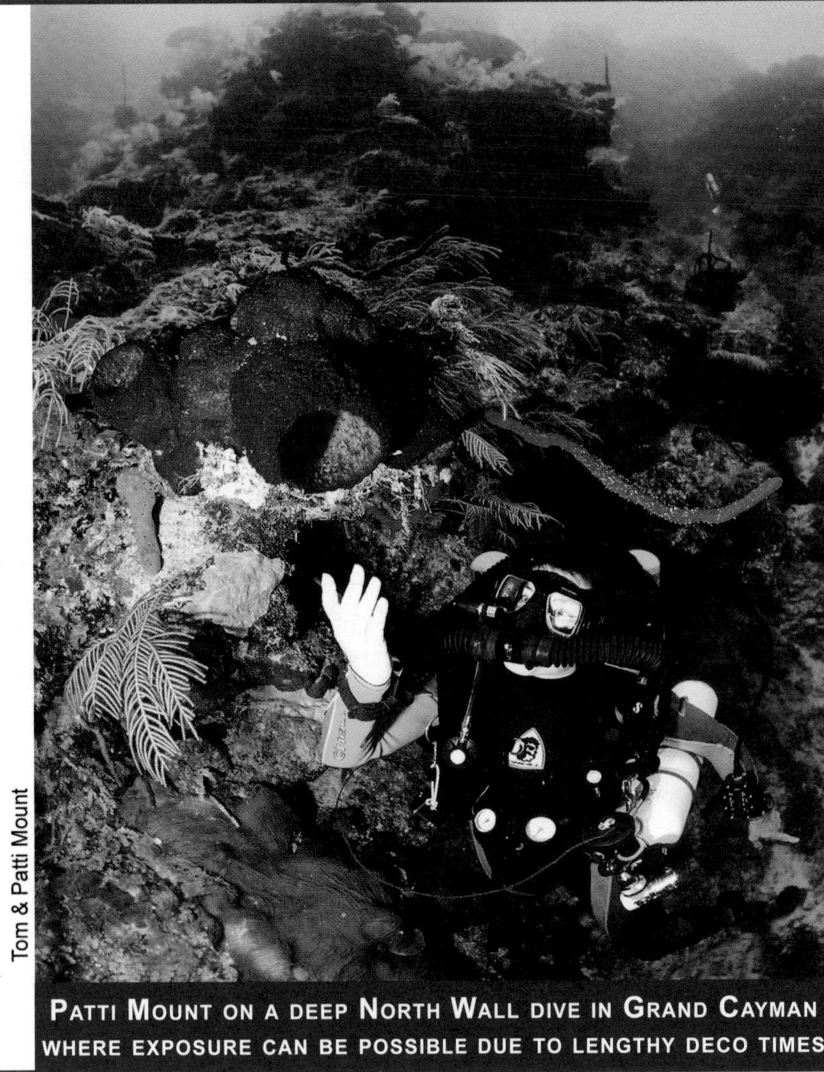

Tom & Patti Mount

PATTI MOUNT ON A DEEP NORTH WALL DIVE IN GRAND CAYMAN WHERE EXPOSURE CAN BE POSSIBLE DUE TO LENGTHY DECO TIMES

- Convection (contact with liquids and environmental conditions, such as water and wind)
- Radiation (infrared rays irradiate from the body)
- Evaporation (mainly through transpiration)

Radiation is considered to be the main heat dissipation mechanism on a resting body. While exercising, 80% of the generated heat is eliminated through perspiration, thus its importance.

Transpiration is essential to control body temperature. For good heat dissipation, the sweat should evaporate from the skin, not simply flow through it.

Hyperthermia can develop on a diver after long term surface activities while wearing an exposure protection suit and without adequate hydration.

Signs & Symptoms

Initially the individual becomes thirsty, tired and develops intense cramps. Some time after the onset of those initial symptoms, the body's thermoregulatory mechanism starts to fail and signs such as nausea, vomit, exhaustion, irritability, mental confusion, loss of self critique, lack of coordination, delusion and loss of consciousness develop. The lack of adequate care may lead to coma or death.

The individual in that condition will have its skin very hot and red, and sometimes shivering may also occur, even in warm environments.

Profuse sweating will take place until the individual becomes dehydrated. At this point, the skin will be dry.

This is a dangerous phase, the absence of perspiration won't allow for adequate heat dissipation, putting the diver at danger.

Once motor activity stops, we can assume that rigorous emergency medical treatment should take place immediately. This treatment should emphasize body temperature reduction (by removing clothes and cooling the victim by cool water immersion).

Divers can prevent hyperthermia by using adequate exposure protection suits for the water temperature they will be diving in, and by cooling down from time to time, by entering the water for example.

To prevent excessive heating, don the exposure suit a few minutes before entering the water and, once the suit is on, keep away from sun exposure. Good hydration is also essential, so have plenty of water or isotonic drinks.

Section Two
Diving Operations

Photo by Andrew Trent

Photo by Jill Hienerth

Chapter Nine
Equipment Configuration

Tom Mount D.Sc., Ph.D., N.D.

Developing a smooth, streamlined underwater swimming style takes practice and an understanding of proper technique. Equally important, however, is the way in which your dive equipment is configured and carried. Improper gear configurations cause excess drag, are more likely to cause entanglement problems, and can make it difficult or even impossible for the diver to access needed back-up equipment. Proper configuration, on the other hand, allows the diver to minimize underwater drag, protects the equipment and allows for immediate access to all primary life support gear and important back-up items.

Beyond these universal factors, there are endless variations on the specifics of proper gear configuration, and there is no single "best" way that dive gear should be worn. Differences in the diving environments and in diving styles place widely varying demands on equipment, and a rig that might be perfect for deep Trimix diving could be totally wrong for confined sump dives.

Safety is the first consideration that must be addressed when planning an equipment configuration. The diving mission often dictates the gear to be carried - and it may have some influence of how that gear is worn. As the diver selects gear to match the dive's requirements, he should analyze each specific piece of hardware, and should select only items that will contribute to the overall safety and performance of the dive. Without a safe system, all other effort is wasted. Before designing a personal system, listen to the experiences of other divers and review accident case studies. By identifying potential problem areas, you can then create a rig that is not only personalized to your needs and habits, but is also created with maximum safety in mind.

Universal Considerations of the Technical Diving Rig

Comfort and fit are key to the enjoyment of any dive, but become increasingly important to diver safety within the context of the longer, more demanding scenarios of technical diving. An uncomfortable diver is more susceptible to stress, will tire sooner and may experience perceptual narrowing caused by the discomfort of the equipment. By contrast, a comfortable diver is more likely to remain alert, relaxed and aware of his surroundings, all of which contribute to dive performance and emergency preparedness.

In addition to providing a comfortable fit, the rig must be stable, even when all the accessories are added. Also keep in mind that your chosen rig should not only be comfortable

20 Essential Aspects of Equipment Configuration
~ Listed in order of importance ~

1. It is safe & dependable
2. It is comfortable for the diver
3. It provides adequate rather than excessive redundancy
4. It fosters self-sufficincy and self-rescue
5. It is simple and user-friendly (*KISS Principle*)
6. Valves and accessories are easily reached
7. Buddy rescue/assist is enabled
8. Customizable to diver's needs and the objectives of the dive
9. Diver feels confident with equipment configuration
10. Presents a low drag profile
11. Equipment schema is balanced
12. Equipment is identifiable by touch
13. Incorporates standard gear placement
14. It is versatile
15. It is stream-lined and clear
16. Updates to the rig are made at a comfortable rate by the diver
17. Decompression stage cylinders feature visual, touch and placement ID
18. Cylinders are labled for intended use
19. The user continues to implement improvements to the gear configuration

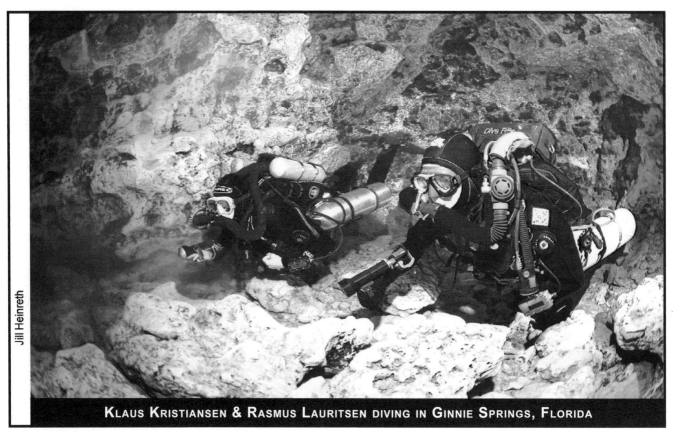

Jill Heinreth

KLAUS KRISTIANSEN & RASMUS LAURITSEN DIVING IN GINNIE SPRINGS, FLORIDA

in the water, but also on land. This is particularly important in cases where you are required to wait before entering the water, or to walk some distance to the dive site. If you are currently using a system that causes discomfort or pain, make an immediate change.

Redundancy is unquestionably technical diving's single greatest safety margin. The philosophy of redundancy dictates that any element of the diving rig that is essential to life support should be backed up by a working spare. Problems arise when divers carry the philosophy of redundancy too far, however. There is seldom any need for multiple back-up systems, and excessive redundancy not only creates configuration problems, but also may actually decrease the overall safety of the diver.

Items that must be backed up include regulators on the primary gas supply and lights in cave and wreck diving. It is also desirable to back-up the buoyancy control system. This may incorporate either a dry suit with one BCD or a wetsuit with two BCDs. Recently, some manufacturers have developed back flotation systems that feature two sets of wings within one cover. These systems do have advantages, as they produce less drag than two independent sets of wings. The disadvantage of the enclosed double-wing systems is that they do not allow the diver the versatility of switching from two to one wing configurations. Another item worthy of back-up is the cutting tool. This may be a small knife, surgical scissors or other form of cutters. For wreck diving the cutting tools must be able to cut wiring and fishing line.

Self-sufficiency combined with the ability to perform self-rescue is the primary requirement of any technical diving rig. The design must allow the diver quick access to any items needed for self-rescue, and should provide the diver with a realistic degree of self-sufficiency. Again, there is no advantage to carrying surplus safety items, and there may be disadvantages. There is a point where too much of a "good thing" may result in decreased performance instead of enhanced capabilities. Treat each dive as if you were diving solo. In other words, do not be dependent upon others for your safety. A self-sufficient diver is a survivor.

Keep it simple, and it will serve you better. Elaborate and complex gear placement leads to confusion. If the configuration is simple and easy to use, then it is ideal. If the complexity causes one to stop and think in order to determine where a needed piece of hardware is located, it will not suffice in a fast-moving, stressful situation. Tank valves must be reachable with a minimum of difficulty, and accessory equipment must be rigged in a fashion and a position to be readily available.

The ability to perform buddy rescue or a buddy assist is a mandatory component of any technical diving rig. One universal feature that allows for this capability is the use of a longer second stage hose attached to either the primary or secondary first stage regulator. This hose should be 5 ft (1.5 m) or longer, with 7 ft (2 m) being the more common length. The hose must also be easy to deploy and hand off to a distressed diver. Before a dive, buddies should familiarize themselves with the location of each other's safety and back-up equipment, and should also check each item to make sure it is functional. Dive teams that work together on a regular basis might wish to go one step further and work towards a common, mutually agreeable means of configuration and positioning of the life support systems involved in buddy rescue.

Out-of-the-box diving equipment seldom meets all the specialized needs of technical diving. As a result, most technical divers have learned to customize their equipment to fit the specific needs of the mission. Before you can effectively customize your equipment for the best possible fit and function, you need to build a basic understanding of each piece of equipment that will make up the rig, and also gain some understanding of how these parts come together as a whole. Therefore, you should be willing to set aside a reasonable amount of time to analyze the components of the system and then determine how you want them to blend into a usable whole.

The backbone of your technical diving rig is the backplate harness - or one of the new technical soft backpacks. For this reason, special care should be given to adjusting the harness of the back plate/back pack for optimum fit. Too often, divers are either uninformed or unwilling to take the time needed to adjust this most basic piece of equipment for optimum fit. Improper adjustment creates discomfort and a loss of diver performance that could lead to errors in judgment or degraded diver performance.

Many instructors devote one to three hours of a course assisting students in arranging equipment. This is a good starting point, but it should not be the end point. As a diver, you should always be on the lookout for a better way. If an item or technique looks to be more streamlined, easier to use or simply more comfortable to wear, then try it. As stated prior, there should be an ongoing search for the perfect rig.

Good technical diving rigs don't just happen; they evolve over time. Don't allow rigid thinking to lock you into a mindset in which you cease to evolve. If you do only one style of technical diving, you may develop an extremely specialized rig matched to that specific environment. If, on the other hand, you find yourself involved in more than one style of diving, you might wish to create a more versatile rig that is easily modified. For example, some of the aforementioned soft backpacks can accommodate single, double or side-mounted tanks with minor adjustments.

Regardless of your customizing efforts, the end result should inspire confidence in your rig, and should allow you to operate with minimal effort and maximum comfort. A streamlined diver creates less drag in the water. By streamlining, you lower the work of swimming and,

Take the Time to Do It Right!

1. Always remain an individual & use your freedom of choice.
2. It is YOUR safety, YOUR life, YOUR comfort!
3. Develop a configuartion based on logical analysis of your needs
4. List the logic for each segment of your configuration
5. Be able to explain why and how you configure your equipment
6. Remember that the final word on configuration must be YOURS

~ Avoid getting stuck in the illusion that only 1 method of gear configuration will work ~ Adopt methods that are applicable to your dive style ~

Be Prudent, Be Responsible, Be Open-Minded, Be Safe, and Take the Time To Do It Right!

in turn, increase your gas supply duration. A streamlined configuration also assists in avoiding entanglement and the possibility of becoming stuck in restricted areas.

Once you have selected and assembled your rig, you must look for ways to streamline and clean up the loose ends. Begin with careful scrutiny of each piece of equipment, looking for ways to streamline it to the point of least possible drag and bulk.

A streamlined rig will have few or no hoses protruding beyond the tank valve handles. Hoses must be stored neatly and gauges must be secured snug to the body. Accessory items should also be attached to minimize drag and the chance of entanglement. In general, you will want to avoid all dangling objects and items attached to the harness by a single clip or strap that allows for excessive movement.

One additional factor to consider when constructing an equipment configuration is the need to create a balanced swim posture. A rig that does not allow the diver to maintain a comfortable horizontal swim position is not suitable for the majority of technical diving applications. Any rig that is inherently unstable or which requires excessive effort to maintain a swimming position should be reconfigured or modified to alleviate the problem.

In summary, an effective technical diving rig should be balanced, comfortable and streamlined. It should provide for a standardized method of gear placement, but must also allow room for improvement or innovation. Each item of equipment should be easily identified by touch and visual identification. In addition, the system should be versatile, allowing you to transition smoothly from one diving environment to another with ease and comfort.

All cylinders used on a dive must be properly labeled. A number of fatalities, including those involving highly trained technical divers, can be directly attributed to a failure to identify and label breathing gasses. When using any gas other than air, you must analyze, identify and label the mixture.

It is obvious that we are all human, and human error is the greatest threat to all of us. Mr. Murphy will capitalize on all events that may lead to a human error. To prevent such accidents, you should take as many precautionary steps as possible. In addition to proper cylinder identification and gas content labeling that includes oxygen content and maximum operating depth, IANTD recommends in all Open Water training situations that gases containing different mixtures and MODs be placed on opposite sides of the diver. The mouthpiece of the highest EANx or Oxygen should either be covered or have rubber tubing wrapped around it. This prevents accidental switches to the wrong regulator(s). The diver cannot breathe from it

Points to Remember

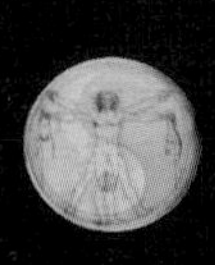

The use of any breathing gas other than air will require specialized training on the part of the diver. If you are using gasses other than air without such training, your are acting irresponsibly, and may be courting disaster.

Points to Remember

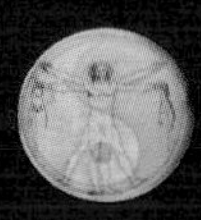

Label your cylinders and always have the gas mixture and maximum operating depth clearly identified on the cylinder.

Ike Ikehara

DAVID MOUNT, MARY BISHOP & MAC FARR CIRCA 1971. NOTE THE EQUIPMENT USED AT THIS TIME COMPARED WITH THE EQUIPMENT IN USE TODAY. IT IS IMPORTANT THAT DIVERS REMAIN OPEN TO CHANGE.

until the cover or tubing is removed from the mouthpiece. This serves as an additional step to avoid confusion of gas cylinders. Do not allow something so simple as a cylinder mix-up to cause an accident.

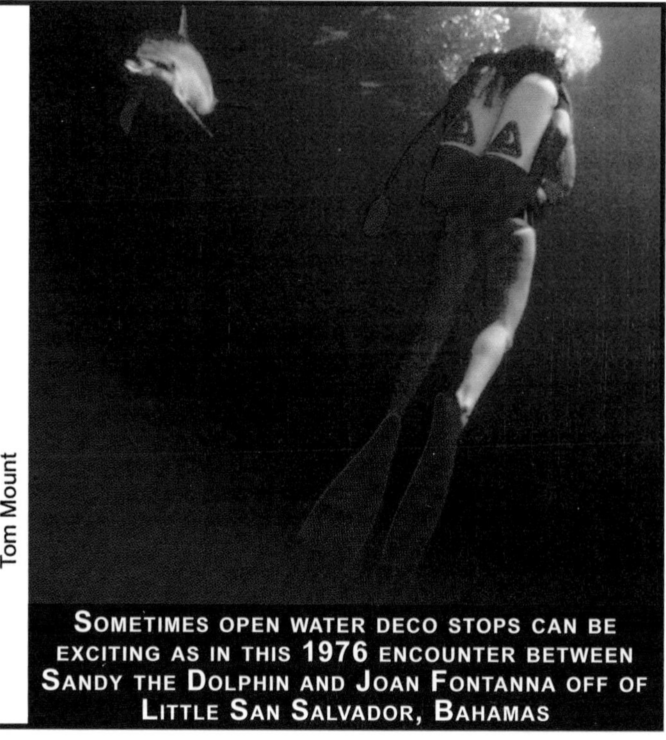
Tom Mount

Sometimes open water deco stops can be exciting as in this 1976 encounter between Sandy the Dolphin and Joan Fontanna off of Little San Salvador, Bahamas

The Background of Technical Equipment

The more you know about the history, attributes, advantages and shortcomings of various pieces of technical diving equipment, the better you will be at selecting the items you incorporate in your personal life support system.

To understand the state of technical diving gear today, and where it might be going tomorrow, let's look into the history and evolution of some of our present day components and systems. In the 60's, the standard deep diving rig was a US Navy harness with a standard single-outlet, double cylinder manifold.

Submersible lights were homemade by any number of jerry-rigged methods that might use motorcycle batteries for power and a plumber's helper for a bulb holder. These and may other off-the-wall ideas were tried, and many worked reasonably well. Around 1966, Frank Martz introduced lights that used a waterproof cylinder as a battery case. These lights proved to be highly reliable, and functioned consistently at depths of up to 300 ft (91 m). Martz also came up with the first dependable safety reels, and the first auto-inflate system. These advances not only increased the diving community's safety, but also stimulated others to design new and improved systems.

In 1970 while exploration diving and filming with George Benjamin, a dive group consisting of this author, Frank Martz, Jim Lockwood, Ike Ikehara and Dr. Dick Williams became concerned with George's use of independent tanks. This concern was prompted by previous body recoveries involving divers using these systems.

The author suggested the tanks be mated together, and Ike Ikehara designed a system to do this. George took this drawing to Tom McCullam who built the Benjamin conversion valves. These were the first dual outlet valves used in technical diving. Shortly thereafter, several others begin to convert standard manifolds into dual valve systems. From this early beginning, the equipment has evolved to the selection of valves we take for granted today.

Not long after the horse collar BC was developed, technical divers began customizing these designs to make them more appropriate for their style of diving. The stabilizing (stab) jacket was developed next, and numerous divers elected to use them. The author's first recollection of the use of a back-mounted BC for technical diving was by Patti-Ann Schaeffer (now Patti Mount) in a cave diving class in June of 1978. The wings had to be taped onto a Cressi-Sub harness, but they performed so well that within a week, the author and Bob Ledbetter had converted some "surplus" street signs into backplates, and used "diving wings" on all dives from that point forward. It is quite possible that someone else may have evolved wings before this time, but that was my first introduction to them.

Today, the back-mounted flotation system has evolved and matured, giving divers a number of styles to select

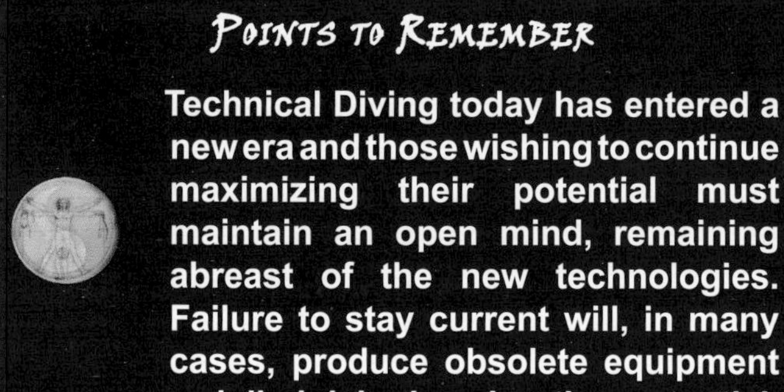

Points to Remember

Technical Diving today has entered a new era and those wishing to continue maximizing their potential must maintain an open mind, remaining abreast of the new technologies. Failure to stay current will, in many cases, produce obsolete equipment and diminished exploration potential.

from. This technology has yielded hard backplates of ABS, aluminum and stainless steel. The hard packs reigned supreme until the mid 90's. Today Zeagle, ScubaPro, Dive Rite and other manufacturers either have, or are in process of introducing, soft packs that may very well be the gateway to the future for technical diving applications. To complement this development, single-bag dual-bladder wings evolved through the efforts of OMS and DiveRite. This evolution of dual wings was the result of numerous reports of BC failure and the need for redundant flotation aimed at divers wearing wetsuits.

Regulator development has also kept pace with the needs of the technical and extended-range diver. In comparison to the equipment of a decade ago, many regulators now on the market offer substantially lower breathing resistance, greater rates of air delivery, higher overall performance and increased reliability.

In recent years, the dive industry has introduced tanks of much greater volume. The ability to carry significantly more gas in such high-volume tanks allows divers to increase safety margins, expand the limits of underwater exploration and open underwater frontiers not considered attainable a few years ago. The introduction of rebreathers to the recreational/technical community in the mid-90's expanded these capabilities to even greater depths and distances with increased safety.

Selecting the Components

Backplates

In your ongoing evolution towards an optimum personal equipment configuration, you must remember to select only those components that will provide safety and fulfill the needs of your dive objective. The best way to begin this selection process is by working outward from the foundation.

On a technical diving rig, the foundation of the system is the mounting platform - the ***backplate***. For the purpose of this discussion, a backplate can mean either a hard pack or a soft pack. To decide which is best for a particular purpose, one should scrutinize the pros and cons of each.

The traditional hard backplate has been reliable and is available in ABS, aluminum or stainless steel. The plate can

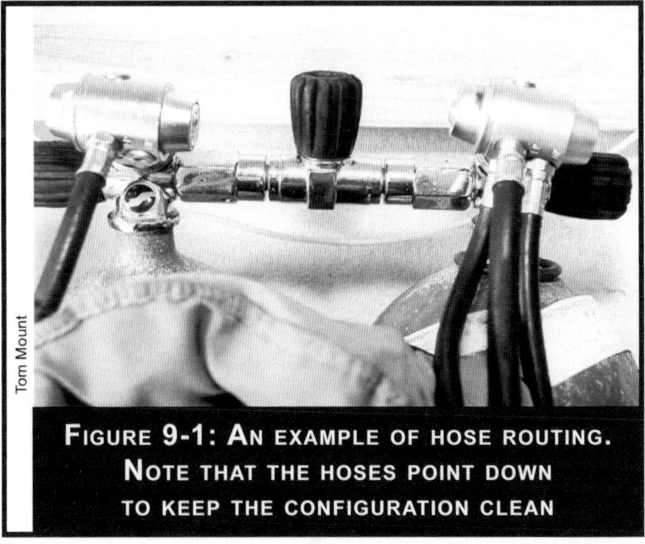

Tom Mount

Figure 9-1: An example of hose routing. Note that the hoses point down to keep the configuration clean

be easily configured and customized to fit all our mounting needs. It has a small profile, and thus creates little drag, and has proven to be very dependable. Due to its simplicity and ruggedness, the hard backplate is, and will continue to be, the foundation of preference for many divers.

The chief limitation of the hard backplate is its lack of versatility for multi-purpose use. The adaptive hardware needed to convert a hard backplate for use with a single tank is awkward at best. Granted, it does work, and is arguably superior to switching from one style BC to another. In addition, the backplate is not convenient for use with side-mount diving, nor is it as comfortable to wear on land as a soft pack. Additionally, hard backplates are a "one size fits all" proposition, and divers who are relatively short or tall will find it to be more uncomfortable than the multi-sized soft pack technology currently on the market.

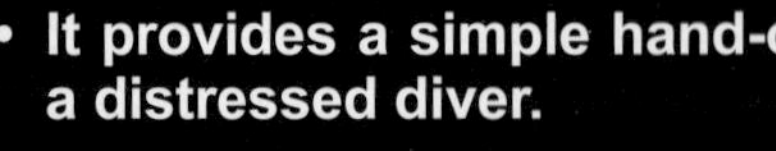

Primary Advantages of Breathing From The Long Hose:

- **It provides a simple hand-off to a distressed diver.**
- **It ensured the out-of-air diver receives a functioning regulator.**
- **In theory, a distressed diver will most likely try to take the regulator from the other diver's mouth.**

Tom Mount introducing his son David to the CIS-Lunar MK5P CCR

Divers have experimented with soft packs for a number of years. In general, the early prototypes did not provide the stability needed to support doubles and stage tanks. For this reason they never gained popularity in the technical diving community. In 1995, two manufacturers, Zeagle and Dive Rite, made dramatic advances in soft pack technology. Zeagle introduced an updated technical pack, and Dive Rite introduced the TransPac. Initially both of these systems had some inherent problems. The Zeagle unit lacked stability with doubles and stages, and the DiveRite was too cumbersome to set up. Both have made improvements that resulted in a usable and suitable system. As a result, there are now several "technical" soft packs on the market.

> **Points to Remember**
>
> **Primary Advantages of Breathing From The Short Hose:**
>
> - **It ensures the diver always has a functioning regulator even in an out-of-air emergency with another diver.**
> - **It takes into account the fact that many divers no longer have the reflex to go for the regulator in the other diver's mouth.**
> - **By connecting the short hose to the left post of the manifold, the diver will know immediately if the valve has been accidentially bumped shut due to contact with an overhead environment. (The valve shuts off clockwise in a foward movement.)**

Whether you opt for a hard backplate or soft backpack, your first action should be to adjust and modify the unit for personal comfort and compatibility. Be sure to streamline this unit to the maximum practical point. No loose ends, no dangling material, and a snug fit are prerequisites.

When rigging a new gear system - either hard or soft - the author typically spends about two initial hours analyzing the pack with regards to personal needs. This includes several trips to a mirror to look at the effect each modification of the system creates. An additional 2 to 3 hours are then spent assembling and re-evaluating the completed configuration. Once the life-support system is optimized, it does not require anything except maintenance and an occasional tweak when a better way is observed or invented.

Regulators

If the backpack is considered the foundation of the technical diving rig, the regulators are the heart of that system. This heart has two parts - the primary and the back-up regulator - and each is of equal importance to the life support system.

One mistake some technical dives make is to settle for a lower performance back-up regulator. Remember, in the event of a problem, that back-up regulator is for you, and you wouldn't want to go from a high-performer to a "hog" in a stressful situation.

Likewise, you don't want to hand a hard breathing, low volume regulator to a stressed diver. Unfortunately, many divers select an ideal primary and then dig out their oldest and lowest performing regulator for the secondary. This is like waving a red flag at Mr. Murphy. The combination of stress and a low performance regulator may lead to an otherwise avoidable incident.

The diver should decide to breathe from the long hose rather than the short hose. The way in which the long hose is stored varies depending on whether the diver breathes from a 5 ft or 7 ft (1.5 m or 2 m) hose.

Tom Mount

ED STANECKI CAVE DIVING IN 1966. ED IS DIVING WITH A MOTORCYCLE BATTERY POWERING AN EARLY UNDERWATER LIGHT & ONE OF THE FIRST SEA VIEW SUBMERSIBLE PRESSURE GUAGES. NOTE THE PROGRESS IN EQUIPMENT.

While in training, a diver should practice with both a five ft and 7 ft hoses (1.5m and 2.1m). Generally speaking, there are two recommended ways to store a long hose. One is to drop the hose back along the back of the wings and then across the body around the left side of the neck with a ¼ turn around the neck.

UNDERWATER LIGHTING

Lights should be evaluated with regards to depth ratings, ease of storage and performance. When diving in overhead environments beyond the point of surface light, the diver must carry a primary light and two smaller secondary lights. If diving within a zone of surface light, a primary and one back-up will suffice.

The physical positioning of the primary light varies widely among divers, but the some popular methods are either waist mounted, backplate mounted, or and on some rebreathers the light canister is inside the rebreather cover, this of course requires a switch on the light head,. Regardless of which method you choose, you should be aware of the advantages and disadvantages of each systems. Additionally, you should be aware of how to use the alternate method, since some situations may be better served by one than another. Safety lights should be carried in manner that minimizes drag while allowing for quick, easy access.

BUOYANCY COMPENSATION

The buoyancy compensation devices of almost universal choice among technical divers are the back-mounted flotation systems typically known as wings. Wing systems conform to the profile of double tanks, while leaving the diver's front free for the attachment of lights, accessories and stage tanks.

When selecting a buoyancy compensation system, make sure it has adequate lift capacity to support you and all the equipment you plan to carry, not only on the surface, but at depth, where compression will reduce the inherent buoyancy of a wetsuit or neoprene dry suit. Generally, technical divers tend to be negatively buoyant because of the double tanks and extra equipment that are part of the technical diving rig. For this reason, most experienced divers feel that some type of redundancy is needed within the buoyancy compensation system. When diving rebreathers, it is much easier to be at neutral buoyancy or possibly even wearing required are trim weights.
For the diver wearing a wetsuit, this may mean wearing a second set of wings, or a system, such as those marketed

POINTS TO REMEMBER

Safety Lights are generally worn in one of three configurations:

- **With a backplate, they can be worn on the lower portion of the shoulder harness and then are placed through a surgical tubing or shock-cord loop, one light on each side.**
- **They can be carried in a pouch worn on the waist.**
- **On a soft-pack like the TransPac, they may be attached to the lower waist d-ring and then secured with loops of surgical tubing or shock-cord. This locates the lights safely near the cylinders and behind the waist d-rings. One light is generally carried on each side.**

by DiveRite and OMS, which provides two bladders within one shell. When diving in a drysuit, the suit itself can fill the need for back-up flotation. In this event, only one set of wings may be needed. In addition, rebreather divers in an emergency can develop additional buoyancy with the counter lungs

Diver error or faulty maintenance causes the majority of buoyancy compensator failures. Common causes of failure include pulling too hard on dump valves, snagging or abrading the air bladder on an environmental feature and allowing sand or debris to clog a dump valve seal. But even if you take exemplary care of your BC system, there is always some chance that an air bladder failure will cause you to lose buoyancy. A second set of wings or a dual bladder system is a small price to pay for the safety they provide.

Lift bags, while not strictly a buoyancy compensation device, are also a needed part of open water technical diving rigs. Bags should have at least 50 pounds of lift, with 100 pounds preferred by many divers, and the uninflated bag should be stored in a manner that minimizes drag and the chance of entanglement.

Cutting Tools

Technical divers carry cutting tools not for the purpose of dismantling artifacts or the environment, but to extricate themselves from entanglements. The cutting tool should be appropriate for the diving environment. For example, a lightweight parachute cutter would suffice in a cave, where the only entanglement potential comes from nylon guidelines, while heavy wire cutters might be needed on wrecks draped in dangling cables, wires and discarded fishing nets. Surgical scissors typically work well in any environment and will cut either wire or line.

Reels

You must carry a safetyl reel on all technical dives, as it is a primary tool of self-rescue. If you become lost, disoriented or separated from a guideline in an overhead environment, the safety reel can be attached to a reference point, allowing you to perform search sweeps without straying further from the point of the initial problem. In open water, the safety reel can be used to deploy a lift bag.

In caves, and on wrecks of major magnitude, you or some member of the dive team should also carry a larger, primary reel, which will be used to form a continuous guideline to open water, either by deploying line throughout the dive, or tying into an existing guideline. Cave dives that call for jumps from one existing guideline to another will require additional small reels known as gap reels. Your dive team should carry one gap reel for every expected line jump, but there is no advantage to carrying more reels than the dive plan calls for.

Pressure Gauges

The large gauge consoles common in open water recreational diving do not find favor with technical divers. Instead, pressure gauges are typically fitted with a minimal cover boot, and are attached to a harness D-ring or stowed close to the diver's body to prevent entanglement. To eliminate the drag and clutter of a dangling high-pressure hose, many divers order shorter hoses that end at waist level or above. For use on stage cylinders, button gauges

Tom Mount

Mark Meadows returning from a 560 fsw (160 m) dive with Tom Mount. At the time, this was the deepest dive completed on a Megalodon CCR with Meg support divers.

Points to Remember

There are several considerations that should be taken into account when rigging and using stage cylinders. Some of these items are:

- **The stage cylinder must be easy to put-on and remove.**
- **The stage must be rigged and worn in a manner that minimizes drag.**
- **The stage bottles must be placed on the diver in a manner that maintains good dive posture.**
- **The diver must be trained in management of stage cylinders.**

are quite popular. Many rebreather divers also rely on the button gauges.

Exposure Suits

Because technical dives typically last much longer than recreational dives, heat loss becomes a concern much sooner. A reduced body temperature is a predisposing factor to DCS, so exposure protection is not only a matter of comfort, but also a safety concern.

In warm or temperate waters, many divers opt for the relative simplicity of a wetsuit, and may include a hood or hooded vest for longer duration dives. As in-water times increase and water temperatures decrease, most veteran technical divers will opt for a drysuit. Before diving a drysuit, you should seek additional specialized training in its use and maintenance.

Accessories

Items such as masks and fins should be selected on the basis of personal comfort, fit and durability. Because your underwater mass and profile are increased by the additional gear you carry on a technical dive, your fins should be large and stiff enough to move you without causing excessive leg fatigue.

Stage Cylinders

In technical diving, additional gas supplies are often needed to either extend the range of exploration or to supply custom decompression mixes. To accommodate these gas needs, divers may carry permanent, semi-permanent or removable stage tanks. Removable stage tanks are the most common option used by technical divers. The term stage implies the use of a specific tank of gas for a specific portion of a dive. Because such tanks are removable, the diver may stage them on sections of the dive.

In exploration diving, this is especially important. Cave exploration entered a new dimension when the concept of stage diving evolved. The practice was initiated by Sheck Exley and named by this author. By using the stage tank on the initial phase of the dive, explorers could extend their diving range. Then, by dropping the stage tank off at a predetermined point - or a point based on gas turn-points of the stage cylinder - the divers could reduce drag and increase their overall swimming efficiency.

Many divers favor carrying stages in a side mount configuration which may keep both cylinders on the same side or opposite sides. The advantage of side mount is

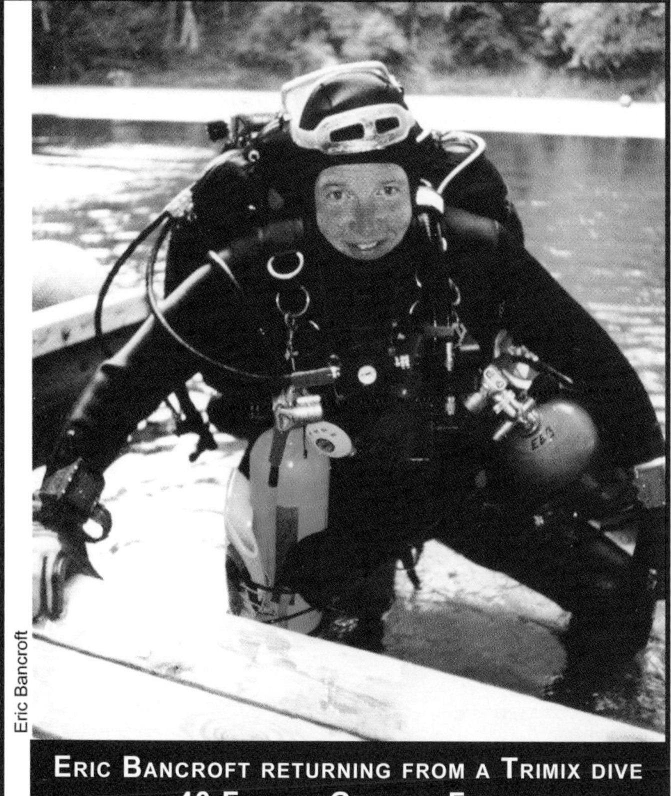

Eric Bancroft

Eric Bancroft returning from a Trimix dive in 40 Fathom Grotto, Florida

reduced drag and is especially popular among rebreather divers.

During wreck penetration dives, the ability to drop decompression stage tanks in open water reduces the risk of entanglement. In addition, the diver may then be able to fit into more confined areas of the wreck. In IANTD technical diving courses, standardized training requirements call for the use of stage tanks.

While stage diving, the size and number of stages may vary depending upon the dive objectives, the abilities of the divers and the presence of support divers. On extensive cave explorations, literally dozens of stage bottles may be used to extend the lead divers' range and to provide bailout capabilities. Conversely, staging done for decompression purposes is usually limited to no more than three tanks.

Proper rigging is the key to the easy handling and removal of stage tanks. A typical stage tank will have a snap hook near the neck of the bottle and at a position even to the diver's waist level when the tank is attached.

One of the simplest and most effective means of rigging stage cylinders is by using a piece of nylon line or parachute cord. With this method, the line/cord is pre-cut to length and then secured around the neck of the cylinder. Next, a snap hook is slipped up to near the neck and tied (a fisherman's knot or half hitch works well). The line is then run under a hose clamp tank band at the middle to lower portion of the tank, and the second snap hook is installed at the end of the line.

For ease of handling, a strap that enables the tank to be carried like a suitcase when it is transported on land can connect the attachment hooks.

If divers are wearing gloves, larger attachment hooks must be used. Many divers argue against the use of boat snap hooks as they tend to attach themselves to wiring and loose lines, and may also allow for accidental disengagement. On the other hand numerous cave divers prefer these and especially when side mounting. On the Eastern Seaboard, many wreck divers refer to boat snap hooks as suicide clips due to this tendency. Large snap hooks typically allow for faster and easier tank removal and replacement - a factor that can save extra minutes of bottom time spent struggling with a difficult stage attachment.

Decompression stages must be configured in a way that

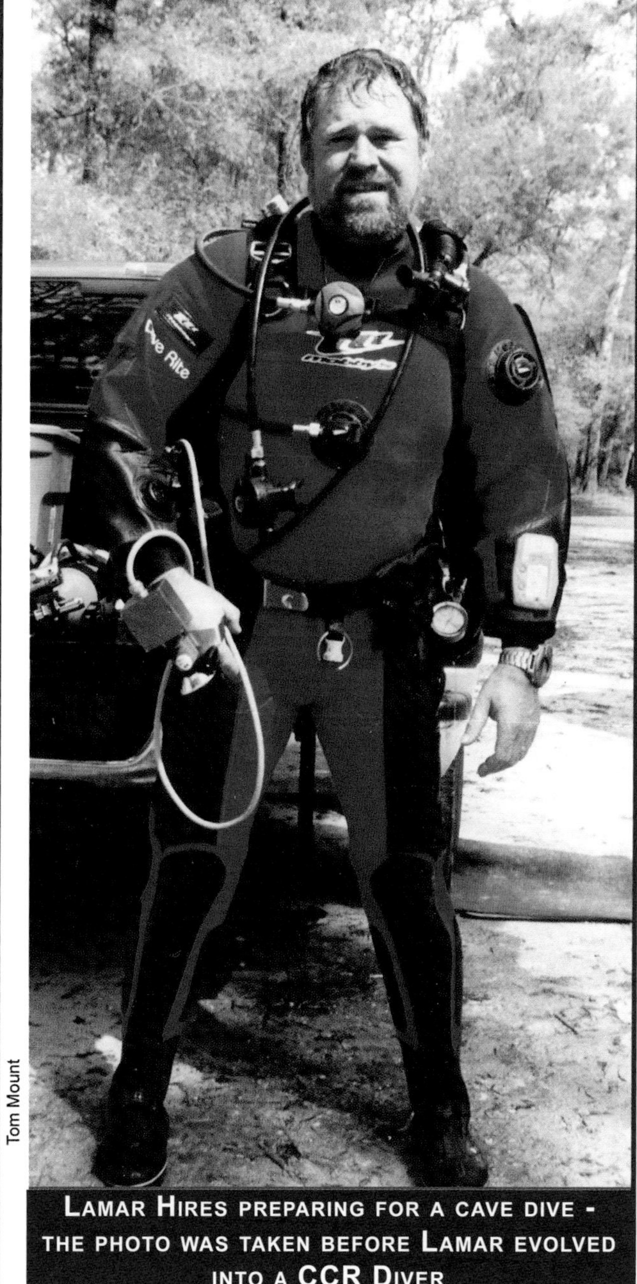
Tom Mount

Lamar Hires preparing for a cave dive - the photo was taken before Lamar evolved into a CCR Diver

allows for identification by touch and by visual reference. Shallow water deco mixe cylinders such as EAN 80 and oxygen should have the mouthpiece of the regulator(s) either covered or wrapped by surgical tubing to prevent breathing from them without at least a conscious move to access the regulator. Surgical tubing, inner tube rings, or commercially available keepers should be placed along the side of a stage tank to secure the regulator hose when not in use.

In addition, the second stage should be attached to the stage tank in a manner to keep it secure. Some methods

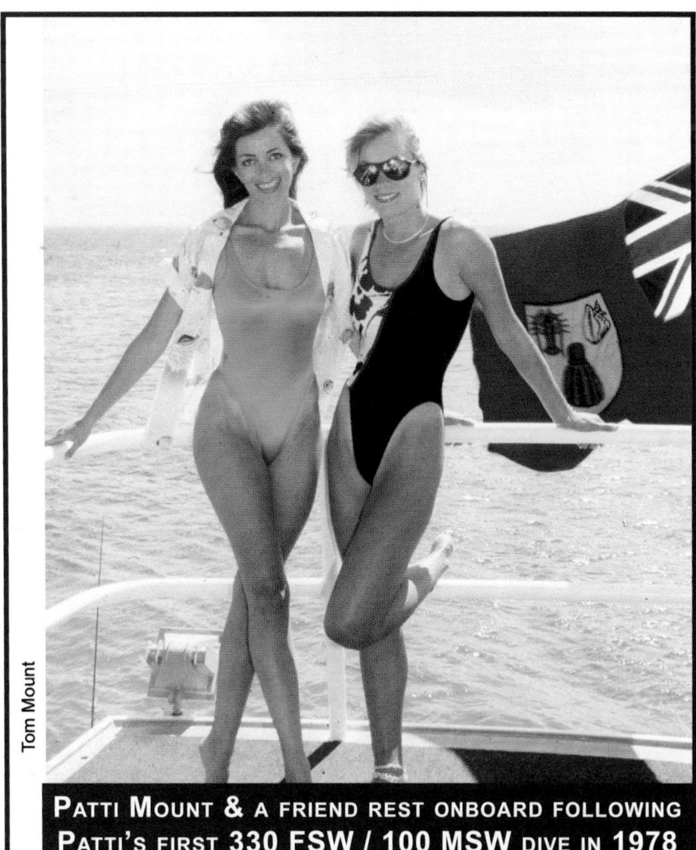
Tom Mount

PATTI MOUNT & A FRIEND REST ONBOARD FOLLOWING PATTI'S FIRST 330 FSW / 100 MSW DIVE IN 1978

of doing this employ the use of snorkel keepers, hooks or secured by surgical tubing. This attachment must be easy to reach, to attach, and to remove while swimming. The physical placement of the stage bottle on the diver can have dramatic effects on his swim posture and drag profile. The majority of divers attach stage bottles on a D-ring high up on the shoulder and a waist D-ring on the harness. The snaps and support attachments are close to the bottle to reduce drag, and are positioned to keep the tank close to the diver's body. Again the side mount configuration for carrying stages provides the lowest drag, but does need precision in use by the diver. Each diver must arrive at a personal balance between a snug, streamlined and flexible configuration that allows for easy access, attachment and removal and possible hand off to a buddy in an emergency.

If the addition of stage tanks leads to marked head-down body trim, the bottom snap on the stage tanks can be moved from the waist band and shifted to D-rings around the primary tanks. This will tend to reduce the head down trim. When making such changes, however, be certain that the tanks don't create a swim posture that brings the feet below the diver's midline in normal swim attitude. This type of head-up trim can cause the diver to stir up silt when swimming near the bottom. Note that in most cases, attaching stage tanks to D-rings on the main tanks will create additional drag, as the tanks tend to hang more loosely in this manner than when attached to the waist strap.

Before using stage tanks, divers should seek formal training in their use. Most respected technical diving courses devote considerable time to stage tank management. Divers should practice removal, staging and retrieval of the tanks until the operation can be performed flawlessly without a change of swim pace. Moreover, the diver must be able to place the proper tank at the correct location even without visibility. This is accomplished by practicing with closed eyes and by ensuring each stage bottle can be identified by the difference in its support attachments or by the difference in regulator design.

In some ways, staging tanks is similar to flying an airplane; one must think ahead of their present position, and anticipate upcoming actions. As a diver approaches the point at which a stage is to be dropped, the tank should already be removed from the harness and held ready to deploy.

Stage bottles should always be rigged and worn in a manner that allows them to be retrieved with ease. As the diver picks up a stage tank, he should be prepared to make buoyancy changes and to attach the bottle with a minimum of delay. The ability to retrieve stages efficiently prevents silting on wrecks and in caves, and also reduces additional bottom time. In too many cases, divers who lacked the necessary stage handling skills have either totally silted out the environment or added significant decompression time to their dive due solely to slow stage retrieval.

DIFFERENCES OF OPINION

If you are new to the sport of technical diving, you can expect to encounter heated debates and widely differing opinions concerning every item and aspect of equipment configuration. Your best course of action is to observe, to examine various rigs with regards to the 20 points made previously, and to determine which is the most comfortable for you and your needs. Ultimately, it is your safety, your diving style and your preference for what works for you that counts!

There are two popular methods of equipment configuration. ***Hogarthian*** which emphasizes breathing from the long hose and being streamlined. In general this requires the simpliest approach to configuration. A second common method is the ***DIR*** system.

Below is an example of the Hogarthian method. This is the manner the author used before he switched 100% to CCR diving or if forced to dive open circuit then side mount.

- The ***doubles*** are manifolded together. If available, an isolator valve is used.
- The ***regulators*** are placed so that all hoses extend vertically downward from the valves. The long hose is on the right post and is the primary regulator. If using a five foot (one and ½ meter hose) it is wrapped under the arm and a ¼ twist round the neck and breathed from. If a 7 ft (2.1 m) hose is used it is wrapped under the wings and, when using my normal waist light placement, underneath it. The hose is simply routed behind the wings, across the body and a ¼ turn around the neck. When diving without a light, the excess hose is tucked into the waist strap. The short hose is the back-up regulator. A permanently attached surgical loop is attached to the back-up regulator; this goes around the neck of the diver. This second stage should be right at the base of the neck just below the chin.
- The ***SPG*** has a custom length such as 24 inches (58 cm) and runs down from the regulator on the left post. It is attached to the left shoulder D-ring or waist D ring.
- The ***BC inflator hose*** coming out of the BC (wings) is a custom length such as 9 inch (22 cm) hose. The ***power inflator hose*** is 15 inches (36 cm) long. This short hose arrangement is ideal for fine tuning buoyancy without a need to raise the hose or to use the lower pull-dumps on the wings. The power inflator hose is attached to the left.
- When diving a wet suit some divers use a ***back-up BC***. On dry suit dives, one set of wings can be used with the dry suit serving as a back-up BC.
- The ***primary light*** for use in cave or wreck diving is normally waist mounted. When diving in areas that are narrow, such as some sections of wrecks or constricted caves, butt mounting is a logical choice. Waist mounting is a simpler configuration for use in less constricted areas and is ideal for long hose configuration.
- The ***safety lights*** are mounted on the shoulder straps with one being placed on each shoulder strap. This allows ease of access to the lights while keeping them removed from busy areas and reducing drag.

Tom Mount

SHAREE PEPPER DIVING IN PEACOCK SPRINGS 1969. SHAREE USED A CLOROX BOTTLE BUOYANCY DEVICE & A MARTZ DIVE LIGHT WITH A DACOR BACK-UP LIGHT. NOTE THAT THE DOUBLES WERE MANIFOLDED BUT ONLY HAD ONE OUTLET. SHAREE WAS ONE OF THE EARLY DIVERS TO LAY LINE IN EAGLES NEST & WAS AN AQUANAUT ON THE NOAA HYDROLAB PROJECT.

- ***Reels*** as needed (use only what you need) are carried on the waist D-rings or on a ring attached to the backplate or back D-ring on the crotch strap. Some favor a side mounted D-ring attached to the crotch strap. This also doubles as the butt plate for side mounting. The lift bag is carried by two surgical tubing loops attached to the base of the backplate.
- ***Stage tank rigging*** is by having a line around the neck of the cylinder and to the point on the cylinder that will align the bottom snap with the waist D-ring. The line is covered with tubing. This can also be with stage straps.

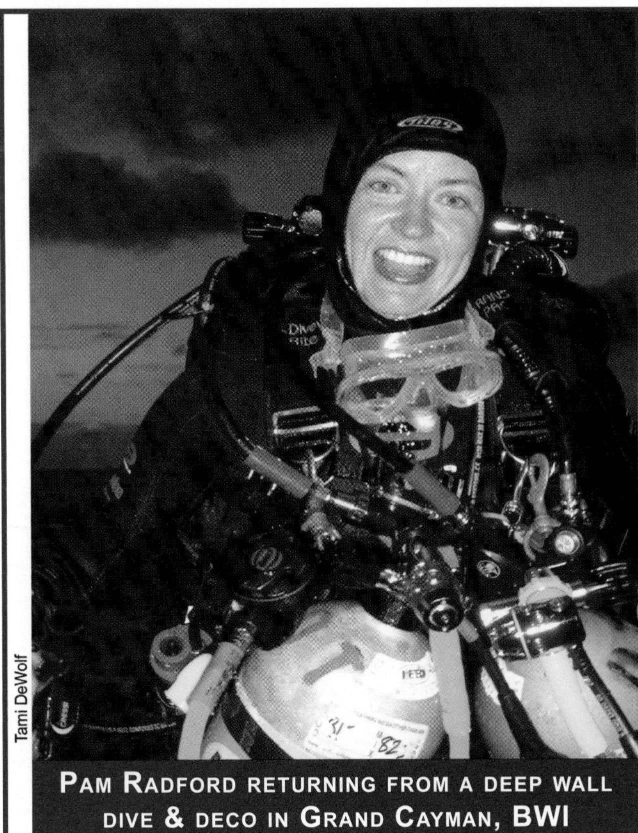

PAM RADFORD RETURNING FROM A DEEP WALL DIVE & DECO IN GRAND CAYMAN, BWI

- The ***back plate*** or ***soft backpack*** chosen will affect the buoyancy of he diver. Many divers prefer a stainless steel back plate with a QD on the lower left shoulder strap. Cutting tools are carried on all dives. A pair of surgical scissors is in a holster on the waist strap. A small knife is placed on the waist strap plus one on the back of my light handle for immediate access.

Equipment Configuration - Side Mount

~ Lamar Hires

The Side Mount System

Side mounting refers to the practice of positioning the primary scuba cylinders on the diver's side rather than on the back. Side mounting may appear to be more streamlined than conventional back mounted cylinders, but this is not the case. It actually presents more drag and increased task loading of equipment management.

This style of cylinder positioning is not new, but has evolved over the years when applied to caves in different areas of the world. I will try to give credit where credit is due, but divers, especially cave divers, are secretive, so someone may have used side mount before the time or place mentioned so please do not get offended.

British cave divers and some Europeans have been using side mount for years. The first need for side mount was established as sumps halted dry cave exploration - underground pools of water in a dry cave possibly leading to a drier cave. Equipment had to be transported by cavers for the cave diver to explore the sump. The distance and terrain traveled inside the dry cave made taking two cylinders configured as twins almost impossible to transport, so singles were preferred for transport. Assembling the singles as independent back mounted doubles required additional hardware, and as sump divers soon learned, the less hardware required, the more likely they were to get dry cavers to assist on more than one trip.

The British use a wide belt with tank cam straps sewn to it to attach the cylinders at one point on the hip. This is functional, but as the cylinders drop in pressure they get buoyant and start to turn perpendicular to the body, increasing drag.

Kiting up was not a one-man job with this style. The diver would assemble the belt, and then lay down while an assistant cinched the waist belt. Cylinders could not be removed and put back on by the diver. This style was acceptable for low to zero visibility diving where trim and body positioning were secondary to the objective of swimming. In some cases, divers would simply walk along the sump in these conditions.

In the United States, most of the easily accessible caves were explored by the early eighties. New techniques were needed to push into deeper, longer and smaller caves. Exploration of the longer, deeper caves is now possible because of new high-powered DPVs, new high-volume cylinders and mixed gasses. Meanwhile, side mounting has opened the door to many low profile caves.

Side mounting gained recognition in North Florida in the late seventies. Woody Jasper started side mounting to explore small caves inaccessible with conventional gear. In the beginning side mount was adapting whatever equipment was handy. This soon proved futile when long-range exploration was part of the equation. Today, side mounting is no longer simply a matter of throwing a couple on cylinders on a backplate, stage style, while leaving the doubles off the back plate. It is a very involved, specialized process, both in terms of equipment and mindset.

FIGURE 9-2: DIVER IN SIDE MOUNTED EQUIPMENT

THE SIDE MOUNT MINDSET

Whatever the reason for using the side mount configuration, the reality of the potential hazards should be understood. By removing cylinders from the back, the diver is more exposed. While riding a DPV, the cylinders are not a bumper, so to speak (divers should not think this way, but it's reality). A collision with the ceiling or wall puts the diver at great risk of injury, and in an overhead environment this could be fatal.

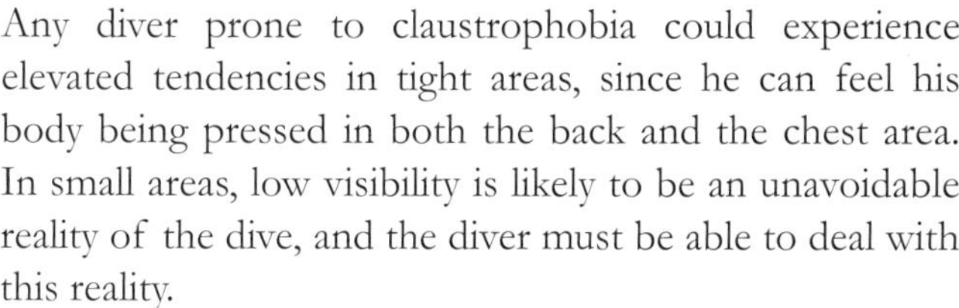

Any diver prone to claustrophobia could experience elevated tendencies in tight areas, since he can feel his body being pressed in both the back and the chest area. In small areas, low visibility is likely to be an unavoidable reality of the dive, and the diver must be able to deal with this reality.

Divers may apply side mount for its convenience of transport down pits, over rough terrain or for in order to manage the weight of one cylinder at a time rather than two. But regardless of the reason, the potential to get into small areas is there, whether planned or not.

Task loading is increased by the need to manage two independent gas supplies, and the position of the cylinders forces all hoses to be run on the diver's chest. Lighting, reels and all back-up equipment has to be thought out carefully, as it must be accessible when the diver is in a confined position.

As I stated earlier, side mount diving has evolved into a specialty. The days of, "This is what I have to work with, so how can I make it work" are over.

SIDE MOUNT EQUIPMENT

Side mount diving has evolved over the years. It began as a method for allowing divers to access remote locations and tight cave passageways. Today, it continues to serve those purposes, yet side mount diving has also become a life style choice for many divers who cannot, or choose not to, bear the weight of double tanks on the back.

Side mounted cylinders give a diver easy access to valves and regulators making it the preferred method for solo divers. With side mounted cylinders there is no need for a "buddy" bottle since the diver has redundancy with independent cylinders and regulators. With today's acceptance of side mount into mainstream technical diving the system has gone through constant refinement as it gains popularity among explorers and trekkers.

New harness systems are available for "out of the box" gear solutions for side mount diving. Two of the most popular systems are the Armadillo and the DiveRite Nomad. These harnesses integrate a back-mounted wing for lift and a buttplate for the lower cylinder attachment. This innovative style pulls the bottle under the arm with the lower attachment point for the cylinders on the hips rather than on the waist. The upper cylinder connection is made with large diameter shock cord. The cord attaches to the harness on the divers back, runs under the arm and secures to chest-mounted D-ring. This allows the cylinders to be "clothes lined" under the arm and run parallel to the body.

Nancy Easterbrook of DiveTech, Grand Cayman

These new generations of side mount gear systems go one step further by also allowing divers to wear back-mounted single or doubles cylinders as well as side mounting stage cylinders. CCR divers have begun to sidemount their bailout bottles to reduce drag and move the bottle away from a cluttered chest, down beneath the arm.

Equipment Considerations

Wing

Divers need to select a wing with the appropriate amount of lift for the cylinders, exposure protection and environment they plan to dive. If a diver needs 50 lbs (27 kg) of lift for back mounted 95 cu ft (15 L) cylinders, then the same amount of lift is required when diving these same tanks sidemount. Redundancy considerations should also be addressed just as if you are using back mounted cylinders use a dual wing or dry suit for back-up buoyancy.

Hoses & Valves

Side mount regulators route under the arms and this tends to make the chest area busy. If side-exhaust second stage regulators are worn, the configuration is less complicated. Each regulator can be secured with a bungee loop high on the chest area. When using conventional, second stages the left regulator should be worn on a hose long enough to route behind the neck. It is secured either with a necklace or clipped to a D-ring on the chest area. The hose length varies with diver size; if it's too long it will roll forward off the neck and into the divers face and if it's too short the diver will lose full range of motion when turning the head. To avoid the hose from coming loose up over the head, install a right angle adapter on the second stage. This will take six inches off the hose length allowing a standard 28" hose to be used by most divers.

The right side second stage should have a right angle adapter as well and be routed down from the first stage and back-up to be clipped off on a D-ring or on a necklace. I recommend only one of the regulators to be on a necklace to avoid confusion with cylinder switches. The SPG on six inch hoses pointing up allow for easy reading, yet are still out of the way.

The exhaust hose on the wing normally comes off of the left side so run the dry suit inflator hose (if applicable) or back-up BC from the right bottle so redundancy is maintained if a regulator is lost on a cylinder. Some divers who select side mount as life style use at least one long hose in the configuration for air sharing among a mixed dive team.

Back-up Equipment

Because sidemount cylinders are worn along the side, they leave little room for back-up equipment. The butt plate is a good platform for reels and back-up lights can be mounted on the harness, but work out better if stowed in a pocket. I recommend suit pockets for all back-up equipment except reels. Primary canister lights can be butt mounted or worn on the waist strap depending on the canister size. Some divers elect to use handheld primary lights instead of dealing with cord routing and canister mounting.

Stage Cylinders

Most of the systems today can carry multiple cylinders on one side. With today's new harness systems like the Armadillo and Nomad divers can carry a third cylinder like a stage bottle clipped at the waist and chest in front of the side mounted cylinder or carry it clipped off to the butt plate and clipped into the shock cord behind the neck of the primary side mount cylinder. Placement depends on cylinder size. I don't recommend putting a cylinder heavier than the primary cylinder in the position behind the primary cylinder because it will push down on the primary cylinder making it very difficult to maintain proper attitude in the water. Since the weight is on the diver's side, the diver is more attune to any offset in balance on each side.

Chapter Ten
Equipment Configuration For Small Divers

Peri Blum Psy. D.

By 2006, I was on the verge of believing what I had been told, verbally or otherwise, by the technical diving world: There was no place there for the likes of me. I would never be in trim, I would not be able to handle the amount of equipment necessary, and I would always have the buoyancy-compensation skills of a life-long recreational diver. My fortune changed, however, when Dr. Tom Mount became my technical instructor.

As Tom and I discovered over three months of replacing, resizing, and rethinking my equipment configuration, the difficulties I encountered learning basic technical dive techniques stemmed from the dichotomy between my size and that of most technical divers. However, with Tom's close supervision and ability to think creatively in conjunction with his familiarity of 30+ years of Patti Mount's gear configuration feats, we eventually solved the equipment configuration problems that were hampering my development as a technical diver. However, in the process, we went through three sets of doubles, six sets of fins, four or five changes in booties, two or three wings, two types of backplates, and a variety of hose lengths of every type.

I stand 5'2" (157 cm) and have a petite frame. Standard-size technical gear literally overwhelms me. The two most common sizes of "double" tanks, LP 80's and 104's, reach down to my hips, extend beyond my back, and rise up past my head. Corrugated low pressure hoses reach almost to my waist, or in some cases, past my waist. Secondary regulator hoses hit me in the back of the head and hang in the middle of my chest. The six foot long hose must be wrapped twice around my shoulder and under my light. The 7 ft (2.1 m) hose is a nightmare come alive; I am trussed like a turkey, with little or no chance of finding my way out to pass it off when necessary. Dry-suit hoses are entanglement hazards. Regulator mouthpieces are too large, creating trans-mandibular joint (*TMJ*) problems. Most low volume technical masks appear high-volume, constantly leak, and obstruct vision. Fins' foot-pockets are so large that buoyancy control while swimming is impossible, as my feet constantly move and shift position. Most harnesses leave me with tanks sliding around to the degree that I don't swim as much as roll through the water. Many well-favored wings stand out so far from my body that they act as entanglement hazards with exceptional drag. Dive computers, bottom timers, and other such gear slides off my arm under pressure, and falls into the depths below. Mounted dive lights take up my entire hand, reducing mobility. Standard closed circuit rebreather (*CCR*) counter-lungs hang past my waist or down to my hips.

The question, therefore, is twofold: exactly how a smaller diver's equipment should be configured, and how small can a technical diver be while still able to perform in a competent, comfortable manner. The answer to the second part of the questions is simpler than the first part; it deals with the myths that surround smaller divers in general and

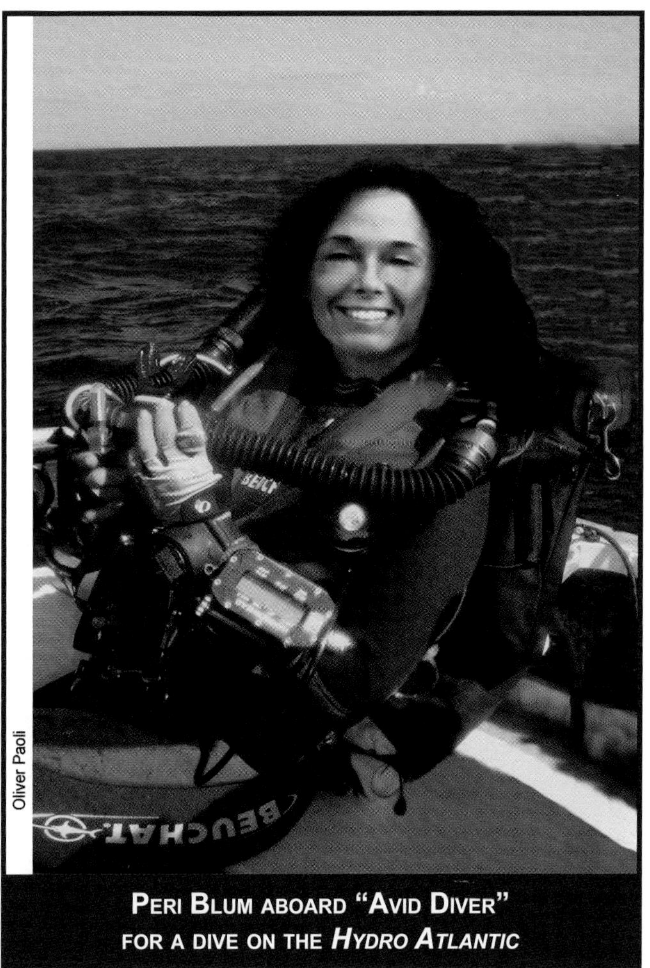

PERI BLUM ABOARD "AVID DIVER" FOR A DIVE ON THE *HYDRO ATLANTIC*

smaller female divers in particular.

Myths: Smaller divers are not able to complete the tasks required of a competent technical diver. They are unable to carry enough gas supply, are entanglement hazards, cannot control their buoyancy, and are useless should a larger diver have any sort of in-water emergency, especially if the situation occurs in overhead conditions.

Truths: The small diver's metabolic rate is naturally lower than that of his or her dive partners. Therefore, given that the smaller diver is in good physical condition and does not smoke or otherwise harm his or her lungs and cardiovascular system, the smaller diver's gas consumption should be significantly less than that of his or her dive partners. With an RMV often half that of most other technical divers, the smaller diver can meet the team gas management needs while carrying significantly smaller bottles. Regarding emergency situations, in most cases, the diver's training, not size, is the most significant variable as to their ability to survive and aid in their partner's survival.

Now that we understand that smaller divers can become competent technical divers, the next step is to review the smaller diver's equipment configuration needs. Each component will be specifically addressed.

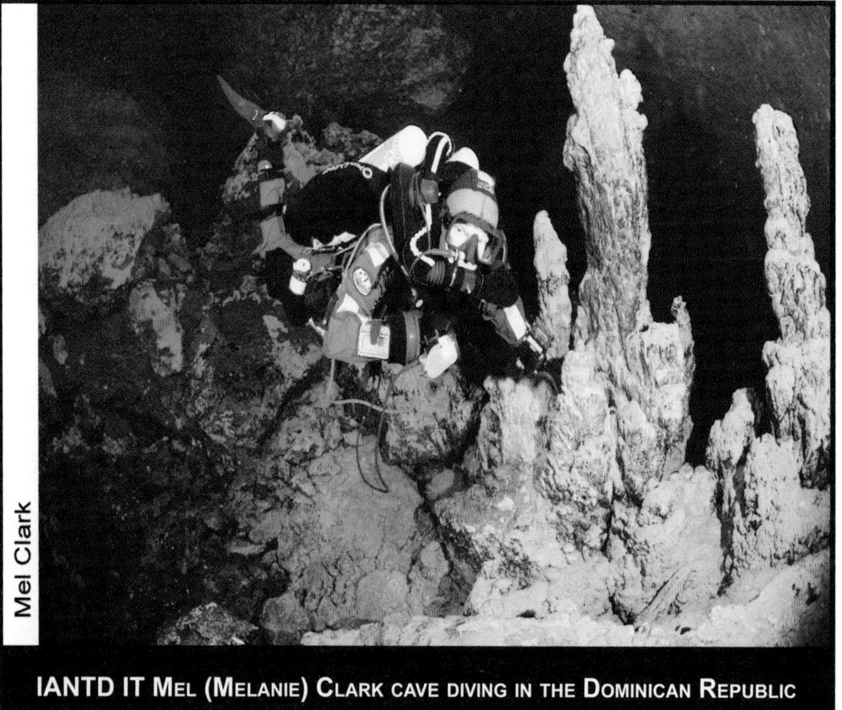

IANTD IT MEL (MELANIE) CLARK CAVE DIVING IN THE DOMINICAN REPUBLIC

BASIC EQUIPMENT CONFIGURATION

MASKS

Smaller divers have smaller faces. Most of the low-volume masks on the market are too large for the small technical diver to wear. Therefore, some effort must be put into finding a mask that fits properly. My masks are approximately 1/3rd smaller than a standard low-volume technical mask.

FINS & FIN STRAPS/SPRINGS

Booties and neoprene socks often solve the problem of overly-large foot-pockets. I use a neoprene sock inside a 5 mm, thick-soled bootie for technical diving. In free, or breath-hold diving, the fin is usually a full-foot type, versus the standard technical open-heel. I use the same bootie and sock combination, and add between one and two layers of neoprene sock over the bootie, and finish with fin keepers, which secure the fin to my ankle.

Another issue with the smaller diver, and most likely the smaller female diver in particular, is the size and strength of the leg muscles. Too heavy fins lead to dropped knees and fin tips down, versus up. As dropped knees and fin tips down can cause a silt-out in an overhead environment, attention needs to be paid to the actual weight of the fin. Dr. Mount solved this problem by using a progression of fins in a step-wise pattern. As I mastered the current fin's weight, I moved to a heavier, and stiffer, fin. Old or inexpensive fins can be used during this process, with less attention paid to fin straps than to mastering the weight and stiffness of the fin. Once the diver is in the correct fin, then springs or straps can be adjusted.

Regarding open-heel fins, fin straps, tightened down, trimmed, and duct-taped to the fin can be used. I prefer fin springs, and learned the hard way that one company's version of "small' is another company's version of "large." Therefore, care must be given to comparing the actual size of the spring to the size of the foot, as an error in this department can easily result in a lost fin.

Backplates & Harnesses

A small diver may need a smaller backplate, as the standard size may ride to high, too wide, and too low. Backplates with extra holes for tank bolts is also beneficial, as it increases the diver's ability to adjust where tanks or rebreathers will settle. Webbing should be trimmed slowly, and fit should be checked after use, while the harness is still wet. If the diver carries little body fat, an aluminum backplate is a better choice overall than a steel backplate due to the difference in weight. A small diver with low body fat content and well-developed muscles may be very negative, even in salt water. Adding more negative weight tends to result in excess drag, as the diver must compensate for the added weight by increasing the amount of gas in the wing, and/or increasing the size of the wing itself.

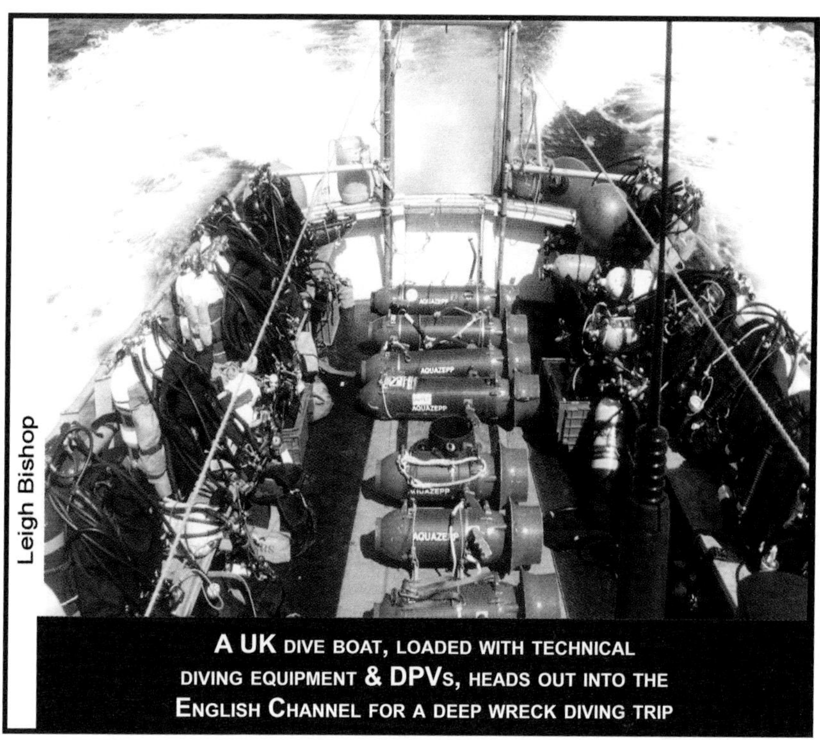

Leigh Bishop

A UK dive boat, loaded with technical diving equipment & DPVs, heads out into the English Channel for a deep wreck diving trip

A number of companies produce soft-pack type harnesses, many with adjustable or exchangeable D-rings. When fitting a soft pack, pay attention to the shoulder, back, and the waistband itself. If the pack's shoulder stands above the diver's shoulder, the harness will shift in the water. The back section should fit similar to a properly-sized backplate, and the waistband should be able to tighten as much as well-rigged webbing on a backplate.

Wings or Air Cells

Fitting wings or air cells, as they are also called, is similar to fitting backplates and harnesses. The usual wing is often too wide and/or too long for the smaller diver, which creates a number of problems. Such wings appear ungainly, create excess drag, confine the diver's movement, and may create entanglement hazards or silt outs due to excess surface area. The wing should be fitted to the diver's width and height. In addition, the smaller diver usually does not need the amount of lift the larger diver requires. Therefore, smaller, narrower wings may well work on doubles, singles with the appropriate valve, and CCR units. However, given the difference in width between the three configurations, the smaller diver may need different sized wings for all three situations.

Tanks, Stage Bottles & Bailout Bottles

Tanks, whether singles or doubles, should reach from slightly below the diver's neck to the lower back. The farthest a tank should reach is the upper part of the tailbone. The tanks' weight is also a consideration: extremely negative tanks may require larger wings, creating a high degree of drag and a poor profile. This is particularly the case with small, lean divers with little surface mass. In addition, the tanks' bands may need adjustment that is not in accordance with standard technical thinking. Raising the band may allow the diver to reach the valves and improve trim by taking weight off of the lower back and improving the diver's ability to flex his or her hips.

Similar to full-size singles and doubles, the smaller diver probably does not require as large stage or bailout (CCR) bottles as the more standard-size technical diver. Again, this does not necessarily affect the team's gas management, as smaller divers usually need less gas than larger divers. Therefore the Rule of Thirds, the Rule of Fourths, or the bailout-bottle rule for CCR divers is not necessarily violated by a smaller diver using smaller-size tanks. Moreover, stage or bailout bottles can be rigged with pockets, thereby supplying handy storage spaces for non-essential equipment or redundant gear, such as a second cutting tool, larger slates, or an extra light.

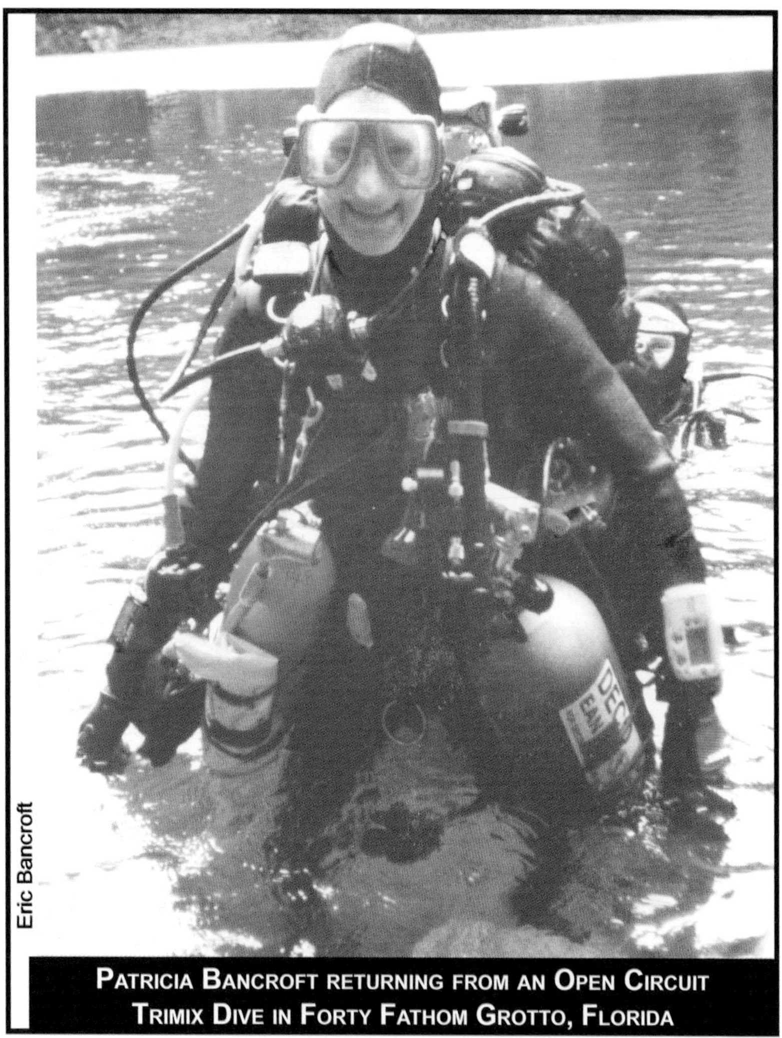

Patricia Bancroft returning from an Open Circuit Trimix Dive in Forty Fathom Grotto, Florida

Closed Circuit & Semi-Closed Circuit Rebreather Units

It is not recommended that the smaller diver purchase a rebreather unit without having the opportunity to try the unit on for size prior to committing a great deal of time, effort, and money into the unit. Rebreathers come in a variety of sizes, shapes, and configurations; such units are not "one size fits all" styles. The diver's size comes into play when choosing the rebreather that will allow for best trim, least drag, and is capable of meeting the diver's needs. There are rebreathers currently being marketed as "recreational" units due in large part to canister size; these units cannot carry enough scrubber material to maintain a larger diver for more than three to four hours at most. In addition, many such units do not have the ability to handle the larger-size diluent and oxygen bottles that larger divers require.

However, as noted earlier, many smaller divers have proportionately lower metabolic and RMV rates. Therefore, they are capable of diving a recreational unit technically, as depth (as in crush rate) is typically not an issue with the latest CCR units. Rebreathers such as the Optima2 FX, Evolution and Titan are some of the more recently-introduced models that serve a dual purpose; they can be dived technically by smaller divers, and recreationally by larger divers. However, care must be taken not to exceed the scrubber unit's safety range. In addition, certain manufacturers offer more customization than others. Dive Rite is able to adjust wing size, counterlung length, low pressure hoses, and various gauges. The manufacturer's flexibility may be the deciding point as to which CCR unit the smaller diver should purchase for technical CCR diving.

Regulators

If you are configuring open circuit equipment for small female divers with little body fat, each item should be considered in relation to size and weight. Certain well-favored technical regulators have first stages that weigh a pound or more; on a small body, each pound counts. Small divers cannot afford extra weight, no matter how minute that weight appears to a larger diver. Therefore, when choosing regulators, it is best to either design a regulator using a lighter-weight first stage, or to choose a regulator with a lighter weight, yet equally strong, first stage. The regulators I tend to use are manufactured by Dive Rite and Apeks; however, there are a number of other manufacturers that design regulators that suit smaller divers.

As will be discussed in a later section, hose length must often be altered to fit a small frame. Again, several manufacturers have well-built technical hoses that can substitute for the original regulator hose. In addition, secondary necklaces should be measured accurately; there is little chance that the smaller diver will be able to use a standard-length necklace. Another part of the regulator that usually needs customizing is the mouthpiece. Most regulators come with mouthpieces that stretch and otherwise irritate small jaws. Slimmer mouthpieces are relatively easy to find; however, they often need to be cut down in order to fit the smaller diver's mouth. Although this may seem to be a minor point, keep in mind that the regulator mouthpiece may be in place I heavy current and for a number of hours. A fatigued jaw may present as ear pain, and as such, often takes quite a while to diagnose the actual problem.

Gauges & Timers

Although it may not be a problem for small male divers, small female divers, by definition, may not have the arm circumference needed to keep gauges in place at depth. I have found that rubber wrist bands, unlike bungee cords or stretch bands can be tightened enough on the surface to maintain tension at depth. This may be somewhat uncomfortable at the surface, however; therefore, I recommend adding gauges as close to the actual start of the dive as possible. Additionally, the bands should be checked regularly for signs of tension tears, which can lead to expensive and unfortunate equipment losses.

Another issue which larger divers seldom face is the question of where, exactly, are these gauges going to fit? As of this writing, one of my forearms and wrists is taken up by a bottom timer and a dive computer. The other forearm is given over to a CCR computer console. Prior to adding my gauges and console, I put my gloves on. This allows me to use the bottom half of my glove, which covers my wrist, to ride under, versus over, my bottom timer. Although this may appear to be an irrelevant detail, try flipping your glove back every time you need to look at an important gauge or dive computer.

As a final note, allow me to remind readers; to gain something, you have to be willing to give something up. In this case, in order to gain the nice warm feeling that comes from knowing my bottom timer will not end up somewhere without me, I must give up the "low profile" bottom timer cases, which are bungeed in place. Instead, I use the older, high-profile wrist strap case and turn the timer in toward my palm. This way, I create a lower profile in the water and ensure that my equipment and I are not separated without my consent.

Hoses

As stated earlier, attention must be paid to hose length versus the smaller diver's height and surface mass. In some cases, the choice in hose length may confound the larger diver: I use a nine-inch corrugated hose on most wings and air cells, compared to the 15-24 inch corrugated hose found on other technical systems. With rebreathers, the hose may need to be slightly longer; I use a twelve-inch corrugated hose on my CCR unit, which I secure inside the harness with a bungee cord. My doubles' long hose is best at five feet versus six feet or more. All other hoses are similarly re-thought, and to date, there has been no need to customize a hose itself; there are enough high and low pressure hoses on the market to suit most diver's needs.

Lights

The smaller the diver, the smaller the lights. Smaller hands translate as less space for a hand-mount, both in width and in length. However, this does not limit the smaller diver to non-technical lights that do not have the ability to "punch" through darkness. Although a diver my size may not be able to swim in trim with a wreck canister, there are 10 watt HID lights, such as the Dive Rite SlimLine™, which takes up little space on a waist band and does not tend to extend into ribcages or interrupt hip movement. From experience, lights worn on a very small hand with a remote battery pack may land in the abyss. However, although a waist-mounted battery pack allows the smaller diver to retain their primary light throughout the dive, it also uses waist-space which the smaller diver may need for other tools or pockets. Some of the soft and hard harness systems have places for extra rings directly below the diver's arm. Battery packs can be mounted on rings with the switch down; this frees the diver from the difficulties that waist-mounted battery packs may create. As a final note on hand-mounted lights, the slimmer the light the better. I prefer the Dive Rite SunSpot™, which is a narrow beam light secured with two elastic bands rather than the more standard metal hand grip.

Backup lights also come in a variety of sizes, and can be connected to the chest-mount D-ring while being held in place using thin strips of bicycle inner tubing. Backup lights can also be carried in pockets on the exposure suit's thighs. The only light that should be placed in a stage or bailout bottle pocket is the diver's third or fourth light. That way, the diver always has access to his or her primary and secondary light. I wear my SlimLine™ on my right, inside of my waist D-ring. I also wear two small, powerful backup lights attached to my chest D-rings in the manner noted above. A small fourth light is carried in a pocket when such quadruple redundancy is called for.

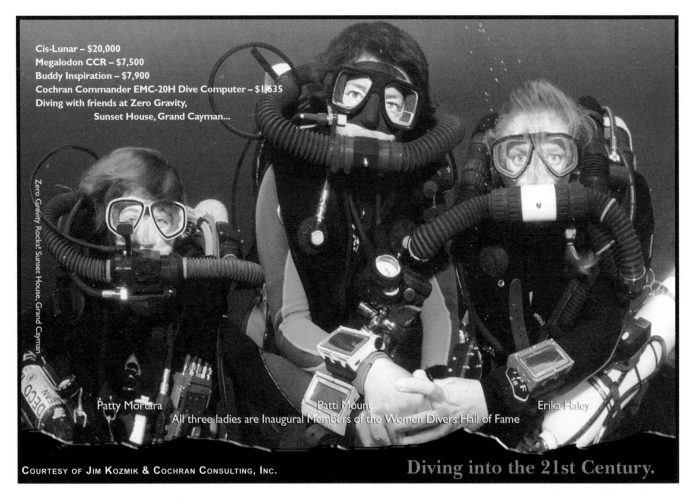

Cis-Lunar – $20,000
Megalodon CCR – $7,500
Buddy Inspiration – $7,900
Cochran Commander EMC-20H Dive Computer – $1,635
Diving with friends at Zero Gravity,
Sunset House, Grand Cayman...

Zero Gravity Rocks! Sunset House, Grand Cayman

Patty Mortara
Patti Mount
Erika Haley
All three ladies are Inaugural Members of the Women Divers Hall of Fame

COURTESY OF JIM KOZMIK & COCHRAN CONSULTING, INC.

Diving into the 21st Century.

EXPOSURE SUITS

The two broad categories of exposure suits are wetsuits and drysuits. In regard to wetsuits, the smaller diver whose body is proportionate to size will probably be able to fit a "standard" suit. However, smaller men with heavily built arms, chests, and/or legs will often find standard sizes overly tight and restrictive in certain areas, and too loose in others. Small women with larger chests or hips may have similar problems. If the issue is significant, the suits may need to be customized; zippers installed, waists taken in, and gussets added are common examples. Certain companies are capable of re-working neoprene; for more information on specific referrals, please contact IANTD World Headquarters in Miami or www.iantd.com.

Moreover, the exposure suits' thigh area is an excellent place for pockets, thereby reducing the amount of gear the smaller diver must carry at his or her waist. In addition, most drysuit manufacturers offer head-to-toe customization for an additional fee. Further, there are certain drysuit manufacturers that have a multitude of available sizes, therefore reducing the need for customization. However, drysuit boots often do not come in sizes that fit small female feet. I use between two and four pairs of thick winter-weight socks to fill out such boots, thereby increasing comfort and fin fit.

In sum, as with all technical divers, the smaller diver must find a balance between utility, force, and trim. Given my experience in the technical diving world, such a balance can be found; it simply may take additional effort and a more unique approach to accomplish the smaller diver's goals. The outcome, however, may surprise the majority of the technical diving community: Even petite female divers may make the type of technical dive partner any diver would want at their side, in front of them as "reel person," or behind them as "second person on the line."

Chapter Eleven
Dive Planning

Tom Mount D.Sc., Ph.D., N.D.

Dive planning is the process by which divers determine and clarify the objectives of a proposed dive, rehearse the specifics of the dive plan, and review their proposed actions in order to eliminate or minimize the associated risks. In order to accomplish these goals, there are four important processes that must be undertaken: information gathering, group planning, personal planning, and contingency planning. These allow for personal and environmental unknowns. Once a dive plan is developed, it should be followed according to the guidelines that will be explained in this chapter.

The basic elements of information gathering include:

- Gathering pertinent data on the dive environment
- Determining the history and qualifications of the participants
- Determining what equipment may be required
- Identifying mitigating or complicating factors

Information gathering, the first step in the planning process, should include all the facts necessary to prepare a safe plan of action on the dive, and should recognize the variables and unexpected contingencies that might occur. In technical diving, detailed information gathering is paramount to the safety and survival of the diver and/or dive team.

When gathering information on a given location, you should refer to all available resources to ensure that both an adequate amount of information is obtained, and that the information is accurate and current. The basic references should include visits to the dive site, conversations with any who have dived the site and collecting any printed reference materials such as cave maps or ship's blueprints.

Once this preliminary information is gathered, a basic dive plan can be formulated. If there are charts or maps of the location, carefully review them and ensure that each person on the dive team is familiar with the specifics of the location. While in the process of planning the route, duration and proposed actions of the dive, you should also discuss the impact your dive plan will have on the underwater environment.

Next, your dive team should determine what equipment would be needed to perform the dive safely, along with any additional specialty equipment that will enhance dive performance. The team should then follow the process of determining the correct gas mixtures to make the dive and to efficiently decompress.

When diving from the beach, for example, divers should determine the wave patterns, the probability of rip currents, the underwater topography and the location of safe areas of entrance and exit points. On cave dives, teams should anticipate the entrance and underwater conditions, including surface hazards, current, silting, passage size, expected depth, and so forth. If there are reversing currents, the team should establish an optimum dive window.

When boat diving, investigate the particulars of water entries and exits from the craft. If the dive will be a fixed anchor dive, be certain you make visual reference and know where the anchor (***upline***) is located. If using decompression stages, do not affix them to the anchor line as the line may break free.

If the stops are to be done as a drift dive, become aware of the procedure used by this particular diving operation/charter. There are numerous methods of securing drift decompression and ascent lines, so insist on having the

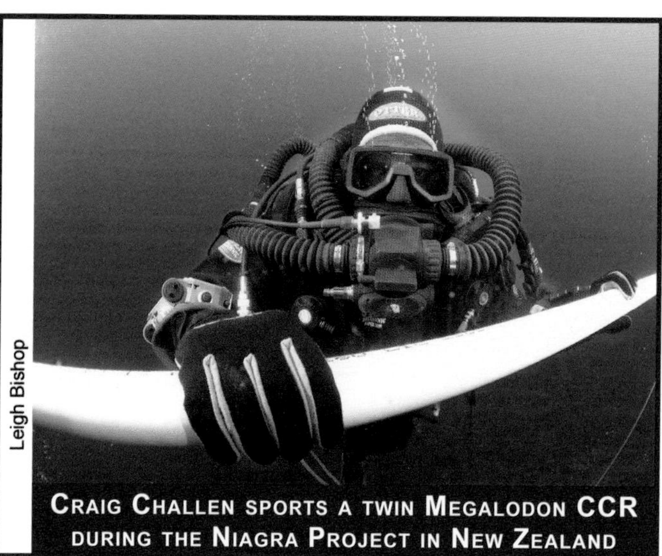
Leigh Bishop

CRAIG CHALLEN SPORTS A TWIN MEGALODON CCR DURING THE NIAGRA PROJECT IN NEW ZEALAND

system explained anytime you are diving from a new boat, are at a new location or are under different circumstances than those you are familiar with. When doing drift dives, be responsible enough to become informed of the procedures used at this location and by the dive operator or the procedures of those who are diving. Do not assume anything. Be informed and be safe. Be certain all divers in the group on open water dives have a lift bag so that if they should become separated, they will have a stable up-line and an indicator to the diving vessel of their location.

Ensure that each diver in the group has the adequate type of equipment and the appropriate amount of redundancy for a safe team dive. Prior to entering the water a safety drill (known as an ***S Drill***) should be performed. During this process, each diver will check their buddy's equipment for functionality and possible leaks. This includes breathing from the long hose, checking lights and seeing if there are any gas leaks in the tanks, valves, and regulators. In cave and shore based diving, the S Drill is to be performed in the water. Even when boat diving, a leak check should be made upon entry into the water if conditions allow.

Gas mix planning is a major concern for technical divers. The factors to be determined during this portion of the planning process include oxygen management, narcosis planning, gas density considerations and decompression planning. In general, the longer the dive or the deeper the dive, the more detailed the dive plan must be. In addition, when making repetitive dives, allowances must be made for tracking residual oxygen in the system.

One of the greatest hazards in technical diving is the risk of central nervous system (***CNS***) oxygen toxicity. Due to this risk, one must carefully plan out the combined risk of bottom mix gases and decompression gas. In most technical diving situations, an oxygen partial pressure (***PO_2***) of 1.4 ATA is the maximum target operating depth (***TOD***). The maximum operating depth (***MOD***) is a PO_2 of 1.5 ATA. For decompression, the maximum PO_2 is 1.6 ATA with 1.55 ATA being the recommended limit. In addition, on long decompressions following lengthy bottom exposures, it is often necessary to reduce the PO_2 to 1.5 ATA at decompression stops with bottom mix exposures well under the 1.4 ATA TOD limit. Environmental and dive performance factors also affect gas planning. In dives involving cold water and/or increased workloads, the bottom mix PO_2 should be reduced by 0.05 ATA per variable and decompression PO_2 reduced by 0.025 ATA for each variable.

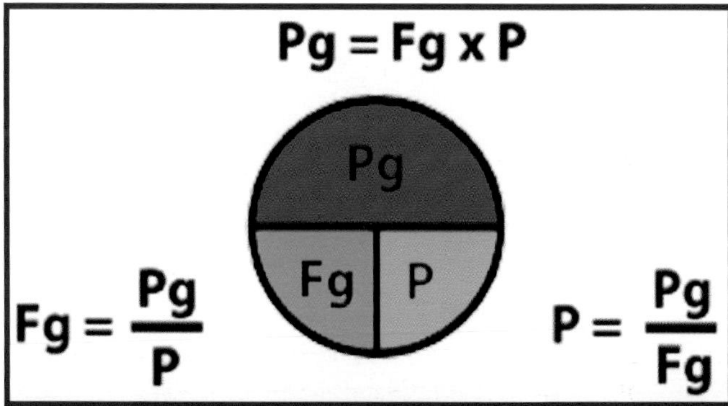

Figure 11-1: The Circle T is used for gas computations using Dalton's Gas Law

In addition to CNS exposure, a diver will need to track the accumulation of oxygen tolerance units (***OTU***), which effect whole body/pulmonary exposure. The OTUs are primarily a concern in saturation diving or when a need for treatment presents itself. As a rule of thumb, if a diver remains within a CNS exposure not exceeding 100% of the allotted dosage, OTUs remain within safe limits. On extended dive programs involving six or more continuous days of diving, the OTU limits may become the controlling factor in oxygen management.

When planning oxygen exposures, the first determination is the PO_2. To do this, refer back to the "*T*" formula, see Figure 11-1, and solve for the best mix. For example assume the dive is to 140 ft (42 m) and will be a combination of hard work, cold water and a bottom time of 50 minutes. To maximize safety, a PO_2 of 1.35 ATA will be used for the bottom mix.

$$\text{Best Mix Fraction of } O_2\ (FO_2) = \frac{PO_2}{P}$$

$$\text{Imperial - US: } \frac{1.35}{(140 \div 33) + 1} = 25.7\% \text{ or } 26\%$$

$$\text{Metric: } \frac{1.35}{(42 \div 10) + 1} = 25.5\% \text{ or } 26\%$$

In the above example, if once the gas has been mixed and the true analysis was EAN 28, the PO_2 at 140 ft (42 m) can be found by using the PO_2 equation.

$$PO_2 = FO_2\ x\ P$$

Imperial-US: $PO_2 = 0.28 \times (140/33 + 1) = 1.46$
Metric: $PO_2 = 0.28 \times (42/10 + 1) = 1.456$

As shown, this is too high of a partial pressure of oxygen to be used on the dive. Thus, the mix would need to be adjusted or the depth limit should be set shallower. To determine the maximum depth with this mix and our desired PO_2, use the MOD formula. The same equation is used for determining the target operational depth (***TOD***). The TOD is the actual planned depth of the dive whereas the MOD is the deepest possible depth available on the dive. Dive plans should consist of both a MOD and TOD for a given mix.

Target Operating Depth

$$TOD = \frac{1.35}{0.28} - 1 \times 33 = 126 \text{ ft}$$

(For **metric**, substitute 1 *x* 10 for 1 *x* 33 & the answer is 38.2 m.)

Maximum Operating Depth

$$MOD = \frac{1.50}{0.28} - 1 \times 33 = 143.7 \text{ ft}$$

(For **metric**, substitute 1 *x* 10 for 1 *x* 33 = 43.57 m)

In the selection of tables, the IANTD EAN 28 Tables would be used incorporating the accelerated schedule at 20 and 15 ft (6 and 4.5 m) using EAN 75.

To avoid mistakes in calculating PO_2, use the IANTD PO_2 Table C-3201B. You may also use the IANTD EAD/MOD Table C-3200 Imperial or C-3204 Metric to determine EAD, CNS %, OTU, and MOD/TOD values in a known mix. Each of the proceeding examples may be determined through use of these tables.

EANx Example

Part One

A dive is planned to a depth of 140 ft (42 m). The dive is on a wreck that has a maximum depth of 170 ft (52 m). The TOD will feature a PO_2 that cannot exceed 1.40 ATA. The MOD must remain at or below 1.50 ATA. Referring to IANTD PO_2 Table C-3201B, the best mix to allow the diver to meet both the TOD and MOD needs is EAN 24 in this case, although the TOD desired is 1.4 ATA PO_2. For safety in event of egress to the bottom, the MOD at 170 ft (51 m) of 1.5 ATA or less restricts the TOD PO_2 to 1.26 ATA. If the MOD requirement had been ignored, the diver could have used EAN 26.

Part Two

For decompression, a gas mix is going to be used that will be no greater than 1.45 ATA PO_2 with a gas switch at 20 ft (6 m). Referring to IANTD PO_2 Table C-3201B or IANTD EAD/MOD Table C-3200 Imperial or C-3204 Metric, we will find that EAN 90 provides a PO_2 of 1.45 ATA at 20 ft (6 m). In order to provide an accurate CNS % and OTU calculations, use IANTD CNS/OTU Table C-3201. To compensate for the oxygen clock during ascent employ the 2 + 2 Rule. This means you should add 2% to the CNS clock and 2 to the OTUs. This is simple and conservative and more than covers the oxygen clock additions on ascent.

To figure out the CNS %/Repetitive CNS % refer to IANTD PO_2 Table C-3201B; begin at the top left column with 100%. Read to the right and after the 30 minute S.I., you will read down the column to see that the diver still has 83% of the CNS O_2 clock loaded, while after 6 hrs. S.I., only 7% of the CNS O_2 clock will remain. All dives should be planned to avoid exceeding 100% of the CNS clock and within the daily OTU units.

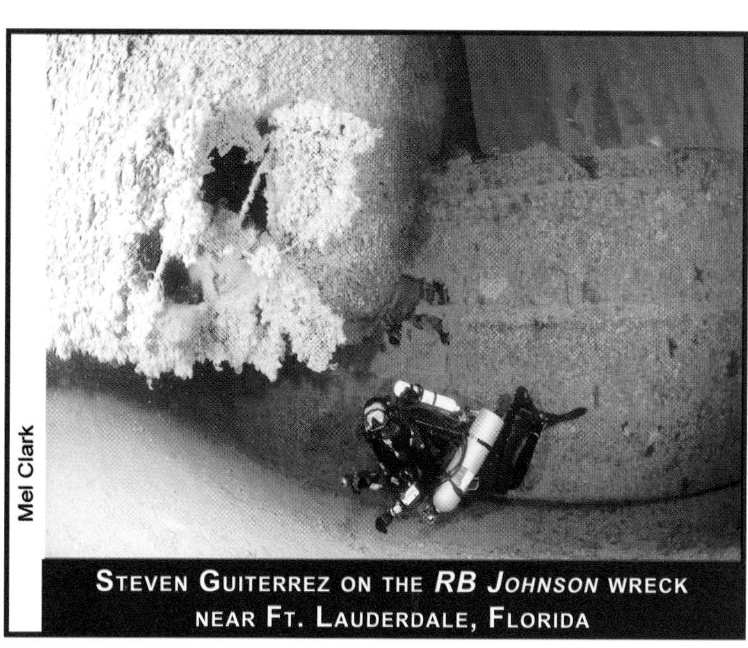

Mel Clark

Steven Guiterrez on the *RB Johnson* wreck near Ft. Lauderdale, Florida

POINTS TO REMEMBER

Waterproof Tables For Use Underwater

The Accelerated Decompression Tables using EAN 75 at 20 & 15 fsw (6 & 4.5 msw) & the Runtime Tables are available in waterproof versions from your local IANTD Facility.

Now, let's put all of the above noted tables plus the IANTD Waterproof Dive Tables to use by planning an actual dive. On this dive, the desired TOD PO_2 is 1.4 ATA. The dive is on a wreck with a maximum depth at the sand of 160 ft (48 m) and the planned dive depth on deck is to 140 ft (42 m). The MOD must be considered as one of the operational parameters even though the diver does not plan to dive to 160 ft (48 m). Thus, we must first determine a mix that does not exceed 1.5 ATA PO_2 at 160 ft (48 m). The second consideration is that the TOD PO_2 is to be no greater than the planned 1.40 ATA. By referring to the above noted PO_2 Table and EAD Table, we discover that at 160 ft (48 m) a mix of EAN 26 presents a PO_2 of 1.52 ATA, and we decide to accept the slight excess oxygen risk.

The second step is to ensure that EAN 26 will not exceed a PO_2 of 1.40 ATA at the TOD. Again, by going to a depth of 140 ft (42 m) with EAN 26, the PO_2 is found to be 1.36 ATA. As this is slightly lower than the planned TOD value, it is acceptable. It should be noted in this example that while we elected to accept the slight (0.02 ATA) excess as a MOD or "***What Ifs***" value, the same acceptance would not apply to a TOD value. The bottom time on this dive is to be 50 minutes. In addition to the IANTD PO_2 Table, the IANTD EAD/MOD Table can be referenced to determine TOD and MOD values at PO_2s of 1.3, 1.4, 1.5, and 1.6 as well as the equivalent air depth. The EAD/MOD Table also lists the CNS % per minute and OTUs per minute.

For the sake of example, we will work this dive in three different methods using the IANTD Waterproof Dive Tables, to reflect the differences in decompression time. The first dive will be on the IANTD C-3502 Accelerated Tables using EAN 26 throughout the decompression. The second will use the same table but follow the EAN 75 schedule at both 20 and 15 ft (6 and 4.5 m). The third method will be using the IANTD C-3602 EAN 25 Runtime Tables using EAN 78. The Runtime Tables do not feature EAN 26; thus, the EAN 25 Tables will be used. If the correct mix is used, the CNS% is given on the Runtime Tables. However, as our mix is EAN 26, we must calculate the CNS and OTU values. Once analyzed, our decompression gas is EAN 80.

Plan the gas actually needed on the dive by assuming the diver breathes 0.6 cu ft (17 L) while swimming on the bottom and 0.5 cu ft (14 L) at rest during decompression. For gas planning, plan the time to the first stop as part of the bottom mix requirements. For example if the ascent takes three minutes for gas planning then plan that ascent as if it were spent on the bottom. This provides a little more safety in the gas management plan. Once the actual gas needed has been determined then plan for the total gas to be carried. Remember that the dive must be made on bottom mix within the rules of thirds. Record the total gas needs under totals at the base of the worksheet or IANTD Technical Diver Logbook along with the CNS and OTU totals.

Please note, when planning the CNS and OTU exposure, do not be surprised if your answers vary slightly from those in the example. It is possible to have a minimum amount of variation depending on if the per minute values of CNS % and OTUs are used or if the set bottom time numbers are added. Calculators will also produce some minor variations based on where they round off.

Following the first dive, a second dive is planned to 110 ft (33 m) 3 hours later for 40 minutes using a bottom mix of EAN 29 with EAN 80 as a decompression gas. The dive will be made on the IANTD EAN 29 Runtime Table C-3603. Please read the following and work through the repetitive dive as you go through the dive worksheets. It is important that you understand these procedures.

POINTS TO REMEMBER

Minimum Gas Needed

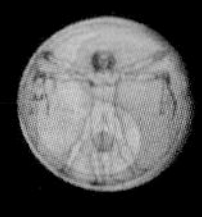

To find the bottom mix needed, multiply the gas needed by 1.5. Decompression planning is not quite as conservative so, multiply the gas needed on decompression by 1.2

In the examples we are working on this series of dives, do the following:

- First Dive to 140 ft (42 m) on the IANTD EAN 26 Table C-3502 for 50 minutes. See the work sheets for decompression schedules, oxygen tracking and gas used. It is recommended that you work these to ensure you understand this phase of dive planning
- Go to the IANTD EAN 26 Accelerated Table C-3502 to get the beginning SIT group. In this case, "K"
- After three hours, a dive to 110 ft (33 m) will be made for 40 minutes on the IANTD EAN 29 Runtime Table C-3603
- Go to the IANTD EAN 28 Accelerated Table C-3503 to get the end of SIT group. In this case, "G"
- On the repetitive dive on IANTD Runtime Tables as the schedule will be an 80 minute schedule, then to convert to the real time runtimes subtract the 40 minutes residual from all the indicate runtime stops and this will correct the schedule for the actual bottom time. (See "IANTD/IAND, Inc. Technical Dive Planners" that follow for corrected runtimes.)
- **RNT:** 40 minutes + 40 minutes actual BT = 80 minutes equivalent nitrogen time/bottom time

When using the the C-3600 and/or C-3700 series of IANTD Runtime Tables, switch to decompression gas at a point that you are actually breathing it upon arrival at the stop requiring the gas switch. Do not wait until arrival to switch the regulator as this may take a minute or so to do. The IANTD Waterproof Runtime Tables are designed for you to leave the stop at the designated time for that stop depth. For instance if a schedule reads a BT 50 minutes it means that you leave that stop depth at 50 minutes. If a stop states 56 minutes you must ascend to the next stop as soon as you reach 56 minutes.

> ***Points to Remember***
>
> **Repetitive Dives Using Runtime Tables**
>
> 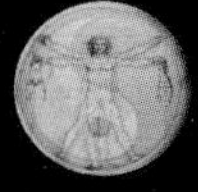
>
> **The procedure is:**
>
> **1. Go to the next lower EANx Accelerated Tables and get the beginning SIT group from that table.**
>
> **2. Go to the next lower EANx Table from the Table the next dive is to be made on for the RNT**

On a runtime table if you are using a 50 minute schedule but leave the bottom at 48 minutes, it is safe to subtract 2 minutes from each of the runtime depths. In other words if your first stop says 56 minutes, leave at 54 minutes. This keeps the actual stop duration the same, as it would be on the 50 minutes schedule.

If you leave the bottom late then you must go to the next greater schedule and subtract the time differences, just as you did in the above example. If the ascent rate is faster than the schedule, stop 10 ft (3 m) below the first scheduled stop for the time difference. If the ascent is slow but within 2 minutes of schedule then add the time to the runtimes at the stops. If the ascent is delayed more than 2 minutes switch to the next greater schedule.

$$EAD = \frac{FN_2\,(0.74)\ x\ [\text{Depth}\ (140_{fsw}) + 33]}{0.79} - 33 = 129.04_{fsw}$$

$$EAD = \frac{FN_2\,(0.74)\ x\ [\text{Depth}\ (42_{msw}) + 10]}{0.79} - 10 = 38.7_{msw}$$

Refer to the IANTD EAD/MOD Table and determine the EAD for this dive. Go to EAN 26, then to the actual depth of 140 ft (42 m), and down the page to the EAD depth. The EAD is 129 ft (38.7 m) for this dive.

This same problem could also be figured out by using the EAD formula.

When planning Nitrox dives, an important consideration is preparing the gas mixture. Detailed procedures for mixing gases are included in the IANTD Gas Blending Courses and the IANTD Gas Blending Student Manual and Workbook M-2116.

Closed Circuit Rebreather Planning

When planning CCR dives two of the greatest hazards are the risk of central nervous system (*CNS*) oxygen toxicity and Hypoxia. Due to these risks, one must carefully plan out the combined risk planned PO_2 plus bottom mix gases

for both diluent and bailout needs. In most technical diving situations, an oxygen partial pressure (***PO_2***) of 1.3 ATA is the maximum target operating depth (***TOD***) while diving on a CCR. When diving on an SCR, it can as high as 1.4 ATA. For decompression, the maximum PO_2 is 1.4 ATA on CCR with 1.6 ATA being the recommended limit for SCR or OC.

When planning partial pressures for the dive, the first determination is the PO_2. To do this, refer to the "T" formula previously presented and solve for the best mix.

For example: Assume the dive is to 160 ft (48 m) the planned PO_2 is 1.3 ATA and the END is planned to be 100 fsw (30 msw). The diluent is planned to have a PO_2 of 1.0 ATA at the TOD. The mix contains 30% helium.

$$\text{Best } O_2 \text{ Mixture} = \frac{1.0_{\text{ATA}}}{(160 \div 33_{\text{fsw}}) + 1_{\text{ATA}}} = .17 \text{ or } 17\%\ O_2$$

$$\text{Best } O_2 \text{ Mixture} = \frac{1.0_{\text{ATA}}}{(48 \div 10_{\text{msw}}) + 1_{\text{ATA}}} = .17 \text{ or } 17\%\ O_2$$

$$\text{EAD} = \frac{FN_2\ (0.53)\ \boldsymbol{x}\ [\text{Depth}\ (160_{\text{fsw}}) + 33_{\text{fsw}}]}{0.79} - 33 = 96.48 \text{ fsw}$$

$$\text{EAD} = \frac{FN_2\ (0.53)\ \boldsymbol{x}\ [\text{Depth}\ (48_{\text{msw}}) + 10_{\text{msw}}]}{0.76} - 10 = 24.88 \text{ msw}$$

Next, plan the END of the dive. Refer to the EAD formula:

$$\text{END} = \frac{[\text{Target END} + 33_{\text{fsw}}\ \boldsymbol{x}\ 0.79]}{\text{Depth} + 33}$$

Thus to find the desired END of 100 fsw (30 msw) for this dive:

So, Helium = 100% – 54% N_2 – 17% O_2 = 29% He

Thus, the mix will contain 29% helium although the actual oxygen in the diluent will only be 17% based on a 1.0 ATA diluent PO_2.

You could also use the IANTD END Table C-3706 for 1.3 PO_2 at 160 fsw (48 msw) to determine the equivalent narcosis depth and FO_2. To determine the exact mix you should look down the END Table to 160 fsw (48 msw), then across until you are below the 100 fsw (30 msw) END value. Note the helium concentration, which would be a mix of 22 23 on the END Table.

For bailout an END of 120 fsw (36 msw) will be used, and a bailout PO_2 of 1.4 ATA will be needed for a dive that is in an overhead environment (in OW a bailout PO_2 of 1.6 ATA could be used).

Referring to the IANTD END Table C-3706, if we look at 160 fsw (48 msw) at a PO_2 of 1.4 ATA we discover the FO_2 is 24% and the helium content for an END of 120 fsw (36 msw) is 13%. Thus the bailout mix will be Trimix 24 13. Obviously, this could also be worked out with the END formula.

To avoid mistakes in calculating PO_2, use the IANTD PO_2 Table. You may also use the IANTD END Table for PO_2 of 1.3 ATA and 1.4 ATA. In addition, tables can be used for tracking of CNS % and OTUs. When they are combined with the appropriate chart the residual CNS % can be calculated as well.

To determine EAD, CNS %, OTU, and MOD/TOD values in a known mix, each of the proceeding examples may be determined by using the various IANTD Tables.

Dive Example

A wreck dive is planned to a depth of 200 fsw (59 msw). The diver will use a PO_2 of 1.3 ATA. The bailout PO_2 cannot exceed 1.4 ATA. On both the diluent and the bailout cylinder the desired END is 90 fsw (27 msw). The dive will have a bottom time of 40 minutes. For decompression, the PO_2 will be maintained at 1.4 from 40 fsw (12 msw) ata, up through the 20 fsw (6 msw) stop. At 15 fsw (4.5 msw), the PO_2 will be dropped to 1.3 ATA. To provide accurate CNS % and OTU calculations, follow the same procedures as in the open circuit examples.

Now, let's put all of the above IANTD Tables (plus the IANTD Constant PO_2 Dive Tables C-3101 through C-3105) to use as part of this dive plan.

By referring to the PO_2 Table, we find that a diluent PO_2 of 1.0 ATA will require a FO_2 of 0.14 (14%) and by using the END equation the nitrogen content is:

$$END = \frac{[90_{fsw} + 33_{fsw}\ x\ 0.79]}{200_{fsw} + 33_{fsw}} = .417 \text{ or } 42\%\ N_2$$

$$END = \frac{[27_{msw} + 10_{msw}\ x\ 0.79]}{59_{msw} + 10_{msw}} = .423 \text{ or } 42\%\ N_2$$

Therefore, the helium content in the diluent will be 100 - 14 - 42 = 44% and the diluent mix is Trimix 14 44. Plan the bailout mix by referring to the END chart. You will discover at 200 fsw (59 msw) a mix of 20 38 will provide a bailout with a PO_2 of 1.4 ATA and an END of 90 fsw (27 msw).

Plan the bailout gas actually needed by each diver as if this is a team of three divers. Base the calculation on the diver who has the highest RMV. In this case we will state the diver with the highest RMV breathes at a rate of 0.7 cu ft per minute (25 L/min). Also assume a bailout EAN 70 cylinder is at 40 fsw (12 msw).

Compute the gas needed, based on the needs of the diver breathing 0.7 cu ft (25 L) multiply ***x*** 1.5 and divide this number by 3.

Note that the diver, by himself, would need 19.6 cu ft (700 L) to bailout and ascend to the first stop at 140 fsw (42 msw). This value was calculated based on the max depth gas consumption which allows for stress at the time of the emergency and during decompression up to the staged deco gas at 40 fsw (12 msw) that the diver would use including the ascent from 200 fsw (59 msw). Thus a total of 66.11 cu ft of gas (2359 L, see worksheet for exact breakdown) is needed. The team would need to carry 66.11 cu ft ***x*** 1.5 or a total of 99.16 cu ft (2359 L ***x*** 1.5 = 3538.5 L) of gas. For safety, round off to 100 cu ft divided by 3 = 33.3 cu ft (3538 L divided by 3 = 1179 L) of gas per diver. The decompression gas needs will require another 114 cu ft of EAN 70 ***x*** 1.5 = 171.16 cu ft of gas (3228 L ***x*** 1.5 = 4842 L). To be staged or carried by the team if broken into individual team member responsibilities then each member would have to stage 57 cu ft (8 L) of EAN 70. In this case, each member could stage a 60 cu ft (8 L) cylinder. (The above gas calculations are for divers using CCR's.)

Points to Remember

Bailout Minimum Gas Needed

To find the bottom mix needed for the team bailout, multiply the gas needed by a diver by 1.5. Decompression planning is not quite as conservative so, multiply the gas needed on decompression by 1.2. These results are then split evenly among the team members.

Points to Remember

Hypoxic Trimix

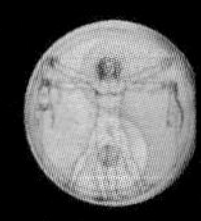

When using Trimix, the starting PO_2 may be a hypoxic mix at the surface. IANTD's EAD/MOD Table may be used for determining the safe depth to breathe the mix as well determining the MOD and TOD values for a given dive.

Trimix Example

Part One

A dive on Open Circuit is planned on Trimix. The target operating depth (***TOD***) of the dive is 280 fsw (84 msw). The maximum depth obtainable is 320 fsw (96 msw), thus the MOD value PO_2 of 1.5 ATA is to be at 320 fsw (96 msw). A PO_2 of 1.35 ATA is selected for the TOD, with the MOD not exceeding 1.5 ATA PO_2. Using Table C-3700B, we will find the mix containing 14% oxygen will provide a TOD of 1.33 ATA PO_2 and a MOD of 1.5 ATA PO_2. From this table, we have determined the bottom mix FO_2 of 0.14 or 14%.

Part Two

To avoid hypoxic mixtures, the dive gas cannot be breathed until the partial pressure of oxygen is at a normal value. To provide a better decompression profile, many times a travel gas will be used. In the current example using the above FO_2 for bottom mix, refer to IANTD Table C-3700B to discover the minimum safe depth to switch to bottom gas.

This is 20 fsw (6 msw) - actually between 15 and 20 fsw (4.5 and 6 msw). For a decompression advantage, we will remain on the travel gas of EAN 40 until we reach a PO_2 of 1.37 ATA. Refer to IANTD Table C-3201B and it will determine that a switch from EAN 40 to bottom mix will take place at 90 fsw (27 msw).

Diving with Trimix produces more variables than diving with EANx mixtures. In addition to selection of the oxygen in the mix, a desired narcosis value must be determined. The amount of helium added to the mix will displace sufficient nitrogen to yield the desired narcosis loading. If we wanted essentially zero nitrogen narcosis, all we need to do is to mix helium and oxygen in the mix. The disadvantage of a mix of this nature would be extended decompression times unless the bottom time exceeds two hours. A second disadvantage is a higher probability of High Pressure Nervous Syndrome (***HPNS***). Typically, a mixture is derived to give an Equivalent Narcosis Depth (***END***) value of 80 fsw (24 msw) to 130 fsw (39 msw). The most recommended and common END is 130 fsw (39 msw) for the TOD value.

Part Three

We will use a Trimix mixture with a FO_2 of 0.14 (14%). The helium content is not known yet. To be safe, an END is desired that will not exceed a maximum of 115 ft (34.5 m) at the TOD depth. As a safety buffer, our MOD END is to be no greater than 160 ft (48 m).

Using the Helium END Table C-3700, it is assumed that the FO_2 is 1.4 ATA. Go across the bottom of the page to the TOD of 280 ft (84 m), then go up the page until you match the desired END of 115 ft (34.5 m); next, follow the diagonal line to the top of the page. This will produce a Fraction of Helium (***FHe***) of .48. Now check that the MOD END will be within the planned value of 160 ft (48 m). Follow the diagonal line at 48% helium until it crisscrosses the depth of 320 ft (85.6 m); at this point, record the END value.

From this we determine that the MOD END is approximately 140 ft (42 m) and is acceptable for the planned dive. The final bottom mix then will be Trimix 14 (oxygen %) 48 (helium %). With this mix, plan a dive for a 20-minute bottom time at 280 ft (84 m). Use the IANTD Waterproof Tables for this dive.

Personal Planning

Personal planning is the most important part of the dive plan. It is the individual and his/her perception and interpretation of the planned dive that yields an acceptable or unacceptable performance. There are many aspects involved in personal planning, and the key is being comfortable with one's role in the accomplishment of the dive. In this area, we will be discussing the key components of a personal plan.

Risk analysis, acceptance and management are the major portion of a personal dive plan. This should begin with an introspective look into oneself to determine how one truly feels about the dive. During this phase, basic questions should be raised and answered honestly.

Each phase of the dive should be mentally reviewed and the following questions answered:

1. What are the specific risks involved in this dive?
2. Do I understand the dive plan?
3. Am I comfortable with the parameters of the plan and my responsibilities within the dive plan?
4. Can I be depended upon - and not be dependent on - others?
5. Have all the "***What Ifs***" of this dive been covered, and have I established a personal management procedure for these variables?

In the process of answering the above questions, all items of the personal dive plan should be reviewed. As part of the risk analysis process, the diver should also review past histories of similar dives. The diver should determine if threatening situations have occurred on similar dives or if accidents have taken place. If either of these has been encountered, analyze what caused those events.

Once the cause has been discovered, develop a reaction response to compensate for the recurrence of a similar situation. List all the possible things that could affect dive safety and develop a response action to these possibilities. Decide if each risk to be encountered is worth the benefit of performing the dive. Prior to the dive, complete the checklist in tabular form on the next page.

When filling out this table, it may be prudent to discuss

your evaluations with other dive team members. Under the Value column, a simple yes or no is sufficient. If the no answers outweigh the yes answers, you may wish to revise the dive objectives. If, in some instances, an overpowering ***no*** is encountered, this may be reason to dismiss yourself from the dive. In addition, listen to your intuitive voice; if you experience bad sensations about the dive, either postpone or cancel the dive, and limit your participation in this type of diving.

Risk #	Risk	Corrective Action/Managment	Benefit	Value
1				
2				
3				
4				
5				
6				
7				
8				
9				
10				
etc.				

Personal comfort must be taken into consideration. While it is true that unfamiliar situations may lead to an expansion of personal capabilities, for safety's sake, a diver should not be pushed too far from his present comfort level. Anxiety from overextending the comfort level of a dive may cloud good judgment. If a diver is forced to function outside his personal comfort level, anxiety will add to the stress and overall risk potential of the dive.

If you are in the process of expanding your comfort level, do it in small and personally acceptable increments. Do not depend on someone else to maintain your safety or establish your limits. Even with the best of intentions, other divers cannot enter your mind and evaluate your mental capabilities for a dive. Dive buddies are limited to watching your performance and your verbal and body language communication for interpreting your comfort level. Remember the three basic ingredients that ultimately evaluate your survival and comfort potential. These are:

Any time you have the slightest doubt in your ability to do any of these three, slow your progression toward more involved dives. A skilled buddy may be able to assist you for a short time if a swimming problem exists, but they cannot maintain that function indefinitely. No one can think or breathe for you, so avoid situations that cast doubt on your ability to complete the dive.

An additional factor that determines a diver's personal comfort level is the combined mental and physical fitness he maintains. A degree of physical fitness is needed to manage the equipment on land, and fitness is needed for propulsion skills.

Perhaps one of the most important aspects of fitness, however, does not become apparent until the diver is faced with adverse conditions. In this type of situation, watermanship and fitness may be the determining factors in survival. Even with superb physical fitness, a diver must also develop confidence and discipline combined with the ability to maintain mental focus. The mental fitness of a diver will be the determining factor in development of these attributes. Be sure you remain within both your physical and mental conditioning.

Individual "What If" situations are in addition to the team plan, but they should also be addressed before the final dive plan is agreed upon. These must be placed in the risk analysis table when deciding how to most efficiently deal with them. Exploration of the "***What If***" scenario includes both the environmental factors and risk associated with equipment dependency.

Listed below are sample "***What Ifs***" that may be encountered on a dive. Analyzing the individual risk associated with a dive can expand these reasons. List these in the Risk Table featured above on this page.

1. ***What If...*** I get lost? Determine a means of finding your way out or in being located by a surface crew/ boat. The exact solution will depend on the type of dive, the location, and the community standard for locating lost divers.
2. ***What If...*** I lose a decompression stage cylinder? In this case, if it is an air dive, you may bail out to an air table or air dive computer. If this is a mixed gas dive, it is recommended that a backup schedule be used, reflecting stops if either deco gas is lost. When tables are not available, then, as a rule of thumb, if the EANx was lost at the stops requiring the higher EANx, double the remaining decompression while breathing the remaining lower EANx mixture. If other divers are present, once they have completed their stops, have them leave the higher decompression mix and complete the stop on this mix. Once on the surface, breathe oxygen for at least 30 minutes. Under ideal conditions, the dive will employ safety divers who may be able to respond to this situation.

In this instance, the support divers would bring decompression cylinders to the diver. In addition, a backup decompression gas supply can be used, such as surface supplied gas on a boat, or, on inshore based diving, safety deco stage cylinders placed at central points along the return path to the entry point. In a worse case scenario, share gas with a dive buddy, provided sufficient gas is available. (The last means is to use up the remaining decompression gas from a buddy once they are finished with his/her personal gas needs for decompression.)

3. ***Think*** and continue this list until you have developed 10 or more personal "*What If*" scenarios.

Once personal "what ifs" are listed, determine the solution to each situation and visualize a method for overcoming them. Once you have identified the problem, developed the solution, and visualized its accomplishment, do not dwell on it. You have achieved the goal of overcoming this specific problem. Dwelling on problems will have two negative effects. First, you begin to worry about it. Worry creates stress and may lead to apprehension and result in either an incident or a dive that you do not enjoy. Secondly, by continuing to think about the problem, with so much emphasis on the problem, the mind may in fact create the circumstance.

Am I confident in my ability to manage rebreather specific emergencies when I am diving on a rebreather? This is the most important question to ask. Survival in an emergency requires a yes to this question. At this point, review and practice all emergency skills and responses taught at earlier levels of CCR training. Any oxygen or carbon dioxide problems will present themselves as confusion. This is one of the major (and usually undetected) symptoms. Considering this, if at any point a diver feels uneasy, first switch to a known safe breathing gas (off board/stage/bailout rebreather) and take a few sanity breaths. It may require more than one sanity breath to relax, or in some instances you may discover it's not a rebreather related problem. Regardless, take the time to determine if there is or is not a problem that needs to be corrected.

Generally, the common reasons for taking corrective actions vary from feeling unusual to recognized symptoms and include the following steps:

1. **Go to a known safe breathing medium and take sanity breaths as required:** A ***sanity breath*** is the act of going to an OC gas or back-up rebreather system, with an acceptable PO_2 and END plus adequate capacity for the depth to be breathed at. The sanity breath allows the diver to take one or more breaths as needed to evaluate any unusual feelings or symptoms they may be experiencing, as well as any suspected problems with the rebreather. Since the first symptom of hypoxia, hyperoxia, and hypercapnia is usually confusion, the sanity breath is a diver's safest reflex in these circumstances. The sanity breath will allow clear thinking; enabling the diver to analyze the problem, determine if one even exists, solve the problem or take other corrective action. At the end of the sanity breath, which may encompass

Formulas In Lieu of Tables

If END Table is not available, the END determinations could be found by working END and EAD equations:

Imperial-US: END = (Target END + 33)(0.79)/(D + 33) -> (115 + 33) (0.79)/(280 + 33) = 0.3735 FN_2

Metric: END = (Target END + 10)(0.79)/(D + 10) (34.5 + 10) (0.79) / (84 + 10) = 0.3739 FN_2

Total gases other than Helium, (37% N_2) + (14% O_2) = 51% -> The balance is 49% (He) Helium

An error of 1% occurs due to the FO_2 actually used being 14% FO_2 versus the chart value PO_2 of 1.40 ATA which provides an FO_2 of 14.8%

For the MOD END on this mix of 14 48 use the EAD formula -> FN_2 = 1.0 - (0.14 O2) - (0.48 He) = 0.38% N_2

Imperial: MOD END = [(FN_2)(D + 33)/0.79] - 33 -> [(0.38)(320 + 33)/0.79] - 33 = MOD END of 136.79 or 137 ft

Metric: MOD END = [(FN_2)(D +10)/0.79] – 10 -> [(0.38)(96 + 10)/0.79)] – 10 = MOD END of 40.98 m

one or several breaths, appropriate problem solving actions will be taken. In some cases you may have to do more than one sanity break to correct a given situation. Once the problem is corrected, return to the loop if a safe PO_2 is been verified. In the event of a canister breakthrough or other uncontrolled hypercapnia event, remain on OC and terminate the dive.

2. **Check the PO_2 and perform a diluent flush as or if needed:** For instance, if you have a set point of 1.3 and note the PO_2 has dropped to 1.1 it would be a good indication that the solenoid is not working and has most likely failed in the closed position. If the diluent PO_2 is 0.8, do not flush the unit. Flushing would drop the PO_2 more and you would need to add more oxygen. On the other hand if you noted the PO_2 was down to 0.4, you would want to flush the unit especially if you have been so careless to allow the PO_2 to drop to this level. It is most likely dropping in a state of momentum; therefore it is possible that the inspired PO_2 is even less than the displayed indication. If you are uncertain as to the accuracy of the PO_2 displayed then flush the system to see if the indicated PO_2 and diluent PO_2 match.

   If you have just made a rapid descent and notice the PO_2 is at 1.45 then monitor the display closely to ensure that the increase is due to spiking from the rapid descent (provided the PO_2 does not continue to increase) simply breathe down to 1.3 where you can dive the unit by either manual control or solenoid control. If the spiked PO_2 exceeds 1.6, flush the system to bring the PO_2 back down to less than 1.6. Then breathe it down to the set point to be maintained and keep it at this value. If the flush does not bring the PO_2 down before you need to breathe, then take a sanity break, return to the loop, and flush the system down to less than 1.6. **When reacting to situations employ common sense.** Remember if the diluent PO_2 is too high you may not be able to flush the loop PO_2 down to an acceptable level. IANTD recommends the diluent PO_2 not exceed 1.0 at the planned depth.

3. **If it is a PO_2 problem, take the appropriate action to manage the particular problem:** For example, correcting a high PO_2 from either a failed solenoid or a leaking manual addition valve may require turning off the supply gas. Once the PO_2 is safe to breathe, manage the problem by going back on the loop and manually turning the oxygen supply valve off and on. At depth this requires ***barely*** cracking the valve and then turning it back off. Caution is required with this procedure. It requires practice and is critical to only open the valve partially. Each CCR requires developing a sense of timing in doing this process. Usually, if a diver waits to see the PO_2 increasing towards the desired upper range of the intended PO_2 they will discover that it overshoots that value. When manually controlling an open solenoid remember you must create a management range. For instance if the desired average is 1.2, allow the PO_2 to go up to 1.4 and then breathe the unit (with oxygen) down to 1.0. This will provide a fairly long interval between valve openings and give a stable, easy to manipulate condition. A second method to control an open solenoid: once the oxygen supply gas is turned off and the PO_2 is at a safe level to breathe, switch to a staged oxygen cylinder or even a diluent with a higher PO_2 than the onboard diluent by connecting it to the manual addition valve. On low PO_2 it is actually a more simple management procedure, since you will monitor the PO_2 closely and manually add oxygen into the loop, maintaing the planned PO_2. For divers who fly CCR manually, or at minimum loop volume, this will be a normal style of diving.

4. **If you have ascertained that you have a canister breakthrough, it is imperative to bailout to OC:** You must be able to problem solve by source management. This ability requires an in-depth understanding of failure points and of the unit as well. The things that lead to emergency situations on CCR all generate from a source. If the diver can identify the source of the problems, they can take a corrective action to manage it. In many cases going

Points to Remember

Personal Planning involves:

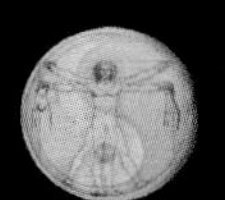

- **Risk Analysis**
- **Personal Comfort**
- **Individual what if situations**
- **Resonisbility**
- **Personal gas planning**

CCR DIVERS INSIDE A WRECK

to the source of a problem may resolve it, and the unit may be "flown" in a normal method. In other situations the problem can be managed so the diver stays on the loop safely.

Source Identification

After you have completed your sanity breaths, and have regained control of the situation, you need to determine the source of the problems:.

Some potential situations include:

1. **Oxygen problems - source oxygen supply:** The first action following a sanity breath is to achieve a safe breathing gas and return to the loop. Use the techniques that you've been trained on and as discussed above.

   The second step is to identify the cause of the failure, while still managing the problem from the source. High PO_2 may be caused by the solenoid failing in the open position; in this case the practical solution is to continue managing the problem by controlling the oxygen supply valve. Second alternatives are turning off the oxygen supply valve and connecting a secondary oxygen supply (or even diluent supply) that has an acceptable PO_2 to the manual oxygen addition connector, and then control the PO_2 manually. A third method is having an extra off-board connector so that either an additional diluent or oxygen supply may be connected into the system. This avoids the need for switching connected gases underwater.

2. **What to do if you have a leak through a Schrader (LPI) valve or other design feature of your particular CCR:** If possible isolate the problem (i.e. disconnect the Schrader valve or other failed component of the CCR design), thus allowing the solenoid to control the set point.

3. **Spiking:** Flush the system down to a safe $PO_{2.}$ This can only be accomplished with a diluent that is low enough to affect a drop in PO_2; it is recommended that the diluent PO_2 does not exceed 1.0.

4. **Improper calibration of the unit:** If you suspect the display PO reading to be inaccurate, either go to SCR mode of operation or bailout on OC or a bailout rebreather. Once on the surface recalibrate the unit. Low PO_2 may be caused by the solenoid failing in the closed position. In this case, the diver must dive the unit by manual oxygen addition. Of course, a safe breathing medium must be insured immediately.

5. **Loss of oxygen supply gas:** There are a couple of options. If an additional oxygen supply has been carried, the diver may hook this source into the manual addition of the CCR and fly manually from the alternate oxygen source. Another option is dependent upon the bailout cylinder mixture. Most of the time divers will plan a bailout gas with a PO_2 between 1.4 and 1.6 at the maximum depth of the dive. In this case (assuming the diluent is a PO_2 of 1.0 or less) simply plug in the bailout cylinder to the manual addition and add the higher PO_2 bailout gas diluent to maintain a more acceptable breathing mixture. At some point it may become necessary to switch to SCR mode and again use the highest (safe) PO_2 gas available. As the diver ascends it is wise to flush the system more frequently. Eventually you may want to switch to OC or a bailout rebreather in order to keep the highest PO_2 for decompression purposes.

An alternate means of control is to plug into a dive buddy's manual addition low-pressure hose and inject

Points to Remember

Personal Planning

Only *you* can swim for you;

Only *you* can breathe for you; *and*

Only *you* can think for you!

enough oxygen to bring the partial pressure up to 1.5 then disconnect. This gives you several minutes before it is breathed down to 1.0, at which time the procedure may be repeated. In order to perform this action you must ensure that LPI connectors are compatible with your CCR's manual inlet port prior to entering the water.

If the oxygen is depleted during the 20 fsw (6 msw) stop, either do as instructed above (2) and inject oxygen from your dive buddy's unit or take a breath of OC oxygen and exhale it into the unit.

The following are some possible causes for low PO_2:

A. Too rapid of an ascent

B. Oxygen supply valve turned off

C. Failure to have the solenoid activated electronically

D. On SCR

- **i.** Rapid ascent
- **ii.** Over-breathing
- **iii.** Breathing the loop down once the gas is turned off or exhausted
- **iv.** Improperly keyed Passive SCR
- **v.** On some Passive SCR inheritance due to over-breathing
- **vi.** Mistake in gas planning for the dive
- **vii.** Diving Active SCR beyond its design limitations

6. **Diluent related problems:** Diluent is continually flowing into the loop. If the unit has a diluent shut-off valve installed in-line, simply open and close it to control the addition of diluent into the system. If it does not have a cutoff valve then control the flow of diluent by opening and closing the diluent valve on the tank.

   If the system only features manual diluent addition and the Schrader valve is allowing diluent to leak into the system, you may address the problem by either disconnecting and reconnecting the diluent quick disconnect or by controlling the supply gas valve. Frequently, the valve on manual additions (this is true of both diluent and oxygen) will be stuck. Once the gas flow is under control the diver may be able to free the push valve and regain normal operation. Also, the Schrader valve may simply have debris in it. Disconnecting and shaking it some will clear this out and the diver may discover it works correctly once reconnected.

7. **Diluent PO_2 is above the planned set point of the dive:** In this case the diluent cannot be added into the system and the dive plan should be modified to shallower dive. If an unplanned event caused the diver to descend below a level where the diluent is at an acceptable level, avoid using diluent as much as possible until you ascend to a safe depth. Preplanning for the correct dive gas mixtures easily avoids this problem. Always remember if the diluent PO_2 exceeds the planned set point limits, it should not be used on that dive. Also, if the diluent is very close to the set point it will make it more difficult to flush the loop down in a high PO_2 situation.

PLEASE NOTE: **Imperial & Metric Examples will be rounded *UP* to approximate real-life tanks and breathing usage for the duration of this chapter.**

8. **Bail-out using onboard diluent:** Using onboard diluent for bailout with an appropriate PO_2 is an acceptable practice in shallow water. However, consider the safety of this practice in deeper water. If a diver breathes 0.7 cu ft (20 free liters) per minute at the surface, and bails out on a 20 cu ft (3 L) cylinder at 200 ft (60 m), then at depth they would be using 4.9 cu ft/min (138.74 L/min). Thus, the 20 cu ft (3 L) cylinder, even if at full capacity, will only last 4.08 minutes. It is apparent on deep dives that a diver should not use onboard diluent for bailout or for sanity breaths. You may wish to remove the onboard bailout system when diving deeper than 130 fsw (39 msw). Many experienced deep CCR divers regard bailout to an onboard diluent supply as suicidal. As an exercise it is recommended that divers compute how long an onboard diluent will last at all depths to 200 fsw (60 msw). Then, decide on the safety or danger of this feature for deeper dives.

9. **Onboard bailout is free flowing through the bailout mouthpiece:** Either block gas-flow to the mouthpiece if possible, or shut off the onboard diluent. If the onboard diluent is shut down, the diver may turn it off and on to satisfy diluent and buoyancy needs or shut off onboard diluent and use

off-board diluent (provided the diluent is acceptable at the depth of the switch). With most CCR designs the onboard diluent may have to be turned on and off for buoyancy control, or switch to the low-pressure inflator connector if it's compatible. An in-line shutoff valve is easily installed and provides the CCR diver with another control feature in the event of free-flowing gas.

10. **Sensor related problems:** Sensors are reading erratically: Switch to a set point that is lower then the diluent PO_2 and then flush with diluent. See if any sensors agree with the diluent. Often the sensors tend to settle down once they are flushed with dry gas. If the sensors disagree, keep the set point low and manually fly the unit based on the sensor(s) that agreed with the diluent flush.

11. **Two sensors read identically while the third sensor reads high or low:** Again, flush with diluent to determine if the two sensors are reading correctly. If the two sensors are correct, the CCR will operate normally based on its averaging circuits. However, one sensor agrees with the dilunet and the other two do not then the one felt to be out of range is in fact the correct one. In this case, one may set a low set point and turn the dive following the correct single sensor by keeping the desired PO_2 manually. If the decision is to fly the single correct sensor then flush the unit periodically to be sure this sensor still agrees with the diluent. The safe option would be to bailout on Open Circuit. On the other hand, if the sensor reading out of range is the accurate one, go to a low set point and fly the unit manually.

12. **All sensors are giving erratic readings:** Most likely this will happen only with either old sensors that are losing sensitivity at higher readings (if the unit has the ability to read MV on the sensors this should immediately be done) or if they are overly damp. Most of the time the sensors (or at least one or two of them) will read correctly at 1.0 or slightly below especially if they were calibrated pre dive. If this occurs while swimming at a constant depth and the diver was employing minimum loop volume, then: First flush the unit to determine the actual PO_2. Then maintain this PO_2 (not the original selected PO_2) by adding oxygen manually, as this should be1.0 or lower as long as safe to breathe the sensors will most likely read accurately. Once depths are changed if the mv or sensor reading still agree the PO_2, they may be safe to dive. If the sensors are becoming erratic, again the diver will have to dive the unit in SCR mode or bailout to OC or a bailout rebreather. Once a continuous ascent begins, the diver must bailout to OC or a bailout rebreather. At the 20 fsw (6 msw) deco, stop flush unit at least three times with oxygen and flush periodically to maintain a high partial pressure of oxygen. Of course, OC bailout or bailout to a bailout rebreather is always the safer choice. So in this predicament one has the following choices, the minimum loop volume maintaining the diluents PO_2 value, SCR or OC bailout. The choice of which, must be a personal decision based on comfort level of the diver. It seems since the unit is not reading correctly across any sensor, adding O_2 to maintain minimum loop volume might be unwise, especially if the O_2 in the loop is already high and/or the correct value is unknown. The only way the diver could calculate the unknown is to perform a diluent flush.

13. **Sensors do not go above 1.2 even if oxygen is added or the set point is at 1.3 and the depth is 160 fsw (48 msw):** Suspect that the sensor voltage is low on all sensors (with units with mv read out check readings) and that they are not capable of reading above 1.2. Thus, the electronics cannot display the true PO_2. Flush the loop until the PO_2 is below the indicated 1.2. The sensors should read correctly if under the output value of the sensors. (It is important to change the set point slightly below the value where the solenoid might fire. Allowing the unit to continue firing the solenoid at the original set point may cause high PO_2 in the loop). Abort the dive and fly the unit at 1.0 to ensure the sensor output will be correct. Alternatively, the diver may do SCR bailout and still monitor the PO_2 when it is below 1.2. At 20 fsw (6 msw), flush the unit with oxygen for decompression. This is a rare event but has happened to at least ten divers I personally know including myself. . Staggering the replacement of sensors, helps prevent this even though some manufactures recommend replacing all sensors at the same time... Frequent checking of sensor output voltage with a meter, or within the system as is possible on some units, will also help avoid false readings. To be prudent do not dive sensors, whether they are staggered or changed at the same time, until failure. Bailing out to open circuit is always an option.

15. **All electronics are lost:** If this occurs while swimming at a constant depth, maintain minimum loop volume and manually add oxygen as it is metabolized. The best option is to use SCR or open circuit bailout. If minimum loop [volume is used the diver may continue the same technique until a depth change is required or ascent is commenced... In this situation at 20 fsw (6 msw) flush the system with oxygen for deco, if a bailout to OC has taken place go back on the loop and flush it with oxygen.

16. **Loop integrity problems:** The counterlung is filling with water: if the design permits it, loosen the counterlung dump valve and then perform a diluent flush while pressing the dump valve. Roll as needed to remove the water from the counterlung. Once the water is dumped remain alert for more water intrusion into the system and be prepared to repeat this sequence. By clearing the flooded counter lung there is a very low probability of having a totally flooded loop inclusive of the canister. If water begins to enter the counter lung a second time the diver should consider aborting the dive. Pre-dives tests and bubble checks at the beginning of the dive help identify problems before they get serious.

17. **The counterlung is filling with water, and does not have a dump valve to eliminate the water egress into it:** Check to see if the source/problem may be corrected. Swim with your feet slightly down to keep the water in the lower portion of the counterlung. If the problem continues it will eventually migrate into the canister. Be prepared to bailout to OC, or a bailout rebreather as the canister becomes flooded, or if breathing resistance becomes too great. It is recommended that divers add a dump valve or other water removal system to units that do not incorporate these. A flood on a deep dive or in an overhead environment can be catastrophic.

18. **The total loop is flooded and you are unable to breathe:** First bailout to OC. If the system is flood recoverable, invert and shake water into counter lung(s). Roll, press manual diluent addition, and purge water from the dump valve. You must bailout to OC or a bailout rebreather if the system is not flood recoverable. In either situation terminate the dive.

19. **The counterlung has been torn allowing water to egress into the system:** Try to pinch off the torn portion of counter lung to stop water entry and terminate the dive. Remain on the loop if possible. Open circuit bail-out is always an option.

20. **Pin-hole leak in counterlung:** In this situation (as long as there is a slight pressure in the counterlung) very little water will leak into the counterlung. The diver may not have to take a corrective action. At the end of the dive, you must repair counter lung.

21. **System has a torn exhalation hose:** Pinch hose together and blow water that has intruded into the counterlung. Terminate the dive. If the intrusion of water is beyond the system's ability to prevent a full loop flood, then bailout to OC or a bailout rebreather.

22. **System has torn inhalation hose:** It is possible the diver may breathe water and the canister may flood. As a preliminary step, pinch hose shut and stay on loop unless the canister floods or there is too much water in the inhaled gas. In this case, you should bailout to OC or a bailout rebreather.

23. **Canister problems:** The diver becomes aware of symptoms of hypercapnia while exerting. First stop activity, switch to OC for sanity breaths, return to the loop, flush the loop and see if symptoms persist. If no symptoms are present, terminate the dive and avoid exertion. If symptoms persist, you need to bailout to OC or a bailout rebreather and terminate the dive.

24. **An acidic taste develops from the inspired gas:** Suspect that water is in the canister, be aware that it is losing its ability to absorb CO_2, and that there is the probability of a caustic cocktail. If the diver elects to stay on the loop, avoid a head down posture. This will increase the possibility of a caustic cocktail. You must also remain vigilant for hypercapnia problems and flush the system at regular intervals. At the first sign of a caustic cocktail (or any unusual feeling such a shortness of breath) you must bailout to OC or a bailout rebreather. The dive should be terminated at the first detection of this situation.

25. **Symptoms of hypercapnia are noticed while swimming at an abnormal pace:** The first step is to switch to OC for a sanity break. Once stable, you may double check for symptoms. Go back on the loop and flush the system. Note how you feel at rest. If any unusual sensations exist, you need to

bailout to OC or a bailout rebreather and terminate dive. Do not try to over-use the scrubber material life expectancy. Change the scrubber material in accordance with manufacturer's guidelines.

26. **The canister is on its second dive with the same absorbent and the diver just does not feel normal:** In this case suspect that the canister was not sealed well between dives and the absorbent material is used up. Bail-out to OC or a bailout rebreather and terminate the dive.

27. **The diver suspects the canister has failed and has symptoms of hypercapnia (even after sanity break, the symptoms return):** In this case the only safe solution is to make a switch to OC bailout or a bailout rebreather.

28. **The canister is flooded:** The diver must bailout to OC or a bailout rebreather unless it is a flood proof canister, in which case the appropriate flood recovery technique may be used.

29. **Bailout gas problems:** Ensure bailout system is rigged correctly to provide low drag, ease of access, and free from being dragged in silt etc.

30. **Leaking o-ring at connection point of first stage and valve:** Turn gas off except while in use. If the gas is being actively used, turn on only when it is actually being breathed or add gas and then back off when inactive.

31. **Second stage is flooding during OC bailout:** In this case the non-return valve failed, there is a hole in the diaphragm or the second stage mouthpiece has a tear in it, so press purge while inhaling and this will blow the water out. You may also need to hold the regulator in your mouth to prevent the tear from opening and allowing water to enter.

32. **Loss of bailout gas supply:** Communicate to your buddy that you have lost the bailout system and the team must terminate the dive.

33. **Bailout rebreather is flooded:** Terminate dive and communicate the problem to the team members. The entire team must terminate the dive.

34. **Bailout regulator OC is free flowing:** Turn unit on while inhaling, and turn it off during exhales. Consider changing with another regulator on one of the other stage tanks.

35. **Gas supply hose failure:** If a gas hose fails turn off the regulator and use an alternate gas supply. If needed, switch regulators form another gas source.

In addition to correcting these problems, also ensure that if you're using a bailout rebreather that it is functioning and pressure is maintained in the loop at all times to avoid flooding. If using a bailout rebreather, frequently check that it has a safe PO_2 and that the END of the diluent for bailout is acceptable. Check functionality of system periodically.

Pre-dive Set Up and Pre-dive Breathe/System Check: These procedures are crucial in avoiding problems with the rebreather or your support systems. The purpose of the pre-dive check steps is to ensure the system is set up and functioning correctly and safely.

Pre-dive set up is the act of ensuring all cylinders are filled and analyzed, and that the system is properly assembled. During the assembly process O-rings must be inspected and lubed as needed. Sealing surfaces should be observed for integrity and all attaching surfaces should be secure. Sensors should be checked for voltage output and response time, periodically. A slow responding sensor is an indication the sensor is aging and may be marginal for diving.

On every third or fourth dive, at 20 fsw (6 msw), flush the system with oxygen and see if it will obtain a PO above 1.55. This will verify the voltage and response of the sensors. This is important. As sensors age, they may have adequate voltage to calibrate at 1.0 but may not be capable of indicating values above 1.2. If this happens a diver may read a display of 1.2 and actually have 2.0 in the loop. The occasional oxygen flush at 20 fsw (6 msw) will alert the diver to any possibility that the sensor output is not adequate to read above 1.0.

Responsibility: Evaluate both your physical and mental conditioning. Determine if you have what it takes to do this dive. This evaluation must be honest. Don't do a dive out of false bravado. Know in your heart that you can deliver 100% effort. Be certain the team can depend on you. The importance of both physical and mental conditioning cannot be overemphasized in technical diving. If you are going to participate, accept and pay the price of staying in good physical and mental condition. Understand in your own mind that you will not be a person that is dependent upon the other team members.

Another important aspect of responsible dive planning involves awareness. Are you absolutely aware of the dive's objectives and the technical components of the dive? While a level of trust is needed for every dive, there's a big difference between trust and a "trust me" attitude. The "trust me leader" expects you to put your life in their hands and follow them wherever they decides to go. Never, ever get yourself in this position.

If a dive is completely or partially exploratory, this fact needs to be established at the outset. If one member of the team is made the leader, their role must be defined. Responsibilities must be established. Conditions for dive termination must be fully defined. And, never forget one simple rule, ***always trust yourself and dive within your personal ability.***

When planning a dive, it's easy to get wrapped up in the technicalities and overlook the reasons why you're doing the dive in the first place. Anticipate the fun you're going to have. Visualize what you may see. Imagine how the members of your dive team will react to these aesthetic elements. As part of this exercise, develop an understanding that you are both a team member and a solo diver. Estimate the abilities of others in your dive team, but always mentally prepare yourself as if you are diving solo. This approach virtually guarantees that you will not exceed your personal limits and expose yourself to extraordinary risks. Besides, if you become separated or find yourself faced with a life-threatening event, you will most certainly face the situation alone. We repeat, when "the chips are down," only you can think, breathe and swim for you. Bearing this in mind, it is obvious that dives must be planned within your personal limits and abilities to rescue yourself. Not quite as apparent, it is also crucial that you remain within your abilities to assist or rescue a dive buddy. As a team member you are responsible to the other divers on the team. In return, ascertain that each of the team members also are capable of rendering help to you.

Personal gas management for OC and bailout for CCR: In this planning stage, the diver will become aware of their Surface Air Consumption (***SAC***) rate and the amount of gas in psig/bar they use when switching tanks. First, one must determine the SAC rate at a moderate swim pace. This can then be used as the normal swim rate SAC. To do this, swim at a predetermined constant depth for a period of at least 20 minutes. It is recommended that this be performed when a tank is between 1/2 and 2/3[rds] of its rated pressure. In addition, this provides a more realistic value if done once the diver has been in the water diving or doing skills for a sufficient duration to add some degree of fatigue.

To calculate a heavy workload modifier, repeat the above drill when swimming at full speed. On this second drill, note the following; Divers who are in good cardiovascular condition will have a slight increase in gas consumption and will be able to retain a more constant swim pace. Divers who are not in good cardiovascular condition will usually have a more dramatic increase in gas consumption and tend to reduce the pace over time.

Group Planning

Group planning is the process used by the overall dive team to determine understanding and acceptance of the objectives of the dive and the responsibilities of each diver. **The specific items addressed include but should not be limited to:**

- Establish gas management procedures
- Decide on the limits of the dive
- Determine the size of team and responsibilities of members
- Determine team member compatibility
- Ensure each diver is aware of the configuration of fellow divers
- Plan for the "***What Ifs***" that affect team safety

Gas management is a crucial portion of any dive. The more involved the dive, the broader it's objectives, the more important gas management becomes. Maturity and judgment reinforce the concept of proper gas management. Most technical divers, and all overhead environment divers, observe the gas management rule known as the Rule of Thirds when diving OC or bailout times 1½ on CCR. The cave diving community developed the Rule of Thirds after analyzing their accident history. The Rule of Thirds is conservative. It was designed to be so. More importantly, experience has taught us it works.

Every gas management rule devised depends on individuals functioning "normally." They must swim normally, breathe normally and function as expected. For a rule to be valid, unanticipated variations caused by the environment or

changes in divers' abilities cannot occur. This means that events such as unexpected currents or having to maneuver through restrictions must not deter the diver's proficiency. If divers are forced to increase their swim pace, they will also increase gas consumption. Other changes in respiratory patterns, such as response to mental and physical stress, will also increase gas consumption. When divers slow their pace, gas consumption is reduced. However, you must never forget that your return speed must match your travel pace. You must cover the same amount of ground in the same time "coming back" as "going to" in order to ensure you won't run out of gas.

Once again, this is where mental and physical conditioning comes into play. With mental discipline and good physical fitness, it is much easier to remain "normal" during a stressful event. A physically conditioned person will have much less increase in gas consumption with increased workloads than an out of shape diver.

A diver who does not maintain good cardiovascular efficiency will experience tremendous changes in his/her gas consumption when going from light effort to harder work loads. A diver who maintains a cardiovascular training program will experience significantly lower changes in his/her respiratory minute volume when switching from light to heavy exertion than a comparable individual who does not train on a regular basis. The diver who is a weekend warrior and a couch potato during the week will also have less endurance and is more likely to experience increased use of gas when fatigued.

Changes in buoyancy will also affect gas consumption. Environmental changes such as silting or changes in current flow and direction will modify the swim pace. Alterations to swim posture can increase drag. Additional gas is needed to anticipate these changes, too. By now it should be obvious that every phase of a technical dive must be anticipated to ensure the effectiveness of the team and personal gas management rule.

Since dive teams are obviously composed of individuals, a "***team gas management***" rule must be established. This rule incorporates all the factors involving individual considerations with another dimension. People working together create this dimension. When you dive alone, you dive differently than you would as a member of a buddy or dive team. To understand these differences, think of dancing. You dance differently when holding someone in your arms. An effective team gas management rule takes time to develop. The team must do a lot more than just shake hands. Each member must learn other team members' dive style and ability. They must also practice emergency management skills.

The size of the dive team will dictate effective gas management. Obviously a two-person dive team is the most efficient from a dive performance standpoint. It needs less communication and requires less choreography. Both divers know where each other are. Swim pace is easier to regulate. A small team reduces the level of environmental management needed. For example, silting is just one of many factors that are easier to anticipate and prevent.

On the other hand, there are strong arguments to support the advantages of a three-person dive team. The group gas supply or bailout gas on CCR can go much further when shared between three people. Two people are usually better able to rescue an individual in trouble.

When computing a team gas management model, compensate for variations in both breathing volume (respiratory minute volume - ***RMV***) and varying tank capacities. In addition, plan out the known gas volumes for the dive. If a dive has a three-person team, the dive gas is matched automatically provided all use an honest Rule of Thirds. If a two-person team is used and the diver who uses the least gas also has the smallest gas supply, the divers must match gas. Gas matching ensures that if a gas failure occurs at the farthest point form the return area, both divers can safely travel on the lowest volume of gas in the team.

Developing a gas management profile for a hypothetical team in OC:

Diver #1, "Jan," consumes 0.37 cu ft (9.9 free liters) a minute. She uses double 100s (twin 15 L) at 3500 psig (232 bar).

Diver #2, "Bill," consumes 1.13 cu ft (32.6 free liters) a minute. He uses 121 cu ft (20 L) steel tanks at 2640 psig (180 bar).

When using the IANTD Gas Matching Table C-3202 & C-3202B, round to the most conservative value. This means round down for the diver who consumes the least gas and round up for the diver who consumes the most gas. In this example, round Jan's consumption down to 0.35 (9.91) and round Bill's up to 1.15 (32.57).

Using the IANTD Gas Management Table C-3202:

1. Follow the left margin side until you reach Jan's RMV, which is calculated at 0.35 (9.91)
2. Go across the top of the table to Bill's RMV of 1.15 (32.57), column #1

At this point, follow Bill's RMV down the column until it's adjacent to Jan's. Note the value 0.81. The number 0.81 represents a conversion factor of 81%. This means that Jan, instead of turning at 66% (0.66) of her gas supply, needs to turn at 81% (0.81). This should provide Jan with an adequate safety margin in case Bill needs to share gas on the way out.

Convert this safety margin into a usable number; Use C-3202 IANTD Gas Management Table:

1. Go down the Starting Cylinder Pressure Column along the left side to 3500 psig (238 bar)
2. Go across the top of the table showing SRFs from 0.67 to 0.81. The last column is labeled 0.81
3. Go down this column until it intersects with 3500 psig (238 bar)

The C-3202 Table shows Jan's turn pressure to be 2,835 psig (193 bar). Normally Jan would turn at 2310 psig (157 bar). The chart shows she must hold an additional 525 psig (36 bar) in reserve to compensate for Bill's increased RMV.

Even with proper gas matching, it is still imperative that all dives remain within normal parameters for these rules to work. When you start diving with new buddies, it's advisable to add a couple of hundred psig (extra bars) to any cutoff point. This practice should be continued until divers have sufficient experience to develop the discipline to function normally under stress. Many experienced divers develop the ability to actually reduce their RMV under stress and to maintain a normal swim pace under the most demanding of situations.

Gas duration required for the dive plan should be figured by anticipating the planned distance traveled, coupled with gas consumption. In this case, let's look at two divers who are planning a dive into a moderate outflow cave. This example employs a cave dive because cave dives generally employ more consistent swimming than open water dives.

Continuing with our example:

- Swimming into a dive, the divers will swim at a pace of 50 ft (15 m) per minute
- From gas planning, it has already been determined that the turn pressure will be 2400 psig (160 bar) from a starting press of 3600 psig (240 bar)
- It has already been determined (through steps explained earlier in dive gas planning) that the divers use 30 psig (2 bar) a minute at the planned dive depth of 90 ft (27 m)
- **To determine the turn pressure time:**
- First, compute the gas available: 3600 psig - 2400 psig = 1200 psig (240 bar - 160 bar = 80 bar)
- **Next, compute the amount of time unto reaching turn pressure:**

o Imperial-US: (1200psig)/(30 psig per minute) = 40 minutes

o Metric: (80 bar)/(2 bar per minute) = 40 minutes

- The divers, traveling at 50 ft (15 m) per minute, will penetrate 2000 ft (600 m)
- If the divers exit at 75 ft (22 m) per minute, it will only take 27 minutes to return. This will increase the safety of their gas management procedures
- However, what happens if the divers slow their return due to an emergency such as a silt-out or gas sharing problem? In this event, let's say the exit speed is at 25 ft (12 m) per minute. The exit will take 80 minutes
- In this delayed exit event, it will take (80 minutes) ***x*** 30 psig (2 bar) per minute = 2400 psig (160 bar) to exit
- If this is a not a gas sharing emergency, there is still a sufficient quantity of gas to exit with reserve. If a gas sharing emergency did take place at the maximum point of penetration, it would require 2400 psig (160 bar) ***x*** 2 = 4800 psig (320 bar), both divers combined gas needs to exit. This is not sufficient gas to return to the surface

Pre-Dive Check

1. Analyze all gases and make sure they are connected to the appropriate regulators.
2. Turn gases on, then off, and record pressure to determine if there is a leak in the gas systems.
3. Check that the inhalation, exhalation hoses, and their non-return valves are installed correctly and functional.
4. Do a positive loop test. Allow at least 5 minutes to observe for any leaks.
5. Perform a negative loop test. Allow it to sit for a minimum of 5 minutes. (Note that some systems require the negative test to be longer per manufacturer's instructions.)
6. Activate electronics. (The electronics are inside of the loop on some rebreathers and need to be activated upon set up.)
7. Check accuracy of all electronic displays and analog displays as relevant.
8. Check if the pressure in the oxygen and diluent supplies has decayed. If there is a leak, fix the leak before proceeding.
9. If applicable, ensure all gases and variables are correctly defined in the electronics and that manual and electronic readouts are consistent with each other.
10. Run check on systems that have an onboard technique for checking sensor voltage and ensure all sensors are within acceptable range.
11. Calibrate system: if doing a manual calibration, flush the system totally for at least 3 cycles. Often 4 or more cycles are required to have a 100% oxygen environment in the loop. While at 100% oxygen, (on systems that have the capability) check the sensor voltage to verify it agrees with the value for a partial pressure of 1.0.
12. When calibration is complete, observe the PO_2 readings. If they tend to drop off sharply, the calibration is most likely in error. In this instance redo the calibration.
13. If the system does not have a two-point calibration you may want (not mandated) to flush with diluent (again three times) and check that the diluent PO_2 is accurate. This also will provide an indication of sensor linearity. Prior to doing this, check that the set point is below the partial pressure of the diluent, that the system is turned off, that it is in manual mode or that the oxygen is turned off and gas is vented from the oxygen supply line. If applicable, check sensor voltage for correct output.
14. Check remaining battery time and be sure it is adequate for the planned dive.
15. On systems that "go to sleep" on the surface, be sure to activate the electronics prior to breathing on the loop. At least one system has a start dive mode that must be activated prior to diving.
16. Ensure that all manual gas control valves or switches are set in their correct position and are functioning.

17. Verify all electronic gas control functions and any switches that may be applicable are in the correct position and operational.

18. Conduct an S drill on the system. Check completely for any leaks or systems abnormalities. Check the bailout system to ensure it is functioning properly. If it is OC bailout, be sure there are no leaks, no free flows etc. Check that the low-pressure inflator hose and fitting will allow you to plug into the manual addition valve if the system is equipped with one. It is advisable to have an interchangeable low-pressure fitting on the counterlung, the BC and dry suit so the source gas may be switched in event of a failure. Check the manual addition valves for smooth and correct operation. Ensure the rigging of bailout systems allows them to be accessible and protected from damage. If a bailout rebreather is used, check its components in the same manner as the pre-dive check on the primary rebreather. If used, check lights and lift bags plus reels.

19. Pre-dive breathing: during this process the canister is conditioned. The diver verifies the solenoid is firing and that the displays are responding to the injection of oxygen. Check the set point is correct and held by the system and that a safe breathing gas is in the loop. The pre-dive check should be performed on a low set point. During the pre-dive check also breathe from the bailout system; check BC inflation, and all systems needed for the dive.

20. The pre-dive breathing sequence should be a minimum of 2 minutes in warm water and 5 minutes in cold water. Note! If a bailout rebreather is used the same procedures must be followed on it!

21. Immediately prior to entering the water verify that the unit is on, that there is a safe breathing mixture, that the automatic diluent addition valve (ADV) (if applicable) works and that any and all manual addition valves respond. Start he dive at the proper set point.

22. At depth, verify a change to the desired set point and that the solenoid still works. Even if controlling the system manually, you should still verify the solenoid fires provided the system uses a solenoid. Some CCRs, like the KISS model, may not use a solenoid as a standard component on the system.

Remember to check your dive log for any faults or developing issues identified in the last dive. Correct these problems before proceeding into the formal pre-dive check!

Another common problem in out-of-gas situations is that the divers' breathing rates increase. Let's assume the divers use some discipline but, due to stress, they increase their combined breathing rate from 30 psig (2 bar) per minute to 60 psig (4 bar) per minute. Let's allow for a normal swim rate equal to the penetration rate of 50 ft (15 m) per minute. The divers will exit in 40 minutes if gas has been matched. It will now take 60 psig (4 bar) per min. *x* 40 min. = 2400 psig (160 bar) per diver, 4800 psig (320 bar) for both divers sharing gas to exit. This is more gas than is available!

From these examples, it is apparent divers must function in a normal fashion even when responding to an emergency. Planning gas needs for decompression is also vital to a safe dive plan. A separate gas supply should be planned for decompression purposes. This gas supply must include the amount of gas needed plus a 1/5th reserve. In this case, determine the gas needed and multiply by 1.2 for the correct volume of gas to carry.

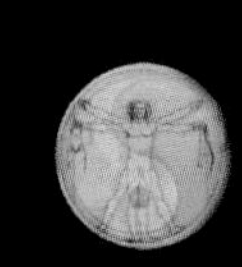

Points to Remember

Technical diving is a hostile environment for dependent divers

Avoidance is a key principle of technical diving. In this case, however, avoidance does not mean ignoring a potential problem. It means knowing what constitutes a small problem and what doesn't. It means knowing that a "tiny" free-flow could become a major problem. It means having the common sense to know if one part of your gas supply is not working properly, turn it off and use your alternate source. It means having the discipline to anticipate, to think ahead, and to immediately neutralize the source of problems.

By taking corrective actions with gas supply problems before those problems escalate, divers can begin sharing gas before the diver with the problem actually runs out. This is good stress management, because it allows the distressed diver to use their own gas whenever a restricted or hazardous point in the dive is reached, and to share air in the long, unobstructed passages.

In a 3-person team, the "out-of-gas diver" should be sandwiched between the two divers with gas. Every few hundred psig (***free liters/bar***), the out-of-gas diver is rotated between donors. This allows the two divers with air to deplete their gas supplies somewhat evenly. When exiting an overhead environment dive, certain problem management techniques have been developed. For example, in three person teams, one of the "donor divers" negotiates a problem area, such as a restriction, ahead of the "recipient diver." Once the lead donor diver has safely reached a clear passageway, the "recipient diver" switches over to their own gas supply and swims to the lead donor diver. They resume sharing the donor's gas while waiting for the third member of the team to join them. This, of course, assumes the "recipient" is not out of gas.

In a true out-of-gas situation, the recipient would share gas with a buddy while the buddy goes through the restriction. At this time, the recipient will go into the restriction to a point where the long hose is dropped and continues until they reach the awaiting second stage of the diver who has already negotiated the restriction.

Two person teams must handle a gas supply problem differently. When negotiating a problem area, the "recipient diver" stops, takes 3 breaths (inhaling slowly and deeply) followed by 3 hyperventilation breaths and waits for the "donor diver" to reach an unobstructed area. Once the donor signals "clear," the recipient swims to the donor and shares gas. There's a good reason why the donor leads. At the point of separation, the recipient has adequate gas in their lungs to reach the donor. Moreover, there's a psychological edge provided by swimming toward a gas supply rather than away from it.

Gas management rules are occasionally modified when conditions warrant a change. Specialized equipment may mean altering normal gas turn around points. **For example:**

- When diving into caves with "siphons" or down-current on wrecks and other circumstances which will require an up-current swim to the exit or ascent point, gas management rules should be modified to account for the challenge of overcoming the in-flowing water. In this case, more conservative rules are implemented. This may be nothing more than adjusting to a different gas turn-around percentage or fraction. A good starting point for mild to moderate siphons is the Rule of Fourths. This is also a good starting reference when you first begin using a Diver Propulsion Vehicle (***DPV***).

- With experience in both technical diving and at a given location, it may be acceptable to make modifications to the basic thirds gas management rules. For example, a diver may use 40% of his gas supply swimming into a dive with a strong outflow. By riding the current out, the diver will not work as hard and will consume less gas. The "turnaround point" might then be adjusted to allow the dive team to adhere to the Rule of Thirds as it applies to this environment.

Such interpretations of gas rules can only be performed by accumulating experience. This experience comes from both the total number of dives logged and the number of dives performed at the specific location where the modifications are being applied. Modifications to gas management rules should be made in gradual increments. Each dive is followed by careful evaluation to determine if the modification did, in fact, allow a true $2/3^{rds}$ reserve gas for exiting the system. Regardless of the current, no more than 40% of the gas should be used when traveling into a dive.

We suggest you be very conservative before making changes to gas management rules. We recommend you make at least 100 total dives and 25 dives at a specific site before considering such modifications. Again, you must be able to prove that the modified turnaround point does provide $2/3^{rds}$ of the available gas is actually available for exiting. This availability is defined within a relationship of time, distance, and duration of gas.

A specific example of a modified Rule of Thirds could involve a dive into a strong current. After completing numerous dives at this location, you realize that upon exiting, you and your buddy team will finish the dive with half your gas. In this example, the management rules can be modified. If, for example, you had started with 3,600 psig (245 bar), the exit would be completed with 1,800 psig (122 bar) remaining in the tanks. Thus, $1/3^{rd}$ of the gas was used going in and only $1/6^{th}$ of the gas was used on return. In psig (bar) this equates to 1200 psig (82 bar) going in and 600 psig (41 bar) exiting. The Rule of Thirds allows for the use of an additional 600 psig (41 bar).

The experienced diver who is familiar with the dive site may now begin to modify the turnaround point to allow for a safety factor of one third. By familiar, we emphasize that it means you have made numerous dives at the site and encountered the same or very similar conditions.

In the above example, if a diver turns with 60% of the gas remaining, a turn around at 2160 psig (147 bar), the dive will reflect 1440 psig (98 bar) used going into the dive. It will require 1/2 of that to exit, or 720 psig (49 bar) with a remaining 1440 psig (98 bar). This works out to more than a 1/3rd reserve as the true "***3rd reserve***" would be 1200 psig (82 bar).

If a diver does not carry extra gas for decompression, it is necessary to plan for sufficient gas supply into the dive plan. In this instance, the diver must incorporate two phases of dive planning into the primary gas supply. These involve bottom gas and decompression gas.

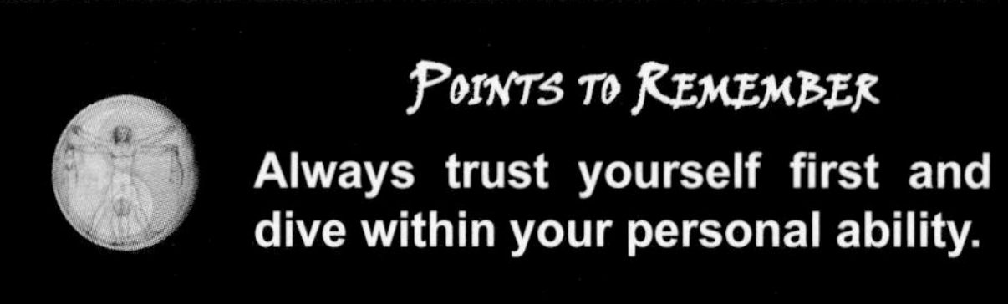

Anticipated need for decompression gas must be planned. When planning the necessary gas, subtract the gas needed for the decompression stops and plan the dive as if that gas did not exist. For example, after careful planning, you determine that 30 cu ft (850 free liters) of gas is necessary for decompression. You would then multiply that value by 1.2 for reserve. Finally, you would subtract the deco gas from your primary gas supply and plan accordingly.

Whenever possible, decompression should be made using Enriched Air Nitrox (***EANx***) of 50% or more. Doppler studies have discovered bubble formation decreases as the oxygen level in the EANx mixture is increased. Many experts consider the practice of decompressing on bottom mix to be unsafe from a DCS standpoint.

Another consideration is the "solo" diver. In this instance, in addition to diving using the Rule of Thirds, it is recommended that the diver must also carry a stage bottle (referred to as the buddy cylinder) that is equivalent to one third of the back-mounted gas. This tank is reserved for emergency use only. It is only used if a failure of the primary gas system takes place. As an example, a diver with double 100s (15 L) has a total of 200 cu ft (38 L) of gas. The safety gas supply must be at least 66 cu ft (12.5 L).

CCR Planning

An advantage for CCR divers is that work rates make little difference on the gas used in the cylinders, thus allowing gas management to be more precise. However, if a diver must bailout then all the things that apply to OC gas usage come back into play. For this reason the team's total bailout gas must be adequate to get 1½ divers to the surface or to another staged dive gas. Each diver in the team must have adequate bailout gas factored into the team's gas to fulfill this requirement. All divers in the team must be competent

in exchanging bailout out cylinders or alternate methods of gas exchange. For team safety, a diver forced off of the loop must surface. Ideally in the future, each diver will have a bailout rebreather for this purpose. If someone is diving in a non-team situation or there is a high probability that team members will become separated, then the diver must personally carry sufficient bailout gat to reach the surface or other staged gas.

In addition to the bailout gas management issue, divers need to plan the dive so that no one has less than one third of their oxygen supply gas upon surfacing or reaching a staged oxygen cylinder. To accurately plan for this, each team member's oxygen metabolism rate must be known. There is a significant variation between individuals with some divers using as much as double the amount of oxygen as their buddy, due to metabolic needs. Another factor is how efficiently he/she dives the unit. If an ADV is always used, you will breathe more oxygen each time the loop reaches a minimum volume because the diluent will add gas. This addition will lower the PO_2 and then the solenoid will fire to restore the PO_2.

In bailout planning, ensure each team member has either a dive computer, dive tables for the dive, a back up computer, and/or back up dive tables. The dive tables should also include the decompression for OC or bailout rebreather needs.

Also, as divers may have more than one style of CCR in the team, be sure the plan includes team bailout management that considers:

1. The valves may not permit gas exchanges between some different CCR designs, so an alternate gas management plan must be developed to deal with this
2. It is possible that all divers may not have the same diluent or bailout gases. In this event the decompression procedure and the ability to use bailout gases other than those the diver may carry must be included into the dive plan
3. If the team dives consistently with each other prior to arriving at the site, preplanning should ensure that the divers have compatible bailout gases and have planned around any inconsistencies in valve variations from one CCR to another. This may require adding extra low pressure hoses to be compatible with a team member's needs, or it each diver may need to add or change valves on their unit so the team is compatible in this area
4. Many divers (including the author) prefer to use all low-pressure fittings that are interchangeable with the counterlungs, BC, and the dry suit. In addition if all team members are of the same philosophy, then compatible fittings can be planned fort he entire team

In a dive team, if a diver has loop failure, the "off the loop diver" will go to their OC bailout. Then once 50% of the bailout gas is used, they will switch stages with another diver until 50% of this gas is used, and so on... This process will be repeated as dictated by the situation, but will ensure all divers have adequate bailout gas to reach the surface or other stages gases. If it is a three person team the "off the loop diver" will be positioned between the other two divers enabling the bailout gas to be rotated between all three divers.

Planning For Mixed Equipment Dive Teams

Diving within a team composed of divers who are using Closed Circuit, Semi-closed Circuit, and Open Circuit systems is definitely an exercise in "Multi-Cultural Diversity!" It can work, but it will ONLY work ***WELL*** if the members of the team display tolerance, understanding, and a willingness to accommodate the "special needs" of the other team members.

Specifically, this will be one of the most complex and difficult dive planning sessions that the team will have to participate in. By following the procedures laid down in this text by Mount, et al, the team members will find that the plan will be simple, easy to follow and above all safe. The key to the project is finding a "baseline," which will be established by the physical limits of the equipment involved (as has been discussed in previous chapters), and begin the mission planning from that point.

Some people take the approach that diving in "mixed" teams should be avoided, but experience reflects that this is not an uncommon practice. When teams are mixed, the OC diver is the one with the greatest disadvantage since he or she usually has limited or no understanding of the rebreathers and their operating requirements.

Logically the first step is to provide the OC diver with an overview of how the rebreather functions (CCR, SCR or both as the case may be). This must include a quick review of issues with the partial pressures of gases, and the fractions of gases in the mix on SCR. The significance of gas supplies, gas duration and canister limitations should also be covered. Then the OC diver should be introduced to recognition of rebreather problems and how they are solved. As many OC divers have great concern with the operating procedures and bailout systems a short course will need to take place explaining these issues. The OC diver in a team that has one or more CCR divers should be aware of the bailout options for the CCR diver should they have a malfunction of the system. Thus it must be explained that the CCR diver has a progression of bailout scenarios.

The options include:

1. If at a constant depth and the CCR diver has been employing minimum loop volume diving, remain on minimum loop until a depth change is encounter
2. Dive the CCR as if it is a SCR
3. Open Loop bailout
4. Bailout to OC
5. Bailout to buddy's OC

Of course this will take a brief description of the process. In some cases, the diver may have a bailout CCR, and if that is the case it will become the first option.

Explain to the OC diver how adequate bailout is predicted and the 1.5 minimum rule is used. Provide the OC diver with an example; How much gas would an OC team need to exit or return to the surface from a maximum point of penetration if one diver has a total loss of gas, requiring them to share gas. The OC diver is diving the rule of thirds, so the plan maintains a gas supply of one third for the buddy to use or to overcome problems on the dive.

Thus an example of planning an OC technical dive includes:

1. The OC dive team determining that the dive would require 85 cu ft (2400 L) to provide a single diver enough gas to complete the dive or return to staged gas or deco gas
2. The next step is to plan the dive so that the Rule of Thirds is included to provide gas for emergencies and gas sharing with team members. To determine the gas needed to incorporate the Rule of Thirds, the OC diver will take the total volume of gas to actually be used (based on highest RMV/gas matching) and then multiply the actual gas used by 1.5, for a total of 127 cu ft (3600 L). That figure equals 85 cu ft (2400 L) for the diver to use and 42.5 cu ft (1200 L) for emergencies and or gas sharing with a buddy

Points to Remember

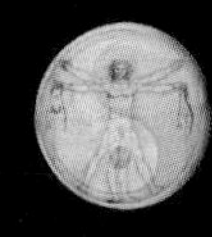

Under stress, divers often slow their swim rate. Gas Matching & the Rule of Thirds rely upon maintaining a constant swim rate!

A disadvantage of gas management rules is they assume the divers will maintain the same exit/ascent rate, the same breathing rate and that there will only be a single failure. If a diver slows down their exit or return to surface swim rate, increases their RMV, or if there is an additional failure to the gas supply of the second diver then the rule will not prevail. When developing gas management rules, it was assumed that each of these variables was under control and that the probability of two people having a total gas supply failure was remote enough to not consider it. Historically these assumptions have worked well enough that the rule of thirds is accepted, it is believed to be a safe approach, and practiced in all OC technical diving circles.

Rebreather bailout principles are based on similar concepts. However when using a rebreather the OC gas plan does not have to include gas for use up to a point of failure (as in OC diving). In its broadest application, it also assumes the same constants the OC rule of thirds does, decontrolled RMV, swim rate and single system failures. The rebreather bailout concept also allows for a solo diver or a high probability of team separation. Each diver, based on their RMV, carries adequate OC gas or a bailout rebreather to surface or get to the staged dive gases. For normal confident diving, the team will remain intact until the end of the dive. Their gas is planned to provide OC bailout to get 1.5 divers out and/or up, or to a staged bailout gas. If we take the same example where we have determined the gas for a single diver in a team, this will be the diver with the highest RMV to return to the surface or other staged that value will be multiplied by 1.5 for the total team gas to be available.

An example of planning a CCR technical dive includes (using the same exit gas reference as on the OC dive):

1. The CCR diver or team will determine the amount of gas needed to exit or reach staged gas by the diver with the highest RMV (unless using a bailout rebreather)
2. In this case we will assume the emergency gas needed for an "out-of-gas" or "off-the-loop" diver is 42.5 cu ft (1200 L) (the same as for the OC example previously discussed). The bailout gas is for bailout or other emergencies and can be given to the OC diver should they have total loss of gas
3. If the team consists of more than one CCR diver(s) and one OC diver, then the CCR team would collectively carry 42.5 cu ft (1200 L) *x* 1.5 or 64 cu ft (1800 L) of team gas
4. In this application, each of the two CCR divers would carry a minimum of 32 cu ft (900 L) of bailout gas. In an emergency the bailout gas would be rotated between the divers. This actually provides an additional 22 cu ft (600 L) of reserve gas
5. If the dive team consists of one OC diver and one CCR diver, the CCR diver must carry adequate bailout gas to exit or reach the staged dive gas. In this case the CCR diver would carry 42.5 cu ft (1200 L) of gas. This provides the same emergency gas, as needed for the team of two OC divers

The above shows that when either diver is forced to go to a gas supply other than their primary gas, the CCR diver could use the OC diver's long hose and the exit would be the same as on any OC dive. If the OC diver is forced off their system, simply go to the CCR diver where they will most likely be given the stage cylinder with the 42.5 cu ft (1200 L) of gas. A stage hand-off to the distressed diver may take a brief moment, but then allows a simpler exit and less time is wasted than with an OC diver on a long hose. The stage hand-off eliminates the slow swim times that a long hose would require and problems associated with narrow openings or restrictions, etc.

Points to Remember

Divers under stress often increase their breathing rates. The results could be life threatening.

Gas Matching and the Rule of Thirds rely upon maintaining a constant breathing rate!

Points to Remember

Once any member of the dive team is using a back-up regulator, the dive should be terminated.

All divers should begin their pre-planned exits.

On some rebreather systems the bailout gas is configured to go directly into the loop. In such a system, the rebreather diver may provide a long hose instead of handing off a stage.

Many rebreather divers, such as the author, prefer to carry two smaller cylinders that can be rotated in a manner to always allow the donor diver(s) to have some form of bailout gas. This also gives more flexibility if more than one diver experiences a system failure, especially considering the probability that two persons would have total system failures at the end of a dive. The 1.5 *x* Gas Needed rule should cover multiple failures and be easily managed if each diver carries their bailout in more than one cylinder. If the bailout is 43 cu ft (1200 L), then carry two 22 cu ft (600 L) cylinders.

Typically on CCR dive teams, once a diver uses 50% of their bailout gas they will exchange cylinders with another CCR diver and once again use 50% of that gas supply. If it is a three-person team, go to the third diver, switch, and repeat each time 50% of the gas in the cylinder is used. If it were a two-person team then the rotation would be between the two persons. On a team with an OC diver, if the CCR diver is the one with the problem they will use 50% of their cylinder, then go to the long hose of the OC diver, use 50% of his share of the OC diver gas, and then back to his cylinder - rotating back and forth in that manner. If another OC diver or rebreather diver is in the team, that diver will also be included in the rotation for gas. If the OC diver has had a problem, simply take the CCR diver's bailout gas. If it is a 2-person team, keep the cylinder until reaching the exit, surface, or other staged dive gas. If the dive has a three-person team the OC diver would follow the same rotational practices as the rebreather divers.

Another method, considering the difference in gas management between CCR and OC divers, is that the OC diver carries bailout gas. Plan the dive in the same manner as the rebreather diver. The primary gas supply will be used for the dive and the bailout stage(s) will be used for emergencies.

Advantages of the OC diver using the bailout concept:

1. Increases dive capability (in this case he would have two primary gas options)
   a. Devote the entire primary gas supply for use on the dive
   b. Use 80% of the primary gas for the dive (includes surface to surface gas) with 20% for emergency use
2. Carry bailout gas in addition to the primary gas based on the same rules as the rebreather bailout
   a. If diving solo or with a high probability of separation, carry adequate personal bailout gas to reach exit or staged dive gas
   b. If confident the team will remain intact, carry adequate team bailout for 1.5 divers. Apply distribution as explained previously
   c. Ideally carry multiple smaller cylinders. In an emergency they can be rotated to always ensure that each diver has onboard bailout

Use this approach especially when multiple cylinders are carried. It allows a better chance of survival in a multi systems failure situation.

An SCR diver using an active (***mass flow***) system is limited by the gas supply, flow rate and canister duration. A diver on a passive SCR will be limited by gas supply based on the ratio of the unit with the diver's RMV factored in, and canister duration. The OC diver is limited by their RMV and gas supply. The CCR diver is limited solely by canister duration.

The biggest issue is that the OC diver must be able to recognize CCR or SCR problems and understand the corrective action taken by these divers. Another point, in this scenario there is a higher probability of each diver being on varying gas mixtures. However, if the dive is planned as a ***team*** dive the bailout gases should be matched to the bottom mix used by the OC diver(s). A bailout by the OC diver to a rebreather diver's stage will not add to the decompression needs of the OC diver.

In an ideal world a rebreather diver will educate the OC diver on the rebreather to an adequate level regarding the different systems between everyone on the team. The OC diver may feel more comfortable if the CCR diver displays his/her PPO_2 read-out. This will ensure that the OC diver knows that the partial pressure of oxygen is acceptable. Also the OC diver may wish to check that the CCR diver is periodically checking his/her displays.

Points to Remember

The key is that all dives must be planned with the diver arriving at the surface with a minimum of one third of the origional gas supply

On decompression, the divers will most likely have variations in the stop times and total run time of the dive. Most likely the CCR diver will complete decompression first, especially on a multi level dive, then the OC diver and last the SCR diver. Additional gas switches by the SCR and OC divers can be scheduled to coordinate the run times.

In summary, prior to commencement of the dive, review all the objectives. During this phase of the plan, ascertain that each diver is aware of the responsibility assigned to him or her. If it is a complex skill, rehearse it through land drills as a team and visualize it. At the same time, discuss the absolute limits of the dive. In addition to gas management, consider factors such as partial pressure of oxygen, narcosis loading, gas density, decompression duration and contingency factors.

For open circuit diving under no circumstance should a bottom mix PO_2 exceed 1.4 ATA, and it is prudent on longer dives to drop to 1.3 ATA. For decompression, a maximum of 1.6 ATA is to be observed. On exceptional exposures, the dive gas design must allow for a total exposure to remain within team and physiological safety standards. Some projects actually limit the bottom mix to less than 1.35 ATA and decompression mixes to 1.50 ATA.

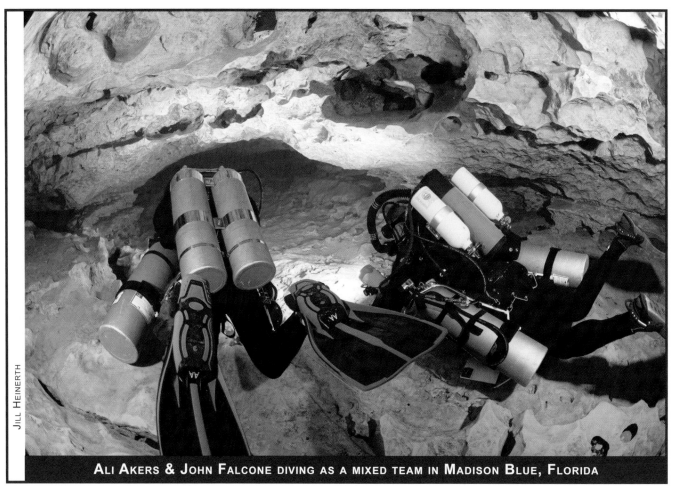

Jill Heinerth

Ali Akers & John Falcone diving as a mixed team in Madison Blue, Florida

Usually, these projects use multiple gas changes on stops and stay close to a range of 1.2 to 1.45 ATA throughout the entire stop times. Remember, to plan both the MOD and TOD (***limits for oxygen, nitrogen narcosis limits***) and gas density.

Define other limits such as penetration on a dive, duration, burn time of DPVs, lights and other support equipment used on the dive. Basically, sit down and detail all the events in the proposed dive and define the minimum and maximum risk values of each. The limits should remain within the agreed on team values, provided they are all within the personal risk acceptance of each individual.

Be careful not to challenge egos when planning complex dives. This is a time when each diver's self and team honesty is paramount to the safety of the project. Be certain the team members are compatible. On technical diving projects, one must be comfortable with the abilities of the team, have trust and respect for the members, and they should have compatible personalities. Remember that each of the members should be self-sufficient, yet aware that in unusual circumstances their lives may depend on a coordinated team effort.

Prior to entering the water, make certain that each diver is totally aware of each other's equipment configuration and its operational parameters. Each portion of the system is to be pre-dive checked and verified by a team member (buddy). When it is possible, do an in-water safety drill to ascertain that all components operate correctly and that each diver can use the buddy system. Divers must breathe from each other's second stage to be handed off and verify the functionality of equipment of the buddy diver. This act is a vital part of pre-dive checks. It should be approached in a checklist fashion.

A list of every "***What If***" that may effect team safety is to be laid out, and the corrective factors defined and rehearsed mentally and physically if possible. This list must include all safety parameters and all possible problem areas the team can identify. Be creative as you make up the list. Once the list is developed and each diver has had input on it, discuss all solutions and develop a "***What If***" plan of action for each. After this, verbally go through each item at least three times and then have the team visualize safely correcting the "***What If***" situations. Once this is accomplished, put it to bed and then visualize and enjoy a safe and productive dive.

In-Water Updates

The final aspect of dive planning is in-water updates. Mr. Murphy is always with us in all endeavors of life. Frequently, dive plans need alternation due to changes in the anticipated water conditions. Therefore, one must remain open-minded when beginning a dive and be prepared to modify the dive performance as dictated by environmental conditions.

Once the dive begins, allow for flexibility in performance. "Mother Nature" is often fickle. The dive may offer the unexpected, and you must be prepared to alter and to modify the dive plan. A degradation of visibility may provide grounds for altering the dive plan while in the water; if so, have that included as an agreed dive plan objective. Changes in the type of, the severity of, or the direction of current may be a sufficient cause for modifications in an existing dive plan. If a boat breaks anchor, or a guideline is broken, or other factors that influence either the exit or ascent of a dive, these are grounds for modification or cancellation of a dive.

You will also need to anticipate behavioral changes within the dive team. Simple things such as one diver becoming uncomfortable will modify the dive plan. Accident potential increases when you fail to modify the dive plan because of a diver's behavioral changes.

Awareness is the critical component in making a command decision to modify the plan of a dive already in progress. As you explore and discover, don't forget to periodically observe the members of your dive team. Set up a plan of intermittent contact.

Observation and communication play key roles. Observation helps you to know when a diver starts slipping. Communication overcomes the hesitancy of divers to tell you they are having a problem.

Guilt associated with failure is a key threat to dive safety. Divers will frequently feel guilty if they cause a dive to be terminated. Feelings of guilt, combined with a "***threatened ego***," produce a potentially dangerous combination if the dive is allowed to continue. When diving not every change is obvious. You must be aware of subtle changes that may occur. These would involve recognizing changes in coordination, swimming style or rhythm, and breathing patterns.

Points to Remember

In-water updates should include provisions for:

- **Changes in Currents**
- **Changes in Visibility**
- **Changes due to upline problems**
- **Changes due to team reaction**

Maturity and sound judgment play key roles in personal success and diving ability. The smart diver knows that cancellation is not the end of the world. Once they learn a dive cannot be accomplished as planned, they will terminate the present dive. They understand that a new plan must be developed to incorporate what has been learned. He or she knows that the price of continuing an unsafe dive skyrockets. It's not only foolish; it's deadly to continue diving with a marginal safety factor.

In summary, a safe dive plan requires divers to gather all information pertinent to the dive site. The entire dive team needs to discuss the dive comprehensively and establish a team plan. Each participating diver must search his or her mind and develop a personal plan of action. This personal plan should be based on self-sufficiency. It must allow for self-rescue ability and team rescue capabilities. Gas Management Rules must be carefully and comprehensively developed from actual field experience.

See Imperial & Metric Worksheets & Pre-Dive Preparation Check Sheets beginning next page...

Dive 1 Using IANTD/IAND, Inc. EAN 26 Accelerated Dive Tables – Imperial-US

FSW MSW	MIX	ATA	END	TIME	PO_2	%CNS	OTU	NEEDED
200 60		7.06						
190 57		6.76						
180 54		6.45						
170 51		6.15						
160 48		5.85						
150 45		5.55						
—	**26%**	5.24	**129**	**50**	**1.36**	**33.33**	**81.44**	**155.00** 3.1 x 50
130 39		4.94						
120 36		4.64						
110 33		4.33						
100 30		4.03						
90 27		3.73						
80 24		3.42						
70 21		3.12						
60 18		2.82						
50 15	**26%**	2.52	**45**	**2**	**.65**	**.32** .16 x 2	**.74** .37 x 2	**2.60** 1.3 x 2
40 12	**26%**	2.21	**35**	**6**	**.58**	**.83** .69 + .14	**1.57** 1.31 + .26	**6.60** 1.1 x 6
30 9	**26%**	1.91	**26**	**11**	**.50**	**0**	**0**	**11.00** 1.0 x 11
20 6	**80%**	1.61		**5**	**1.28**	**2.78**	**7.39**	**4.00** 0.8 x 5
15 4.5	**80%**	1.45		**26**	**1.16**	**12.38** 9.52 + 2.38 + .48	**34.37** 26.44 + 6.61 + 1.32	**18.2** 0.7 x 26
	26%			3		2	2	9.30 3.1 x 3

Add travel time to first deco stop into bottom time and use 2 + 2 Rule for CNS and OTU calculations.

TOTALS (include residual values): CNS%: 51.64 OTU 127.51 Run Time 103 Gas Needed: Bottom Mix (155+2.6+6.6+11+9.3) x 1.5 = 276.75 Deco Gas: (4 + 18.2) x 1.2 = 26.64

Dive 1 Using IANTD/IAND, Inc. EAN 25 Runtime Accelerated Dive Tables – Metric Version

FSW MSW	MIX	ATA	END	TIME	PO_2	%CNS	OTU	NEEDED
200 60		7.0						
190 57		6.7						
180 54		6.4						
170 51		6.1						
160 48		5.8						
150 45		5.5						
140 42	**26%**	5.2	**38.7**	**50**	**1.36**	**30.30**	**77.67**	**4400.0** 87.79 x 50
130 39		4.9						
120 36		4.6						
110 33		4.3						
100 30		4.0						
90 27		3.7						
80 24		3.4						
70 21		3.1						
60 18		2.8						
50 15	**26%**	2.5	**13.4**	**1**	**.65**	**.16**	**.37**	**35.0** 35 x 1
40 12	**26%**	2.2	**10.6**	**8**	**.57**	**1.11** .69 + (.14 x 3)	**2.09** 1.31 + (.26 x 3)	**248.0** 31 x 8
30 9	**80%**	1.9		**6**	**1.52**	**6.67** 5.56 + 1.11	**11.11** 9.26 + 1.85	**162.0** 27 x 6
20 6	**80%**	1.6		**4**	**1.28**	**2.24** .56 x 4	**5.92** 1.48 x 4	**88.0** 22 x 4
15 4.5	**80%**	1.45		**25**	**1.16**	**11.90** 9.52 + 2.38	**33.05** 26.44 + 6.61	**507.5** 20.3 x 25
	26%			3		2	2	**264.0** 88 x 3

Add travel time to first deco stop into bottom time and use 2 + 2 Rule for CNS and OTU calculations.

TOTALS (include residual values): CNS%: 54.38 OTU 132.21

Run Time 97 Gas Needed: Bottom Mix 4947 x 1.5 = 7420.5

Deco 757.5 x 1.2 = 909.0

Dive 1 Using IANTD/IAND, Inc. EAN 25 Runtime Accelerated Dive Tables – Imperial -US

FSW MSW	MIX	ATA	END	TIME	PO_2	%CNS	OTU	NEEDED
200 60		7.06						
190 57		6.76						
180 54		6.45						
170 51		6.15						
160 48		5.85						
150 45		5.55						
140 42	**26%**	5.24	**129**	**50**	**1.36**	**33.33**	**81.44**	**155.00** 3.1 x 50
130 39		4.94						
120 36		4.64						
110 33		4.33						
100 30		4.03						
90 27		3.73						
80 24		3.42						
70 21		3.12						
60 18		2.82						
50 15	**26%**	2.52	**45**	**1**	**.65**	**.16**	**.37**	**1.30** 1.3 x 1
40 12	**26%**	2.21	**35**	**8**	**.58**	**1.11** .69 + (.14 x 3)	**2.09** 1.31 + (.26 x 3)	**8.80** 1.1 x 8
30 9	**80%**	1.91		**6**	**1.53**	**6.67** 5.56 + 1.11	**11.11** 9.26 + 1.85	**6.00** 1.0 x 6
20 6	**80%**	1.61		**4**	**1.28**	**2.24** .56 x 4	**5.92** 1.48 x 4	**3.20** 0.8 x 4
15 4.5	**80%**	1.45		**25**	**1.16**	**11.90** 9.52 + 2.38	**33.05** 26.44 + 6.61	**17.5** 0.7 x 25
	26%			**3**		**2**	**2**	**9.30** 3.1 x 3

Add travel time to first deco stop into bottom time and use 2 + 2 Rule for CNS and OTU calculations.

TOTALS (include residual values): CNS%: 57.41 OTU 135.98

Run Time 97 Gas Needed: Bottom Mix (155 + 1.3 + 8.8 + 9.3) x 1.5 = 261.60

Deco (6.00 + 3.20 + 17.5) x 1.2 = 32.04

Dive 1 Using IANTD/IAND, Inc. EAN 25 Runtime Accelerated Dive Tables – Metric Version

FSW MSW	MIX	ATA	END	TIME	PO_2	%CNS	OTU	NEEDED
200 60		7.0						
190 57		6.7						
180 54		6.4						
170 51		6.1						
160 48		5.8						
150 45		5.5						
140 42	**26%**	5.2	**38.7**	**50**	**1.36**	**30.30**	**77.67**	**4400.0** 87.79 x 50
130 39		4.9						
120 36		4.6						
110 33		4.3						
100 30		4.0						
90 27		3.7						
80 24		3.4						
70 21		3.1						
60 18		2.8						
50 15	**26%**	2.5	**13.4**	**1**	**.65**	**.16**	**.37**	**35.0** 35 x 1
40 12	**26%**	2.2	**10.6**	**8**	**.57**	**1.11** .69 + (.14 x 3)	**2.09** 1.31 + (.26 x 3)	**248.0** 31 x 8
30 9	**80%**	1.9		**6**	**1.52**	**6.67** 5.56 + 1.11	**11.11** 9.26 + 1.85	**162.0** 27 x 6
20 6	**80%**	1.6		**4**	**1.28**	**2.24** .56 x 4	**5.92** 1.48 x 4	**88.0** 22 x 4
15 4.5	**80%**	1.45		**25**	**1.16**	**11.90** 9.52 + 2.38	**33.05** 26.44 + 6.61	**507.5** 20.3 x 25
	26%			**3**		**2**	**2**	**264.0** 88 x 3

Add travel time to first deco stop into bottom time and use 2 + 2 Rule for CNS and OTU calculations.

TOTALS (include residual values): CNS%: 54.38 OTU 132.21

Run Time 97 Gas Needed: Bottom Mix 4947 x 1.5 = 7420.5

Deco 757.5 x 1.2 = 909.0

Dive 1 Using IANTD/IAND, Inc. **EAN 26** Accelerated Dive Tables **EAN 26** used for deco – Imperial-US Version

FSW MSW	MIX	ATA	END	TIME	PO_2	%CNS	OTU	NEEDED
200 60		7.06						
190 57		6.76						
180 54		6.45						
170 51		6.15						
160 48		5.85						
150 45		5.55						
140 42	**26%**	5.24	**129**	**50**	**1.36**	**33.33**	**81.44**	**155.00** 3.1 x 50
130 39		4.94						
120 36		4.64						
110 33		4.33						
100 30		4.03						
90 27		3.73						
80 24		3.42						
70 21		3.12						
60 18		2.82						
50 15	**26%**	2.52		**2**	**.65**	**.32** .16 x 2	**.74** .37 x 2	**2.60** 1.3 x 2
40 12	**26%**	2.21		**6**	**.58**	**.83** .69 + .14	**1.57** 1.31 + .26	**6.60** 1.1 x 6
30 9	**26%**	1.91		**11**	**.50**	**0**	**0**	**11.00** 1.0 x 11
20 6	**26%**	1.61		**7**	**.42**	**0**	**0**	**5.60** 0.8 x 7
15 4.5	**26%**	1.45		**57**	**.34**	**0**	**0**	**39.9** 0.7 x 57
	26%			**3**		**2**	**2**	**9.30** 3.1 x 3

Add travel time to first deco stop into bottom time and use 2 + 2 Rule for CNS and OTU calculations.

TOTALS (include residual values): CNS% 36.48 OTU 85.75 Run Time 136

Gas Needed: Bottom Mix (155+2.6+6.6+11+5.6 + 39.9 + 9.3) x 1.5 = 345.0 Deco gas needed ______

Dive 1 Using IANTD/IAND, Inc. **EAN 26** Accelerated Dive Tables **EAN 26** used for deco - Metric Version

FSW MSW	MIX	ATA	END	TIME	PO_2	%CNS	OTU	NEEDED
200 60		7.0						
190 57		6.7						
180 54		6.4						
170 51		6.1						
160 48		5.8						
150 45		5.5						
140 42	**26%**	5.2	**38.7**	**50**	**1.35**	**30.30**	**77.67**	**4400.0** 88 x 50
130 39		4.9						
120 36		4.6						
110 33		4.3						
100 30		4.0						
90 27		3.7						
80 24		3.4						
70 21		3.1						
60 18		2.8						
50 15	**26%**	2.5		**2**	**.65**	**.32** .16 x 2	**.74** .37 x 2	**70.0** 35 x 2
40 12	**26%**	2.2		**6**	**.58**	**.83** .69 + .14	**1.57** 1.31 + .26	**186.0** 31 x 6
30 9	**26%**	1.9		**11**	**.50**	**0**	**0**	**297.0** 27 x 11
20 6	**26%**	1.6		**7**	**.42**	**0**	**0**	**154.0** 22 x 7
15 4.5	**26%**	1.45		**57**	**.34**	**0**	**0**	**1157.1** 20.3 x 57
	26%			**3**		**2**	**2**	**264.0** 88 x 3

Add travel time to first deco stop into bottom time and use 2 + 2 Rule for CNS and OTU calculations.

TOTALS (include residual values): CNS% 33.45 OTU 81.98 Run Time 136

Gas Needed: Bottom Mix 6528.1 x 1.5 = 9792.15 Deco gas needed ______

Dive 2 (repetitive dive) Using IANTD/IAND, Inc. EAN 29 Runtime Accelerated Dive Tables Imperial-US Version

FSW MSW	MIX	ATA	END	TIME	PO_2	%CNS	OTU	NEEDED
200 60		7.06						
190 57		6.76						
180 54		6.45						
170 51		6.15						
160 48		5.85						
150 45		5.55						
140 42		5.24						
130 39		4.94						
120 36		4.64						
110 33	**29%**	4.33	**96**	**40 actual**	**1.26**	**22.22**	**59.09**	**104** 2.6 x 40
100 30		4.03						
90 27		3.73						
80 24		3.42						
70 21		3.12						
60 18		2.82						
50 15		2.52						
40 12		2.21						
30 9	**80%**	1.91		**7 (50)**	**1.53**	**7.78** 5.56 + (1.11 x 2)	**12.96** 9.26 + (2 x 1.85)	**7.00** 1.0 x 7
20 6	**80%**	1.61		**5 (55)**	**1.28**	**2.78**	**7.39**	**4.00** 0.8 x 5
15 4.5	**80%**	1.45		**27 (82)**	**1.16**	**12.86** 9.52 + 2.38 + (.48 x 2)	**35.69** 26.44 +6.61+(1.32x2)	**18.9** 0.7 x 27
	29%			**3**		**2**	**2**	**7.8** 2.6 x 3

Add travel time to first deco stop into bottom time and use 2 + 2 Rule for CNS and OTU calculations.

TOTALS (include residual values): CNS%: 47.64 + 12 residual = 59.64 OTU 117.13 + 85.75 = 202.88

Run Time 82 RNT 40 (80 minute schedule)

Gas Needed: Bottom Mix 111.8 x 1.5 = 167.7 Deco 29.9 x 1.2 = 35.88

Dive 2 (repetitive dive) **Using IANTD/IAND, Inc. EAN 29 Runtime Accelerated Dive Tables - Metric Version**

FSW MSW	MIX	ATA	END	TIME	PO_2	%CNS	OTU	NEEDED
200 60		7.0						
190 57		6.7						
180 54		6.4						
170 51		6.1						
160 48		5.8						
150 45		5.5						
140 42		5.2						
130 39		4.9						
120 36		4.6						
110 33	**29%**	4.3	**28.7**	**40 actual**	**1.25**	**20.51**	**56.00**	**2920.0** 73 x 40
100 30		4.0						
90 27		3.7						
80 24		3.4						
70 21		3.1						
60 18		2.8						
50 15		2.5						
40 12		2.2						
30 9	**80%**	1.9		**7 (50)**	**1.52**	**7.78** 5.56 + (1.11 x 2)	**12.96** 9.26 + (2 x 1.85)	**189.0** 27 x 7
20 6	**80%**	1.6		**5 (55)**	**1.28**	**2.78**	**7.39**	**110.0** 22 x 5
15 4.5	**80%**	1.45		**27 (82)**	**1.16**	**12.86** 9.52 + 2.38 + (.48 x 2)	**35.69** 26.44 +6.61+(1.32x2)	**548.1** 20.3 x 27
	29%			**3**		**2**	**2**	**219.0** 73 x 3

Add travel time to first deco stop into bottom time and use 2 + 2 Rule for CNS and OTU calculations.

TOTALS (include residual values): CNS%: 45.93 + 12 residual = 57.93 OTU 114.04 + 81.98 = 196.02

Run Time 82 RNT 40 (80 minute schedule)

Gas Needed: Bottom Mix 3139.0 x 1.5 = 4708.5 Deco 847.1 x 1.2 = 1016.5

Dive 1 Using IANTD/IAND, Inc. VPM B Constant partial pressure Dive Tables – This example is for CCR using the CCR tables also includes bailout.

FSW MSW	MIX	ATA	END	TIME	Set point	%CNS	OTU	18 / 38 Team deep bailout 100 cubic feet (33 each) 3538.5 L (1,1795 L each)
200 60	**14** **44**	7.06	85 26	30 CCR BO	1.3			
190 57		6.76						
180 54		6.45						
170 51		6.15						
160 48		5.85						
150 45		5.55						
140 42		5.24						
130 39		4.94	33 (1)					
120 36		4.64	34 34 (1.) (2)					
110 33		4.33	**35** **(1)**					
100 30		4.03	**36 36** **(1) (2)**					
90 27		3.73	**37 38** **(1) (2)**					
80 24		3.42	**39 41** **(2) (3)**					
70 21		3.12	**42 44** **(3) (3)**					
60 18		2.82	**45 49** **(3) (5)**					
50 15		2.52	**49 56** **(4) (7)**		**CNS** **1.3.** **26.88**	OTU 1.3 71.04	
40 12		2.21	**54 60** **(5) (4)**	**1.4** **E 70**			EAN 70 bailout 171.16
30 9		1.91	**60 66** **(6) (6)**				
20 6		1.61	**64 71** **(4) (5)**		**CNS** **1.4** **16.25**	**OTU 1.4** **40.75**	
15 4.5		1.45	**84 93** **(20) (22)**				
Total			**84 93**		**43.13**	**111.79**	

This example is worked in the classroom with your IANTD Instructor and uses IANTD Waterproof Table C-3104. The IANTD Waterproof Bail-out Table is C-3717.

A repetitive dive is planned for two hours later to the same depth again for a 30-minute bottom time

Dive 1 Using IANTD/IAND, Inc. VPM B constant po2 table repetitive dive. Use the CCR tables 14/ 44 dil for repetitive dives.

FSW MSW	MIX	ATA	END	TIME	PO_2	%CNS	OTU	NEEDED
200 60	**14** **44**	7.0	85 26	30	1.3			18 / 38 Team deep bailout 100 cubic feet (33 each) 3538.5 L (1,1795 L each)
190 57		6.7						
180 54		6.4						
170 51		6.1						
160 48		5.8						
150 45		5.5						
140 42		5.2						
130 39		4.9		33 (1)				
120 36		4.6		34 (1)				
110 33		4.3		**35** **(1)**				
100 30		4.0		**36** **(1)**				
90 27		3.7		**37** **(1)**				
80 24		3.4		**39** **(2)**				
70 21		3.1		**42** **(3)**				
60 18		2.8		**45** **(3)**				
50 15		2.5		**49** **(5)**				
40 12		2.2		**54** **(5)**	**1.4** **E 70**			
30 9		1.9		**61** **(7)**				
20 6		1.6		**66** **(5)**				
15 4.5		1.45		**97** **(31)**				
				97				

**Add travel time to first deco stop into bottom time and use 2 + 2 Rule for CNS and OTU calcul

TOTALS (include residual values): CNS%: 48.61 OTU 117.13 Run Time 103

Gas Needed: Bottom Mix 5217.93 *x* 1.5 = 7825.5 Deco 637.8 *x* 1.2 = 765.36

Trimix Dive Using IANTD/IAND, Inc. Runtime Trimix Dive Tables – Imperial-US

FSW MSW	MIX	ATA	END	TIME	PO_2	%CNS	OTU	NEEDED
280 84	**14%** **48%**	**9.48**	**118**	**20**	**1.33**	**12.12**	**31.07**	**114.00** 5.7 x 20
200 60		7.06						
190 57		6.76						
180 54		6.45						
170 51		6.15						
160 48		5.85						
150 45		5.55						
140 42		5.24						
130 39	**14%** **48%**	4.94	**46**	**1 (24)**	**.69**	**.18** .18 x 1	**.47** .47 x 1	**2.50** 2.5 x 1
120 36	**14%** **48%**	4.64	**41**	**1 (25)**	**.65**	**.16** .16 x 1	**.37** .37 x 1	**2.30** 2.3 x 1
110 33	**14%** **48%**	4.33	**36**	**2 (27)**	**.61**	**.32** .16 x 2	**.74** .37 x 2	**4.40** 2.2 x 2
100 30	**36%**	4.03	**75**	**1 (28)**	**1.45**	**.72** .72 x 1	**1.70** 1.70 x 1	**2.00** 2.0 x 1
90 27	**36%**	3.73	**67**	**2 (30)**	**1.34**	**1.22** .61 x 2	**3.10** 1.55 x 2	**3.80** 1.9 x 2
80 24	**36%**	3.42	**59**	**2 (32)**	**1.23**	**1.02** .51 x 2	**2.8** 1.4 x 2	**3.40** 1.7 x 2
70 21	**36%**	3.12	**51**	**4 (36)**	**1.12**	**1.76** .44 x 4	**4.96** 1.24 x 4	**6.40** 1.6 x 4
60 18	**36%**	2.82	**43**	**4 (40)**	**1.01**	**1.48** .37 x 4	**4.32** 1.08 x 4	**5.60** 1.4 x 4
50 15	**36%**	2.52	**35**	**6 (46)**	**.91**	**1.88** 1.57 + .31	**5.50** 4.58 + .92	**7.80** 1.3 x 6
40 12	**36%**	2.21	**27**	**8 (54)**	**.80**	**1.77** 1.11 + (.22 x 3)	**5.22** 3.27 + (.65 x 3)	**8.80** 1.1 x 8
30 9	**80%**	1.91		**11** **(65)**	**1.53**	**12.22** 11.11 + 1.11	**20.36** 18.51 + 1.85	**11.00** 1.0 x 11
20 6	**80%**	1.61		**6** **(71)**	**1.28**	**3.34** 2.78 + .56	**8.87** 7.39 + 1.48	**4.80** 0.8 x 6
15 4.5	**80%**	1.45		**45** **(116)**	**1.16**	**21.43** 19.05 + 2.38	**59.50** 52.89 + 6.61	**31.50** .7 x 45
	14% **48%**			**3**		**2**	**2**	**17.18** 5.7 x 3

**Add travel time to first deco stop into bottom time and use 2 + 2 Rule for CNS and OTU calculations

TOTALS (include residual values): CNS%: 61.62 OTU 150.98

Run Time 116 Gas Needed: Bottom Mix (114 + 2.5 + 2.3 + 4.4 + 17.18) x 1.5 = 210.57

Travel gas (2 + 3.8 + 3.4 + 6.4 + 5.6 + 7.8 + 8.8) x 1.2 = 45.36 Deco (11 + 4.8 + 31.50) x 1.2 = 56.76

Trimix Dive Using IANTD/IAND, Inc. Runtime Trimix Dive Tables – Metric Version

FSW MSW	MIX	ATA	END	TIME	PO_2	%CNS	OTU	NEEDED
280 84	**14% 48%**	**9.5**	**35.7**	**20**	**1.32**	**12.12**	**31.07**	**3200.0** 160 x 20
200 60		7.0						
190 57		6.7						
180 54		6.4						
170 51		6.1						
160 48		5.8						
150 45		5.5						
140 42		5.2						
130 39	**14% 48%**	4.9	**13.6**	**1 (24)**	**.69**	**.18** .18 x 1	**.47** .47 x 1	**69.0** 69 x 1
120 36	**14% 48%**	4.6	**12.1**	**1 (25)**	**.64**	**.16** .16 x 1	**.37** .37 x 1	**64.0** 64 x 1
110 33	**14% 48%**	4.3	**10.7**	**2 (27)**	**.60**	**.28** .14 x 2	**.52** .26 x 2	**120.0** 60 x 2
100 30	**36%**	4.0	**22.4**	**1 (28)**	**1.45**	**.72** .72 x 1	**1.70** 1.70 x 1	**56.0** 56 x 1
90 27	**36%**	3.7	**20.0**	**2 (30)**	**1.34**	**1.22** .61 x 2	**3.10** 1.55 x 2	**104.0** 52x 2
80 24	**36%**	3.4	**17.5**	**2 (32)**	**1.23**	**1.02** .51 x 2	**2.8** 1.4 x 2	**96.0** 48 x 2
70 21	**36%**	3.1	**15.1**	**4 (36)**	**1.12**	**1.76** .44 x 4	**4.96** 1.24 x 4	**172.0** 43 x 4
60 18	**36%**	2.8	**12.7**	**4 (40)**	**1.04**	**1.48** .37 x 4	**4.32** 1.08 x 4	**152**00 60
50 15	**36%**	2.5	**10.3**	**6 (46)**	**.91**	**1.67** 1.39 + .28	**4.98** 4.15 + .83	**210.0** 35 x 6
40 12	**36%**	2.2	**7.8**	**8 (54)**	**.80**	**1.77** 1.11 + (.22 x 3)	**5.22** 3.27 + (.65 x 3)	**248.0** 31 x 8
30 9	**80%**	1.9		**11 (65)**	**1.53**	**12.22** 11.11 + 1.11	**20.36** 18.51 + 1.85	**297.0** 27 x 11
20 6	**80%**	1.6		**6 (71)**	**1.29**	**3.34** 2.78 + .56	**8.87** 7.39 + 1.48	**132.0** 22 x 6
15 4.5	**80%**	1.45		**45 (116)**	**1.16**	**21.43** 19.05 + 2.38	**59.50** 52.89 + 6.61	**913.5** 20.3 x 45
	14% 48%			**3**		**2**	**2**	**480.0** 160 x 3

**Add travel time to first deco stop into bottom time and use 2 + 2 Rule for CNS and OTU calculation

TOTALS (include residual values): CNS%: 61.37 OTU 150.24

Run Time 116 Gas Needed: Bottom Mix 3933.0 x 1.5 = 5899.5

Travel gas 1042.0 x 1.2 = 1250.4 Deco 1342.5 x 1.2 = 1611.0

PRE-DIVE ESSENTIAL DIVE PREPARATION VERIFICATION

Complete prior to boarding vessel or preparing to don equipment. Checks to be completed early enough to be able to fix problems if any exist without becoming stressed or rushed. All checks on this sheet to be completed by each diver and cross referenced between dive team members.

- ☐ **Verify self & buddy completed mfg. equipment set-up and mfg. Check Sheets.**
- ☐ Verify gas delivery system CCR & Bailout operational.
- ☐ **Verify system continues to hold during both positive & negative pressure checks.**
- ☐ Verify analysis of all gases to be used on dive.
- ☐ **Verify calibration.**
- ☐ Verify cylinders are labeled for use.

CCR "S" Self & Buddy Check (S = Safety = Survival)

Team safety depends on teamwork; safety and survival are enhanced by S drills completed for each dive. It is the team's responsibility to KNOW all systems are functional for everyone.

Note! Always do "S" Drill on surface. Environment dependent if possible repeat applicable steps in-water!

Within 15 minutes of starting ANY dive:

- ☐ **Reaffirm adequate bailout gas available. Self & Buddies**
- ☐ Reaffirm gas pressure of all cylinders to be used on dive. Self & Buddies
- ☐ **Confirm ALL gases are turned on. Self & Buddies**
- ☐ Confirm no detectable leakages of gases or loop integrity. Self & Buddies
- ☐ **Confirm gas addition oxygen (solenoid ECCR or orifice MCCR). Self & Buddies**
- ☐ Confirm manual oxygen addition. Self & Buddies
- ☐ **Confirm A.D.V. activates and manual operation. Self & Buddies**
- ☐ Confirm bailout gas delivery system functional. Self & Buddies
- ☐ **Confirm breathing loop delivery. Self & Buddies**
- ☐ Confirm pre-breathe/PO_2 held & scrubber canister functionality on surface. Self & Buddies
- ☐ **Confirm all electronic systems agree - primary, secondary, etc. Self & Buddies**
- ☐ Confirm D.S.V. or B.O.V. functional -> Self & Buddies
- ☐ **Confirm ability to switch to a bailout -> Self & Buddies**
- ☐ Confirm compatibility of "pluggable" off-board gases in the dive team. Self & Buddies
- ☐ **Confirm on completion CCR is functional (Gases on – Safe PO_2 in loop) – do not turn electronics or gases off until post dive. Self & Buddies**
- ☐ Confirm support equipment (lights, reels, etc.) functional. Self & Buddies
- ☐ **Confirm divers are familiar with each others systems & configuration. Self & Buddies**

Always Know Your PO_2 - Verify Buddy's PO_2 Frequently

Always Know Your Scrubber Canister Contents Is Within Safe Usage Limit

IANTD® THE LEADERS IN DIVER EDUCATION

Immediately prior to every submergence or water entry

Quick Individual Safety Check

- ☐ Reaffirm all gas delivery systems on and functional.
- ☐ Reaffirm safe PO_2 self & buddy - O_2 delivery working.
- ☐ Reaffirm A.D.V. is on if applicable.
- ☐ Reaffirm manual addition working.

In-water "S" Check

- ☐ Upon entry in water, if possible, leak check buddy if environment does not allow a surface check - leak check on descent or immediately upon completion of descent.
- ☐ Confirm self & buddy switch to desired PO_2 and maintain it.
- ☐ If practical, check bailout to ensure that it is completely functional.
- ☐ Be observant for any abnormal behavior in dive performance.
- ☐ Know and avoid the causes of accidents.
- ☐ *Enjoy the dive!*

Accidents don't happen by themselves
Be prudent and study common causes
Be responsible and choose not to create them
Practice survival skills and survival habits, ideally with dive partners
Go beyond drills, complete the intent of training; turn it into learning = knowing

Always Know Your PO_2 - Verify Buddy's PO_2 Frequently

Always Know Your Scrubber Canister Contents Is Within Safe Usage Limit

IANTD Isobaric Counter Diffusion Chart ~ Side 1

5:1 Ratio permits 1% increase in N_2 for each 5% decrease in He

	% He																			
FO2	**90**	**85**	**80**	**75**	**70**	**65**	**60**	**55**	**50**	**45**	**40**	**35**	**30**	**25**	**20**	**15**	**10**	**5**	**0**	**FO2**
.7	3	8	13	18	23	28	33	38	43	48	53	58	63	68	73	78				.7
.8	2	7	12	17	22	27	32	37	42	47	52	57	62	67	72	77				.8
.9	1	6	11	16	21	26	31	36	41	46	51	56	61	66	71	76				.9
.10	0	5	10	15	20	25	30	35	40	45	50	55	60	65	70	75				.10
.11	0	4	9	14	19	24	29	34	39	44	49	54	59	64	69	74	79			.11
.12	0	3	8	13	18	23	28	33	38	43	48	53	58	63	68	73	78			.12
.13		2	7	12	17	22	27	32	37	42	47	52	57	62	67	72	77			.13
.14		1	6	11	16	21	26	31	36	41	46	51	56	61	66	71	76			.14
.15		0	5	10	15	20	25	30	35	40	45	50	55	60	65	70	75			.15
.16			4	9	14	19	24	29	34	39	44	49	54	59	64	69	74	79		.16
.17			3	8	13	18	23	28	33	38	43	48	53	58	63	68	73	78		.17
.18			2	7	12	17	22	27	32	37	42	47	52	57	62	67	72	77		.18
.19			1	6	11	16	21	26	31	36	41	46	51	56	61	66	71	76		.19
.20				5	10	14	20	25	30	35	40	45	50	55	60	65	70	75		.20
.21			%		9	13	19	24	29	34	39	44	49	54	59	64	69	74	79	.21
.22			N			12	18	23	28	33	38	43	48	53	58	63	68	73	78	.22
.23			I			11	17	22	27	32	37	42	47	52	57	62	67	72	77	.23
.24			T			10	16	21	26	31	36	41	46	51	56	61	66	71	76	.24
.25			R	→			15	20	25	30	35	40	45	50	55	60	65	70	75	.25
.26			O					19	24	29	34	39	43	49	54	59	64	69	74	.26
.27			G					18	23	28	33	38	42	48	53	58	63	68	73	.27
.28			E						22	27	32	37	41	47	52	57	62	67	72	.28
.29			N						21	26	31	36	40	46	51	56	61	66	71	.29
.30			(FN_2)						20	25	30	35	39	45	50	55	60	65	70	.30
.31										24	29	34	38	44	49	54	59	64	69	.31
.32										23	28	33	37	43	48	53	58	63	68	.32
.33								%		22	27	32	36	42	47	52	57	62	67	.33
.34								N			26	31	35	41	46	51	56	61	66	.34
.35								I			25	30	34	40	45	50	55	60	65	.35
.36								T			24	29	33	39	44	49	54	59	64	.36
.37								R	→		23	28	32	38	43	48	53	58	63	.37
.38								O			22	27	31	37	42	47	52	57	62	.38
.39								G			21	26	30	36	41	46	51	56	61	.39
.40								E			20	25	29	35	40	45	50	55	60	.40
.41								N				24	28	34	39	44	49	54	59	.41
.42								(FN_2)				23	27	33	38	43	48	53	58	.42
.43												22	26	32	37	42	47	52	57	.43
.44													25	31	36	41	46	51	56	.44
.45													24	30	35	40	45	50	55	.45
.46													23	29	34	39	44	49	54	.46
.47													22	28	33	38	43	48	53	.47
.48													21	27	32	37	42	47	52	.48
.49													20	26	31	36	41	46	51	.49
.50													19	25	30	35	40	45	50	.50
.55													18	20	25	30	35	40	45	.55
.60													17	15	20	25	30	35	40	.60
.65													16	10	15	20	25	30	35	.65
.70													15	5	10	15	20	25	30	.70
.80													14	0	0	5	10	15	20	.80
.99																0	0	0	1	.99

NOTE: increments of 5 ↓

Designed by Jeff Johnson IANTD Instructor/IT

1) Start on Chart Side 2 determine Max PO_2 1.6 for depth **2)** Go to Side 1 & locate the corresponding FO_2 line **3)** Slide across line to N_2 < or = N_2 of previous gas **4)** Look at top of column for appropriate % He -> N_2 may be increased by 1% for each 5% reduction of He **5)** Subtract N_2 increase from He to yield 100%

Example: 200 fsw / 60 msw make another gas switch from 12/60/28 (O_2/He/N_2) **1)** Go to Chart Side 2 to determine Max FO_2 in PO_2 section **2)** At 200 fsw /60 msw line cross to Max Safe PO_2 of 1.6 to find 22% O_2 **3)** Side 1 in O_2 column find 22% and slide right **4)** Our last N_2 was 28, if we slid right on the 22% O_2 we find 28 which is < or = our last gas N_2 **5)** 28 N_2 is in the 50% He column **6)** He has been reduced by 10% so N_2 can be increased 2% **7)** 28 + 2 = 30% N_2 **8)** Remove the 2 extra % from the He for a **22/48/30** (O_2/He/N_2) mix = 100%

Depth	END For use with IANTD Isobaric Chart													END
Depth	140	130	120	110	100	90	80	70	60	50	40	30	20	10
fsw / msw	42	39	36	33	30	27	24	21	18	15	12	9	6	3
400 / 120	31	29	27	26	24	22	20	18	17	15	13	11	9	7
390 / 117	32	30	28	26	24	22	21	19	17	15	13	11	9	8
380 / 114	33	31	29	27	25	23	21	19	17	15	13	12	10	8
370 / 111	33	31	29	28	26	24	22	20	18	16	14	12	10	8
360 / 108	34	32	30	28	26	24	22	20	18	16	14	12	10	8
350 / 105	35	33	31	29	27	25	23	21	19	17	15	12	10	8
340 / 102	36	34	32	30	28	26	23	21	19	17	15	13	11	9
330 / 99	37	35	33	31	28	26	24	22	20	18	15	13	11	9
320 / 96	38	36	34	32	29	27	25	23	20	18	16	14	11	9
310 / 93	39	37	35	32	30	28	26	23	21	19	16	14	12	9
300 / 90	41	38	36	33	31	29	26	24	22	19	17	14	12	10
290 / 87	42	39	37	34	32	30	27	25	22	20	17	15	12	10
280 / 84	43	41	38	36	33	31	28	25	23	20	18	15	13	10
270 / 81	45	42	39	37	34	32	29	26	24	21	19	16	13	11
260 / 78	46	43	41	38	35	33	30	27	25	22	19	16	14	11
250 / 75	48	45	42	39	37	34	31	28	25	23	20	17	14	12
240 / 72	50	47	44	41	38	35	32	29	26	24	21	18	15	12
230 / 69	51	48	45	42	39	36	33	30	27	24	21	18	15	12
220 / 66	54	50	47	44	41	38	35	32	29	25	22	19	16	13
210 / 63	56	52	49	46	43	39	36	33	30	26	23	20	17	13
200 / 60	58	55	51	48	45	41	38	34	31	28	24	21	17	14
190 / 57	61	57	54	50	47	43	40	36	32	29	25	22	18	15
180 / 54	64	60	56	53	49	45	41	38	34	30	27	23	19	15
170 / 51	67	63	59	55	51	47	43	40	36	32	28	24	20	16
160 / 48	70	66	62	58	54	50	46	42	38	33	29	25	21	17
150 / 45	74	70	66	61	57	53	48	44	40	35	31	27	22	18
140 / 42		74	69	65	60	56	51	47	42	37	33	28	24	19
130 / 39			74	69	64	59	54	49	45	40	35	30	25	20
120 / 36				73	68	63	58	53	48	42	37	32	27	22
110 / 33		FN2 →			73	67	62	56	51	45	40	34	29	23
100 / 30						73	67	61	55	49	43	37	31	25
90 / 27							72	66	59	53	46	40	34	27
80 / 24								72	65	58	51	44	37	30
70 / 21									71	63	55	48	40	32
60 / 18							FN2 →			70	62	53	45	36
50 / 15											69	59	50	40
40 / 12												68	57	46
30 / 9													66	53

Depth	PO2							
fsw / msw	1.6	1.5	1.4	1.3	1.2	1.1	1.0	
400 / 120	12	11	10	9	9	8	7	
390 / 117	12	11	10	10	9	8	7	F
380 / 114	12	11	11	10	9	8	7	O
370 / 111	13	12	11	10	9	9	8	2
360 / 108	13	12	11	10	10	9	8	
350 / 105	13	12	12	11	10	9	8	
340 / 102	14	13	12	11	10	9	8	
330 / 99	14	13	12	11	10	10	9	
320 / 96	14	14	13	12	11	10	9	
310 / 93	15	14	13	12	11	10	9	F
300 / 90	15	14	13	12	11	10	9	O
290 / 87	16	15	14	13	12	11	10	2
280 / 84	16	15	14	13	12	11	10	
270 / 81	17	16	15	14	13	11	10	
260 / 78	18	16	15	14	13	12	11	
250 / 75	18	17	16	15	13	12	11	
240 / 72	19	18	16	15	14	13	12	F
230 / 69	20	18	17	16	15	13	12	O
220 / 66	20	19	18	16	15	14	13	2
210 / 63	21	20	19	17	16	14	13	
200 / 60	22	21	19	18	16	15	14	
190 / 57	23	22	20	19	17	16	14	
180 / 54	24	23	21	20	18	17	15	
170 / 51	26	24	22	21	19	17	16	
160 / 48	27	25	23	22	20	18	17	F
150 / 45	28	27	25	23	21	19	18	O
140 / 42	30	28	26	24	22	20	19	2
130 / 39	32	30	28	26	24	22	20	
120 / 36	34	32	30	28	25	23	21	
110 / 33	36	34	32	30	27	25	23	
100 / 30	39	37	34	32	29	27	24	
90 / 27	42	40	37	34	32	29	26	
80 / 24	46	43	40	37	35	32	29	
70 / 21	51	48	44	41	38	35	32	
60 / 18	56	53	49	46	42	39	35	
50 / 15	63	59	55	51	47	43	39	
40 / 12	72	67	63	58	54	49	45	
30 / 9	83	78	73	68	62	57	52	
	1.6	1.5	1.4	1.3	1.2	1.1	1.0	

Designed by Jeff Johnson IANTD Instructor/IT

Side 2

Helium REQUIRED for any mix with FO2 less than 21 percent

1. On Side 2 enter line at proposed gas switch depth: example: 200 fsw / 60 msw
2. Find FN2 of proposed gas switch from Side 1 example of 28 + 2 = 30% N2
3. Now go back to Side 2 & look up column to check END: in this example END is less than 60 fsw / 18 msw
FN2 and FO2 listed should not be used for mixing. They are rounded down to remain within safe parameters of field e.g., FO2 is inside the safe PO2 as listed and FN2 is within limits of END

Gas 1

We are planning a dive to 400 fsw / 120 msw utilizing 8/60/32 (O_2/He/N_2)
Determine isobaric shift that is within 5:1 Rule
We'll calculate a bailout from CCR to OC which will, after initial bailout, be applicable to either OC or CCR

For every 5% Helium dropped, the N_2 can be raised 1%

1. Leaving 8/60/32 look at Isobaric Chart Side 2; PO_2 of 1.6 @ 400 fsw / 120 msw permits FO_2 of 12%
2. Chart Side 2 determines that Max PO_2 1.6 is 12% FO_2
3. Go to Chart Side 1 for isobaric determination
4. In O_2 column at 12% line slide right to 60% He column
5. Intersecting lines of O_2 and He fractions yields N_2 less than that in the previous mix for a safe isobaric switch from 8/60/32 (O_2/He/N_2) to **12/60/28** (O_2/He/N_2) at 400 fsw / 120 msw

At 200 fsw / 60 msw make another gas switch

Go to Chart Side 2 to determine Max FO_2 in PO_2 section
1. At 200 fsw / 60 msw line slide right to max safe PO_2 of 1.6 to find 22% O_2
2. Return to Chart Side 1
3. In O_2 column find 22% and slide right
4. Our last N_2 was 28; if we slide right on the 22% O_2 we find 28 which is equal to or less than our last gas N_2
5. 28 N_2 is located in the 50% He column
6. He has been reduced by 10% so N_2 can be increased by 2% --> 28 + 2 = 30% Nitrogen
7. Remove the 2 extra % from the He for a **22/48/30** mix (O_2/He/N_2) at 200 fsw / 60 msw

Next, we would like to perform another gas switch at 100 fsw / 30 msw
1. Check Chart Side 2 for Max PO_2 of 1.6 yielding an FO_2 of 39%
2. Go to Chart Side 1 and O_2 column, FO_2 line of 39%
3. Our last N_2 was 30; if we slide right on the 39% O_2 we find 30 which is equal to or less than our last gas N_2
4. Look up to the top of Column to find the He content of 30% which is a reduction of 18% He permitting an increase of 3% N_2 (per 5:1 Rule). This would yield **39/28/33** (O_2/He/N_2) at 100 fsw / 30 msw
5. Reduce the He % content by the amount that we increased the N_2% content
6. In this case due to rounding on the chart we only need to decrease He by 2% (39 + 28 + 33 = 100%)
7. Note, the slower tissues control the shallower depth deco stops and are less susceptible to isobaric counter diffusion issues. The 5:1 Rule is also a guideline to limit the possibility however it is ***not*** an absolute

Gas switch desired to 50% FO_2?
1. Check Side 2 for Max PO_2 of 1.6 depth
2. We see that the switch can be made at 70 fsw / 21 msw
3. Go back to Chart Side 1 & slide right across 50% FO_2 line to find last gas N_2 or less (33%)
4. 30% N_2 is found in the 20% He column for a reduction of 8% He
5. We can increase the N_2 by 1% to 34%
6. Because we added 4% to the Chart N_2 of 30%, we will now subtract 4% from the He %
7. This yields a 50/16/34 (O_2/He/N_2) mix. Perhaps this is not the best mix so let's look for a better mix

Let's look at EAN 80
1. Chart Side 2 demonstrates that at a PO_2 of 1.6 a 30 fsw / 9 msw switch is possible
2. Chart Side 2 in the FO_2 column line of 80% shows that we have 20% N_2, which is less than the N_2 in our last mix thus permitting a safe 5:1 Rule switch with **EAN 80** at 30 fsw / 9 msw

The above example illustrates a CCR dive implementing 4 OC bailout gas switches beginning at 400 fsw / 120 msw all the way to the surface effectively managing PO_2 levels and isobaric counter diffusion issues.

Chapter Twelve Gas Management For Rebreathers

Kevin Gurr &
Tom Mount D.Sc., Ph.D., N.D.

Rebreather diving presents new challenges for technical diving gas management protocals. At the CCR diver level, it is simple enough for a CCR diver to plan their bailout gas supply based on the amount of gas necessary to get to the surface if solo diving. In technical diving, the process is more involved due to the emphasis on buddy teams, and the need to ensure that adequate gas is carried to meet team needs. In contrast, solo divers simply carry adequate gas for a safe return to the surface based on their respiratory minute volume (RMV). For the solo diver, the amount of gas carried is independent of whether they are diving on OC or on CCR. This chapter is broken into two sections, the first by Kevin Gurr and the second by Tom Mount. Both Gurr's and Mount's views emphasize diving with the minimum amount of safe bailout gas necessary to safely reach the surface, whether as a team or as a solo diver.

Section One ~ Kevin Gurr

Open-circuit cave diving has given us the basic set of rules that we deem a minimum requirement for safe diving in overhead environments.

The prime rule for gas management used in this environment is the ***Rule of Thirds*** states that you will finish the dive with 1/3rd of your gas remaining.

This rule assumes the following:

- Gas matching calculations conducted should take into consideration the following:
  - o Individual breathing rates
  - o Water flow (high flow, siphon/spring)

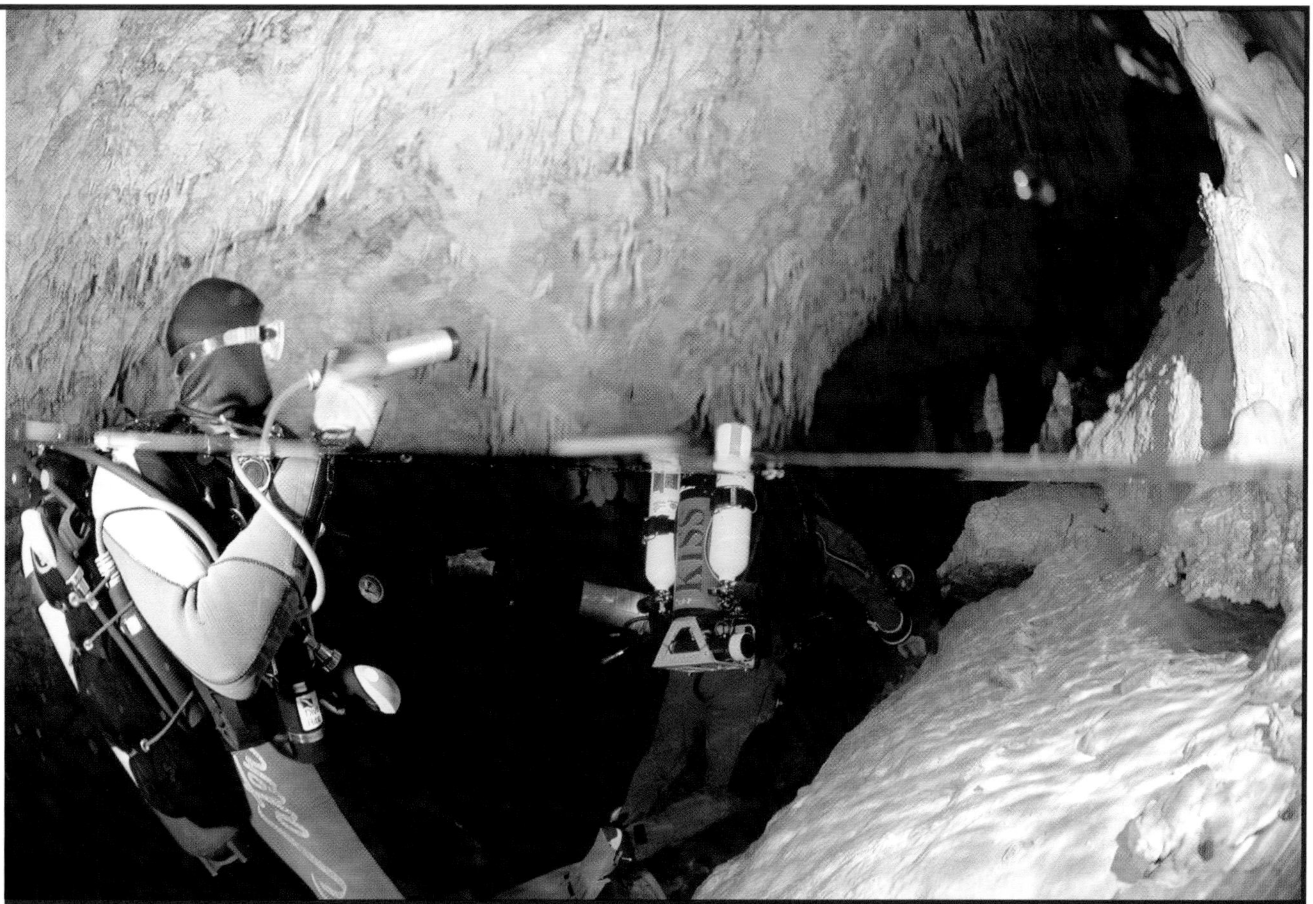

Mel Clark

Francisco Marte & Curt McNamee entering a cave in the Dominican Republic

- Conditions, i.e. visibility, silt, etc.
- Total volume of gas available
- Distance/time of travel
- Equipment redundancy

The concept of equipment redundancy is often "glossed over." While divers appreciate the basic concept, the subtlety of how it affects the gas management rules is often misunderstood.

For the rule of thirds to work, the equipment assumptions are two-fold:

1. In a 2-man team emergency, where another diver has an equipment failure and has to share your gas, you (having used gas matching calculations) will have enough gas for them and you to exit (ignoring excessive stress/gas usage)
2. Where you are solo or separated and you lose one of your two primary regulators/gas supplies, you have one breathing system remaining and (assuming fast enough reactions) at least 50% of your gas remaining to finish the dive

Hence, both of these scenarios assume a fully functioning secondary system with enough gas for you or anyone in your team to safely exit the dive. Obviously, the worst case scenarios occur most frequently when solo diving or when a 2-man team is separated.The Rule of thirds works for both of these.

This concept is basically the result of a historical Failure Mode and Effect Analysis (***FMEA***). This is a standard engineering principle. I do not believe it was ever ***officially*** tested, but has merely evolved.

While the rule of thirds has proven to be a safe minimum, many divers will testify that is a ***minimum*** and often barely enough to exit safely.

Let's look at the gas volume issues as we move on to Closed Circuit Rebreathers and the concept of ***Team Bailout***. Team bailout assumes that the team will carry 1½ times (1½ ***x***) the gas needed for anyone to exit. Hence if a team (having used gas matching rules) finds that it can penetrate for 30 minutes, then the team will carry 45 minutes of gas between them.

As an example of ***team gas management***, if either gas management rules or, in a 2-person team, the diver with the highest RMV deems that 8 L, or liters (a metric measurement referring to the amount of unpressurized gas a tank will

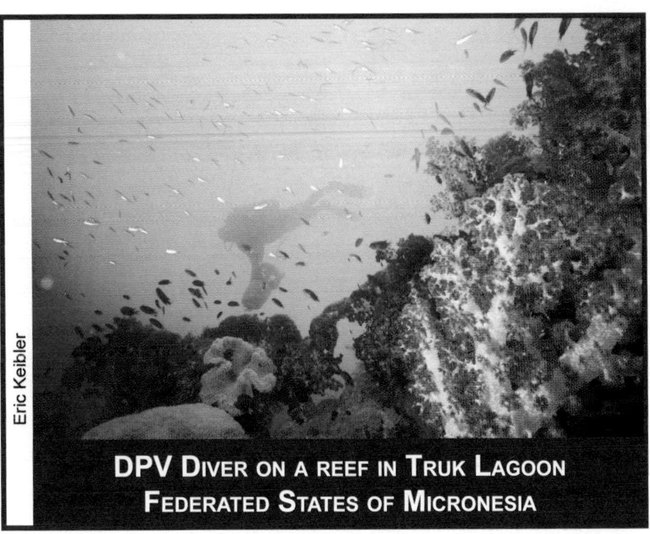

Eric Keibler

DPV Diver on a reef in Truk Lagoon
Federated States of Micronesia

hold) of gas is needed to exit, the divers will carry 12 L between them. An additional safety factor often added is that no matter how many people are in the team each diver will carry one half of the required 88 cu ft (12 L) bailout (rather than dividing the 88 cu ft (12 L) by the number of divers in the team as is the basic concept) in other words each diver will carry 37.5 cu ft (6 L) of gas.

Hence, in a 4-man team, each team member will have 37.5 cu ft (6 L) of gas to share or exit alone. Bear in mind 63 cu ft (8 L) will be needed for one diver to exit; it is assumed cylinder switching/long hose sharing will be needed.

This rule further assumes:

- Any off-board connections are cross-compatible
- If used, wing/suit inflations systems are compatible
- Bailout cylinders can be swapped and divers are proficient in the practice
- The environment is suitable for good communication and has enough room for divers to manoeuvre
- The out-of-gas diver does not become separated during the exit

When diving solo, the diver always carries enough gas to exit (***plus stress reserve***) as they only have themselves to worry about. The advantage that rebreathers give us in overhead environments (for example, assuming 30 minutes of bailout gas) is that you could firstly do a 30 minute penetration, then travel towards the exit for a period (say 10 minutes) and then explore in another direction for the period you spent swimming towards the exit (10 minutes). This process can be done repeatedly towards the exit, given that canister durations are not exceeded. With CCRs, the canister and gas supply usually results in longer dives than on open-circuit.

Team Bailout does not work in situations where the team becomes separated. In the above example, the separated diver is carrying a portion of the team bailout gas supply. If a team member must bailout at the maximum point of penetration or even near to it, the team will not have enough gas to exit.

This is where Team Bailout breaks the Open Circuit FMEA rule established above.

Again the Open Circuit FMEA assumes you have a fully redundant secondary system with a suitable gas volume to exit safely alone, whether in a team or not.

The current FMEA for rebreather designs assumes an open circuit system will be used in the event of a catastrophic failure. This is applicable as no commercially available designs currently have redundant breathing loops, making this a single point of failure that should be backed up.

So where the OC diver switches to another open circuit system, so does the rebreather diver. This fulfils the FMEA. Where the FMEA rule for a rebreather team bailout does not match the "**1½ *x*** gas needed" rule is in the amount of gas carried by the team in case of emergency.

So given the same failure scenario and corrective action, why should the gas management rules change?

The reasons are often voiced as:

1. The need to keep the rebreather diver streamlined
2. In a team gas failure scenario, other team members have more time to assist the out of gas diver

While item 2 has some validity, the following must be considered:

- The donor divers end up with less gas for their own subsequent emergencies during the exit
- Separated divers may not have enough gas to exit in an emergency

Gas Management Rules

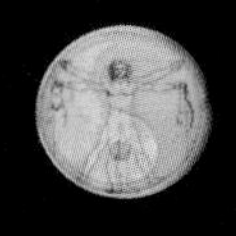

All Gas Management Rules are based on maintaining "normal" behavior in an abnormal situation

So in summary, we adhere to one rule for open circuit diving but appear to break it for closed circuit on the following assumptions:

1. We will never exit alone, having started the dive in a team configuration
2. Other team members have more time to assist the out-of-gas diver
3. The environment will always allow for good (visible) communications and allow enough room to manoeuvre
4. All team members have compatible gas connection systems
5. All divers are proficient in cylinder swapping drills

While developing safe diving systems and "rules" can just be a function of maths and logic it can also be a function of probability. In other words in the "real world" how many times do all the elements of the problem actually manifest themselves and in the Team Bailout example, mean we exit alone or are subject to the other variables above.

While the rule of third's over time has given us statistics and hence probability to work with, the "Team Bailout" concept may require more real-life appraisal before it can be deemed "probability sound."

In the end we should be able to set a minimum standard which may have acceptable, more conservative adjustments for environment/equipment variables. That said, we must be careful not to break rules we have already set either for convenience sake or because we forget why they were set in the first place.

Section Two
~ *Tom Mount*

The CCR **1½ *x*** bailout gas needed to bailout from the maximum distance, time or depth of a dive endorsed by IANTD Standards was experimented with for two years in both cave and OW. These took place in depths up to 400 fsw (120 msw) and penetrations of 4000 ft (1333 m) in caves. Over 20 instructors on actual dives tested the CCR 1½ ***x*** bailout rule. These rules have been used in major explorations by many including me, Martin Robson, John Jones, etc. Members of Michael Barnette's Association of Underwater Explorers (AUE) also used the 1½ ***x*** bailout gas rule when they were relining Eagles Nest, part of a Central Florida cave system, as well as on numerous deep wreck and other cave dives. In addition, once they were validated, they

were voted in to the IANTD Program by the international Board of Advisors, Licensees and the BOD of IANTD. These rules have also been adopted by the NSS-CDS based on IANTD's extensive testing.

Whereas the CCR bailout rule underwent rigorous testing the rule of thirds was introduced based on a logical thought process with out actual testing. The rule was introduced by Deperni, Wolf and Dickens and came to popularity through the efforts of Sheck Exley. Many reading this, most likely are not aware of how this history came to be as only a few of us who were cave diving at that time are still active in cave diving today. Due to its history, it was accepted throughout OC diving as we know it today. The following discussion will explain and compare the rule of thirds and the more modern rule of 1½ *x* bailout gas.

Open Circuit Rule of Thirds

If we analyze accepted gas management procedures, we discover the following:

1. In open-circuit diving using the rule of thirds, if an emergency occurs at the time the matched gas divers are the farthest point from the surface, there will be adequate gas to exit
   - a. However, this will result in an exit with exactly zero gas left in the cylinders
   - b. If the gas has not been matched based on differences in RMV then there will not be adequate gas to exit
   - c. With matched gas, should the divers have an increase in RMV due to stress (which is quite likely) there will not be enough gas to exit
   - d. If the diver team slows down during the exit, it is quite likely that there will not be enough gas for the team to exit safely
   - e. If the divers become separated and one has a total failure, then that diver will most likely die
     - i. If the dive is one that has a high probability of the divers becoming separated, using an additional bailout cylinder or larger stage bottle is recommended; it is as if the divers were solo diving. (It has been observed that many solo dive fatalities may have been avoided if the divers had used additional, or larger, bailout cylinders.) The additional gas is only to be used in event of a total gas failure when separated or diving solo. The extra gas supply is therefore functioning as a "dive partner" in regard to emergency-gas availability
   - f. In the highly unlikely event that all divers on the team experience a total rebreather failure, then all team members will most likely die. However, this type of incident is virtually unheard of, and only addressed herein due to questions some OC divers posed regarding this particular scenario regarding CCR diving
     - i. Cautious divers may consider carrying a bailout cylinder similar to that used by a CCR diver
     - ii. There may be merit in using the CCR 1½ *x* bailout gas rule (review below) for OC divers
   - g. The relative merits of the 1½ *x* bailout gas rule may bring up the question as to why the rule of thirds is considered safe for OC diving. **The answer, which is outlined i. - iv., is simple:**
     - i. The probability of an emergency at the maximum distance or time from the surface is low
     - ii. The probability of a dual total gas failure is also low
     - iii. The rule assumes the divers will not become separated, as they are diving as a team
     - iv. Statistically, the rule of thirds has worked and has a history that enables it to be accepted as safe. I feel it is a safe rule and it is the industry standard. As can be seen in a worst-case scenario, it most likely has drawbacks

CCR 1½ *x* Bailout Gas Needed Rule

1. The team gas management CCR 1½ *x* bailout rule works like this: The team takes the highest RMV among team members and multiplies the amount of gas needed for that diver to execute a safe exit from the maximum point of penetration, distance, or depth by 1½ and then divides that number by two. (The rule actually allows a division by three, which in testing worked on maximum distance predictions and in depths up to 400 fsw, or 120 msw.) However, it is recommended that no matter how many divers are on the team, the division is made as if there were only two divers. As an additional safety factor, all team members carry this amount of gas (½ the amount needed based on two divers using the CCR 1½ *x* bailout gas rule). The bailout cylinders are exchanged once the diver who has bailed out uses 50% of the gas in a cylinder. The process is repeated each time 50% of the gas is used per bailout cylinder
   - a. The rule of thirds is designed so that upon exiting or surfacing the dive team will have 33% of the total gas remaining. This enables each diver to have

bailout gas (16.5%) upon reaching the surface

i. ***Example:*** 100 cu ft (15 L) of gas is needed by the diver with the highest RMV to exit from the most extreme point of the dive. Using the 1½ ***x*** bailout gas rule, the team will carry 1½ ***x*** 100 cu ft (15 L), which equals 150 cu ft (21.5 L). Each diver in the team will then carry 75 cu ft (11 L) of bailout gas.

Should a catastrophic gas emergency (total loss of "onboard," fully integrated CCR gas cylinders) occur with the diver who has the highest RMV, and if this emergency takes place at the maximum point from the surface or exit, there will be 50 cu ft (7 L) of team bailout gas remaining upon reaching the surface (given the OC rule of thirds, there would be zero gas remaining). If it is a 3-diver team, there will be more gas remaining, given that each team member carries 50% of the amount of gas deemed necessary when using the 1½ ***x*** bailout gas rule for a 2-person team (similar to OC diving, given favorable conditions, there is additional safety in a 3-person team than a 2-person team)

b. The divers are less likely to experience a slowdown in travel towards the exit or surface, as they are not tied together by the long hose

c. Less stress develops, as the out-of-air diver is still independent and is not physically or psychologically dependent on other team members gas supply as the only source of a breathing medium

d. Even if a slowdown occurs or RMV increases the reserve third of the bailout gas is beyond what is needed to exit as a team, and should be more than adequate to insure a safe exit or surface return. There will be even more gas if this is a 3-person team. Whereas given the OC rule of thirds, the divers die due to lack of sufficient gas

e. Should the divers become separated (unless the separation is at maximum time or distance) the out-of-gas diver has enough bailout gas to exit safely

i. If separation takes place at the maximum point, the out-of-gas diver who manages his or her gas wisely still has a high probability of a safe exit. In addition, if the divers separated, there is still a high probability of reuniting with the other team member(s)

Note: Given the same situation as outlined above, should the separated OC diver lose their backgas supply he or she will die. This has happened more than once

ii. If team separation is considered highly likely, IANTD recommends that the CCR diver, like the OC diver, plan for the separation. In this case, the CCR diver carries the necessary amount of gas needed to exit safely and individually. Thus the OC diver who agrees to a dive plan with a high likelihood of separation from team members should carry a ***buddy cylinder***

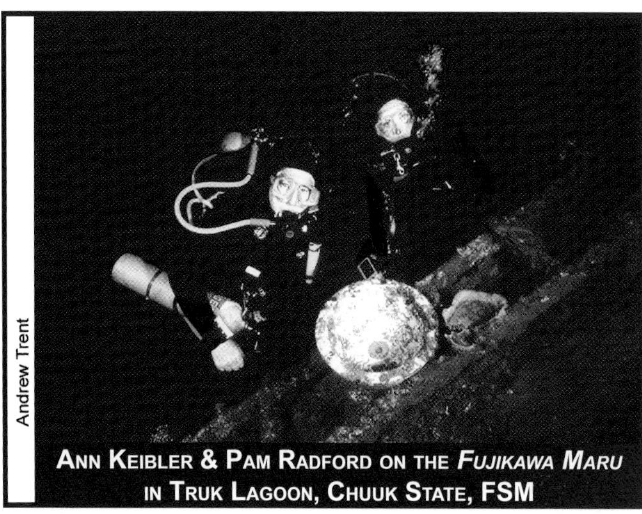

ANN KEIBLER & PAM RADFORD ON THE *FUJIKAWA MARU* IN TRUK LAGOON, CHUUK STATE, FSM

iii. If a diver who requires 50 cu ft (7 L) to exit at the maximum point of penetration and his or her dive partner is carrying 1½ ***x*** that amount, or 75 cu ft (7 L), then each diver will have 37.5 cu ft (6 L) available in case of an out-of-gas emergency. Should the partners separate, it is highly likely they will reunite during the course of the dive, and if not, with a little discipline, the amount of bailout gas each partner carries can be used for a safe exit. In the same scenario on OC, if a buddy cylinder is not used, the out-of-gas OC diver will die.

f. In the event of a dual CCR failure, there is bailout gas unlike the same scenario on an OC dive. If this failure occurs at a point, less than the maximum distance or time from the exit or surface more than enough gas should be available to both divers. If the event takes place at the farthest point or time there is at least a chance to survive by wise management of the gas supply. This is another advantage of the CCR 1½ ***x*** bailout gas rule over the OC rule of thirds in which dependence is on the back gas of the divers

i. ***It should be noted*** that on CCR the only thing that would mandate bailout to OC is a canister failure, and the probability of canister failures on two CCRs

is far more remote than a dual OC failure, which is highly unlikely

ii. If an electronics failure occurs, the CCR diver may dive the unit as if it were a passive SCR. Divers skilled in minimum loop volume might also dive it as a fully functioning CCR until the divers change depths.

g. On CCR dives, unlike OC dives, should a dual catastrophic gas loss occur, there is still gas to bailout out on.

Note! Based on the added safety of the CCR 1½ x bailout gas rule, OC divers may wish to incorporate this rule into their own dive safety parameters.

3. For exploration-type OC divers there may be much merit in experimenting with the CCR 1½ ***x*** bailout gas rule due to the added danger and chance of separation inherent in this type of activity
4. For mixed team dives one may wish to employ the CCR 1½ ***x*** bailout gas rule to balance gas for both divers. In this event the OC diver may elect to allow ½ of the reserve third of back gas to be used on the dive. This is possible as the OC diver is now carrying a separare stage cylinder whose volume is based on the rebreather diver's 1½ ***x*** bailout gas rule
5. IANTD Standards require CCR divers to bailout for a set ascent in OW or for a specific distance in a cave during training. The CCR student's gas needs are then calculated based on how much gas is used. OC divers seldom practice this skill

In closing section two of this chapter, the CCR 1½ ***x*** bailout gas rule exceeds the safety of the rule of thirds in many areas. If someone is more conservative, they may carry all the gas they are comfortable with. It is true that no one has died from too much gas, although the diver has to work harder to carry the excess load, and thus may experience more in-water resistance as well as more stress from the excess weight and drag. However, we are each responsible for our own safety so make all gas management and other risk decisions based on your comfort and experience level. But, at least, do meet the CCR 1½ ***x*** bailout gas rule. For me, the this rule is conservative, but I honor it based on its extensive testing. Moreover, if it makes you nervous to only carry the amount of bailout gas designated by the CCR 1½ ***x*** bailout gas rule, then carry additional gas. You can try this rule to see if it fits your diving style in any IANTD technical course. As the old adage goes, "Try it, you might like it." Then decide which rule you think is safer overall for YOU.

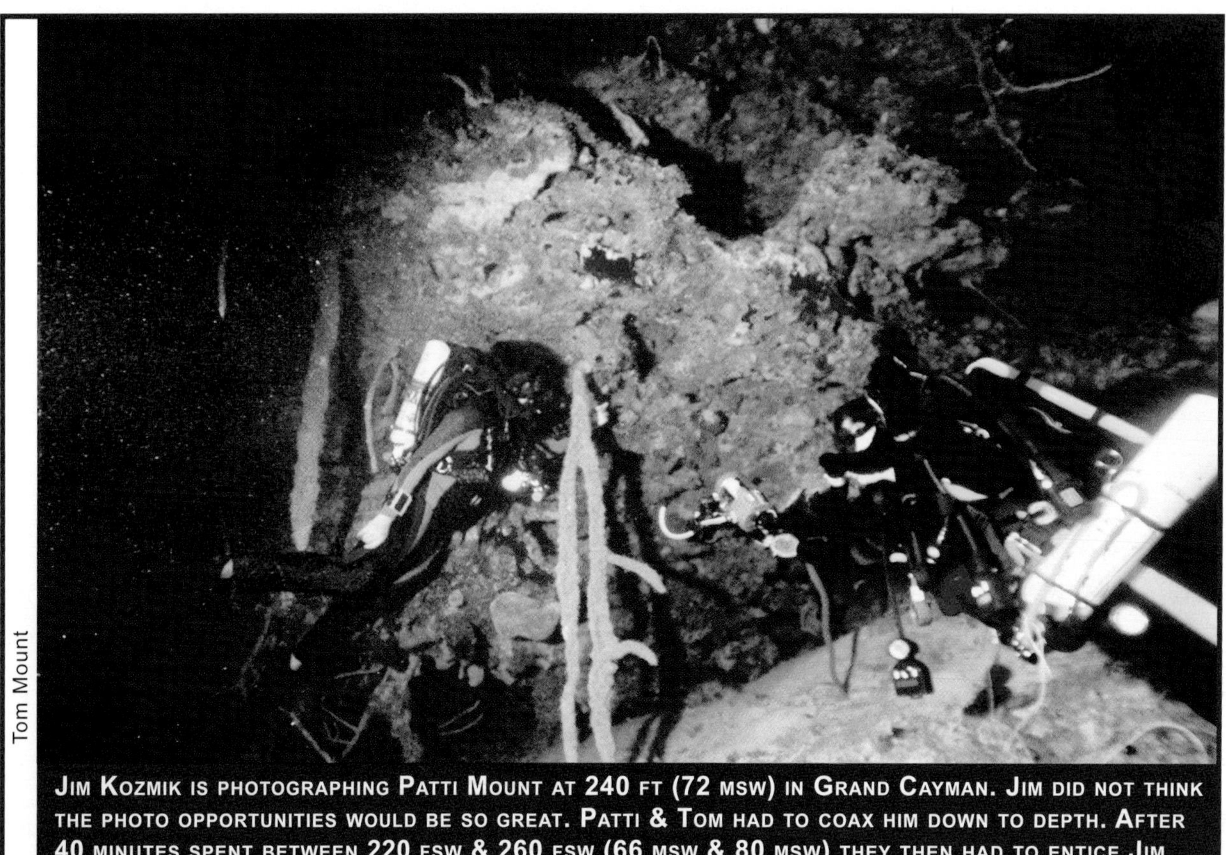

Tom Mount

Jim Kozmik is photographing Patti Mount at 240 ft (72 msw) in Grand Cayman. Jim did not think the photo opportunities would be so great. Patti & Tom had to coax him down to depth. After 40 minutes spent between 220 fsw & 260 fsw (66 msw & 80 msw) they then had to entice Jim into ascending! Jim shot several magazine shots on just this one dive.

Chapter Thirteen
Operational Safety

Kevin Gurr

Safety, while it should be of primary concern to all divers, becomes increasingly important as one venture into technical or extended range diving. In these more advanced forms of diving, the increased duration and scope of the dive plan will cause a corresponding increase in risk exposure. A simple analogy might be; ***If I stand in the street long enough I am more likely to get run over.***

The longer a diver remains underwater the more the effects of equipment reliability; diver error and environmental changes become an issue. Complex dives often involve extended decompressions, depth outside of the accepted sport limits, large amounts of gas and support equipment as well as sophisticated dive platforms such as boats and underwater habitats. The following is offered as a general guide of questions to be addressed when planning such dives.

Safety Divers

Historically ***safety*** or ***stand-by*** divers, as they are known in commercial diving, have been in the front line of diving safety. In the commercial diving world the stand-by diver often remains fully kitted for hours on deck waiting for an incident to occur, only being ***launched*** when required.

With the advent of technical diving, especially with deeper and deeper wrecks and caves being explored using Trimix, the safety diver has crept into the recreational diving world. So who is this group of divers, trapped between the surface and the draw of exploration being undertaken by those they protect? What does it take to be a safety diver and why would you ever want to be one?

As many Trimix dives are undertaken without safety divers why do we need safety divers?

Probability is the answer. The longer you stay submerged the more risk of incident. It's like if you walk in the middle of the street for long enough. You ***will*** get run over. Decompression dives can be long and complicated. More time spent submerged means nature has more time to ruin your day. Short projects or weekend Trimix dives often "get away" without using additional dive support such as ***Safety Divers***, ***Dive Supervisors*** or ***Medical Technicians*** simply because they're not "out there" long enough. That doesn't mean to say they will always remain safe. History tells us differently. Safety divers can at the very least improve your day and at best save lives. I have witnessed it on several occasions.

To be a safety diver takes as much skill and knowledge as it does to go to the bottom. Very often on extended projects, the most experienced members of the team elect to be the safety divers on the high-risk dives.

The skills list of a safety diver will include:

- IANTD Service Technician (for that exploding kit above and below the water)
- IANTD Diver First Aid and Oxygen Provider qualifications
- An in-depth knowledge of the dive profile and what to do if it changes
- Equipment capability (you will often carry as much or more cylinders and gear that any team member)

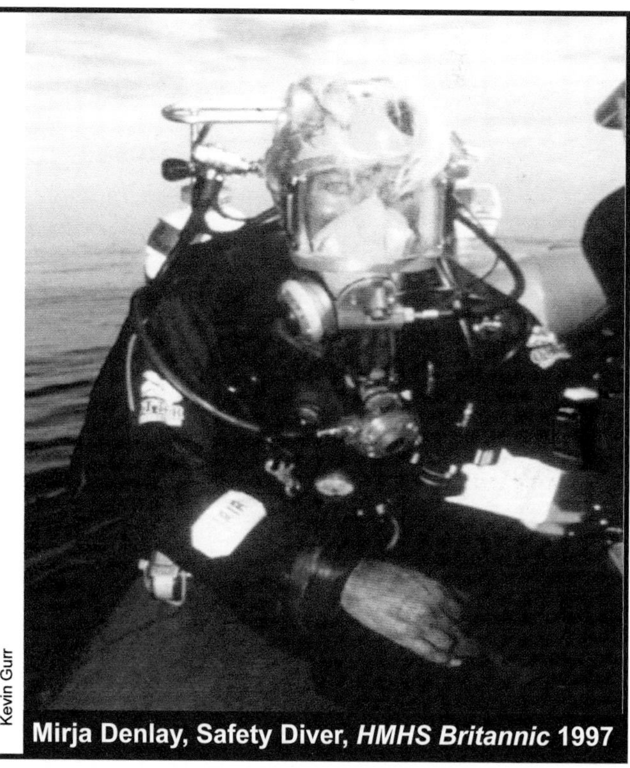

Kevin Gurr

Mirja Denlay, Safety Diver, *HMHS Britannic* 1997

- The mental ability to work alone underwater
- A sixth sense of what will happen next
- Boat skills necessary to understand how the changing environment can affect boat/sea conditions and overall team safety
- Cook/tea person
- Insomniac

So safety divers need to be a bit more than 'one of your mates' who doesn't fancy going to the bottom.

What Does a Safety Diver Do?

Depending on the depth of dive (and team size) anything up to four safety divers can be easily used. I'll give a practical example of the work we did on the *HMHS Britannic* in 1997. Due to the high current and shipping lane we had one safety diver who stayed on the boat. His job was to launch if any of the divers became separated from the decompression system or if someone needed to be recovered close to the surface. They would be equipped with a twin set of air with a 6 ft (2 m) sharing hose and an emergency decompression line.

The second safety diver was to meet the divers at their deepest decompression stop. They would take any heavy equipment, such as scooters and cameras and clip them to a recovery line. They would also carry a twin set of the appropriate bottom mix (air if the stops were above 170 ft (50 m)) and decompression gases the same as the dive team. They would stay with the dive team during the deep-water decompression and handover at the next gas switch depth, usually 100 ft (30 m) to the next safety diver. The ***deep safety*** was the only safety diver allowed to get into decompression. After ***handing over*** they would complete their decompression and return to the surface ready to take over a shallow safety diver role later in the six hour decompression.

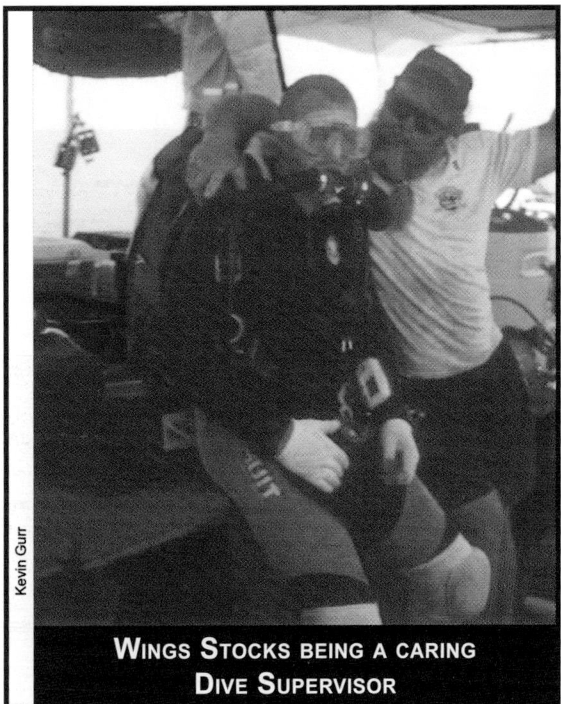

Wings Stocks being a caring Dive Supervisor

The safety diver at 100 ft (30 m) would stay out of deco and be in the water with the deep safety diver ready to take an injured diver directly to the surface (the deep safety diver only being able to ascend to 100 ft [30 m]). They would carry a twin set of nitrox and the bottom diver's mid range deco gas and oxygen. This mid-range safety diver would hand over to another safety diver at the next gas switch 30 or 20 ft (9 or 6 m). This safety diver (and the shallow one) would have wireless communications equipment with a link to a surface supervisor.

Finally, the shallow stops would be covered by two safety divers rotating, as time permitted.

Basically, there is a safety diver in the water at all times and by staggering their decompression schedules, a casualty can be taken directly to the surface at any time.

So, a summary of the work involved might include:

- **During the planning phase:** Dealing with some of the logistics. This could range from ensuring fluid is available for a simple dive to defining and assembling sufficient gas quantities and its management for an extended operational period
- **During preparation:** Ensuring all equipment is in place and that support is correctly loaded; assembling any emergency equipment and verifying its functionality

Prior to diving:

- Checking and tagging all decompression and dive gases
- Assisting the divers to "kit up." Deploying of the decompression station and any in-water emergency equipment

- Ensuring divers safely enter the water and all shallow water checks are conducted successfully

During the dive:

- At least one safety diver descends to the first gas switch point to ensure emergency gas is staged and functioning
- If possible, they wait until all divers have returned safely past the first gas switch point. The safety diver should then make sure all divers are safely on the decompression station prior to setting the station loose (if applicable)
- In a simple operation requiring two safety divers, one remains near the surface. In the event that a rescue has to be performed the "shallow water" safety diver is best suited to this role. Also, if one of the team becomes separated this safety diver is deployed to define the extent of the problem and assist where possible. (See other notes on deep and mid-range safety divers)

Post-Dive: Maintaining records. Assist the team with exiting from the water and de-kiting. Provide fluids and any surface gas for the team; stow equipment; help with an overall assessment of the operation and provide useful input for next time

In short, safety divers are essential parts of the dive team and team members rotate through the safety diver role.

Dive Supervisor

The designated Dive Supervisor remains on the surface during all dive operations. The Dive Supervisor may elect to nominate a replacement Dive Supervisor from within the team at any point during diving operations if they have tasks to perform which will take them away from the deck.

The Dive Supervisor is in overall control of the dive and rigging operations. The Dive Supervisor in conjunction with the safety divers is in control of all record keeping and final equipment checks prior to divers entering the water. The Dive Supervisor also reviews any safety issue after the day's diving operation with the team. The Dive Supervisor is responsible for controlling all emergency situations.

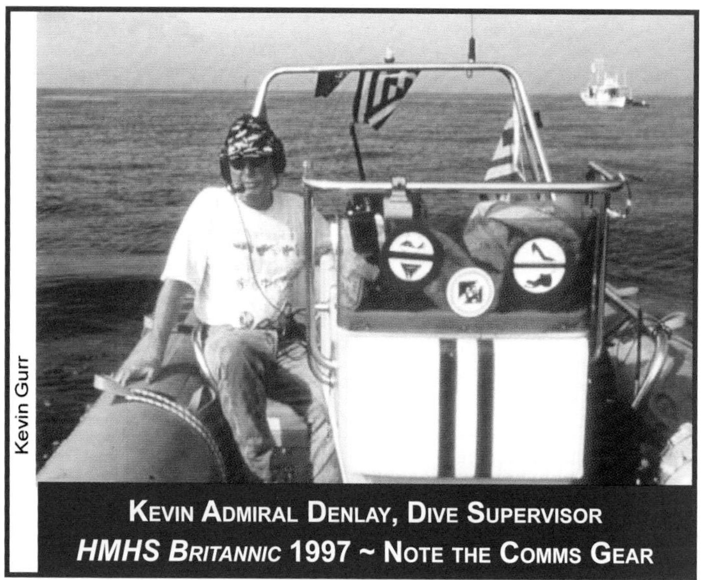
Kevin Gurr

Kevin Admiral Denlay, Dive Supervisor
***HMHS Britannic* 1997 ~ Note the Comms Gear**

Other Elements to Consider

Communications

The vessel must have VHF radios. In addition, short wave headsets are used between key members of the team during any rigging operations. This is ideal between the main vessel and any tender as they can be hands free units and provide an element of privacy. The operation will 'log-out' with the Coast Guard on leaving port and contact them when on-site providing details of the day's operation. Upon completion of the working day, the operation will log back in on arriving at port.

Documentation

The Dive Supervisor will be responsible for keeping the daily dive log and completing a daily risk assessment plan. (See below.)

Points to Remember

One of the best weapons in your arsenal is you, provided that you are a prepared and practised, logical, thinking diver.

Project Plan and Generic Risk Assessment.

Generic Information for the Project

Review Date:

Contractor		Supervisor/instructor	Print	Sign	Surface personnel	Print	Sign	Equipment not required (pool operations etc)
Project/course start date		Rescue diver	Print	Sign	Location of emergency Eqp.			
Emergency services numbers/radio channel		Area of operations			First Aiders.			
Coastguard		Expected visibility						
Recompression		Expected water temp			Pollution (note any)			
Police/ambulance		Course type						
Pre course equipment checks (Comment on any failures/replacements for loaned/hired equipment or just sign for checks completed).								

Students Name	Contact	Emergency Contact	Last Qualification	Medical (student initial)	Waiver (student initial)	Own Equipment serviced (initial)	Equipment issued	Issued Equip. Serviced (instructor initial)

Daily Dive Log and Dynamic Risk Assessment

Side one of a paper log or plastic slate. *One completed per dive.* ***All data must be transferred to the paper Operations Log***

Location		Dive Description		Planned depth		Planned time		Bottom mix PO_2	
Date									
Wave Height		Notes.						Communications check (Initial)	
Bottom Type									
Sea state		Casualty Recovery System.							
Wind									

Divers name	Gas 1			Gas 2			Gas 3			Deco algorithm.				
	Mix	Gas in	Gas out	Mix	Gas in	Gas out	Mix	Gas in	Gas out	Actual depth	Actual time	Canister start	Canister end	Changes to project plan

Daily Dive Log and Dynamic Risk Assessment

Plastic slate or paperwork, side two. *One completed per dive.*

Skill list	Risk Briefings (conduct and tick)		Hazard (additional to briefing list and Project Plan Generic Risks list)	Preventative action
1.	Access			
2.	Egress			
3.	Pairing/team order			
4.	Dive turn limit (1/3rd etc)			
5.	Signals (U/W)/Abort			
6.	Signals (to/from surface)			
Notes:	Special equipment (guidelines etc.)			
	Separation Rules			
	Entanglement Hazards			
	Deco. System			
	Silt			
	Gas on/manifold setting			
	Lights test			
	Reels			
	Buoyancy/inflation			
	Regulator check		Generic Risks from Project Plan Review. (Instructor to sign as students informed)	
	Current		Name	Initial
	Navigation			
	Emergency gas location		Notes:	
	Buddy Check			
	Bubble check (submerged)			
	Brief conducted (Initial)			

Decompression Systems

Introduction

As decompressions become longer and more complex, there is a need to use systems which improve individual and team safety and comfort. Long decompressions can be hazardous if conducted in shipping channels, tidal areas and cold environments. The decompression itself, as an additional hazard, can necessitate long uses of high oxygen mixtures. Well-constructed and planned decompression systems significantly reduce the risk.

When to Use a Decompression System

A good rule of thumb is any decompression that requires multiple decompression gases and/or is more than approximately 30 minutes long (meaning that single or pairs of divers surfacing on marker buoys would become significantly separated) requires the use of a decompression system. Let's look at the problems in turn.

1. Multiple decompression gases: the use of multiple decompression gases usually means long and possibly deep dives. In certain situations (especially on Trimix dives where deep-water decompression gases are needed) if a diver loses a deep-water decompression gas he/she may not be able to complete the decompression on their remaining gases. In open water this normally applies to dives over 260 ft (80 m) in depth (given "recreational[1]" bottom times). Hence, some kind of decompression system is used to stage safety gas for this phase of the dive. Better

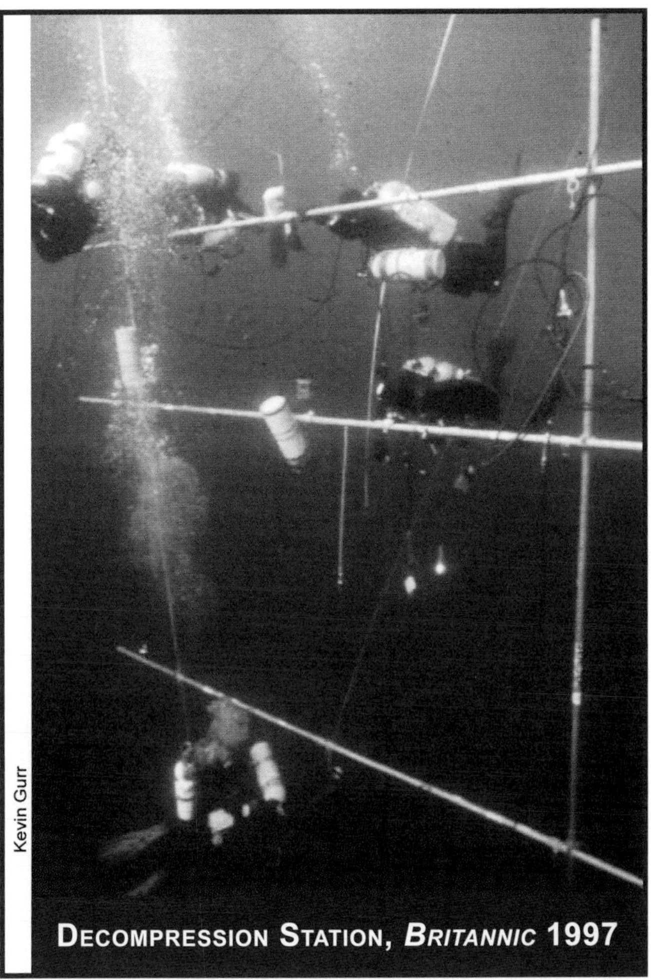

Decompression Station, *Britannic* 1997

still, this scenario is further covered by using safety divers who carry additional gas

3. Long decompressions: long duration decompressions, especially in tidal waters, means that individuals deploying surface marker buoys (SMB's) to decompress under will become separated. **This is a hazard for three reasons:**

   a. In the event of any one (or several) divers having an incident and surfacing, the boat skipper may just be in the wrong place at the wrong time and assistance may not be rendered quickly enough. Also, should an incident occur, the skipper may be forced to leave the vicinity with injured divers making the probability of loss of the remaining divers still in the water high

   b. In surprise adverse weather, divers can become lost

   c. In shipping channels, large vessels may try and avoid another boat but individual divers will not be seen on a boat's radar

Decompression Stations & Habitats

The function of a decompression station or habitat is to provide a stable platform on, or within, which the team can complete the decompression phase. Advantages and disadvantages of such systems are:

Advantages:

- A place to stage emergency equipment
- Allows the team to stay together in a tidal environment
- Provides a visual reference to assist with buoyancy control (stations)
- Allows the team to exit (or partially exit) the water (habitats)
- Provides extra safety in the event of an oxygen incident or where oxygen durations need to be extended. Use habitats because the casualty is dry. Use station because casualty can be assisted by the other divers or recovered by the safety divers.
- Reduces the effects of cold (habitats)
- Provides a common communication point

Disadvantages:

- High level of individual discipline required to act as a team
- Divers have to be able to return to the shot/anchor line/station
- Habitat set-up may be complex

Varying environmental conditions require different adaptations to the decompression station concept. Three basic layouts of decompression stations will be discussed as well as simple and complex habitats, although there are others.

System 1

Use area: Low to medium tidal flow, good in water and generally good surface visibility. Small or large dive teams. Possibly heavy shipping traffic.

Method: This system normally involves the support boat being tethered into the wreck/reef on a fixed single point bow mooring. The boat then deploys a weighted drop- line under the stern of the boat which joins a horizontal line or bar at 20 ft (6 m) connected to the bow mooring line. In good visibility, where a return to the mooring line is simple, decompression cylinders may be staged on this 6 metres line or at a point on the mooring line where they will be first needed. The boat may also provide surface supplied O_2 or indeed any decompression gas. In current, divers may use Jon-lines to clip off to the mooring line.

One alternative to the single weighted drop line for larger groups of divers is to assemble a solid trapeze which is suspended on its own buoys and tethered to the boat. The base of the trapeze is again attached to the main down line by another horizontal line.

Safety Systems: Each diver carries an inflatable surface marker should they lose any of the lines. A dual color-coded system is used, one for ***alone but OK*** (orange) and one for ***Help, Need gas, etc.*** (yellow). Unless a return to the mooring line is guaranteed, divers will always carry all their own gases. Divers should carry some form of surface

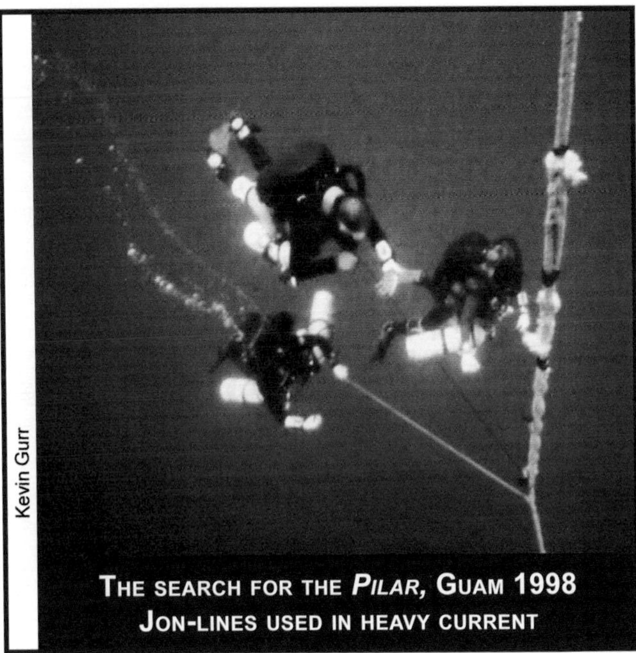

THE SEARCH FOR THE *PILAR*, GUAM 1998
JON-LINES USED IN HEAVY CURRENT

signalling device (flares/EPIRB).

System 2

Use Area: High tidal flow. Low in-water visibility. Possibility of poor surface conditions. Small or large dive teams. Possibly heavy shipping traffic.

Method: The main buoy line is sunk (shot or grapnel) to the site with a large surface buoy. The boat is not fixed to this line and works as a safety boat at all times. At the end of the dive the anchor or shot is retrieved and tied up the line several metres and hooked in place allowing the line to free-float with all divers using it as a visual reference. With Trimix diving, safety, travel or deep-water decompression gas may be staged at various gas switch points.

Safety Systems: Each diver carries an inflatable surface marker should they lose any of the lines. A dual color-coded system, one for ***alone but OK*** (orange) and one for ***Help, Need gas, etc.*** (yellow). Divers will always carry all their own gases. Divers will carry some form of surface signalling device (flares/EPIRB). The surface vessel will carry emergency gas to be deployed on measured and buoyed depth lines, (dependant on the dive plan) in the event of an emergency buoy being deployed. Slates can be attached to buoys for additional information. Boat must be equipped with radar and radios.

System 3

Use Area: High tidal flow. Low in-water visibility. Possibility of poor surface conditions. Small or large dive teams. Possibly heavy shipping traffic.

Method: The main buoy line is sunk (shot or grapnel) to the site with a large surface buoy. Two 30 ft (9 m) lines with a buoy at the top and a weight of 4.5-9 lbs. (2-4 kg) at each base. Each line will have loops every 10 ft (3 m). The lines are joined as in a trapeze with a movable bar 7 to 10 ft (2-3 m) long. This station is attached to the main buoy line by a ***jump*** or ***travel*** line. Dependant on the amount of tide expected, this line will be 20 ft (6 m) or longer than the point to the deepest decompression stop, allowing for the angle on the line due to the tidal effect. With Trimix diving safety, travel or deep-water decompression gases will be staged as appropriate. Adaptations to this system for larger groups may include several down-lines and a triangular bar system.

Safety Systems: Each diver carries an inflatable surface marker should they lose any of the lines. A dual color-coded system is essential for communications with surface support divers, one for ***alone but OK*** (orange) and one for ***Help, Need gas, etc.*** (yellow). Divers will always carry all their own gases. Divers will carry some form of surface signalling device (flares/EPIRB. The surface vessel will carry emergency gas to be deployed on measured and buoyed depth lines, dependant on the dive plan, in the event of an emergency buoy being deployed. The boat must be equipped with radar and radios.

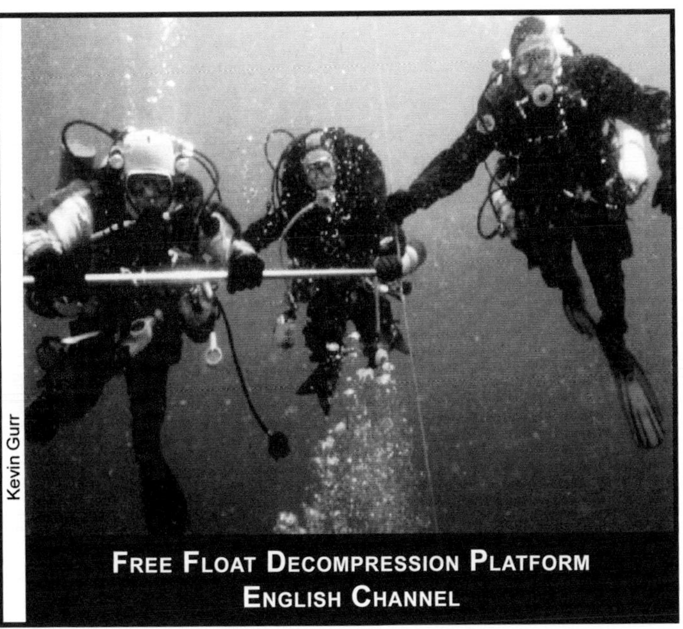

FREE FLOAT DECOMPRESSION PLATFORM
ENGLISH CHANNEL

System 4

Use Area: Good underwater and surface visibility, low volume surface traffic, small teams and minimal decompression schedules.

Method: Each diver or pair is allowed to deploy their own surface marker as the decompression starts.

Safety Systems: Each diver carries an inflatable surface marker should they lose any of the lines. A dual color coded system, one for ***alone but OK*** (orange) and one for ***Help, Need gas, etc.*** (yellow). The surface vessel will carry emergency gas to be deployed on measured and buoyed depth lines, dependant on the dive plan, in the event of an emergency buoy being deployed. Divers will normally carry some form of surface signalling device (flares\EPIRB).

Team Management

With the use of Systems 2 and 3, as noted above, and in extreme tidal areas, team management is vital. If team members are late arriving back at the station the current may be so strong as to drag down the surface buoys and therefore sink the station. Should this situation occur the only option is to deploy the individual surface markers (orange) and commence solo decompression. To ensure team members return to the station within a safe tidal window, it is vital that tidal conditions are assessed and a team plan devised. The key is to define what is often known as a "cut-off time" or the time point in a run time schedule when the jump line will be disconnected from the main line, thus allowing the station to free float. This can either be a fixed time of day in the team plan or a time point in the runtime schedule of the last pair to enter the water (i.e. entry plus 30 minutes). Each team member signs in on a slate positioned where the jump line joins the main line. Should the majority of divers return within the time and other team members not yet be returned, the ***on station*** team has the option to disconnect the jump line at the station end (rather than descending again) at the cut-off time. Each team member must be able to navigate back to the line or be prepared to use a line reel.

Members not managing to return by the cut-off time will realise this and simply deploy their markers and not waste energy or gas trying to return to the station.

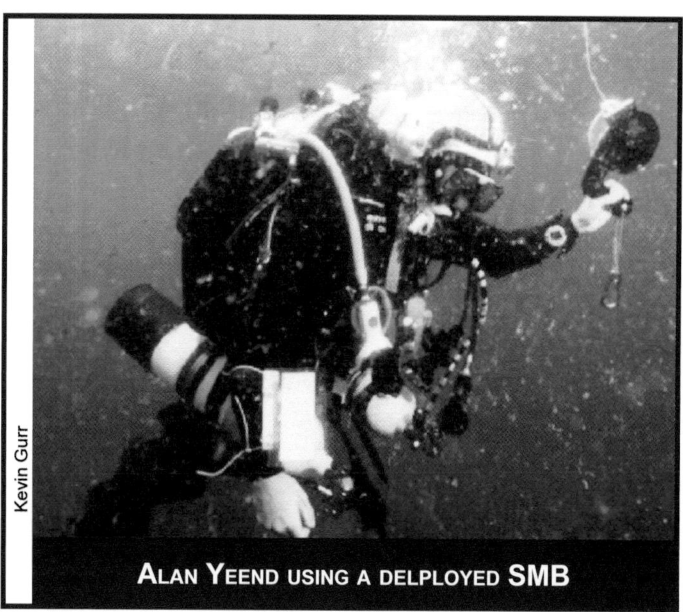

Kevin Gurr

ALAN YEEND USING A DELPLOYED SMB

There may be several adaptations to this system. Whichever is employed, teams are advised to practice all eventualities before settling on a system.

The above systems are primarily focused on open water use. Cave or quarry dives have their own specific problems but generally involve the staging of gases and emergency equipment at fixed points. The use of any system that requires a return to a fixed point should employ visual markers such as strobes, reels or lights attached near the bottom to ensure a safe return.

Emergency Procedures

The main point of using any decompression system is to avoid team separation and improve safety. However, this does not always happen. To help reduce further problems as a result of separation, ***decompression drop stations*** are used.

Drop Stations

These are used when an emergency signal is seen from a diver at the surface. These are usually a specific color (yellow) SMB or two SMB's together. The drop station will be a line as long as the deepest planned gas switch. The line will have on it at least a cylinder of each of the deep-water decompression gases tied on at the maximum operating depth (MOD) of each gas. Cylinder valves will have been pressurised and turned off to prevent free-flows. In some

cases the shallow decompression gas will also be on the line, but usually as there is more time to correct a problem when shallow, this safety gas will be carried on the boat and only dropped if the safety diver deems it necessary, or if an additional pre-arranged signal is seen. Too many cylinders make the drop station unwieldy and prone to tangling.

Often the drop station is launched with a safety diver descending with it to ascertain the problem. Whatever the problem the first assumption should be a gas failure and the station is always launched.

This system covers individual becoming separated from the main up-line or divers using individual SMB's.

Safety Boats

Where decompression systems are employed that require the vessel to be locked in to a down line and station, then a ***safety boat*** should also be used. This is a small, fast vessel capable of following and recovering drifting divers and in an emergency being able to take a casualty to shore or the nearest Medi-Vac point. **The checklist for a safety boat might include:**

- Radio
- First Aid Kit
- Oxygen Resusciation equipment
- Diver recovery system
- Emergency drop station with appropriate decompression gasses
- Navigation equipemtn (for relaying position)
- Drinking water
- Standard boat safety gear such as flares, tools, etc.

Habitats

Dependant on the climatic conditions, extended decompressions (where there is either cold or a risk of oxygen toxicity) should involve decompression habitats where the divers may partially or totally exit the water to complete the decompression phase. Habitats can be simple affairs that allow a portion of the diver to exit the water (almost like an up-turned bucket) or more complex arrangements that allow a complete team of divers to totally exit the water[2]. Habitats reduce the possibility of hypothermia as well as help control the risk of drowning should an oxygen convulsion occur.

Habitat construction can be a detailed science especially when one is designed for open water use. If a unit is to be constructed that is capable of allowing a team of divers to fully exit the water, this will take considerable engineering skill and resources.

Habitats have become popular with cave divers, mainly because exploration cave dives tend to be very long and the environment is more static than the open ocean, making habitat deployment and anchoring relatively simple. In cave diving the types and size of habitats vary considerably. From the large-scale Wakulla Project[3] unit to upside down plastic waste bins often found in places like the Emergence du Russel Cave system in France, each is correct for its task.

Operational Safety

Safety should be something we are all concerned about. With technical or extended range diving, where the diver is more likely to stay submerged for longer periods of time, there is a higher risk of problems occurring. A simple analogy might be: "If I stand in the street long enough I am more likely to get run over." The longer a diver remains underwater the more the effects of equipment reliability - diver error and environmental changes become an issue. Complex dives often involve extended decompressions, depth outside of the accepted sport limits, large amounts of gas and support equipment as well as sophisticated dive platforms such as boats and underwater habitats. The following is offered as a general guide to questions to be addressed when planning such dives.

To define a safe operating procedure we must first look at several specific issues:

1. The type of dive and it's associated hazards
2. Risk
3. Safety planning
4. Dive platforms
5. Safety divers
6. Rescue management and equipment

Types of Dive

The range of dives available to recreational divers is almost limitless. Over recent years the concept and scope of recreational diving has expanded into the realms of what has become known as technical diving. So there is recreational diving and there is technical diving, but what is the difference? Divers are often diving for fun past the recreational norms of 130 fsw (40 or 50 m), so depth is not necessarily the issue. It is now fairly common in certain parts of the globe to see divers hiring boats to take them out into 240 fsw (70 m) of water and do a ***recreational*** Trimix dive. So where does recreational diving really stop? Should the analogy be that as long as the diver is doing it for fun it is still recreational diving irrespective of depth and time submerged? What makes diving ***technical***?

Perhaps the difference is based on the functions of time and exploration. Exploration is going somewhere no one else has been before (which generates its own risks) and extending submerged times at any depth exposes us to risks outlined above. Taking open water diving as an example, this generally means going past the sport diving limits of 130 fsw (40 m+) ***and/or*** spending significant time at any depth, hence generating a considerable decompression obligation.

So a description of *technical diving* might be:

> "Technical diving is a range of knowledge, skills and suitable equipment which, when combined correctly, allow recreational divesr to increase their safety whilst underwater. This information may be employed in either shallow or deep-water, may be used to safely extend the divers submerged duration well into the realms of extended decompressions and is often used as a tool for exploration."

As readers are mainly interested in technical diving, this type of diving will be the focus. It is not to say that any dives planned would not benefit from some of the topics discussed in this chapter, of course they would.

Put broadly types of dives include:

1. Shore dive
2. Boat Dive
3. Cave Dive

Whilst all types of diving (especially at a technical level) are generally similar; cave diving should and does command the most respect. Many of the techniques employed in technical diving were first used in caves.

The cave environment is both fascinating and challenging; both from a mental and a technical standpoint. Caves, although initially appearing benign, can soon turn into a diver's worst nightmare. As such, cave diver training is some of the most rewarding. If you think you are a good open-water diver, take a cave class! Cave diving is not the same the world over. Cave diving in the UK is a million miles apart from cave diving in Florida. However, most of the basic skills employed are generic and are covered within this text. Do not stray into caves without the correct training.

Diving Hazards

Items 1 & 2 can be subdivided in to ***reef*** or ***wreck***. All dives can obviously be fresh or salt water and may be at altitude or at night and there are a variety of different cave dives. Looking at each one in turn (and in order to identify the risk involved) let's list some of the hazards, see Figure 13-1. The table shows some, but not all the general hazards (both physical and environmental) which might occur. This should be completed for the specific dive being planned and where necessary, corrective actions defined for any high risk scenarios.

SOME EXPEDITIONS GET VERY TECHNICAL WITH A CHAMBER BEING INSTALLED ON THE PROJECT

Risk

Looking at all of the above, the overall risk for each item can be defined as a combination of the probability of any event occurring and how life threatening it is. As all dives involve risk, they should have varying levels of safety planning. In some cases such as gas supply failure where the probability of failure is potentially low (due to reliable regulators) but the life threatening potential is extreme - the combined risk is high and hence detailed safety plans should be made. In another situation the probability of losing a safe egress from a shore dive in bad weather is fairly high but the potential for rescue and hence the life threatening factor might be low, making the overall risk minimal.

In general, low-risk dives normally have their safety requirements covered by standard diving equipment and practises such as those often employed on a normal recreational dive. High-risk dives need specific emergency plans for any highlighted hazards. So how do we assess risk and define which scenarios need more planning than others?

We can generate a table to assess the risks. **The probability of a hazard occurring should be graded as:**

1. Not likely
2. Possible
3. Probable

Life threatening factors should be graded as:

0. No risk
1. Low
2. Medium
3. High

For example, looking at the table in Figure 13-2, in the first example a diver uses a single high quality regulator and a loss of gas is the defined hazard. This regulator however has a low failure probability of 1, but if it does fail (as there is only one) the potential for loss of life is high due to drowning, etc. Hence the overall risk is high (3). In this instance the most practical safety plan for this scenario would be to carry a backup or redundant regulator. The same type of assessment can be made for the other examples and a safety plan generated.

In summary:

- Define each hazard
- Define the probability of the risk occurring
- Define how life threatening it is
- Grade the probability and life-threatening factor to define the overall risk
- Plan for the specific safety procedure to instigate should the combined risk score be 3 or above

As all dives do involve risk the need to execute them must be balanced against that risk and the potential reward. In some cases the reward is worth the ultimate risk. The focus of this chapter is to make you think about the hazards and define which require detailed safety planning to reduce the overall risk.

Kevin Gurr

Entrance to George Cave, Dordoigne Vally, France

Risk is reduced by proper planning, training and equipment.

Safety Planning

Having defined the hazards which require detailed safety planning (scoring 3+) it is important to review the environment's affect on those hazards, after which a safety plan may be generated.

The world's diving environments are not only varied across the globe but may vary from day to day and even hour to hour at any one site. Each type of dive has its own specific environment due to its location. Especially in open water, dives that require extended decompressions or long submerged durations may be affected by a range of changing environments. It is important to plan for these changes and include them as part of a risk assessment.

Type Of Dive	Scenario	Hazard
Shore -> Reef	Enter / Exit Point	Physical Injury
	Current	Swept Away From Safe Egress
	Marine Life	Physical Injury
	Boat Traffic	Physical Injury
	Sea State	Physical Injury, Inability To Safely Egress
	Weather	Changing Sea State, Reduced Visability
	Gas Failure	Drowning
	Underwater Visability	Loss Of Dive Partner
Shore -> Wreck	All Of The Above	All Of The Above
	Entrapment	Drowning Or Other Physical Injury
Boat -> Reef or Wreck	All Of The Above	All Of The Above
	Underwater Visability	Loss Of Line To Surface
Cave or Wreck Penetration	Line Loss	Inability To Find Exit
	Silt Out	Inability To Find LIne Or Partner

Figure 13-1: General Hazards
This table shows some of the general hazards (both physical & environmental) which might occur. These should be assesed for each specific dive being planned. Where necessary, corrective action should be implemented for any high rish scenario.

As the dives' environment and any physical hazards affect our overall safety, let's now include both of these in our safety plan and define possible corrective action to reduce any risk. This will be completed for a range of dives.

Scenario / Hazard	Probability	Life Threatening Factor	Overall Risk
Loss of Gas	1	3	4
Loss of Boat	1	2	3
Loss of Partner	1	0	1

Figure 13-2: Example Of A Probability Table

Shore Diving

Shore diving generally requires that a diver has good navigational skills especially when ocean diving along cliffs, where specific access/egress points are limited. Where drift dives are to be performed with an extensive floating decompression, ensure boat cover is adequately equipped.

With all diving, but especially where land is to be crossed, remember: always respect the environment and landowners' wishes.

Boat Diving

Boat diving presents a number of unique challenges. See Figure 13-4 for some examples of boat diving risk.

Cave Diving

We have looked at a range of dives and their possible hazards. We have defined the probability of a hazard occurring and the life threatening potential if it happens. As well as defining the risk we have looked at how the environment may produce its own problems and how to plan safely to reduce those problems. **It is worth noting at this point that the three most common causes of diving fatalities can be defined as:**

1. Not planning for proper gas reserves (***Rule of Thirds***) especially on penetration dives.
2. Not carrying a truly redundant gas source.
3. Not using a continuous guide line to the exit on penetration dives.

Hazard	Safety Procedure
Difficult Access / Egress To Site	Carry kit in stages - employ sherpas - Use ropes & slings
Ocean Swells	Submerge ASAP to identify U/W hazards - Deploy exit line & floats - Use shore cover personnel
Ice	Always use a line to the surface and shore personnel - with thick ice, ensure surface cover has safety cutting equipment
Poor Surface Visibility	Carry surface signalling equipment - Sonic Alerts or EPIRB'S work in most instances
Poor U/W Visibility	Use buddy lines and compasses
Boat Traffic	Use surface marker buoy
Nets & Lines	Carry cutting equipment
Current	Where long dives are planned in a tidal area, tidal planning to predict an egress point is vital - Shore and probably boat cover will be needed - Drifing divers should always use a surface marker

Figure 13-3: Examples Of Shore Diving Hazards

Hazard	Safety Procedure
Rough Seas	Deploy diver pick-up and kit drop lines with buoys tethered to the boat - Do not attempt to egress in full kit
Current	In the event of being swept away carry signalling equipmentsuch as flares, EPIRB, Sonic Alert, etc. - Plan for a Lost Diver Drill and Search Pattern at a predetermined time/ point where the divers should surface
Other Boats	Never surface without a marker or being on your boats shot line
Entrapment	Avoid penetration - Check structures for safety before entering - Dive with a partner who may be able to assist
Nets & Lines	Carry cutting equipment
Poor U/W Visibility	Use strobes or reels on the down line to ensure a safe return

Figure 13-4: Examples Of Boat Diving Hazards

Hazard	Safety Procedure
Current	In extreme cases work against the flow going in - Test for changes in current and tidal effects before entering - Lay strong lines - Correct & strategic planning should prevent tidal problems
Low In-Water Visability	Always use continuous exit lines - Remain in touch contact
Collapse / Entrapment	Dive as part of a team - Do not enter unsafe structures

Figure 13-5: Examples Of Cave Diving Hazards

Surface Dive Support Platforms

Dive platforms can be subdivided into those that remain on the surface and those that stay submerged during the dive. In the simplest form these range from shore safety personnel, the boat, through to decompression stations and habitats. Shore personnel must be aware of the team plan, carry safety equipment such as oxygen and ropes and slings and have good communications (phone/radio).

Boats

Let us first define the functions of a boat in a technical diving operation. **Briefly, these can be listed:**

- Safe transport to and from site
- Protection from the elements
- Accommodation
- A dive-support platform
- A rescue platform

The first three categories of the above list are almost always defined by the physical size of the boat. Boats as operational platforms tend to fall in four size-related categories. These categories will also define the range of the vessel and possibly its suitability for a specific operation.

Whilst each of the above may be suitable for technical operations, each has its own problems. Because weather will often decide the range and type of diving undertaken on the smaller vessels, larger boats also generate problems in strong weather particularly ith diver egress. Even though larger vessels may take divers comfortably to site in strong weather, diver safety may still be compromised during the entry and exit phase because of poor ladders/ high sides, etc. In short, anything much above a force 5 on the Beaufort scale will preclude safe diving. Extended decompressions in strong seas also become uncomfortable unless precautions are taken[4].

Accommodation will only normally be found on the larger live on board/expedition size of vessels. Find out as much about the boat as possible prior to chartering. Three things that can make a trip miserable above all others are poor or inadequate food, inability to rest comfortably and poor sanitation. All of these also affect team safety.

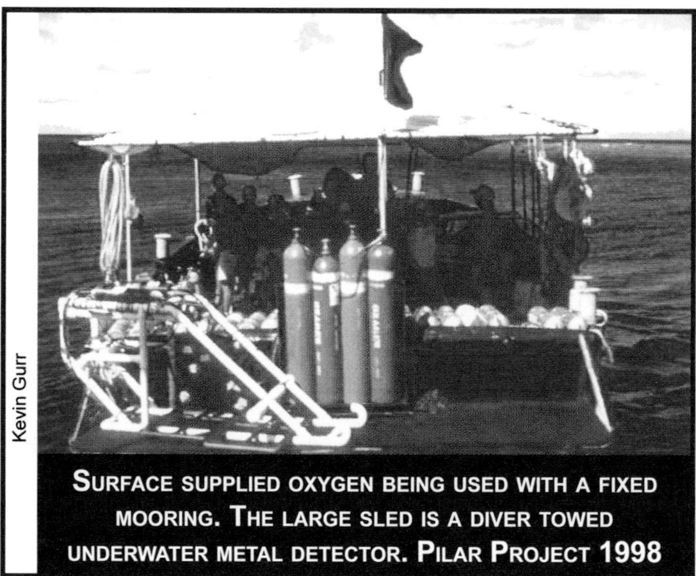

SURFACE SUPPLIED OXYGEN BEING USED WITH A FIXED MOORING. THE LARGE SLED IS A DIVER TOWED UNDERWATER METAL DETECTOR. PILAR PROJECT 1998

BOATS AS DIVE SUPPORT PLATFORMS

The boat is used to deliver the divers to and retrieve them from the water, to allow an area for kiting and de-kiting, to provide protection while they are submerged and to transport equipment specific to an operation. The following is a list of practical suggestions to overcome some of the associated problems.

ENTRY & EXIT

Smaller vessels allow the diver to roll backwards to enter the water and once in, clip on additional equipment and cylinders (if boat space is limited). Exit at worst will involve removing the equipment prior to returning into the boat. This is especially true of the inherently stable inflatable technology. Larger vessels may have a similar entry method although stern entry doors are becoming more popular and do provide more safety and less potential for physical injury with multiple cylinder set-ups. With larger vessels, re-entry to the boat will often be via some form of ladder. Whilst side ladders are extensively used in some countries, on non-cathedral hull boats (where the pitching of the vessel can be extreme) this type of exit can be hazardous. In general, stern platforms provide for a much more stable base for entering and exiting the boat. In any event one of the safest ways to re-enter any vessel is to remove excess equipment prior to so doing. **Two proposed methods for achieving this are:**

1. Use a small support boat (inflatable) to retrieve heavy equipment (side mounts, etc.)
2. Deploy a kit retrieval line. This is a long line of 15-33 ft (5-10 m) with brass rings positioned along it and a large float at one end. The other end is tied to the stern of the boat, preferably at a high point away from the propeller using floating line. If surface conditions are slight, simply return to the line, remove one side mount clip at a time and clip it to the line. (This stops accidental dropping and loss of the cylinder)

If conditions are severe, undo the rear side mount clip whilst still submerged (at the last stop) rather than in the surface swell. Attach one clip at a time to the line to prevent loss. Pull yourself back to the boat using the line, allowing the skipper/support crew to retrieve the cylinders. If twin sets are to be removed, provide a firm anchor point on the set by which it can be lifted (not the manifold). Some boats may have winches to assist with this.

KITING & DE-KITING

Whilst kiting areas on smaller boats may be limited, on larger vessels there can often be too much space leading to confusion on the boat. Boat loading plays a crucial role especially if an emergency occurs.

IN SUMMARY:

- Ensure personnel team equipment is accessible in the order of which it is to be used. The first pair of divers in the water should have their kit nearest the kiting area or exit point

Type	Construction	Size	Suitability
DORY / BOSTON WHALER	GRP or Aluminum	Up to 20 ft (6 m)	In-Shore Open Boat Work Can Be Used For Small Team Technical Operations
INFLATABLE	Rigid or Soft Hull Inflatable	Up to 30 ft (9 m)	In-Shore & Off-Shore Work - All Levels of Technical Ops
DAY BOAT	GRP, Wood or Steel	Up to 50 ft (15 m)	As Above
LIVE ABOARD	As Above	Up to 80 ft (24 m)	As Above + Expeditions

FIGURE 13-6: TYPES OF MARINE DIVING PLATFORMS

Kevin Gurr

THE M1 SUBMARINE CONVERTED LANDING CRAFT WAS USED FOR THE 80 METRE DIVE PROJECT

- Ensure that all safety equipment is easily accessible and make space to treat a casualty
- Where possible, make a separate kiting up to travel area for equipment. In rough seas equipment tends to move around and should be firmly locked in a stowage area to prevent damage. It is often far safer to fully rig equipment on land prior to loading and then firmly secure it in the boat rather than trying to assemble and test it in a pitching sea. This also reduces the number of kit bags required (freeing valuable space). Simple benches or a central table make good kiting areas once on site, empty bags being stowed underneath
- If support divers can be used, employ them to kit team members. If they are not available, educate your boat skipper!
- When re-entring the boat, de-kit as quickly as possible and stow equipment
- Employ team planning to reduce pre-dive stress. Each member has an assigned task and each pair helps the previous pair to dress in and out

Operational Check Lists

A vital part of operational safety is ensuring that all equipment is loaded prior to leaving base. In order to achieve this it is prudent to generate checklists. Figure 13-7, is offered as a typical checklist that might be employed.

Similar checklists can be generated for shore and cave-diving activities.

Protection Whilst Submerged

Whilst the dive is being conducted, it is the boat's function to protect the dive team. The vessel its self can offer physical protection from other sea users by employing such things as radar and communications equipment. Its ability to do this for the whole team relies on the divers acting as a unit. In tidal areas it is just not acceptable that extended decompressions be carried out on an individual basis where there is a possibility that the group will become fragmented. **Separation of the team is hazardous for the following reasons:**

- The boat cannot offer protection from other vessels for all team members
- If weather and sea states change, divers may become lost at sea

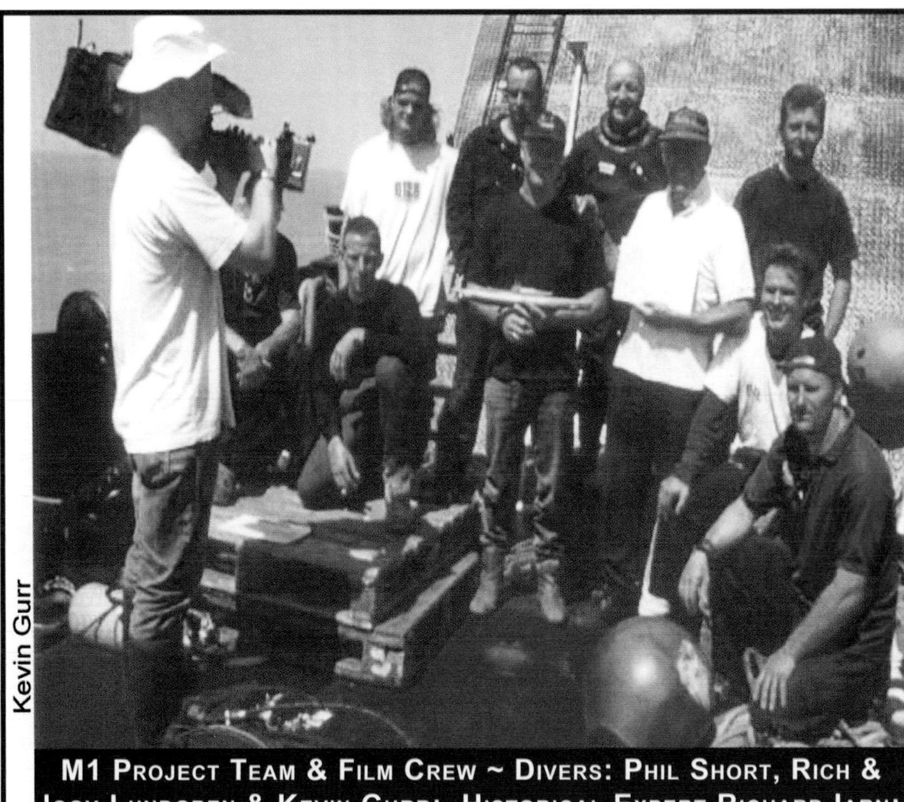

Kevin Gurr

M1 PROJECT TEAM & FILM CREW ~ DIVERS: PHIL SHORT, RICH & IGGY LUNDGREN & KEVIN GURR; HISTORICAL EXPERT RICHARD IARN; CHAMBER OPERATOR RUSSEL CATELY

Personal Equipment	Boat Equipment	Emergency Equipment
Cylinders	Shot Lines	Surface Oxygen
Regulators	Navigation Gear	First Aid Kit
Suit Inflation System	Decompression Station	Casualty Recovery Equipment
Harness and Wings	Emergency Deco Gas	Fluids/Hydration Supplies
Primary Light	Radio and Cell Phone	
Primary & Back-up Reel(s)	Anchor	
Lift Bags	Tools and Spares	
Dive Computer	Kit Recovery Lines	
Back-up Dive Timer/Guages		
Dive & Run Time Tables		
Communications Slate		
Emergency Buoys		
Marker Strobe		
EPIRBS/Flares/Sonic Alert		
Knife and Net/Line Cutter		
Tools/Spares		
Suit and Underwear		
Fluids/Hydration		
Mask/Fins/Gloves/Hood		
Compass		
DPV		

Figure 13-7: Sample Operational Checklist

- If a pair of divers or an individual has a problem, the boat may not be in the right place at the right time
- If separated pairs of divers or individuals have problems, the boat cannot be in two places at once
- In emergencies, organised team help is more efficient than buddy assistance

The only real answer to this problem is the use of decompression stations or habitats as described in a previous chapter.

Whichever boat platform is used there are several golden rules which should not be broken:

- Never leave the boat unattended
- Carry a 100% oxygen supply system
- Carry a medical kit
- Carry communications equipment (radio, phone, flares, etc.)
- As a minimum carry a compass and/or more suitable electronic navigational aids

Helicopter Rescues

Important points to remember are:

- Remove all obstructions (aerials, etc.) from pickup point
- Always follow the pilot's instructions
- Never touch the winch man, lines or stretcher until a ground wire has touched the boat or sea. There is a risk of electric shock
- Do not attach any lines from the helicopter to the vessel

Deep Research Submarine on Grand Cayman with underwater photographer/technical divers

- Do not haul on the winch line
- Attach detailed written information about the incident to the casualty
- Position the boat into the wind at an angle of 30 degrees off the port bow. You may be asked to slowly motor (5 knots)

In the event of a lost diver scenario the dive boat should mark the last known position prior to leaving the incident site.

Insurance

International medical insurance to cover diving incidents and any subsequent treatment can be covered by taking out Divers Alert Network (DAN) insurance or Dive Assure. DAN can also advise on chamber locations and rescue facilities.

Conclusions

The safety planning of any single dive or series of dives may range from the simple to the extremely complex. Remember, define the hazards, assess the risks, plan for the specific scenarios and stay in practice.

One of the best weapons in your arsenal is you, provided that you are a prepared and practised, logical, thinking diver.

Notes & References

[1] 30 minutes maximum

[2] Dr William C Stone. *The Wakulla Springs Project*

[3] *The Wakulla Springs Project* book is an excellent reference for would be habitat designers. See Bibliography.

[4] P. 155

Chapter Fourteen
Tracking Absorbant Through Oxygen Consumption

Jeff Gourley

Oxygen is taken into the body via the lungs and ultimately used for the production of ATP in the mitochondria of our cells. Carbon Dioxide (***CO_2***) is a by-product of this cellular metabolic process and is carried away by the blood to the lungs. Few body cells are close enough to the surface to have any chance of obtaining oxygen and expelling carbon dioxide by direct air diffusion so the gas exchange must take place via the circulating blood. The blood is exposed to air over a large diffusing surface as it passes through the lungs. When the blood reaches the tissues, the small capillary vessels provide another large surface where the blood and tissue fluids are in close contact. Gases diffuse readily at both ends of the circuit and the blood has the remarkable ability to carry both oxygen and carbon dioxide. This system normally works so well that even the deepest cells of the body can obtain oxygen and get rid of excess carbon dioxide almost as readily as if they were completely surrounded by air.

In order to determine how much CO_2 we are producing we must first determine our VO_2 and our $MaxVO_2$.

Oxygen consumption (***VO_2***) is the amount of oxygen taken in and utilized by the body. Because most of the energy in the body is produced aerobically, VO_2 can be used to determine how much energy a subject is expending. VO_2 can be reported in absolute terms (***L/min)*** or relative to body mass (***ml/kg*min***). Oxygen consumption is dependent on the ability of the heart to pump out blood, the ability of the tissues to extract oxygen from the blood, the ability to ventilate and the ability of

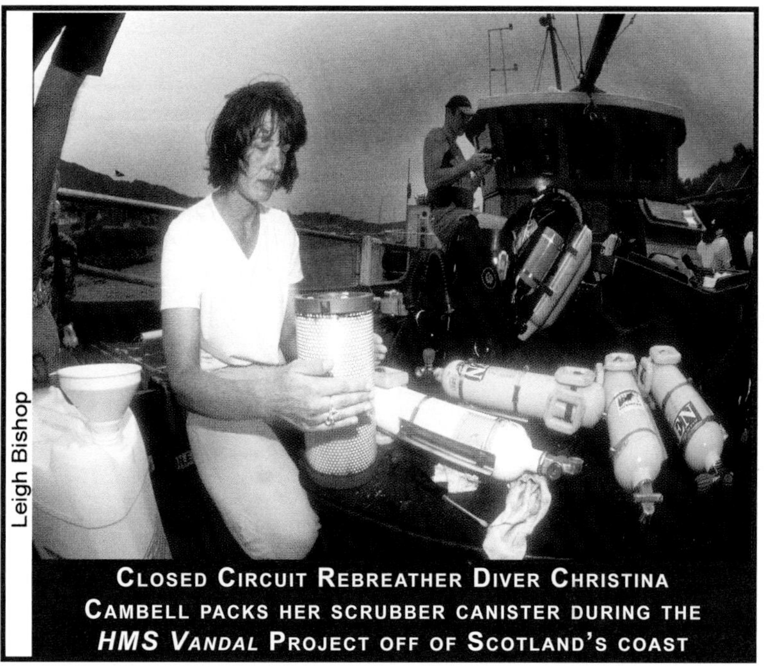
Leigh Bishop

Closed Circuit Rebreather Diver Christina Cambell packs her scrubber canister during the *HMS Vandal* Project off of Scotland's coast

At the alveolar level the exchange of O_2 and CO_2 takes place and is known as the RER or Respiratory Exchange Ratio. This is the ratio of carbon dioxide production to oxygen consumption (***VCO_2/VO_2***) and a direct correlation between the amount of O_2 consumed to the amount of CO_2 expired can be made. The majority of the CO_2 expired (approx. 2.5-6% CO_2) comes from cellular respiration, however during high intensity exercise some of the CO_2 that the subject is blowing off comes from buffering of the blood (in order to maintain proper PH).

the alveoli to extract oxygen from the air. Resting absolute values tend to be around .2-.5 L/min in men and .15-.4 L/min in women. The approximate resting relative VO_2 for all individuals is 3.5 ml/kg*min. Oxygen consumption is

	VO_2 (lpm)	RMV (acfm)	RMV (lpm)	Work Level
Rest	0.24	0.35	10	--
Sitting,standing quietly	0.40	0.42	12	Light
Walking in tank, min. rate	0.58	0.53	15	Light
Light activity in chamber	0.70	0.64	18	Light
Walking, muddy bottom, minimum	0.80	0.71	20	Moderate
Walking in tank, max. rate	1.10	0.99	28	Moderate
Walking, muddy bottom, maximum	1.20	1.14	32	Moderate
Swim, 0.8 (average speed)	1.40	1.34	38	Moderate
Swim, 1 knot	1.70	1.59	45	Heavy
Swim, 1.2 knots	2.50	2.12	60	Severe

Figure 14-1: US Navy Duration Chart

Eric Keibler

DIVER CHUCH GERLOVICH EXITING THE ENGINE ROOM IN THE *KENSHO MARU*, TRUK LAGOON, FSM

Activity	VO_2 (lpm)	RMV (acfm)	RMV (lpm)	Work Level
Rest	**0.24**	**0.35**	**10**	---------
Sitting, Standing Quietly	0.40	0.42	12	Light
Walking in Tank, Minimum Rate	0.58	0.53	15	Light
Light Activity in Chamber	0.70	0.64	18	Light
Walking, Muddy Bottom, Min. Rate	0.80	0.71	20	Moderate
Walking in Tank, Maximum Rate	1.10	0.99	28	Moderate
Walking Bottom, Maximum Rate	1.20	1.14	32	Moderate
Swim 0.8 Knot Average Speed)	1.40	1.34	38	Moderate
Swim, 1 Knot	1.70	1.59	45	Heavy
Swim, 1.2 Knot	2.50	2.12	60	Severe

Figure 14 - 1: US Navy Duration Chart

most frequently determined using open-circuit spirometry. Open-circuit spirometry can be used not only for the determination of oxygen consumption, but also for the determination of metabolic rate.

Maximal oxygen consumption (***VO_2max***) is the highest VO_2 value recorded during maximal exercise. VO_2max is thought to be the best indicator of aerobic capacity and therefore of aerobic fitness. It is also a relatively good predictor of endurance performance. VO_2max tends to be higher in men than in women. College age males have an average VO_2max of 45ml/kg*min and college age females have a VO_2max of about 35ml/kg*min. The highest absolute VO_2max values recorded have been in large endurance athletes, such as elite heavyweight rowers (values of over 7 L/min have been recorded), whereas the highest relative VO_2max values are typically recorded in small endurance athletes such as cross-country skiers, cyclists, and distance and middle distance runners (values of up to 90ml/kg*min have been recorded). VO_2 varies from day to day for many reasons; type of food consumed, temperature, health, environmental conditions, etc… and can vary greatly between individuals so only averages can be used.

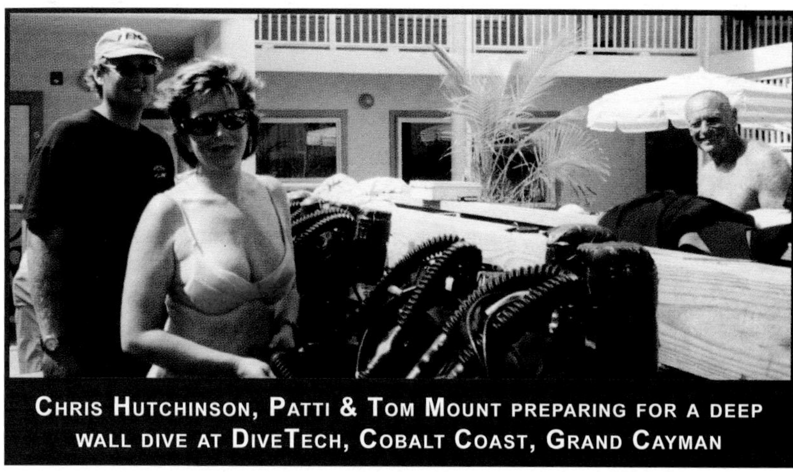

CHRIS HUTCHINSON, PATTI & TOM MOUNT PREPARING FOR A DEEP WALL DIVE AT DIVETECH, COBALT COAST, GRAND CAYMAN

Once you have approximated your VO_2 use that to calculate your Respiratory Quotient (***RQ***). RQ is the ratio of the amount of carbon dioxide produced to the amount of oxygen consumed during cellular processes. RQ values used to determine scrubber duration range from 0.7 to 1.0 depending on the study: Schreiner uses RQ = 0.8, HBOT Online uses RQ = 0.84, US Navy uses RQ = 0.9, and Bühlmann uses 1.0.

Figure 14-1, is a chart that the U.S. Navy uses for duration calculations. (***Note***: the ***Navy Diving Manual*** uses a VO_2 of 1.4 for planning.)

Now let's look at an example of how we can use these calculations, instead of time, to more safely determine how long our scrubber could last. For comparison take a CCR with a 3000 psi 27 cu ft (764 liters) oxygen tank and a CO_2 cartridge that can absorb 382 liters of CO_2. Apply the numbers that the Navy uses to calculate how long it could last. With an RQ of .9 when we use up that tank we will have created approximately 687 liters of CO_2. Using the Navy estimation the effectiveness of the cartridge would be unsafe after you used up half of the O_2 (687 ÷ 2 = 382) so you would need to change the cartridge every 1500 psi of O_2 consumed.

Any gas loss during ascent, or resulting from O_2 flushing, serves as an added safety buffer in your calculations. Increasing your activity during the dive results in higher VO_2 and therefore higher VCO_2.

FIGURE 14-2: OXYGEN CONSUMPTION

OTHER FACTORS THAT CAN EFFECT THE SCRUBBER DURATION

When exhaled gas passes through a scrubber a series of chemical reactions occurs. CO_2 gas is converted into calcium carbonate (***CaCO3***) a solid. For this reaction to occur there must be water present $CO_2 + H_2O \leftrightarrow H_2CO_3$ in fact, before proper scrubbing can occur there must be water already in the absorbent bed (not just humidity in the exhaled breathing gas). This water is not visible as a liquid but has been incorporated by the manufacturer during formulation. The improper storage of new or used absorbent can result in too little or too much water present in the material, and scrubber will be affected.

DISCLAIMER: The opinions and conclusions represented in this article are solely that of the author and not

DiveTech

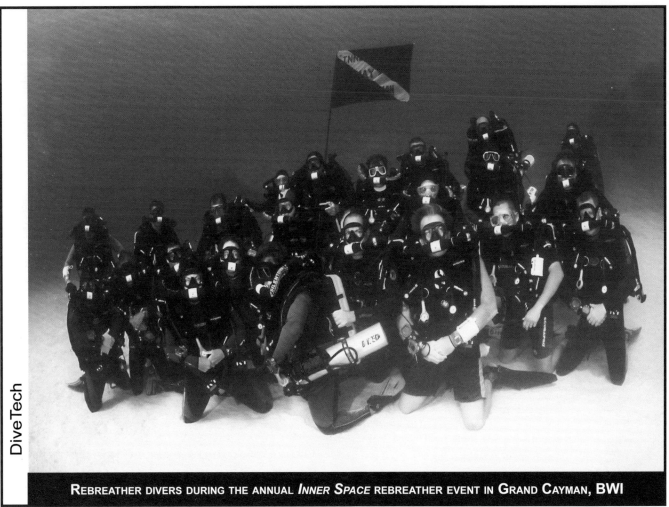

REBREATHER DIVERS DURING THE ANNUAL *INNER SPACE* REBREATHER EVENT IN GRAND CAYMAN, BWI

the texts cited. Determining personal VO_2, VCO_2, and the actual capability or duration of the scrubber for any given dive profile is the sole responsibility of the diver.

References

1. JD MacDougall, HA Wenger, H Green, eds.: Physiological Testing of the High-Performance Athlete, 2nd Ed., 2nd edn. Champaign, IL: Human Kinetics; 1991.
2. American College of Sports Medicine., BA Franklin, MH Whaley, ET Howley: ACSM's guidelines for exercise testing and prescription, 6th edn. Philadelphia: Lippincott Williams & Wilkins; 2000.
3. RA Boileau, CA Horswill: Body Composition in Sports: Measurement and Applications for Weight Loss and Gain. In: Exercise and Sports Science Edited by WE Garrett, DT Kirkendall. pp. 319-338. Philadelphia, PA: Lipincott Williams & Wilkins; 2000: 319-338.
4. SE Gaskill, BC Ruby, AJ Walker, OA Sanchez, RC Serfass, AS Leon: Validity and reliability of combining three methods to determine ventilatory threshold. Med Sci Sports Exerc 2001, 33:1841-8.
5. J Svedenhag, B Sjodin: Physiological characteristics of elite male runners in and off-season. Can J Appl Sport Sci 1985, 10:127-33.
6. Jeffrey E. Bozanic: Mastering Rebreathers. 2002 pp.158-183.
7. Navy Diving Manual: Chapter 3.
8. HBOT Online.

Chapter Fifteen ROVs & Hard Suits For Expeditions

Joseph Dituri M.S.

As a growing trend, technical dives are becoming longer and deeper. As many of you well know, the deeper the dive, the greater the decompression penalty for getting to the bottom even if the diver finds they are not near the wreck, or that this spot is not what they thought it would be. Remotely Operated Vehicles (***ROV***), drop cameras and Hard Diving suits may assist expeditions in reducing the amount of unnecessary bottom time.

In expedition diving, the exact location of the wreck or site may not be known or due to the current or a storm the site may have moved. If it were always in the same place it probably would have been dove. When looking for an item on the bottom, side scan sonar may be useful. Side scan sonar is specialized Sound Navigation and Ranging (***SONAR***) system used to search for objects on the seafloor. Similar to other SONAR, a side scan transmits sound energy and analyzes the return signal (***echo***) that has bounced off the seafloor or the object. The Side scan sonar system's transducer is housed in a towed array or tow fish, which is towed through the water several meters above the bottom at 2-4 knots. The transmitted energy is formed into the shape of a cone that sweeps the seafloor from directly under the towed array to either side, to a distance of between 16-45 ft (5-50 m) although other ranges can be used depending upon the size of the object being sought.

The strength of the return is continuously recorded creating a "picture" of the ocean floor. Objects that protrude from the bottom create a dark image and shadows from these objects are light areas. Most side scan systems cannot provide any depth information so must be used in conjunction with a depth sounder to ensure the towed array does not impact the bottom. Side-scan sonar is also called side looking sonar and bottom classification sonar. While towing, specific areas of interest are often marked with GPS as possible target areas. Although the resolution of the side scan image is generally good, it may be difficult

Oceaneering International

ROV ON THE PROPELLER OF THE *TITANIC*

to determine if the dive spot is what you are intending and it may useful to scout these areas with a "pre-dive" where a something descends to the bottom for a look.

ROVs or drop cameras are excellent for searching large areas and save divers for direct mission-oriented dives. How many of you have dove using a depth recorder on the boat that has shown a "great dive spot" with dramatic drop offs, which upon diving is only a gentle sloping pile of sand? The price for this drop to 400 ft (121 m) could be hours of decompression and a wasted dive day for at least two divers. An added feature of the ROV is the ability to take digital footage for review by experts who can provide oversight without actually being on site.[1]

Joe Dituri

JOSEPHINE AMY DITURI WITH A SMALL VIDEO ROV

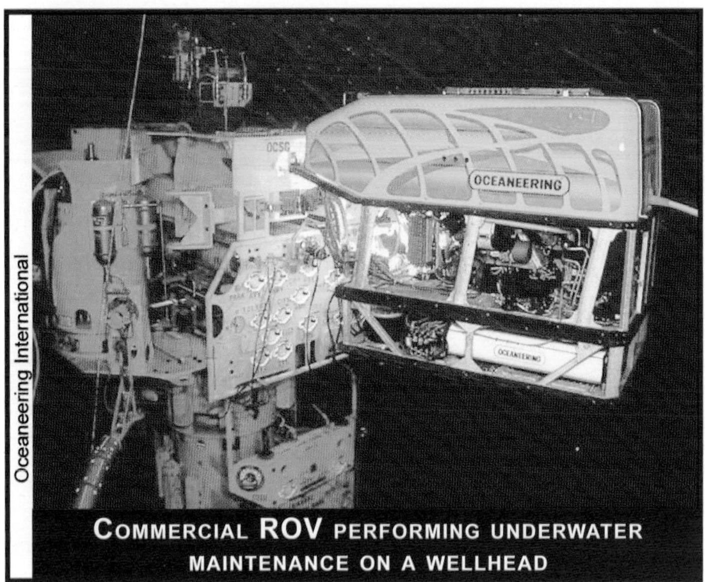

COMMERCIAL ROV PERFORMING UNDERWATER MAINTENANCE ON A WELLHEAD

There are many classifications of ROVs, some of which are more practical for technical expedition diving. Working class ROVs generally have large control vans and are as large as 12 ft (4 m) square. These systems require a large crane or complex Launch and Recovery System (***LARS***) that prohibits their use from normal dive boats. Additionally, these working class ROVs are overkill for the quick look required in expedition diving as they have multiple thrusters and manipulator arms. The working class ROVs require a control van usually the size of a conventional CONNEX box to house the video reproduction equipment and control sections. They are generally cost prohibitive as well.

The most economical class of ROV is the video class. One can be purchased for under $10,000 and provides digital video that is shown on a small liquid crystal display screen or can be recorded by a laptop or other digital video recorder. Their LARS is a person lowering it into the water by hand and these systems do not take up much room on a boat. It is generally operated using 110 V AC and can be fitted with a converter to use DC (***battery***) power.

One downfall with the video class ROV is that they generally do not have a significant amount of thruster power. It is difficult for it to haul the lengths of tether required for expedition depth diving. One solution is to tie a clump weight 70 ft (20 m) from the ROV onto the umbilical. Then lower the clump into the water with the ROV. Once the clump weight hits the bottom, the ROV will be able to search a 130 ft (40 m) diameter circle around that spot. This increases significantly the ROVs ability to maneuver through the water by effectively eliminating the excess tether required to be carried by the ROV although it does limit range. Bottom visibility is generally no greater than 130 ft (40 m), so this system does not hamper the ability to obtain a quick look. If required, the weight and ROV could be picked up, dive boat moved into a new position and the weight and ROV re-deployed.

Drop cameras are just that - video cameras (protected from the pressure in a case) that are dropped to the ocean floor and connected to a surface monitor. Generally these cameras have no thrusters and what you see is what you get. You can maneuver the boat around to look around the ocean floor, but they have much less efficacy than the video class ROV and generally cost a little less. This author's experience has them limited to well know positions of wrecks.

Another benefit to both the ROV and the drop camera is they allow the surface support team to video the dive and observe from above. This could significantly increase safety by allowing someone who is not involved in actually diving to monitor the dive. A threat or concern can be communicated to the diver by flashing the ROVs lights on and off and pointing with the ROV. Light signals would have to be discussed prior to dive. Additionally, the ROV tether could be used to drop a note to the diver with a carbineer. The ROV's tether can also be used to lead the diver directly to the wreck or site there-by decreasing dive time. These ROV or camera lights also function as an additional source of lighting and the video could be used to complete a record of the dive.

One atmosphere (also called Atmospheric Diving Suits [***ADS***]) hard suits, WASP suits or Newt Suits (after their conceptual designer Phil Nuytten) are pressure vessels (diving suits) where the pilot is completely isolated from the sea pressure by the aluminum of the suit and is not affected by the increasing pressure with depth. Contrary to popular thought, these suits maintain a slight pressure vacuum and the pilot is not under any external pressure. One atmosphere suits are a superb method of exploring very deep areas without requiring decompression. The suits have on board digital cameras and light that allow all the pilot's motions to be recorded with a topside digital video recorder. These commercial off the shelf suits allow a diver to visualize first hand the life or wrecks at 1200 fsw (366 msw). Some units made to a different standard for the U.S. Navy have the capability to go to 2000 fsw (610 msw). Opponents of one atmosphere suits claim the same job can be done with an ROV, but anyone who has worked with ROVs know that with a monocular view provided by a single ROV, depth perception is difficult. Some mini submarines have the same human input capability as well.

The pilot gets in a hard suit and the surface support team seals it. These suits are tethered to the surface by an umbilical. All functions such as thruster control and manipulator control are accomplished by the pilot from inside the suit. Special clothing must be wore inside that has been tested to ensure it does not emit are harmful smell once enclosed in a single atmosphere. There are multiple back ups systems to the communications system in the unlikely event there is a problem with communications.

These suits require significant surface support, atmospheric monitoring and are generally very heavy. Similar to a working class ROV, weighing almost 1500 lbs, they may require a LARS to get them in the water. They are generally considered cost prohibitive,

Left & Right: Joe Dituri in various Hard Suits preparing for 2000 fsw (600 msw) dives

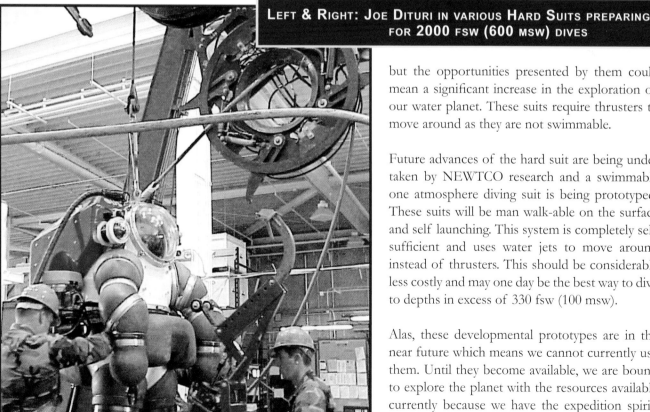

but the opportunities presented by them could mean a significant increase in the exploration of our water planet. These suits require thrusters to move around as they are not swimmable.

Future advances of the hard suit are being under taken by NEWTCO research and a swimmable one atmosphere diving suit is being prototyped. These suits will be man walk-able on the surface and self launching. This system is completely self sufficient and uses water jets to move around instead of thrusters. This should be considerably less costly and may one day be the best way to dive to depths in excess of 330 fsw (100 msw).

Alas, these developmental prototypes are in the near future which means we cannot currently use them. Until they become available, we are bound to explore the planet with the resources available currently because we have the expedition spirit. Using a video class ROV or drop camera is a cost

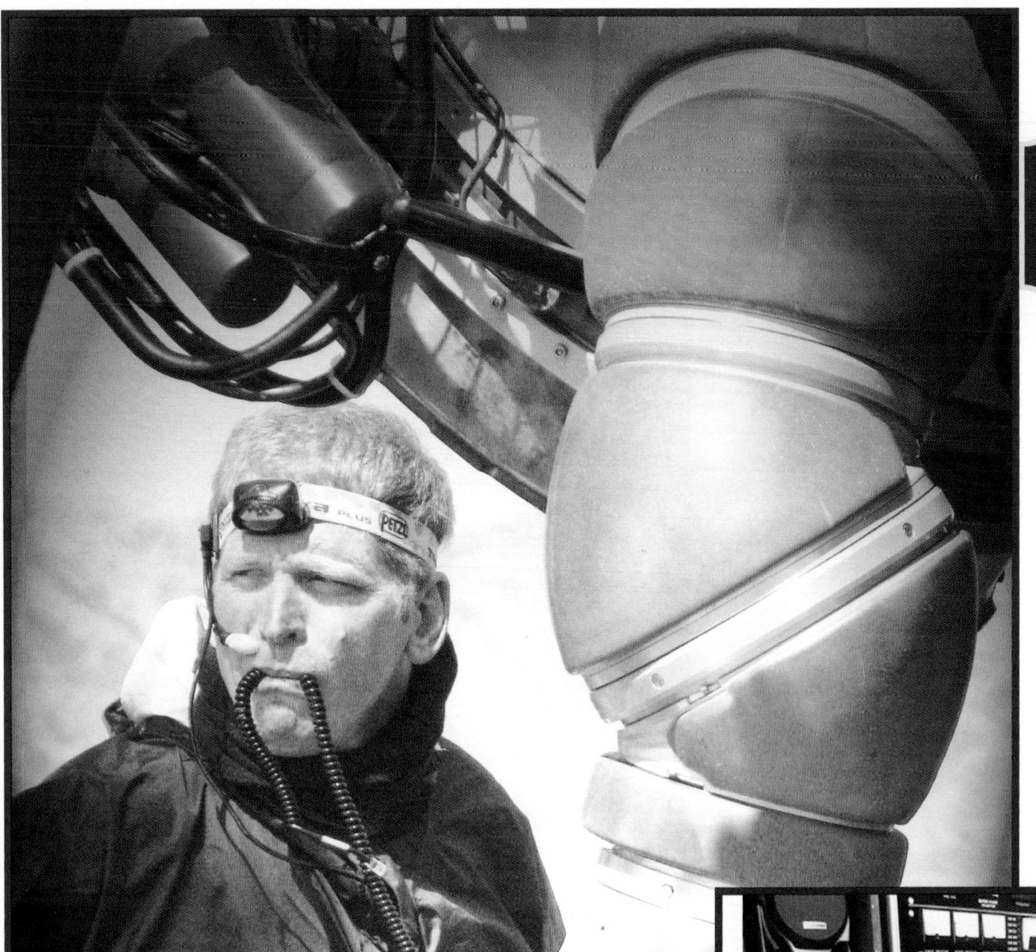

LEFT:
JOE DITURI AFTER A TRAINING DIVE WITH A HARD SUIT

Oceaneering International

OPERATOR FLYING AN ROV INSIDE A CONTROL VAN

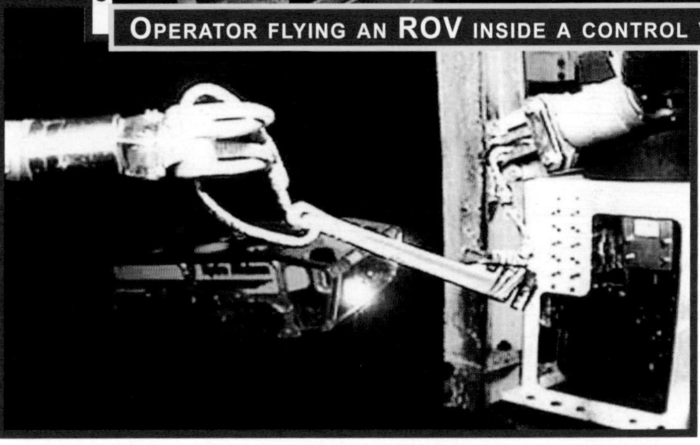

effective way to increase safety of expedition dives and will maximize the time a diver spends diving directly on the site vice looking for it.

Footnote

[1] Remotely Operated Vehicle Use Within Shipyards, Joseph Dituri, ***Journal of Ship Production,*** Volume 19, Number 4, 1 November 2003, pp. 205-206(2)

Section Three
Psychological Aspects & Survival Strategies

Photo by Kevin Gurr

Photo courtesy Mel Clark

Chapter Sixteen

Spiritual, Mental & Physical Training For Safe Diving & A Better Life

Tom Mount D.Sc., Ph.D., N.D.

Spiritual, Mental and Physical development processes enable us to become better people and enjoy life more. Each process covers a wide variety of issues and in itself could be a stand-alone article.

Most people think of diving as a purely physical pursuit, when in reality it is much more than that. Diving, like Martial Arts, offers spiritual and mental growth. For many of us, our dedication to diving and "inner-space," or the realms beneath the water, is similar to ours, or others, devotion to religious ideas and concepts. The practice of being at peace within and looking into ourselves has a traquil and soothing effect on us, thus making it ideal to be at ease spiritually and mentally, opening the gate to greater understanding of these realms. Looking into oneself is a conscious decision which requires self-discipline, self-acceptance and the ability to forgive. Self-evaluation also encompasses the willingness to receive "universal energy," which is often defined as attuning and channeling for specific energy for healing the body and mind. However, the rewards of seeking and discovering internal balance in our spiritual, physical and mental lives are well worth the effort, as such an undertaking is a major step towards individual peace and personal happiness. The path to this level of self-harmony often uncovers buried, yet innate, healing abilities and leads us toward the realization of self as "holistic," or spontaneously evolving through the parallel action of mind and body working as one, creating a version of self that is at once whole and greater than the sum of its individual parts.

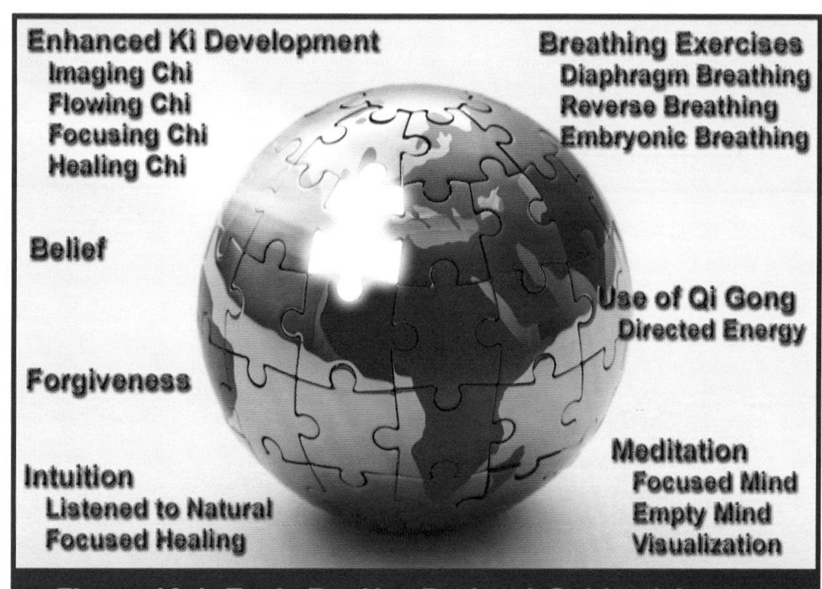

Figure 16-1: Tools For Use During A Spiritual Journey

Seeking internal balance has additional compensations: Increased health; enhanced self-healing; greater happiness; enhanced self-esteem; stronger will power; heightened immune system; maximized survival skills and a more peaceful life on the physical plane in which we exist. Our relationships will be enhanced, our attitudes will become more positive, and we can dissolve negativity from our lives. Through this growth process we gain more respect in the communities in which we live. If these rewards entice you, then prepare to journey deep into yourself and discover your personal path to enlightenment.

First, let's discuss the tools and vehicles for this internal trip and define terms that will be used during this exploration.

You will find a partial list of tools that may be used during the Spiritual portion of our journey in Figure 16-1.

As you can see, it is evident that our quest will demand developing the spirit to attain the rewards previously mentioned. It is an exciting path we're on and one with immediate rewards. ***Let's begin...***

Spiritual & Mind

The spiritual realm is the one that actually directs our life. This is the realm where we are connected with God or universal energy, and it is the one least explored by many. Others vastly misunderstand it. This discussion has no bearing on religious beliefs but rather focuses on the energy we gather and use to sustain our lives.

Let's begin with breathing exercises. At first, some may question how breathing is considered spiritual. The answer is simple: ***breathing gaps the spiritual, mental and physical realms*** as it is the sum of all energy and information in the universe, and as such, it provides the energy for our life form. In

FIG 16-2: TOM DEMONSTRATES CORRECT BREATHING

this context, understand that breathing is the essence of the spirit when manifested in the physical body. It gives the body energy to survive; it empowers our mental abilities, uniting the brain with the spirit and thus creates the mind. It is interesting to note that the mind is neither the brain nor the spirit and in western culture has no specific definition. But, the mind contains the sum of all information if it is receptive. Breathing is the ***biofeedback*** path for unity of spirit, mind, and body.

Correct breathing is done through the diaphragm. In Daoism, philosophically, a contributor to aging is the breath (source of all energy thus life). Breath moves upwards from the diaphragm and center of our being towards the throat, resulting in less exchange of energy via the lungs, which deprives us of the energy attained with diaphragmatic breathing. In fact, correct breathing provides more oxygen to the blood and tissues. According to Eastern medical beliefs, incorrect breathing speeds up the aging process and predisposes one to stress and disease. It is notable that current Western medical thought often acknowledges stress as a major contributor to disease. But, the mind contains the sum of all information if it is receptive. Breathing is the biofeedback path for unity of spirit, mind, and body.

POINTS TO REMEMBER

Stress changes our breathing or energy patterns creating a base for abnormalities in our physical and mental being that may lead to ailments, including cancer, kidney, and heart disease.

Correct breathing is done through the diaphragm. ***Daoism***, or ***Taoism***, as it is often called in western culture, is an Eastern philosophy emphasizing, among other concepts, nature, vitality, peace, modesty, and humility. Daoist thought relates breathing to aging, as correct breathing links the self with the source from which energy and life derives. Breath moves upwards from the diaphragm and center of our being towards the throat, resulting in less exchange of energy via the lungs, which deprives us of the energy attained with diaphragmatic breathing. In fact, correct breathing provides more oxygen to the blood and tissues. It is easy to understand that incorrect breathing speeds up the aging process and predisposes one to stress and disease. Many, in both eastern philosophy and western medicine today, acknowledge stress as a major contributor to disease.

In Eastern philosophy, breathing is also the source of ***Chi***, or life energy. Chi allows us to balance the negative and positive aspects of the body and mind, and as such enables us to realize our true physical and mental strength.A person with strong Chi, derived by proper breathing can accomplish the seemingly impossible. A person with good Chi may remain calm in the midst of chaos.

GUIDELINES FOR CORRECT (NATURAL) BREATHING

Concentrate on breathing through the diaphragm. To do this you must relax the stomach area and chest; otherwise correct breathing cannot take place. Perform slow deep inhalations followed by slow long exhalations. Most people in western society breathe between 15 to 20 times per minute. Those who practice correct breathing average between 5 and 10 breaths a minute. The author breathes between 3 and 5 breaths a minute, varying with workload. Why is this slow breathing so beneficial? It maximizes the exchange of gases in the lungs providing more oxygen (***energy***) for the blood and tissues.

If we look at the lungs we discover two-thirds of the blood is in the lower one third of the lungs. Therefore it becomes apparent that if a person is a ***chest breather***, or one who inhales and exhales via the upper two thirds of the lungs they most likely have inefficient gas exchange, which negatively affects their energy levels. If diaphragmatic breathing is used, a dual effect occurs: Gas travels to all portions of the lungs, allowing more oxygen (or in Eastern terms, ***energy***) to enter the circulatory system, and increasing carbon dioxide, or waste, removal.

Learn to maintain the same slow breathing rate even while

working. This takes time and practice but is worth the effort. You will learn to pull in more air volume in a given breath under heavy workloads, rather than increase your respiratory rate. It is obvious to see the benefit of this in martial arts environments. Make your breathing a continuous action. Only hold your breath during specific breathing exercises or for breathhold diving.

Anytime you feel stressed, first do a complete exhalation then follow this with natural (***slow, deep***) breathing. If you are upset due to a threatening event, anger, fright or emotional stimuli, this will calm and allow you to deal more effectively with the situation.

Always remember, breathing and the way we breathe controls the direction, force and effect of the energy we are bringing into ourselves, or extending outward from ourselves.

On land, breathe through the nose. Avoid chest breathing. It is shallow, thus causing a higher rate. This changes the acid to base balance. The O_2 binding becomes too tight with RBC and the body becomes energy starved. It also restricts blood vessels causing cold feet, hands, etc., and may lead to damage of the heart and brain.

Dantien breathing incorporates both the stomach and lower back; on inhalation they expand outward and on exhalation they both will contract towards each other. This is an ideal way to loosen muscles and to relieve stress.

This exercise should be practiced regularly. This exercises all of the internal organs filling them with Chi (***internal energy***) and at the same time massages the organs, which leads to better health.

Embryonic breathing is easy and gentle. It leads to a feeling of serenity. It is very slow and very relaxed, allowing us to totally release if the mind is quiet. This is an advanced stage of breathing and, like Dantien breathing, is a combination of 4 stages: inhale, the turnaround and relax, exhalation, and a slight natural pause before the next breath.

These breathing techniques should be done as effortlessly as possible; do not offer "strength" while doing this. At the same time feel the 5 qualities of the breath. It should be slow, long, deep, smooth and even - with no one part of the breath being favored. Practice this in 10 minute sessions. Continue to practice until this becomes your normal breathing habit.

Reverse breathing is an exercise where we actually reverse the action of the diaphragm while breathing. This technique develops breathing efficiency, focusing power and/or healing energy. This is not a normal way of breathing, but as an exercise it increases Chi and works the diaphragm muscles. It is used in some martial arts applications and should be practiced for 5-10 minutes, a couple of times a week. On inhalation, the tongue raises up against the roof of the mouth. It is important to form an image of drawing energy into the lower back. On exhalation, lower the tongue and exhale from the mouth. Visualize your breath leaving from your lower abdomen. Thus, the energy enters via the lower back and exits the front of the lower stomach. This strengthens the kidneys and brings healing into the entire lower body.

Meditation is the key to unlocking the sprit and uniting it with the physical body. When meditating the mind is free; all blocks are removed and the sprit can absorb the energy of the universe. This is when the mind and brain communicate with the sprit. During meditation one becomes relaxed, may experience inner vision, intuition, perception, and even clairvoyance.

Focused mind is a meditation method where one focuses on a single item or group of single things. This can be an object, a color, light, or even a void. This develops concentration, healing techniques and psychic protection. It also develops discipline, concentration and internal power. It is ideal in focusing and achieving our goals in life.

Empty mind meditation is actually a method of not allowing distracting thoughts to interrupt us during meditation. In

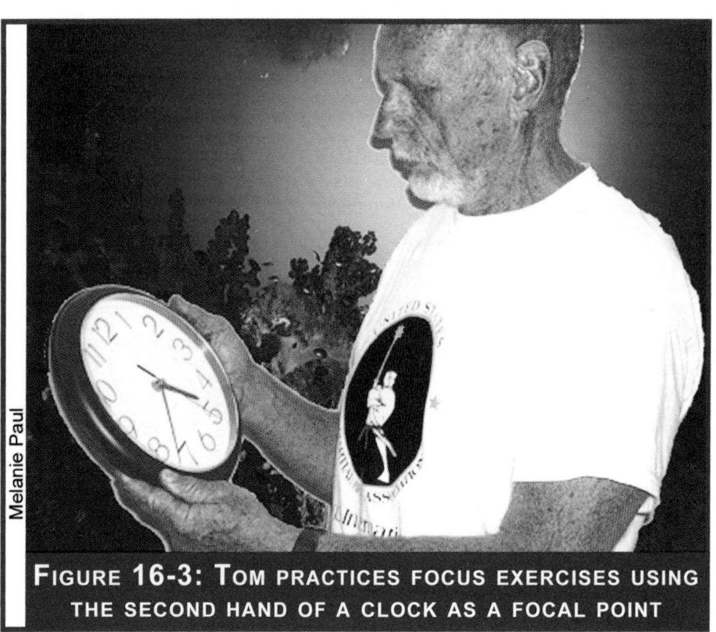

Figure 16-3: Tom practices focus exercises using the second hand of a clock as a focal point

this form of meditation we may actually focus on an open vision or on a single purpose. This is ideal for learning to avoid having feelings, emotions or images that may distract us from our meditative objective. This carries over into the everyday as we learn to vent thoughts that may derail us from our purpose in life.

Visualization meditation is a strong meditative tool and the most commonly practiced discipline. This is exemplified by pre-sparring visualizations, survival visualizations or goal achievement. A major form of visualization meditation occurs in fighting and over-coming disease or the achievement of lifelong goals. It enhances our belief system as we see ourselves doing the things we seek, as if already accomplished.

Points to Remember

Meditation allows us to see and experience what we desire, enables us to believe and pray during this time, and otherwise achieve those things we believe in.

Many people advocate and practice visualization meditations in conjunction with ***affirmations***, or positive self-statements such as "I will succeed..." that are mediated on and/ or repeated in order to implant the thought as a viable, obtainable goal. Affirmations are of the most powerful tools available to us and everyone should practice it. It is now used by most world-class athletes and is responsible for numerous sports world records. It also leads to healing both chronic and acute disease. In my own experiences I have used it to survive an airplane crash, control pain, stop bleeding from a gunshot wound, control pain and bleeding when a finger was bitten off, to control bleeding and pain from a knife wound and overcome a prostrate problem. It is remarkable that this type of visualization is so effective in improving performance and enhancing our immune systems.

Overall, meditation is the most effective tool we have to prepare us for survival and success in life. It helps us develop a stronger belief system and reap the benefits of our prayers. As is stated in most doctrines in one form or another, ***what so ever you ask for, ask for believing and you will receive it.***

This goes well with, "***What the mind believes it can achieve.***" Also avoid the "***I Want;***" a syndrome that has a lack of belief and little probability of achievement. Meditation is the tuning fork that unites us with our higher spirituality and the power of the universe, our God. It allows us to meet our guardian angels and become more intimate with our spiritual direction. Meditation leads us to question and then discover our own beliefs. This deepens the belief and personalizes it, creating a greater foundation and inner growth. It may transform you into a greater spiritual leader, a more content person, a more deeply religious person, or an independent view of life and eternity. It will make you a stronger person, as you will discover your impersonal self.

Grand Master Tom Mount demonstrating Qi Gong energy building

Enhanced Chi development fosters our abilities to focus, become stronger and even to become a healer. ***Chi*** is the use and transfer of energy through the breath and universal energy gathering into a resource to be used by the individual.

Chi also enables us to accomplish the seemingly impossible and difficult. Since Chi is gained from drawing energy into our spirit, we are more able to focus on our mental being and physically display its power. Keep in mind that Chi is a mystical quantity that is manifested by using breathing techniques and the universe's omnipresent flow of energy. We all have the ability to employ Chi, but for most it takes years to develop the trust in ourselves to manifest its usage.

Points to Remember

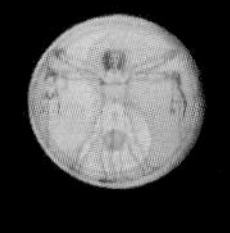

Once it is incorporated into ourselves, we can control our mind and physical being through the spiritual energy achieved by pulling Chi into us.

We access Chi through numerous techniques, which are linked to breathing. We can imagine it as pure energy, light or a flowing body of water. Chi can be focused into a single body part. Those who have mastered its use can distribute it throughout the body

Martial arts practitioners demonstrate Chi through acts such as resisting choking, getting out of a body lock, and controlling an opponent's grip. Chi is also used by martial artists to maintain their stance and push through their sword or knife which, based on simple physics, is thrusting them backwards when they attempt an attack with the blade and are met with resistance. It seems mystical, yet it is simple in manifestation. To use high levels of Chi requires practice, breathing control, belief and concentration combined with energy-gathering.

Chi can also be used for health maintenance, as a healing entity and pain control mechanism. ***Qi Gong*** is a practice that emphasizes building, nourishing and directing Chi. Accomplished Qi Gong practitioners can direct Chi as a healing agent when injured and even assist the healing of others. Chi can be directed into the palms, for instance.

Energy passed from the mid-point of the hand towards another being helps to heal them. It can also be used in the same fashion to increase strength and balance. Qi Gong incorporates a combination of visualization, forms (***frolics***), and energy gathering exercises. It is frequently used in conjunction with or by other martial arts. Qi Gong is a part of Chinese Medicine that dates back thousands of years. Traditional Chinese

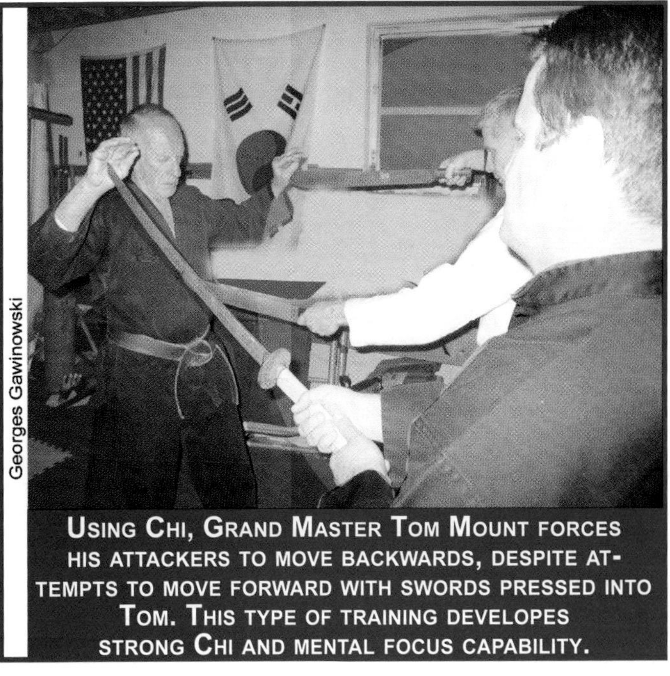

USING CHI, GRAND MASTER TOM MOUNT FORCES HIS ATTACKERS TO MOVE BACKWARDS, DESPITE ATTEMPTS TO MOVE FORWARD WITH SWORDS PRESSED INTO TOM. THIS TYPE OF TRAINING DEVELOPES STRONG CHI AND MENTAL FOCUS CAPABILITY.

Medicine uses Chi, acupressure, acupuncture, herbs and many other energy techniques to treat disease.

> **POINTS TO REMEMBER**
>
> What the mind believes, it can achieve

Intuition is a valuable asset of our minds. This is that little voice that somehow knows or sees without a conscious reason for why. Intuition is enhanced when incorporated with meditation or Qi Gong. Today there is also a growing population of Medical Intuition practitioners. These folk become so tuned into their intuition and their ability to sense the distress in others that they average on first time diagnosis, as high, or higher than medical doctors do. Many also have the operability of intuitive healing which has been more effective than traditional western medicine in some cases.

While all of us are not skilled in medical intuition we can use it to avoid mishaps in life. For this reason, the author advocates pre-exercise/diving/activity visualizations allowing the mind to sense any bad vibrations about the activity. Visualization also relaxes the body prior to activity. It is interesting that on all of the tragic accidents I have thoroughly reviewed over the last 40 years, at least one or more people have had

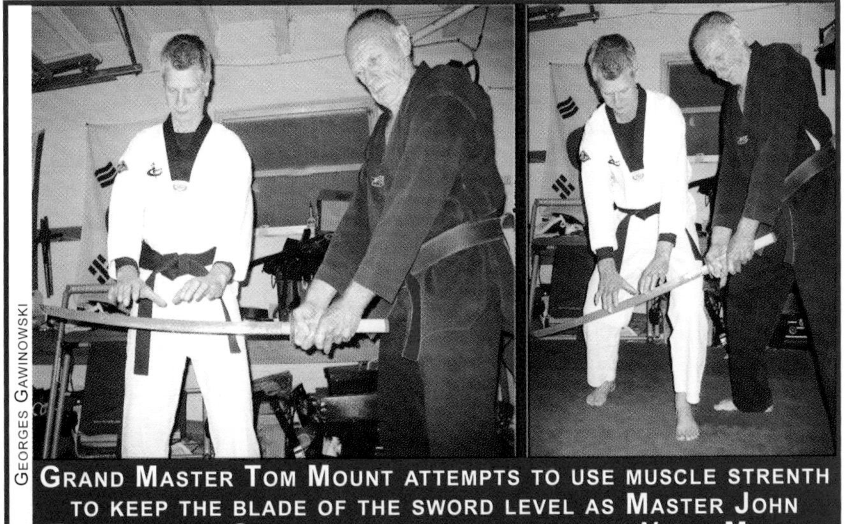

GRAND MASTER TOM MOUNT ATTEMPTS TO USE MUSCLE STRENTH TO KEEP THE BLADE OF THE SWORD LEVEL AS MASTER JOHN TIMINSKI USES CHI TO FORCE THE BLADE DOWN. *NOTE*: MASTER JOHN NEVER ACTUALLY TOUCHES THE BLADE WITH HIS HANDS

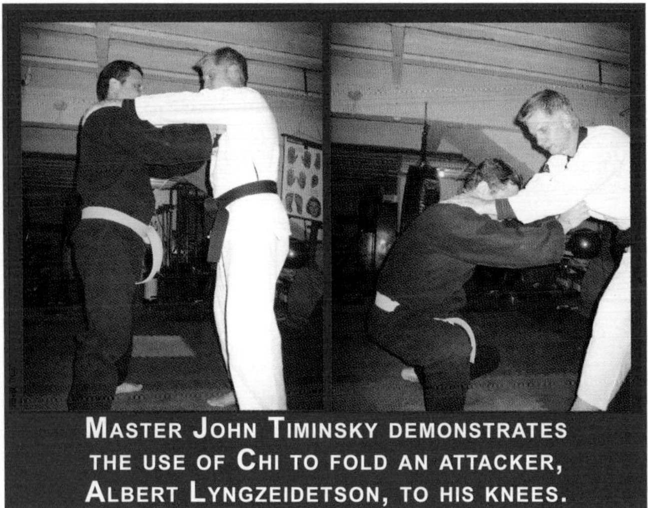

Master John Timinsky demonstrates the use of Chi to fold an attacker, Albert Lyngzeidetson, to his knees.

a "bad feeling" about the situation or person(s) prior to the incident. If we train ourselves to listen to these feelings we can avoid many accidents.

Belief is the foundation for all accomplishments. Belief is developed through reinforcement combined with faith. To truly believe one must have faith, and faith is essential to becoming a believer. Our minds and our sprits can partake in miracles if we have faith, trust in our abilities and believe in them. But, for many, it takes a long process to develop and tune in to these essential parts of the human spirit and mind

Indeed teaching martial arts and diving has taught me this lesson. New students have the capacity to do many of the feats that an experienced martial artist (real martial artist not just those who kick and punch, and expert divers) can do except they do not yet have the faith, trust or belief to do these skills. Even at the black belt level or dive instructor level they are still developing these areas and although they exercise many examples of Chi, some still doubt it.

We must first believe, have faith in ourselves, and in the power of the universe before we truly experience the internal power in our lives. Once we believe and accept these points, all else will follow in natural order.

Martial artists and divers alike need to develop their inner beliefs, trust and faith to survive the seemingly impossible or to realize their full potential.

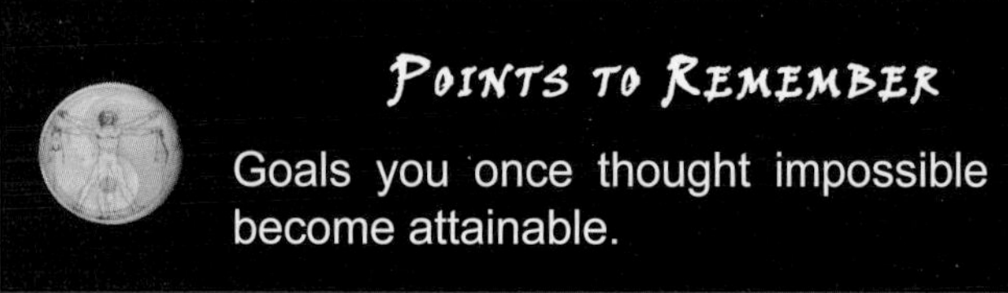

Points to Remember

Goals you once thought impossible become attainable.

Forgiveness is the most difficult of tools to master for advancement in life. Yet forgiveness is the true key to gaining spiritual power. Without forgiveness we tend to spiritually stagnate. It is also a prerequisite to enable one to love fully. Forgiveness is essential to develop a belief system, faith and trust. Everyone has something or someone in his or her past or present lives that must be forgiven. This act of forgiveness is essential for us to grow spiritually, mentally and physically. This is perhaps the hardest of the tools for us to develop and utilize yet is so vital to our growth and health.

Failure to forgive leads to fear, anger, frustration, distrust, insecurity, hate and numerous other roadblocks to personal success, growth, achievements, goals, health and happiness. It can create stress and reduce health, both mentally and physically.

It is essential that we learn to forgive. Meditation is an ideal tool to assist us on this path. Without forgiveness we tend to get bogged down into a sea of negativity, confusion, anger and frustration - ***and that's no way to live***.

Mental & Mind

The ***mind*** is the most powerful tool we can use to become mentally and spirituality in tune. When we discuss mental aspects, we include our mind as an inner link between our brain and our spiritual being.

Our ***brain*** is an amazing and narrowly understood entity. One human brain contains enough energy to fulfill the power requirements of Los Angeles County for 24 hours. The average person uses less than 5% of it. When you consider what is accomplished using only 5% - 10% of our brain, it is astonishing to comprehend a fully activated brain. Special exercises can help us develop and use more of our brain.

Some of the ways we develop and use our brain include our ***spiritual body*** - the ***brain, mind and physical body*** together. We can set ***goals*** and use their power to achieve them. Goals give us mental direction, influence our strategies to attain things we desire, and reinforce our beliefs. Goals are vital to lift ourselves to any level we seek yet most people do not do it.

When setting your goals, think long-term and imagine your ultimate desires. Then divide the goals into segments building towards the ultimate ones. Goals should span a lifetime - ten year, five, four, three, two, one, six months, and finally monthly (up to six months). Short-term goals are easy to achieve. As you complete your goals set more demanding goals. Begin with the simple ones. You will strengthen your belief system. As they become more demanding, your belief system will flourish.

Always write down your goals, map their course and visualize accomplishing them fully. ***Visualization*** is an important tool and works best with short-term goals. Performance improvements in sports are well documented among athletes who use visualization. It expands your horizons and personal capabilities beyond your wildest dreams. Visualization also increases Chipower,which has beneficial side effects i.e. a stronger immune system, less anxiety, increased emotional balance and it enhances your life overall.

IANTD LICENSEES (L) JANG-HWA HONG (KOREA) & (R) PAUL LIJNEN (BENELUX) CHECK & FOCUS ON EACH OTHER AS A TEAM TO PRE-BREATHE THEIR CCRs.

Affirmations are also helpful. To review, an affirmation is stating a goal as if it has been accomplished. Healers and successful business people use this technique. Affirmations may be verbal, written or incorporated into mental pictures. Try using affirmations in each form. Looking in a mirror and stating positive affirmations will accelerate your goal accomplishments.

The most extreme sin is not having a ***goal in life.*** This leads to a subdued and unbalanced state. It places someone in limbo so they just drift with the tides. People without goals get lucky and have short-term wellness but typically live in turmoil. They rarely find lasting happiness or peace, and frequently wind up jealous of those who appear to have the traits and success they desire but lack the energy to achieve.

POINTS TO REMEMBER

Having an open mind is an imperative step towards accepting others and true happiness

Gaining focus is a major step towards developing concentration, full potential and self-actualization. Begin to focus the mind. Sit and look at the second hand on a clock. Discard any thoughts and focus 100% on the movement of the second hand. This may seem difficult in the beginning but skill develops rapidly. With practice you can totally focus for five or more minutes. Try these exercises combined with visualization techniques. When we face threats of any kind, we must focus. In life or death situations, people who focus their minds and energy fully on survival can overcome what's threatening them-regardless of what it is. Focus speeds up learning, enhances intelligence, recognizes intuition and makes better decisions.

Open-mindedness is another aspect of mental development that is ignored. It teaches us new concepts and knowledge, tolerance and acceptance, and honesty. This helps us actually see the symbolic self in others and us. We can share this understanding, be calm, and omit expectations

POINTS TO REMEMBER

Exercise is not an option for physical health. It is mandated.

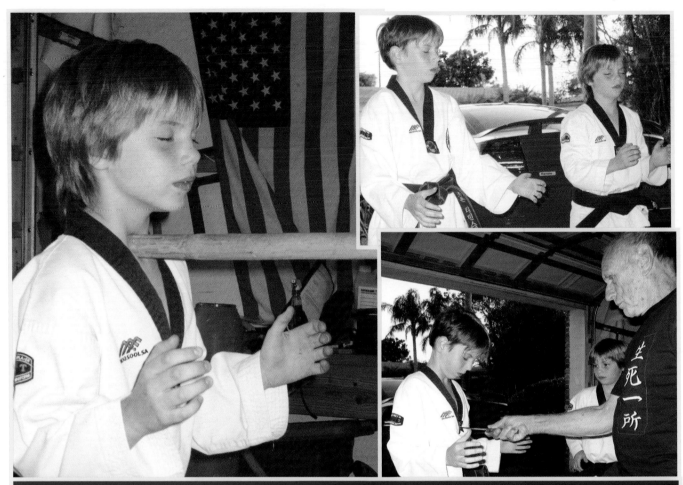

Jordin & Chase Timinsky focus on building energy & then channel their Chi to defend themselves against the knife & staff. Grand Master Tom Mount, using muscle strength only, is pressing against them. In both examples, the boys are able to actually push Grand Master Mount backwards while the weapon is held against them. Jordin, age 12, and Chase, Age 8, have received special energy training from Grand Master Mount in order to perform these skills.

Please Do Not Try This Without Receiving The Proper Training!

or attachments that weaken our being. This allows us to give and receive feelings more fully, without selfish expectations.

Maintaining an open mind throughout life is a most rewarding goal. Always study your own existence and the sources of life. Engage in research about the earth and universe that provide more internal knowledge. This brings true wisdom and better equips you to deal with life's changes. It will even give you personal power to enact positive changes in your life.

Understanding means looking deep inside your higher self for life's true virtue. Be analytical, yet trusting of your intuitive values and ascend into a more peaceful existence with greater confidence. Understanding enables us to respond proactively, removes doubt, builds confidence and allows us to ignore negative influences. It also leads to acceptance.

Attitude is the summation of everything above. It is the quality that shapes our lives. It makes things happen, attracts our success, and reflects our soul. Developing a good attitude brings good things to life and success in areas we value. A bad attitude will ultimately bring misfortune. Attitude is controllable and changeable through our evolution as previously discussed. We can change and indeed should always continue growing and making consistent changes in our attitudes.

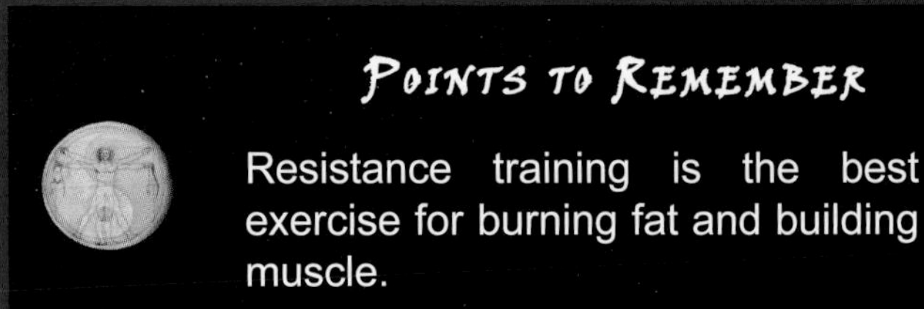

Points to Remember

Resistance training is the best exercise for burning fat and building muscle.

TOM USES CHI TO ACTUALLY PUSH JOHN BACKWARDS.

PHYSICAL & MENTAL CONDITIONING

As we progress into the physical dimension it is worth noting that once again we are united with the mind. The mind interacts with the physical body as much as it does with the spiritual and mental body. It gains wisdom and function from each of these areas. In fact, each of these areas functions as a giant biofeedback network. You cannot ignore any one area and expect to gain in another area.

This is one of the challenges for people in healthcare. As in many disciplines, a practitioner will focus on one part and ignore the others. A truly healthy individual has to maintain balance in spiritual, mental and physical realms thus leading to sustained health. Drugs, remedies, herbs and energy practices have limited effect if any of these realms are ignored.

With all the known benefits many people still jeopardize their health by avoiding exercise programs. Even more amazing is that many people claim to be deeply interested in health and do not perform proper exercise.

It is astonishing that a large percentage of people in healthcare choose not to include exercise in their regime. Many MD's, PhD's in health-related fields, Homeopaths, aging Martial Arts Masters, Dive Instructors, Coaches, etc. do not perform scheduled exercise programs, even though by education they recognize its importance.

Your body needs regular exercise to function properly. Exercise builds muscle and burns fat. Anyone on a proper routine is improving his/her lean muscle mass to fat ratio. Improving the ratio of lean muscle tissue to fat enhances circulation and oxygen transport ability therefore increasing the energy levels Exercise builds collateral circulation providing better gas transport in the body. Exercise also increases our red blood cell (RBC)/hemoglobin count, aiding in the removal of carbon dioxide. Moreover, exercise increases our ***VO_2max***, or our aerobic capacity, which enables us to exercise better. It also stimulates the production of human growth hormone (***HGH***), which is a foundation for keeping or building muscle mass, bone density and slowing the aging process.

It is of great concern that so many senior citizens do not have a balanced exercise program. We (the author turned 69 in March 2008) lose our ability to produce HGH and exercise stimulates its production, even in the elderly. Indeed as important as an exercise program is for young people it is even more critical as we age. Exercise is a well-documented stress-reliever. Therefore, reducing stress enhances our immune system and helps us avoid disease. In addition, many theorists consider disease in itself to be a reaction to one form or another of stress. This concept takes the approach that exercise has benefits well beyond that of improving our bodies and minds. We could easily devote this entire article on the benefits of exercise without even getting to the subject of how to exercise, but in this paper exercise is only a part of the whole so we will limit the discussion.

So, what kind of exercise should we do? This question created many debates, and as a result, numerous theories evolved around this issue. Today we have such a vast scientific understanding of the effects of the different types of exercise, that we can explain the benefits of each type.

Aerobic exercise stimulates good cardio-vascular conditioning, so it should be a part of any routine. The more immediately accessible aerobic routines include jogging, running, fast walking, swimming, cycling, Pilates, skating (such as rollerblading), and home-or-gym related aerobic exercise machines such as stair-machines, treadmills, and aerobic programs available on video or DVD. All of these are good for some people, just as each may be bad for other people. I enjoy jogging with one of my dogs, but jogging is not for everyone, as it is hard on the knees and is classified

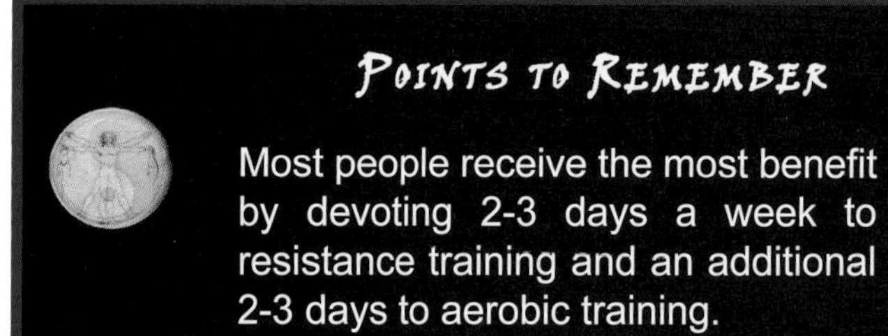
POINTS TO REMEMBER

Most people receive the most benefit by devoting 2-3 days a week to resistance training and an additional 2-3 days to aerobic training.

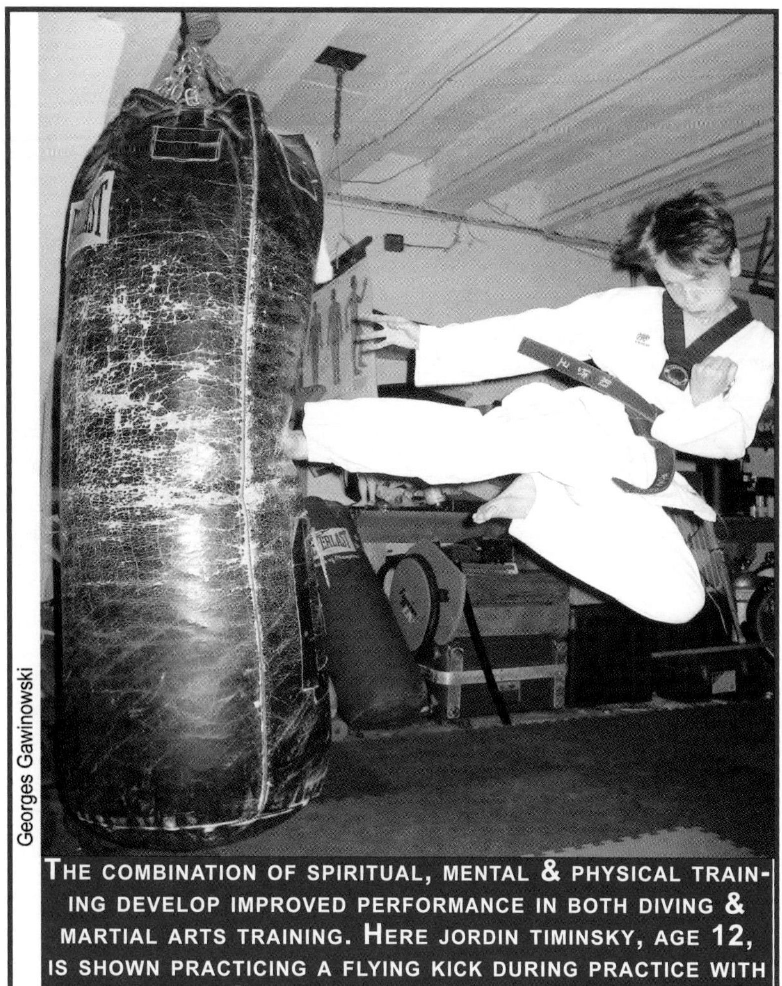

THE COMBINATION OF SPIRITUAL, MENTAL & PHYSICAL TRAINING DEVELOP IMPROVED PERFORMANCE IN BOTH DIVING & MARTIAL ARTS TRAINING. HERE JORDIN TIMINSKY, AGE 12, IS SHOWN PRACTICING A FLYING KICK DURING PRACTICE WITH GRAND MASTER TOM MOUNT.

as a ***high-impact*** exercise. The same conditioning effects may be gained from numerous low-impact machines or aerobic routines.

Swimming is an ideal cardiovascular program as it uses the majority of our muscles; in fact if we change strokes or styles (for example, ***free style*** to ***breast stroke*** to ***butterfly*** to ***back stroke***) we hit every muscle in the body along with a great cardio workout. For variety, to burn more calories and build leg strength, do cardio swimming with fins on. For those who have discipline, go to a gym and enroll in their aerobic program. This will provide the professional supervision for correct technique when doing the exercise combined with matching the best form of activity with a persons needs. Whatever activity you select, it should be done a minimum of 2 to 3 times weekly. It is also advisable to do cross-training; for instance, swim one day then jog on another day. Also, do not limit your program to aerobics only.

Points to Remember

Fitness is the marriage of lifestyle, a balanced workout program and proper nutrition. Complete fitness will also include our mental and spiritual outlook.

Resistance training is the best for increasing bone density and avoiding osteoporosis. The most common form of resistance training is ***weight lifting*** with free weights or using resistance machines that duplicate this action. When deciding what type of resistance routine to do, identify your training goals. If you wish to simply ensure good muscle tone with some strength improvements then opt for circuit training. For the majority of people this is the best solution. Circuit training builds stronger muscles, achieves the health benefits of resistance training and can be performed at a near, if not at, an aerobic pace (thereby taking advantage of both types of training). For those with time-management problems this is a faster moving program. As a rule, it does not build the mass of a body-building or sculpturing routine or the raw strength of a power-lifting routine.

If you desire somewhat bigger muscles or enhanced body sculpture, then a body-building type of workout is beneficial. Do not be worried that you will have massive muscles if you do this routine. For most people to become massive, a more intense workout is involved, and requires considerably more time than most people will dedicate to physical training.

The difference in a ***circuit-training*** program and a ***body-building*** routine is basically that in a circuit you will go from one exercise directly to a different exercise until you have completed all of your routine. Then, in most circuit programs you will repeat it. There is little to no rest between the exercises. In circuit training, a lighter amount of weight is lifted than in body building, as there is little muscle recovery time between exercises. You most likely will discover on a circuit program you actually are doing the same exercises as the body-builder, just laid out in a different fashion and accomplished at a faster pace. A good circuit program can actually be accomplished in as little as 30 minutes of training.

A ***body-building routine*** is designed so the person will do an exercise, then rest and repeat for 2 to 3 or more sets then they will move to the next exercise. The routine also is broken into muscle groups, such as 2-3 chest exercises; followed by shoulder exercises, then back exercises... until all the muscle areas have been individually worked. Typically a body-building routine will allow 30 seconds to 2-3 minutes between sets, and a longer time-lapse exists between body parts. Some people actually do a body-building type routine at the same pace as a circuit routine. This does not allow adequate time for muscle recovery when using heavier weights, and will not build as much muscle mass. Many people on body building regimens do a "***split routine***," where different muscle groups are worked on different days. A typical routine of this sort would exercise the muscles that "push" on one day (i.e. shoulders, chest and triceps) and then on another day work the muscles that "pull" (i.e. back, biceps and legs). The most serious body builders split the routines even more by adding a day of leg-work only. Some even do a single muscle group each day. This is well beyond the interest to the majority of us.

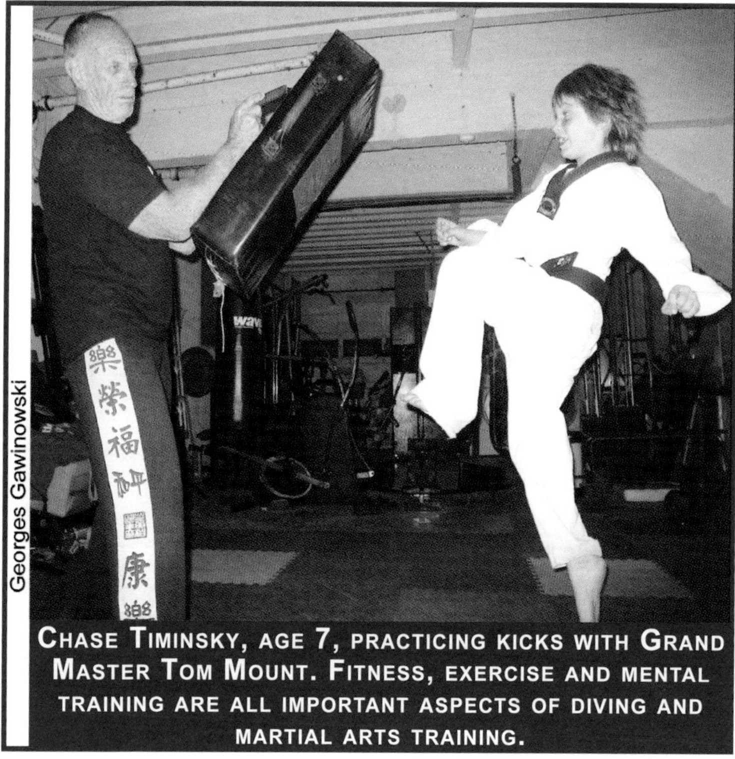

CHASE TIMINSKY, AGE 7, PRACTICING KICKS WITH GRAND MASTER TOM MOUNT. FITNESS, EXERCISE AND MENTAL TRAINING ARE ALL IMPORTANT ASPECTS OF DIVING AND MARTIAL ARTS TRAINING.

Power Lifting will most likely build more muscle mass. It encourages the use of extremely heavy weights, but for those who desire maximum strength it is the most efficient. However, like all sports when the intensity becomes more extreme there is a paradox: we may get more benefit, but we may also sustain more injuries.

Another form of resistance training is ***calisthenics***. This includes push-ups, pull-ups, using muscle against muscle, dips and a wide range of other exercises where we use our bodies as the resistance. There are also programs such as ***dynamic tension*** and ***isotronics*** that fit into the resistance training agenda. Dynamic tension is a self-resistance type of exercise routine where the muscles in a given part of the body are tensed, and then the tensed muscles are moved as if the person were lifting weights. Isotonics, or isometrics, on the other hand, involves the static contraction of a muscle group without visible movement in the body's angle or joints. A good target is to exercise 60 minutes a day with 1-2 day(s) a week total recovery time. For those pressed for time, it may be easier to devote 3 days a week and do both aerobic and resistance training in the same session.

Then of course we have other forms of exercise. Many of these incorporate elements of both resistance training and aerobic activity. I personally practice and teach ***Martial Arts***. My first form of martial art was boxing, which I started as a child. I then expanded my knowledge of martial arts to include ***Judo***; then I started to practice ***Karate***. I furthered my martial arts education by learning the ***Tae kwon Do***, ***Hapkido***, ***Mauy Thai***, ***Dim Mak***, and kick-boxing forms. Later, I developed ***Chi Survival Systems***. I also practice ***Qi Gong*** and use various aspects of martial arts in my energy-healing work. Overall, I have been practicing martial arts for over 50 years (since 1948 starting with boxing). In addition to excellent physical training it also teaches us to be more spiritual and forces us to use our minds. In olden days, the oriental martial arts masters were both the defenders/warriors and the healers, thus many concepts in oriental medicine were developed through martial arts. Some of us have been fortunate enough to have some of that information passed on to us. Dedicated martial artists do much research and study into the links between the spirit, mind and body to make them a more balanced person. Martial arts are not only a way to work out, but also a lifestyle, providing many of us with our philosophies on life and a religion.

Yoga is yet another discipline that is of great benefit, providing flexibility and strength. The reason older people tend to get more muscle, tendon and ligament injuries are due to loss of flexibility. Yoga allows one to maintain or gain more flexibility, which results in a lower probability of injuries. Yoga is an activity that may be practiced solely on its own or cross-trained with other sports. Most athletes who train for strength find that yoga often reduces injuries and muscle pain. Additionally, yoga, like martial arts, has a deep spiritual aspect.

As we all know, there are numerous activities we can practice to provide us with aerobic and resistance training. For overall training, one of the best sports is ***gymnastics***. Here one uses resistance combined with balance and stretching to aid in physical health.

All of us should have some kind of physical maintenance program. Due to our differing personalities and interests there is no one program that is best for everyone. The primary focus for someone just beginning an exercise routine is to discover something enjoyable or at least an activity that you will maintain a training schedule on. Many of you will enjoy participating in a variety of activities.

Diet is another critical area of health maintenance. The saying, "***We are what we eat,***" is true. Our diet has a tremendous influence on our health and feeling of well-being. In today's rushed society many sacrifice eating well with eating what is fast and convenient. This is a process that may eventually lead to various forms of disease. It is almost better to skip a rushed, valueless, unhealthful meal than to ingest the toxins in fast and over-processed foods for the momentary gratification of your appetite. You should take time out to enjoy food and to eat foods, which are nutritious and nurturing for your body and soul. What is really sad is that, with a little planning, good food can be attained as easily as fast junk foods.

Dim Mak combines fitness, mental training, Chi and understanding energy which, in turn, helps you comprehend your nutritional needs. Your activity levels should influence both the types of food you eat and the quantity. Another good suggestion is avoid the standard Food and Drug Administration's (FDA) "healthful eating" pyramid. Instead, turn it upside down.

The ***food pyramid*** as endorsed by the FDA until this time has led to an epidemic of diabetes, heart disease and an alarming obesity rate. When you look at the FDA recommendations and then look at the Farm Bureau's suggestions for fattening cattle and pigs, you will find the resemblance in the two diets disquietingly similar. Given the congruity between the two organization's approaches to food planning it is easy to understand why much of North America is obese. However, there is still hope. The food pyramid is now being revised and supposedly this year new recommendations will be made. Meanwhile, it is worth reading two textbooks to gain insight into a correct diet: ***The Zone*** and ***Radiant Health Beyond the Zone***. These books tie food needs to cell physiology, explaining what is necessary for health from the cellular level up. ***Fitness*** is more complex. Many feel, "Oh, I work out so I'm fit." Some of these same people eat hurried and terrible diets. While they may have great muscular tone and even a good lean muscle to fat ratio, they may not be truly fit.

An individual who is "fit for life" combines all the elements mentioned above. Such a person is truly healthier than his or her cohorts, and will most likely have a better quality of life throughout their years on earth. So ask yourself, am I truly fit? Review, and see if you do include the whole fitness package or just one or two areas of it. Evaluate what you need to include in your lifestyle to be truly fit for life and incorporate it into your daily living.

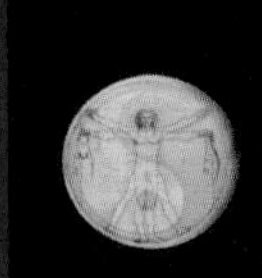

Points to Remember

Survival training teaches you not to quit, regardless of the odds.

Another very important area of mental and physical fitness is our ability to ***survive*** in everyday life and when faced with a physical, health, mental and/or spiritual threat or stressor. For purposes of this discussion we will call this ***survival body and mind***.

Survival body and mind is a method of increasing your willpower to survive physically and mentally during extraordinarily taxing situations. It forces you out of your comfort zone. This type of conditioning starts with setting up a survival training regime and following it. Regarding personal survivability, a large factor is having the discipline to continue training on those days when you really don't want to workout. Don't give yourself excuses, "***Oh, I'm too tired. I just do not feel good today.***" Or, "***I'm not in the mood to workout today.***" Instead, just go out and do it. This moves you beyond your comfort zone of quitting into not quitting! As simple as it sounds, this is an immense step toward physical and mental survival and toughness. The same applies to maintaining meditation practices and other areas your life. When you maintain your training program on the days when you really do not want to, most of the time you will feel much better once you have accomplished your fitness goal. Even though the change may be subtle, you have grown as a survivor.

Training skills to increase your survivability may be

incorporated into your workout schedules. It is good to use an exercise machine that provides a measurement capability. On these systems (Stepping-machines, elliptical trainers, treadmills, etc.) use the level of performance attained as a measurement. For instance, if a given machine measures distance and time, then set two goals - one for time duration and the other for your distance traveled. You will have to experiment with your capability and fitness level to determine your maximum performance. Set a time such as a half-hour or up to an hour. Note your short-term maximum rate of performance. Then score yourself as to how close you can match your maximum performance over the duration of the time selected. The most critical part is that you complete the time you have planned. The second most important aspect is to be as close to maximum performance as possible. This last goal is well beyond a daily cardiovascular workout, so limit it to 1-2 days each week.

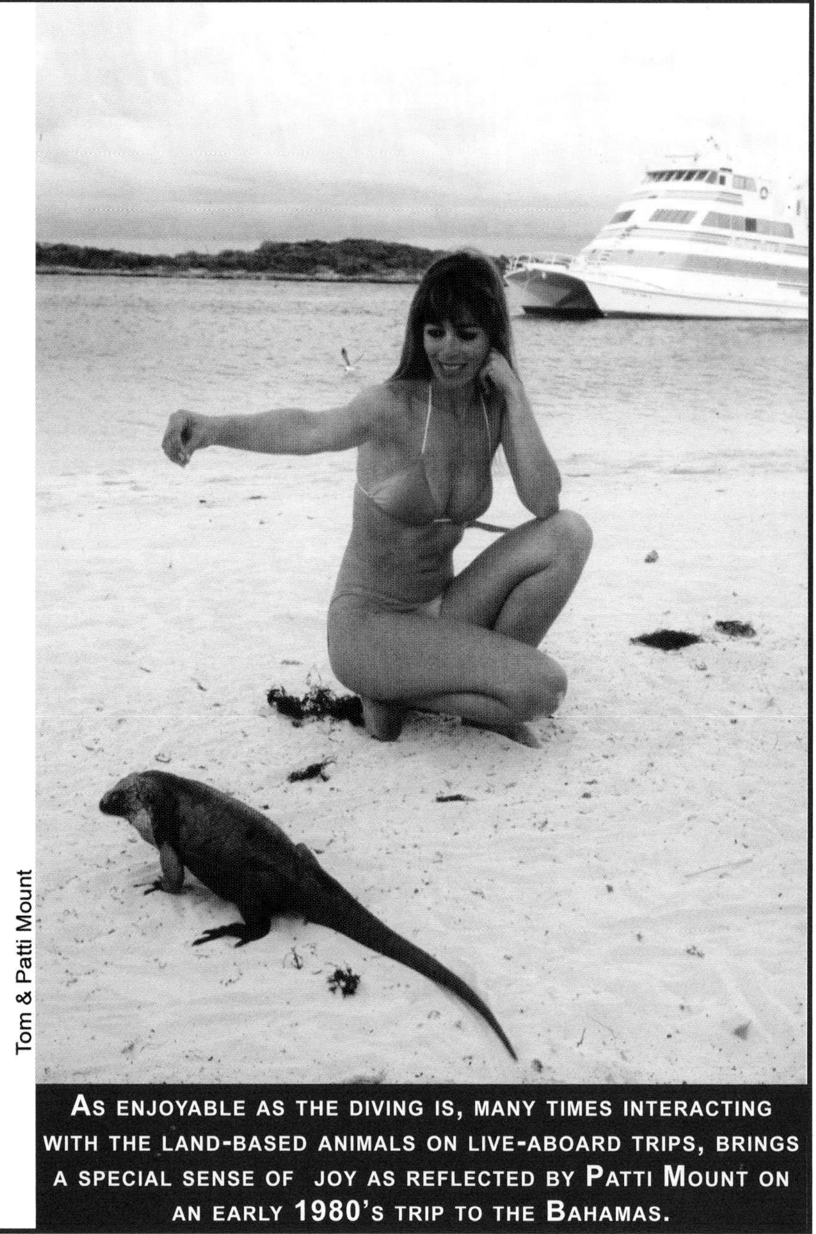
Tom & Patti Mount

AS ENJOYABLE AS THE DIVING IS, MANY TIMES INTERACTING WITH THE LAND-BASED ANIMALS ON LIVE-ABOARD TRIPS, BRINGS A SPECIAL SENSE OF JOY AS REFLECTED BY PATTI MOUNT ON AN EARLY 1980'S TRIP TO THE BAHAMAS.

Develop your ability to maintain the same breathing rate as if at rest, instead of giving into the stimulus to breathe faster. Faster breathing will result in ***turbulent gas flow*** and chest breathing, therefore reducing efficient gas exchange. This process may eventually lead to ***hyperventilation*** and ***blackout***. Concentrate on maintaining a normal breathing rate. Allow more volume of gas in each breath. This is where your breathing exercises come into play and why it is important to learn to breathe correctly. If you practice, you will be amazed how much your performance will increase. You will also expand your ***will to survive!***

Another method of survival training is similar to what Special Operations Forces in the militaries of the world do. ***Simply push limits*** to a point that the body screams for relief but do not give in to the urge to quit.

As a person becomes involved in more adventurous lifestyles this type of discipline and survival training may very well save a life. In my own life, survival skills have saved the life of others and my own on more than one occasion.

In many accidents, ***quitting or fleeing*** is the real reason for the accident or death. Survival training will make a difference for all of us

Many of the ideas that we have discussed so far play a role in survival. The ability to focus, build Chi, breathe correctly, develop a belief system, have faith, and use discipline all are tied together when the "chips are down." Although these techniques are employed when faced with physical threat, they also apply to emotional, psychological, and mental survival. It even applies to our business life and our personal relationships.

Reflex development is a by-product of training. Survival

Amy Dituri

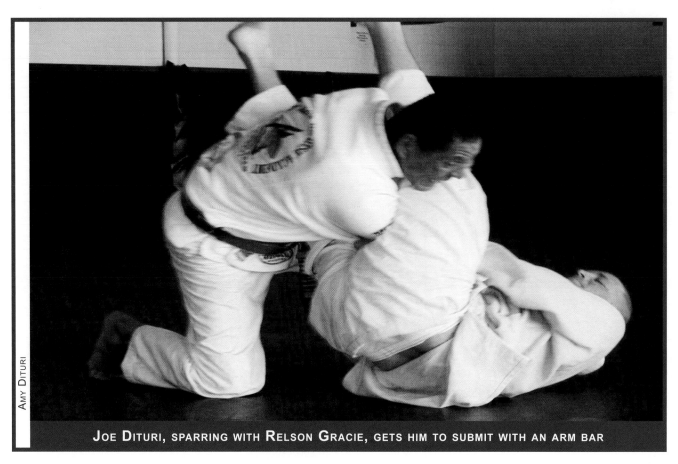

Joe Dituri, sparring with Relson Gracie, gets him to submit with an arm bar

reflexes are honed by training and skills maintenance. In emergencies, diving or otherwise, our reflexes will have a great effect on our reaction and the outcome. While some may have superb reflexes when checked during a physical, these are not necessarily the reflexes that provide a safe outcome to a physical, mental, spiritual or emotionally life-threatening situation.

The responses we want to develop are those associated with the activities we pursue in life. We need good physical reactions, but more importantly, we need to develop and reinforce intuitive, mental and skill reflexes. The old saying, "***Use it or lose it,***" is very true here. This is why divers periodically practice fundamental skills and why martial artists cover the basics routinely - to allow them to face and overcome the seemingly impossible.

Nurture and care for your body so it can be healthy. Up to this point we have discussed exercise, diet, fitness, survival… and some may think all of these sound like torture. However, it is unwise to abuse your body as it is a holy temple, and should be cared for accordingly. Everything we have covered is needed to develop health, live longer and enjoy a better quality of life. ***Give yourself rest and recuperation time, so your body can replenish itself.*** Muscles, when worked at high intensity, need a full day to recover. This is one reason to workout different body parts or types of exercise on different days, so the physical body can maintain itself. Go one step beyond and reward yourself with a massage, soak in a hot tub, or a steam room. Occasionally, just take a day to be lazy and allow your cells to rejuvenate.

In closing, we realize that discussing these subjects under the headings of mind, body, and spirit is a little misleading. Hopefully we have developed an understanding that the mind is our greatest treasure, as it is linked to the spiritual, mental and physical being. I believe we are one with each of these aspects of self, and are also one with the universe, as we are created with the energy of God. To be whole we must be aware and willing to develop our selves in these areas. The reward is better health, greater ability to deal with the world and increased contentment in life. ***Be healthy and live long...****

*Reprinted from IANTD's ***Nitrox Diver*** magazine

Chapter Seventeen
The Diver's Mind

Joseph Dituri M.S.

Generally speaking, divers are not risk adverse people; they simply have a certain zest for life. A smaller and still more extreme group of divers are technical divers. As Psychologist Frank Farley of the University of Wisconsin notes, many of the world's ***daredevils, doers and delinquents*** share a common personality, ***Type T*** (for thrill seeking). Whether scientists or criminals, mountain climbers or extreme skiers, says Farley, they are all driven by temperament, and perhaps biology, to a life of constant stimulation and risk taking. These people are ***pursuing the unknown, the uncertain***. It is my contention that the most valuable piece of equipment these thrill seekers take with them on each diver is their brain. Potential superfluities and detractors to the health and welfare of your ***brain power*** include, but are not limited to: diet, sleep, memorization techniques, and the physiological changes that occur in stressful situations. This chapter is an exploration of Type T people as well as a hypothesis of how they can improve their brain function and consequently chances of survival in a high stress situation.

Diet

For years Tom Mount and IANTD have been extolling the virtues of proper diet and nutrition for these extreme series of dives. Recently, a Cambridge study confirmed Dr. Mount's opinion. The study indicates good eating habits have proven to increase productivity and aid in memorization ability. Most importantly, Omega 3 makes it easier for your brain to ***jump*** gaps between brain cells. These ***gaps*** will be described in greater detail below. Many other memory aids, in the form of pharmaceuticals, have been developed and show great efficacy of improving memories in laboratory rats. However, most of these drugs have side effects ranging from headaches to death. As we were all told in our open water classes, it appears that drugs and diving do not mix, but eating well is a good way to get a solid head start.

Memory aid substances have flooded the supermarket and television info-commercials and have been marketed

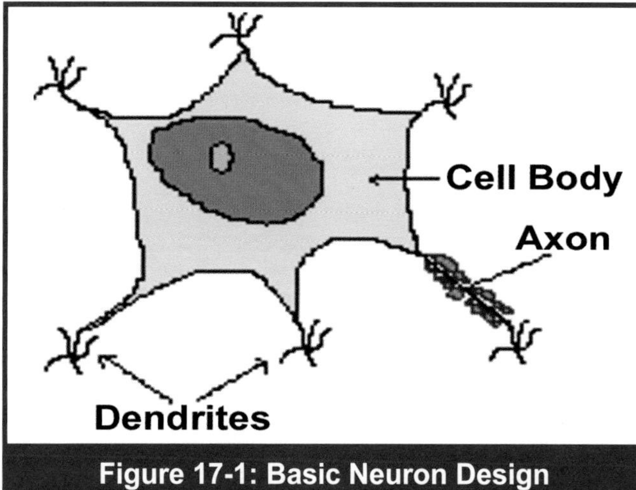

Figure 17-1: Basic Neuron Design

as drugs that assist the brain in its paramount function. The efficacy of these drugs remains questionable and for the most part, should be avoided unless a compatibility test for diving has been conducted. Before choosing one of these memory aid substances, it is important to understand what happens within your brain with respect to the memorization process.

The brain is made of approximately 100-billion nerve cells called neurons. These neurons have the ability to gather and transmit electrochemical signals. They are like the wires in a computer along which signals are transmitted. Neurons have similar characteristics and parts to other cells, but the electrochemical feature lets them transmit signals over long distances and pass messages. The neurons in the brain have axons (cable-like projection of the cell that carries the electrochemical message along the length of the cell) that are very short because of the relative closeness of the other neurons. The neurons make links that connect the sensory inputs and motor outputs with centers in the various lobes of the cortex. There are also connections between these cortical centers and other parts of the brain.

Sleep

Most people have heard the axiom that a good night's sleep aids in concentration. It is assumed that a good night's sleep allows the diver to be clear in the morning and gives him or her the maximum advantage when performing these technical dives. Moreover sleep aids in memory formation. A Harvard study suggests memory accuracy increases as much as 30% with a good night's sleep. This increase is due to the fact that when we sleep, our minds deconstruct the day's events. In an assiduous manner, our

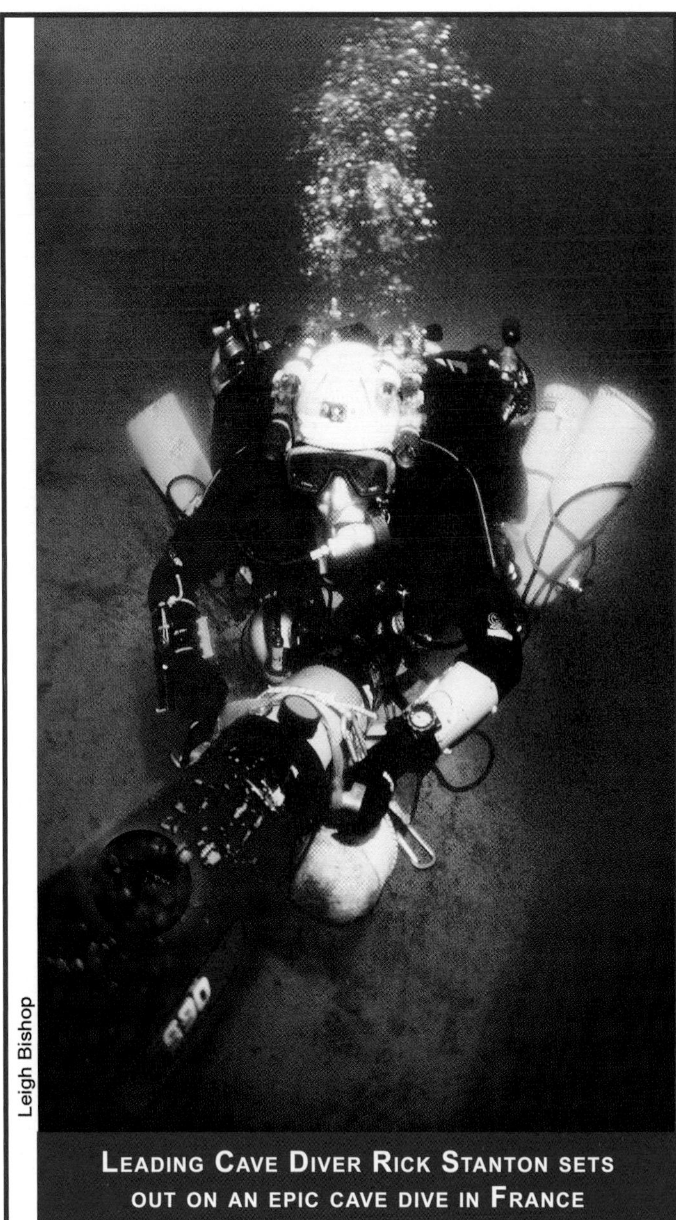

LEADING CAVE DIVER RICK STANTON SETS OUT ON AN EPIC CAVE DIVE IN FRANCE

brains spend the "***down time***" during sleep attempting to associate the events encountered in the day to those with which the brain is familiar. Sleep allows the brain time to catalog the learned events of the day. Cutting short the sleep cycle shortchanges the body's ability to strengthen the connections between brain cells.

Memorization Techniques

There are several techniques individuals can use to train their minds to recall items. For instance in order to recall the order of a deck of 52 playing cards in three minutes some people use a technique called "***association***." These memory experts break up the stream of information and put it in smaller packets. Then they associate the smaller memory with something they have already cataloged and remember easily. They build a story with those easily remembered associations to recollect the stream of information.

An example of this is the number seven. While seven is a rather innocuous number, James Bond is a particularly memorable figure and modern icon. To remember the number seven, one merely has to associate it with James Bond's agent number 007. By correlating the number requiring memorization with your favorite Bond, one would easily recall the number seven. By stringing together several of these associations, one could build a story and, for instance, easily recount that it takes seven turns of a knob to turn the bottle from open to closed. This is the method by which some Type T people perform progressive penetration into wrecks. They continue to look back and make a mental picture of the retreat while associating it to some other memorable situation.

Most divers already make similar types of associations. ***ConVENTID*** is a mnemonic device using letter association. It remains a group of unrelated letters that do not form an intelligible word. However, divers know it stands for: Convulsions, Visual disturbances, Hearing disturbances, Nausea, Twitching/Tingling, Irritability, and Dizziness. Our brains have formed the association between this seemingly meaningless word and its alternative significance.

Stress

Stress hormones have been shown to have a marked increase in solidification of learned events. The memory gained from the stress of surviving the traumatic event is well engrained enough that the traumatic event is not repeated. This is why people generally only make significant mistakes once. A recent study showed people could duplicate this effect by voluntarily exposing themselves to a traumatic event after a point of erudition. Something as subtle as immersing your arm in ice-cold water for as long as you can stand was enough to solidify events and provide a 25% increase in recollection of facts.

Before we utilize this extreme methodology with our students or ourselves a disclaimer for the Type T individuals is appropriate. You need not subject yourselves or your students to extreme measures to solidify your salient points.

When you are at the point of information saturation, you could, for instance, take a very cold shower. As seems evident, this should be in a controlled environment to ensure safety.

The mind is a powerful tool. It can be used to promote safety. Although much of the focus in technical diving is gear-related association, there are many other concerns of equal or greater value. Most injured divers have received proper training and knew the way to avoid their unfortunate situation. The supposition that the brain is the determining factor in technical diving injuries is not the primary focus of this article. The fact remains that most divers who suffer injuries were properly trained at one time and ***failed to respond or prepare*** for the stressful situation.

Physiological Changes That Occur During Stressful Situations

When a diver goes through times of significant stress, myriad physical changes occur within the body and the mind that help the person overcome the situation. Physical power is increased with the release of adrenaline among other changes in physical ratios, but physiologically, the flow of information in-and-out of the prefrontal cortex is reduced. This abridged mental acuity seems contradictory to the initial premise that the brain is the most important piece of equipment a diver has, but it is the reality of our physiological being. The prefrontal cortex controls the willed actions as well as higher thinking functions. Willed actions can be interpreted as the survival skills that divers should be working towards during high stress situations such as regulator recovery or valve shutdown during a catastrophic tank neck o-ring failure.

The prefrontal cortex control allows divers to prevent the flight part of the ***fight or flight*** syndrome. While fear and stress can account for a decreased flow to and from the prefrontal cortex, an increase in parasympathetic systems activity can account for an increase in flow to the prefrontal cortex. There are many ways to stimulate the parasympathetic systems, but the ***most profound*** results seem to be correlated with yoga and meditation.[1] Many of these mind control methods have been empirically tested at great length. During transcendent states of consciousness as have been found during meditation and yoga exercises, the brain activity shows a marked increase in prefrontal cortex activity.

This indicates some of these meditation and yoga exercises may actually increase people's ability to remain cool and calm in a situation. Before learning yoga or seeking the console of a meditation guru, temper this information with some balance. Many busy people may not have the time or desire to absorb yoga or adopt the philosophy behind meditation in order to perform these actions correctly. While meditation and yoga yield the best results, a compromise is breathing slowly and deeply and gazing off into the distance while not focusing on any particular object. This action can achieve a portion of the benefits of meditation and yoga. The supposition around this premise is that the mind becomes confused with no change in visual input and turns its recuperative power elsewhere. This results in a stimulation of the body's recovery systems, one of which is to restore normal brain function. Obviously a diver cannot break into a meditative trance during a high-pressure situation. However, evidence suggests that repeated exposure to this transcendental state increases an individual's ability to remain calm in a highly stressful situation. The diver can effectively train the involuntary response. ***What was once considered an unchanging set of neural pathways is now believed to be pliable and modifiable.***[2] As discussed earlier, if Type T people can improve their neural pathways, they will increase their intellect and consequently their safety.

As suggested meditative practice or similar return to this state can ***re-wire*** the brain during high stress situations. This re-wiring could facilitate retention of higher brain function throughout the experience, which would benefit the diver and allow him/her to think and reason. This meditation can potentially change a person from someone who merely reacts to someone who is proactive.

The average divers spend 30 minutes prepping their technical diving gear and upward of 60 minutes prepping a rebreather for a mid-range technical dive. Spending 15-30 minutes each day in a deep state of relaxation will aid you psychologically to ease daily life stressors as well as reduce the magnitude of your physiological response to a dangerous or stressful situation. This seems like an easy decision. If the brain is the most important piece of equipment on a dive, divers would be spending the same amount of time working on it as would be spent prepping other gear; 15-30 minutes could amplify your level of safety.

At this point in a diver's continuing education, a diver can dive in many different environments. In his book, ***Caverns***

Measureless to Man, Sheck Exley discusses hazards of diving, which seem apropos. **A relevant passage is recounted below:**

> "When asked how I have survived so many years of diving I replied, controlled paranoia. This forces me to take the time to examine all of the potential hazards of each dive, and devise ways to surmount them as well as conjure up backup procedures in case those ways don't work. Lots of divers have the self-discipline to go through that process, and have the ability to perceive the hazards and weigh the risks so they can decide whether or not they can dive with an acceptable degree of safety. But to survive a long-term career of diving, you can't afford to stop at that. You have to convince yourself that the ocean is a fickle friend, harboring malevolent thoughts. If you leave any danger un-addressed, no matter how remote, the ocean will definitely and gleefully kill you."

Sheck confirms that divers need to think and be proactive with their safety and well-being.

What Sun Tzu, the author of ***The Art of War,*** said in his book has direct application to the mind of our Type T individuals: ***Warfare is the greatest affair of state, the basis for life and death, the way to survival or extinction.***

It must be thoroughly pondered and analyzed. This is true for technical divers as well; they must concentrate, visualize and analyze the situation at hand. Add an adequate night of sleep, good diet and proper training of your mind to maximize memory of the training you have received and a well-equipped diving warrior emerges. Treat the extreme sport of technical diving like warfare and prepare yourself with all possible tools to ensure your survival. If you know both yourself and your ***enemy***, you will come out of one hundred ***battles*** (with the ocean) with one hundred victories.[3]

Footnotes

[1] Brian Germain, "Skydiving and the Mind," *Parachuting*, (Jan 2007): 42.
[2] Brian Germain,"Skydiving and the Mind," *Parachuting*, (Jan 2007): 43.
[3] Sun Tzu, Translated Into English by Samuel B. Griffith, USMC (Ret), *The Art of War*, (1963): 38.

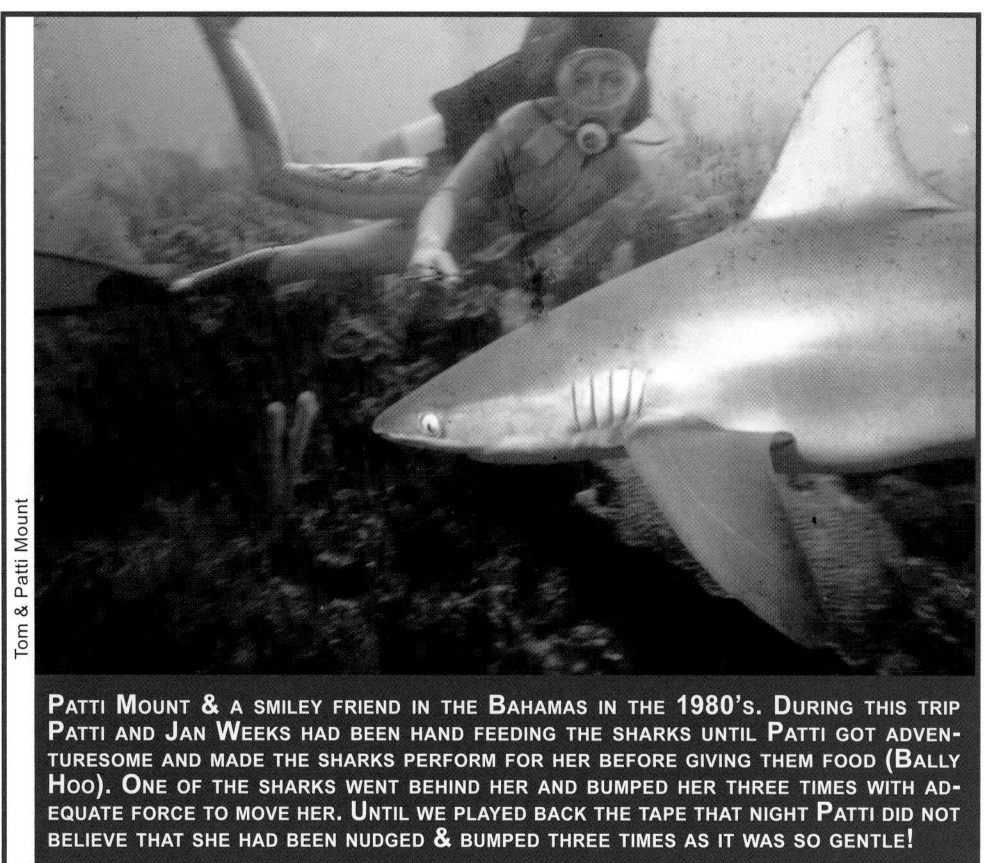

Tom & Patti Mount

PATTI MOUNT & A SMILEY FRIEND IN THE BAHAMAS IN THE 1980'S. DURING THIS TRIP PATTI AND JAN WEEKS HAD BEEN HAND FEEDING THE SHARKS UNTIL PATTI GOT ADVENTURESOME AND MADE THE SHARKS PERFORM FOR HER BEFORE GIVING THEM FOOD (BALLY HOO). ONE OF THE SHARKS WENT BEHIND HER AND BUMPED HER THREE TIMES WITH ADEQUATE FORCE TO MOVE HER. UNTIL WE PLAYED BACK THE TAPE THAT NIGHT PATTI DID NOT BELIEVE THAT SHE HAD BEEN NUDGED & BUMPED THREE TIMES AS IT WAS SO GENTLE!

Chapter Eighteen Psychological & Physical Fitness For Technical Diving

Tom Mount D.Sc., Ph.D., N.D.

Introduction

Today's explorers push and often exceed limits that would have been thought impossible a decade ago. In fact with all the advances in dive technology many non exploratory dives now completed exceed the most adventuresome of exploration projects in the past. This is in large part due to exciting advances made in dive technology such as the use of Rebreathers, smaller brighter and more durable lighting systems, and the uses of DPV's to name but a few. While these new technologies have extended diver capability, they have also produced new challenges and exposed divers to potentially more psychological stress full conditions. To top this off the new tools even allow us to exceed many physiological parameter that have been safe before. Such areas are decompression, for ultra deep or long dives, or a combination of both. In the past the equipment kept most divers with in known safe ranges. Today's advances allow us to enter a "new frontier" in regard to various physiological issues and physical Stressors due to greater depths and distances. By entering a realm where we may exceed the validity of dive tables and additional envirometal stressors that we previously understood, the modern explorer must adapt to new circumstance if he/she is to survive. These physiological and mental/psychological challenges require behavior modification - a process that requires the diver to develop a unity of the mind, body, and spirit.

Factors that influence the way in which a diver reacts to the demands and hazards of his environment include his attitude, awareness, physical fitness, self-discipline and the ability to separate perceptions from reality. To understand this phenomenon, an in-depth overview of the various mental and physical stimuli that influence a diver's attitude and performance must be examined.

Stress in Technical Diving

Underwater, one's reaction to stress can easily determine the difference between an enjoyable dive and an accident that may lead to death or disability. Stress is a phenomenon that if unchecked may, lead to panic. Wrecks and caves present us with challenges of overhead environments. Caves and wrecks are dark. In many it is easy to stir up silt and reduce visibility to zero, thus they often present us with "tough" choices. Deciding which passage or companionway to take in a seemingly endless maze can create its own sources of stress. As we review each stress source, it will become apparent how these environmental hazards add to stress.

Time-pressure stress is present in a wide number of scenarios. In its most simple form, time-pressure stress involves matching the gas supply to the duration of the dive. This expands into a major problem when a dive plan has been exceeded and the gas supply is running low. In this instance, uninformed or unskilled divers may actually

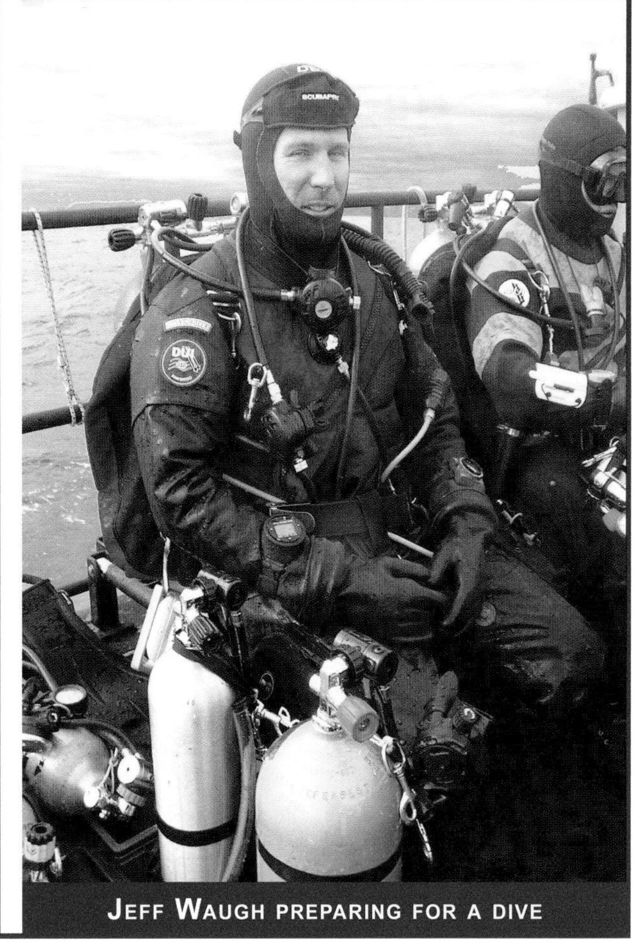

Jeff Waugh preparing for a dive

compound the problem by increasing their breathing rates. Time-pressure can also build when a diver looks at his/her decompression "***clock.***" Another contributor to time pressure is with the use of CCR's. Divers can easily extend penetrations to a point that bailout situations may easily bring on extreme time pressure stress. And on deeper dives the rebreather opens new capabilities. When problems arise, may contribute greatly to time pressure stress. Being rushed prior to a dive is a huge time pressure stimulant and may easily lead to adverse diver reactions and thought processes. One should always prepare equipment early to avoid the last minute rush and trying to cope with equipment related or personal issues.

Distance presents a major time-pressure stress. The greater the distance to open water, the more time stress has to build. The greater danger in distance-related stress is the perceived time-pressure threat. In this case, the perception is usually greater than the actual threat. There have been numerous instances when divers have become so distressed they forgot basic, but important, rules for diving.

If stress is not controlled, it may lead to panic. Panic is a life threatening event!

Confinement is an obvious source of stress. This is usually lurking in the recesses of the mind and comes into play when other stresses are introduced. Confinement couples time-pressure stress with the distance factor. The reaction to bolt toward the surface must be overcome by overhead training that discourages thinking about the "traditional escape route". In addition training must emphasize avoidance of the "***freeze***" reaction to stress. In this way, confinement stress is managed.

Task loading stress occurs when divers must perform more tasks than they feel they can handle. Task loading can happen when a diver is trying to do three simple things at once – manage a reel, manage two cylinders and swim in a normal, correct, and relaxed manner. Add this to a Diver Propulsion Vehicle (***DPV***) or other specialized items, and the diver's ability to function on a normal level may be impaired. The increasingly popular use of CCR's adds to this equation as well. For divers with minimal experience on the CCR, the skills involved in its use combined with the skills diving specialized environments, such as cave and wreck, may be overwhelming at first. Fortunately with experience these new skills become as reflexive in nature as Open Circuit skills had been. With experience, divers will learn to handle multiple tasks with greater ease, but each time an additional action or responsibility is added to the diver's task load, stress will increase.

Incorrect breathing patterns are tied to stress in a two-way cause/effect cycle. Incorrect breathing patterns will create stress, but stress will also cause incorrect breathing, which will in turn compound the diver's original stressed condition. Once a pattern of incorrect breathing has begun, a vicious cycle develops. The pattern is often so subtle a diver may not even recognize it.

To break this negative cycle, a diver must become aware of and regain control of his/her breathing. Divers should practice diaphragm-breathing exercises and, when diving, should concentrate on breathing slowly and deeply until it becomes a natural reflexive reaction. A good recommendation is to practice either Yoga or Qi Gong and thus also gather energy as well as perform correct breathing.

When a diver first becomes aware of stress or a feeling of discomfort, it's important for the diver to stop all activity, exhale slowly and fully, and then inhale slowly and fully. This breathing pattern should be repeated at least three times before resuming the dive. The diver should then continue breathing slowly and fully using the diaphragm muscles. Discomfort can almost always be alleviated by this method.

A good way to avoid breathing stress is to develop a swim pace that allows acceptable forward momentum while maintaining a correct, comfortable respiratory pattern. Accelerating one's swimming stroke will frequently lead to uncontrolled breathing, and can even produce a sensation of uneasiness.

Points to Remember

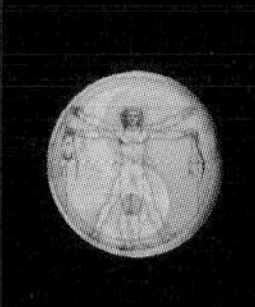

The most serious form of stress is compound stress. It occurs when more than one stress source is involved. Compound stress is more difficult to manage than individual sources of stress. However, in reality, it is very common to have more than one source of form of stress on a dive.

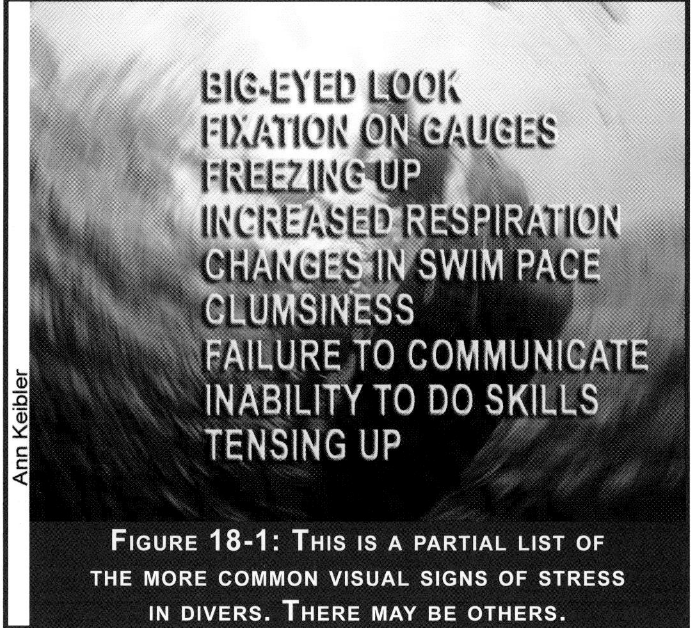

BIG-EYED LOOK
FIXATION ON GAUGES
FREEZING UP
INCREASED RESPIRATION
CHANGES IN SWIM PACE
CLUMSINESS
FAILURE TO COMMUNICATE
INABILITY TO DO SKILLS
TENSING UP
Ann Keibler

Figure 18-1: This is a partial list of the more common visual signs of stress in divers. There may be others.

Divers who maintain good physical conditioning will discover that the human body is much like a boats hull. Once a boat reaches hull speed, doubling the power produces little or no increase in forward momentum. Divers bodies behave similarly. Human bodies like boat hulls, come in different shapes. Some shapes pass through the water easier and faster than others. Exceeding our "hull speed" takes more work and produces a minimal increase in performance. Unwanted respiratory induced stress will result.

Unlike boats, divers can change the shape of their "hulls". A lean profile generally produces less drag and is more efficient in water. Divers should be encouraged to maintain a lean personal profile through exercise and proper diet, but a lean profile also involves the diver's swim posture and equipment configuration.

Poor swim posture may lead to stress, and will require more energy to maintain. This increased energy demand, and in turn, makes increased demands on our respiratory system.

Exertion and thermal imbalance produce stress, as the diver is either too hot or too cold. An aware diver should be able to control these stressors simply by monitoring his comfort level and using adequate and appropriate thermal protection.

Ego threats, or peer pressure, are indirect sources of stress, particularly if they cause a diver to attempt feats beyond his/her own personal ability or comfort level.

Disorientation is always a problem when exploring overhead environments or deep water. Most overhead environments feature multiple passages. Deep water allows little time for correction of navigational errors. Both environments create the very possibility of becoming lost. The proper use of navigation aids such as visual referencing, compasses, and in overhead environments, line arrows and guidelines can offset the stress of disorientation and the risk of becoming lost. One of the leading causes of deaths in overhead environment dives is the failure to follow a continuous guideline.

Darkness or loss of visibility produces stress due to sensory loss. This can be a result of a light malfunction, low visibility, turbid water, or silt outs. While this should not be a major concern in and of itself, when combined with other stresses and performance inhibitors, loss of visibility can lead to threatening situations.

Other stresses include buoyancy problems, excessive dependency on another diver, and real or perceived physical threats. Early recognition of the telltale signs and symptoms of stress can help reduce or prevent the escalation of the stress reaction. Personal indicators of stress often include an uneasy feeling, unusual anxiety, apprehension or irritability. Our intuitive hunches will attempt to tell us if there is a reason for stress. Becoming tuned in to our inner self is an important stress-free diving. Developing such a degree of awareness requires training and the use of mind control techniques.

Stress control can be accomplished through self-awareness. Frequently, the stressed diver is unaware of an increase in respiration. A buddy, who notices his dive partner breathing quickly or unusually, should immediately alert him to remain at rest until his breathing has returned to a normal rate. For us to control stress, we must first be aware of it and then execute a corrective action. When dealing with stress, we must remember that while its cause may be either real or perceived, the results are equally dangerous. Also keep in mind that stress frequently manifests itself by a change in respiration.

As divers, we must learn to recognize some common behavioral modifications that can result in "mental narrowing," or more aptly stated, becoming unfocused as

it relates to problem solving. By becoming overly focused, the diver may lose the ability to correctly analyze situations and to perform both newly learned and well-known skills. Mental narrowing can compound the problem because of falsely perceived task loading. This type of behavioral change, if not corrected, may lead to panic.

The body's physical reactions to the psychological trauma of stress may include increased respiration, increased heart rate, abnormal adrenaline release, and the instinctive urge to flee.

For survival, it is imperative that we compensate for behavioral and physiological change. The tools that will enable to control stress in all its manifestations include awareness, adequate training and the application of newly acquired skills. In addition, we must develop a new discipline (or attitude). We must be able to instantly recognize a real threat as opposed to a perceived one, and we must instinctively make the appropriate corrective action in order to avoid disaster.

The need for intensive, repetitive training of all pertinent skills becomes apparent when a situation takes a critical turn. Poorly learned skills will be forgotten in times of duress, and only those skills that were practiced to the point of becoming virtually instinctive will remain with the diver.

An indirect source of compound stress is a form of mental narrowing which leads to distraction from the dive itself and creates a focus on either a skill to be practiced or when reacting to an actual emergency. At first, one would say of course that is the way to learn a skill or correct an emergency procedure. However if teaching a skill the intent is for the student to focus on how to and then to convert the skill into not being a separate event but apart of the dive. In many situations either while doing skill practice in a class or when actually responding to a true emergency, divers focus so hard on the event that they lose contact with dive performance. This may evolve from attempting to resolve the problem but due to loss of focus on the dive, it may result in creating a second emergency. As an example imagine a diver is in a cave or wreck, they are retrieving a stage cylinder and in the process of getting the stage and preparing to switch to it they forget for a moment the importance of dive technique due to being totally focused on the stage and the gas and the switch of regulators, thus while doing the skill they go into a fin down attitude, this in return creates silt and possible a silt out and a risk of becoming lost. It may even create a situation that separates the team members. Another perspective of the same or similar situation would be that by focusing on the stage and change of regulators the distraction might resole in the diver swimming into another passage again resulting in potential to become lost and in a silt out. To avoid this type scenario all skills and emergence must be performed as a part of the dive thus the diver maintains awareness and technique and deals with whatever the issues they have as a part of the dive. Provided a diver has gas to breath, all problems can be solved. With a good the attitude and reaction to emergencies as being a part , of the dive survival is almost certain.. In numerous accidents the type of distraction discussed above have created unmanageable situtations in an otherwise easily managed event.

Points to Remember

The overall applications of risk recognition and management was stated aptly by psychiatrist Gil Milner MD: ***If known, you have the responsibility to fully explain the risk of any activity to all who choose to pursue this endeavor. As an individual, you must be responsible for discovering all of the apparent risks in activities you want to pursue. Once all risks are fully understood, you have the right to subject yourself to whatever degree of risk you chose even if it is life threatening.***

Risk Management

Risk management and understanding risk management is an essential key to becoming a good technical diver. By employing the concept of risk management, divers learn to establish realistic objectives. They can then decide what kind of diver they really want to be - a recreational diver, a technical diver or an explorer.

As we continue to emphasize, there are many risks in diving. There are also various solutions to most of the risks. Once you decide to accept a given level of overall risk, you must also consider what compromises you will need to make. You must, for example, weigh efficiency with safety. You

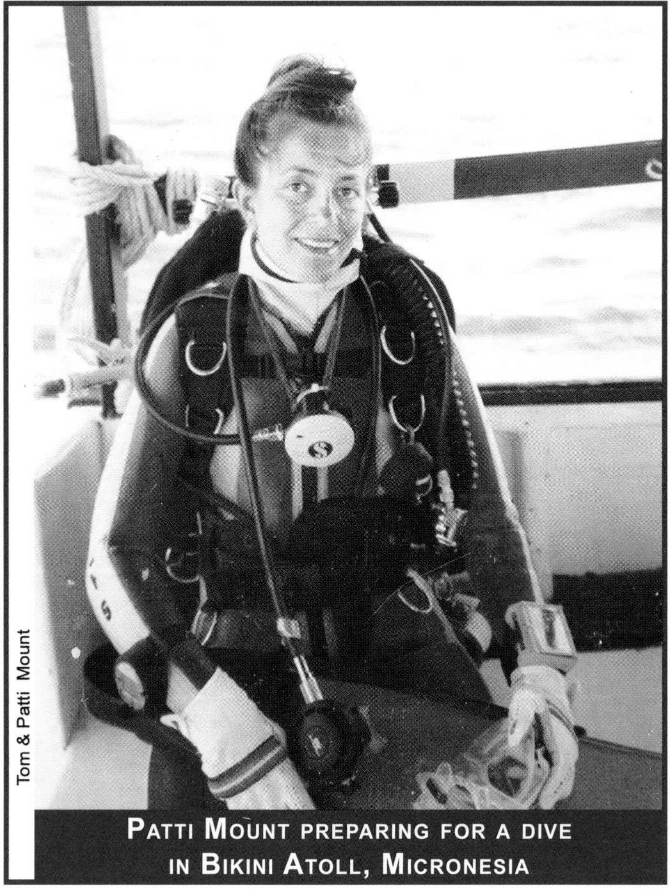

PATTI MOUNT PREPARING FOR A DIVE IN BIKINI ATOLL, MICRONESIA

must recognize the hazards as well as benefits and deal with the positives as well as the negatives.

Various factors will enter into these compromises, including the size of the dive team, equipment configuration, individual diver capabilities, the degree of decompression risk and the level of acceptable discomfort. As technical divers, we must review all of these factors and determine the limits of your personal control zones. Many paths lead to the same destination in exploration or enjoyment. The quickest path often yields the greatest risk, but may produce a more immediate return. The more deliberate path may take longer to arrive at the same destination, but will provide greater safety. It all comes down to individual risk management and how much risk you're prepared to take.

You must opt for a level of risk you can live with. The best determination is, perhaps, one, which you feel, allows you control over your own destiny - worded another way, a profile that acknowledges, "Only you can breathe for you, swim for you or think for you." A dive plan determined by you as survivable is a matter of personal choice.

If this is your first or 1000th dive, you should approach risk management the same way for every dive. The ***first*** step is to list all the anticipated risk(s) associated with the dive. Once this list is completed, define how each risk can affect safety. ***Second***, prepare a plan of action to cope with known stresses on the dive. ***Third***, determine which risks are acceptable to you. ***Fourth***, outline your equipment needs (for dive accomplishment and for your feelings of personal safety). ***Last***, develop an operational plan providing a set of limits which makes you comfortable.

Regardless of what you decide, expect others to probably challenge your decisions. The debate of risk management vs. efficiency is an eternal one. There are minimums all should agree on, but the specifics are totally individual.
Mind Control

Behavioral Failure: In this presentation we will discuss diver capability failure points and also some suggested variations and approaches based on whether one is cave or open water diving certified. Safe diving depends on many variables that can be classified as failure points. What exactly is a failure point? Is this a breakdown in the diving system, diver behavior and/or education that may lead to an accident?

DIVER CAPABILITY

Herein lies the critical point in being a safer diver. There are many issues that contribute to this and offer increased performance. Life support systems, equipment configuration, equipment reducing failure points, all can enhance performance but it is the raw capability of the diver that will determine the safety foundation.

To discuss diver capability, some definitions must be established. Capability is defined as having ability or competence. It includes qualities that may be used or developed, thus one's potential can be determined. So, to have or to develop capability then is a combination of becoming aware of the environment, becoming skillful in specific diving technique for efficient swimming, developing detailed techniques for specific environments, evolving to a good body attitude and, of course, practicing. Experience is a valuable contributor to diver capability. Experience may also be a positive contributor by continued use of correct skills and techniques. However, experience may also be a negative influence if the diver's early experience did not lay a firm foundation in basics skills, technique,

body attitude and risk awareness. If one routinely practices a bad technique, then this bad technique is "perfected"and becomes a stumbling block for growth as a diver.

Diver capability begins in the first open water class and evolves through continuing education and practical application of diving skills, and knowledge. It is therefore important that the initial training be strict in the basics of diving. In most sports, optimum performance is gained by mastering technique first, then concentrating on "going for it." Technique is everything. I (also) teach martial arts and one of the most difficult things to tell people is to relax, breathe out as they strike or prepare to get hit, and develop proper technique.

The same is true in diving: relaxed and correct breathing combined with relaxed (untensed) muscles when executing correct form and even calculated movements is how performance is improved. For instance, as regards kick technique, just ensuring the toes are pointed in a relaxed manner makes a world a difference in power on a flutter kick. With a frog kick, technique is the difference between the kick being almost useless or having a strong and efficient tool to move through the water. During this kick, being relaxed as the leg spread out and then cupping the toes followed by an inward thrust that brings the toes together is very important. If one is flexible enough, this thrusting before the heels touch provides the majority of forward momentum. When a diver does not bring the fins together, they are quite inefficient in realizing the full potential of this technique. Learning ascent techniques, especially in dry suits, also adds to diver capability.

Thus, in diver education the primary goal at all levels is to increase diver capability in the environments she/he is trained in. The secondary goals will include equipment selection and configuration that will enhance performance. But remember, these will be wasted if a capable diver is not using them.

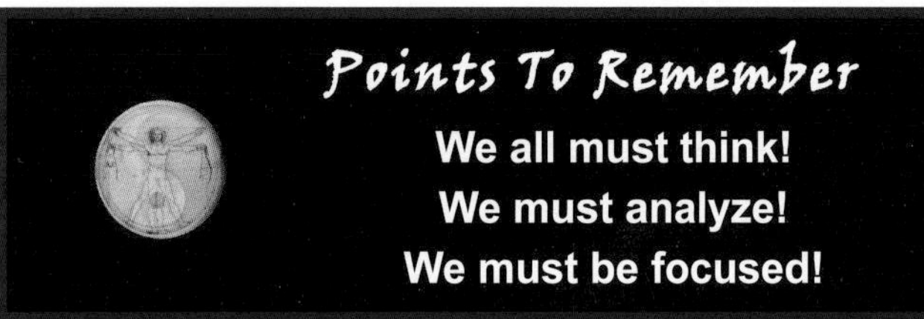

Points To Remember
We all must think!
We must analyze!
We must be focused!

A capable diver, once efficient in technique, must also become capable of managing stress. Diving is an activity

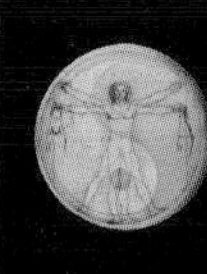

Points to Remember

In my own experience when investigating accidents, I have found that when accidents occur, one or more team members had bad feelings or premonitions about the dive.

~ Tom Mount

that removes us from our natural habitat; therefore, one must anticipate that a stressful event will occur at some point someday on some dive. A diver trained is stress management will not yield to a perception of stress but will in fact automatically respond with a corrective measure. To ensure this type of response, the diver must be exposed to simulated reality-based situations during training. The most serious are gas failure problems. Other areas include equipment failure and most importantly, behavior failure. IANTD programs emphasize these areas as diver capability is the single most important aspect of diver safety.

A capable diver is one who has a foundation in good diving technique and skills. They continue training either in formal programs or by self-improvement. The capable diver employs a good attitude and has self-confidence. This individual defines a personal safety envelope of limits and establishes goals and direction as a diver. Once capable, this person reaches out to find avenues to increase performance, thus extending accomplishments while still maintaining a safety envelope.

Our mind is the most powerful tool we possess. Scientists believe the power of the mind may be infinite. They say most of us use less than 5% of our brain's potential. Imagine for a moment what you might accomplish if you could suddenly tap into your brain's total potential.

Thoughts direct our conscious mind. In fact, we are what we think. Each and every one of us is a product of our thoughts. Our happiness, our success, and our health are all influenced by what we think. These though patterns have been embedded in our minds from the moment we began to think. They were shaped by our upbringing, past experiences, and education. If we want to improve ourselves, the first step is to improve our outlook and, perhaps, our beliefs and thoughts.

By controlling our minds, we have the potential to improve our lives. Sound simple? It is. However, few of us have developed the discipline to think strategically. It appears most people seem to merely respond to their environment. Being ahead of the game, people with foresight and judgment plan and shape their world. Yet, developing mental discipline and the ability to think strategically takes time. It requires you to exercise your mind. The mental exercise techniques I use include meditation, affirmations, goal setting, breathing exercises and concentration.

I am convinced that a physically conditioned body is necessary for creating a health mind. For the body to experience outstanding health, the mind must remain healthy. The mind, body and spirit all work in unison. We are, indeed, what we think. In time, we can probably make our life what we want it to be by using mind control. Some people have called it the "***right stuff.***" Perhaps it is. Having the right stuff means having increased self-confidence. It means being able to accomplish important goals. Moreover, it means being able to survive when mentally and physically challenged.

In mind training, there are numerous facets to be considered. It is often necessary to overcome ingrained negative beliefs. Self-confidence is a major component in making the right decision, especially when faced with unforeseen adverse situations. A positive self-image and self-confidence go hand-in-hand.

Points to Remember

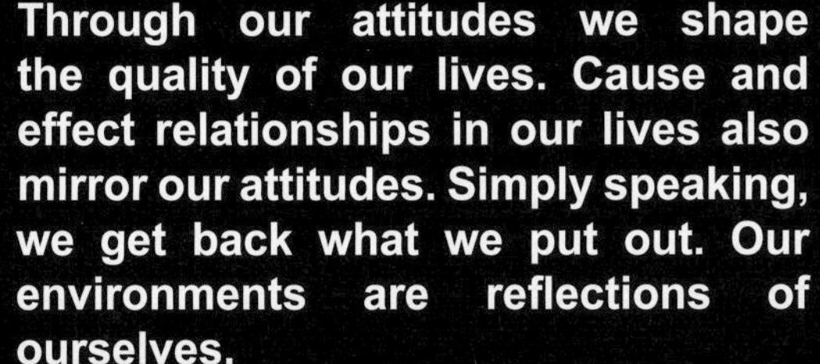

Personal attitudes are a controllable part of our philosophies. They determine our outlook toward life and how we believe the world looks at us.

Through our attitudes we shape the quality of our lives. Cause and effect relationships in our lives also mirror our attitudes. Simply speaking, we get back what we put out. Our environments are reflections of ourselves.

A positive attitude produces great results. A poor attitude produces nothing except, perhaps, thoughts of inadequacy and self-doubt.

Often in our society, people are "brainwashed" more by what they can't accomplish rather than by what they can achieve. Many people live their lives in fear. They fear the unknown. They're afraid to walk out their homes at night. All of these are negative thoughts. When you were younger, how often did someone say you couldn't do such and such, or that you were a bad person?

These statements, direct at us during our formative years, became embedded in our minds. Over time, this conditioning evolved into a belief system. **To produce a positive belief system, it is often necessary to recondition our inner beliefs:**

1. "It is our attitude at the beginning of a difficult task that will bring about its successful outcome."
2. "Our attitudes toward others determine their attitude towards us. Our success depends largely on how we relate to others."
3. "We must think, act, talk and conduct ourselves in all affairs as if we were the person we wish to become. We must keep a mental image of that person in front of us throughout the day."
4. "Note, the more successful a person, the better the attitude, and that attitude is not the result of success rather success is the result of attitude."
5. "Recognition and self-esteem represent the major need of our lives. To provide this, develop a habit of making all thoughts constructive and positive. Do not waste time discussing negative values."

As we've said, when it comes to becoming a good technical diver, we must develop an "***I Can***" belief system. We must program our minds. We can accomplish this with techniques of visualization and affirmation.

These powerful mechanisms change and improve belief systems. They also provide the most clear cut approach for helping us to accomplish all our desired diving goals. As stated by Tom Ford, "Believe you can, believe you can't either way you are right." As stated in the bible, "Whatever a man thinketh, so he is." Our total being is a reflection of what we think we are. Our thoughts are our reality.

Visualization is an excellent tool for developing mental control and changing belief systems. The process is quite simple. Here's how it works: Close your eyes and concentrate on breathing slowly and deeply. You are going to slowly relax every muscle in your body. You will begin with your feet. Once these muscles feel relaxed, you'll move to the calves of your legs. Then, continuing this relaxation technique, you'll move slowly upward relaxing each and every muscle group from your big to the top of your head. As soon as you feel totally relaxed, form an image in your mind. This image may involve the performance of a given skill or the completion of a goal. These are the first steps to becoming your own master.

Most champion athletes and many successful business people use visualization to manage their lives. It is merely a part of their total training program. If you to achieve grater success, we strongly recommended you begin a program of mental conditioning, if you aren't already doing so.

To visualize an upcoming dive, use this relaxation and visualization technique. Picture in your mind the entire dive from beginning to end. Include all dive team members. Visualize what you might see as well as what challenges you may face. Be thorough. Do the dive step by step in your mind. Once this dive has been mentally rehearsed, it's easy for your body to duplicate this performance.

When you are in a relaxed state, it's easy to communicate with your subconscious mind. If your mind "tells you" something can go wrong during your upcoming dive, sort it out. Talk to your buddies. Tell them, about your concerns. Go back and run the dive through your mind again. If you still get "bad vibes," bail out. If you're the team leader, cancel the dive.

There are numerous self-help tapes available to guide you to learn the technique of visualization. They include, for example, self-image improvement, correct breathing, goal setting, and increased concentration. While tapes are excellent materials to help you get started, eventually you'll need to customize your training to include your specific needs. No tapes are available to help you visualize an upcoming dive. The tapes will show you how to do the visualization, but after that, you're on your own.

Your pre-dive visualization can be as brief as three minutes or up to half-hour. The more serious the dive profile, the greater the detailed you should devote to the visualization. I visualize all my dives. When possible, I try to do one meditation session daily. I usually average about three sessions a week, plus pre-dive visualizations.

Once you incorporate a meditation program into your lifestyle, you'll find yourself becoming more relaxed and able to handle stress more quickly and easily. You should also see immediate improvements in your dive performance. When diving, you should feel more relaxed and have a greater sense of confidence. Gradually, you'll discover not only your lifestyle has changed, but your entire belief system has changed as well.

When you begin the process of visualization, be patient. Negative feelings, or a sense of inadequacy, which have been a part of your life for years, cannot be changed overnight. Improvements will come gradually. Before you laugh or dismiss this idea, remember the process does work. I use it, as do most of my friends and dive buddies.

Visualization enables you to increase your self-confidence.

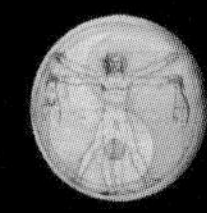

Points to Remember

- It is our attitude at the beginning of a difficult task that will bring about its successful outcome.
- Our attitudes toward others determine their attitude towards us. Our success depends largely on how we relate to others.
- We must think, act, talk and conduct ourselves in all affairs as if we were the person we wish to become. We must keep a mental image of that person in front of us throughout the day.
- Note, the more successful a person, the better the attitude, and that attitude is not the result of success rather success is the result of attitude.
- Recognition and self esteem represent the major need of our lives. To provide this, develop a habit of making all thoughts constructive and positive. Do not waste time discussing negative values.

It permits you to see yourself as you really are. Being honest with yourself is very important, not only with your abilities as a diver, but in your life as well. It is excellent for expanding awareness and for becoming more intuitive. It enables us to get to know our own selves. For the serious diver, visualization is an essential part of the dive planning process. This is the means by which you can go within yourself and make a major life commitment. Importantly, it is in these moments when we discover our real feelings about life's meaning. When this energy is channeled toward dive planning, we are able to reach new levels of excellence and control.

Affirmation is the concept of stating something as if it has already happened. It is another means of communication with the subconscious mind. Affirmation can be spoken, written, or repeated during the process of visualization. A great deal of research on the effective use of affirmation s has been performed in recent years. Psychiatrists, psychologists and social workers, as well as self-help tapes are now using the results of this research. All of these are using the findings of this research to successfully help patients establish realistic goals and belief systems.
Verbal affirmations are quick, beneficial, and efficient. They play role in helping you re-program your mind. Written affirmations are more effective than verbal ones. Writing down what you want to accomplish is the best way to reach your brain's subconscious realm. Any time is good to do affirmations, but many researchers conclude that the best time is about 30 minutes prior to falling asleep.

It's good idea to keep a ledger to log your affirmations. The best way to do this is to divide your log into three sections. First, set personal goals. Second, each night write down the steps you have made to accomplish each goal. Third, log the affirmations reflecting accomplishment of an individual goal. Stating an affirmation while visualizing it is probably the best way to create an accurate personal goal or objective.

The right attitudes cause us to be responsible and expectant. We expect our actions to produce pleasant experiences. Our attitudes cause us to receive what we expect. Attitudes reflect our "inner person." Success in diving, or in business, is simply a reflection of our attitudes. Luck happens when preparedness meets opportunity. A positive attitude causes good luck. A person with a winning attitude expects and achieves success. Winning attitudes don't just happen. We create them through practice. Remind yourself daily to ontinue to develop and sustain a good, positive attitude.

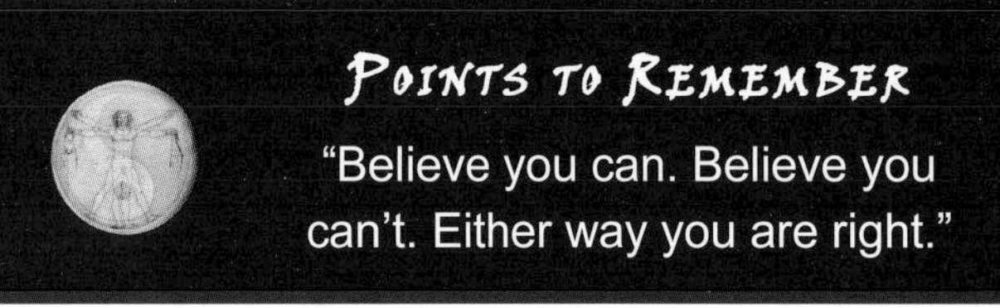

Points to Remember
"Believe you can. Believe you can't. Either way you are right."

As our attitudes develop, we begin to learn more about ourselves. We become honest with ourselves and, more importantly, we begin to believe in ourselves. As this belief strengthens, it is easy to exhibit self-discipline. Thus, as our attitudes develop, our ability to know ourselves becomes a natural outcropping, and the ability to be true to ourselves becomes a reflex. A winning attitude helps us deal favorably with stress. Most importantly, it helps us conquer the impossible!

A winning attitude causes life's energy to flow positively. As divers, we can accomplish more. As individuals, we become happier and more content. Five statements summed up by Earl Nightingale, the renowned motivator, bet explains the role of attitude: "When it comes down to it, all life is just a matter of thoughts and belief we are simply acting out our thoughts. The mind is capable of achieving everything it can conceive and believe. Realistic beliefs originate from thought and are improved by exercise. In the process, some minor goals evolve providing a path to achievement of major goals. Overall, long term goals are ultimately accomplished."

All the world's major philosophies and doctrines share fundamental beliefs. The Christian Bible says, "Whatsoever you ask for, ask for believing and you will receive it." If you ask with disbelief or doubt, it is unlikely your prayers will be fulfilled. Confucius ironically stated, "Do not unto others what you would not want done to you." Taoism teaches universal duality, the Ying – Yang. Over two thousand years ago, the Chinese philosopher Lao Tzu noted, "For every positive action there is a positive reaction." He also taught, "If a tree does not bend with the wind, it will break." For us, this means we need to open our minds, be receptive to new ideas, and be willing to change for the better! **Thomas Ford, the inventor of the automobile, sums up the idea of "belief" most aptly,**

> "We do, in fact, achieve what we believe in. This includes survival in a life threatening situation or success in any of life's ventures. Our only limit is the depth of our belief system. Our outlook is the greatest influence on that belief. If we do not believe it can be achieved, we

POINTS TO REMEMBER

We must think!
We must analyze!
We must be focused!

will not achieve it unless we can change our attitude."

The material discussed in this chapter will help you develop a positive belief system. By developing positive attitudes, we can change our thought patterns. When we change our thought patterns, we change our belief systems. When we change our belief system, we change our lives. When we believe we can, we accomplish all we wet out to do. Success, survival, happiness, honestly in self and with others, self-discipline, and good relationships all depends on positive attitudes.

Another key ingredient necessary for success in technical diving, or in life in general is goal setting. This is the process of defining an objective we desire to accomplish. Success is simply the achievement of our goals. To effectively utilize the technique of setting and realizing goals, we must follow a three step process. First, we must define exactly what we want. Second, steps must be defined to consummate the goal. Third, we must develop a belief in the attainment of the goal.

Goals are achieved one step at a time. When we accomplished one step, we move on to the next. A belief system also develops in the steps we pursue. Once the mind believes in a realistic goal, it can be fulfilled. Steps taken in orderly progression allow the mind to fully believe in success.

It's a smart idea to write down your goals. In business, it's common to set long-term goals. The long-term goal is then broken down into short-term goals, usually annual goals. Accomplishing each intermediate goal brings long-term success much closer.

The same process works in diving. This is true whether your goal is to simply be a good diver or a record-setting explorer. Once written, the subconscious mind begins to program itself. The use of affirmations and the act of visualizing the goal will speed up its occurrence. Once a given goal is attained, new goals should be envisioned.

The ability to focus, a talent, which is mainly developed through meditation, can be enhanced by a few simple exercises. One of the best exercises is simply observing a clock's second hand sweep and concentrating on its movement. The key to this exercise is to dismiss all other thoughts that may present themselves during the exercise.

This type of control is essential when facing threatening situations. The key is learning to focus and direct the mind in selective fashion.

Survival depends on being capable of rejecting negative thoughts. A diver who masters the ability to focus can overcome nearly all threatening situations. Under duress, negative emotions and thoughts will flow in an unconditioned mind. If these negative thoughts are allowed a mental audience, they lead to worry, which amplifies, stress and can lead to reactions that culminate in death.

Several years ago, I read an article praising some diver who died. The name of the publication or that of the diver doesn't matter. The article described how the dead diver was found, dive slate in hand. It went on to say that the diver wrote a letter in wonderfully long and articulate prose to his loved ones. A touching story was presented, one of love and concerns for those dears him. While it's admirable that this person could devote the last moments of his life to those he loved, it also brought up another thought. In his perceived moment of tragedy, it appears the diver stopped fighting. I think, perhaps, the diver died because he simply gave up instead of trying to solve his problem. In this case, I think it is quite possible that had the diver spent the time swimming and ***THINKING***, he would most likely be alive today!

As I was completing this book, I came across a true story I thought you'd like to read. It gives a good example of the desire of a very disciplined individual to survive. A cave diver in his late 40's was diving in a popular North Florida site. He was in extremely good physical condition and worked out every day. On the day of the incident, he

POINTS TO REMEMBER

"When faced with dying or achieving the impossible, some people choose to live."
~ Bob Smith

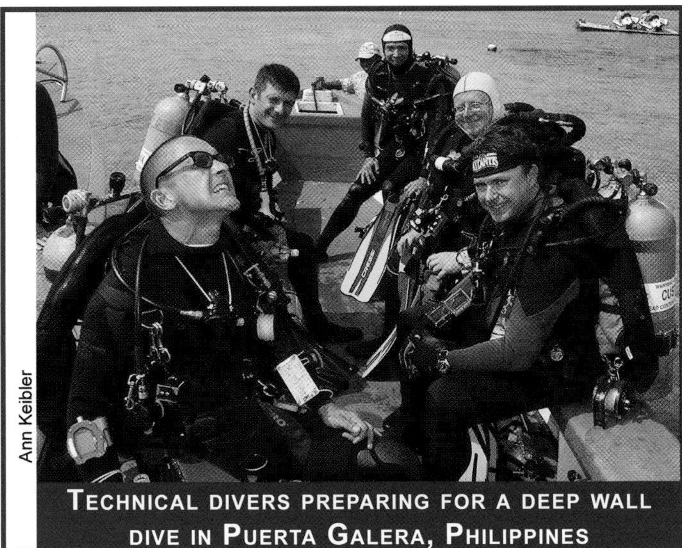

TECHNICAL DIVERS PREPARING FOR A DEEP WALL DIVE IN PUERTA GALERA, PHILIPPINES

was driving with two buddies. The three divers became separated. During the ensuing events, our diver found himself separated and disoriented.

When he finally figured out where he was, 2000 ft (610 m) back in the cave, he only had 400 psig (27 bar) in his primaries and he was 200 ft (61 m) away from his stage bottle. When he was 100 ft (30 m) from his stage bottle, his air ran out. Through sheer willpower and a desire to survive, our diver swam the last 100 ft (30 m) with only the air in his lungs.

There are two points to this story. First, by all accounts, the dive team followed all the rules. What happened to them could happen to anyone. Second, our out-of-air diver survived because he kept his head together by fighting stress and panic. He never stopped thinking! He analyzed the situation and he remained focused throughout the ordeal. And, most importantly of all, he didn't stop to write us a letter. He did not quit. He kept on kicking and kicking, and as a result, he's still alive and able to tell the story!

If all the steps and procedures referenced in this chapter are incorporated in you habits, you will achieve any goal you set providing that you develop a positive, realistic belief in these processes. Saying, "I wanna do it" does not accomplish anything. It is kind of like the Janis Joplin song, "Oh Lord, won't you buy me a Mercedes Benz?" Want and belief are not the same thing.

Wanting something does not produce it. Belief accomplishes all. You must program your mind to believe. You must *THINK* and mentally picture the goal continuously. You must train and make whatever sacrifices are needed to realize your goals!

SURVIVAL TRAINING

To merely say that survival training is extremely important would be an understatement. In fact, it's necessary if you want to keep on living! Survival training's benefits are summed up in the book ***Safe Cave Diving***, which I wrote with several contributing authors in 1973. **Bob Smith, a contributing author, stated in the Stress Chapter:**

> "Survival training enables divers to exemplify Bob's very apt statement. In fact, it teaches you how to focus your mind on the job of staying alive while, at the same time, making wonderful discoveries. And, importantly, it teaches you how to be physically tough and mentally disciplined through a winning attitude."

This training program addresses the risk of technical diving for both recreational and exploratory divers. We have learned it is essential to be able to make informed decisions. A problem 2000 ft (610 m) into an overhead environment is far more difficult to manage than a problem in open water. By reviewing the accidents in diving, it is apparent that technical diving does have risk. We must be aware of the risks and how to evaluate them.

POINTS TO REMEMBER
IN DIVING, QUITTING IS THE UNFORGIVABLE SIN!
QUITTING IN A LIFE THREATENING CIRCUMSTANCE LEAVES ONE ALTERNATIVE – DEATH!
CONTINUING, REGARDLESS OF THE ODDS, PROVIDES THE OPTION OF SURVIVAL!

Several years prior to his death, Sheck Exley introduced the merits of breaking down accidents into steps and analyzing the mechanisms that produced the incident. The majority of accidents are the results of diver's mistakes. In other words, your life may depend on your ability to think fast and to get it right the first time. If you're tired, or hurt, a buddy may be able to help you swim for a little while, and, if necessary, share gas; however, you're the only

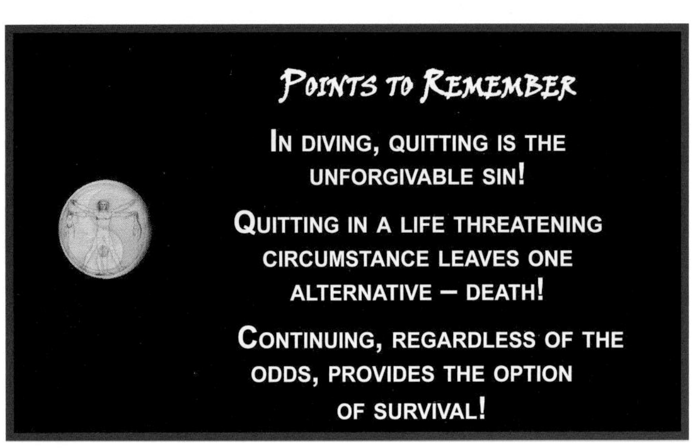

KIM SMITH ASCENDING FROM A LONG SWIM WALL DIVE ON GRAND CAYMAN, BWI

one that can really control your breathing rate. And, when your "you know what" is in a sling, ultimately ***only you*** can save it!

To react favorably in the face of a physical threat, your mind must be preconditioned to as many uncomfortable yet life-dependent variables as possible. A good example would be your ability to survive in the event of a real gas-sharing emergency. In a real emergency, your buddy is going to be more than an arm's length away. Your buddy is probably swimming and not looking directly at you.

In your mind, visualize this scenario: you're 60 ft (18 m) down. Everything beyond you beam of light is pitch black. What's worse, you're just a "mere" 1000 ft (305 m) from the upline. You've had a total gas supply failure. Perhaps your regulator has broken. Picture yourself not panicking. All you have to do is just swim nonchalantly over to your buddy and tap on their shoulder to get their attention. They signal, "What's wrong?" You casually indicate, "I'm out of air. Notice how blue my face is?" They acknowledge that you've indeed looked better. You go onto inquire ever so meekly, "Would you please let me share your air?" They say, "Sure. No problem!"

Gas sharing rarely goes as smoothly as the above scenario. In fact, gas sharing requires precision teamwork to work smoothly. All team members involved must know their roles and be able to execute them without making mistakes. Not only is the life of the out-of-air diver at stake, but probably those of the team members as well. After all, it's their air that's being shared.

The best way to ensure that buddy breathing never becomes a nightmare is through the regular practice of out-of-air drills that stimulate the stress of a "real" situation. Prior to implementing gas sharing and breath holding survival skills, begin by swimming a set distance underwater without breathing. If this is hard, remind yourself of the importance of being able to cope with the feeling of needing to breathe.

Keep in mind that in real situation, your buddy will be swimming. You will have to get their attention and/or overtake them in order to find an air source. In these drills, the actual breath holding duration rarely exceeds 35 to 45 seconds. There is no real danger of blackout and no true physiological demand for air. There is a psychological scream as the mind and body exceed the time at which it is conditioned to breathe. This skill is paramount for divers who may be exposed to real out-of-air situations. It is not, and is not approached as, a fitness test or "toughness skill"

The gas sharing exercise involves swimming without air 60 to 75 ft (18 to 23 m) to a buddy, gaining their attention and initiating gas sharing. Both divers will then remain at rest for at least three breaths to allow the out-of-air diver to regain respiratory control. Both divers then perform a timed swim. The timed swim is not for speed. The divers must maintain a normal swim pace. If the divers swim too fast, additional stress is developed and gas consumption is increased. This, of course, may inhibit them from making it to the surface. On the other hand, if the pace is too slow, they may not have enough gas to reach the surface. The key is that the timed swim be based on a normal swim pace.

Now, let's analyze why this skill helps divers develop survival instincts. If faced with a "real" out of air situation, the subconscious mind "knows" it can deal with it. The mind has been preconditioned to handle the emergency. It means that the diver knows how it feels to need and really want air without being forced to "turn blue." It means being disciplined and in control when faced with adverse conditions.

Additional training skills include the performance of other life support and equipment familiarity skills. A few essentials include: gas shutdowns, use of safety lines, lost diver procedures, and navigating a line in blacked out conditions (simulated by closing the eyes). Training and certification, if done properly, prepare divers for the stress that coincides with in-water emergencies.

The Importance of Fitness

The ideal technical diver is a finely tuned individual, both mentally and physically. Good physical fitness allows the diver to handle his equipment without staggering under its weight. It permits him/her to swim long distances without tiring. Even the diver who uses a DPV must be physically fit. Indeed, this diver is at special risk if unfit should the DPV malfunction during the course of a dive.

Out-of-shape divers are prone to cramps, unable to control respiration, and incapable of providing physical assistance in an emergency. Their work and resting RMV is dramatically different. Fit divers tend to develop coordination as part of their training. This enables them to become more skillful diving technicians. Mental fitness is a must for maintaining self-discipline. Much of the training in a technical program is aimed at developing mental control.

It is appropriate to say that physically unfit divers should avoid technical diving. The non-thinking diver is not qualified for technical diving. Serious deficiencies in either mental or physical fitness place a diver at much greater risk in the diving environment.

A diver needs to be physically fit to prevent injury. Cardiovascular fitness provides the stamina to be comfortable while swimming extended distances in SCUBA gear. It has been documented that unfit divers may retain up to 50% more CO_2 than physically fit divers. This is important. CO_2 build-up induces early fatigue, decompression illness, inert gas narcosis and oxygen toxicity. In other words, excess CO_2 may hurt you. Increased CO_2 may also lead to uncontrolled respiration. It is a major factor in loss of consciousness with resultant drowning.

The first step on the road to survival training involves getting a complete physical at your doctor's office. The second step is to begin a physical conditioning program. The initial training should incorporate some exercise for muscular toning and a graduated level of cardiovascular conditioning. In selecting the muscular toning exercise, resistance with weights or machinery is effective. This part of the regime should simulated actions using muscles that you will need for your style of diving. (For example, high pull-ups will simulate the act of lifting tanks.)

Resistance training needs to be balanced. Extending and contracting muscles prevents an imbalance by working both groups of muscles. Unbalanced musculature may lead to injury when an overdeveloped are creates excess tension on its opposing muscle. Special attention should be placed on stomach and lower back muscles. These muscles groupings are subjected to strain in technical diving environments. This is especially true when managing equipment in and out of the water.

POINTS TO REMEMBER
Points to remember for safe diving:
"Only YOU can think for you.
Only YOU can swim for you.
Only YOU can breathe for you."
In short, no one but YOU
can guarantee your survival.
YOU must be a responsible diver.

Believe it or not, this two-step approach to fitness is also the first level of survival training. The survival benefit

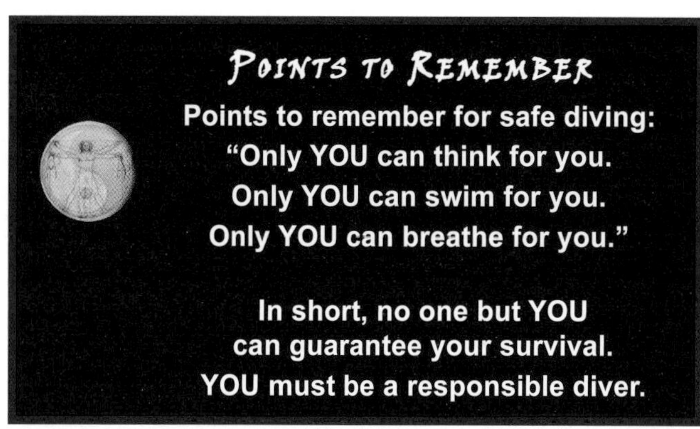

Mel Clark

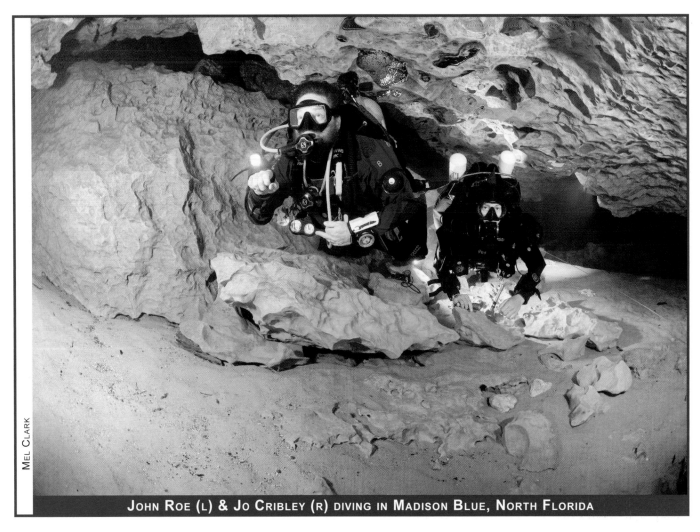

John Roe (l) & Jo Cribley (r) diving in Madison Blue, North Florida

is developing the discipline to enter and maintain a fitness program. Even the most devout athletes require discipline. There are days when excuses abound to avoid a training session. There will be days when you literally drag yourself into a workout. Getting the job done means you are developing a good survival instinct. It is on these days you are going beyond your comfort zone. The days you give in and do not workout can be viewed as diminished survival days.

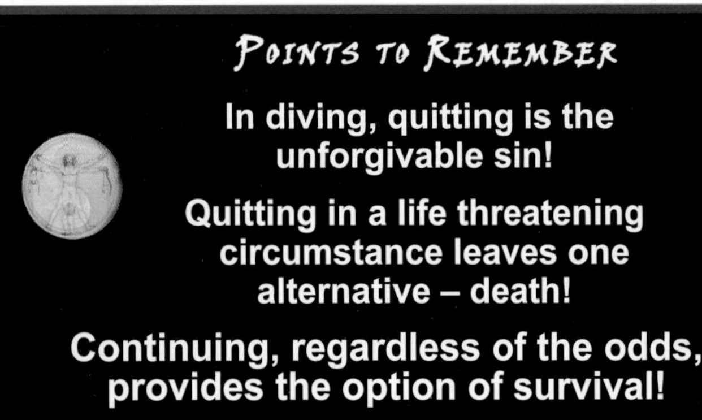

Points to Remember
In diving, quitting is the unforgivable sin!
Quitting in a life threatening circumstance leaves one alternative – death!
Continuing, regardless of the odds, provides the option of survival!

Once the first two basic steps have been initiated and a reasonable degree of fitness has evolved, it's time to begin the third step. Hard-core survival training takes all you can muster mentally and physically. This is an ongoing, increasingly tough and demanding pace. The benefits will greatly enhance your ability to overcome adversity and to survive. In this training, we select a given exercise and assign three goals. The first goal is a time factor. The second is a distance or performance measurement. The third separates us from the pack. We will accomplish these goals at all cost! Keep in mind, this is a gradual process. Training becomes addictive once current goals become less challenging. Mentally these must be viewed as life or death achievements.

Survival abilities can be developed, enhanced and maintaining on lad even more conveniently and effectively than underwater. The programs to develop survival conditioning, however, go beyond the level of cardiovascular training. Many physical trainers and physiologist define

cardiovascular-level training as the point where an elevated pulse is maintained for at least 20 minutes. During this period, the individual should be able to carry on a conversation without interrupting the exercise pace.

Eric Keibler on a wreck in Truk Lagoon Chuuk State, Federated States of Micronesia

However, when performing survival training, exercise should be well beyond the "conversation level." When you've reached this plateau, the only voice you'll be able to muster is the one in your mind that says, "Don't quit. Keep on going!" This is unquestionably a maximum level performance. The entire program is aimed at functioning beyond your comfort level and maintaining that level. The parameters involve maintaining maximum, sustained effort while maintaining a constant respiratory rate. To function in this manner requires discipline to allow increased volume without a corresponding increase in respiratory rate. Obviously, it takes more than a few training sessions to master.

Controlling the respiratory rate under stress means overcoming interfering message generated by the autonomic nervous system (***ANS***). Efficient respiration is vital for developing good discipline when using SCUBA gear. As divers, we deal with an assortment of variables requiring us to maintain a slow inhalation and exhalation rate. A few of these variables include a regulator's breathing resistance, drag while swimming, and the density produced by the depth and/or gas mixture. By controlling our respiratory rates, we have taken the first step in mental control. In this instance, limited control of the ANS has been gained.

A stair climber, or step machine, is an excellent tool for survival training. This is an exercise I personally use and recommend. I begin by establishing the maximum comfortable level I can maintain. Next, I gradually boost the level exercising a minimum of 40 minutes.

As your fitness improves, you can incorporate interval training. After the first 2 minutes on the climber, boost the level by one. Remain at this level for 2 minutes. Then, resume the previous level and repeat every 2 minutes. Throughout the exercise, maintain a constant slow respiratory rate. A good initial respiratory rate is achieved by inhaling approximately 6 seconds. Pause no more than 3 seconds. Finally, exhale 6 seconds with an exhalation pause of 3 seconds or less.

Once you've mastered the initial step in interval training, increase your work level to the absolute maximum that can be maintained for 20 minutes. Next, reduce the level by one and complete 5 additional minutes at this level. Start increasing the intensity of interval training. After 3 minutes. Return to the next higher level for 3 minutes. Finally, repeat this procedure for 30 minutes and set the "bump up" intervals to 5 minutes in length.

This concept of maximum exercise should be maintained throughout the entire exercise session. Gradually increase the total time from 20 minutes to 40 minutes. When you've reached the upper level and can maintain it, it's time to begin survival training.

Survival training exceeds the limits of normal interval training. It means your workout session is a maximum effort from beginning to end. I do the following. On my stair climber I set the upper level at 12. This translates to 20.3 flights of stair-per-minute. I do the entire 40 minutes at this level. My performance goal is 40 minutes and 820 floors, or an average of 20.5 floors-per-minute. The acceptable range is from 770 floors to 820 floors.

On those days when I maintain this level, my survival ability is rated as certain. On days when I climb less than 770 floors, I score myself as having reduced survival abilities. In my scoring system, as long as I complete the time and remain between 725 and 750 floors, a good survival probability exists. If less than 725, but more than 675 floors are completed, the survival probability is average. When the total floors climbed are between 650 and 675,

the probability of survivability is low. With less than 650 floors, the rating is poor. When I'm unable to complete the exercises, I rate my odds for survival at zero. In my training philosophy, I "***die***" on those days.

When accomplishing these drills, attempt to complete all goals. Even on those days when you cannot maintain the accelerated rates, at least complete the time objective. Occasionally, it will be necessary for you to actually stop (just as in a stressful diving situation), regain respiratory and/or mental control, then resume exercising. Going the full time limit is paramount. The survival probability is lower when only two or more objectives are completed. However, going the distance greatly increases discipline and improves your possibility of survival. Quitting too soon means you probably won't survive. Every one of us has read about divers who quit trying. When they quit trying, they died!

The level of intensity in survival training varies from person to person. Everyone should be able to discover a personal system and rating code. The tougher the training, the greater the survivability factor will be for you. Jim Lockwood, for example, has survived near impossible situations. His workouts on the stair climber last over 1½ hours. He goes "flat out." He also finds time for a 70 to 100 mile (112 to 161 kilometer) bicycle ride 2-3 times per week. In season Jim combines swimming and kayaking with the same degree of intensity.

Experiment with a level of exercise that will force you to become more mentally and physically disciplined. This combination of mental and physical self-control is paramount to your survival. While training, your body and mind will often cry out for relief. When this happens, visualize yourself in a critical situation. Your only hope of survival is to keep going. When you want to stop and rest, dig deep within yourself and produce that extra burst of mental power to drive your physical body to success. On those really tough days, give yourself a reward for completing a survival session. Getting the job done when it's the hardest improves your survivability factor. On the easy days, and they are few, you simply maintain and reconfirm your abilities.

Cross training is an excellent tool to help you increase fitness and prevent boredom. Swimming, especially with fins is an excellent way to improve stamina and endurance. When cross training, set up your program for maximum effort. This may sound extreme. It is. However, it also conditions both your body and mind for a better survival level. I know this to be true from dozens of personal experiences, including a plane crash.

Both Patti Mount and I survived a plane crash with multiple injuries. We were in the water fighting for our lives for over 3½ hours. Patti was semi-conscious and unconsciousness for much of this time. The entire 3½ hours was spent swimming, as our raft sank faster than our plane. The only flotation device I could think of involved using my blue jeans, which I made into a float for Patti. Thanks to our survival training, we are both alive today.

The importance of physical fitness should be evident by this time, but as it relates to both mental and physical discipline, we will take a more in-depth look at the benefits of fitness for technical divers.

By incorporating the survival training I have described, a positive belief system evolves. Inner awareness is created. We become in tune with our "intuitive selves" as well as with our physical and mental abilities. We accomplish what our belief system dictates. People achieve their beliefs, not undirected daydreams. However, through some of the above practices, it is possible to turn daydreams into belief systems.

References

Mount T, *The Art of Safe Diving,* 1973, NACD Gainsville, FL

Mount T, *Proceeding of IQ 10*, 176 Naui California

Mount T, *Practical Diving*, 1976, Univerisity Miami Press, Miami, FL

Mount T, *Mixed Gas Diving* 1993, Watersports Publishing, San Diego, CA

Mount T, *The Technical Diver Encyclopedia*, 1996 IANTD, Miami, FL

Mount T, *Tek Lite*, 2005, IANTD, Miami Shores, FL

Smith, Stress in Cave Divng from the *Art of Safe Cave Diving*, 1973, NACD, Gainsville, FL

Smith, R, from *Practical Diving*, 1976, Univerisity Miami Press, Miami, FL

Chapter Nineteen
The Psychology Of Survival

Tom Mount D.Sc., Ph.D., N.D.

On the occasion of every accident that befalls you, remember to turn to your self and inquire what power you have for turning it to use.

~ Epictetus

When reviewing dive accidents, one of the more complex questions is: ***Why did this incident take place?*** Out of the dive accidents that result in fatalities, many of the divers seemed to have died in manageable conditions, and for no obvious reason. In contrast to this set of divers, there are those who survive events that in retrospect appear nearly impossible to live through. The above two scenarios repeatedly present themselves to those who analyze dive accidents, injuries and deaths. **As a result, the question of *Why?* is broken down to:**

- What led to this series of events?
- How did this diver narrowly escape death? ***And...***
- What occurred to change an easily solved problem into a deadly problem?

Moreover, as divers, we tend to view ourselves in a separate box and find all the solutions with in this small parameter. In reality, the negative events that take place within diving are similar to negative events in other sports and our daily lives. Once we accept that the core problems found in diving are not unique, we are able to review the wealth of available accident and fatality data outside of the dive world and apply this newfound information to the way we dive, live, and care for our body. An excellent source for data such as mentioned above and detailed descriptions of accidents is found in the book ***Stress and Performance in Diving*** by Bachrach and Engstrom. The knowledge gained from reading this text may be used as a first step in understanding accident and consequence.

In their book, Bachrach and Engstrom say:

"In virtually all cases, the term accident is used synonymously with injury, or casualty (***fatality***). In recent years, a school of accident methodology (Bachrach: Licht, 14, 116) has developed in which a different approach to defining and reporting accidents has come about. In this approach, an accident is unforeseen, unplanned event in which control is lost.

An accident occurs the first time the individual loses control. Thus, if you are driving your car, hit an icy patch and skid out of control, you have had an accident The important distinction here is that the consequences of the accident characterize the event. If you regain control and bring the car back to a normal path, there are no major negative consequences. If you do not regain control and the skid leads to a crash, then there may be major negative consequences such as injury or death. In either event an accident has occurred.

To regain control in an accident, the person must be able to quickly and accurately obtain information about the environment and the hazardous situation. Moreover, this information must be processed in a timely manner to allow an effective and appropriate response. Both the event and the response in an accident are time constrained."

Accident Mitigation

If an accident is an unforeseen and unplanned event, then to speak of accident prevention is not meaningful. **What we need to address is accident mitigation which takes two basic forms:**

Leigh Bishop

CARL SPENCER PAUSES TO EXAMINE THE AWESOME GUNS OFF THE ***HMS AUDACIOUS*** IN THE NORTH ATLANTIC

- Trying to foresee what might possibly happen and prepare as best we can for the unplanned event, and…
- Trying to mitigate the consequences if an accident occurs (pp. 23-24).

From the above quote it is easy to understand that each of us may experience an accident; however, the key component that determines who survives is the individual's reaction to the accident and its' consequences. There is a vast difference between ***learning*** and ***training***; training exposes the individual to situational possibilities and on occasions to situational probabilities. Learning, on the other hand, is instilled into muscle memory through training and life experiences. While on a surface look these seem similar the difference between learning and training is ***who survives*** and ***who does not*** survive. This chapter will, among other issues, focus on the role of surviving possibly life-threatening accidents. For additional information and more in-depth accident assessments the reader is encouraged to review the references cited in this chapter.

One characteristic that is found in survivors is a survival-orientation, or in other words, the ability to accept that each day may produce unforeseen and unplanned incidents that may result in an accident. In order to adapt to such possible negative events, our attitude and thought processes must be highly flexible, and we must understand, at a very profound level, that we may live or die based on the outcome of our reactions to these occurrences.

The belief that we may die in a given situation is, at a visceral level, unacceptable to most individuals. Instead, there is often a covert, or occasionally overt, belief that death or severe trauma occur to other people. The conviction that ***bad things happen to others*** often masks the reality that we may be that other person. However, this cognitive twisting of reality works against the survivor mentality. To survive situations in which our life depends on our ability to accept reality and act quickly and rationally, we must possess an innate understanding that the choice between life and death may occur any time, any place, any day, and during any activity.

While there is little need to spend time worrying about the possibility of facing life or death scenarios, the alert person accepts the truth of the above statement. Failure to do so may lead to denial that such threats exist, which in turn may prevent a survival response from developing quickly enough to overcome the physiological impact of the accident. **In the book *Survival Psychology* Leach elaborates on this concept:**

1. The most frequent psychological response encountered under threat is denial. The most common action is inactivity.
2. During the pre-impact period denial and inactivity prepare people well for the roles of victim and corpse.
3. During the period of impact ten to twenty percent of the population will remain relatively calm. They will be able to think, make decisions, and act. Approximately 75% will be stunned and bewildered. They will not be able to think effectively and will act in a semi-automatic, almost mechanical manner. The remaining 10-15 percent of a population will show a high degree of uncontrolled and inappropriate behavior (p. 29 - Summary).

In another section, Leach discusses most individual's reaction to a traumatic event:

> "There is very little doubt that the most commonly observed reaction shown by people before, during and immediately following a disaster is that of disbelief and denial (p. 39)."

To continue with Leach on the subject of denial:

> "Denial can also appear as a form of perceptual distortion. In such cases the information which is impinging on our senses (sight, sound, smell, touch, and taste) is incorrectly processed to give a false result or conclusion (p. 42)."

This chapter also explores the core of living or dying, and reviews factors that increase or decrease a diver's ***survivability potential***. Accident analysis and other research indicate that, in similar in-water traumas, there is often little difference in actual skills between divers who die as a result of the event, divers who experience serious injury as an effect of the incident, and divers who survive the occurrence without severe harm. In situations that lead to death, many of the problems faced by the diver are easily overcome, leaving the diver's peers wondering as to why a simple, easily resolved condition led to death. In part, such deaths occur due to the diver's inability to accept that anything can happen at any time, and plan accordingly.

It is imperative that the response to a diving emergency is not a rushed, unfocused attempt at resolving the problem. Many divers who are unprepared for the unexpected do not perceive that an underwater accident is developing. Moreover, when faced with a possibly critical situation, ignoring the need to act in a quick, calm and direct manner often leads to chaos, severe trauma, and possible death.

It should be noted that there are a plethora of books relating to survival in specific environments and conditions, such as disease, Prisoners of War (*POW*), and the ***Holocaust***, a term used to describe Hitler's mechanized, inhuman extermination of those that did not follow or fit into the Nazi world view. However, although reading such works may be considered as a positive ***first step*** on the road to increasing survivability, the act of simply reading such material does not ensure survival. Training, as noted earlier, is a controlled exposure to certain skills and actions designed to assist the diver in managing a possible catastrophe.

Training is an exposure to skills and actions that are designed to assist us in dealing with a survival situation. It is up to us to transform training into learning. The military has a great deal of expertise in training combatants to respond appropriately to life-threatening situations. However, many of the physically and mentally fit individuals who train for special warfare operations who fail to meet standards train as an exercise. They do not, or are not capable of, internalizing the learning aspect of their training, and therefore do not develop the survival response that the weeks or months of training intended them to learn, and which they must have in order to face critical situations. **Thus the reason this group of recruits wash out of the programs can be attributed to the following:**

> "Not learning, and therefore not internalizing, the intent of the training and not possessing the physical or psychological discipline to withstand the challenges the recruits are faced with."

Similar to elite combatants, it appears that divers who survive and those who do not may be equal in many attributes. Yet when placed in similar situations, some will live, some will die, and some would die or experience serious injury if not rescued. The difference between the two groups as proposed in this chapter is that the divers who survive learned from what they were taught and trained in, or were able to draw on past learning.

Just as the degree and type of physical fitness required for one sport does not necessarily translate to another sport, our instinctive responses may not adapt to other environments. Different mind-sets as well as separate skills are often needed in changing from, for example, a land-based sport to an in-water sport. Separate schemas and diverse emergency skills are also necessary when altering levels within sports, such as moving from open-circuit diving to closed circuit diving. **In the book *Deep Survival*, the author Laurence Gonzales explains:**

> "I believe everyone should learn about basic survival skills and the survivors' frame of mind, because they come in handy when the trappings of civilization (or even financial or emotional support) that we take for granted drop away for what ever reason. Instructors at survival schools are finding that more and more business people are taking their courses, not because they want to survive in the wilderness but for the other qualities that grow out of knowing how. Here are some suggestions, fist for staying out of trouble, then for dealing with it when it comes.
>
> Perceive, believe, and then act. Avoiding accidents, avoiding survival situations, is all about being smart. Horace Barlow, a neurobiologist, says that intelligence is a matter of "***guessing well***." Guessing well involves a natural tendency people have to predict. Training is an attempt to make predictions more accurate in a given environment. But as the environment changes (and it always does), what you need is versatility, the ability to perceive what's really happening and adapt to it. So the training and prediction may not always be your best friend… (p. 279)."

The final sentence in the above quote underscores the crucial difference between training and learning, and as such, can be applied to diving. The diver is taught skills and emergency procedures that may be simple or complex. Methodologically, the diver's instruction progresses in a step-wise fashion, which continuously builds on and increases the diver's capacity to perform should certain incidences occur. However, the environment may produce an emergency in a manner not rehearsed in training; thus the diver who accepts training as the equivalent of learning may respond to the novel emergency in a way that is more suited for other situations. In contrast, the diver whose training led to actual learning adapts his or her cognitive map to include the new information. This in turn allows for "generalization;" the diver may innately

Courtesy of Don Shirley

DON SHIRLEY WAS THE BACK-UP SAFETY DIVER 746 FT (220 M) ON A TEAM WHOSE MISSION WAS TO RECOVER THE REMAINS OF DEON DREYER, A DIVER LOST IN THE BOESMANSGAT SYSTEM PREVIOUSLY. DURING HIS ASCENT DON SUFFERED A VESTIBULAR DECO HIT, WHICH AFFECTS THE INNER EAR. DURING HIS 13 HOUR DECO SCHEDULE, DON HAD TO DEAL WITH EXTREME ROTATIONAL VERTIGO AND NAUSEA AS WELL AS A LOSS OF BALANCE AND DIRECTION. DON'S IS ONE OF THE GREATEST UNDERWATER SURVIVAL STORIES. ~ JANUARY 13, 2005

modify survival techniques taught during training to meet environmental demands. This diver, who does not confuse training with learning, has a higher probability of survival than the diver who believes that training and learning are merely different words for the same process.

The above paragraph helps explain the more subtle differences between equally trained divers who, when faced with the same situation, have completely divergent responses, leading to circumstances in which some of the divers live and some die or experience severe trauma if not rescued. Most likely, the divers who survived without the need for rescue drew on past learning, or internalized the intent of their training and exercises, and were able to generalize survival procedures and responses to include similar, yet still novel, emergencies.

It is also possible that some individuals are born with greater survival skills than others; such traits may be based on genetics or from ***past lives,*** which, as defined by Dr. Morris Netherton, is ***any second from this moment back into the past.*** In contrast, there are people who have a very low ***survival index***, or as some state, a poorly developed will to survive. Following accidents in which some gain control of the situation and survive whereas others do not, observers and researchers often note an apparent ***willingness to die*** in those who failed to live through the incident. Cody Lundin, a rather plain-spoken author, suggests that the psychological and cognitive loss of any desire to survive the current situation kills people more frequently than the actual, physical danger or trauma that they face. **In his book, *Keeping Your Ass Alive*, Lundin states:**

> "Survival is 90% psychology. When the chips are down, it doesn't matter what you have buried in the back yard or how many books on survival you've read. If you're a mental and emotional basket case during your survival episode, you're toast (p. 25).
>
> Training in the physical skills necessary to survive is rather easy when compared to the psychological aspect of survival. People who die in survival situations experience psychological death long before their physical bodies check out. Fear, anxiety, embarrassment, anger, frustration, guilt, depression, confusion, boredom, and loneliness are common reactions to emergency stress. All will attempt to strip you of hope, coercing you into giving up the fight for life. As we will soon explore, in life threatening situations, the line between a survivor's physiological and psychological responses becomes rather transparent (p. 26)."

According to the author Al Siebert, Ph.D., World War II POWs called the willingness to die ***give-up-itis***, or the fully acknowledged mental and emotional loss of any desire to survive the current situation. Siebert discusses this concept in terms of the Bataan Death March. The Bataan Peninsula is a rocky extension of the Zambales Mountains on the island of Luzon in the Philippines that separates Manila Bay from the South China Sea. In 1941, the Japanese surprised the American military with a powerful attack on Luzon's main United States airbase. In a desperate attempt to save America's hold on the island, General Douglas MacArthur directed the American and Philippine troops to engage in a dual action which forced the soldiers to leave necessary stockpiles of food and supplies behind.

After three months of brutal battles, a painful decision on the part of the American military was made, and the American and Filipino warriors were told to stand down and surrender. The POWs then began the 65-mile trek later known as the ***Bataan Death March***. The atrocities committed against the American and Filipino soldiers both during the march and throughout their confinement were as despicable as unnerving. Following Japan's surrender in 1945, an Allied commission convicted the Japanese General in charge of the Death March of war crimes against humanity, leading to the General's execution in 1946. To this day, the Bataan Death March is recognized as one of the greatest displays of horror and heroism (adapted from the website www.bataan.navy.mil).

According to Dr. Siebert in his book *The Survivor Personality*:

> "In those conditions it was easier to die than to live. Staying alive was something a person had to choose to do every day, even every hour. Thousands of men did give up and die. The POW's called it "***give-up-itis***." To stay alive was an act of personal will; to die, all a person had to do was reach the point of deciding, "I can't take this anymore." Some members of the American Defenders of Bataan and Corregidor told me that dying was, "...as easy as letting go of a rope." Once a man had decided to give up the struggle to stay alive, he was usually dead within a few hours (p 219)."

Survival, therefore, is as much a psychological decision as an emotional and physical issue. In the preceding discussion ***just giving up***, or what I refer to as ***quitting***, was addressed and defined as a lack of desire to do whatever it takes to live.

A related, yet somewhat different, response to stress or threat is panic to the point of immobility, and is often referred to a ***freezing up***. The person essentially ceases to respond to external stimuli. This reaction to a possible life-threatening situation does not appear to be so much of a loss of interest in survival and an autonomic reflex that renders the individual incapable of self-rescue. **John Leach, the author of *Survival Psychology*, explains the concept of freezing up when he writes:**

> "There are occasions when anxiety in a life threatening situation becomes so overwhelming that it induces a form of paralysis. This condition of being frozen to the spot can be considered as a form of panic. Certainly a freezing action or a paralysis is grossly ineffective and will often lead to self destruction. (p. 35)."

Leach later notes:

> "Further analyses and debriefings strongly suggest that there are two basic forms of freezing behavior which the author terms deadlock and live lock. Deadlock refers to the first type of behavior in which the victim's muscles show intense rigour (even violent assault may not move them) and an apparent cessation of mental processing. Livelock produces in the victim a muscular tension which is within normal range and although mental processing is occurring it is not being converted into action. This seems to be because the thinking process is engaged in a decision dilemma (p. 36)."

It is easy to understand how quitting, freezing and *give-up-it is* might contribute to dive accidents, as the initial flaw that lead to death, severe trauma, or the need to be rescued may be deeply imbedded in the diver's psychological profile. It is also possible that the genes of a diver may contain clues as to why some will react in such ways. The author Robert Scaer explores the possible role of genetics on trauma responses in his text, ***The Trauma Spectrum: Hidden Wounds and Human Resiliency*. In it he writes:**

> "In his book ***Nature via Nurture,*** Matt Ridley (2003) explored the complex nature of the gene versus experience debate from the personality structure concepts of free will. Ridley noted a rather obscure scientific finding that a specific gene may predispose its owners to personality traits of depression, self-consciousness, anxiety, and vulnerability – traits that fall under the psychological definition of neuroticism. The degree that these traits find expression in the life of their owner, however, is determined by the life experiences of that individual. The genes, in other words, are "***switched on***" by nurture. The absence of trauma even in the face of the neuroticism genetic template may minimize the expression. In the face of trauma, however, the individual with this genetic pattern may be much more likely to develop the personality traits that we associate with neuroticism, some of which correlate with the late symptoms of trauma. (p. 86)."

From the above quote, it is apparent that researchers are exploring the concept of genetic coding as it relates to an individual's response to real or perceived threat. In addition, our personal experiences from childhood through adulthood appear to exhibit a strong influence on how we react to threat.

For those of us who believe in reincarnation, karma most likely plays a deciding role in our behavior under stress, as

our reaction to threat may be based in past life events. In this regard, Past Life Therapy (***PLT***) can be considered a valuable tool in our quest to discover factors that inhibit or enhance our ability to survive. As stated earlier, Dr. Morris Netherton's definition of a past life experience is any second prior to the one we currently inhabit. If we accept Dr. Netherton's theory, PLT may prove to be an excellent tool for discovering and modifying our cognitive map by rectifying past experiences. Following this line of reasoning, our reactions to a traumatic situation in the ***now*** may have been formed during birth, conception, a previous life, or a prior death.

Past life events are considered embedded in the individual's ***soul memory*** which in part affects current behavior. Therefore, soul memory may play a major role in how a person responds to life in general, and the ability to survive and remain healthy in particular. **Regarding the effectiveness of PLT in resolving past life traumas that inhibit the survival instinct in the current life, Dr. Morris Netherton states in *Strangers In a Land of Confusion:***

> "The mind is drawn to situations that contain the unconscious perception that we will not survive. The fears of survival are eliminated when unconscious experiences, which contain pain, trauma and confusion, are resolved and questions answered. In the process of discovery, the mind first asks the questions, and then provides the answers. The mind is the ultimate source of survival... (Note: page numbers are not available; e-book.)"

If one accepts the concept of past lives, it is reasonable to postulate a correlation between genetic memory and soul memory. Moreover, both types of memory may possess an embedded predisposition toward a flight-or-fight response to threat. Once the fight-or-flight response is initiated, panic in its various forms may rule. The individual may experience a profound need to leave the threatening situation as quickly possible, resort to mind-numbing and possibly deadly, inactivity, or other actions that are detrimental to survival. Conversely, the memories deep within the gene or soul memory may precondition us to become survivors. Although it is quite likely that these last two categories are more common than the freeze or quit responses in most individuals, tools will be introduced later in this chapter to help transform those who may be prone to the flight or fight impulse, such as bolting, freezing, or experiencing "give-up-itis" into survivors, as well as increasing the survivability of natural survivors.

As noted, our emotions and beliefs play a major role in our ability to survive. This is an area in which response is difficult to predict, as emotions may vary day to day and from event to event throughout our lives. Paul Valent, who authored ***From Survival to Fulfillment***, explored the emotional factors that affect automobile accidents. It should be noted that similar factors may play a role in diving incidents. **In the above-mentioned book, Valent noted the following:**

> "With regard to stress, M.R. Weinstein (1968) and Hirschfield and Behan (1969) showed that accidents could serve as means of resolving relational stresses and unacceptable emotions, especially in people who could not think through their conflicts. In addition Chan (1987) found emotions immediately before incidents to be important. Such emotions were frustration, hurt, anger, fear, anxiety, inadequacy, and depression (p. 35)."

Figure 19-1-A: Surrogate muscle testing allows us to understand how the energy of team mates may affect our survival capability. In these two illustrations, Grand Master Tom Mount muscle tests Lucie Gawinowski while John Timinisky simply lays his hand on Tom's shoulder. In this illustration Lucie's arm is strong and remains readily outstretched.

It is apparent that all of these emotions would have a negative effect on a diver's mental state. However, many dive while feeling one or more of these emotions. If a diver thinks back to his or her mental state at the beginning of a dive that did not have the intended outcome, there is a high probability that the diver started the dive in an emotionally unbalanced condition. It is notable that, when divers are interviewed following a diving accident, one or more of the divers admit to experiencing a negative or depressive mood pre dive. With this said, it is also important that the diver not block his or her emotions. It is imperative that divers accept, understand, and learn to use emotions in ways that help, versus hinder, the diver. It is a major tragedy that cultures advocate blocking or negating emotional responses rather than acknowledging, understanding, and learning to use emotions in a beneficial manner. Further, it is important to know how to transform certain emotional issues so that their effect helps motivate us into appropriate action, increases our survivability, and positively affects our long-term health.

In order to increase one's understanding of how emotions alter human performance, try the following exercises, which use a technique known as ***muscle testing***. Refer to Figure 19-1-A and 19-1-B.

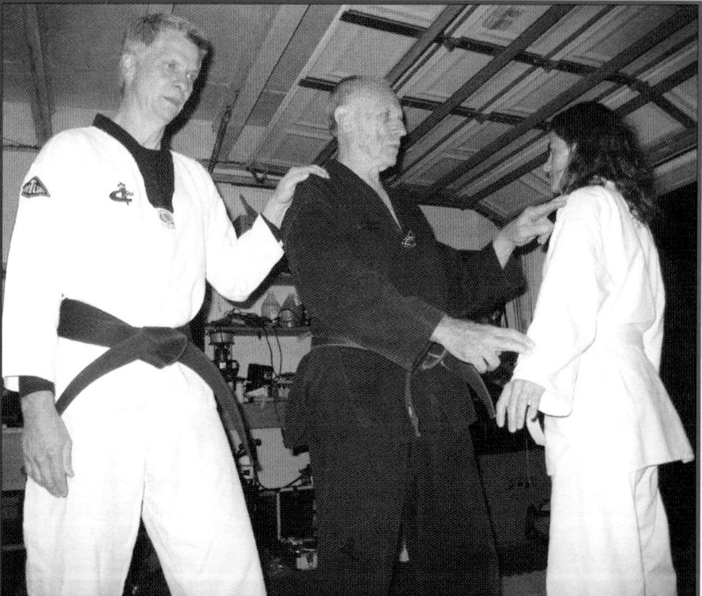

FIGURE 19-1-B: LUCIE'S STRENGTH & SURVIVAL CAPABILITY REACT TO A NEGATIVE THOUGHT JOHN IS HAVING & HER STRENGTH WAS ALMOST INSTANTLY GONE. THIS IS THE REASON WHY IT IS SO IMPORTANT TO KNOW YOUR BUDDY & TO KNOW WHAT THINGS IN THEIR LIFE MAY BE AFFECTING THEM AT ANY GIVEN TIME. OUR ATTITUDES, EMOTIONS & THOUGHTS MAKE THE DIFFERENCE IN NOT ONLY OUR SURVIVAL BUT ALSO CAN AFFECT THE SURVIVAL OF TEAM MATES AS WELL. IT ALSO DEMONSTRATES THAT EVERY THOUGHT IS A PRAYER THAT PUTS AN ACTION INTO MOTION. PROJECT THOUGHTS WISELY AS THEY ARE OUR MOST POWERFUL TOOL.

Have a partner muscle test you:

- Think a negative thought and have your partner muscle test you again; note any change
- Think a positive thought and once again have your partner muscle test you; note any change
- Repeat above steps except have your partner be the one doing the thought projections
- Repeat the steps with you checking your partner this time

The importance of this exercise is to illustrate how you and your partner's emotions affect each other as individuals and as a team. Muscle testing also exemplifies the classic ***feedback loop***; the changes noted affect mental status, and as a result, affect outcome. In other words, your physiological response to threat or pleasure can adversely affect your emotional state, the emotional state of those around you, and your physiological abilities. As a corollary, the more capable you are of controlling your reaction to real or perceived threat, the greater your probability of surviving the incident.

Once you have completed the muscle-testing exercises and reviewed your results, prepare to learn another mental technique: ***How to protect yourself against the effects other's negative emotional output has on your emotional state.*** For this exercise, draw a mental line down the center of your body. Now, take you finger and place it directly below your navel, and centered on your pelvis. Move your finger up toward your collarbone, ending at the base of your bottom lip, staying on the center line, otherwise known as the central meridian or conception vessel. While engaging in this process, visualize a zipper running along the central meridian, and you are closing and securing the zipper from outside influence. Once you have completed this step, have your partner project negative thoughts. If your meridian is ***sealed***, chances are that you will not be emotionally affected, or be affected to a lesser degree, by your partner's negativity.

The ***zip up*** (without having your buddy test it) line visualization, is an excellent technique to incorporate pre-dive.

Another part of your pre-dive repertoire is learning to increase your internal energy while developing a greater resistance to others' negative energy. Although there are a number of complex exercises that can be done, the technique presented here is simple and easy to master. **To begin:**

- Place your hands about six inches out from your body, at the level between the waist and pubic bone
- Now imagine a spring between your hands
- With palms facing in, exhale and press the ***spring*** tighter
- Just before your hands touch, inhale and pull the spring outward by moving your hands away from each other

You should begin to feel some tingling, which is a sign of internal energy buildup, shortly after starting this process.

These drills exemplify the need to choose buddies based

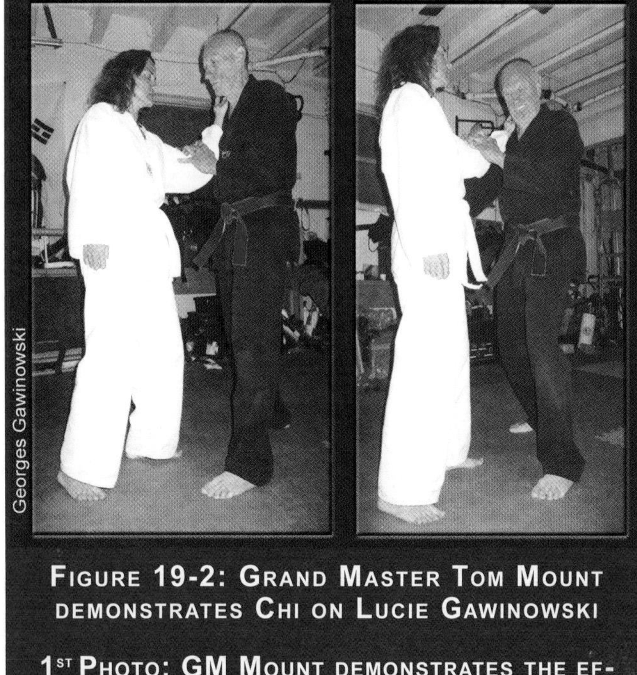

Figure 19-2: Grand Master Tom Mount demonstrates Chi on Lucie Gawinowski

1st Photo: GM Mount demonstrates the effects of negative thoughts on Lucie's locked arm, which she is unable to keep locked.

2nd Photo: Lucie is able to keep her arm locked despite GM Mount's efforts to move her arm. In this case, after thinking good thoughts she sealed her meridian from outside emotions, applying the zipping technique as taught by GM Mount.

Figure 19-3: Tom Mount demonstrates muscle testing on Lucie Gawinowski using a traditional health care method

on emotional status as well as diving skills, as a buddy team is synergistic: It potentiates both the negative and positive effects of each individual's survivability, energy level, and thought processes. Therefore, the difference between a pleasurable dive and a miserable one, or the dichotomy between an appropriate, survival-oriented response to an emergency and a rushed, panic stricken response to a crisis is often based on the team's interactions above and below the water. Although there are numerous other ***energy tools*** such as ***Aura expansion*** that can be used by divers to increase positive energy and immunity from negative energy, which in turn amplifies survivability, such techniques are beyond the scope of this chapter.

When discussing the capacity to survive trauma and ways in which survivability is increased or decreased, addressing the attributes of a natural survivor furthers our understanding of what ***survivability*** means. Most research on the subject has found that the natural survivor tends to adapt to the moment. In other words, such the natural individuals are not locked into a ***black and white, wrong or right*** belief system. Instead, the natural survivor's thinking processes are highly flexible, in that the natural survivor is capable of immediately reassessing a situation and adapting to any novel information presented. These individuals are able to change ***schemas*** or known and accepted ways of functioning, in order to fit the world around them. This process is called ***accommodation***. Those who are not natural survivors tend to assimilate new material into an already extant schema, changing important aspects of the new material rather than altering their view of what they expect to find.

Unlike those with a rigid belief system that relies on assimilation, the natural survivor accepts that nature creates challenges, makes accommodations in their thought patterns which lead to the immediate development of a new schema that includes the present danger, and devises reality-based ways in which to meet the current, unexpected, threat. Therefore, the survivor adapts to any given emergency, and recognizes the emergency no matter how the crisis is presented.

When faced with possible trauma, the natural survivor adds cognitive flexibility in order to increase the effectiveness of other highly developed skills such as forethought, knowledge of the environment, an in-depth grasp of human reactivity during an emergency and technical expertise. This combination creates a positive synergy, which allows the natural survivor to modify learned responses in order to correctly address the current emergency, and control the degree of trauma as the crisis unfolds.

However, the personality characteristics that create the natural survivor often appear contradictory, and may frustrate or appear psychologically abnormal to those who maintain a more rigid system of beliefs, practices, habits, and behaviors. **According to Al Siebert:**

> "Survivors puzzled me at first. They are serious and humorous, hard working and lazy, self confident and self critical. They are not one way or the other, they are both one way and the other.
>
> This was a hard mental barrier to break through. Most tests of personality view a person as either one way or another not both... Many authors write about people as being "optimists" or "pessimists," as type A personalities or type B. Yet many survivors are optimistic and pessimistic, hard-working as well as lazy... (pp. 27-28)."

Siebert continues to assess the survivor personality in when he writes:

> "When I ask survivors if there is any quality or attribute that contributes most to being a survivor, they usually answer with out hesitation. They say either "flexibility" or "adaptability" (p. 28)."

Siebert synthesizes the above information and notes:

> "Biphasic personality traits increase survivability by allowing a person to be one way or its opposite in any situation. To have biphasic traits is to be more adaptable rather than being "either one way or another." It is to be proud and humble, selfish and unselfish, cooperative and rebellious...
>
> Pairs of biphasic, paradoxical, or counter-balanced traits are essential to a survivor style because they give you choices about how to respond (p. 29)."

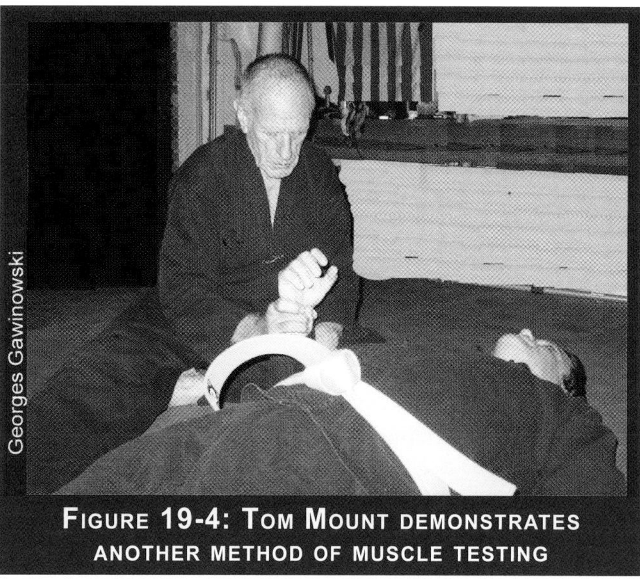

Figure 19-4: Tom Mount demonstrates another method of muscle testing

John Leach devotes several chapters in his text to exemplifying and elaborating on the various traits needed for survival. Similar to Siebert, Leach's observations are based on a lifetime of studying survivability in numerous and highly varied environments and circumstances. **Leach sums up the necessary components for survival when he states:**

> "At this stage it is more useful to identify and decompose those observable factors underlying survival and to seek their source in human development. The key psychological factors found in survivors have been described both in this chapter (establishing a mission, tasking, attachment, prayer, personal character, humor, active-passiveness, adaptation and consolidation) and in earlier chapters (training and preparation). In a survival situation these factors all come to the aid of the victim but they will not work in isolation. They must be integrated one with another and it is perhaps this degree of integration which is being observed and labeled as the will to survive. That is, the greater the fusion within an individual of these factors the greater is his chance for survival and it is the fusion which reflects

the will to survive. Furthermore, this integration must become pseudo-instinctive. It must, when called upon, produce the behavior which is second - nature to the victim. This is essential because thinking and reasoning will already have become hostages to the disaster (p. 174)."

Most people who either studied survival or who are survivors agree on the traits that natural survivors possess. As a survivor of numerous traumatic events in my life, such as being shot with a gun, wounded by a knife, nearly killed due to a plane crash, as well as various life-or-death situations encountered while diving, in the military, performing high-risk underwater rescues, and undergoing surgeries, I agree with the traits described by Siebert and Leach. However, I would also emphasize the importance of prayer to whichever god is of one's choosing.

Based on personal experience, I further agree that there are many times in which one makes a conscious decision to live or die. Once the choice is made, the survivor will manage whatever issues are at hand. Should I die underwater, it is my intent to be in a swim position, with my mouthpiece intact in my mouth, my mask on my face, and a look of conscious effort on my face. When rigor mortis sets in, I plan to be found with one fin raised and ready for the next kick.

When teaching diving or martial arts, I demonstrate a variety of skills in order to remind my students of the abundance of techniques available that, when added to their current survival skills, will increase their ability to act accordingly to whatever nature presents. Teaching offers an excellent platform from which survivability and what contributes to survivability may be addressed. To increase survivability, habits that contribute to our personality and behavior must alter. In order for such profound change to occur, formal training in handling emergency situations followed by personal skills practice is essential, as these techniques affect the mechanical aspects of survival. Visualization techniques, affirmations, and meditation also aid in modifying habit. Rehearsal and role-playing helps address the physical and psychological aspects of survival, and also serve to aid the student in developing the discipline necessary for going beyond their current level of comfort. However, the carefully structured discomfort felt during training should not be confused with unacceptable risk-taking, such as diving beyond one's limits.

Outside of an actual course, or as an addendum to a course, personal survival training can begin with something as simple as exercising when one would rather do something else, such as watching television, reading a book, or taking a nap. The discipline necessary to exercise is related to the ability to overcome one's own desires, which is one of the building blocks of survivability, as in certain circumstances, the desire to live may not be as powerful as the desire to die. Going beyond one's comfort level by exercising may eventually translate into going beyond one's comfort level by continuing to press forward and live instead of lie down and die.

Moreover, self-competition aids in adopting a ***can do*** versus a ***cannot do*** attitude, and there are ways to incorporate self-competition into a survival-oriented regimen. For instance, when jogging or cycling discover your best ***time***, and grade yourself as though you were undertaking, and surviving, a high-risk activity. In the future, grade yourself on your ability to meet this time whenever you engage in the activity. This form of self-competition often causes the individual to exceed their comfort zone in an effort to reduce their ***time***. If you are able to achieve a better time or go a longer distance than your bench-mark, give yourself a superior score in survivability for that day. In contrast, if you are slower subtract ***survivability points*** for that day's performance. However, as long as you do not quit, and you complete the distance be sure to give yourself at least a ***passing grade***.

If for some reason you are overwhelmed and must stop, or believe you cannot continue, allow yourself to stop, exhale, and breathe deeply and slowly. While recovering, analyze why you had to stop, or why you felt you needed to quit. Then continue the forward motion until the activity is complete, and remember to give yourself points for ***surviving***, despite the need to stop or the urge to quit. However, should you actually terminate the activity prior to it's' completion, give yourself a failing score on survivability for that day. The concept behind the failing score is that had the situation been life-threatening, you chose to give up, which translates as choosing to die.

Be aware that this is not a program for designing training objectives; it is a tool for survival-based learning. This technique forces our bodies and minds to accept that performance is a key to survival. When taking a diving course, look at each skill taught and analyze that skill. Learn why the skills are vital to increasing your chanced of surviving a life threatening event, and master what you are taught. One of the dangers in a dive course is the tendency to view the successful completion of the required skills as a means to receiving a certification card. Realize that these skills evolved from the techniques used by earlier divers who survived catastrophic events, and are taught to new dive students in order to increase their chance of survival. In IANTD's courses, many of the skills introduced and practiced during confined and open water drills are actual tools that can be used to manage the stress of a true underwater emergency. Recognizing the skills' value helps in learning from the skill, not simply training in the motions necessary to complete the skill.

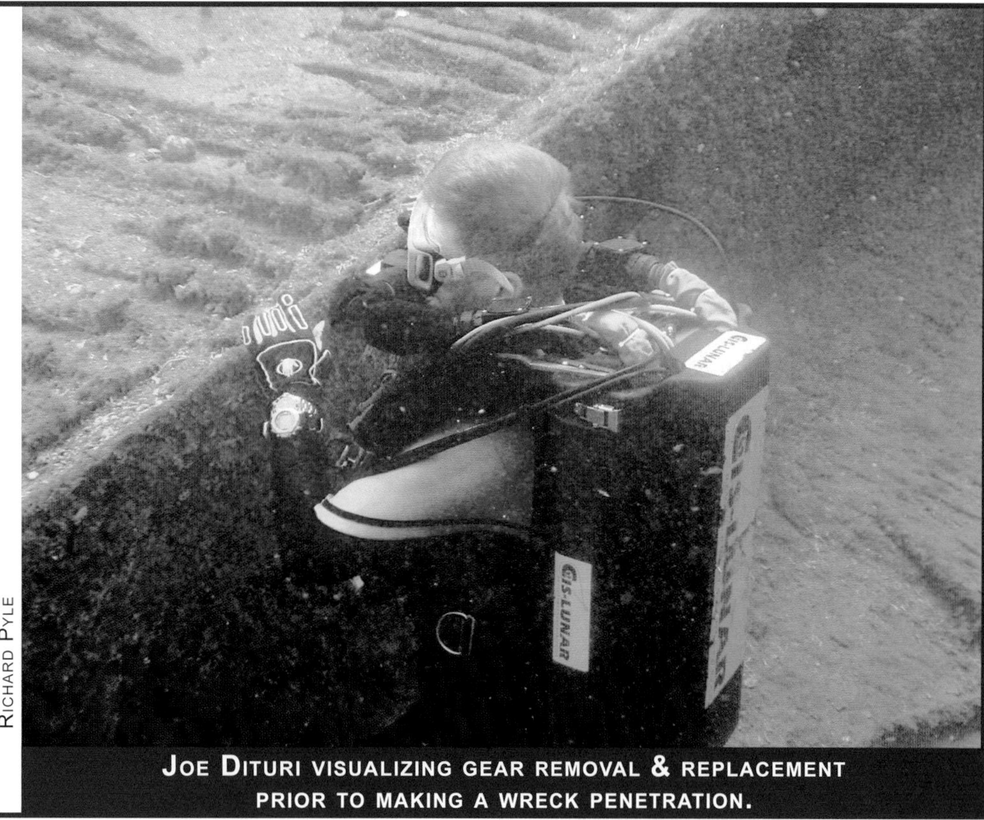

Richard Pyle

JOE DITURI VISUALIZING GEAR REMOVAL & REPLACEMENT PRIOR TO MAKING A WRECK PENETRATION.

Once a course is completed, continue practicing the skills, and become creative in performing the drills. This will keep you in a state or preparedness, as a dive emergency can occur on any dive, at any time. Resolve to be in control and to be the one that can be depended upon. Surround your self with dive partners and teams who share this same philosophy of survival. Further, when the "Sh_t Hits the Fan" do not be surprised; simply respond appropriately and maintain your focus on the objective: survival, with as little physical and mental trauma as possible.

Another survival technique is to list your feelings about the dives you are performing. Work to understand your emotional responses, so that you are able to use your feelings and intuitions as a tool, rather than becoming a slave to your emotional status. Emotions are intended to form the foundation of our survival. However, if allowed to run rampant, emotions may be the cause of our death. Once the equipment is set up and checked, go inside yourself and meditate, visualize, or practice relaxed breathing techniques to eliminate stress that built up while preparing for the dive.

Further, do not allow yourself to be lulled into the belief that diving, especially technical diving, is risk free or simply a recreational activity. Diving is a high-risk sport. Billy Deans, a good friend and accomplished diver and survivor, once expressed the risk of a dive as, "The risk doubles for every atmosphere of depth, or in overhead environments, for the amount that the distance to the surface is increased. This risk is not something to be afraid of; it is something to plan and prepare for."

Be aware that in true life-threatening emergencies both your mind and your body must be fine-tuned by on-going practice and constant vigilance or you cannot rely on your skills in overcoming the situation. Statistics reflect a large percentage of diving deaths where the victim, no matter how highly skilled, was not aware or had not maintained the physical and psychological fitness necessary to survive. It is very easy to become complacent in the water, as dive upon dive goes smoothly and without incident. Keep in mind that nature has a habit of lulling those who are vulnerable into a false, and possibly deadly, sense of security.

If faced with a life-threatening situation in-water or on land, it may be wise to use a mnemonic formula advocated by Cody Lundin: ***STOP A***, which stands for ***Stop, Think, Observe, Plan*** and ***Act***. Once the first step, ***Stop*** is utilized, exhale, as when under stress, breathing patterns become abnormal; often fast and shallow, which in itself can trigger the fight-or-flight response. Exhaling allows

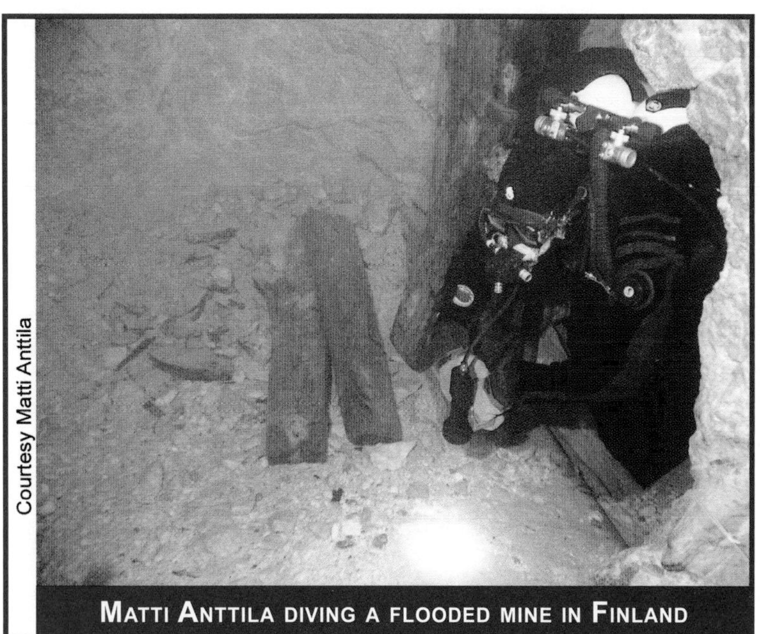

MATTI ANTTILA DIVING A FLOODED MINE IN FINLAND

you to reestablish normal breathing patterns, or go into a slow, deep breathing sequence. By slowing down your breathing, you are signaling your brain that there is no need to fight or take flight. Also, and very importantly, listen to your inner voice; do not ignore intuition, just as you do not disregard emotion. During graduate school, I wrote a paper pertinent to this topic. **In it I wrote the following lengthy excerpt:**

"Most of my life I have had intuitive flashes, used intuition for making decisions on exploration diving projects, sports and climbing up the proverbial business ladder. My earliest encounter was at the age of 15 when two of my best friends, age 16 and twin brothers, had the use of their dad's new convertible and invited me to go out with them. What a dream for a 15 year-old! A night out with friends and a brand new convertible, but I had a bad feeling about going, so I asked for advice from my Grandmother. My grandmother explained that the feeling I had was "G_d's voice" telling me not to go for some reason, and as much as I truly did want to go out, I called back and told the brothers I could not join them. The next morning, the first news I heard was about a convertible running under the back of a semi truck and killing two twin brothers… From this early introduction I started to hear and most often respect that deep inner voice.

On another occasion at age 16, I had a bad feeling about taking my motorcycle out one night, and attributed it to the fact that a friend wanted to go and I did not like having a rider on the seat behind me. We went out, stopped to get gas, and as we entered the road which appeared to be clear, a speeding car that had its headlights turned off struck us from behind. My friend was hit directly on the leg and thrown about 10 ft (3 m) into a gully, and broke his leg in two places. The bike rolled over me, peeling much of the skin from my back. Oddly, the motorcycle sustained very little damage.

In sports, most athletes including myself rely on intuition but tend to label it reflex action. As a martial artist and extreme sports enthusiast, I realize it is much more than reflex that allows us to know someone is going to attack before they actually do. Or that an offensive action will happen.

On many occasions I have had premonitions of accidents and also of danger to avoid. At one point following a very tragic event, I tried to suppress this intuitive process as it frightened me. This took place in 1971 in the Bahamas while doing a cave exploration of the Blue Holes just off Andros Island.

During this project we were to divide out time between working on a film documentary with and about George Benjamin by the Canadian Broadcasting Company and the deep cave diving exploration we were currently involved in. One morning, my best friend (Frank Martz) and dive partner for many years and I arrived at the boat to prepare for the days activities. Upon arrival Frank announced he was going to explore a deep passage we had located on our last trip. I informed him that this was a filming day. Frank began to argue that the filming could wait. This discussion became quite heated, and we became angry at each other for the first time in all the years we had dived together. I was angry because the film crew was on board and ready to film and Frank because he really wanted to do the exploration dive. To stop the argument, George agreed to allow the dive. I then had this terrible feeling that if we did the exploration dive one of us would die. But I let logic override this, attributing it to the emotionality of the argument, and went ahead with the dive. We broke into two teams - Zidi, another diver and team member, and I would explore the North Passage, while Frank and Jim, the other team member, would go to the new offshoot in the South Passage and drop down to the new lead, which started at a depth of 280 ft (84 m) and was about 1000 ft (300 m) back into the cave. About 25 minutes into the dive I had this weird sense of sorrow and relief, as I knew someone had died and it was not Zidi or I. As we swam back towards the cave opening and began our decompression, I had this heavy feeling in my heart; I knew one of my best friends would no longer be alive. As we arrived at the opening where the two passages divided, I saw Jim and realized Frank must be dead. When Jim saw me he indicated he and Frank had become separated in a silted-out tunnel at a depth of 320 fsw (96 m) and he had assumed Frank had gotten out of it and exited. So Jim and I decided with what gas (air) we had left we would go back to see if we could find Frank, hoping he was out of the deep tunnel and could be rescued. But evidently he was still in the deep passage. We had pushed our gas reserves to the point that should anything unplanned occur, we were in jeopardy, so we exited the cave. We both ran out of gas at the time we reached our decompression cylinders. To this day Frank's body has not been found.

For a period of time following the accident I struggled to suppress the intuitive messages, as it always seemed to be informing me of accidents and tragedy. Once past this roadblock to intuition, I have listened to this voice and it has served me well. Later I discovered that when investigating dive accidents at least one team member had a "bad feeling" about the dive. The same has held true in climbing, motorcycling, power boat racing, flying, martial arts and all areas of activity I have been involved in or investigated.

On several occasions I have been at a dive site and had a bad feeling about someone as they entered the water and went in check on them. One time, two divers went into a cave and I told my buddy, "Let's suit up and go in. I just feel these people are in trouble." When we got there, one diver was out of air and they were in a struggle over the air the other diver had, so we gave them our extra second stages. Since they now had ample gas, and we were able to take them out of the cave. Further, there have been times when I have seen people in high risk activities that I sensed would die in the given activity, and they did. On numerous occasions I was called in to recover their bodies.

On a night dive in Roatan, Honduras, I had this feeling someone was in trouble, and moments later I heard a scream. I immediately and instinctively went to an undercut at 90 ft (27 m) underwater (sort of a mini-cavern) and found a girl lying in the fetal position but breathing. I pulled her out and made sure the regulator remained in her mouth as we begin to ascend. At around 40 feet she returned to functionality and a safe ascent was completed.

After teaching a YMCA SCUBA instructor program in Grand Cayman in 1979, a group of us went free diving (breathholding) and at first teamed up and did some dives in the 100 to 130 ft (30 to 39 m) range. After awhile we moved into the 60 ft (18 m) range and started diving individually. At one point I had this terrible sensation something was wrong. I swam about 150 ft (45 m) from where I had been free diving to discover a good friend lying on the bottom in 60 fsw (18 m) of water convulsing. I immediately free dived to him and started to bring him up, but by this time he had swallowed enough water to be extremely heavy. Luckily another diver had the same dark sensation, free dived down, and gave me a hand. On the surface the diver had no pulse and was not breathing. We did an impromptu Heimlich maneuver, which caused him to spit water out, but he still required mouth to mouth resuscitation. By the time we got to the boat he was OK and climbed on board under his own power. When we reached shore he insisted on getting off the boat on his own, but then collapsed.

We took him to the hospital, which at that time did not have a drown unit, or staff familiar with drowning and near drowning incidents. After we left him at the hospital I started to have weird feelings again, so Patti Mount, John Ely and I returned and went to his room to discover he was blue and not breathing. Again we administered mouth to mouth since his pulse was OK. He revived and we alternately stayed with him for the next few days. He developed pneumonia from the near drowning but recovered completely, and is a well known dive resort manager today.

On another occasion my then-girlfriend-now-wife Patti Mount, had a "***very*** bad feeling" about a trip to Grand Cayman, flying in my Cessna 310C. On the trip down the weather was great and all was perfect. On the return we crashed into the ocean from 10,000 ft (3000 m) high. On this occasion I had not had psychic

warning for some reason, but Patti had and insistently voiced it several times. I was the pilot and chose to fly regardless. We experienced a vapor lock in the fuel system when changing from the auxiliary tanks back to the mains which stopped fuel flow. I managed to get the right engine started twice but could not keep it going even with Patti furiously reading sections of the Owner's Manual to me. As this was happening we were just clearing into American airspace from flying over Cuba, and through the whole incident, which is on tape, we performed all emergency procedures correctly but still crashed into the Atlantic ocean. The plane sunk immediately and by the time I got the door open and pulled Patti out, she was unconscious and we were at least 30 ft (9m) underwater. I pulled the tab on our life raft and it sank even faster than the plane.

I managed to get us to the surface and Patti revived for awhile, but of the three hours we were in the water she was either unconscious or only semi-lucid for 1.5 hours. I kept her afloat by inflating pants and jackets, converting them to flotation devices. As we were bleeding, we also had interesting interactions with Oceanic White Tip Sharks. (These are credited with the most deaths by shark attack following plane crashes and ship sinkings.) And I actually had to punch one to keep it off Patti's legs. At one point I remember really wanting to close my eyes and just let go and die. But then looking down into the ocean depths with the mesmerizing light rays criss-crossing below, my mind asked, "***Do you want to live or die?***" I made a decision to live and I also vowed to keep Patti alive. We were finally located and plucked out of the ocean by two Navy Fighter planes and two Coast Guard Rescue Choppers just at sunset.

They flew us to a hospital in Key West, and quickly transferred Patti to Miami, as she had 2nd and 3rd degree burns on 60% of her body (from raw aviation gas literally eating at her) plus she was pronounced "drowned." Medical staff did not believe that Patti could survive. My injuries were 240 stitches in the head, 6 broken ribs, a concussion, a neck injury and a back injury. Once I was released from the hospital I went to Miami to Patti's hospital room and one of the few things she remembered was my marriage proposal, which I made while we were waiting for rescue; she said, "***Yes!***" And remains my beloved wife to this day.

Patti also experienced a concussion, possible embolism on the ascent out of the plane to surface, required 100's of stitches to her head, had the base of her nose torn off, and her tongue was close to severed. Patti also had a broken molar, her face suffered nerve-damaged, her spine and neck also had severe nerve injuries, horrible bouts of vertigo & tinnitus ensued, multiple cuts, bruises, and her right collar bone shattered and shoulder broken. She also had aspirated a significant amount of water, leading to lung and stomach drowning. For three years Patti had little use of her right arm, even though she started back diving within a few months after her release from the 6 month hospitalization. She had severe short-term memory loss for the next year and fairly intense short-term memory loss for over 2 more years.

Interestingly, Patti was supposed to be scarred for life. However, we both meditated together and she was on long-term dosing of Vitamin E. Today it is very hard to even discern where she was burned. However, from March 19, 1984 till about August 2000 Patti could no longer sweat and endured numerous bouts of heat prostration. Then after taking the homeopathic remedy Sulphur, Patti had a wonderful reaction and began to perspire again and she has also experienced a great deal of nerve "regeneration," and her severe level of pain, tinnitus, and vertigo dissipated. Patti then studied to become a practicing homeopath, received her Master's Degree, is now an ordained minister as well as current CEO of IANTD."

On other occasions I have received calls from divers expressing their intuitive "***hits***," such as one from Jim Lockwood in the 1970's. He and Sheck Exley were doing some "pushes" at Sally Ward Sink and another diver was going to join them. Jim called and told me he felt that if the other diver did these dives (Deep Air to 290 fsw/89 msw) he would die. Jim decided to leave, and two days later I was called to recover the other diver's body. Sheck had tried to rescue him, but could only swim with him so far and had to leave him. The recovery was made by Paul Deloach and me.

In another situation we were doing a body recovery at Ponce De Leon Springs in the mid-60's when a psychic started calling the sheriff and predicting things that would happen to us on dives. At night when we recalled the events, the sheriff would look at his notes and say, "Yes, that's

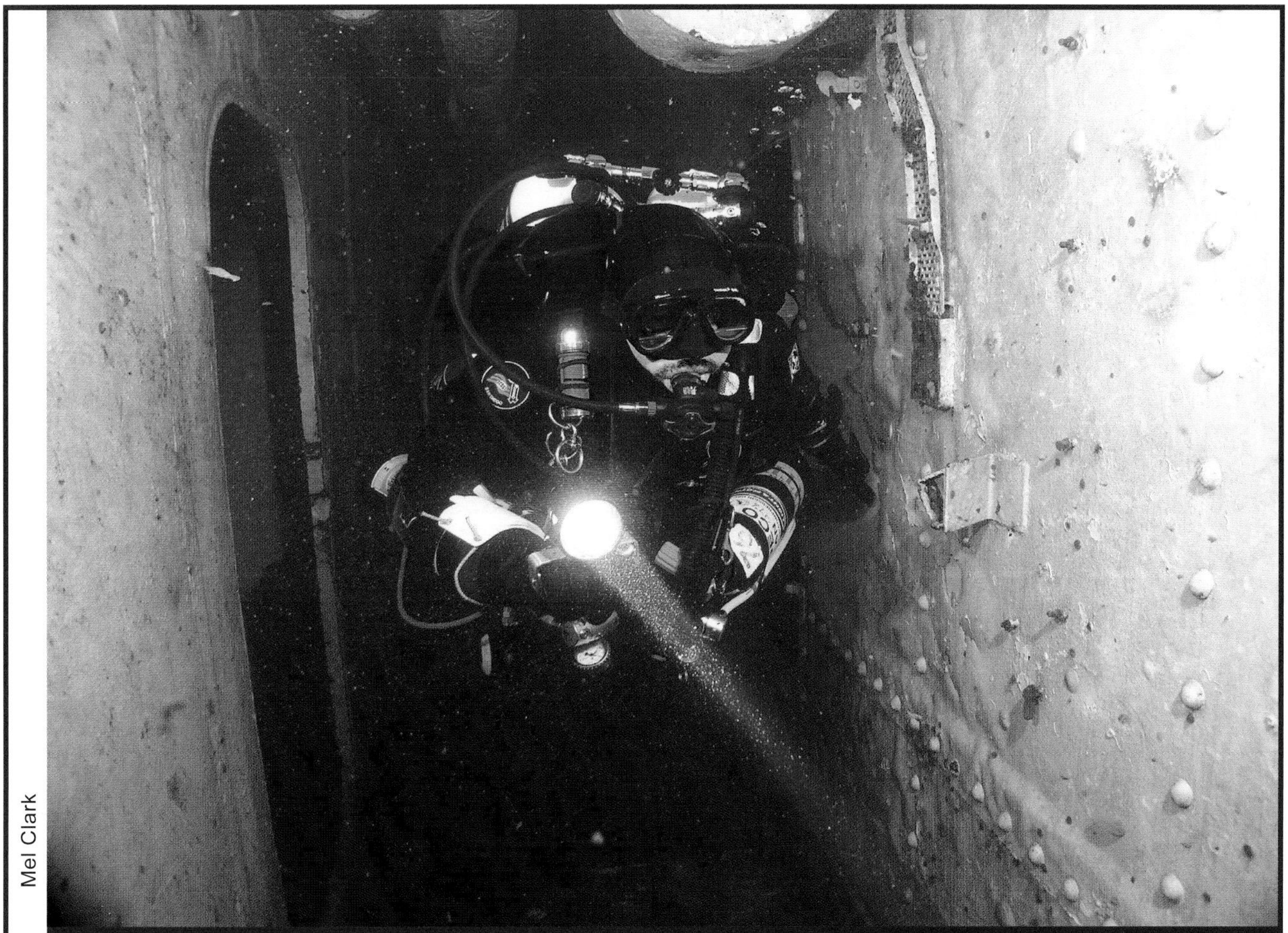

Mel Clark

CRAIG MILLER EXPLORING *CAPE BRETON* ENGINE ROOM IN NANAIMO, BC, CANADA

what she predicted." One morning the sheriff met us and called the operation off. He was reportedly told that a soul had contacted the psychic and informed her that he would remain on this plane, since if we continued diving one of us would die. Perhaps the soul was planning on helping the dead diver's soul cross to another threshold of existence. The sheriff did as the psychic suggested, and halted the operation. On another body recovery at Tarpon Springs, we had a similar incidence where following a couple of close calls while trying to locate the deceased divers the sheriff had a psychic contact him, which resulted in the Sheriff closing down the recovery attempt.

To bring this chapter to a close, I would like to present the following guidelines for survival:

- Train
- Learn the intent of the training
- Personal training, as in skill and drill repetitions: remember the old adage, "Practice, Practice, Practice."
- Do some form of survival training so you possess the discipline necessary to deal with what nature chooses to throw at you
- Know the environment, or if it is a novel environment, ask those who may have knowledge of the environment questions regarding the situation
- Be aware
- Listen to your intuition and from others, too
- Check both you and your team's emotions, and dive only when they are in balance and positive
- Use visualization and meditation for both skill performance and relaxation
- Understand the bodies reaction to stressors and manage them

- Avoid peer pressure
- Do not act on impulse alone
- Analyze the situation: This is where your "practice, practice, practice" and knowledge comes in handy
- Deal with issues as they occur, and do not worry about the end result; problems must be solved one at a time and worry only leads to more stress
- React as calmly as you can; this helps avoid making potentially serious mistakes
- Be willing to "turn" a dive any time for any reason; If you perceive the need, act on it
- If you are not comfortable during a dive, let your buddy or team know, and bailout of the dive immediately
- Plan for the "What Ifs" and resolve them ahead of time; this is often called be prepared
- Be decisive: Do not be "wishy-washy" in life threatening situations; once you make a decision or a decision is made, do not hesitate to follow through with it
- Trust yourself: This comes from confidence created by formal and personal training, knowledge, and practice
- Rejoice in each step of survival, as each step is toward the ultimate goal of living to dive another day
- Be mindful of your breathing and gas supply: Remember, as long as you can breathe you can most likely solve whatever problem you face
- Stay within what you define as your personal limits
- Recognize fear as a method of alerting you, but do not allow fear to control you: Use it only to appraise whether and to what degree danger may exist
- If you chose to place yourself in a risk zone then be responsible enough to maintain good physical and psychological conditioning, as this is the key to living or dying
- ***Always!-Always!-Always!*** Remain in the dive while solving problems. Do not become so absorbed into the problem that you lose the awareness of the dive
- When faced with the impossible ***Choose To Live***

References

Al Siebert, Ph.D., *The Survivors Personality*, 1996 The Berkley Publishing Group NY, NY

Arthur J. Bachrach Ph.D.-Glen Egstrom Ph.D., *Stress and Performance in Diving*, 1987 Best Publishing Co. San Pedro, CA

Cody Lundin, *98.6 Degrees the Art of Keeping Your Ass Alive*, 2003, Gibbs Smith Publisher Salt Lake City, NV

John Leach Ph.D., *Survival Psychology*, 1994, Macmillan Press Ltd. London, UK

Laurence Gonzales, *Deep Survival*, 2003, W.W. Norton NY, NY

Morirs Nethereton Ph.D., 2004, *5 Strangers in A Land of Confusion*, E -Book http://www.apple.com

Paul Valent, *From Survival to Fulfillment*, 1998,Brunner/Mazel, Philadelphia, PA

Robert Scaer M.D., *The Trauma,* Spectrum-Hidden Wounds and Human Resiliency, 2005, W.W. Norton Co.. Inc. NY, NY

Roger Walsh M.D., *The Physiology Of Human Survival*, 1984, Shambhala Publications, Boulder, CO

Chapter Twenty Response Training & Failure Points ~ The Importance Of Developing Response

Tom Mount D.Sc., Ph.D., N.D.

In the majority of cases, it is seldom a single event that causes a diving accident, but rather a chain of escalating incidents and reactions. Moreover, there is the actual event and the diver's subjective view of the event. The diver's mental reaction is often based on his or her perception of the initial incident, which in turn leads to a behavioral response. This response is based partly on objective fact and partly on subjective experience. In many cases, it is the diver's reaction to the immediate situation that causes the accident, rather than the actual event. If a diver has a basic fear of darkness, in the diver's mind, the loss of an underwater light may be considered a serious emergency. This scenario leads to fear, and in some, to full-fledged physical and mental panic. In the same situation, another diver might simply switch to a backup light and exit the dive.

Sadly, most diving accidents are avoidable. Analyses indicate that most accidents would either not occur or be significantly minimized if the diver had followed certain simple steps designed to prevent minor mishaps from escalating into life-threatening situations. "***Response Training***" is the term used to identify the type of teaching that helps prevent relatively innocuous problems from developing into catastrophic events, as well as potentially controlling negative outcomes in true emergencies. Response training should be an integral part of every diver's education, as it is a key to safe diving practices. Response training begins with the identifying and understanding the causes of dive-related stress. Through discussion and practice, the diver is encouraged to develop an analytical attitude to adversity or unexpected events. Response training culminates with mental conditioning and physical drills designed to develop virtually instinctive mental and physical reactions to potentially threatening circumstances.

Through research supported by the University of California (*UCLA*), Glen Egstrom, Ph. D., determined that humans require repetitive practice in order to retain and recall learned skills while under duress. For example, it is not very likely that a person shown a single demonstration of CPR technique will remember the necessary skill in the chaos of an automobile accident. On the other hand, a person who has practiced CPR drills repeatedly will typically remember the correct skill sequence, even in a moment of stress. Just as CPR training involves multiple repetitions of the chained skills comprising CPR coupled with ongoing CPR practice sessions and refresher courses, technical diving programs should provide the repetitive practice needed to develop emergency response skills. Ideally, divers rehearse the skills most important to survival using a variety of methods and under a variety of conditions. In addition, divers should practice such skills both during and outside of formal training sessions.

The old adage "***use it or lose it***" definitely applies to emergency response capabilities. A single demonstration, practice, or explanation of a skill provides the diver with a general idea as to how the skill is performed; it does not create the over-learned response necessary for using, or possibly even remembering, the skill itself. Unfortunately, some instructors do not provide needed practice in response training, and few students realize they are not receiving necessary skills practice.

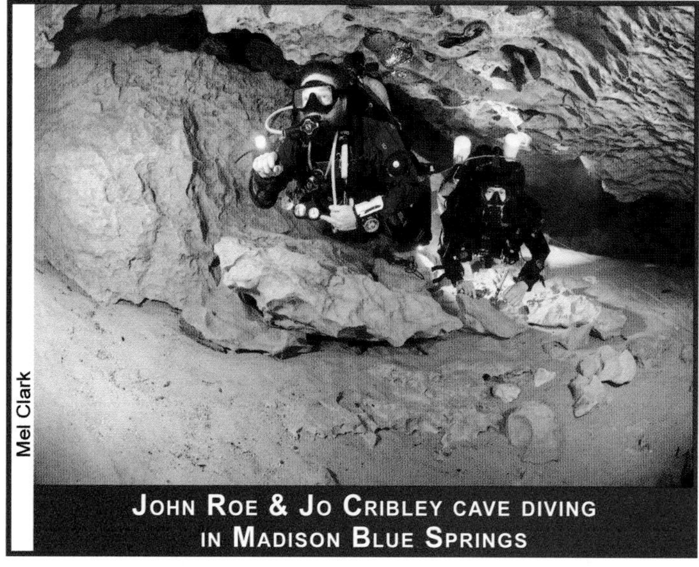

Mel Clark

JOHN ROE & JO CRIBLEY CAVE DIVING IN MADISON BLUE SPRINGS

Emergency Response Skills to Master

Over the years, IANTD identified certain emergency response training skills that should be a necessary component of a comprehensive training program. Emergency response training and practice should be in effect for each of the following areas: Valve manipulation, out of gas and gas sharing procedures, stage and decompression tank management. Moreover, based on the diving environment, skills such as guideline and lift bag use may be highly valuable.

One cause of underwater accidents is the diver's reaction to gas supply emergencies. This includes true gas failures, perceived failures, and accidental valve shutdown. As simple as the emergency drills for such situations appear, each of the above situations has produced a number of accidents. Regarding perceived or true catastrophic gas loss, the first response skill that must be overlearned is the ability to open and to shut down valves during a dive. A dual valve manifold has little advantage if the diver cannot reach the valves to shut them down in event of a regulator failure. In addition, most dual valve outlet manifolds have a design dysfunction enabling the valve on the left post to shut down if it makes contact with the roof in an overhead environment, or in some instances, even a descent line. Training divers to recognize and appropriately respond to this situation by immediately reopening the valve effectively stops the "snowball effect," in which a minor emergency becomes a major catastrophe.

In IANTD courses, manipulating valves and practicing in-water regulator switches begins in confined water and continues in each open water training session thereafter. This skill is practiced until the diver is able to shut down the primary regulator, switch to the secondary, open the primary, and shut the secondary while switching back to the primary quickly and efficiently. Upon completion of the drill, the diver is responsible to ensure that both valves are on. Divers practice this drill, in one form or another, on almost all dives in the applicable courses. One may ask, "Why so much emphasis on valve manipulation?" The answer is that your life could depend on a quick, correct, valve shutdown. ***Valve shutdown is the proper response to a number of common gas delivery or gas failure problems, and experience has proven that divers who do not practice this skill fail to make appropriate corrective action in real life occurrences.*** In addition, many divers with limited shoulder flexibility find this skill quite difficult to perform, and should therefore take every available opportunity to gain proficiency at reaching and manipulating the valves.

In Closed Circuit Rebreather (***CCR***) diving, the ability to open and close valves is also important. This skill may be required in the event of an oxygen solenoid failure or issues with diluent addition. CCR divers must rehearse and overlearn responses to hyperoxia, hypoxia, hypercapnia, canister floods, solenoid failures, and gas loss events. The CCR diver must practice each of these at regular intervals to remain competent in each of these situations. The CCR diver must also be highly skilled in bailout and in switching cylinders with a dive partner at critical gas pressures.

The correct out-of-gas response is a multi-task skill divers should practice until it becomes second nature. To understand the importance of this skill in real-world diving situations, remember that divers typically are not within touch contact of each other, and when an out-of-gas emergency occurs, both divers are usually swimming. This means that under the duress of an out-of-gas situation, the distressed diver must develop the ability to maintain composure while swimming to his dive partner, get his or her partner's attention, and then commence gas sharing in an orderly fashion.

The actual physical actions involved in gas sharing are straightforward, as are the training exercises. What is considerably more difficult than mastering the physical actions is training the mind to react to the stress of an unplanned, unexpected gas emergency during an actual dive. This is why it is so important to provide the diver with a conditioned response in the event of a real emergency, and why conventional training, which does not emphasize overlearning through continuous practice often fails the diver in the most critical of situations. In conventional recreational dive training programs, divers simply start gas sharing while positioned side-by-side. This procedure, while teaching the basic physical technique of gas sharing, does not simulate the stress of being out of gas. In addition, recreational courses frequently teach divers to escape to the surface in a gas sharing situation.

In technical diving, where there is typically an overhead environment and/or a multi-stop decompression ceiling to contend with, escape to the surface is not a valid option. Thus, the technical diver's training must include developing deeply embedded responses to out-of-gas emergencies, and conditioning the diver's ability to control emotional responses in possibly life-threatening situations. O n e drill used by IANTD to promote such skills is to have divers swim 60 to 75 ft (18 to 22.5 m) without gas. (***Note:*** The regulator should remain in the ***out-of gas*** diver's mouth, as it is better to breathe and repeat the exercise than to drown.) When the "out-of-gas' diver reaches his or her partner, the divers commence sharing gas, with the "***distressed***" or "***out-of-gas***" diver taking the second stage with the long hose. The divers remain at rest for a minimum of three breaths to simulate regaining their composure, and then the divers swim a specified distance while sharing gas within a given time limit.

When we analyze this training skill, we find that the out-of-air swim simulates the distance an out-of-gas diver typically swims in order to reach his partner, taking into account the extra distance created by the continued movement of the partner, who does not yet know of the emergency. The timed swim that follows is at the divers' average swim pace. The reasoning here is that if the divers swim too fast, they will increase both stress and gas consumption. On the other hand, if they swim too slowly, they run the risk of running out of gas before they reach the surface.

With CCR divers, the emphasis is on switching to the "distressed" diver's bailout stage breathing from it. In addition, they are also taught how to exchange stages with the dive partner, in a manner that allows for close to normal swim pace and body posture. The importance of trying to maintain normal swim pace and posture is to avoid the creation of additional emergencies due to situations such as silt, disorientation, and changes in exit speed that may affect duration of the gas supply. In an actual CCR gas emergency, the divers make the exchange when the "distressed" diver's bailout gas is at the half-way point. This practice ensures that each team member exits with remaining bailout gas.

Stage and decompression tank management is another area that calls for response training. These drills develop the diver's ability to remove and replace the tanks quickly, and to position them on the body for minimum drag. For deep diving, at least one of the stage bottles usually contains a decompression gas. In these applications, it is important to develop a consistent order for tank placement, along with a profound awareness as to the location and identity of each tank within the arrangement. In addition to learning standardized stage bottle placement, the diver must practice the physical act of removing and replacing the stage tanks, with special attention given to positioning. A slow recovery of a stage tank increases the dive's bottom or stop time, creates confusion, and may add to the chance of entanglement. This is even more important for the CCR diver, as part of the gas management procedures in a bailout situation depends on proficiency in stage exchanges between divers. Moreover, tank placement for minimal drag is important on any dive, but especially so on swimming dives, such as cave and wreck penetration dives. Another area that requires practice is learning how to deal with malfunctions in gas delivery systems such as:

1. **Non-return valve leaking, thus allowing water into the divers breathing medium:** Lightly "ride" the purge immediately before and after inhalation resolves this issue. However, a diver who is not educated in this technique may not be able to identify and problem-solve this issue while under duress

2. **Leaking O-rings at the regulator or cylinder interface**: Divers can manage leaking regulator or cylinder o-rings by repeatedly opening the cylinder valve when inhaling, and closing the valve when exhaling. This technique ensures that the duration of gas will be similar to that of a normal functioning gas supply

3. **Loss of a decompression gas:** Divers should be taught how to modify their decompression schedules and how to switch to a dive partner's decompression cylinder once the dive partner's decompression obligation is complete. In this instance, emphasizing teamwork and team safety is critical

4. **CCR divers must be proficient at managing open solenoid failures and free flowing or leaky Auto Diluent Addition Valves (*ADV*).** If the diver is controlling the CCR unit manually, the diver must be able to deal with and, if possible, correct ADV failures. Such ADV failures result in diluent being added at such a rate that the dive becomes overly buoyant. Moreover, If the solenoid (or shrader valve is adding oxygen, the PO_2 level will be getting continioously higher. In sum, the diver must be able to handle ***both explosive*** and "***creeping gasses***" from either the oxygen or the diluent side of the breathing loop.

5. **CCR divers must be proficient in manually controlling their gas supply when solenoids fail**

in the closed position. Failed closed solenoids prevent the automatic injection of oxygen into the breathing mix when the PO_2 level drops below the diver's setpoint. CCR divers should likewise be able to handle failed orifices in manual CCR units. In addition, CCR divers should be capable of plugging in off-board gas given gas loss occurring in either the on-board diluent or oxygen supply.

6. **Experienced CCR divers should learn how to dive their units as if they were "passive" Semi-Closed Rebreathers (*SCR*).** Although the appropriate drills and techniques may be introduced in the CCR diver course, it is imperative that such drills be practiced in Normoxic or overhead CCR programs provided the CCR unit can be dived in SCR mode.

Additional areas that require response training would include the use of guidelines within overhead environments and the deployment of lift bags in open water scenarios. A full discussion of these and other related drills and techniques is beyond the scope of this chapter. At this point, the reader should be aware of the importance of response training, as it relates to one's survival as a diver, and to the survivability of a dive team. The reader should also understand the need to seek out responsible, competent technical or CCR instructors who practice emergency response skills, and who are certified by reputable agencies such as IANTD.

Once the diver attains the appropriate degree of response training, the second phase of response training begins; training the diver to keep the emergency response integrated into the dive. In many situations, the diver focuses on the emergency response to the point of removing themselves from the dive. This is actually an unwanted effect of response training and other survival skills; the distressed diver becomes hyper-focused on overcoming the current emergency that he or she ignores or forgets the safety objectives built into the dive itself. When this occurs, even though the distressed diver may react correctly to his or her situation, other emergencies involving the diver and or the team itself may arise due to the diver's, and possibly the teams', tendency to ignore critical components of the dive itself, such as orientation, buoyancy control, silting and simple dive performance. ***The ability to perform a correct emergency response yet remain focused and attuned to the dive performance is one of the major challenges in response training.***

The purposes of response training:

- Provide recognition of emergency situations
- Develop conditioned responses to specific emergencies
- Rehearse responses to the point that they become reflexive
- Develop recognition of risk benefit for all dives
- Train the diver to focus and block negative thinking
- Produce a survival-oriented diver
- Develop skill levels to the point of constant exemplary performance
- Instill an "***I can do***" attitude
- Train a diver to be self-reliant
- Produce a diver who recognizes self-defined limits, is responsible, and who fully appreciates and enjoys all dives due to self-confidence, mature judgment, enhanced skill levels and an awareness of his or her surroundings

Failure Points in Life Support Systems

The key point of equipment is that it functions as a safe and reliable life support system. The equipment we wear supports our very lives when underwater. It is imperative that we are sure a breathing gas is available, we have the ability to perform self-and-partner rescue, and are capable of surfacing safely. It is evident that the equipment we elect to use is our life insurance, so we must use the best equipment we can find. Do not shortcut your safety by using inferior equipment. The old saying "the right tool for the right job" is "right on" for SCUBA diving. The more sophisticated the diving, the more profound this statement becomes.

First, we must choose the correct equipment for the type of dive we are making. Be careful to be neither over nor under equipped. Further, equipment needs vary according to depth and possible overhead conditions. Being in open water versus overhead environments significantly affects equipment choices, and the extent of a dive also contributes to what type of gear is necessary. Obviously, on a 60 ft (18 m) open water dive in relatively calm seas, the equipment requirements are minimal. A mask, fins,

Steven Gutierrez in the engine room of the *RB Johnson*, South Florida

buoyancy compensation device (*BC*), regulator with an octopus, exposure suit, depth gauge and timer or computer is adequate. At 100 ft (30 m), or in an overhead environment, a prudent diver will look at failure points and realize that unless they are quite experienced, a completely safe emergency swimming ascent is difficult. They will realize that while the octopus is a good safety device for shallow water it can be a diver's worst enemy on deeper dives.

The octopus is for your dive partner's use; it is not a self-rescue device. If you develop a free-flow on an octopus, you are losing your gas supply. This may lead to a rapid ascent, and even prevent a safety stop, or if diving beyond no-stop limits, cause a diver to omit a decompression stop. On the other hand, the aware diver will elect to use a dual outlet valve (***H-valve***) instead of the common "***K***" valve on the cylinder. With an H-valve, the diver is able to connect two regulators with shut-off valves to his or her cylinder. This allows the diver to shut down the free-flowing regulator and switch to the remaining operative regulator.

An alternate and much safer procedure would be to use a pony or stage cylinder in lieu of the H-valve; a pony bottle usually mounts on the tank, while a stage bottle connects to the backpack or backplate with clips. Open water divers using a pony or stage cylinder, as a safety gas supply should configure the bottle so it can be easily removed in situations such as entanglement or the need to hand the cylinder off to an out-of-air diver.

A dual outlet manifold, which is used with "doubles," is a third option. Doubles is the term used for two tanks banded together. The manifold connects the two tanks; however, each tank has its' own original shut-off valve. Either tank can be shut down if the regulator connected to it free-flows, or in any other situation that causes a loss of gas in one of the two tanks. Many manifolds also have a third shut-off (isolation) valve in the center of the manifold, allowing the diver to shut off gas exchange between tanks. The options discussed in the last few paragraphs serve as examples of risk management and avoidance of failure points in the life support system. The paragraphs also emphasize a main theme; considering the diver, and the diver's situation, location, dive plan, and needs are all part of risk management and response training.

If diving in current or in areas where it is possible to become lost, the thinking diver will add a lift bag and reel. In technical diving, a lift bag and reel is required when diving in open water environments. This practice allows the diver to have a stable ascent platform and, more importantly, may prevent the diver from being lost at sea. If the diver increases depth or explores overhead environments such as wrecks and caves, the diver's equipment needs again change. Be responsible enough to accept this and ensure

the right tools are used. Failure points may vary in an open water environment versus an overhead environment. For instance, let's look at quick release devices (***QD***) on a backpack or harness.

If a cave penetration is the dive objective, quick releases may not have an in-water need. However if the unusual chance a diver is required to remove equipment it may expedite this process. In an open water (***OW***) environment, the quick release may also make the difference between life and death during a rescue attempt.

In our rescue programs, we teach that regardless of how carefully the diver configures is or her equipment, there is a significant difference in the time it takes to remove dive gear from a "victim" on the surface who does not have a QD compared to one who does. In the author's opinion, QD's are one of the greatest safety assets in open water diving offered in modern day diving. Even the old navy harnesses and early backpacks used QDs. The history of diving and diving accidents bears out the importance of QDs in open water rescue situations. With quick-disconnect failures being as rare as they are (one manufacturer states once in 5000 dives, and most often due to other divers damaging them by placing heavy equipment on top of them), it is worth considering using QDs in both open water and overhead environments. The QD's value in open water as a safety factor for rescue and for ease of removal on the surface or a boat is well recognized. However, many cave divers view it as a failure point; however, this author does not agree with this analysis. In contrast, this author, who has seen the inside of many a cave and wreck, believes a single QD is an advantage in all diving environments.

The equipment a diver chooses and the configuration of said equipment may easily be an accident in the making if incorrect equipment and poor equipment configuration rules the day. The following discussion will not address overall configuration: it will identify and discuss potential failure points in the type of equipment and the configuration of the equipment used. With this in mind, the diver should snap consoles or pressure gauges to the BC or waist strap so they do not dangle and remain easy to access. Moreover, a diver should carry a depth gauge, bottom timer, and dive tables as their primary or back-up decompression guide. Although many dive computers have integrated bottom timers and depth gauges, divers may wish to consider wearing an independent bottom timer and depth gauge as a "back-up" in case of computer failure. Some technical divers opt to carry two dive computers, thereby affording them a computerized decompression profile given a primary dive computer failure.

In recreational open water diving, the alternate second stage should not to dangle loosely beside the diver. Instead, the diver should stow or clip off the alternate in a safe and efficient manner. Avoid Velcro enclosed octopus pockets, as they often bond quite tightly, and may be hard to open. In an emergency, any difficulty releasing the alternate may become a life threatening failure point. The spare second stage, be it an octopus or alternate regulator, should be stored in an easy-to-access method. Ideal set-ups have the primary with a four-to-five foot hose wrapped around the neck; in this configuration, the diver hands off his or her primary regulator. The diver secures his or her alternate second stage in a "necklace" often made of bungee cord below the neck, so that he or she can easily switch to the secondary when handing off the primary. This method insures, among other issues, that the distressed diver will receive a functioning secondary stage.

An additional method adopted by some divers is using an integrated second stage. An integrated second stage usually consists of a usable regulator mouthpiece attached to the BC's low-pressure power inflator. In this configuration, equipment keeps to a minimum by eliminating the octopus' hose. If a diver chooses this system, the non-distressed diver hands off his or her primary regulator's second stage to the distressed diver and switches to the integrated alternate. If a diver chooses to use an integrated alternate octopus, I personally recommend that his or her primary regulator's mouthpiece be attached to a four-to-five ft (1.2 to 1.5 m) long second stage hose. A diver configures a primary regulator attached to a long hose in a certain way; the hose routs under the shoulder to avoid entanglement. If the diver chooses a five ft (1.5 m) length, the diver should also make a ¼ turn around the neck with the long hose.

It is considered good practice to have low pressure cutoff valves "up line" from the alternate air source second stage. Many divers attach low pressure cutoff valves on all second stages. If the diver incorporates such valves into their configuration, the diver must train on opening and closing the valves, and to be certain they are open if handed off or switched to during a dive. Dive partners must be aware of such modifications, so that if the diver who passes them a second stage fails to have it in the open position, the receiving diver is capable of adjusting the valve to get gas.

Another important point concerns surface self-rescue. A common behavioral failure point is that divers frequently forget to drop their weight belts when in trouble on the surface. All BC's on the market will allow a diver who becomes unconscious to float with the face partially or wholly submerged. To offset this situation, which could lead to a diver drowning, some recommend steel cylinders or attaching a weight to the back of the cylinder. In theory, these techniques will force the diver who is unconscious at the surface to roll over on his/her back, provided the BC be fully inflated. If either of these methods is to be used, care should be taken not to overweight the diver.

In technical diving, hose configuration is a major decision; a long hose on one of the diver's second stages is required in technical diving as a dive partner assist option. Generally, the long hose is between 5 and 7 ft (1.5 and 2 m) long. The chosen length depends on the type of dive and the local community standard. Keep in mind that some divers overuse the longer hoses. As the length becomes excessive, there is an increase in entanglement potential and difficulty in storage. Most of us view a hose over 5 ft (1.5 m) as a potential failure point.

Where the long hose is stored can also create a failure point. Hoses wrapped along the outside side of a cylinder can and do become entangled with wiring, fishing lines, lures, and other obstacles in wreck diving. This in itself may become a threat to the diver's safety. In addition, hoses configured in this manner create "hose chaffing," which shortens the life of the hose. If you must store your hose on the cylinder, place it in close proximity to your back, rather than on the outer side of the cylinder. Wrapping a hose across the back of the tanks below the manifold is another potential failure point. It may cause confusion when you reach for the valves, or if the manifold itself is entangled with the hose, the initial problem may easily escalate into two or more problems.

The hose configuration IANTD recommends, and is the most popular with IANTD instructors and divers, is to simply run it down diver's side (usually behind the wings), across the divers body, and then wrap the hose ¼ around the diver's neck. This particular hose storage system prevents entanglement and chaffing potential. Further, all hoses leading off the regulators should be routed as straight down as possible. Avoid hoses that stick out from the sides of the diver, especially those that actually go beyond the width of the tank valves. This creates a failure point in that it increases the entanglement potential when diving on wrecks or in caves. Two common means of hose routing are the "criss-cross" method advocated by a supposed *do-it-right* (***DIR***) methodology and the original Holgarthian DIR approach, which consists of running the hoses straight from point to point, thereby extending the hoses downward and avoiding criss-crossing the hoses. Please note that the diver should decide which approach suits his or her needs best and adopt that hose configuration.

Back-plates and harness/backpacks is another area where potential failure points can and do occur. This is also an area where strong opinions exist. There are two issues offering the most debate and that is the choice of a back-plate or a technical backpack. In this discussion, we will leave this debate to the individuals, as both are safe and efficient. However, the design of either may produce failure points.

The quick release is where points of contention exist. In the cave community, many consider a quick release a failure point. The argument is the quick release creates unnecessary risks during a penetration dive, as QDs occasionally break or disengage. In actual practice, most divers find that should a quick release unhook, the cylinders still tend to remain stable. When one analyzes the history of quick release failures, it becomes obvious that such occurrences are extremely rare and tend to occur on land rather than in the water. The advantages of a quick release include an ease of equipment removal either on land or in the water. Although this is normally considered simple convenience, in emergencies the quick release can make a tremendous difference in the time it takes to remove the disabled diver from the water.

A harness or backpack without a quick release usually has to be cut from the distressed diver on the surface. In choppy seas, this can become a complex situation and the extra time either cutting the webbing to free the diver or the time spent wrestling the diver out of the gear may very well complicate the rescue. While the distressed diver is in the water, it is likely, especially in choppy seas, that he or she may aspirate seawater or become more anxious and panicked. A diver can readily open a quick release, and remove equipment from the distressed diver in seconds.
The time saved by using a quick release speeds up and simplifies the rescue, which may make a critical difference in whether the distressed diver survives. Moreover, the quick release also decreases the chance of creating another victim: the diver desperately trying to cut an entire rig off

Fabio Amaral

Patti Mount geared up for her first OC Trimix dive in Bikini Atoll

his or her partner. Given the difficulty involved in cutting through webbing, possible poor sea conditions, and fighting to control a panic-stricken diver, the rescue diver may reach a point of exhaustion, become entangled with the distressed diver or float lines, and at worst create a double drowning.

Rigging the back-plate or backpack is also an important consideration. In general, the more simple the configuration, the better the configuration. The back-plate or back-pack system should have an adequate number of D-rings placed appropriately, as well as whatever other accessories are needed for the dive. However, "more" is not necessarily "better." Some recreational manufacturers, who are not overly familiar with technical diving yet are interested in gaining market shares, as well as certain "technical" manufacturers, appear to be following the trend of "the greater number of bells and whistles, the better." Such companies are promoting systems that are overly bulky and quite confusing.

Remember the back-plate and backpack is the foundation of a technical diving system. If the foundation starts as a simple apparatus then the remainder of the system is easy to keep simple and clean. Either a back-plate or backpack can fulfill the needs of the diver. Beyond that, the diver should put a great deal of thought into the number and way to rig backup light placement, reels, and other accoutrements. The goal is simplicity and functionality. To produce an ideal system, combine simplicity and functionality with the concepts of minimizing failure points while still providing rescue capability.

Redundant flotation devices and air cells, also known as wings, are worth review. Given the weight and complexity of technical gear, a bladder failure within a wing or air cell poses a potential problem. Divers who use drysuits may have the dry suit provide the necessary redundancy. CCR divers can use their counter lungs as redundant flotation devices. When wetsuit diving, if the diver cannot swim in and/or ascend safely in his or her gear given a wing failure, the diver may wish to consider a redundant wing. Some feel using a single-bladder BC when diving wet on open circuit (**OC**) is a potential failure point. However, it is the diver's obligation to weigh the risk of the failure point and the corrective action necessary to survive a BC bladder failure and make his or her decision based on an objective assessment of available information. With this information, the diver can then decide whether to offset the failure point by using a redundant BC.

Reel storage and backup lights often present failure points. A misplaced light or reel can lead to entanglement or be lost without the diver being aware of it. In this author's opinion, the greatest failure potential exists when divers place safety lights and reels on tank D-rings. This configuration increases the likelihood of entanglement and essential gear loss more than any other configuration. Other failure points occur due to swivels, which result in more O-rings in the diver's configuration. When setting up equipment, the diver should take the time and effort necessary to analyze the failure potential of each portion of his or her life support system.

Once the diver has completed the evaluative step outlined above, the diver should return to the configuration

and determine methods for reducing all failure points. Bear in mind those items critical to survival rate additional redundancy, and the diver minimizes all other items. In other words, the diver uses what is necessary and reduces what is unnecessary. Unneeded items increase the number of failure points within the system.

The very number of items causes an increase in failure points, and unnecessary complexity may over-task a diver's reactions in critical situations.

Deciding how to store stage cylinders is also an important part of the diver's configuration. Two common methods are the "standard" way of attaching the stages to a top shoulder D-ring and a waist D-ring. Another method that is becoming increasingly popular is to place the stages in a "***side mount***" configuration. Whatever the choice, the diver must become proficient in removing and replacing the stage bottles, as well as in exchanging the stage bottles with other team members. often side mount systems incorporate a butt plate. However, many technical divers prefer to eliminate the butt plate, as it is awkward to store on boats. A set of side mounted D-rings attached to the crotch strap works extremely well in lieu of a butt plate. These side mounted crotch strap D-rings also serve as excellent places to store reels. For CCR diving, this type of configuration seems to be ideal.

Gilberto Menezes De Oliveira prepares for an in-the-water recompression treatment for a 600 ft (180 m) dive in Brazil.

After surfacing, Gilberto developed Neurological Decompression Sickness Symptoms. Since a recompression chamber was not close at hand, he elected to perform a successful in-the-water recompression profile.

Regarding stages and CCR diving, the CCR diver secures the stages so they can easily be handed off to a CCR diver who is "off the loop" for the duration and has used a specific portion of their own bailout gas. Moreover, the stages may also serve as an alternate gas supply for a distressed OC diver. Practicing removing and securing stages, handing off stages, and related drills is necessary to ensure that regulators are easily accessed, and a quick hand off is possible. Some CCR divers opt to use 40 inch (1.25 m) to 5 ft (1.5 m) hoses on their bailout cylinders' second stage. This configuration mandates that the diver accomplish a regulator handoff before the bailout cylinder is passed to the distressed diver.

Dive planning and team responsibilities are the core of a safe dive. The dive plan does not need to be an elaborate and complex deed. A dive plan, though, must ensure that the divers are aware of individual responsibilities. In

addition, in order to become responsible as a team member, the diver must be proficient and self sufficient in the type of dive conducted. At this point, he or she can be a responsible team diver. A team should support and assist one another; they should be efficient in rescue technique and skilled in the needs of a particular dive.

Failure points in a dive team exist when one or more divers are dependent upon the abilities of the other divers instead of being working partners. In complex exploration dives, each team member has to depend on the fulfillment of each individual's assigned task. This is not a place for the dependent diver. ***A failure point in team responsibility can lead to disaster.*** To avoid failure points in a dive plan, be sure to understand the objectives of the dive and have confidence in your ability to perform your task on that dive.

Potential failure points on a dive plan and team effort include:

- The team or team leader does not define dive objectives
- The team members cannot meet the dive objectives
- One or more divers do not understand objectives of the dive
- Dive objectives are beyond one or more team member's ability; therefore, the divers' missions cannot be completed
- Dive objectives are too stressful for one or more team members
- Dive objectives are not completed by a team member
- Dive objectives are modified during the dive by a team member, thereby placing the team's safety in jeopardy
- The dive plan does not call for sufficient back-up support such as safety gases on a penetration dive or adequate decompression gas
- Dive objectives are not verbalized or do not exist; both situations lead to confusion and mistakes
- The dive plan does not insure that each individual is functioning within their limits, which may prevent the divers from being confident in their ability to swim, think or breathe for themselves

The solution for all of the above failure points is team communication and comprehension. Most accidents occur due to failure points in dive systems, diver behavior, and a lack of diver education. By reviewing dive-related failure points, incorporating response training, and insuring the capability of the team's members, divers will enjoy safer dives by minimizing the potential for accidents.

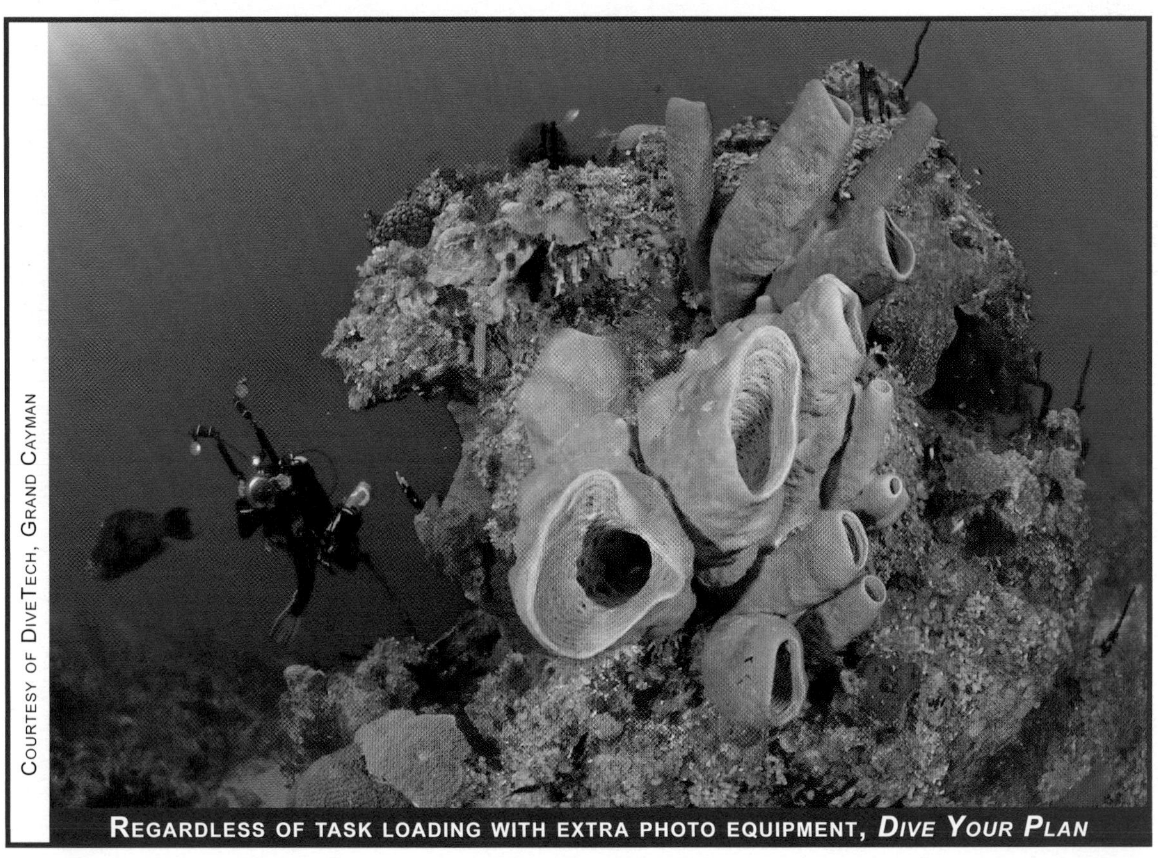

Courtesy of DiveTech, Grand Cayman

Regardless of task loading with extra photo equipment, ***Dive Your Plan***

Section Four

Deeper Exploration & Decompression Strategies

Photo by John Gavin

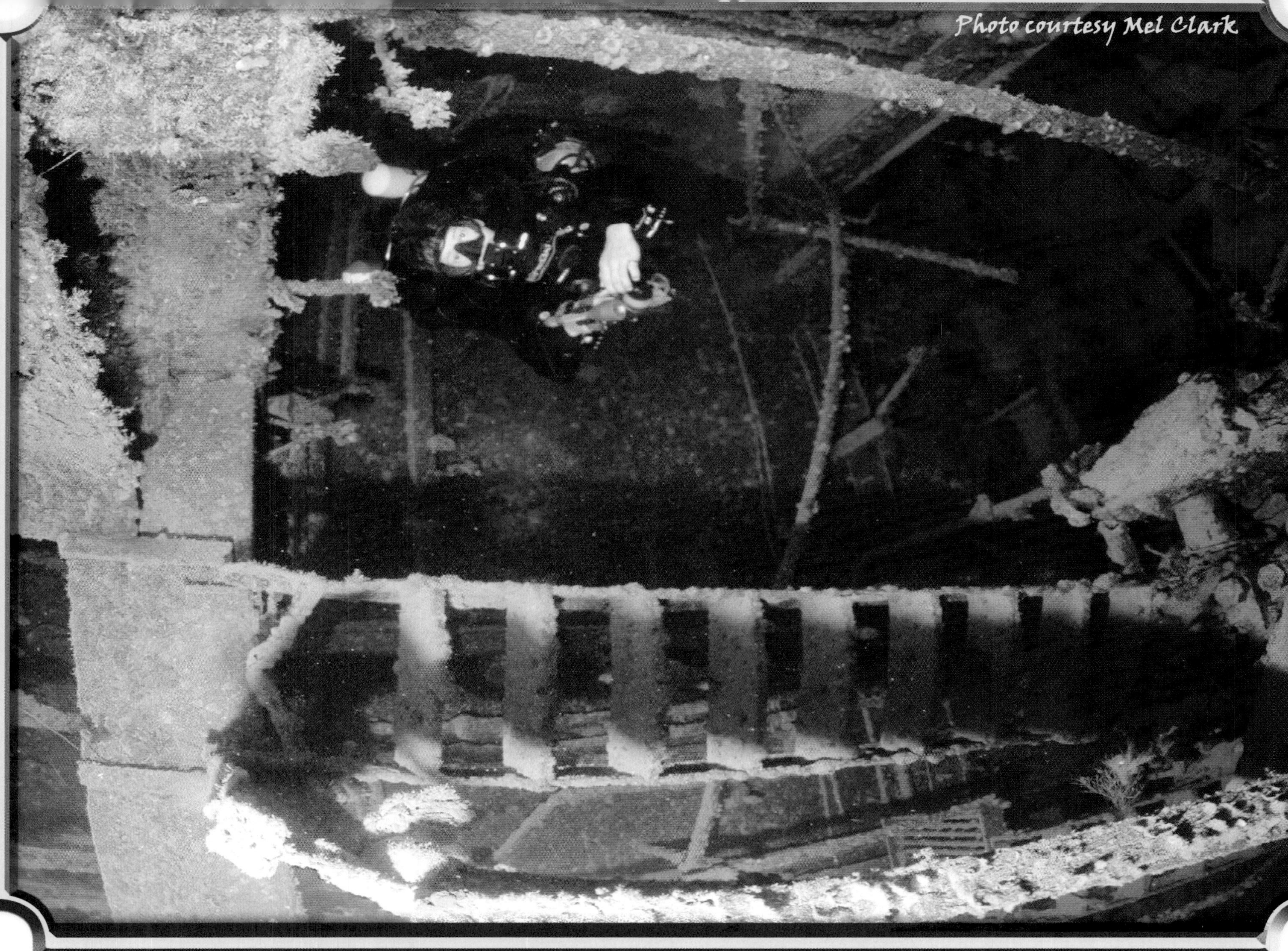
Photo courtesy Mel Clark

Chapter Twenty One

Deep, Deeper, Deepest & Further Back ~ Ones Man's Personal Quest & Staying Alive To Do It

Tom Mount D.Sc., Ph.D., N.D.

Fools venture where wise men fear to go - but fools reap, the rewards of having done it, not looking back and saying if only I had ~

A deep diving philosophy ~ Tom Mount

Caution! The information in this chapter may or may not be applicable for use for all divers - it is strategized from a "what works - works" experience-based protocol for my personal physiology and psychological outlook on diving. Experiment at your own risk!

When I was nine years old, I read a book on diving and was totally fascinated by it. Around 1952 I saw the movie ***Navy Frogmen*** with Richard Windmark and knew I had to dive. Upon my first ocean dive in 1957 in Key West, Florida - the moment my face was underwater - I had this immense desire to go deeper. Of course, at that time, I had no definition of deep but whatever it was I wanted to go deeper than I had been. This continued with each dive I made. It continues today with each dive I do. The difference is, though, that today I have a sense of what is deep and I have developed a respect for depth. I have also quietly accepted the depth that I consider as acceptable for me which is deeper than some would go and more shallow than others have gonc.

The fist dive I made once discharged from the United States Navy (***USN***) other than a couple of lake dives playing with my new equipment was into a cave. I had read a book by Dr. Eugenie Clark and Colonel Bill Royal in which they discussed a near-death experience for Bill in Ponce De Leon Springs, FL that had intrigued me. Being young, dumb, and indestructible (at least in my mind-set at the time), this was my gotta-try-it dive. Even though I carefully followed the advice given and took care not to get stuck on the ceiling by use of a weight belt, I too experienced a similar dive as Bill's had been. Even at that I was eternally hooked on cave diving. However, I did conclude that wearing a weight belt to avoid being stuck on the cave roof was not good advice so I discarded the idea and quickly evolved it into a neutral buoyancy quest for all diving including cave.

My next adventure was a 200 ft (60 m) dive and oh G_D. What a thrill! Now I had two addictions in my life - cave diving and deep diving. To solve the buoyancy control problem I borrowed Hal Watts's "discovery of the decade" methodology - an empty Clorox bottle - to provide buoyancy control. The nig advantage was if you forgot it; simply find a junk dump enroute to the dive site and one could be acquired. At worst case buy a bottle of Clorox and empty it... Soon my companions and I improved upon this by utilizing Jerry cans (5-gallon gas cans) and found that if we placed them under our hips, they were excellent for both buoyancy control and body posture. Aha, the new silt avoidance secret of the time. ***Note! Remember that we did not have BC's nor SPG's. However, the SPG was developed and then, a couple of years later, the Horse Collar BC evolved.***

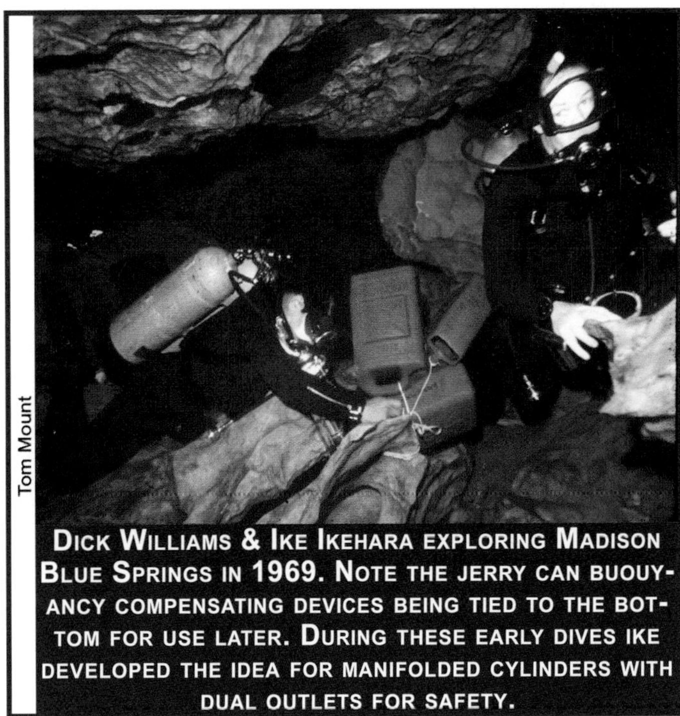

Tom Mount

DICK WILLIAMS & IKE IKEHARA EXPLORING MADISON BLUE SPRINGS IN 1969. NOTE THE JERRY CAN BUOUYANCY COMPENSATING DEVICES BEING TIED TO THE BOTTOM FOR USE LATER. DURING THESE EARLY DIVES IKE DEVELOPED THE IDEA FOR MANIFOLDED CYLINDERS WITH DUAL OUTLETS FOR SAFETY.

The next application of my addictions was discovering Deep Cave diving - now I had become an incurable addict for sure. These addictions had complete control over my life. As all our dives were on air at the time I felt some of the addiction was due to narcosis, so warm so cozy that warm glow and meaningless time passage. In the early days, we believed we could develop tolerances to both narcosis and oxygen poisoning so had to be committed to frequent deep dives to maintain it. For example my addiction was such that while doing commercial work diving I would depart from the barge (usually following a week at sea), say hello and good-bye to my wife and son, then depart to do a deep night cave dive or 40 Fathom Sink dive. The dives got deeper, we started using oxygen for decompression and guess it is true G_d does protect fools and drunks, as we were diving to and beyond 300 fsw (91 msw) then decompressing on oxygen commencing at 30 fsw (9 msw).

(***Comment*** - We had discovered that the 300 fsw (91 msw) USN exceptional exposure air tables were not the most reliable [A discovery that is true even today of all models, if tables or dive computers are used in pure form on extreme dives] thus the use of oxygen - in those days the oldest most rusted cylinders and the crappiest of our regulators were used for the oxygen decompressions - again G_D was watching over these fools.)

The oxygen decompression worked when we used the USN air decompression times or when used with the old SOS decompression meter known as the ***Benzomatic*** by its devoted followers. It used a piece of brick to simulate tissue absorption - just think, if they had used Parapene it may have been the development of the VPM model in an early stage. Oh well not to speculate! In fact eventually we had Gene Melton develop a set of repetitive dives for them as we were frequently doing two to three deep dives a day (long days of course more like a day and half a night). Wonder if this is why I and some of my friends squeak when we walk today. Looking back, the oxygen decompression most likely worked because we were essentially doing a treatment on our selves. Maybe we should think of this as In-Water Recompression, without ever leaving the water. If you follow the oxygen decompression profiles we used they were not far off from the Australian IWR treatment tables. But it was a "***what works, works***" approach to a symptom free decompression. In my case, I continued to use oxygen at 30 ft (9 m) until 1989, when we started using Bill Hamilton's tables for Trimix that used EAN 36 at 100 ft (30 m) to 20 ft (6 m) where we switched to oxygen.
My next new discovery was using my recently acquired cave skills I entered a wreck and now I had yet another must do activity in my life. They say drug addiction begins by experimenting with one drug and progressing to other drugs. Evidently, this same process applies equally to diving addictions.

With so many diving addictions surely there can not be more, yet, due to my contracts putting cables in throughout the Atlantic missile range, I discovered wall diving. Oh-Oh! Gee whiz, had I died and gone to heaven? What a sensation! What a thrill! To look over the wall and be invited by the dark blue water to go just a ***tiny ever so tiny*** bit deeper. Umm how about that next ledge? It looks so close.Wow is it possible that was another 50 ft (15 m) away. I felt and still feel like this big hand is just beckoning me to go deliciously deeper.

When we first started diving gas, I thought it would be less addictive to sink into the arms of this serene temptress, thinking that the urge had always been due to the effects of narcosis. Hmmmm, I got that wrong! If anything the urge is even stronger as I presume that because we can think more clearly the desire bacame stronger. So now, here I am preoccupied with all of these addictions and no desire whatsoever for a cure! Alas I remain a hopeless addict. Please, please somebody ***HELP*** me! Ah Ha, my split personality comes out - don't you dare take my glow away.

It was natural that, like most addicts, conflict within the family developed and by 1967, I found myself single. While this did create emotional discomfort, sadness, feeling of loss, feelings of guilt, the bright side was that it afforded me more freedom to cave and wreck dive and pursue my love affair with depth. Therefore, after all, **life** was good. (As I said I was truly addicted to cave and deep diving - they were the most important things in my life in those days - I think they are second to a "***few things***" today? Umm, yes they are - aren't they? Oh well!) I did have another addiction to going fast and this was true on or off the road, car, truck, motorcycle, or boat, which led to one of my companions Gil Milner a MD and psychiatrist (one of the craziest dive buddies I ever had and that says a lot) to comment, "Tom, you are just going to buzz along at 90 miles an hour in everything you do in life, until you just suddenly drop dead." I could not understand why he described this at such a slow speed! As to Gil's sanity? Well,

last I heard from Gil he had left his family and medical practice and went to Tibet to become a monk.

Around 1964 I met Frank Martz and we became close friends and constant dive partners. When we were in the water it was as if our minds were one and thus no need for any form of formal communication. We just knew what the other thought and what they wished to do. Even on major dives we simply looked at each other took lines to add and dived. We functioned as if two bodies were tied together with one brain, one mind, and one spirit. We survived numerous narrow escapes as these were the days of learning by survival in both deep and cave diving. (***Note! The advantage of learning by survival is the lessons are well learned; the disadvantage of learn by survival is many did not and do not survive.***) We learned a lot and developed techniques that rewarded us with additional safety both in dive performance and decompression. Deeper diving decompression schedules then and now was as a crap shoot. Frank was a very quiet, methodical person and an equipment genius. His diving skills were beyond excellence and as we survived many situations in which we could easily have died, we developed confidence in each other. One of our major explorations was Eagle's Nest mixed in with sneak dives at numerous other deeper springs in Florida that were closed to divers at the time as some still are. We also spent many hours exploring more shallow caves and had some great accomplishment for that error of time. In 1965 Frank and I made a record deep air dive to 360 fsw (110 msw), which beat Hal Watts' record to 355 fsw (109 msw) in 1963. Hal returned in 1967 to push the record to 390 fsw (114 msw) that set the stage for numerous future deep diving records. This is a pursuit by some that continues today on both air and Trimix.

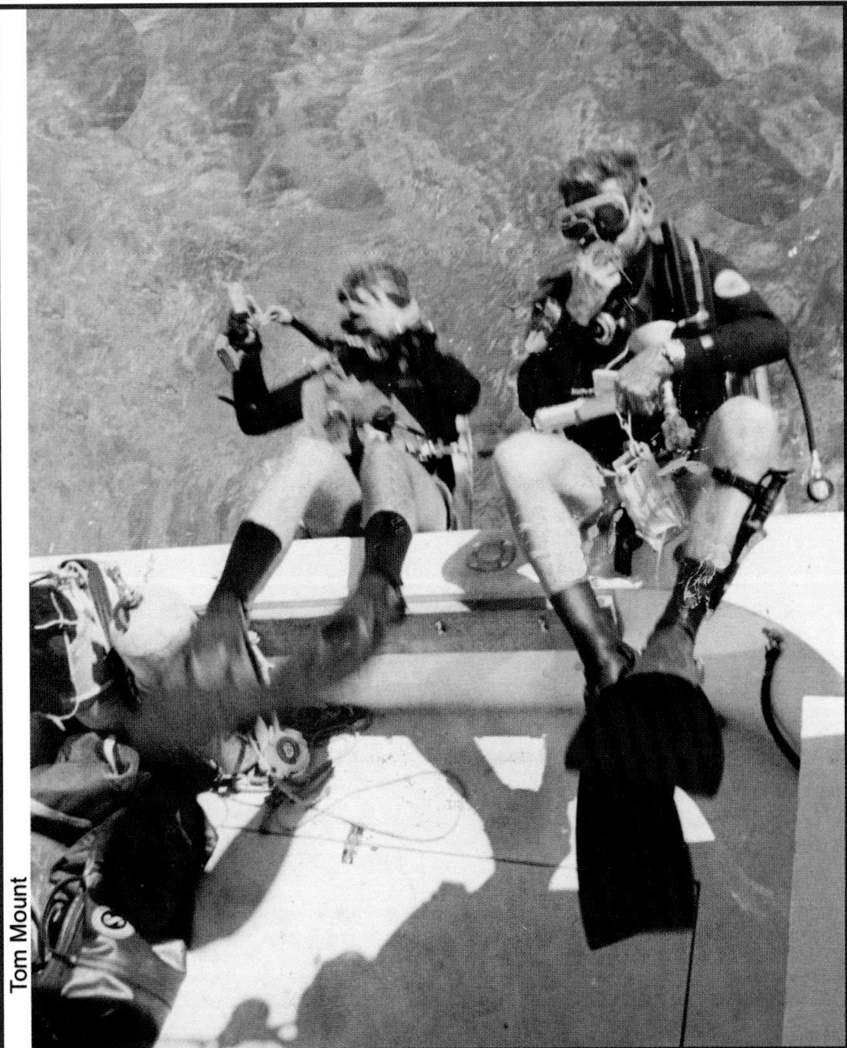

Tom Mount

CIRCA 1973, FRANK MARTZ (R) & JIM LOCKWOOD (L) BEGIN A DEEP EXPLORATION DIVE INTO BENJAMIN'S CAVE, ANDROS, BAHAMAS

THIS DIVE WOULD PROVE TO BE FRANK MARTZ' LAST DIVE. I HAD A PREMONITION ABOUT THIS DIVE. IT WAS ALMOST A FEELING THAT EITHER SOMONE IN FRANK'S TEAM OR MY TEAM WOULD DIE ON OUR RESPECTIVE DIVES. I DISMISSED IT BECAUSE I FELT IT WAS A RESULT OF A DISAGREEMENT FRANK AND I HAD EARLIER ABOUT THE OBJECTIVES FOR THE DAY. ON THIS DIVE ZIDI AND I ADDED LINE AND WALLED OUT THE NORTH PASSAGE OF THE CAVE. JUST AS WE DID, I HAD A FEELING OF CERTAINTY THAT SOMEONE WAS DEAD AND ON THE RETURN TO THE TEE, WHERE YOU COULD HEAD NORTH, SOUTH OR TO THE EXIT, WE WERE GREETED BY JIM ALONE. WE RETURNED AND ATTEMPTED TO FIND FRANK BUT HAD TO STOP WHEN AIR BEAME CRITICAL, TO A POINT THAT WE BOTH RAN OUT OF AIR AS WE REACHED OUR DEOCMPRESSION GASSES. MY FRIEND AND DIVE PARTNER FOR MANY YEARS STILL RESIDES IN THIS CAVE, BOTH IN HIS PHYSICAL REMAINS AND HIS SPIRIT.

~ TOM MOUNT

Starting in 1969 we begin to explore the Blue Holes in Andros Bahamas which ranged anywhere from 120 fsw (36 msw) to in excess of 330 fsw (100 msw). These are some of the most dramatic dives imaginable. It was the temptation of these unexplored deep, dark and intriguing passage that resulted in Frank's death in 1971. His final dive ended in a passage he discovered on an earlier trip located in Benjamin's Cave (Blue Hole #4) and had vowed to return too. This passage begin about 600 ft (180 m) back into the cave and was entered through a tight restriction at 280 ft (85 m) where it opened to a huge chamber at 320 ft (95 m) and reportedly the bottom was not in site. While alive Frank revolutionized cave diving equipment and produced cave diving's' first modern lighting systems, including adjustable beam halogen lamps - some of the best reels that exist even today. He also developed the first auto inflator for a BC (the old horse collar type which were the first available around 1970). With his death I lost one of my best friends and dive buddies and cave diving lost the most innovative manufacturer of the decade. Frank's life contributed a wealth of information on dive technique, dealing with ultra-deep diving situations, mental survival strategy for extreme events and he provided the foundation and standards for innovative equipment for cave and deep diving. Frank is gone but his spirit lives on. We thank him for the gifts he gave us to better understand deep exploration. In addition, his foundation for the development of lights, reels and inflators for BC's. We miss you Frank - but I know you are with me on all deep cave dives.

In 1967, at the time of my divorce, I had a dive shop and commercial diving operation which specialized in putting communication cables in up and down the Atlantic Missile range via NASA contracts, it also was involved in salvage and any other commercial diving venture that came along. In early 1968 I and one of my friends , former dive student and dive buddies as well as fellow martial arts enthusiast Ike Ikehara, planed on taking off (I would sell - and did sell - my business) we planned on bumming around the world diving - raising hell, whatever. So in early 1968 while planning to "get away" another friend, Bill Hulet M.D., Ph.D., approached me about taking on the responsibility of the Diving Officer position at the University of Miami Institute of Marine Sciences (later renamed Rosensteil School of Marine and Atmospheric Sciences, ***UM RSMAS).*** Funny the influences of donations! At the time, I was more interested in travelling around the world but did agree to an interview. Dick Williams, a Medical Student now M.D., also encouraged me to take the job. Dick had become one of my crazier dive buddies as well. He joined Frank and me along with other cave divers as we explored many new and existing systems.

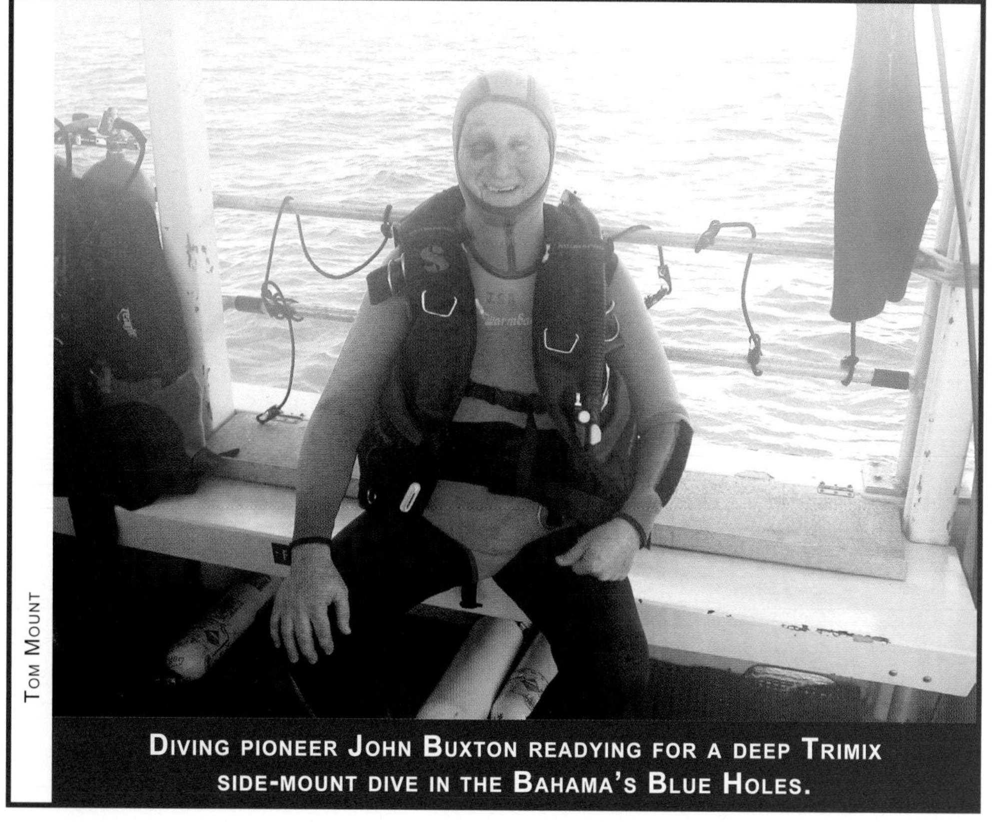
TOM MOUNT

DIVING PIONEER JOHN BUXTON READYING FOR A DEEP TRIMIX SIDE-MOUNT DIVE IN THE BAHAMA'S BLUE HOLES.

After the interview, I was tempted but still desired to travel for a while. However, Dick got down and dirty in an effort to get me to take the job. Knowing I was single and that in Titusville their were few single available women at the time, thus he introduced me to some nurses, so being practical (or maybe something else) I rethought my decisions and took the job. Strange the influences we make that our most important life decisions are

Bob Friedman's wife, Sue, on a cave dive in 1973

based on. My tenure as the Diving Officer at UM RSMAS was a very enjoyable and rewarding challenge; it was one of the best decisions, if not the best in my life even if due to somewhat dubious reasons. While there, I discovered many new adventures, and gained knowledge to contribute back to my addiction and true loves deep, deep walls, wreck and cave diving.

Again, as fate would have it a wider door of diving pursuits was opened. I brought Ike Ikehara down as my Assistant Diving Officer and we developed one of the most advanced university diving programs of all times. We were able to build hyperbaric chambers to support our operations. It did not take long to develop a deep diving interest in scientists at the lab. Thus a scientific diver program that featured Deep Air diving to 240 fsw (72 msw) , scientific cave diving, a limited Heliox program to 330 fsw (100 msw) with no was Trimix known or available to blend at that point time. And wow! With the chambers in my back door of the office, I could get my deep narcosis fix weekly if weather or schedule prevented diving. Yes, Life was good! Spending many days a year at sea and doing deeper dives on each trip kept my appetite wetted for the deep deeper and deepest pursuits and a formal excuse to do the dives. With Ike and Dick Williams on hand we made numerous Friday PM departures to go cave diving. When it was only Dick and I in his Mustang or my car, and then later we had access to a Van, we competed to see who could set the best time from the door of my office to cave country (Believe me - Gil had been way off base with his ***only*** 90 mph statement!) We allowed one pee stop only. (Oh! For younger kidneys again.)

Then even as good as it already was we managed to become involved in Tek Tite II, in 1971 a Man Undersea Technologies project. This was a saturation diving program in St Johns Island. While the project was great being introduced to the GE MK 10 CCR and the protype CCR 1000 really made the adventure complete. This opened the door to multi year projects doing saturations dives on Hydrolab where I had the privilege of being on the first government sponsored co-ed saturation dive with Dr. Sylvia Earle Mead. She is a dedicated scientist, "diveacholic," and deep diving enthusiast. Therefore, we made some good dives and some that may have been just a *tad* bit deeper than the project limits. After all, we were sitting on the wall in Grand Bahama – what is one to do? This then led to my supervising the diving on the FLARE Saturation project. These sat dives also allowed me to bring down and use as support or safety and even sat divers many of my cave diving friends including Jim Lockwood and Sheck Exley, my other cave buddies Dick Williams were the three rotating hyperbaric physicians's and Ike Ikehara rotated with me as supervisor on FLARE. On the FLARE Project, one of the divers I used was Randy Hilton who was both one of the best cave divers I knew and the strongest person I have ever seen underwater. Unfortunately, on a day off, Randy went to Eagle's Nest for a dive and did not come back up.

Some say timing is everything, thus my life and pursuit of understanding cave, wreck and deeper has had perfect timing. I managed to be at the infancy of cave diving, as we know it today. In 1968 myself and a group of us from a cave diving club we had formed, the Aqua Marine Cave Dwellers (later renamed the Florida Cave Dwellers), Hal Watts of the Forty Fathom Scubapros, Dave Desautles of the Barnacle Busters, Dale Malloy also of the Barnacle Busters, Larry Briel at the time a graduate student, and Jim Sweeney united to form the NACD, the United States first cave diver training agency. The philosophy was that we and the groups we represented seemed to be surviving where many others were dying, thus maybe if we combine our talents we can prevent deaths and develop safe cave divers. Informally most of us had already been training others, primarily to have someone safe to dive with thus there was

SHECK EXLEY AND TOM MOUNT DISCOVER OLD REEL IN ZOO HOLE, ANDROS, BAHAMAS CIRCA 1971

tried and true information to share. We had managed to solve many issues peculiar to both cave and deep diving. Both Hal Watts and I were teaching Deep Air diving (no formal certifications existed and Hal had been teaching it since 1960). Thus we had special areas to contribute for deeper cave diving pursuits. History reflects the results of this combined effort.

As knowledge evolved and ideas were exchanged, technical diving developed into a mainstream pursuit. Hal formed PSA as a deep diving association. Later when Dick Rutowski appointed me as the president of IAND (1990) and we decided to change the name to include technical diving, IANTD, we developed standards for all venues of what is called technical diving today. This included the first ever Trimix certification courses. Much of the knowledge of the mixed gases is derived from an early Heliox program I had developed at UM RSMAS. This coupled with the experiences of Billy Deans teaching Trimix in open water from 1988, Sheck Exley's practical experiences on deep record dives including his Trimix Cave training programs which originated in 1987, decompression knowledge contributed by Dr. Bill Hamilton and many early classes that consisted of informal idea exchanges rather than the formal training we have today. It is interesting that the first two people who attended IANTD Trimix class, which I conducted as an evaluation of what we had learned so far, are still diving today. One of these is Joe Citelli who has authored another chapter in this text. Prior to the Trimix course Joe and I had been diving with each other for quite awhile and still do from time to time. Little did we fully understand the challenges that this first step would open as the sport grew and our quest to go deeper evolved.

Another program was the first official wreck penetration course. Again we drew experienced wreck divers together including myself, Billy Deans, Gary Gentile, Wings Stocks, Jim Baden and contributions from others to build the foundation of the IANTD Technical Wreck Diver program which continues to evolve both practically and knowledge-wise.

As we already had many of the most experienced cave divers within IANTD, the development of the cave diver education programs was actually our easiest quest. The politics around it in the early days were more of the challenge.

With growth came needs for new programs and IANTD once again led the way with the first Intermediate Trimix program now called Normoxic Trimix and later another first introduction of Aadvanced Recreational Trimix, and even Recreational Trimix diver. These levels grew into the curriculum to support most divers. At the same time, it became apparent there was a need for education of divers seeking to go yet deeper thus the introduction of another first for IANTD; the Expedition Trimix program with training to 400 ft (120 m).

About three weeks before Sheck Exley died on his record attempt in Mexico we got together to dive Die Polder. Prior to the dive I had asked Sheck what mix did he wish for us to use. His answer was "***just air***" as we would not dive deep. That sounded great as even at that time I was still diving to 200 ft (60 m) on air. One of the goals of the dive was that Sheck was testing some modifications he had made to the Poseidon regulators he would use on the record dive he was planning. So, yes, it would be a fun dive, but Mary Ellen (his former wife and very closest friend) and I would also be safety divers for him if the modified regs failed.

When we got to Die Polder the water was black on the surface, so Sheck asked me to lead and if it did not clear up at a reasonable depth we would call the dive. Well, descending on the line we could not see our hands on the line so, to say it was less than ideal would be an understatement! However, ***bingo*** at 165 ft (50 m) it was as if someone suddenly turned on the light bulb. We had an instant shift from zero visibily to crystal clear, blue water. We looked at each other after swimming awhile and then Sheck turned, grinned at us and headed into deep space. Oh well, what can I do as I went head down and power stroked into the blue behind him. Mary Ellen, much to her credit, descended slowly and stopped around 250 ft (75 m) while Sheck and I continued the free fall to 290 ft (85 m). Here Sheck put the first regulator through its paces, resting, and then shifted to the second one and tested it. Satisfied with the results he gave the up signal and we started our ascent. For depth and time, we both had Aladdin dive computers so we more or less followed these up adding in our own individual modifications to decompression based on experience. As Sheck had dived much deeper than I had already having two mixed gas records beyond 800 ft (240 m) I adopted his even-deeper-than-my-stops on ascent. However using oxygen up from 30 ft (9 m) to the surface, I would have cut deco in half, but Sheck, insisted we do the entire lengthy Aladdin air duration decompression. Post dive Sheck explained that he agreed we had over-decompressed, but this close to his planned record dive, he just wanted to be careful and not take a hit. Little did I realize that in three weeks Sheck, like so many other excellent divers and good friends of mine, would be dead!

Mel Clark

CCR Wreck Diver

This day we had a great and enjoyable dive. At dinner while eating catfish, we even recalled a body recovery we had made many years before. Following that recovery we had been eating cat fish at a local restaurant with friends and Sheck without thinking blurted, "This reminds me of the catfish that was actually eating one of the divers faces we had recovered." This had an unexpected affect on some of the others at the table who suddenly did not appreciate the value of an all-the-catfish-you-can-eat dinner we were gorging on any longer. Sheck and I had more than enough catfish that night. However, we certainly did not get warm and friendly vibes from our friends at the table. Later Mary Ellen remarked to me that she had tried to talk Sheck out of this dive or agree to make it the last record attempt. I had commented back to her that from the time I first met Sheck when he was still in college he had a goal of doing a 1000 ft (300 m) cave dive. We had discussed it numerous times, as we both wanted to dive to that depth. Sheck wanted to do it as a record setting dive and I had ambitions of being able to do it from a bell, submarine or habitat. I felt he would continue setting depth records until that goal was obtained. I have often wondered if Mary Ellen had a premonition about the dive. In every accident I have investigated someone involved in the dive or project or close to the person has had a premonition. Post accident in this case I was not comfortable asking about it.

After the accident, some commented, "What a waste!" and that really upset me. Was it tragic? Of course. It was sad to have a person as full of life and energy with so much knowledge to share as Sheck die. Nevertheless, to insinuate that someone died while doing the one thing in life they enjoyed most, a life style they had pursued since their teens, was a waste is stated out of sheer ignorance. Makes one wonder if those who think that way would rather be sitting in their rocking chair at age 90 in an old folks home saying. "If only I had." Now that to me would be a waste. ***It is quality of life and living life that is most important, not the quantity of years survived.***

Timing again, as CCR came into being, I had the good fortune of being the Dive Officer at UM RSMAS when Walter Starck developed the Electrolung, and unfortunately, he was leaving just as I was hired. Later Dr. Pat Colon (at the time a graduate student at UM RSMAS) developed a homemade CCR. Pat still makes his own CCR, which he uses for studying deep-water sponges for cancer research. This makes Pat among the most experienced, even if not known by most recreational divers of today, CCR divers in the world. The next CCR exposure was the UT 240, which

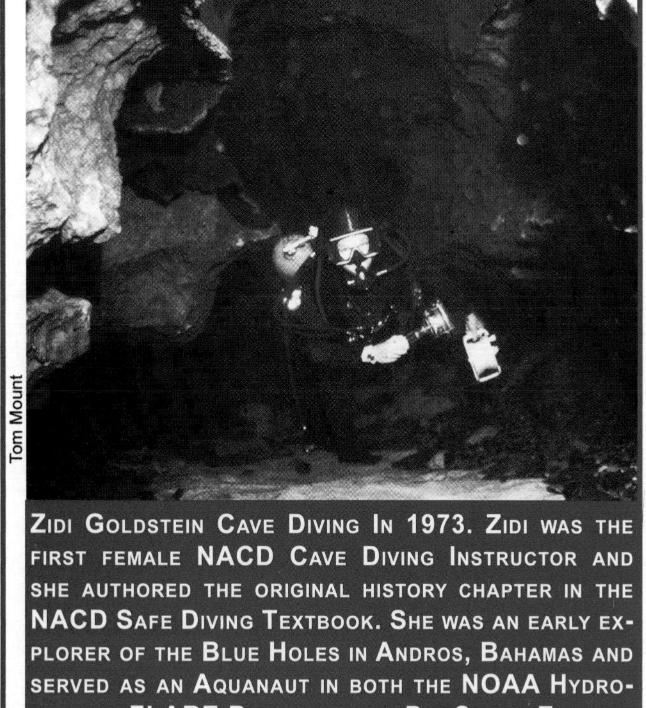

Tom Mount

ZIDI GOLDSTEIN CAVE DIVING IN 1973. ZIDI WAS THE FIRST FEMALE NACD CAVE DIVING INSTRUCTOR AND SHE AUTHORED THE ORIGINAL HISTORY CHAPTER IN THE NACD SAFE DIVING TEXTBOOK. SHE WAS AN EARLY EXPLORER OF THE BLUE HOLES IN ANDROS, BAHAMAS AND SERVED AS AN AQUANAUT IN BOTH THE NOAA HYDROLAB AND FLARE PROJECTS WITH DR. SYLVIA EARLE.

proved to be ideal for program development but a bust as to functionality. The program was conducted at IANTD HQ in Miami and was attended by Ed Betts of ANDI. Both ANDI and IANTD benefited from the exposure by discovering ideas to include in all CCR diver programs.

Meanwhile, Dr. Bill Stone was developing the Cis-Lunar CCR. As it evolved, Richard Pyle, then a graduate student at U of Hawaii, Bishop Museum, begin to test it in protype form. Later Kevin Gurr also worked with the protype MK4 followed by the protype MK5. Eventually the unit was to come to market. IANTD was the selected Training Agency and I went to Boston to be trained on it along with Larry Green. Things did not go as planned as upon arrival we discovered the units were not completed thus our "training" became help assemble them. Upon completion of putting the units together, Richard Nordstrom told us our window for training had passed. Larry went home to await delivery of units for Wakulla II and the development of the formal program. Richard pulled me aside and said here is your unit, you have enough back ground with rebreathers to use it and to develop the Cis-Lunar training program, Then bomb shell one; "Incidently we have a class schedule for 2 months from now." Of course, my reaction was, "OH SHIT!" As if that was not enough pressure bombshell two developed. "By the way, there is no operational manual for the MK5. Richard Pyle is developing one that should be ready in a month or so. Please give me your feedback on how things go with the unit." At this time I asked myself, "Just how insane am I, to take a very complex CCR, with no operations manual or anything to reflect how it works?" Of course the answer to myself was, "Since when have you used sanity as a guideline in your life, so go do it."

I happily took my MK5 and boarded the plane to Miami. The next few weeks were spent in the pool with the MK5 combined with long phone calls to Richard Pyle at night. Comments such as, "Rich, why is it doing x, and other comments... Rich, that may be what the MK5 prototype did, but this one is not." Thank G_d Rich's unit arrived and he now had the production unit as well as the protype to dive and base the manual on. (His is serial number one, mine number two, but as I brought mine home, it was actually in my possession before his arrived due to being shipped from Boston to Hawaii.) Much to all of our surprise Rich completed the manual (ahead of schedule) and I was able to develop the foundation-training program and the course started on time. Wow! What a diverse group of students! A Film Maker, a few wreck divers used to solo wreck diving, a deep-water fish collector who only dives solo plus two almost-sane divers. The first, Andrew Driver who at least has some military background on rebreathers (***LAR V***) and was used to teaching diving thus not so inclined to disappear. The second "sane" diver was Nick Jewson, from the UK. Our protocol became Rich Pyle and I teaching skills with Richard Nordstrom acting as the "cowboy" rounding up all the strays as they tried to desert the "herd." The course was successful because everyone lived through the experience in spite of attempts to disappear! We recognized Richard Nordstrom as the Cowboy of the Year and life was rosy again. The friendship of this group was enhanced by all night repair jobs during the course.

While CCR is ideal for film work and behavior studies, to me the most apparent advantage of course is the ***Oh Boy - deeper and longer duration***. Yes, life was even sweeter than before. Indeed, the primary reason for development of the Cis-Lunar was for deep cave exploration, which it was immediately used for during the Wakulla II project and on cave expeditions to Mexico.

From this foundation CCR, diving has grown to mainstream. Additional formidable units soon entered the recreational dive market such as the Inspiration which is very close on the heals of the MK 5 and with more capability to deliver thus being the trend setter in bringing CCR diving to the recreational forefront. Today AP Valves has introduced the even more capable Vision electronics for the Inspiration and the Evolution. The CCR 2000 has unfortunately became unavailable, KISS and Sport KISS, Megalodon (plus Mini Meg and Copis Meg), the Ouroborus, O2ptima (and O2ptima FX), Prism Topaz and many more units are appearing such as the rEvo, Titan, Menshes, Pelegian and rumors of many more entries into the field that may already be on the market by the time this book is published. To say the least, the CCR diving generation has arrived!

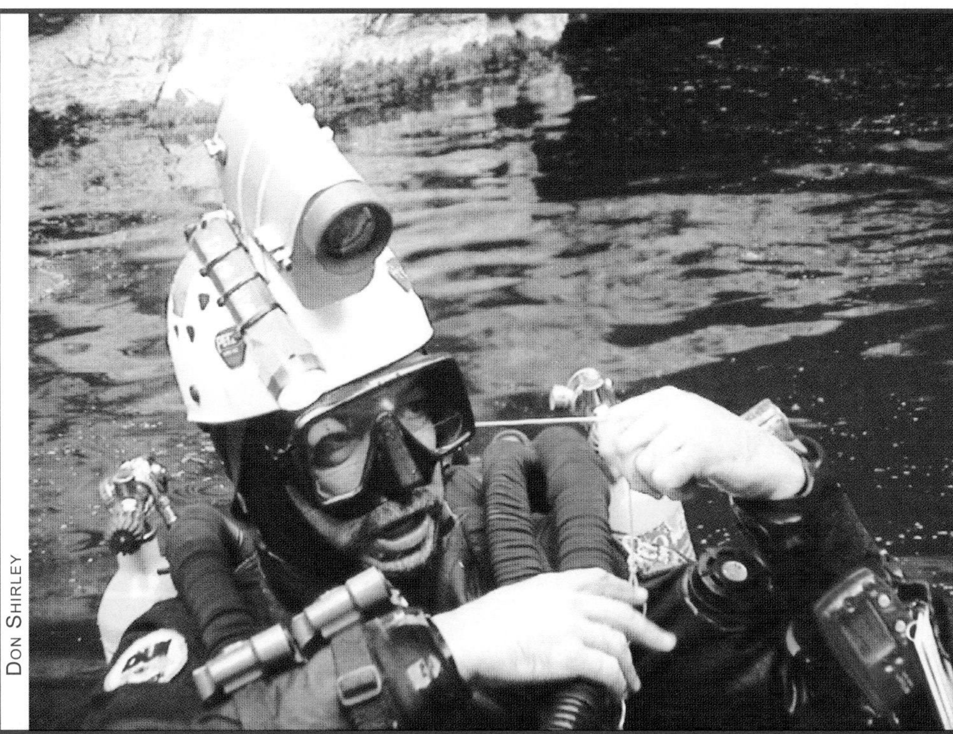
DON SHIRLEY

DAVID SHAW PREPARES FOR A DEEP CAVE DIVE TO OVER 800 FT (244 M) IN BOESMANSGAT, SOUTH AFRICA, ON 13 JANUARY 2005

THE TEAM WAS ASSEMBLED TO RECOVER THE BODY OF DEON DREYER, A DIVER LOST IN THE SYSTEM PREVIOUSLY. THE PLAN ALLOWED FOR FIVE MINUTES AT THE BOTTOM TO RECOVER THE BODY AND THEN RETURN TO 720 FT (220M) TO RENDEVOUS WITH DON SHIRLEY, THE BACKUP SAFETY DIVER. AT 26 MINUTES INTO THE DIVE, ALL BREATHING AND COMMUNICATIONS BY DAVID SHAW CEASED AND DON SHIRLEY, AFTER TRYING TO HELP, MUST RETURN TO THE SURFACE WITHOUT DAVID SHAW.

Timing is all; timing has been good and I have become a kid in a candy store. The CCR allows us to exceed any goals we may have had as open circuit divers. In addition, many of us in the dive community have pushed OC to and beyond any reasonable limit.

My personal deepest OC dive was not planned and was on air to a depth of 450 fsw (127 msw). The purpose of the dive was to rescue a girl who was narked out and dropping over the wall. On this dive, I had a potent O_2 hit and my vision became a red field with black dots. (I have had this experience twice - this time and once at a graduate students' party while I was the Diving Officer at UM RSMAS.) I managed to ascend with the girl by literally climbing the wall and my vision began to reoccur in small blocks beginning around 250 fsw (75 msw). Following that episode I have made OC dives on Trimix to 400 fsw (120 msw) which is a reasonable maximum limit for OC diving. Many of us now consider CCR as the only alternative to obtain our diving goals. At the time of this publication, my deepest CCR dive is 560 fsw (170 msw).

Also a great advantage of CCR is until its' appearance the big improvement in technical diving each year had been, introducing the new and larger X cylinder and the new and larger with longer burn times lights. Now we can do the biggest of dives with a CCR on our back that weighs around the same as a single cylinder with weights, a light that is small and gives 3-4 or even 8 hours of burn time and DPV's that actually do last for 2 hours or longer. For a diver of my age (and any age) this is truly welcomed.

The down side of CCR is, by being able to go deeper or further back, we now push tables, and many physiological and psychological parameters. Decompression is one of the areas of concern on both deeper and longer dives. As the depth and duration increased, many had higher hit rates than exposed to on shallow dives. In fact, in a survey of divers who explore deeper than 330 fsw (100 msw), it became apparent that in order to be symptom free, at least most of the time, the majority of experienced extreme divers have made moderate to major changes worked into the decompression model used. This same learning process applies to exceptional duration dives at lesser depths. Thus our new found capacities challenge us to find a better "what works - works" method to overcome

DIVERS ON THE *HMS VICTORIA* DISCOVERED IN 2005 OFF THE COAST OF LEBANON

deep water and very long duration dives.

Many of the approaches to surviving these are covered in other chapters, I will in the conclusion address profile changes I have made that work for my physiology but realize they may or may not work for yours. I feel these are useable to at least 600 fsw (180 msw). But it is one venue to consider until a validated model comes along to solve the problem. Within the content of his text, JP Imbert discusses a model that may just do the trick, but until we have input from field users it will be difficult to comment on. It is my belief that the deeper we go, the more critical it is to develop decompression strategies that are more adaptable to the individual's physiology. Even then, no one can predict the impact of emotions or psychological reaction on decompression profiles. However, we do know our physiology responds to our emotions and psychological event in our life. So one aspect of modeling has to be for us to know ourselves - and be in control of emotions and our psychological reflexes. When we cannot control these, we must be disciplined to say no. My what works for me may or may not work for you. With deeper or longer dives, we have truly entered the zone of intuitive decompression planning.

Joe Dituri joined IANTD as its Training Director many years ago and has brought his wealth of information and background as a Naval Diving Officer, and as a fellow deep diving addict. He along with Dr. Richard Pyle and their team of explorers also discovered the inadequacies of decompression models for deeper diving. They too have developed strategies to cope with this. Within IANTD, we are fortunate to have so many explorers who are not only exploring but who are willing to share their experiences so we can all enjoy safer deep adventures. It is our joint goal to be able to discover and recommend methods to provide increased safety for all deep-water addicts such as ourselves.

One of the major points to be made is my addiction and possibly your addictions to deeper or loner dives has proven to be fatal many times to many divers. Earlier I causally mentioned deaths to great divers on air- well we also have the deaths of great divers on Trimix too. So if you desire to fall prey to the deep addiction be sure your accept the risk of such an addiction. You will be entering a very unforgivable world. One in which your discipline to survive may be the only thing to get you back to the surface alive, due to a combination of our physiological reaction, psychological reactions and mechanical induced problems we may face and be forced to deal with or die. If you think the term, dying is too harsh then you have no business dong the extreme dives. An unfortunate part of the new technology is it opens the extreme door to many who can afford it, but have to develop the physical, mental and practical skills to deal with potential disasters.

I would recommend every budding extreme diver carefully review the video in which Dave Shaw died at over 800 ft (240 m). It is sobering but provides many lessons on how to survive deep diving. It also exemplifies the most supreme discipline and survival will that one can imagine as performed by Don Shirley. So this video, if used as a learning tool, may be a key to understanding what it takes to survive the seemingly impossible. It also illustrates the factors that did lead to the death of a remarkable explorer, Dave Shaw, who was also a survivor personality.

For my addictions to reward me, there are some simple rules to survive by and they may allow you to also be rewarded for your efforts in extreme environments underwater. Accept or reject them; it is your choice and living and dying is based on choice. You choose your path - you chose how to avoid accidents or you chose to blindly invite them, you chose to prepare for the dive or to just go with the flow it is all a matter of choice so choose wisely - yours and your buddies life depend upon it.

1. First and foremost, learn to listen to that little voice inside of you, before, during, and post dive. Trust it

because it is your intuition and it can keep you alive and will help you avoid bad incidents. If you ignore it, be prepared to test all your skills on how to survive

2. Realize that some of the best divers and explores who ever lived have died diving. To name a few, Frank Martz, Randy Hilton, Sheck Exley, Rob Palmer, Rob Parker, Steve Berman, David Shaw, John Bennett, Parker Turner, and the list goes on and on. Many who read this will dwell on trying to say, "They died due to such and such, thus as I'm above this and it will not be my issue." Regardless of your analytical findings for the cause of death, ***always*** accept that it was caused by a mistake, that is something we, as humans, seem to have in common with one another. Due to our common ability to make mistakes, in acknowledging this, we can work towards reducing the number of mistakes we make and this is a mandatory process as the world of the ultra-deep or ultra-distance is unforgiving and uncaring so mistakes are not tolerated. This should allow you to get beyond any feeling of immortality you have. This is good because, once you recognize risk and the possibility of death, you are better equipped to deal with those factors that could contribute to both yours and your buddies death or injury.
3. Never rush. Regardless of how critical you may sense the situation, react calmly and deliberately
4. Avoid being distracted from the dive itself. ***Even emergencies must be taken in stride and dealt with as part of the dive.*** Therefore, while we do problem solving our focus must also remain on dive performance, least we begin a series of actions that then create additional emergencies. Distraction and rushing are serious competitors that kill
5. Solve the challenges as they appear. Do not dwell on the end result. Accomplish the step to survive now - once it is accomplished deal with the next level of threat. Failure to deal with the immediate issues may inhibit your capability having the luxury of solving the final step, and surfacing alive
6. Be very selective in who you chose to dive with. A wrong decision may kill you. Dive only with those who are self-sufficient and you can trust under any situation and in return be equally as self-sufficient and trust-worthy. The self-sufficient team finds solutions to the most extreme of challenges and are able save each other if need be
7. Be competent and confident in your abilities. Progress your dive goals at the rate your competence increases physically, technique-wise, knowledge-wise and discipline-wise ***with*** emphasis on ***wise*** at each step of the way
8. Listen and learn from the experiences of others who have been there. Incorporate their learned survival skills and avoid the mistakes they made in which they were forced to survive or die
9. Accept that the extreme environment is little known and outside the norm. The science is weak to non-existent so you must create a safe profile or behavior. For many of us this is most likely the challenge that keeps us in the game; The unknown frontier. Nothing could be more exciting, and nothing could be more life threatening, thus a worthy challenge. It is a way to ensure quality of life but may have dramatic affects on quanity of life

LEIGH BISHOP USING AN OUROBOROS CCR DURING THE FILMING OF DEEP SEA DETECTIVES

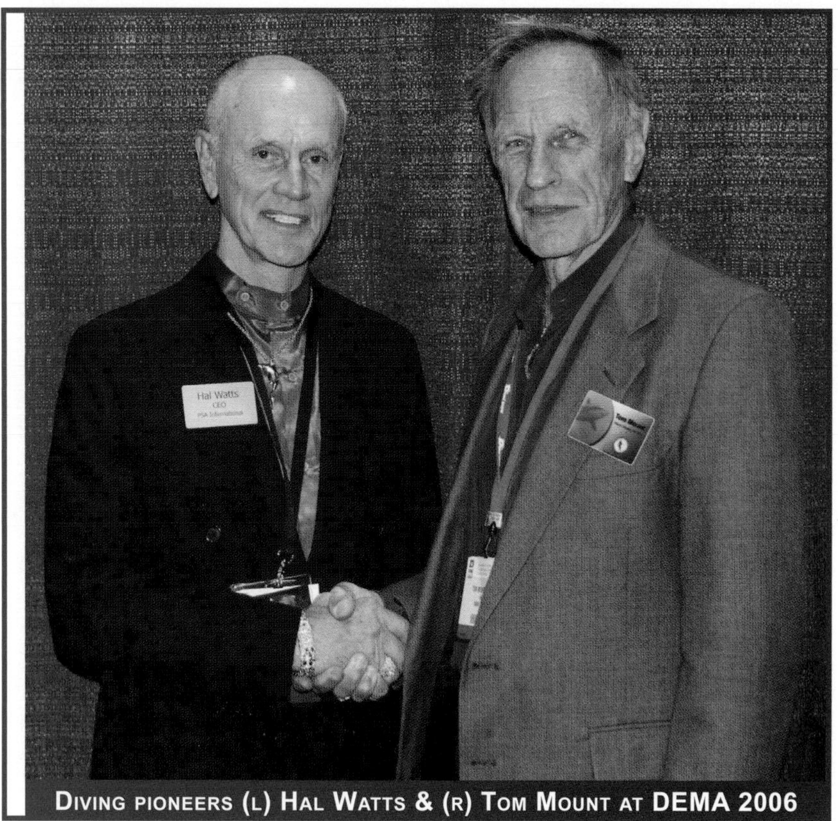

DIVING PIONEERS (L) HAL WATTS & (R) TOM MOUNT AT DEMA 2006

10. Proceed to the extremes only if you are skill full and have incrementally gained the needed experience to do so

11. Avoid the BS of those who talk the talk but do not walk the walk (***the internet is full of them***)

12. Always realize only you can survive the "impossible" no else can do it for you

13. When faced with danger weigh the probabilities by doing such and such against the certainties of dying. ***Example:*** You have just drawn your last breath of bottom mix, the only gas you have left is a high PO_2 one. There is a very high probability of dying if you use the high PO_{2}, but if you do not there is a certainty of dying with nothing to breathe. Apply this strategy to every level of your diving. In fact apply it to every level of your life

14. Adapt to your situation and once again trust your inner voice to see you through a crisis

15. Adopt my attitude: If I die on a dive, may I be found with one foot up and the other foot down in kick position and in perfect posture when rigor mortis sets in. ***Do not quit!***

16. Remember: If you manage to breathe - you can think if you can think - you can solve problems - if you solve problems - ***you survive***

17. Always do relaxation and visualization pre dive

18. Be informed as to the environment you explore

19. Avoid negative energy, distance your self from those who are negative, least they fill you with the same negativity. This kind of energy can lead to bad decisions, and death

20. Keep learning, knowledge empowers, knowledge and knowing allow us to incorporate the phrase "Don't worry, be happy" as we are now able to fully enjoy the richness of what we wish to explore as we know our selves, we know the critical factors of the environment, we know how to react, we have practiced our reaction skills, we neither expect nor deny the existence of threat so we are happy and enjoying our experiences yet if Murphy appears we can and ***we will*** deal with it

If any of the above is harsh or unacceptable to you, then it is in your best interest to remain in non-extreme environments.

If you are willing to experience the thrill, the rush, the personal achievement, even the possibility of facing death and walking away, to see what is next , to feel the adenine in your blood welcome to my addictions and G_d help you. May you live in excitement and die in peace. Not in a rocking chair saying if only I had done such and such – instead live every moment as your last and regret nothing, not even the bad experiences you may have to overcome in life. Even the bad things provided we survive teach us and make us more knowledgeable of our selves and the events. And if we do not survive think was it worth it - for me the foregone conclusion is ***YES***, every minute of it. Dying is not nearly as terrible as having not lived.

A works for me decompression approach. I happen to believe in deep stops and have since reading Brian Hills book ***Thermodynamic Decompression*** back in 1971 and follow up, papers on this concept by Dr. Fife over several years. In OC, diving the required depths of stops had been an issue that was difficult if not impossible to utilize due to the volume of gas needed. With the use of CCR the process was worth investigating. JP Imbert's original chapter in the first version to the technical encyclopedia added much in the discussion on practical management of profiles combined with decompression models. In addition, experience forces the adaptation to personal modification in order to arrive symptom free (including such symptoms as fatigue beyond what one normally experience). For me deeper stops built into models seems to have accomplished this to what I think is acceptable to 600 ft (180 m).

SUSAN DASHER (L) AND DORA VALDEZ (R) ON A DEEP NORTH WALL DIVE IN GRAND CAYMAN, BWI

So, as promised decompression that works for me and a few of my friends until a better model comes along. But if you use this approach do so with no science of validation behind it. **Accept or reject or modify to your needs the below:**

"Knowledge is essential, Survival is practical."

~ *Tom Mount, 1999*

On dives to or deeper than 300 ft (91 m):

- Do not ascend more than 30 ft (9 m) before doing a brief deco stop of up to one minute
- Upon completion of the first stop ascend no more than 20 ft (6 m) and do a one minute stop; Repeat his until you have reached the required stop depths of a VPM (or RGBM or carefully selected gradient factor) model - then follow that table or dive computer from that time to the surface (some of my friends do the shallow stops per Bühlmann - but I get too cold). Hopefully the ABM model will resolve these issues
- Consider surface oxygen breathing for 10 to 30 minutes and avoid any strenuous activity for two plus hours. Avoid hard work withing 2 hours of the dive pre or post. By the same token I workout to some degree 5 to 6 days a week, diving or not. Be your own judge on this. Exercise is another of my addictions
- My dives are made with a bottom PO_2 of 1.2 as maximum and decompression no greater than 1.4 - typically, I stay at 1.2 until I arrive at a 4 minute stop or longer then shift to 1.3 PO_2. Upon arrival at 100 ft (30 m), I go to 1.4. From this point on, I will stay at 1.4 PO_2 with a lesser 5 minute breathing period every 30 to 40 minutes of the dive
- Complete the required decompression at 20 ft (6 m)
- Upon completion of decompression ascend to 10 ft (3 m) drop PO_2 to 1.0 and do a safety stop for a few minutes (***to be honest, the time depends on how cold and tired I am***)
- Remain on the CCR (if OC remain on high mix) and keep PO_2 between 0.7 and 1.0 until seated on the boat or arrival to land
- Consider the use of high PO_2 (0.5 or higher) breathing for 10 to 30 minutes post dive. with minimal activity
- When diving a CCR it is very important to keep the PO_2 consistent. Many who try and maintain higher PO_2's have them bouncing up and down thus it provides the same physiological affects as doing yo yo dive profiles as the inert gas loading is constantly changing and spiking then dropping. This also acts similar to cavitation effect. Not maintaing a tight PO_2 is an excellent way to develop DCS

On dives between 200 and 300 ft (60 and 91 m) I'm comfortable following a deep stop GF - VPM or RGBM schedule - but

(L to R) IANTD Training Director Joe Dituri & wife Amy with BOD members Patti & Tom Mount in 2008

do ascend somewhat slower. I take the stops 6 ft (2 m) deeper than indicated if I am using a computer. Diving tables specifically I remain with the indicated depths but use 2 minutes of the allowed or planned bottom time to observe a slower ascent rate.

Above 200 ft (60 m) to 100 ft (30 m) I follow the model being dived, usually VPM - RGBM or a 35 90 GF as this seems to be close to VPM or RGBM profiles. At least as reflected on the IANTD Tables (VPM) and the Explorer dive computer using RGBM with conservative factor 1.

For me most models work about equally well above 100 ft (30 m) with the exception of USN and DCIEM tables as they still tend to begin deco too shallow.

Also as controversial as it may be I tend to workout on the days I dive. Being as the dives are exercise on dive days I work out easier but maintain my schedule unless the dive is 4 hours or longer or deeper than 330 ft (100 m). Then I skip the work out. I also stretch and do mini exercise while at decompression again a very controversial practice.

I hydrate starting the day before. In the past when I have had symptoms, it has usually been linked with improper hydration levels.

Anyway, the above is what works - works - for this person and a few of my friends. A similar process may or may not work for you so by sharing my strategy with you I do not endorse this procedure as safe nor effective for every one. ***Extreme*** dives require the development of intuitive decompression and practical adaptation of models. Also listen to your intuition many times you know it is safe to surface (but be conservative and follow your schedule) other times even though in theory you have completed decompression if that little invoice talks to you - listen and obey it.

In closing, I thank G_d for the good timing in my life. I feel quiet privileged to be exposed to all the exciting venues of diving as they evolved and to be privileged to be a part of IANTD and its' list of first programs developed for divers by divers.

Below are just a few of the IANTD First's:

1. EANx introduced to recreational divers by Dick Rutkowski in 1985 when he founded IAND, Inc. currently known as IANTD
2. Recreational Trimix Diver
3. Advanced Nitrox Diver
4. Advanced Recreational Trimix Diver
5. Technical Cave Diver which combines cave diving with extensive technical diving knowledge
6. Technical Wreck Diver
7. Trimix Diver
8. Inermediate levels of Trimix Diver
9. Open Water Nitrox Diver
10. CCR Diver includes all levels from the most basic level of Open Water CCR Diver to CCR Expedition Trimix Diver
11. Expedition Trimix Diver
12. EANx and Trimix Gas Blender programs
13. In addition, of course, many other programs that other agencies feature
14. And some of the most advanced text materials, such as this one, in the dive industry
15. And, of course, IANTD was the first agency to acquire Technical Instructor Insurance for its' members to enable them to teach all of these programs

Safe diving, Tom

Chapter Twenty Two
Going Past The Edge

Joseph Dituri M.S.

If you are considering the performance of dives in excess of 330 ft (100 m), there are a few things you must know. Most divers I know have between 10-40% bends incidents on dives deeper than 350 ft (106 m). This includes all symptoms; some which remain unexplained. Significant risks are associated with this type of diving. It should not be considered without good reason, and then only after the diver has performed Operational Risk Management techniques and risk mitigation. I have some knowledge in this area as the CEO for the Association for Marine Exploration (***AM-E***), and I have been involved with planning and executing several different expeditions; looking for new species of fish, locating wrecks, exploring caves and searching for new geological samples. A great deal of this information comes from a AM-E projects involving many dives between 250-410 ft (76-125 m) in several; different countries and with varying configurations of diving.

Medical

Medical attention may be problematic in remote locations. At least one member of your team should be trained in advanced first aid. The advent of lightweight and portable AEDs is an affordable means of reversing ventricular fibrillation. All expedition personnel should be trained in basic life support, including basic first aid and CPR.

Considering the depths of these expeditions and the weight of a standard recompression chamber, a portable recompression chamber seems apropos. These units have come a long way from the scary "chambers in a bag," and now are very useful and reasonably safe. They are capable of recompressing a diver to 165 ft (50 m) and completing a treatment table four when incorporating a small chest-mounted rebreather. Approximately 90% of all Decompression Illness (DCI) respond immediately if the diver is compressed to 60 ft (18 m). The other alternative for treating DCI is in-water recompression. This requires significant planning, training and practice. I am an advocate of in-water recompression (because it saved my life at least once), but I do not suggest people do it without training and a great deal of practice. There are a number of considerations to take into account if in-water recompression is planned; such as severity of

John Gavin

Olivier Isler descending into Doux De Coly, France during his record setting sump dive of 13,304 ft (4,055 m)

symptoms, possibility of the diver losing consciousness and hypothermia. Sometimes in-water recompression might be the only alternative if recompression facilities are quite distant and time is of the essence to treat the DCI symptoms.

Some adjunctive therapies to assist with DCIs are normal saline solution or lactated ringers (provided you have a person trained to insert an IV catheter). Introducing additional drugs, such as steroids, has shown little evidence of assistance, especially considering the hassle to obtain and administer. Never underestimate the recuperative power of adequate hydration.

Additional prior planning should be made with respect to other potential wounds such as shark bites, cuts, abrasions, stings and tears. A lack of anti-biotics and limited medical supplies in remote locations might turn a hike out of the jungle or 150-mile boat ride to civilization into an arduous task. Antiseptics and antibacterial ointments must be a basic part of your medical kit.

If you are making dives to depths greater than 300 ft (91 m), between 30 and 50% of all divers can expect compression pains. In 1973 & 1974 Duke University found this ailment in 33% of all divers diving to greater than 350 ft (106 m). Compression pains are usually in joints and only experienced at depth. As depth limits are pushed lower by greater numbers of technical divers, more people are experiencing these pains at depth. Any pain that persists following ascents to normal diving limits may be a DCI and should be treated as such. Compression pains are a bit of an enigma as the patho-physiological mechanism is unknown. We know they tend to manifest themselves at dives deeper than 300 ft (91 m) and can intensify with depth. Compression pains could be linked to hydration levels because a rapid in rush of gas causes an osmonic shift potentially leaving a joint without lubrication. These pains tend to decrease or disappear upon ascent. The residual of these pains, that is to say the damage from the pain may not decrease as your depth decreases. Differential diagnosis is indicated to differentiate between DCI and compression pains. Compression pains are more common in areas with a history of injury. Additionally, the pain in one joint may cause the diver to alter muscular movements, creating a different pain in another. Care should be taken, if a diver experiences compression pains, to ensure the diver does not adversely affect another muscle group by overcompensating.

Prepare to deal with divers suffering from High Pressure Nervous Syndrome (***HPNS***). HPNS manifests itself in many manners of physiological and psychological effects. The most obvious effect of "***Helium Tremors***" is where the hands or head shakes uncontrollably with symptoms similar to that of an overdose of caffeine. HPNS normally does not occur shallower than 300 ft (91 m), but often occurs deeper with a potential link to the amount of helium in the breathing mixture. Our group has limited the helium content to an Equivalent Narcotic Depth of between 60-80 ft (18-24 m). Our experience shows that breathing pure helium gives us the "***willies***" which are literally translated to mind-race or lack of ability to concentrate. We feel this may be the predecessor to HPNS. A little nitrogen added into the mix "***normalizes***" everything.

Rapid descent rates can contribute to HPNS and compression pains. As you know, descent time is bottom time. Rapid descents are required for this type of diving, but should be moderated to ensure HPNS is not a factor.

Surface Support Selection & Logistics

These people are your link to a safe return to the surface and their importance to the mission should not be minimized. It may be beneficial to select a person who coordinates the overall expedition. Often this responsibility falls upon the lead diver. Most times, it should be a separate person. The divers have significant responsibilities without the responsibility of mission coordinating. A surface coordinator allows divers to concentrate on their mission, which is getting back safely.

Logistics is the Achilles heel of any expedition. Every aspect of an expedition must be planned. Seemingly small inconveniences become extremely complicated on an expedition, such as tending to dietary needs as well as waste disposal. Many tasks we routinely perform, such as air travel may be difficult with technical diving gear. Most airlines have cargo limitations of 50-70 lbs per bag, and they have issue with transporting hazardous materials and compressed gas containers. Careful coordination with the cargo operator or airline is necessary when you attempt to ship rebreathers, booster pumps and sodasorb. Most airport security personnel are unfamiliar with these items and could mistake them for a bomb or other potentially hazardous devices. Significant interaction prior to team deployment is required to ensure all gear arrives at the destination on time or slightly ahead of schedule. Ensure all oxygen/diluent cylinders are drained and scrubber material has Materials Safety Data Sheet and paperwork accompanying the shipment.

Local sherpas (***transport guide***) may be beneficial to transport gear through the woods. Invest in reputable transportation and pay them generously. Remember, this is your life support equipment they are carrying.

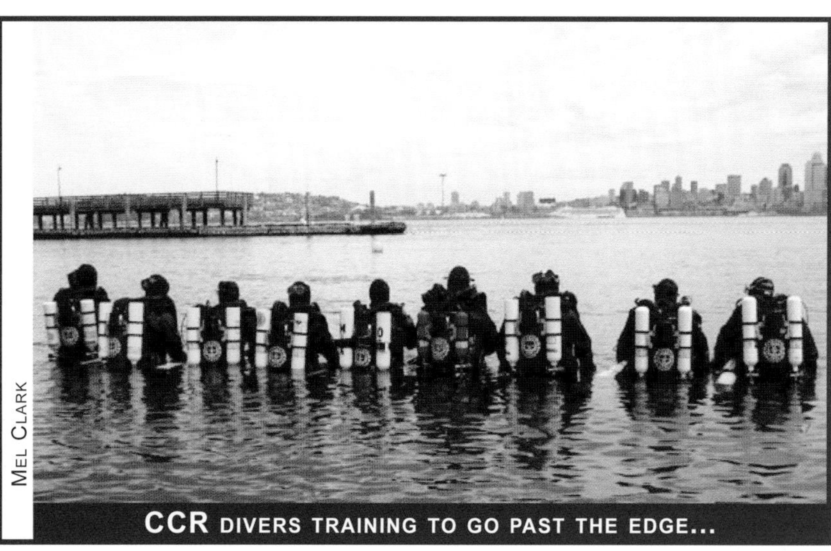

CCR DIVERS TRAINING TO GO PAST THE EDGE...

Redundant or bailout rebreathers offer a lightweight alternative to OC bailout. Additionally, oxygen rebreathers significantly extend the duration of minimal oxygen supplies and reduce the overall expedition footprint. These oxygen rebreathers are perfect for in-water recompression and for extending the limited supply of oxygen even on the surface. If oxygen rebreathers are to be used then it is imperative that each member of the dive team be trained on the units to thoroughly understand the mechanics and proper use.

If your expedition is in the open ocean, the boat captain is vital. This person can be the difference between life and death. Someone experienced in technical diving and surface support is a must. A chase boat is also helpful. If the expedition is from a large live-aboard vessel or in a remote pond or cave, a small boat can give surface support crews a more timely response to any potential emergency.

We use through-water communications and surface marker buoys (***SMBs***) in combination to signal the surface. The boat captain or surface coordinator can listen to conversation on comms and coordinate a recovery/pick up. If the comms fail, every diver should carry two different colored SMBs. One should be red and one yellow. Yellow buoys are for non-emergency situations. In the unlikely event that the surface team sees a red SMB, they are trained to immediately drive to it in the chase boat and clip on a weighted bailout tank that slides down the line to the divers below. Following the bailout a diver is immediately deployed to ascertain the problem. Practice reactions to emergency situations regularly. While expedition planning does not lie solely with surface support, surface support personnel usually perform the lion's share.

Obtaining sponsors is a large part of any expedition. The best thing is to try is gain one single benefactor who will sponsor your cause. Because there are not enough philanthropists in the world, you may have to seek assistance of several sponsors. Most diving manufacturers would be glad to support a worthy cause. Manufactures typically do not want to be associated with an expedition that has a limited chance for success. A well thought-out plan will help you succeed. Additionally, sponsors do not want to be associated with "***loose cannon***" divers. Manufacturers prefer to support expeditions that further their company's goals such as conservation, exploration or preservation. Alignment to similar goals will help you. Do not be afraid to offer publicity in return for a discount or donation. Web pages are an excellent place for publicity and a good avenue to get your word out.

Dive Planning

This is a touchy subject. Many people swear by certain profiles or algorithms. To quote Bill Hamilton, "What works...works." It is not my intention to tell you how to decompress or whether to use VPM, Bühlmann or RGBM models. The information presented herein is only to enlighten you to a tried and true method that works for me. Clearly, this type of diving is a risk, which you alone assume.

AM-E generally dives the rebreathers in the most basic onboard configuration. This means oxygen and air for diluent. The reason is because this configuration is how we dive most frequently. Our people are most familiar with this configuration. We plumb off board oxygen and Heliox 10 to our gas block. The Cis-Lunar and MK-15 rebreather

we use all have the ability to convert all diluent addition locations to the onboard or off-board gas with one switch. The 10% oxygen diluent allows us to purge the breathing bags with diluent at depth to check our sensors. At 400 ft (122 m) Heliox 10 applied directly to the sensors equals 1.3 PPO_2. If this is applied to the sensor and all sensors do not read 1.3, we know where the problem sensor is located. Additionally, the diluent applied directly to the sensor discourages the water vapor from forming on the sensor face.

Upon descent, we start with the rebreather in on-board mode (air as the active diluent and on-board oxygen) and a 1.0 PO_2 set point. Between 70 and 100 ft (21 and 30 m), we slow our descent and all team members signal a gas switch to off-board oxygen and diluent. We do not flush the loop with our off-board diluent at this time, which fixes our equivalent narcotic depth between 60 and 90 ft (18 and 27 m). At this time, we perform a bubble check as well. Significant communication is the key on descent. My experience dictates that if something will go wrong, it happens on descent. Our communication and coordination are practiced on every dive until they are second nature. We also adjust PO_2 to 1.4 for the duration of the bottom time and initial ascent. If you start with a 1.4 PO_2 and descend quickly, your solenoid would fire continuously which could lead to a dangerous oxygen spike at between 300 and 400 ft (91 and 121 m).

Rick Freshee

SHECK EXLEY IN BEN'S HOLE, ANDROS, BAHAMAS 1970'S DURING THESE DIVES, TOM MOUNT & SHECK EXLEY BELIEVED THEY HAD WALLED OUT THE SYSTEM ONLY TO LEARN LATER THAT OTHER EXPLORERS WERE NOW ADDING THOUSANDS OF FEET OF LINE YET MORE!

We continue our descent and complete the mission. Our ascents are gradual in deeper depths, commonly referred to as "***Pyle stops***", we return to our first true decompression stops. We normally do not "stop" per-se, rather we decrease our ascent rate to between 10-20 ft (3-6 m) per minute. At this point of decompression, we may adjust PO_2 or manually maintain set points at 1.5 PO_2. We continue decompression in the usual manner emphasizing "active decompression" (***movement***) as opposed to passive decompression (***just hanging***). We find this procedure increases off gassing and warmth. Divers should be careful not to perform too much exercise at depth because it could lead to bubble formation.

When we reach 70 ft (21 m), we reduce the set point on our rebreathers to about .7 or disable the solenoid. We then switch back to onboard air as a diluent. We purge the breathing bags three times, which (according to our calculations) is sufficient for purging the loop of all helium. If you do not adjust set point down or disable the solenoid, you will waste a great deal of oxygen during the inert gas switch. Upon completion we re-adjust our set point to 1.5 PO_2 and switch our computers to indicate our switch of active diluent. We switch at 70 ft (21 m) formally having done it at 130 ft (39 m) because this makes us feel more energetic post dive. We remain helium-limited for a longer time if we switch at 70 ft (21 m), but the 30 and 20 ft (9 and 6 m) stops wash out the helium well.

We often have a safety diver at the switch point to bring hydration, food, check time to surface, and remove our Trimix bailout cylinders, cameras and whatever else needs to be sent to the surface. A very important item to consider on these longer dives is hydration and caloric intake. A ¼ turn twist-top "Gatorade" bottles work well for underwater re-hydration, with a 50/50 solution of Gatorade to water. Gatorade alone will actually dehydrate you because it will suck all the liquid from your cells to your stomach. Some prefer water to a sports drink, but water is hyper-osmolar and your body has a difficult time retaining it. Take great care not to get saltwater in the drink. Expel air into the bottle to keep its shape. Ingestion of seawater can lead to an upset stomach, which could be mistaken for CNS oxygen toxicity.

A good source of caloric intake is "squeeze" packages of carbohydrate energy boosters. The better ones contain amino acids and polymerized glucose, which regulate the body's sugar processing rate for an even energy boost over longer durations. These squeeze energy boosters also contain anti-oxidants, which we all know hasten the onset of CNS Oxygen toxicity. They are also reasonably easy to ingest. Regardless of the delivery method, divers should remain hydrated and stave off hunger. This will increase circulation and warmth. I notice significant warmth following ingestion of food and liquid. Be careful not to consume too much liquid underwater. Given pressure immersion dieresis, fluid levels in the body move more evenly and spread throughout the body more so than on the surface. There is a possibility that the increase in fluid levels under reduced gravity could lead to pulmonary edema. My personal experience indicates 20 oz of fluid is adequate for me.

For additional warmth, divers should consider heating packs. These can be activated when the divers are starting to get cold on decompression. The heater pack contains sodium acetate, a form of salt, which under normal conditions in an open container will change from a liquid to a solid (freeze) at 130°F (54°C). By placing this solution in a sealed container, the solution can be cooled well below this temperature (as low as 14°F) (-10°C). This sealed container also allows submersion without concern for the effects of pressure. Flexing the stainless steel "trigger" within the sealed container causes a single molecule of liquid to crystallize which starts a chain reaction causing the entire solution to change from a liquid to a solid. This phase change causes the pack to heat to approximately 130°F. Great care should be given to placement of this pad. Do not place it directly against the body because the extreme change in temperature could burn the skin. These packs generally last about two hours.

Do not use heat packs that are activated by air. The increased partial pressure of oxygen can cause these heat packets to over heat and cause serious burns. Not being able to remove the packets while underwater simply increases the length of time the tissue is damaged and can cause third degree burns. There have been at least two instances of fatalities recorded when this type of air activated heat pack was taken into a recompression chamber during a patient's treatment. In Italy, during the first incident, the heat packet caused an explosion and eleven people died. The second incident in Japan claimed the lives of the patient and his wife.

We decompress according to our plan and computers to 20 ft (6 m) where we perform the bulk of our decompression. On rebreathers, it may be very hard to obtain a 1.5 PO_2. Your solenoid could keep firing and waste oxygen trying to maintain a high set-point. We solve this in two ways. Sometimes, we decrease the set point to 1.4 PO_2. Another option is to shut the active diluent and purge the bag with pure oxygen. This raises the PO_2 to about 1.52, effectively turning your rebreather into an oxygen rebreather. Turning off the active diluent also gives an RMV driven alarm for an inadvertent increase in depth. Do not descend below 20 ft (6 m) on pure oxygen! The risk can be mitigated with planning and practice. If you plan on purging the breathing loop with pure oxygen and turning the unit into an oxygen rebreather during decompression, do not forget to accurately track the CNS percentage and take air breaks as necessary. It doesn't take long at 20 ft (6 m) to increase CNS exposure beyond 100% of your daily allotment.

Consideration is being given currently to switching this decompression strategy in favor of continuing with helium based inert gas as the diluent for the entire decompression vice switching to nitrogen based (***air***) diluent. Helium seems to be more "kind" to the body and diffuses 2.67 times faster than nitrogen. However, the "jury" is still out on this. Since we are breaking ground on this type of diving and there are no studies of these profiles, careful planning and small steps should be taken whenever deciding to

MEL CLARK DESCENDING PAST THE EDGE IN LAKE CRESCENT, WASHINGTON

change the method of decompression that is currently working well. We are also considering switching to an on board diluent that is breathable on the bottom. This would eliminate the nitrox shift at 70 ft (21 m) or push it to an even more shallow depth. Additional considerations would allow us to dive from and return to the surface without shifting gasses sands an oxygen flush at 20 ft (6 m).

On many occasions we spend the last five minutes of our 10 ft (3 m) stop actually at 10 ft (3 m) (instead of the usual 20 ft) (6 m) breathing air. This is a way to purge the high PO_2 from my blood before the final ascent. Sometimes we perform this "air stop" following completion of all required decompression. Most of the rebreather divers we know see no benefit to completing a 10 ft (3 m) stop, and I tend to agree. However, following an expedition dive, we have set protocols in place that require us to stop at 10 ft (3 m) and gradually decrease our depth until we surface. The final ascent is crucial. Do it very slowly because the largest change in pressure of the whole dive is from 20 ft (6 m) to the surface.

We have found breathing surface oxygen impairs communication, increases risk of vascular PO_2 swings (when taking the regulator out to talk to someone) compounded by effects of dehydration and evaporative cooling in the lungs. In short, we find it to be more a hindrance than help. Our current practice is to surface and breathe air while still floating in the water. We allow at least 5-10 minutes before we get in the boat.

This allows abatement of O_2-induced vasoconstriction while we are in a gravity-free environment, and when we're least likely to do any nuclei-inducing physical activity. We keep the O_2 at the ready, in case someone doesn't feel right and/or wants to do in-water recompression.

We never perform dives of this magnitude more than one time per day. Additionally, varying inert gas content on long missions could limit the amount of inert gas stored in the slow tissues.

Out of necessity, deep diving has been a trial and error process. Not enough people are performing deep dives to justify massive studies and still fewer are performing these deeper dives on rebreathers. The protocols herein are not recommendations. They are non-imperially derived set of procedures that work for us. We do not advocate divers use these procedures, but seek training from a reputable training organization such that they can arm themselves with the information required to survive and have fun while going past the edge of technical diving.

Chapter Twenty Three
Expeditions - Wrecks

Joseph Dituri M.S.
~ Contributions from Kevin Gurr
and Christina Young

Information Gathering

History is important to divers. When launching an expedition to a wreck, history and historic perspective, with respect to the sinking of a ship or method of deployment, is extremely important. Expedition planners need to conduct background research, which may consist of historical renditions as well as eyewitness accounts. Excellent places for this type of information are the National Archives, the Internet and the Naval Institute Press. Additionally, public libraries may have applicable newspaper articles. Shipyards where the vessel was built or modified may also prove valuable when searching for deck plans, construction information and last modified pieces of machinery. Such plans may make penetration easier and less dangerous.

Treasure hunting or salvaging all or part of a vessel may fall under Admiralty law, which is the distinct body of law (both substantive and procedural) governing navigation and shipping. Topics associated with this field in legal reference works may include: shippingnavigation, commerce, insurance, and recreation.

The courts and U.S. Congress wanted to create a uniform body of admiralty law both nationally and internationally in order to facilitate commerce. The federal courts derive their exclusive jurisdiction over this field from the Judiciary Act of 1789 and from Article III § 2 of the US Constitution. Congress regulates admiralty partially through the Commerce Clause. American admiralty law now extends to any waters navigable within the United States for interstate or foreign commerce. Admiralty jurisdiction includes maritime matters not involving interstate commerce as well as recreational boating within these waters.

Unlike land-based volunteer acts to save property, the person who saves property at sea is entitled to a reward, which is computed in light of the fundamental public policy involved. When the property has been abandoned, anyone may become a "salvor." If the owner wants to reclaim his property in the future, he would take it subject to a lien for the salvage claim. The owner in possession of the property does not have to accept an offer of salvage. Some examples of a typical act of salvage are; recovering a ship's bell, recovering art or china from a ship, or removal of part of the ship's structure.

As was noted earlier, certain factors must be met for an act to qualify for salvage. For property to become subject to salvage it must be in the water or on a beach or reef.

Mel Clark

Leon Scamahorn in the engine room of the *Speigel Grove* in Florida

James Rozzi

ANDY DONN SHOOTING VIDEO ON THE THREE MASTED SAILING SCHOONER *ARBY MAID* IN THE DRY TORTUGAS

With respect to what concerns the amount of a salvage award, a court opinion from *The Blackwall is often cited: "Courts of admiralty usually consider the following circumstances as the main ingredients in determining the amount of the award to be decreed for a salvage service:"*

(1) *"The labor expended by the salvors in rendering the salvage service*

(2) *The promptness, skill and energy displayed in rendering the service and saving the property*

(3) *The value of the property employed by the salvors in rendering the service, and the dangers to which such property was exposed*

(4) *The risk incurred by the salvors in securing the property from the impending peril*

(5) *The value of the property saved*

(6) *The degree of danger from which the property was rescued"*

The ship, freight and cargo are taken into account in assessing the value of the property. The salvage award can never be greater than the value of the salved property and will most often be lower, except in the case of abandoned or derelict property. From what the author has seen in court cases here substantial values are involved, awards tend to be under 20% of the value of the property.

It is important to consult local laws and research ownership of a wreck. It may also be necessary to obtain permission from state or federal groups to perform dives on "their assets." You can research permits when looking at vessel registry. Many complicated laws exist to protect owners from sea thieves. The Internet is an excellent resource to research these laws fully. The bounty you seek and recover may be plundered by law enforcement officials or a court if you fail to follow the rules.

Surface Support Selection & Logistics

This selection is very important. These people are your link to the surface. It may be beneficial to select a person who coordinates the overall expedition. Often this responsibility falls upon the lead diver. Most times, it should be a separate person. The divers have significant responsibilities without the responsibility of mission coordinating. A surface coordinator allows divers to concentrate on their mission, which is getting back safely.

Logistics is the Achilles heel of any expedition. Every aspect of an expedition must be planned. Seemingly small inconveniences become extremely complicated on an expedition, such as tending to dietary needs as well as waste disposal. Many tasks we routinely perform, such as air travel may be difficult with technical diving gear. Most airlines have cargo limitations of 50-70 lbs per bag, and they have issue with transporting hazardous materials and compressed gas containers. Careful coordination with the cargo operator or airline is necessary when you attempt to ship rebreathers, booster pumps and sodasorb. Most airport security personnel are unfamiliar with these items and could mistake them for a bomb. Significant interaction prior to team deployment is required to ensure all gear arrives at the destination. Ensure all oxygen/diluent cylinders are drained and scrubber material has Materials Safety Data Sheet and paperwork accompanying the shipment.

Redundant or bailout rebreathers offer a lightweight alternative to OC bailout. Additionally, oxygen CCR units significantly extend the duration of minimal oxygen supplies and reduce the overall expedition footprint.

The boat captain is vital. This person can be the difference between life and death. Someone experienced in technical diving and surface support is a must. A chase boat is also required such as a Rigid Hulled Inflatable Boat (***RHIB***) or a small open cockpit boat. Minimally one boat is required, but two affords you the ability to chase after more than one lost diver at a time and improves safety. If the expedition is from a large live-aboard vessel, a small boat can give surface support crews a more timely response to any potential emergency. The boat captain needs to be briefed on the overall expedition and then briefed to know what to expect on every dive. This charter is not a normal one wherein the captain has been to the sight and knows the current and bottom conditions. Expedition environments are generally ground breaking and often the surrounding surface areas are treacherous.

The boat should be large enough to accommodate all the divers sleeping comfortably as well as enough room for equipment and gearing spaces. Additional consideration should be given to boats that have compressors and gas fill stations. The time, effort and energy it takes to mount an expedition will pale in comparison to the disappointment if you are required to leave station because you do not have adequate bailout or gas to complete the expedition. Gas boosters have become more available and with the advent the mini-booster, no expedition should be without one. Additionally, portable chambers have debuted and are extremely effective. Prior to chartering a boat, significant dialog should occur between the owners/operator and the clients.

Finally, ladders need to be suitable for the divers laden with expedition level equipment to enter and exit.

As an expedition leader, you have a fiduciary responsibility of care for those on the expedition. The paperwork of the boat should be up to date as well as a current U.S. Coast Guard safety inspection. Any captain for hire is required to have relevant qualifications and the boat should be insured. Significant practice is required to get

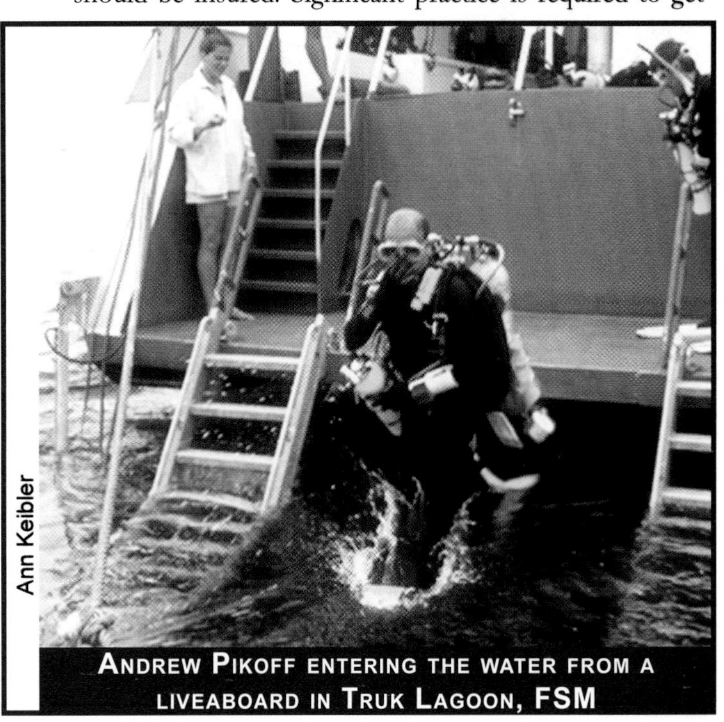

Andrew Pikoff entering the water from a liveaboard in Truk Lagoon, FSM

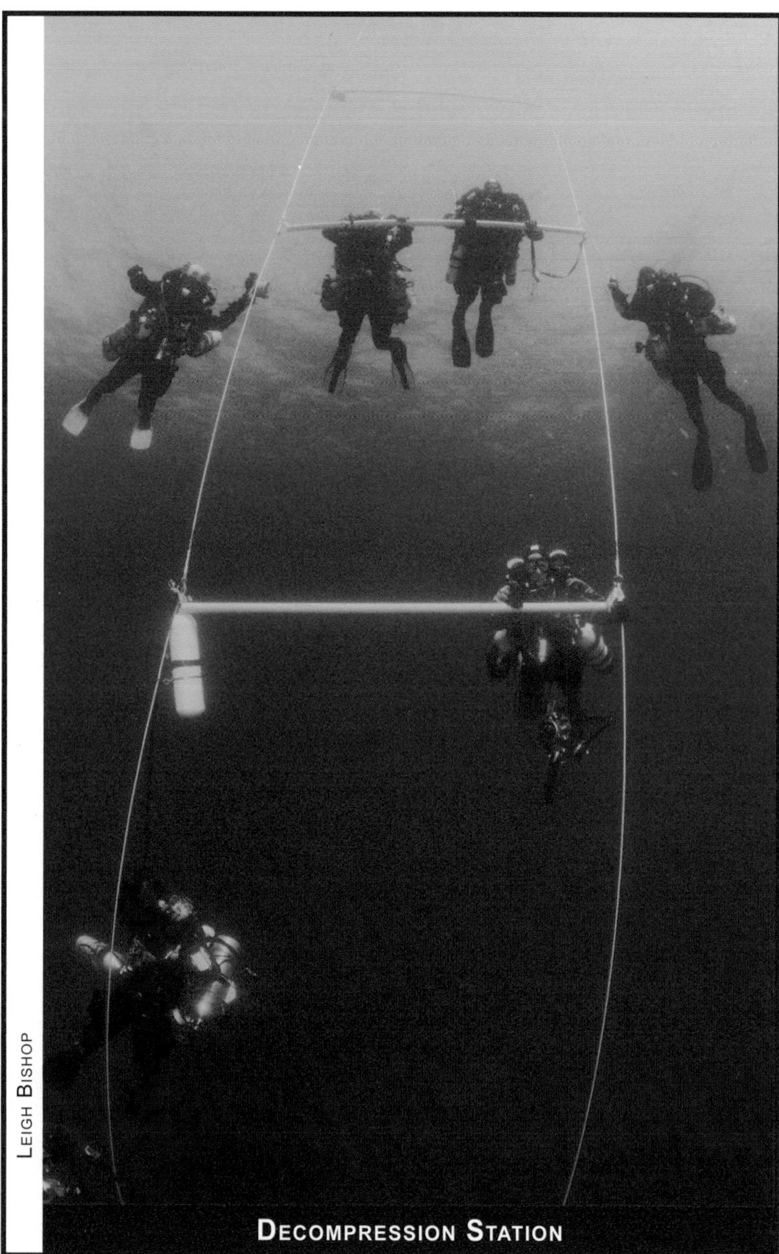

Decompression Station

every expedition should have a primary and a back up for location of teams and the sight of the wreck.

Prior to the expedition, emergency drills should be practiced and hard spots identified. This includes in water and surface support positions. It is as important to know what happens if a diver sends up a red marker indicating low on gas as it is to know how to abandon ship and where the life rafts are located. Moreover, all positions should be practiced by all personnel such that people can multitask on different days. This reduces the overall number of people required to come on the trip.

Sponsorship

Obtaining sponsors is a large part of any expedition. The best thing is to try is gain one single benefactor who will sponsor your cause. Because there are not enough philanthropists in the world, you may have to seek assistance of several sponsors. Most diving manufacturers would be glad to support a worthy cause. Manufactures typically do not want to be associated with an expedition that has a limited chance for success. A well thought-out plan will help you succeed. Additionally, sponsors do not want to be associated with "loose cannon" divers. Manufacturers prefer to support expeditions that further their company's goals such as conservation, exploration or preservation. Alignment to similar goals will help you. Do not be afraid to offer publicity in return for a discount or donation. Web pages are an excellent place for publicity and a good avenue to get your word out.

the team used to the required safety procedures and daily boat operations. Practice is required to ensure the team functions well together.

Weather services such as National Oceanic and Atmospheric Administration (***NOAA***) are helpful to determine tides, currents, prevailing winds and bottom types. Additionally, local vessel traffic may be monitored on a VHF radio. Most boats have VHF radios, but if you are not in direct line of sight with land or another vessel, communications may be difficult. The team should consider a ham radio or satellite phone capable of communication at the maximum range. Finally, GPS systems are so light and portable now that

Liability

If you are planning an expedition and soliciting the assistance of others, give considerable thought to your responsibilities and potential liability. All personnel attending and assisting with the expedition should sign liability releases or waivers. It is well worth the money to have this formatted by a professional with your interests at heart. Contracts should be arranged between all parties so everyone knows his/her responsibilities and expectations.

Expeditions are pushing the envelope. Risk is inherent. Everyone should be aware of the risks beforehand. Additionally, include liability releases for your sponsors and the owners of the property on which (or from which) you are conducting the expedition. As a method of protection, it is wise for EVERYONE to carry some kind of decompression insurance that will allow them to expedite treatment if they are bent…such as DAN diving insurance.

Decompression Stations

The function of a decompression station is to provide a stable platform from which a dive team can complete the decompression phase. **Advantages and disadvantages of these systems include but are not limited to:**

1. A place to stage emergency equipment
2. Allows the team to stay together in a tidal environment
3. Provides a visual reference to assist with buoyancy control (stations)
4. Provides extra safety in the event of an oxygen incident or where oxygen durations need to be extended.
5. Provides a common communication point

Disadvantages:

1. High level of individual discipline required to act as a team
2. Divers have to be able to return to the shot/anchor line/station
3. Habitat set-up may be complex

Changing conditions may require different adaptations to the decompression station concept. To help reduce further problems as a result of separation, decompression "drop stations" are sometimes used.

A method of underwater communication should be developed. We use through-water communications and surface marker buoys (***SMBs***) in combination to signal the surface. The boat captain or surface coordinator can listen to conversation on comms and coordinate a recovery. If the comms fail, every diver carries two different colored SMBs. One is red. One is yellow. Yellow buoys are for non-emergency situations. In the unlikely event that the surface team sees a red SMB, they immediately drive to it in the chase boat and clip on a weighted bail-out tank that slides down the line to us. Then, they immediately deploy a safety diver down the line. Practice reactions to emergency situations regularly. While expedition planning does not lie solely with surface support, surface support personnel usually perform the lion's share.

Drop Stations

These are used when an emergency signal is seen from a diver at the surface as described previously. The drop station will be a line as long as the deepest planned gas switch. The line will have on it at least a cylinder of each of the deep-water decompression gases tied on at the maximum operating depth of each gas. Cylinder valves will have been pressurised and turned off to prevent free-flowing of regulators. In some cases the shallow decompression gas will also be on the line, but usually as there is more time to correct a problem when shallow, this safety gas will be carried on the boat and only dropped if the safety diver deems it necessary. Too many cylinders make the drop station unwieldy and prone to tangling.

Connecting to a Wreck

Once over the wreck site, an important consideration is how to get divers to the wreck from the dive boat. There are several methods, and some are favored over others depending on ocean conditions, environment, and regional customs. The most prevalent three methods are described here in. When deciding to grapnel a wreck or use a shot line, factors to consider include: visibility, conditions of wreck/deep holds and depth of relief.

Hooking a Wreck - When visibility is less than 10 ft (3 m) it is best to grapnel into the wreck (hook the wreck) rather than use a shot line. If the shot lands more than 10 to 20 ft (3 to 6 m) from the wreck, a whole dive might be spent trying to find the wreck. Conditions of the wreck are important such as weak structure or fishing nets. A grapnel could get caught in a net but a shot line might go through the net and would be hard to retrieve. A shot landing in a deep hold is much more difficult to pull out do to the weight of the shot. If using a grapnel on a wreck with relief, letting out only enough line to reach the top of the wreck can give the diver the option of diving shallower.

(L to R) Jeff Manor waits as Jerry Whatley exits the Patrol Bomber Lockheed PV-2 Harpoon's fuselage in Lake Washington. This plane was ditched in 1947

Shotting a Wreck - Shot lining a wreck is the preferred method if the visibility is greater than 10 ft (3 m), the condition of structure/no deep holds and the wreck is low lying. A shot can be any type of heavy object (preferably stainless) to which an anchor line can be attached and should weigh 40-50 pounds. Using a heavy duty locking carabineer, the chain and anchor line is attached to the shot. When the captain is over the desirable location over the wreck, the shot and line is tossed over the side with a large float attached at end. There should be 75 to 125 ft (22.5 to 37.5 m) of extra line to allow for current, wind and/or choppy seas.

A team of two divers should "tie in." The lead diver detaches anchor line from shot and secures chain and line to the wreck. The second diver can send shot up with lift bag for the boat to retrieve. If the boat has a windlass the shot may be attached to anchor chain once the lead diver has tied in. The lead diver signals crew by sending up a signal that the crew can spot immediately. The boat then motors up to float and ties off. Another advantage of using a shot line, the captain can "tie into" virtually any place on the wreck.

Parachuting a Wreck - Have the vessel captain drop the shot line. Then use a depth sounder to verify that it is on the wreck. Next the boat takes divers up current and drops them into the water. The divers free fall to the wreck in the direction of the current. This method is excellent if the current is far too strong to directly pull yourself down a fixed line. In fact it is the only safe way to get down in deeper water with a high current running

There is a possibility that divers might miss the wreck, but experience and knowing how fast the current or tide runs is a must to ensure delivery on top of the wreck. At the end of the dive the last dive team pulls the shot line loose so they can all drift and sometimes the remainder of the team needs to ascend using their personal lift bags

Documentation

When locating archaeological specimens, specific artifact documentation is required, along with tagging the finds with unique numbers and pinpointing their position with triangulation and photo grids. On larger vessels the position of off-ship wreckage may be of use in establishing a cause of sinking. For instance with the ***HMHS Britannic*** and some of the sunken U-boats a large section of wreckage is located away from the main site.

Chapter Twenty Four The Practical Aspects Of Deep Wreck Diving

Joe Citelli

Deep wreck exploration originated as the genre of adventuresome groups of divers who became enamored with the mysteries hidden in the shipwrecks beneath their local waters. Quickly labeled "cowboys" for their defiance of all convention, these men and women boldly ventured where few were willing to go. Paying a heavy price in lives and injuries, they paved the way for those who would follow in their footsteps. Simultaneously, their subterranean counterparts were pushing limits by refining both technology and technique and using it to explore underwater caves. Advances in decompression theory, willingness to experiment, and mainstreaming the use of mixed gasses enabled them to attain previously unheard of depths and distances.

Eventually, curiosity won out and the two groups became interested in each others methods. ***Wreckers*** became ***cavers*** and ***cavers*** became ***wreckers***, each borrowing and learning from the other. Fraught with controversy over style and technique, they ultimately selected the best each had to offer, resulting in the marriage of two distinct styles of diving and giving birth to the modern techniques in use today. This chapter will define and describe the fundamentals of the methods borne of this marriage. It will address the psychology, methodology and mechanics of deep wreck expeditions from the inception of the mission to its execution. While not intended to be a how-to guide, hopefully the reader will gain an understanding of this subject matter before engaging in serious deep wreck exploration. Topics covered will be the psychology and state of mind necessary to successfully engage in deep exploration plus the basic mechanics so often ignored but crucial to mission success.

MEL CLARK

JO CRIBLEY CCR DIVING ON THE *HYDRO ATLANTIC* ANCHOR WINDLESS

Psychology

Contrary to common belief, deep exploration is a mental discipline rather than a physical endeavor. Successful missions are the product of multiple components, the most important of which are discipline and organization. One must possess the mindset and confidence that planned missions will be safe and successful and have the organizational skills to make them happen according to plan. This begins with imaginary rehearsals and visualizations of potential problems and how they will be successfully overcome. Careful planning to the smallest of details must be used to eliminate any doubt or indecision, placing extra emphasis on matters of safety and self rescue. Mentally rehearsing all possible scenarios enhances the

Divers at 250 fsw (77 msw) on the *Carrie Lee*, Grand Cayman, BWI

confidence necessary to overcome problems when they arise. A successful mission depends on a dynamic between the mental and the physical. Explorers must possess the skills necessary to execute a plan and the discipline to follow it. They must identify their personal limits and those of their teammates. Confidence in abilities preserves calm and averts panic in an adverse situation but cannot compensate for exceeding personal limits.

Diver training programs typically encompass both physical and mental rehearsals for a variety of staged emergencies. During these drills it is always assumed the diver is at least reasonably calm and able to function. Real life experience has taught us that fear management is a personality trait unique to the individual. Training can somewhat modify uncontrolled reactions but does so only to a limit. Surpassing that limit ultimately allows fear and anxiety to emerge, often times uncontrolled. Identification of all participants' personal limits is essential to a successful mission. Facing certain disaster is not the time to discover one's innate inability to function under high stress. A little fear is a healthy thing but indecision born of fear and anxiety has no place in deep exploration.

Self Confidence

Deep wreck exploration also requires independent thought and confidence in ones' abilities. The capacity to allow personal instincts to overrule established protocol when circumstances require it is an essential for survival. A bad situation can be exacerbated by strict adherence to a learned protocol that does not address the problem. For example, remaining at depth to complete deep stops in accordance with training makes little sense when gas supplies are limited. Failure to put risk in proper perspective and fear to deviate from training sometimes encourages divers to make choices that do not solve their immediate problem. Deep wreck exploration requires its participants understand their training is a continually evolving tool they must personally develop, not a panacea for every situation.

Emergency Management Planning & Crisis Management

All team members must maintain a reasonable degree of personal fitness to minimize the potential for injury, be it Decompression Sickness (***DCS***) or other. They must also be physically able to effect a rescue if need be and deal with any emergencies that may arise. The boat should be equipped with all of the appropriate marine communication and navigation equipment including an operational satellite phone. Additionally, all participants should be familiar with In-Water Recompression (***IWR***) and be comfortable with the idea of using it as it may well be the only option. To that end, an adequate supply of emergency oxygen and a full-face mask should always be available and readily accessible.

Ideally, one expedition member should be an Emergency Medical Technician (***EMT***) and another should be trained in the use of a portable chamber, if available. This would enable the administration of IV fluids while recompressing in the case of severe DCS. Inclusion of an EMT and a portable chamber with a qualified operator should be given serious consideration when planned locations are remote. This is especially true when diving in colder water where IWR may not be feasible.

Deep wreck explorers must have the basic tenets of crisis management ingrained in them. The most fundamental of these is to focus on and solve the immediate problem at hand, and deal with future problems when and if they present themselves. They must also use caution and not become so completely consumed by the problem they are trying to solve that they fail to address the rest of the dive. This can result in effectively solving the existing problem while simultaneously creating a greater one. Usually, the initial event, while serious, is but a small part of the complete picture. Becoming completely immersed in it and ignoring the rest of the dive can have dire consequences. A misguided, singular focus on a specific problem is detrimental to all else, and is at best counterproductive, usually resulting in things devolving into a far more serious threat.

Mission Control & Organizational Structure

Deep explorers must always remain in control of their mission. Decisions to dive or not dive must be made without influence or pressure from sources outside the team or even overzealous team members. Completion of the mission must be second to all matters of safety. Sponsors' needs can sometimes conflict with this. Time and monetary considerations will often be used in an attempt to influence the decision making process. These can never be permitted to justify an otherwise bad decision.

A well organized expedition must operate using a team concept. Independent buddy teams comprised of individuals whose abilities complement each other is the preferred situation. These teams are responsible for their own safety and self rescue. All teams need to maintain a high degree of situational awareness and be available to assist other buddy teams should the need arise.

Points to Remember

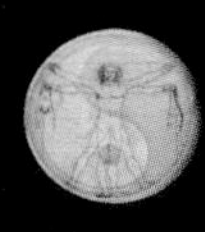

Buddies are self-reliant and self-sufficient and do not require each other to do the dive, but rather, their association enhances their abilities and mission safety.

Much has been written about buddy diving. All too often experienced divers will opt to dive solo because they think a buddy will interfere with their personal mission. Nothing could be further from the truth. To function as a buddy team it is only necessary for buddies to maintain a constant awareness of each other. They are not required to remain side by side. The decision to explore a cabin or passageway simply requires they inform one and other. In the event one encounters difficulties and does not return within a reasonable time they know where to look. Buddy diving also requires all entry and exit phases of the dive be done together.

Buddies are not a crutch to permit diving beyond ones' abilities or to facilitate otherwise reckless actions. They are a tool to be used towards the safe and efficient achievement of a mission goal. ***Buddies are self reliant and self sufficient and do not require each other to do the dive, but rather, their association enhances their abilities and mission safety.***

Buddy teams should be selected with an attempt to match experience levels, personalities, and abilities. Individual

James Rozzi

200 fsw (60 msw) Japanese destroyer *Oite* in Truk Lagoon

strengths and weaknesses should complement each other. Pairing two equally skilled and experienced divers, one of whom is bold and the other more conservative can be a good match since they may nicely balance each other.

Good team mates must also be good ship mates. Close quarters at sea demand all team members understand that basic boat etiquette is critical to a successful expedition. Participants must be aware of their surroundings and the needs of other divers and the boat crew. Teammates should know not to block passages with either their person or their equipment. They should be vigilant and ready to assist in all phases of the operation, such as the preparation of lines and the deployment of the grapnel or anchor.

Equipment

Uniformity in equipment configuration is essential to mission safety and success. Expedition members must be similarly equipped and configured with compatibility in mind. To facilitate rapid emergency response everyone should carry similar equipment in a similar place on their person. Interchangeability of all life support and safety equipment is a must, and any non-standard equipment should be disallowed. Since most deep exploration is now being done on Closed Circuit Rebreathers (***CCR***), uniformity is even more important. On CCR expeditions, dissimilar quick disconnects should be prohibited. The inability of divers to "plug into" each others' gas supplies defeats the team bailout concept. At a bare minimum, in addition to whatever bailout and decompression gasses are required, each diver should have two lift bags, two reels, and a light for signaling plus whatever equipment may be required to effect safe penetrations.

Team members should be minimally equipped with:

- A suitable primary light for both illumination and signaling
- Back-up lights in the event of a primary failure during a penetration
- A knife
- Shears capable of cutting wire leader
- Two lift bags
- Two reels as previously described
- Any special equipment specific to the task at hand

For remote area exploration a Personal Locator Beacon (***PLB***) is recommended. This is a small Emergency Position Indicating Radio Beacon (***EPIRB***) one can store in a canister carried on the waist harness similar to that used for a light. When activated, the EPIRB transmits an emergency signal and Global Positioning System (***GPS***) coordinates to a satellite and relays this information to local Search and Rescue (***SAR***) authorities. Sudden weather changes and the potential for boats to become disabled make this is a good addition to each buddy team's kit. Additionally, a few flares and a signaling mirror may also be beneficial and can be stored in the canister with the PLB. Each independent buddy team should be so equipped to insure survival in the event of a lost at sea emergency.

Extreme depths require the use of a reel rather than a spool for marker deployment. Reels should be a simple open design so the line is easily accessible should it slip off the spool. Divers must be skilled in reel use so they can confidently deploy it without fear of it "***bird nesting***" (tangling). They must also possess the special skills necessary to deal with the challenges of extreme depth, some of which are quick reactions and the ability to think creatively. Some times current *shear* (opposing currents at different depths) will drag a marker horizontally and play out all of the line on a reel well before it reaches the surface, dragging the diver past his first deco stops. A second reel must be ready and the diver adept enough to clip the second reel to the first to avoid this problem. Minimally, divers need at least two reels, each of which carry heavy line long enough to reach the surface (minimum #24 braid although #36 is preferred). They also need at least two marker buoys in the event one fails or is lost. Buddies should be equipped similarly such that each team has no less than four reels and four markers.

At depth, work contributes to CO_2 buildup, DCS, and on open circuit accelerates gas consumption. It is your enemy and should be avoided if at all possible. To that end, probably the most valuable tool a deep explorer can have is a Diver Propulsion Vehicle (***DPV***). Of course, it must be one capable of tolerating extreme depths or it will quickly become a huge liability. A flooded DPV becomes extremely negative and can easily drag a diver to the bottom if it is not dealt with properly. A lift bag dedicated to DPV rescue must be readily available so it can immediately be used to send a flooded vehicle to the surface. Inside a wreck, a DPV can also become a very efficient silt generating machine. Only highly skilled operators should ever consider penetrating a wreck using a DPV.

There are three modes of water entry when DPV diving. The ***first*** and simplest method is for the diver to get in the water and have someone hand the DPV off to him. This only works in no or very low current situations.

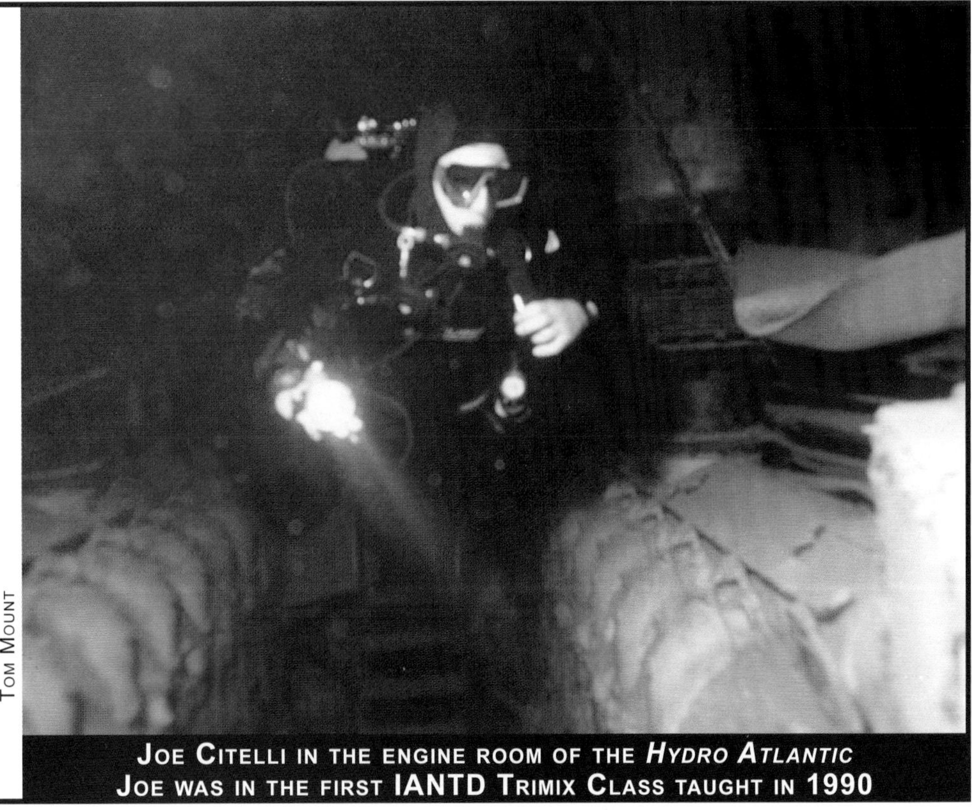
TOM MOUNT

JOE CITELLI IN THE ENGINE ROOM OF THE *HYDRO ATLANTIC*
JOE WAS IN THE FIRST **IANTD** TRIMIX CLASS TAUGHT IN **1990**

The ***second*** method is to stand on the swim platform or at an exit point with the DPV standing on its shroud and the tow rope clipped to the crotch strap D-ring. Holding the DPV by its nose cone or body handle the diver lifts it and jumps into the water, using his free hand to hold his mask and mouth piece. As soon as the diver hits the water the DPV is manipulated into position and he begins his descent.

The ***third*** method is actually the easiest but requires the most skill and a bit of upper body strength. The diver sits on the gunnel with all stages, deco bottles and any other hanging paraphernalia over the outer edge to avoid it being caught. He then lifts the DPV sideways onto his lap so that the battery compartment is resting on his thighs and holds the nose with one hand and the propeller shroud with the other. When the captain gives the go ahead a back roll is executed. Mid-air the diver pushes the shroud away from his body and towards the hand that is holding the nose handle while that hand is pulling the nose of the DPV down and into position. The diver turns to the direction he needs to be traveling and begins his descent. This is a very effective method if done in a continuous fluid motion and facilitates the rapid descents necessary for high current exploration diving.

Dive Execution

There are two basic methods of executing a wreck dive. The ***first*** and most common is anchor diving. The boat anchors into the wreck and a "***tag***" line is tied to the anchor line so that divers can enter the water and pull themselves along side the boat to the anchor line and pull down to the wreck. This works well in low or no current situations. Since the dive boat is anchored and immobile it absolutely requires that a chase boat be in the water with a crew ready in the event of an emergency.

When anchor diving, the first team in the water sets the anchor and does the tie in so that the boat can not break loose and drift away. The last team undoes this and frees the anchor.

The ***second*** method is live boating, of which there are ***three*** variations. The ***first*** is to free drop the wreck. The captain marks the wreck on the bottom finder, calculates the current and the team dives when the captain gives the go ahead. This method requires highly experienced captains and divers.

Divers must be able to descend rapidly, pick a depth to drift at and watch the bottom while monitoring their depth, time and compass. By estimating the current they need to know when the drop was bad and they missed the wreck. They cannot search for the wreck for more than a predetermined time, after which they must deploy a surface marker buoy from the bottom so the captain will be able

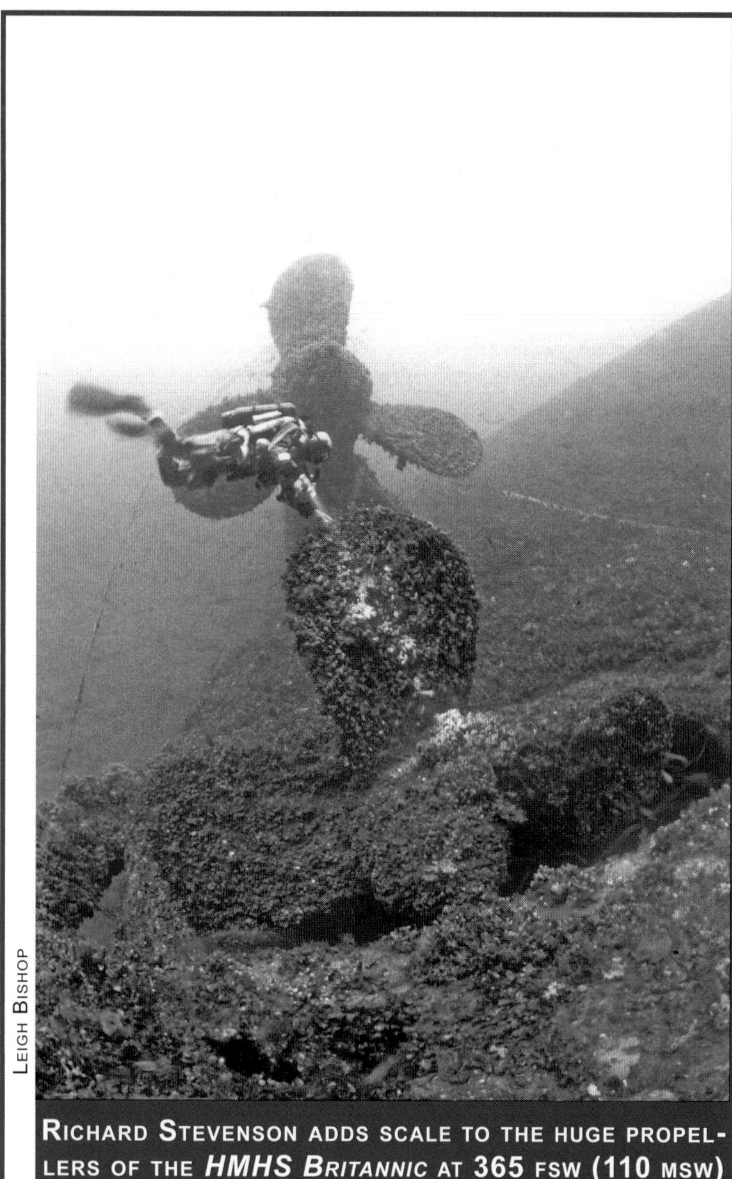

LEIGH BISHOP

RICHARD STEVENSON ADDS SCALE TO THE HUGE PROPELLERS OF THE ***HMHS BRITANNIC*** AT 365 FSW (110 MSW)

to find them. Any undue delay in deploying a marker can make it extremely difficult if not impossible for a captain to find divers. This is of absolute importance and must be completely understood by all team members.

The captain and crew must be ever vigilant for surface markers because they are the only means of communicating whether or not the team is on the wreck. They must be confident that a marker will be deployed as planned and know how many markers the team intends to deploy. This allows them to know when a diver is missing or something has gone awry. Usually, early marker deployment is indicative of a bad drop while no marker after a specified time passes indicates the team is safe and on the wreck.

All team members must know that leaving the bottom at their predetermined times both in the event of a bad drop and with respect to planned bottom times insures that the boat crew is looking for them in the right place and at the right time. Any delay in deploying a surface marker buoy will make the captain's job that much more difficult and unnecessarily jeopardize the divers. Whenever possible the marker must be deployed from the bottom as soon as you leave the site. Lost at sea is not much fun.

The ***second*** variation of live boating, which, in this author's opinion, is the preferred one, makes use of a poly ball, shot line, and grapnel. The captain marks the wreck with the bottom finder and GPS, motors upcurrent and drops the hook into the wreck. If the hook is caught solid the divers can opt to pull down the line (and risk inadvertently freeing it), but most will opt to free drop the wreck. The captain can use the poly ball as a line of sight marker to aid in making the drop. In high current situations it is critical that he align the drop with the wake behind the ball so the divers drift at the correct angle.

The ***third*** variation of live boating occurs when the divers jump into the water holding the end of a line attached to a poly ball. The captain motors an appropriate distance upcurrent, deploys the poly ball with a proper length of line attached to it and the divers jump holding the end of the line to which a carabineer is usually attached. This method requires significantly more skill and team work on the part of all participants. The captain must be able to accurately drop the divers far enough upstream so they can ride the current with the line and the ball. The divers must be able to descend quickly enough to prevent the ball from getting too far ahead of them. This technique requires the lead diver to hold the end of the line while the second diver stays about thirty feet behind and slightly above him, pulling on the line to give the lead diver some slack. As the divers approach the wreck the lead diver must find a tie off point and quickly wrap the line around it securing it with the carabineer. Meanwhile the second diver assists by making sure there is enough slack in the line so the wrap can be made. If necessary, he may have to deliberately snag it on something to buy the first diver more time. In a strong current this can be risky

because getting a limb caught between the line and the hull of a wreck can be quite painful.
The advantage of liveboating with a poly ball and grapnel becomes obvious at the end of the dive. The last divers to leave the wreck free the grapnel (or the chain in the last variety described). They must foul it high enough off the bottom so it will not snag anything or, by employing a quick release, separate the grapnel from the chain and send it to the surface with a small lift bag. Simultaneously, a carabineer is used to secure the remaining chain high enough off the bottom to prevent it from snagging anything. The divers can then ascend drifting with the line and not have to contend with current, a much easier, more pleasant way to decompress, especially in high current areas.

As previously stated, deep wreck explorers must understand the importance of immediately deploying a surface marker buoy when they leave a wreck or if they become separated from the ascent line. This topic is a very serious matter and deserves special attention. Deep waters often have varying currents at different depths. A boat captain may be experiencing a north current with an easterly wind push while the divers on the wreck may be experiencing a southwest current. The only fixed reference in this equation is the wreck. Divers can easily drift a considerable distance from where the captain is expecting to find them if they leave a 300 ft (91.5 m) deep wreck and wait until the 150 ft (46 m) stop before deploying a marker. This makes it quite difficult for them to be located, especially in rough seas. All too often divers fail to recognize how essential surface marker deployment is to their safety and survival and that it is one of the most important skills for them to master.

Ideally, a marker should be deployed as soon as the team leaves the wreck. Sometimes varying currents prevent this. In that instance a specific closed marker buoy should be deployed. This serves as a signal to the captain that the team is making their ascent without benefit of a line and a second marker with a line attached will be deployed as soon as conditions permit. By viewing where the first non tethered marker surfaces in relation to the wreck and looking at the decompression schedule the captain will know where to look for his divers. Failure to observe this protocol almost guarantees becoming lost at sea.

An individual diver or buddy team who fails to observe the established surface marker buoy protocols effectively jeopardizes the safety of everyone by distracting the captains' attention from the group to search for them. Anyone unwilling or unable to deploy a marker per protocol should be excluded from the team.

Another use for the surface marker buoy is that of a distress signal. A specific marker is often designated as an emergency signal indicating there is a problem. A slate can be attached so the exact nature of the problem can be communicated. Otherwise it is a signal to send a safety diver or backup team.

Water Entry & Exit

Too often ignored, coordination of water entry and exit is critical toward mission success and safety. Entries should be in synch with planned bottom times. This permits the buddy team releasing the grapnel to do a head count and insures they leave no one on the wreck. The first buddy team to enter should be the one doing the longest bottom time. They have the responsibility of assuring the surface marker, grapnel or anchor line is properly tied in and secure. All following teams should stagger their entry so that their dives end at approximately the same time as the first team. This permits everyone to ascend together, enhancing safety during the most dangerous phase of the dive, the time when the risk of toxicity, embolism and trouble with predators is the most likely.

Wreck Penetrations

Much has been written about wreck penetration methodology and there are primarily two schools of though on the matter. The first method, embraced by many Northeast Atlantic wreck divers, is called ***Progressive Penetration***. As the name implies, wrecks should be penetrated gradually over a series of dives without benefit of a guide line. The idea is to learn the wreck well enough and be familiar enough with it so you can safely exit using your memory and familiarity with the wreck and her passages. This method is dangerous unless used in conjunction with a guide line as a hedge against the unforeseen such as silt outs caused by other divers or even marine creatures.

The next method is to use a reel and guide line. A reel with a heavy gauge braided line (#36 nylon braid is preferred) is run from open water along whatever passages you explore. Critics of this method claim that it is flawed because if the line breaks the diver has no familiarity with his surroundings

which he could use to find his way out. For that reason, line placement must be done with great care to avoid any sharp edges which could easily sever the line.

In a perfect world, both methods should be combined. Divers should not attempt maximum penetrations of wrecks until they have some familiarity with them, nor should they use familiarity to justify not using a line. A guide line should always be deployed when making a penetration, no matter how familiar you are with the wreck.

The deep explorer has a rather unique circumstance. Typically diving in remote places, he does not have the luxury of returning tomorrow. Multiple dives for familiarization with the wreck are usually not possible. The utility of every dive must be maximized, making the reel and guide line the only viable choice. For that reason the deep explorer must be very skilled in the use of a reel and in line placement. He must also learn to pick out features that will be remembered and be identifiable by feel in the event of a light failure or silt out. Line placement must be done in a manner that allows a zero visibility exit with minimal problems.

Why We Do It

Deep wreck exploration requires a melding of skills and techniques learned over a long period of time. It demands a deep well of experience from which its enthusiasts can draw. Participants must be well versed in a variety of subjects which include mathematics, physics and physiology. A better than average understanding of decompression theory is requisite as is the ability to put technical "book" knowledge to practical use. They must also be blessed with the gift of common sense and have the aptitude to be inventive when necessary.

The deep wreck explorer must also be the adventurer, seaman and scientist possessing the commitment and dedication necessary to accomplish the mission. He must be highly disciplined, willing to endure long, harsh boat rides and accept risk well beyond the norm. Sharks, murky waters, swift currents and remote locations do not deter him. His motivation is the desire to know the unknown, to solve the mystery. Conversely, his rewards can be amazing. There is no description for the feeling one gets dropping into the gloom and viewing a ship which no other human being has seen for 100 years or more. Like a snapshot in time, a virgin wreck will coyly tease your imagination and yet only yield a small part of her mystery. Intrigued, you wonder what happened. Your mind races as you monitor depth and time while wondering what the captain did the day she went down. Coal intended to fuel the boilers covers the bottom as you ponder what might have happened to the crew? Perhaps remnants of a binnacle lead you to speculate on what her intended destination may have been. Some answers come in the form of artifacts. They tell part of a story, giving a glimpse of what life at sea was during her era. An old oil lamp or rotted out cabin latch come into view. They bear testimony to the lady's former glory making you wonder whose eyes last saw light from the lamp, whose hand last turned the latch. Those who can understand this will also know why we do it. The extreme effort, risk and expense of deep wreck exploration are miniscule when compared to the unique rewards its enthusiasts enjoy.

James Rozzi

Divers on the *Arby Maid*, Dry Tortugas

Chapter Twenty Five Expeditions ~ Caves

Martin Robson

Introduction

The purpose of this section is to provide a simple set of guidelines for planning and conducting a diving expedition, in particular looking at those factors which are relevant to cave diving. This does not mean that the content cannot apply to other types of expedition diving. Whilst this section is not intended to be the definitive document for those wishing to plan and conduct their own expeditions, it is hoped that there will be information and advice that expedition planners, leaders and participants will find useful.

There is no set way to plan and conduct an expedition because each one is unique. New ideas are a source of constant updating and change, however, they must build on lessons learned from experience.

Expedition Goals

All expeditions should have a purpose or a mission the participants want to achieve. Regardless of how big and ambitious or how low key your project is there needs to be a clearly defined purpose or aim. A well defined set of objectives may also act to attract team members and possible sponsorship.

Each member of the team must agree with the project mission statement, its aims and objectives and how this will be achieved.

There are many possible goals for a Cave Diving Expedition. The most obvious is the exploration of a new site or new passage within an existing site, however, there are many other opportunities including cave surveying, re-lining a cave, geological, hydrological or other scientific research, photography/videography or simply fulfilment of a personal goal even though the dive may have been done by many divers before you.

Without a laid down plan it will be more difficult to bring success to the expedition or measure this.

Objectives should be:

- Simple
- Measurable
- Achievable
- Realistic
- Set to a Time Frame

Personal needs and ambitions should not be allowed to overtake the needs of the project.

Forward Planning

Research

Some amount of time needs to be spent researching the project. You need to gather all the information you can find to establish current knowledge of the site. There is no point setting out to see if a particular point in a cave can be passed if it has already been done, mapped and visited by hundreds of divers. Research should include all available resources such as web based information, cave diving publications, local caving and cave diving groups, maps, surveys and visits to the site where possible. Don't forget that it is easy to overlook resources in languages other than your own.

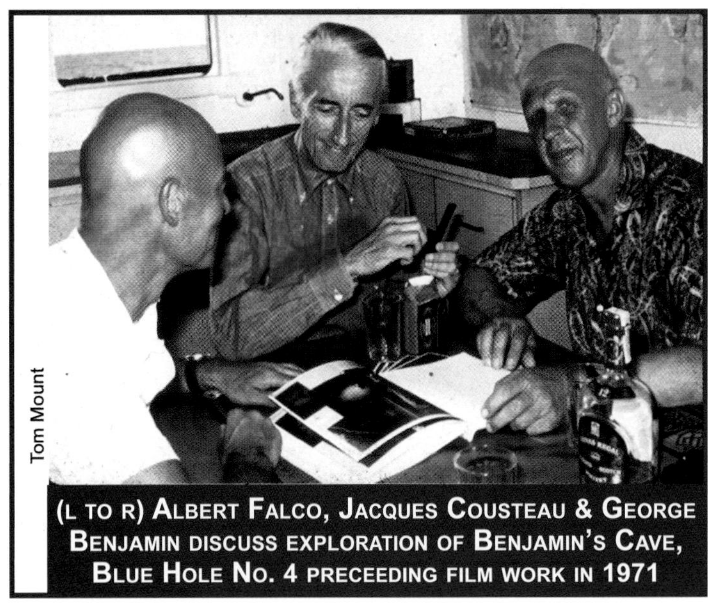

Tom Mount

(L to R) Albert Falco, Jacques Cousteau & George Benjamin discuss exploration of Benjamin's Cave, Blue Hole No. 4 preceeding film work in 1971

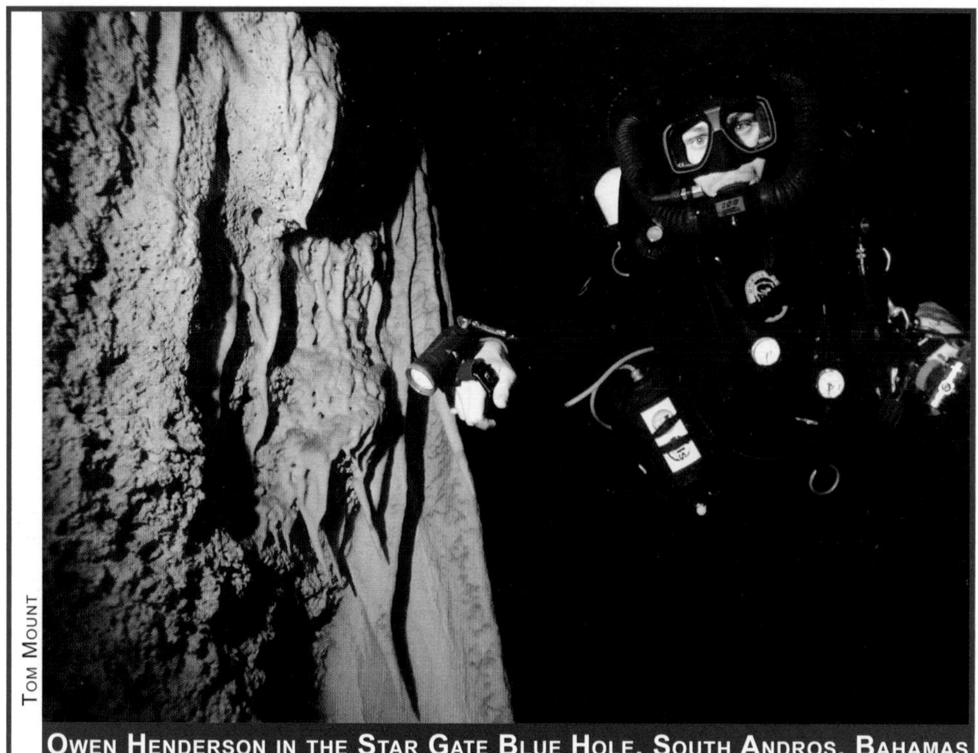

Tom Mount

Owen Henderson in the Star Gate Blue Hole, South Andros, Bahamas

Information pertaining to the actual diving objective may include your own or team members dive experience of the site, limits of current exploration, latest surveys, verbal description from other divers, scientific reports, photos or videos, annual weather patterns and rainfall, water levels and flow, water temperature, visibility and depths.

A certain amount of general information on the site and the area will also prove useful. This information should include items such as transport links, local medical care, accommodation availability and specific information on vehicular access, rights of way, land access and ownership and the local language.

We stood at the gate with an angry farmer and two rather nonplussed local police. None of them spoke a word of English. If we hadn't had someone in the group whose French was fluent we would still be there now, arguing over whether the permissions we had to dive the site were legitimate.

Access

Access arrangements in cave diving are often a delicate issue. At all times diving teams must be aware of land ownership issues and be sensitive to the wishes of private or state land owners and possible access arrangements already negotiated by cave divers local to the area.

Ignorance is no excuse and can lead to loss of access for everyone. In some countries police are empowered to arrest divers, confiscate dive equipment and vehicles if you are caught at a dive site without the appropriate permit

In checking access it is also considered to be good manners to make sure that the cave(s) that are the target of the expedition goals are not already being actively explored or surveyed by another team of divers. If this is the case it does not necessarily meant that the trip will need to be abandoned, but it may need to be postponed until the current team are "finished" with the cave site. This will need to be discussed with the divers currently exploring the chosen site.

Obviously if a team say they are exploring a system it would be reasonable to expect them to be active in doing so. It is not unheard of for a team to publicise the fact they there is an ongoing exploration or survey, yet not dive the site for a number of months or even years. If this is the case it will be up to the project manager, lead divers and team as a whole to decide if the trip will go ahead.

Once sufficient information has been gathered it will be possible to make a basic plan of requirements and overall schedule.

Personnel

Often the first decisions will be to do with expedition personnel. How many? What diving qualifications and experience do they need? Is non-diving support necessary? What non-diving skills will be required or useful? How will the team be invited or chosen to participate? Will there be a need for team-training prior to the expedition and if so, how, when and where will this take place?

Dates & Time Frame

When will the expedition take place? This must be based on a time when local conditions are likely to be favourable and team availability. How much time does the expedition need including travelling to and from the site? Does this allow sufficient preparation time?

Equipment

Determine necessary personal diving equipment, team diving equipment, safety equipment, vehicles, surface and support items. Who will supply the equipment? On a small scale trip the team members will supply equipment but some things including safety equipment and compressors can be hired. Ground breaking projects often attract sponsorship from manufacturers in the form of equipment given or loaned for the duration of the project. Equipment must be in good service at the start and well maintained throughout. Who will do this and what spares, parts & tools must be taken.

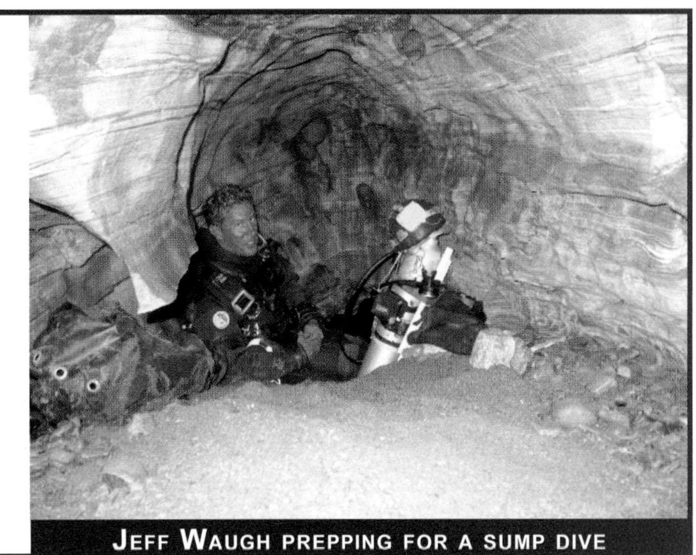

JEFF WAUGH PREPPING FOR A SUMP DIVE

Four of us stood around wondering what the next move should be. The immigration authorities were allowing us to enter the country but there was no way they were letting us take our rebreathers in with us!

Local Services

Caves are often in remote locations. There are usually no dive centres. Hotels and restaurants can be seasonal, shops close some days and fuel stations may only have deliveries one a week. Campsites may not be willing to accommodate compressors or have the capacity to charge batteries from DPVs and lights. You should determine what, if any, local diving services are available, locate the nearest fuel stations, find and book accommodation for the team, check out restaurants and supermarket opening. If you can find a local contact they will be of immeasurable help in local logistics planning.

Travel & Transport

This may be as simple as booking flights/ferries or arranging a simple package holiday or could involve shipping large amounts of kit to remote areas with difficult access. There are companies who will do this for you but the cost is often prohibitive. Either way time should be allowed for delays, immigration and damage during transport. Local advice on how to bring items into the particular country will be invaluable.

Finance

Most small expeditions are financed by the team but the amount/items each member funds may not be equal. Each diver may be responsible for their own costs, support divers or non-diving support personnel's costs may be subsidised by lead divers or the team leader, team costs should be estimated and clarified. Team members should be aware of financial commitments prior to the expedition including what financial penalties there will be if they drop out of the trip. Some expeditions may be lucky enough to get sponsorship, scientific grants or be televised. Equipment items donated, grant money or profit earned should be allocated and agreed upon by all parties.

A Risk Assessment should be carried out to identify potential problems and ways of preventing or solving them.

Team Roles

Deciding who to take or invite on an expedition can make the difference between success or failure, team harmony or a stressful, fractious dive trip.

In choosing a team for the trip interpersonal skills are as important as diving skills. It also helps if each team member can bring something more that just diving to the

overall project. A support diver who can blend and mix gasses or repair regulators as well as provide dive support would be a genuine asset to the team. For large projects pre-assessment dives may be appropriate but often divers are invited because they are already known to the team leader.

Lead Diver(s)

Generally these will be the divers who will have decided on the scope of the project and whose aims and ambitions are the driving force behind the expedition. It may be, however, that the lead divers have been asked to join the team to help that team meet its aims.

Obviously lead divers must be highly qualified, experienced and motivated to the success of the mission lead divers, however, they still need to be a member of the team and mindful of the fact that the dives they are hoping to do cannot happen without the team supporting them.

Support Divers

Support divers do not have to be the best divers in the world but they must be comfortable and capable at the level of dives they are undertaking. A diver giving shallow water support to a decompressing lead diver does not need to be an experienced trimix diver. Common sense and being a team player are as important as diving skills.

As mentioned earlier, if support divers can bring more to the project than just their diving skills they will be a real asset to the team.

We chose our team not just because of their skills as divers, but because we got on well together as people, and they each brought something a little extra to the group. SR, being a police officer was used to dealing with people and working under stress. AA and TS were both accomplished trimix divers, had experience in diving in very harsh conditions and of servicing & maintaining compressors in those environments. JC was an engineer and regulator service technician. NS was a doctor with training in hyperbaric medicine. Every support diver had extra skills that could be of value to the project.

Surface Support

If a willing volunteer is available then the luxury of having surface-only support personnel will allow the divers to concentrate on their own role within the team and can take time pressure away from having to do the day to day tasks needed for the smooth running or the operation.

Typically surface cover roles can include:

- Gas blending
- Equipment maintenance
- Medical cover if suitably trained and qualified
- General dive site logistics
- Back-up and/or reserve team manager

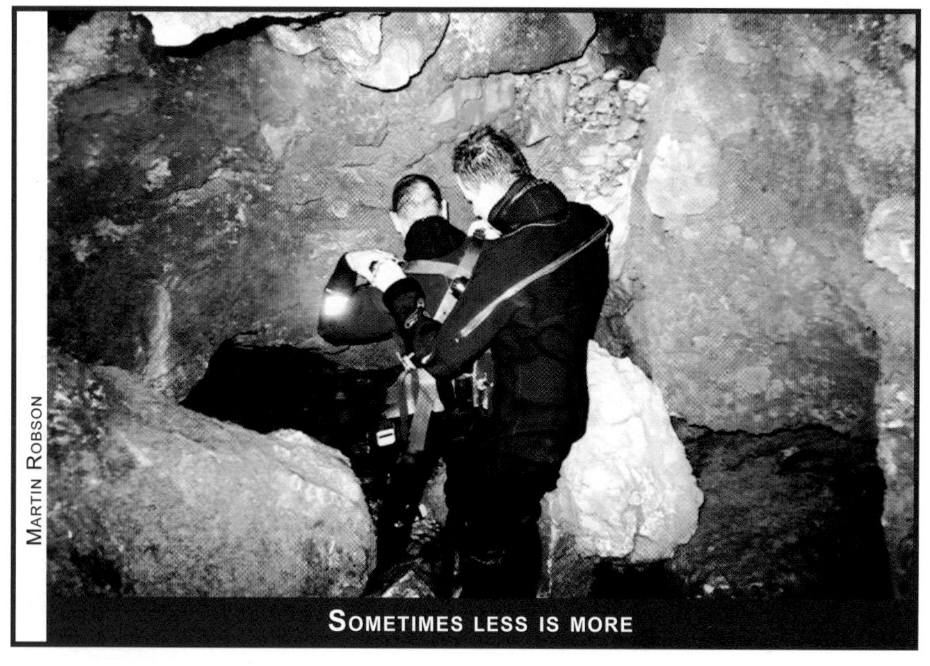

Martin Robson

Sometimes less is more

Another important role for anyone on the surface is that of photographer. Whilst it may be a luxury to have someone dedicated to that alone, a photographic record of the project can be anything from an invaluable addition to magazine articles or publicity shots expected by sponsors to a personal memento of the expedition for all of those involved.

Team Manager

The role of team manager is not

always ideally suited to be undertaken by a lead diver. The team manager needs to be in a position to co-ordinate the activities of the divers and the overall day-to-day running of the project. If the lead divers will be submerged for lengthy periods then they might not be able to fulfil these roles. Often the team manager role will be fulfilled by one of the more experienced support divers. This will allow the manager to take part in the diving operation without the commitment to the potentially more serious lead diving.

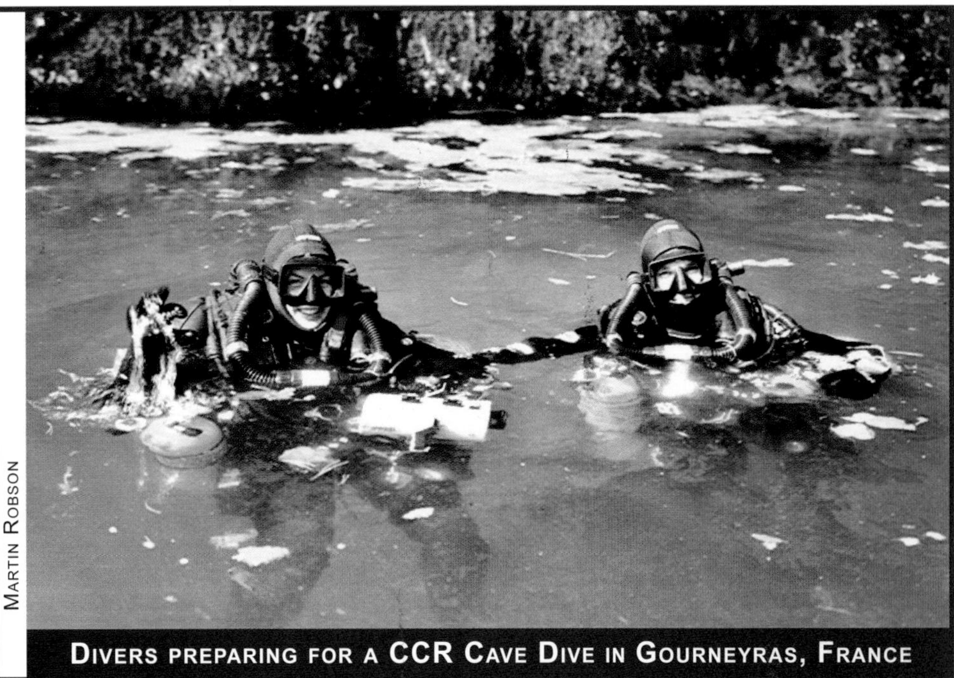
Martin Robson

Divers preparing for a CCR Cave Dive in Gourneyras, France

The team manager must have good organisational skills, be diplomatic, patient and capable of motivating the rest of the team, sometimes in circumstances that are less than ideal.

The lead diver was by now a long time overdue back at the 20 ft (6 m) stop near the cave entrance. The very narrow entrance leading in to the cave made entering and exiting difficult and nerve racking, and meant that a diver had to physically be in the cave to monitor the decompressing diver. The support team had been on the go for over twelve hours and were understandably tired but I had to ask one of them to kit up and accompany me on a search for the overdue diver. As we started to kit up our surface manager shouted back to the support team that they could see the bubbles of a rebreather diver flushing his loop. I dived into the cave just to be certain and was relieved to see the diver back and safely decompressing, but the need to spur the support team into a possible search and recovery had not been a pleasant experience

Team Planning

Once the team is chosen everyone should know who is doing what and how decisions will be made. Will they be made by the team leader or voted on by the group? Everyone needs to understand and agree with the overall goal of the expedition and their role in it. It is also prudent to ensure that those you have asked to join the trip are fully aware of the risks and hazards, have discussed them with and have the support of their partners and family. At this level divers should have a diving medical from a recognised physician within the last year.
Participants may wish to release all other parties from legal liability by signing release forms.

Team members' availability can be easily overlooked. In planning your expedition take enough time in advance to ensure that everyone you want to join the trip is free and in a position to participate.

Team Training

Scheduled training for the team will enhance performance and minimises the number of warm up dives required on site. Individuals are also responsible for maintaining dive and personal fitness in the run up to and throughout the expedition.

Team Meetings are vital to update members on logistics and training schedule. They can be used to ensure individual responsibilities have been carried out on schedule, brief members on the next phase, answer questions and prevent problems. They should be run by the project manager/ leader to ensure that the meeting is kept on track and discussion or questions are relevant. With internet technology available to all it is no longer necessary for divers to meet physically or even be in the same country

Diver checking access pre-dive

prior to the expedition.

Dive Planning/Logistics

Schedule

The expedition needs to have a schedule for advanced planning, team meetings and training and an on-site schedule for any warm up dives, set up dives, the mission dives where the expedition goals will be achieved and any clean up dives needed afterwards.

Gas Planning

Gas requirements will vary greatly depending on the nature of the dives and scope of the project. Open circuit, SCR or CCR dives will affect the overall gas plan, as will availability of gas at local dive centres (if any).

Suffice to say more is better than not enough and the team should always plan to have additional gas both in the water and in reserve.

Decompression Considerations

In cave dives depth is not always the most important variable. Distance from the entrance can have just as much impact on dive planning and how the dives and support dives will be conducted. Dives should be planned with a realistic swim pace/scooter pace and sufficient gas staged to cover any emergencies. If the dives planned are exploration dives it will be impossible to know in advance the exact depth, distance, time that lead divers will undertake so a series of dive plans encompassing the most likely possibilities should be worked out. These will form the base line for planning subsequent dives once more information from reconnaissance and initial push dives has been gathered.

If available and dive site conditions allow, the use of a decompression habitat should be considered. This will allow the divers to decompress in greater comfort than in-water decompression and is safer if long decompression exposures are expected.

Actual decompression planning has similar considerations to any other dive and is discussed in another chapter. It should be remembered that the divers may be subjected to aggressive dive profiles where the accepted normal safe dive profile is just not possible. Caves may be found situated at elevated altitudes and this is another variable to be thought through when planning decompression. Dive plans and decompression schedules should be generated with all of this in mind to make sure sufficient decompression is done by all the team.

For deeper dives or where long duration dives are expected it is not uncommon for normal safe diving parameters to be exceeded. CNS Toxicity and OTU exposures may well be above recommended limits.

Safety precautions such as the use of a decompression habitat, lower PO_2 decompressions and regular low FO_2 or air breaks should be employed to help minimise the risks.

By the time I had got close to finishing the deco my CNS was up to around 465%! Although the nature of the cave had precluded the use of our habitat, I was monitored throughout the deco and had no adverse affects from such a long in-water exposure. Even underwater I had regular drinks breaks, regular air

breaks, I was warm even in the 10°C water and felt comfortable.

With all of this in mind the model used to calculate decompression obligations should be tried and tested and have a proven track record. For deeper or more challenging profiles divers might wish to make adjustments to predicted decompression obligations.

These can be slower ascent rates (especially as the diver approaches shallower water), a system of deeper stops than calculated by the model being used, or high PO_2 decompression where safety is not overly compromised.

Depending on dive depth and exposures we have tried a number of variations to our deep diving deco schedules. These have included stopping every 33 ft (10 m) for a minute on dives deeper than 400 ft (120 m), a progressive slowing of ascent rates as we get shallower and higher than usually accepted PO_2s. We increase PO_2s progressively during ascent and have on occasion finished our deco on 1.85 Bar PO_2. None of the divers have ever had any adverse symptoms from elevated PO_2 or increased CNS or OTU exposure and none have had any DCS symptoms at the end of the dive.

Any techniques that are out of the ordinary should not be undertaken lightly and should be researched as much as possible, with information gathered from other diver's experiences and techniques.

The factors that affect susceptibility to DCS, CNS Toxicity, OTU exposure, HPNS or any other diving related physiological effect should not be overlooked as they can have a profound impact on the diver, especially if divers are ***pushing the envelope***.

Physical fitness, diving fitness, hydration levels, fatigue and thermal comfort should be considered of vital importance for this level of extreme exposure. This type of diving should not be undertaken by those without the self-discipline to maintain the highest levels of personal fitness.

Thermal Considerations

The nature of cave diving often leads to prolonged dive times and exposure to cold water. Regardless of the water temperature, unless it is at body temperature levels, exposure will have a cooling affect on the body. Care must be taken to ensure that all divers have suitable thermal protection for the dives they are undertaking, including how much extra in-water time may be incurred in an emergency scenario. This needs to be integrated into the dive planning process to ensure the comfort and safety of the dive team.

(L to R) Vikki Batten & Martin Robson decompressing in the Ressel, France

Emergency Procedures

A comprehensive plan should be prepared for dealing with any emergencies. This should include out-of-water incidents; anything from a minor cut to a more serious medical emergency should be discussed in advance of the trip and a plan made to deal with this. Team equipment should include first aid supplies and team members must be familiar with the equipment and be capable of giving first aid. A plan of action should also be ready in case of in-water emergencies.

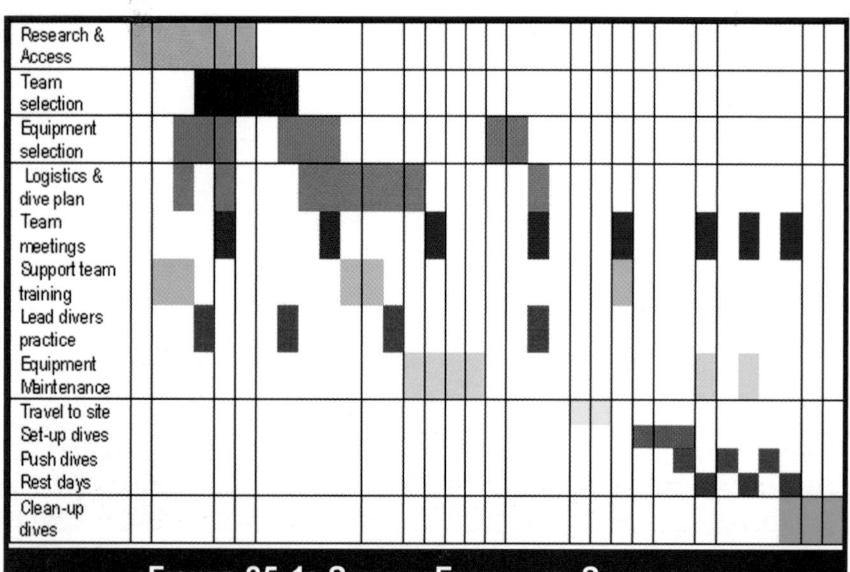

Figure 25-1: Sample Expedition Schedule

Operating in remote areas means that the normal response to diving, or any other emergency is unlikely to exist. Time to treatment may be hours or even days therefore on site first aid must be available.

In the event of a life threatening emergency, an evacuation plan needs to be in place. Contact with local emergency services during the planning phase could prove invaluable. Prevention is better than cure so a system of post dive checks and re-hydration is recommended.

The Expedition

It may be that not all of the team will assemble at the same time. Logistics, transport or personal needs might mean the team arrive over a period of days, especially if not everyone will be needed straight away.

The first priority, assuming a reconnaissance trip has been done by some members of the team, will be to familiarise everyone with the dive site and any other facilities available locally. This first on-site team meeting should include a reminder of the outline and schedule for the expedition and a more detailed briefing for the next days diving. The team should then turn to the task of equipment preparation.

On site each day:

- Site briefing and check of diving conditions
- Daily briefing - should be just a quick reminder
- Safety equipment preparation
- Team equipment preparation
- Personal Kit checks
- Diver Team check before entering the water. There should be a system in place to ensure that each diver has prepared the equipment needed for the dive and is not missing any essential items needed for their safety or a particular task
- Surface personnel log dive teams in to the water – gas, run times etc.
- Surface Co-ordinator runs the timetable ensuring support divers enter the water on schedule for the safety of other members of the team and that they surface when expected
- If safety divers are appropriate they should be ready to enter the water if needed
- Divers doing repetitive dives must ensure they have sufficient gas and dive time to re-enter the water.
- Log divers out of the water
- Post dive equipment maintenance

It is vital that the safety and welfare of all the members of the team be considered when scheduling a days diving. Support divers in particular can often be asked, sometimes inadvertently, to do multiple dives in one day.

The day of the last push dive started with a team meeting and breakfast at 7 am. By 9 pm all of the support divers had done multiple dives (mostly shallow but some to 40 mfw/130 ffw) and the lead diver still had 4 more hours of deco!

PAUL HEINERTH

JILL HEINERTH IN REMOTE NORTHWEST SECTION OF DOS OJOS CAVE SYSTEM, TULUM, MEXICO

POST DIVE

The mission of the project will determine how post dive activities are catered for. For example a survey project will need data to be carefully recorded and collated as well as the normal post dive activities of gas replenishment and equipment maintenance.

A large exploration project may require a number of team members to be actively involved in the stripping and reassembly of rebreathers and DPVs, filling cylinders, charging of battery packs, etc.

Sometimes the occasional willing volunteer can be a real bonus. We were staying in a small local hotel. Having been carefully watched for several evenings by the hotel owner, who had kindly let us use his underground garage for kit storage, took it upon himself to take over stripping out all our primary light batteries and put them all on charge. By the end of the fourth day we were more than happy to let him do the same for the scooters.

At the end of each day of diving a meeting should be held to make sure that all the divers are fit and well, information from the dives has been gathered in and any problems discussed and resolved. The following days schedule and dive plans can then be reviewed.

POST EXPEDITION

An assessment should be made as to whether the project aims and objectives were actually met. Once the pressures of the expedition are over it will become apparent whether the expedition was unable to meet it's goals, was successful, exceeded all expectations or discovered new goals. Will the team require a return trip to meet the original or new goals? If the project becomes an ongoing exploration the return trip may well have been discussed before even finishing the current trip.

MEL CLARK

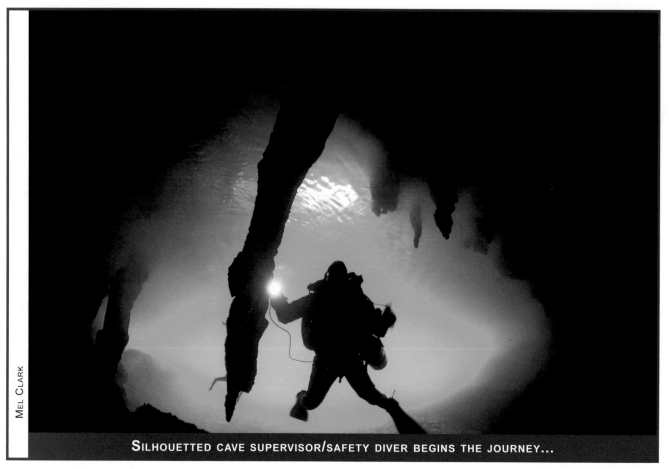

SILHOUETTED CAVE SUPERVISOR/SAFETY DIVER BEGINS THE JOURNEY...

Information and survey data will need to be collated and interpreted. Photographs and film will need to be processed and edited. Equipment loaned or provided by sponsors will need to be returned.

The results of the exploration should be published. This may be on a personal website, by writing articles for publication in journals or magazines, as a television program or combination of media.
Whilst not related to a specific project the table below outlines the way in which time frames can be integrated when planning and conducting an expedition

SUMMARY

Every expedition is different. Individual and team goals will shape the way in which the project is planned and conducted almost as much as the dive site itself. Equipment choices and gas choices will vary from team to team, and from cave to cave.

This information is not all encompassing but it is hoped that there is enough to offer guidance and insight for those planning their own expeditions or eager to join a team.

Cave diving expeditions increase our knowledge of individual geographical locations, have led to the safety rules we dive by today, expanded technological development and new equipment, increased scientific knowledge and environmental awareness that affects the way governments plan, how water is used and highlighted environmental issues.

Cave expedition diving brings unique challenges and rewards. Whatever the aims of the project or motives of the divers the way in which expeditions are planned and conducted, and the information these projects bring back is essential to the future of the caves and cave diving.

Chapter Twenty Six ~ Expeditions ~ Arctic Ice Diving

R. Todd Smith
Contributions by Joseph Dituri, M.S.

Note: This topic references ocean diving in the Arctic and Antarctic regions. There are a number of sub-arctic areas that seasonally may provide excellent open water or ice diving in the ocean or in alpine environments that are not covered here. Additionally, specific ice diving training is a text volume on its own thus only key considerations are addressed here. Seek proper training and experience.

Where To Go: How & When

Arctic

The geographic extent of the Arctic is loosely defined in a number of ways. One common definition is everything north of the tree line (north of which the climate is too severe for trees to grow) often called the Low Arctic. Beyond that is everything north of the Arctic Circle at Lat. 66°33'. This is the line north of which there is at least one 24 hour day of total sunlight and at least one 24 hour day of total darkness each year.

Most diving in the Arctic takes place along or within the countries that are located there including Russia, Canada, Demark (Greenland), USA (Alaska), Norway, Sweden and Finland. Several popular destinations are located in the Arctic Archipelago in Canada. This group of islands covers a large that lies north of the Arctic lowlands and roughly between Alaska and Greenland that includes the large islands of Baffin Banks, Ellesmere, Prince of Wales and Victoria as well as smaller, but well known islands such as Cornwallis (Resolute Bay) and Beechy Island, the grave site for Franklin Expedition members. A number of commercial operators offer diving expeditions for adventurous divers.

The best time to dive in the Arctic depends on where you are going and the weather during that particular season. High Arctic travel is ill-advised before April or May as it is simply too cold and after the end of June the prospect of ice break-up can make travel difficult. Resolute Bay, a popular destination, is certainly best from Mid-May to the end of June in a typical year.

Antarctic

Unless you are lucky enough to take a month long circumnavigation cruise of the continent or spend a season at one of the handful of research stations, you are most likely to take a ship from Tierra Del Fuego (either Chile or Argentina, but most often Ushuaia in Argentina) at the tip of South America to the Antarctic Peninsula.

The Antarctic Peninsula is sometimes referred to whimsically as the "banana belt" of the Antarctic for is relatively mild temperatures in summer, hovering around freezing in the late austral summer (February-March). The west side of the Peninsula is dotted with thousands of islands that offer excellent wildlife habitat, excellent diving and most importantly protection from the relentless storms that pound the region.

(L to R) Anita Rigassio & R. Todd Smith

In Port Lockeroy diving amongst Gentoo penguins

How to Get There

Where you go and how you get there often depends on your plans: land based or boat based. Unlike many types

of expedition diving, you will definitely be largely dependent on the operator you choose for lodging, logistics and certain equipment. Boat based options provide divers with a variety of choices, but since they are basically run as group tours may not be ideal for expedition support. Land based operations are typically better able to support true technical expeditions, but are harder to find and limited in geographical coverage.

Traveling to the Arctic

Arctic travelers can often get to key destinations such as Alaska, Resolute Bay and Svalbard directly with air travel. This usually requires a connection from a standard continental air carrier to an obscure regional or local carrier. These can be quite expensive. A recent check of flights from Montreal to Resolute Bay showed tickets pricing out at nearly $3000 USD.

From resolute Bay it is possible to charter a Twin Otter to the geographic North Pole for $150,000. Additionally, there are significant weight and materials restrictions that vary greatly. If you need to take a compressor you may be able to but it typically takes planning months in advance to arrange.

Traveling to the Antarctic

Most people believe that the way to the Antarctic is by aircraft via New Zealand since this is the way many scientists get to McMurdo, but this is not commonly used by "tourists." Some expedition ships do leave from NZ.

Travel to Antarctica from the Northern Hemisphere is a technical adventure in and of itself. It is 5253 miles (8454 km) from New York to Buenos Aires and an additional 1490 miles (2398 km) to Ushuaia. Again, significant weight and materials restrictions are in play. From there a ship is taken for the 600 mile (1111 km) trip through one of the world's most perilous stretches of ocean, the Drake Passage. Here gale force conditions prevail over 250 days per year and storm force is common. In 2007 we experienced Force 8 to Force 9 wind conditions for the entire 72 hour passage. 30 ft (9 m) waves were common. This truly is the end of the earth.

Preparing for the day's ice diving activities...

Necessary Skills & Experience

Unless you are going to an area that is definitely ice free, you will need to ensure that you have specific training and subsequent experience in ice diving. Cave or wreck training is no substitute for the unique challenges faced in the harshness of the polar ice environment. Additionally, ice training in "southern" lakes is not a complete preparation and first time polar divers need to be thoroughly briefed on not only the polar diving environment in general, but in the specific considerations and hazards of the local area.

Fitness

Maintaining adequate fitness is drummed into

technical divers over and over, but in polar diving it takes on an even more important priority. Not only is the exertion a factor, but the basic increase in metabolic activity for heat production requires a higher level of fitness to avoid discomfort, exhaustion and poor performance. Regardless of the comfort of your accommodations, long days in the arid polar climate will take an insidious toll on your energy level and you must be in excellent shape to stay on top of your energy demands and your diet. The good news is that you will likely eat more with little change in weight. Some individuals, this author included, intentionally gain weight (while conditioning simultaneously) for polar trips to provide extra warmth above and below.

R. Todd Smith

Anita Rigassio Smith with Sea Star in Paradise Bay

Divers should be well rested, have a meal high in carbohydrates and protein, and should not consume any alcohol. Alcohol dilates the blood vessels in the skin, thus increasing body heat loss.

Bathing is an important health measure to prevent infectious diseases prevalent in cold environments. If necessary, the body can be sponge-bathed under clothing. After bathing, a soothing ointment or lotion should be applied to the skin to keep it soft and protect it against evaporation caused by the dry air. Shaving and washing the face should be done in the evening because shaving removes protective oils from the skin. Shaving too close can also remove some of the protective layer of the skin, promoting frostbite.[1]

What to Take

It is a challenge to balance equipment with weight and space restrictions. On a 2007 expedition to Antarctica two divers packed carefully and ended up with 275 lbs of diving equipment, personal items and photographic supplies. The amount of spares must be balanced with weight and space restrictions.

Packing is complicated but a necessity for bringing adequate protection for both the diving as well as the surface exposure. Even in the polar summers you need to dress as though you were winter skiing or camping.

Be sure to bring heavy duty motion sickness remedies if you are traveling by ship as you may need them. Try them at home fist to ensure they do not cause adverse reactions. Also bring a sleeping mask to cover your eyes and be careful to maintain proper sleep patterns because the circadian rhythm of the body is interrupted given the longer days and shorter nights.

Special attention should be given to the type of regulator. The U.S. Navy diving manual suggests that special regulators are required if the water is less than 37° F (3° C). The potential is issue is free flow of the regulator. While the concern is cold water diving, in reality, it is a combination of the cold water and air temperature that will have ice crystals forming in places where they should not. Ensure the regulator functions well in a warm environment and reframe from breathing it in the cold air prior to dive. Once underwater, the likelihood of frees up is reduced. Divers should avoid pressing the purge button while diving because sustained free flow cold cause freeze up.

Diver should consider having regulators equipped with an antifreeze cap, which is a special first-stage cap that can be filled with liquid silicone available from the manufacturer. Correct maintenance and application of an approved lubricant to the appropriate points are also essential. Extra precautions should be taken to ensure that scuba cylinders are completely dry inside, that moisture-free air is used, and that the regulator

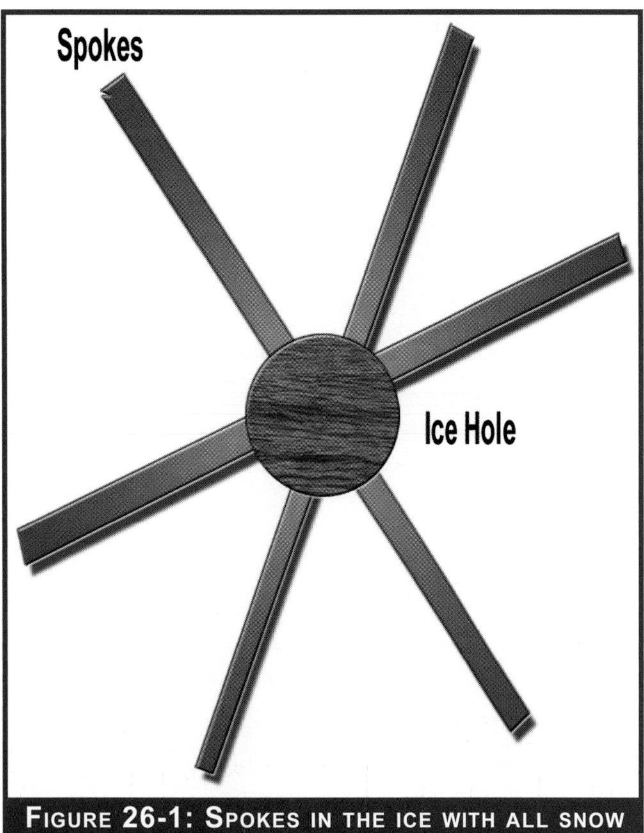

FIGURE 26-1: SPOKES IN THE ICE WITH ALL SNOW COVER REMOVED ALLOW THE LIGHT TO PENETRATE THE SURFACE SO ALL BRIGHT RAYS OF SUN IN THE WATER SHOULD LEAD TO THE EXIT HOLE

is thoroughly dried prior to use.

The diver's mask may show an increased tendency to fog in cold water. An antifog solution should be used to prevent this from occurring. Saliva will, in most cases not prevent cold water fogging. Additionally, great care should be taken when and if it is required to remove a mask or full face mask under water. The drastic change in temperature will cause a diver to gasp and may be problematic.

Because of the environment, batteries tend to not last as long and a magnetic compass is not very accurate or useful in the face of the magnetic field of the North or South Poles.

Diving Logistics

If diving from ice, there are commonly large piles of broken ice as far as the eye can see. It is also full of large fractures and ice ponds. Travel on this type of terrain can be accomplished most easily by foot towing your gear on a sled, or by sled towed by a snowmobile. Foot travel must be undertaken with great care to avoid twisted ankles or even broken bones. Do not carry anything heavy on you back or shoulders as it will only increase the chances that you will fall and be injured. Watch for Polar Bears in the Arctic.
To get through the ten foot thick ice, first, try to reduce the labor by looking for readily available opening in crack that can be widened to a safe size. Also, look for large black dots on the snow. These are seals, or in the Antarctic seals or penguins who have already found open water. Chainsaws fail quickly in salt water and are not long enough to reach through think ice. You will likely have to chip and hack your way through with axes and ice chippers unless you have the resources for a steam hole borer.

Post a bear watch (only if diving in the Arctic; the Antarctic does not have Polar Bears). This needs to be a person with no other responsibilities or distractions, well armed and capable of dealing with a bear if the need arises.

Diver should consider making "spokes." This is accomplished by clearing a layer of snow and making smooth the light penetrating surface so the light will better shine through the ice under water. If done in a spoke centered at the hole (see Figure 26-1), all bright rays of sun in the water should lead to the hole. If a diver is lost or fails to go in the water with a guide or tending line, the way back will be marked sufficiently.

Additional consideration should be given to the surface support or preparation area. If possible, wood or rubber should be placed on the ice to insulate the divers as they prepare for entry and the surface support team (if used) from the temperature of the ice.

Finally, that swirling water in the hole indicates current. Whether or not you see it, always assume there is current and always use a tether, not a guideline. Even the slightest current is difficult to swim against for any distance.

Diving from a boat will normally involve taking Zodiacs from a main ship. The advantage is a great platform to manage your gear on the ship. The disadvantage is that most Zodiacs are not terribly roomy and getting back in with technical equipment takes care to ensure that nothing is lost or damaged.

General Polar Diving Rules

1. Always dive with a tether or a continuous guideline
2. Take an ice diving course before you go to a polar region and get some additional experience ice diving after the course. (Specific ice diving technique is beyond the scope of this section.)

3. Train and dive in the gear you plan to take
4. Use cameras in advance to get adjusted to photography with a tether in the way
5. Do not dive under or around moving ice!

Tether or Guideline? Which is Better & When?

A tether is the overall safest option for most ice diving and the only reasonable choice when any current is present. However there are a number of situations where experienced ice divers may opt for a continuous guideline that they are ***not*** attached to. This practice is increasingly favored the longer the penetration distance where entanglement and line fouling become greater risks. This practice must be undertaken with extreme care and should not be the first option for divers new to the ice environment. It goes without saying that conditions must me very good: visibility better than 33 ft (10 m), no current, no moving ice and have suitable places to place the guideline along the way. If not, use a tether!

While general statements do not cover every eventuality, a good rule of thumb is to opt for a guideline over a tether if the following conditions or logistics apply:

1. All divers should have both significant cave/wreck training and standard ice training and experience
2. Frozen lake environments during winter when the ice is fast and stable and there are no currents to deal with (so inlet/outlet or river diving would be a poor choice)
3. In polar marine environments when ice is fast and stable and currents are low or predictable. Theseconditions can occur in bays or other restricted areas, but out on the open ice sheets there almost always seems to be a tidal current to deal with that is difficult if not impossible to predict
4. The dive is more than 200 ft (66 m) total underwater distance from the entry point
5. Deep dives below 130 ft (40 m) or cases where the dive needs to be carried out a long lateral distance from the entry hole where a long tether would be required and potentially difficult to manage. A dive of this nature should be conditional on the team first meeting Item 1 and the conditions meeting Items 2 or 3
6. There is significant risk of entanglement hazard if a tether is used

Divers may also opt to use a guideline for the primary part of the dive and "clip in" to a tether for deco as currents are usually strongest near the surface. Regardless the risk envelope is increased substantially with ice diving. In caves or wrecks you can use feature referencing if you get blown off of your line. You don't have that in featureless lakes in particular and often the visibility is fairly poor in Polar Regions due to algae blooms and sediment load. Additionally, the ice environment is inherently more unstable than most cave or wreck environments and inclement weather can turn everything upside down.

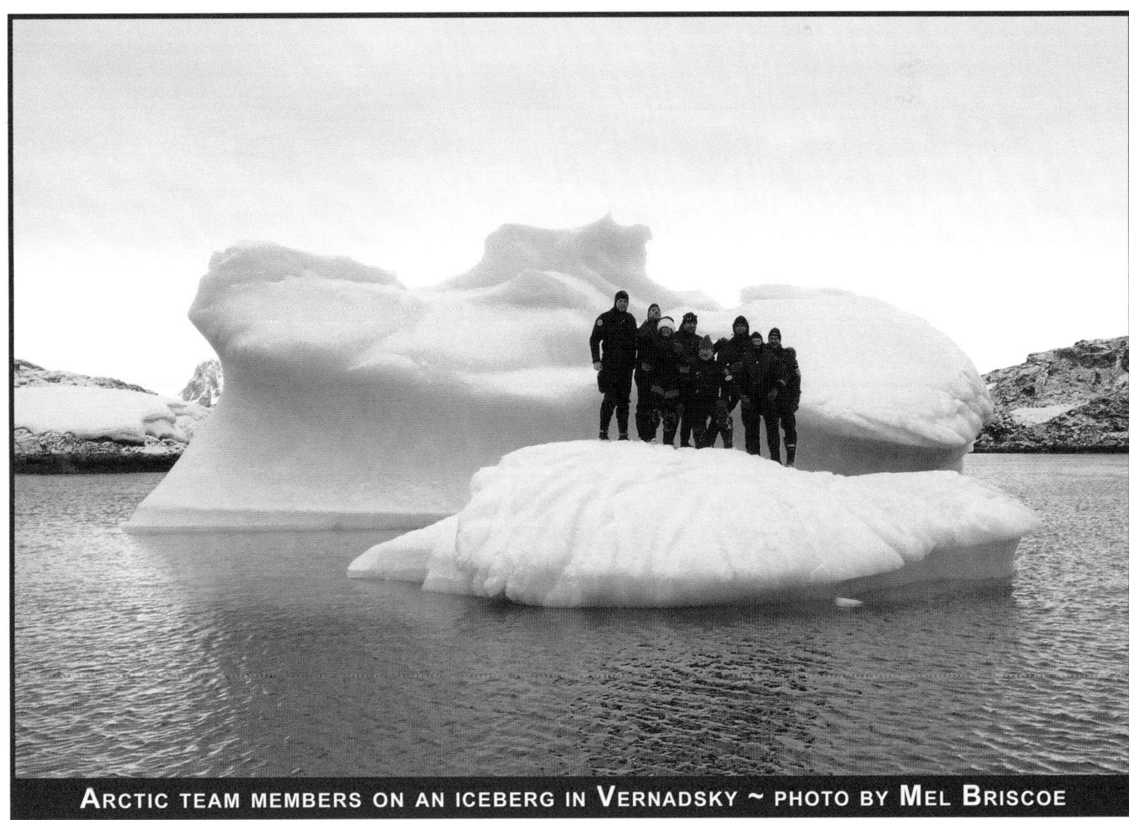

Arctic team members on an iceberg in Vernadsky ~ photo by Mel Briscoe

R. Todd Smith under the ice of Cuverville Island

Rules for Diving Around Ice Bergs

1. Never dive under or around moving ice!
2. Never dive around a berg that is "shedding" ice, chunks or crystals as this can reduce visibility
3. Icebergs can roll without warning spurs can hit you with great force. Try to dive on only grounded stable icebergs
4. Never dive into fissure or caves in bergs as these are often the most unstable areas of the formation. They are the underwater equivalent of glacial crevasses
5. Never dive under overhangs where ice could calve and fall onto you
6. Be aware of sharp protrusions that can catch equipment

Recommendations for Diving to Depth

Decompression diving in Polar regions is quite risky. Especially in Antarctica, there are no recompression chambers and no chance of aircraft evacuation. Even with drysuits and battery powered heat packs, immersions of over 1 hour in 28.3° F (-2° C) water can get very uncomfortable and inhibit proper decompression.

Do not use the small yellow "Iron" heat packs. If they are placed near the skin and get wet under pressure in conjunction with the increased partial pressure of oxygen at depth, they can cause severe burns.

Check In / Check Out

No solo diving. My concern is for the rescuers who would put themselves at risk trying to find you. Stay in pairs. This is particularly important in large groups aboard ships where it would be easy to miss a lone traveler.

Hazards & Challenges

Challenges to your safety in the Polar environment can be listed in the following priority:

1. Your abilities: planning, fitness, conditioning and diving skills (dry suit, cold water, ice diving experience and ability)

Many technical divers take it for granted that if they are skilled and trained in technical cave or wreck diving that they have all the requisite skills and equipment to handle ice diving. While many of the basic premises are the same, there are a number of significant skills and operational procedure that are quite different and need to be learned and practiced as in any other technical discipline. Paramount among those are use of tethers and an strong working knowledge of ice formations and ice behavior along with a healthy respect for polar climate, wildlife and weather.

2. The Polar Environment

On a sunny summer day with temperatures above freezing, a day on the ice sheet may feel like a summer vacation. However, technical divers need to be cognizant of everything from fast changing weather patterns to the "jet lag" effects of unending sunlight that can precipitate a number of exhaustion related problems if not handled properly. One thing is for sure: polar ice moves in the summer and the later in the summer you are there, the more it can move. Moving ice is not something to dive around. It is really as crazy as diving in a wreck that is collapsing around you.

Despite the low incident sunlight in the polar areas, the reflection off of the snow, ice and water and the prolonged if not unending presence of the sun each day necessitates great care in exposure protection. Severe sunburn and snow blindness are a real risk. In Antarctica this issue takes on a particular urgency when accounting for the large hole in the protective ozone layer. In 2007 the research scientists at Vernadsky station (formerly Faraday Station) told me directly that ***ten minutes*** was the maximum safe exposure time, even on cloudy days. Stay covered up, wear high SPF sun block on your face and use glacier glasses or other high UV filtering glasses.

Types of Ice

The biggest danger in polar ice is that it ***always*** has the potential to move. This can be as inconvenient as creating an open water lead that forces you to make a long detour to get back to base, or it can be as catastrophic as closing off the only open avenue to the surface. Couple that with the fact that you are indeed diving in the ocean and all oceans have tidal currents and you have to be doubly careful that you can always reliably return to your entry point. Calving ice should be observed from a distance, in a Zodiac or from a ship. Do ***not*** dive around it, period.

Icebergs and Bergie Bits are famous for rolling and movement. See above.

Fast ice and currents can be shifty. Solid pack ice still groans, creaks, shudders and cracks particularly when there is current or temperature changes. Pay attention to the ice noises on the pack and get used to what they mean.

Dangerous Wildlife

The stories about polar bears are all basically ***true***. Polar Bears are essentially 880 pounds (400 kilograms) of bad intentions driven by insatiable appetite in a land with little food. They know no natural predators and they are crafty and patient. Adult males will even kill young cubs to remove competition. They have been known to stalk polar travelers for days. I have seen scars on Narwhals where a polar bear tried to ambush them from above. Human attacks are rare, but that is only because there are limited amounts of human visitors and they are very cautious. No encounter with a Polar Bear is a safe encounter.

As a result, any group traveling in the High Arctic should be equipped with firearms. The best way to do this is to hire a local, usually an Inuit native in the Canadian Arctic. This accomplishes two major objectives. First you have a skilled hunter (the Inuits are often Polar Bear hunters as well) who can assess the real threat of an encounter and determine the best course of action. Wildlife authorities take a dim view if they find a dead polar bear that has been shot in the back. Second, using the Inuits' knowledge solves one major equipment logistic nightmare. Should you find it absolutely necessary to bring your own firearms, you need to check with local regulations for import, declaration and carrying rules, but above the Arctic circle it is common practice. In fact there are areas on Svalbard where the carrying of rifles is compulsory. Do not travel with handguns as they are illegal in most parts of the world, including Canada. An additional safety measure can be for each traveler to carry "bear spray" which launches an irritant into the bear's eyes, if you can get it out and aim it in time.

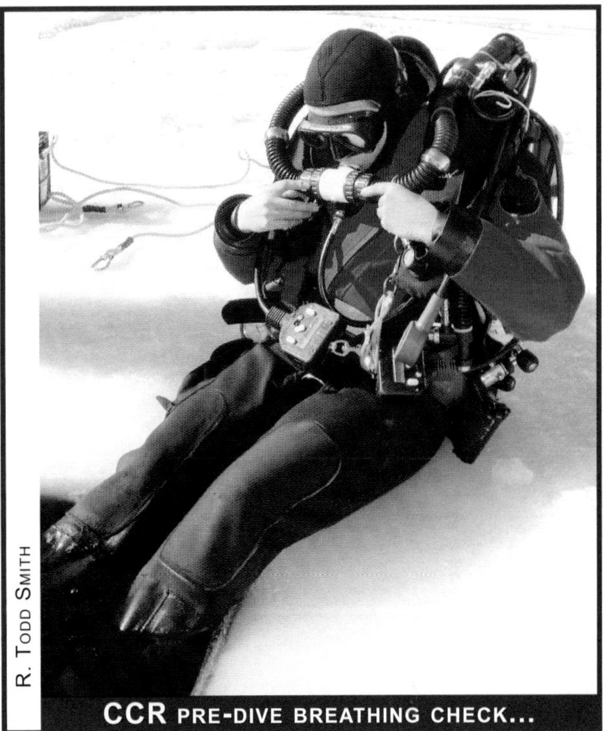
R. Todd Smith

CCR PRE-DIVE BREATHING CHECK...

Leopard Seals are common in the Antarctic and are often found around penguin colonies, which is their main food source. These are like over-sized Sea Lions weighing as much as 990 pounds (450 kilograms) and possessing amazing strength and speed as well as a mouth full of teeth that rivals a Polar Bear's. Aggressive encounters are rare, but on July 22, 2003 a young female research biologist was snorkeling around a seal with a partner when the seal grabbed her and dove to a depth of 230 ft (70 m). When rescuers reached the site they observed the seal holding the woman on a shelf at about 33 ft (10 m). The seal eventually released her, but resuscitation efforts were unsuccessful. Since then, many of the expedition ships have discontinued their diving and snorkeling options. The bottom line is most animals in the Antarctic have no fear of humans and since they are vicious hunters, have little concept of play versus injure.

It is advisable to ***get up close*** to Leopard Seals from a bergy bit or a Zodiac. They will come quite close, but you will

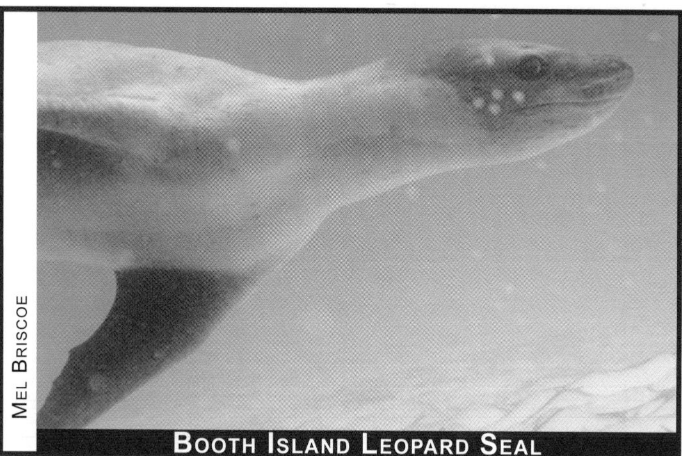

Mel Briscoe

Booth Island Leopard Seal

not be in as vulnerable a situation as when in the water with them. **When encountering Leopard Seals in the water observe the following safety guidelines:**

1. Dive/snorkel in small groups and do not crowd the animal or corner it near the shore or an ice berg
2. Do not attempt to pet or touch the seal if it comes close. Keep you hands next to your body
3. Only dive/snorkel around solitary animals. If two or more seals are present, leave the water as there is no way to keep your attention on the behavior of multiple seals at the same time
4. Swimming up close may only be a sign of "playfulness" or curiosity, but repeated passes and false charges may indicate irritation or aggression
5. Leave the water immediately if the animal shows the following signs of aggression: charging with an open mouth (may be playful but there is little way to tell the difference); the seal blows bubbles in tight circles while bobbing its head: any nervous or quick movements, especially with its head

Walrus encounters are rare, but these "slothy" animals can be aggressive when provoked and they are over twice as large as a Leopard Seal. Give walrus's a wide berth.

Safety Considerations

I never travel to these remote ends of the earth without my own integrated GPS Emergency Position Indicating Radio Beacon (***EPIRB***, aka ***ELT*** if you are a pilot) that is properly registered with SARSAT and a friend back home so that everyone knows it is not a false alarm if it is deployed. I have found that units on ships in remote regions are often out of date, poorly maintained and likely improperly registered. Do not activate except as a very last resort when you are certain that your very survival depends on it.

It should be obvious that an EPIRB is not the AAA automobile club, or really even a 911 emergency rescue service. These are both services that are actually trained and waiting for your call. If activated an EPIRB is picked up by the COSPAS-SARSAT system, (Google it) verified as legitimate and resources if available may be deployed to your aid. These resources are very often ***NOT*** emergency personnel, but rather military, commercial or research personnel who are proximal to the location of the distress call. This means that not only are they not necessarily prepared or equipped to rescue you, but that you may very well place them into grave peril by forcing a response, since response by commercial vessels to directed to assist COSPAS/SARSAT is compulsory. It is extremely important that you register your beacon with your government agency. In the USA this is **www.beaconregistration.noaa.gov**

You must be extremely careful to avoid false alarms and never activate the beacon unless self rescue is impossible and death is imminent.

There are several different types of EPIRBs. Older 121.5 MHz are not precise or reliable enough and have been discontinued in favor of 406 MHz units. These have a 48 hour battery life. Do not use a Personal Locator Beacon (***PLB***,), as these are cut down versions with only 24 hours of battery life. If possible get a unit that has a built in GPS receiver as this will transmit your precise location to the satellites within 15 minutes and within 100 ft (30 m) of your true location. A non-GPS integrated unit can take an hour to provide a fix of only a mile.

Footnotes

[1] ***U.S. Navy Diving Manual***, Volume 2, Chapter 11, Page 11

R. Todd Smith

Divers with tethers to the surface

Section Five
Decompression Models

Photo by Ann Keibler

Photo courtesy Andreas Fritz

Chapter Twenty Seven ~ Modeling ~ Multi-Model Approach

JP Imbert

DIVERS ON A WW II ERA AIRPLANE WRECK

You do not need to know how an engine works to drive a car. You could say therefore that we do not need to know more about decompression than what is written in our dive computer manual. But dive computers have limitations, and technical diving often takes us beyond these limits. Behind the sump there is another sump ... after the wreck there is a new one that we have just discovered ... we always need another table to help us reach that next challenge.

Algorithms provide us with tables that are as good as their assumptions. Our understanding progresses slowly as one good constructive idea comes along approximately every 20 years. The last good idea was the ***Arterial Bubble Assumption***. Now it is gas nuclei which fit into the picture like a piece of a puzzle. They provide a three level explanation from microbubbles to big fat bubbles and an overall picture emerges.

Microbubbles

Dr. Alf Brubakk is a professor at the University of Trondheim in Norway. He was running a project with his students on fitness and decompression. He used rats as a model and separated them into two groups. The first was a group of fat and sedentary animals, well fed in small cages. The second group was comprised of athletic rats, trained on treadmills by his students to Olympic levels. He then sent the two groups through some bad rat decompression and measured, as expected, a higher rate of survival among the fit rats. However, to his surprise, when the experiment was conducted on a Monday morning, the population of both fat rats and fit rats was equally decimated.

Dr. Brubakk recalled that his students went home on the week-ends leaving the fit rats to rest, and concluded that it was not only the fact of the exercise but the timing of the exercise that made the difference. This led to the formulation of his gas nuclei theory.

Gas nuclei are pre-existing tiny pockets of gas attached to the wall of the blood vessels. At the surface, they are harmless. During a decompression, they grow and become microbubbles, the precursors of bubbles. Exercise mechanically induces the release of these microbubbles into the blood stream. Exercising rats had fewer microbubbles than the unfit rats and better resisted the decompression. But apparently the gas nuclei were regenerating over the weekend while the fit rats rested and on the Monday morning they all died, just like the unfit rats.

Since this discovery, converging experiments have further supported Brubakk's findings. During a study performed by the French Navy, trainee divers performed light jogging in the morning before a long dive in the afternoon. Doppler bubble detections showed that exercise prior to a dive significantly reduced the incidence of circulating

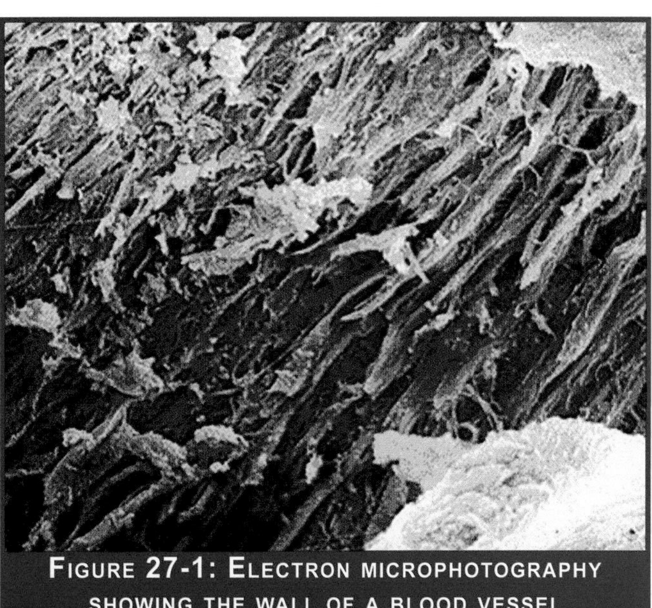
FIGURE 27-1: ELECTRON MICROPHOTOGRAPHY SHOWING THE WALL OF A BLOOD VESSEL
THE IRREGULARITIES ON THE SURFACE PROVIDE SHELTERS FOR A POPULATION OF GAS NUCLEI

bubbles. More surprising, Dr. Ballestra of the Divers Alert Network (***DAN***) recounted the story of an old diver who explained that when he went diving he always drove at full speed in his Zodiac inflatable on his way out to the dive and returned at an idle. This gave Ballestra the idea of putting divers on vibrating beds before a dive. He also measured significantly lower levels of bubbles after the decompression.

Thus everything starts on the blood vessel walls prior to the dive. The following scenario applies to the first part of the dive:

- Small gas pockets called gas nuclei are located in cracks on the blood vessel walls. They are only a few nanometers in size
- When the decompression starts, these nuclei start growing with the surrounding dissolved gas
- They are released in the blood stream and serve as precursor to microbubbles
- The number of microbubbles influences the safety of the decompression
- One must try to reduce the number of gas nuclei available before the dive
- Nuclei can be released mechanically by exercise, vibrations, etc.
- Nuclei can also be released bio-chemically, in particular by NO, a free radical that regulates vasodilatation, and thus modifies the blood vessel surface

This is consistent with the fact that fitness in general, and light exercise before the dive in particular improves decompression safety.

This also explains why older divers tend to produce more bubbles than younger divers for the same dive, as reported in Doppler monitoring studies. Effectively, an aging diver can be expected to have damaged blood vessel walls and cholesterol clusters, and thus more gas nuclei.

There is a possibility that simple vasodilatators, such as the ones used by people with cardiac diseases, could open the road to bio-chemically improved decompression. I believe that the diving community would be interested in any study on a particular vasodilator with spectacular side effects, i.e. Viagra, but this remains to be tested.

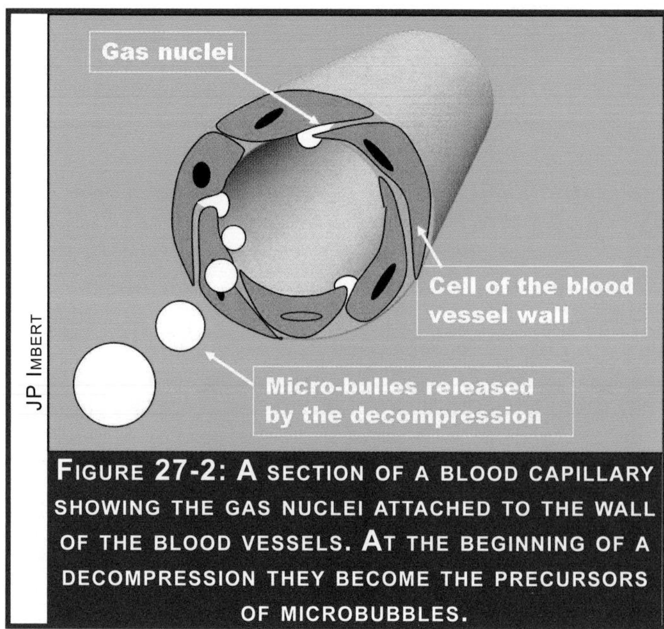

Figure 27-2: A section of a blood capillary showing the gas nuclei attached to the wall of the blood vessels. At the beginning of a decompression they become the precursors of microbubbles.

Tiny Bubbles

Let us consider now the first few minutes following the start of the decompression. The diver is traveling to the first stop or beyond. The microbubbles released in the venous blood have grown to the size of tiny bubbles (around 1 micron). They are collected by the venous system in the right heart and directed to the lung.

A normal decompression produces numbers of these bubbles that are commonly detected by Doppler. They enter the lungs and are trapped by size filtration in the capillaries. They rapidly transfer their gas into the alveoli and collapse. This is why we survive decompression.

If by chance, one of these bubbles crosses the pulmonary filter, it will be dumped in the left heart and injected into the arterial system. The tiny bubble may be recycled but if it passes through a desaturating tissue, it may grow, especially in the brain. The brain is a high consumer of oxygen and its blood "piping" is very direct. When the tiny bubble is accelerated into the aorta, it is likely to be centrifuged into the carotids and straight into the brain.

The brain is also a fatty tissue and a large inert gas reservoir. As a rapid tissue, it is supersaturated at the beginning of the ascent and can feed a tiny bubble passing by. The bubble can then reach a size big enough to block the capillary. Local tissue beyond the capillary will be starved of oxygen supply and die. This is the scenario for the onset of a central neurological decompression sickness, in the early part of

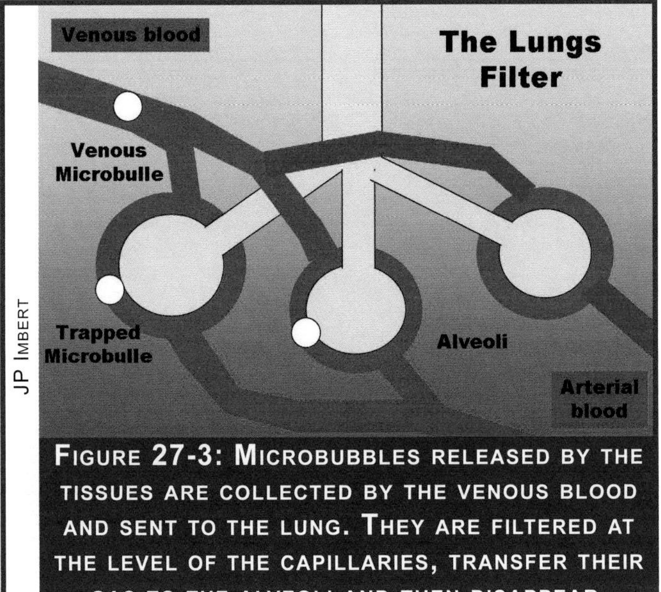

FIGURE 27-3: MICROBUBBLES RELEASED BY THE TISSUES ARE COLLECTED BY THE VENOUS BLOOD AND SENT TO THE LUNG. THEY ARE FILTERED AT THE LEVEL OF THE CAPILLARIES, TRANSFER THEIR GAS TO THE ALVEOLI AND THEN DISAPPEAR.

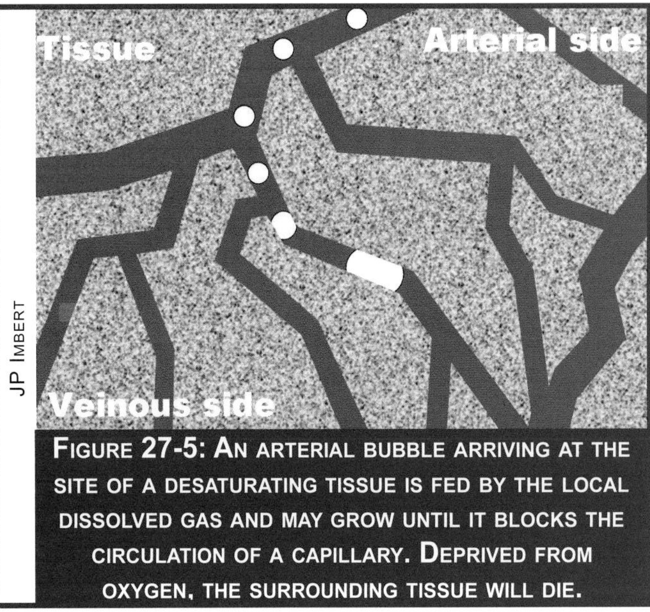

FIGURE 27-5: AN ARTERIAL BUBBLE ARRIVING AT THE SITE OF A DESATURATING TISSUE IS FED BY THE LOCAL DISSOLVED GAS AND MAY GROW UNTIL IT BLOCKS THE CIRCULATION OF A CAPILLARY. DEPRIVED FROM OXYGEN, THE SURROUNDING TISSUE WILL DIE.

the ascent. It is called the "***arterial bubble assumption***" and was published by Tom Hennessy in 1987.

The same assumption applies to vestibular hits that are also related to bounce dives with a short bottom time and long ascent to the stop depth. It is believed nowadays that the bubble site in vestibular problems is more likely to be the brain than the inner ear. Apparently, the area of the brain responsible for balance is a terminal zone for perfusion. If a tiny bubble arrives there, it will grow.

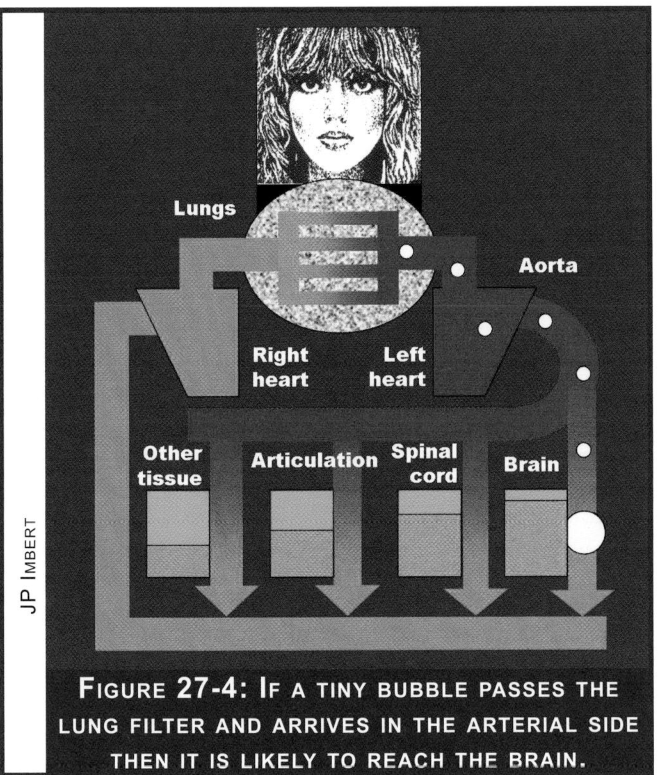

FIGURE 27-4: IF A TINY BUBBLE PASSES THE LUNG FILTER AND ARRIVES IN THE ARTERIAL SIDE THEN IT IS LIKELY TO REACH THE BRAIN.

We now have the second part of the scenario:

- Tiny bubbles are normally produced during a decompression and transported by the venous system to the lungs
- Lungs work as a filter and stop these bubbles in their capillaries. These bubbles further exchange gas with the alveoli and vanish
- Some bubbles may pass through the lung filter and arrive in the arterial blood system
- The brain is readily accessible to arterial bubbles
- The brain, being a fast tissue, is expected to be saturated at the beginning of the dive and will feed these bubbles with gas
- Growing bubbles will block the tissue capillaries, depriving the surrounding tissues of oxygen and causing tissue damage and DCS symptoms

The arterial bubble assumption explains how the decompression outcome depends both on the diver and his dive profile.

A diver must be a good bubble filter. There is individual variability at the level of the lungs. Some divers have cardiac or pulmonary shunts. Recent publications have shown that in nearly 90% of the cases treated in chambers for central neurological symptoms, there was a permeable

foramen ovale or pulmonary shunt detected.

Some dive profiles may favor neurological symptoms. We have already seen how deep short dives with long ascents to shallow stops tend to produce central neurological and vestibular hits. The same applies to yo-yo diving and short interval repetitive dives. They are suspected to pass arterial bubbles during the multiple recompressions, purely as a result of Boyles' law.

Large Bubbles

Let us finally consider the last part of the decompression, with the divers reaching long stops close to the surface. The off gassing process has lasted long enough for some bubbles to grow to a significant size. By absorbing the gas dissolved in the surrounding tissues they have reached 50 microns in diameter or more. One could see them with the naked eye. They have spread over several capillary areas and now deserve the name of "tissue bubbles", although historically, they traveled via the arterial bloodstream and started growing in the vascular bed. Because of their size, they can have a mechanical effect. It takes a large bubble to produce pain. The pain is caused by the bubble tearing tissues and compressing nerve endings. We suspect these bubbles located in connective tissue, tendons or bones are responsible for articular pain.

Type I pain only symptoms are typical of long/deep dives with a lot of dissolved gas. They tend to occur at end of the decompression or just after reaching the surface, because of the increase in their volume, Boyle's law again.

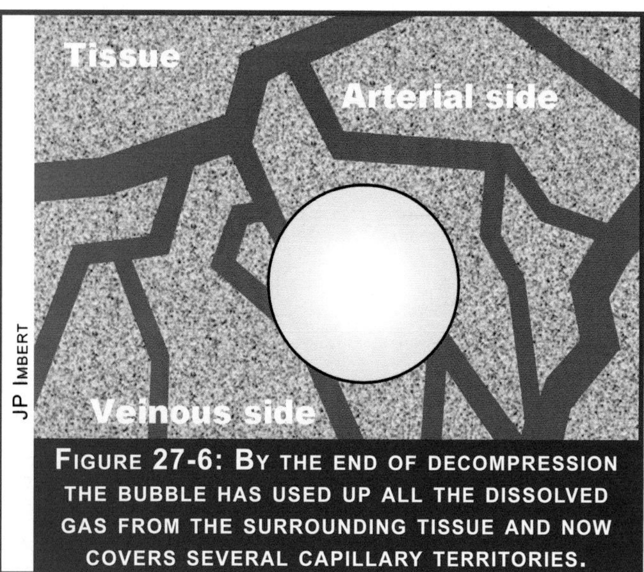

Figure 27-6: By the end of decompression the bubble has used up all the dissolved gas from the surrounding tissue and now covers several capillary territories.

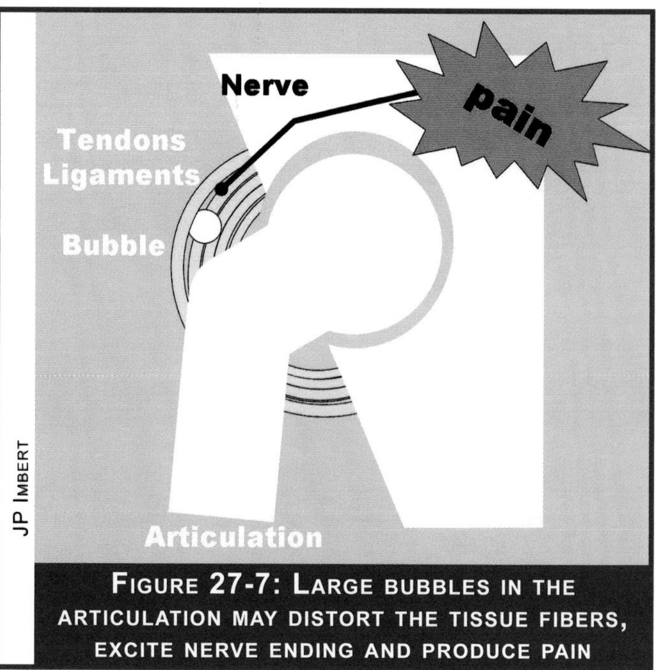

Figure 27-7: Large bubbles in the articulation may distort the tissue fibers, excite nerve ending and produce pain

Large bubbles might also be involved in the "***venous damping***" effect advocated by Dr. Allenbeck. After a series of experiments with dogs he postulated that the mechanism of spinal neurological symptoms was the down stream damping of venous blood by large bubble populations. He was able to show on film that reduced blood flow caused the development of local bubbles in blood vessels of the marrow. The blood supply in the spinal cord is very different from that in the brain, and it seems difficult to send an arterial bubble there by centrifugation. Effectively, there is no correlation in the literature between heart shunts and spinal symptoms. It seems reasonable to associate neurological spinal symptoms and large bubbles through the venous damping assumption.

We finally get to the last part of the scenario:

- Close to the surface, the combined action of a long off gassing process and Boyle's law allows bubbles to grow to a size of over 50-100 microns
- This size gives them a mechanical effect
- They might cause pain in connective tissues and tendons at points of articulation
- They may block the venous bloodstream and reduce blow flow in the spinal cord causing local production of bubbles and medullar neurological symptoms

The scene is now complete. From microbubbles at the

beginning of the dive, decompression produces tiny bubbles and finally large bubbles. Each type of bubble is associated with different symptoms at a different location. It thus seems obvious that modeling a decompression requires at least three different models, each working at a different scale. The solution to decompression safety must be multi-model based.

Algorithms Used In Decompression Modeling

Unfortunately, the multiple models required for the solution to safe decompression are not yet available.

Working on a small scale, we do not know enough about gas nuclei to give them either shape or size. We suspect there are populations of various shapes and sizes. Solutions exist to get around the difficulty such as fractal calculations but they remain to be developed fully. If we only had a tool, we could deduce the effect of exercise, the consequences of age, the limits of repetitive diving, etc. from measuring the initial gas nuclei populations. We just need more Nobel prizes.

On a medium scale, the arterial bubble assumption opens new possibilities to mathematical approaches. **In the *ABM algorithm* described in a next chapter, the critical situation corresponds to:**

- A tiny bubble that has just arrived from the arterial side into a tissue capillary.
- The tissue is super-saturated at this moment during the decompression
- It offloads gas into both the capillary and into the bubble
- The bubble in turn off loads gas into the bloodstream
- By controlling the rate of ascent, one controls the various gas fluxes and can manage to prevent the bubble from growing

Similar algorithms working on the control of tiny bubbles are called "***bubble growth algorithms***." Their particular characteristic is to slow down the first part of the decompression by displaying deeper stops than in a classic table.

On a large scale, we have more models than required. Since Haldane, the classic approach has been to express the safe ascent criteria as a relationship between the ambient pressure and the dissolved gas tension. Haldane's criterion was only a ratio:

Ptis < C Pamb

Where Ptis represents the dissolved tissue gas tension and Pamb, the diver's ceiling pressure for a safe ascent. A simple improvement to the Haldane equation gave us the linear expression that has now become the fundamental criterion for safe ascent:

Ptis < A Pamb + B

Where A and B are empirical coefficients attached to each tissue compartment. The US Navy tables designed by Workman were based on six tissue compartments and their respective M-values and yield exactly the same linear expressions:

Ptis < DeltaM Pamb + Mo = M-value

The success of the US Navy tables made M-values very popular. The French Navy, the Norwegian Navy and later the Canadian Forces also used M-values to design their own tables. Comex and other diving contractors took the same approach for developing their offshore tables. Most decompression experts worked consistently with linear

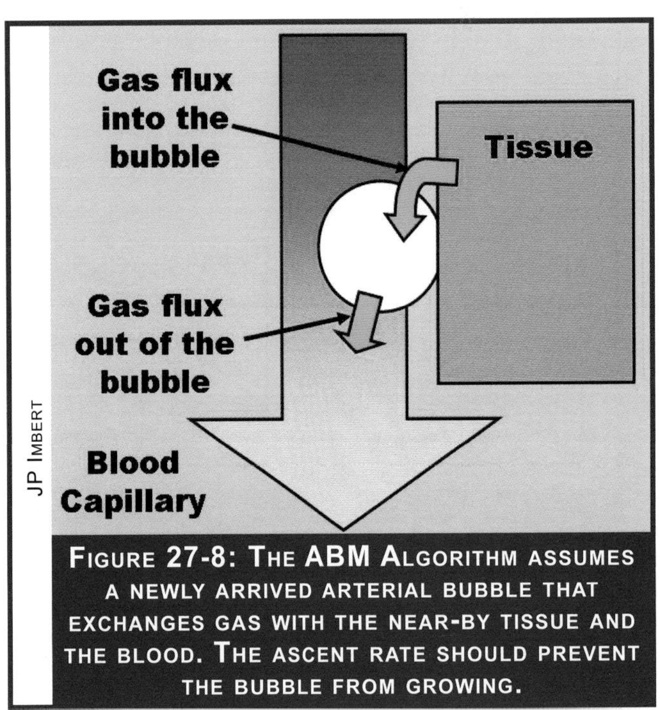

Figure 27-8: The ABM Algorithm assumes a newly arrived arterial bubble that exchanges gas with the near-by tissue and the blood. The ascent rate should prevent the bubble from growing.

criteria. **Dr. Bill Hamilton had linear relations in his DECAP model and Dr. Bühlmann's formula mimics the same expression:**

$$\text{Ptis} < \frac{\text{Pamb}}{a} + b$$

M-values have been used because they are mathematically friendly but their meaning has remained hidden for years. In 1977, Dr. Hennessy and Dr. Hempleman of the Royal Navy showed that this formulation expresses the fact that a large tissue bubble should not exceed a critical volume. They named it the ***critical volume assumption***, something we call the ***large bubble scenario***.

If we turn the story around, it appears that 60 years of decompression research have led to the finding of a linear criterion for computing decompression. This criterion only states the condition to control large bubbles that would produce pain in the points of articulation. Pain only symptoms merely represent 20% of the reported cases of DCS in technical diving. The major concern is Type II neurological DCS. It is ironic that we have followed tables that were only designed to prevent symptoms that rarely occur with the profiles we use, while being fully exposed to the real threat, Type II DCS.

No wonder that leaders in technical diving such as Richard Pyle soon realized these limitations and published empirical methods to slow down the initial ascent of traditional tables with deep stops. Others dug out old models that give deep stops, such has the VPM algorithm. Others started twisting classical models such as the GAP algorithm, in an attempt to produce the desired decompression profiles.

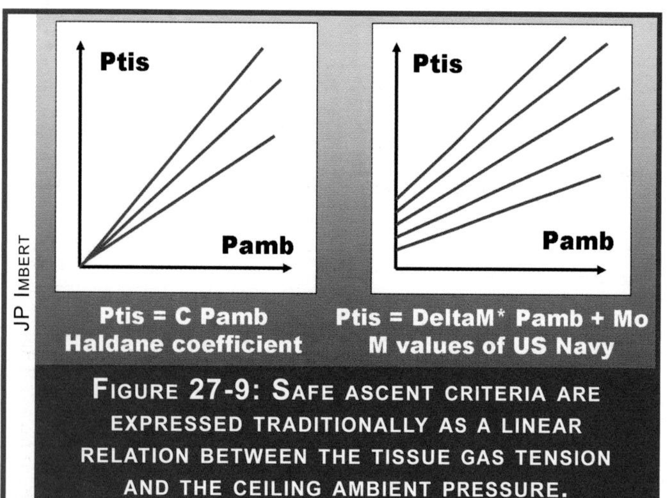

Figure 27-9: Safe ascent criteria are expressed traditionally as a linear relation between the tissue gas tension and the ceiling ambient pressure.

Strategy For A Decompression

Because the three algorithms we have identified as required for the complete description of a decompression are not yet available, the best we can do is to combine the ones we have. And as we lack scientific data, there is room for personal views and opinions. Incantation replaces demonstration.

The one to start with is the Bühlmann algorithm, today's well accepted reference. It has been amply validated and we are all familiar with its tables. It is important to know that Bühlmann spent his life tuning up his air tables, which are excellent, but he had great difficulty with Heliox. As a consequence, Bühlmann Heliox tables have longer than the air tables time-at-deco-depth limits and make Heliox diving unattractive. His Heliox coefficients are ***very*** conservative. His Trimix tables too. I have used the waterproof IANTD Trimix 20 25, 19 30 and 16 40 tables (derived from the Bühlmann algorithm) a lot in my Trimix courses. My students and I have accumulated more than 1250 exposures without any problem (***touch wood***). We have run bubble Doppler detection experiments on deep dives and found very few circulating bubbles. The Bühlmann algorithm is a definitively good reference.

However, I believe the Bühlmann algorithm is only valid for the last part of the decompression where large tissue bubbles control the ascent. A good table should look like a Bühlmann table in its last stops as one approaches the surface. However, the initial part of the decompression should be different, because at this stage in the dive it is arterial bubbles that control the ascent.

Software, computers and internet gurus propose a variety of alternatives for the initial part of the decompression.

One way of slowing down the initial ascent is to introduce a series of intermediate stops as in the classic version of Delta P Technology's ***VR3 dive computer***. The computer uses a classic Bühlmann table and bolts some arbitrary deep stops on it. If these deep stops are omitted, the computer falls back on to the initial Bühlmann tables without any change in the ascent.

The danger with empirical deep stops is that there must be a limit not to cross. They may work on microbubbles but excessive ascent time also increases the tissue gas uptake. In 2002, the French Navy published results on some experimental tables with deep stops and showed that they

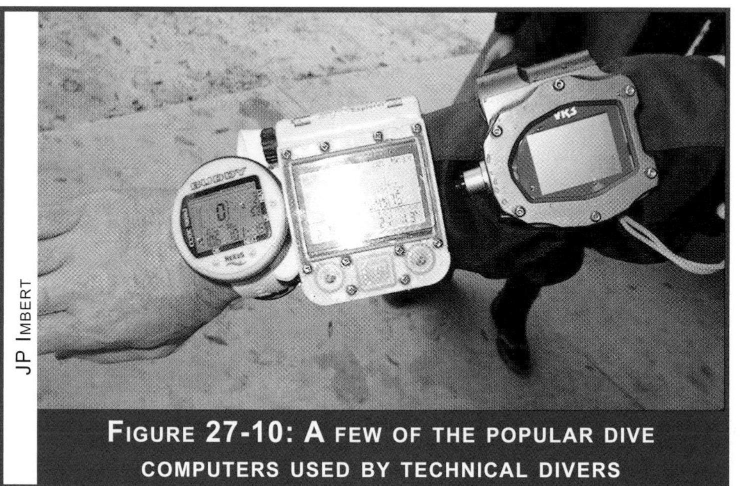

Figure 27-10: A few of the popular dive computers used by technical divers

can produce severe DCS if the stops are badly adjusted. A complete solution must be worked out, taking into account bubble growth and gas exchange.

Another way of slowing down the initial ascent is by changing the coefficients of the linear criteria. The principle is implemented in GAP software and in the Vision computer for the Inspiration rebreather. Two factors permit changing the slope and the origin of the line to obtain progressive mutations of the Bühlmann tables. This works if you are given the right values for a given dive, but the system has no predictive capability because the factors have no meaning. If you were to dive deeper or longer, the coefficients would have to be changed. How? You would need to have spent 20 years of your life in hyperbaric medicine to work out an answer.

The last option relates to the family of Variable Permeability Models (***VPM***) algorithms. The original VPM came from work carried out by Dr. Yount. He spent his life at the University of Hawaii studying gelatin tubes that he compressed in a small chamber. Through the porthole, he could see, count and measure growing bubble populations. He wanted to explain the bubbles' surprising stability during compression. He knew surface tension tended to shrink bubbles and he introduced surfactants to prevent bubbles from shrinking too much. Modern views on surfactants would challenge his findings but nevertheless he started using his model to trace the growth of an entire bubble population during a decompression. With Dr. Eric Maiken and Dr. Erik Baker, they computed surprising decompression tables with extremely deep stops which were never tested. History would have forgotten these tables if, as part of the quest of the technical diving community into deep stops, Ross Hemingway had not implemented the VPM into a well designed piece of software named "***V Planner.***" Supported by V Planner, the VPM algorithm became well-known and widely used. As it was getting used, V Planner underwent a series of modifications to replace the dramatically short shallow stops by some "Bühlmann-like stops" more acceptable to our culture.

Dr. Bruce Wienke also produced a commercial version of VPM called ***RGBM***, implemented for instance in the Suunto dive computers, but he never published it in a scientific journal with peer review, so we do not know how it works, we cannot reproduce it and, therefore, we cannot discuss it.

Understanding VPM requires several evenings reading, sending away the wife and children to ensure calm and concentration. But at the end I found it extremely disappointing as the safe ascent criteria reduces to a certain volume of gas not to exceed after surfacing. There is no physiological analysis of the possible different sites and scenarios, no understanding of the fact that different profiles would result in different symptoms. One could say that VPM is good for gelatin tubes as this is how it started. I would say that VPM certainly describes a part of the arterial bubble scenario but that it should not be used for the complete decompression. Effectively, if VPM is asked to reproduce some commercial Heliox dives with

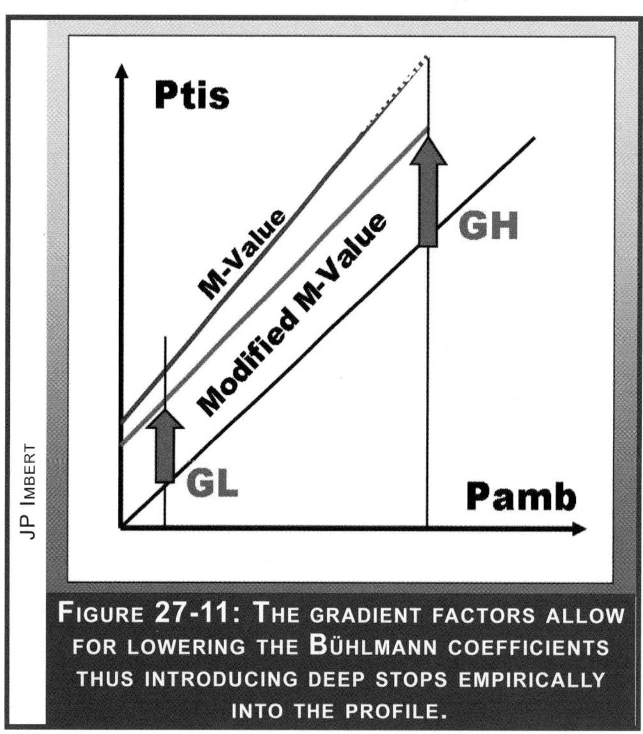

Figure 27-11: The gradient factors allow for lowering the Bühlmann coefficients thus introducing deep stops empirically into the profile.

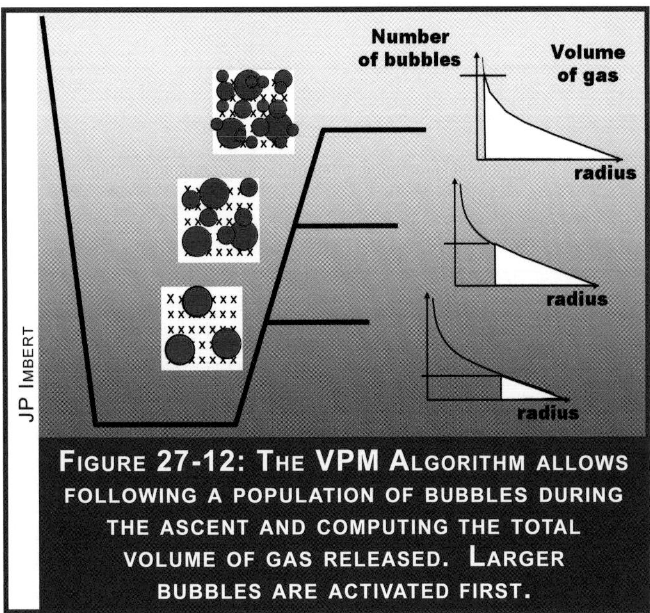

FIGURE 27-12: THE VPM ALGORITHM ALLOWS FOLLOWING A POPULATION OF BUBBLES DURING THE ASCENT AND COMPUTING THE TOTAL VOLUME OF GAS RELEASED. LARGER BUBBLES ARE ACTIVATED FIRST.

significant bottom times, its predicted decompressions fall dramatically short of the actual procedures in use.

In conclusion, at the moment the best that we can do is to combine large bubble algorithms with a bubble growth algorithm to get reasonable tables. The future belongs to models that will permit a full description of the bubble story and enough physiology to account for the various symptoms and scenarios. In its way, the ABM algorithm with its smooth transition between the tiny bubble and the large bubble might be a precursor.

In any case, the difficulty in the future will be to validate new algorithms. The Navies of the world and the offshore industry did the work before but they are now operating ROVs and manipulating arms and will no longer spend money on research into diver safety. The technical diving community is not sufficiently well organized to support scientific research and expensive validation programs. There will never again be official bodies and scientific authorities to back-up table development programs. The best we will get is a consensus of opinion. ***Be prepared to use more empirical and questionable tables.***

GREG WOLKFILL

(L TO R) LYNN PARTRIDGE, MEL CLARK & PAUL RAYMAEKER ACCUMULATING BUBBLES AT THE OLD SEATTLE PORT I-BEAMS DURING CCR TRAINING DIVES...

Chapter Twenty Eight ~ Modeling ~ Arterial Bubble Model

JP Imbert

History of the Arterial Bubble Model (ABM) Algorithm

At the turn of the 80's, the diving industry changed its way of operating in the North Sea. The construction phase was over and operations continued with inspection and maintenance jobs. As inspection work is generally shallow, commercial diving changed from Heliox saturation to air diving. At the time, the decompression tables in used in offshore industry were based on the US Navy tables. With the increased number of air diving jobs, poor safety performances became an industry concern.

In the early 80's, I was working at Comex, a large diving contractor, and I operated a diving database that contained more than 100,000 exposures from commercial diving. With these data I documented the limitations of the air tables used offshore and obtained a research contract from the French government to improve their performances. Using statistical analysis and data fitting techniques I developed a first model that I now call the ***ABM-01 algorithm***. The algorithm already used a criteria expressed as a continuous function of the compartment time period and calculated tables that looked very much like the Bühlmann ones.

The algorithm produced a complete set of tables, both with air and Heliox, for SCUBA, surface supplied and bell diving operations. The tables were sent for evaluation on selected worksites under monitoring of the Comex database. Two years later, I ran comparative statistical analysis and demonstrated the improvements made over the former procedures. The tables then became the new Comex procedures.

The complete set of tables was later included in the 1992 revision of the French commercial diving regulations and became official tables, freely available to any one. (See reference at the end of the chapter.) The tables are still largely used by diving contractors in France and the Comex database (maintained until 1995) shows that they were very safe.

However, when calculating the deep Heliox tables with the ABM-01, I had to use three sets of different coefficients to cover the full range from 160 to 600 ft (48 to 180 m). This proved that the mathematical expression was inadequate. After discussing with Tom Hennessy who published the ***Arterial Bubble Assumption*** and Dr. Philip James, who

Curt Bowen & DiveTech

Decompressing in tranquility... DiveTech shore dive, Grand Cayman

was at the time the Comex Medical Advisor in the North Sea, I started investigating the concept of a multi model approach to decompression tables. The formulation was long. The mathematics was very heavy as usual with bubble thermodynamics and I needed a simple solution because extensive data fitting was going to follow to validate the algorithm with the database. Finally, starting from Comex deep experimental dives, I "reverse engineered" a solution that gave the ***ABM-02 equation***. This formulation immediately proved very successful because I could describe my complete set of Heliox tables from 160 ft to 600 ft (48 to 180 m) with only four parameters. However, it took me sometime to found a justification to it.

Since then I have worked on further research contracts that permitted the development of the ***ABM-02 algorithm*** and its validation with air, then with Heliox and finally with Trimix. Cave divers Olivier Isler and Pascal Bernabé used some ABM-02 tables during some deep push dives. I am presently involved with the French Navy on designing a set of Trimix and Heliox tables for deep rebreather missions with the ***ABM-03*** revision. The ABM-02 model derivation is presented hereafter.

Definition of the ABM Algorithm

Using a multi-model approach to decompression safety as defined in Chapter 27, we developed a new algorithm using the arterial bubble assumption. The assumption is summarized in Figure 28-1. The algorithm was thus called the Arterial Bubble Model or *ABM* ***algorithm***.

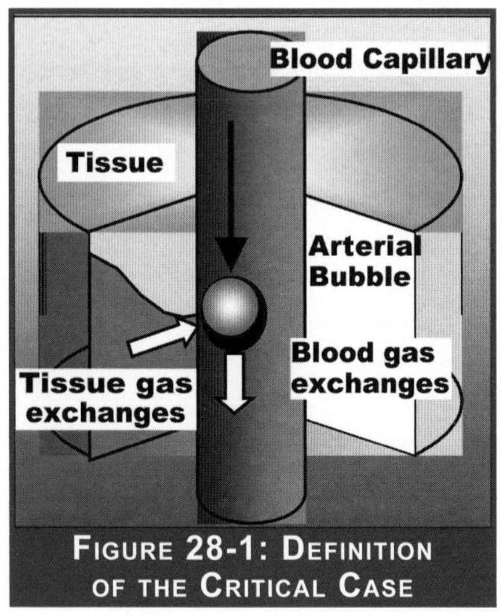

Figure 28-1: Definition of the Critical Case

The Critical Case

The critical case is defined as the arrival of an arterial bubble in a tissue compartment (see Figure 28-1).

Again, a series of simplifying assumptions was introduced:

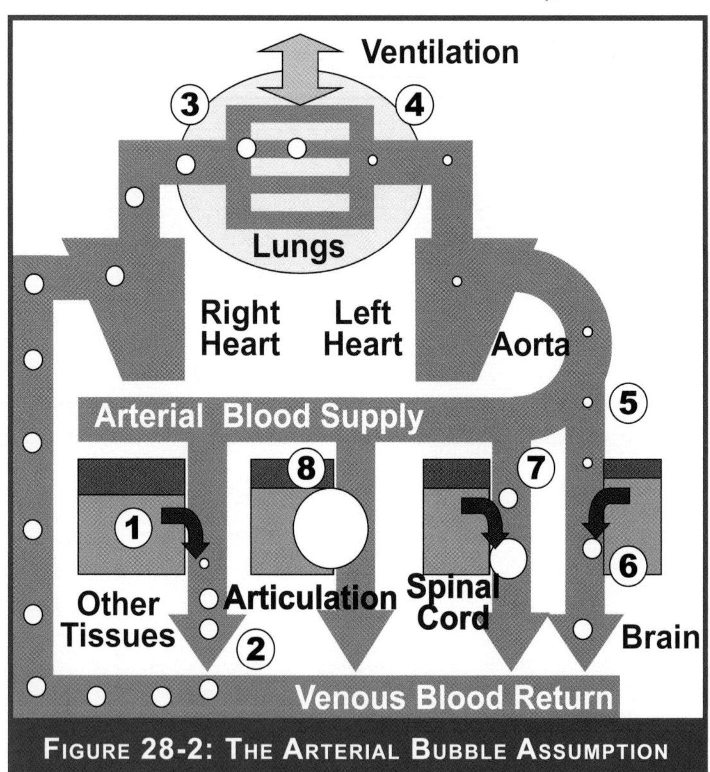

Figure 28-2: The Arterial Bubble Assumption

- The bubble was formed elsewhere. Its growth does not modify the local tissue gas load
- The bubble is reputed to be small when compared to the tissue gas capacity, at least at the beginning of the decompression process. It does not change the tissue perfusion time response
- Stuck in place, the bubble exchanges gases with both blood and the adjacent tissue
- However, the bubble is stable and keeps a critical volume
- It is expected it will not disturb the tissue blood supply and eventually will vanish into the arterial side

Additional assumptions could be added that will generate a family of solutions. However, as the validation of these models is done by data fitting, the mathematical expression should remain simple and the number of parameters was to be kept minimal.

Referring to Figure 28-2, you will see Points 1-8:

1. Diving requires breathing a compressed inert gas that dissolves in the various tissues during the bottom exposure. When the ascent is initiated, the

compartments off-load the inert gas as soon as a gradient is created

2. Bubbles are normally produced in the vascular bed and transported by the venous system to the lung
3. The lung works as a filter and stops the bubbles in its capillaries by an effect of diameter. Gas transfer into the alveoli further eliminates the bubbles
4. The critical issue is the filtering capacity of the lung system. Small bubbles may cross the lung and passes into the arterial system
5. At the level of aorta cross, the distribution of blood is such that the bubble is likely to reach the brain
6. The brain is a fast tissue and is likely to be in supersaturated state in the early phase of the decompression. It acts as a gas reservoir and feeds the bubble that starts growing. The bubble may just proceed to the venous side for another cycle. It may also grow on place causing major alteration of the blood supply and finally ischemia. The consequence will soon be central neurological symptoms
7. Much later in the decompression, bubbles may reach a significant size and produce a venous damping effect that might be responsible for spinal neurological problem
8. Finally, large bubbles may exert a local pressure, specifically in dense tissues such as tendons and ligaments that excites nerve terminations and produces pain

Structure of the Decompression Algorithm

Decompression models are all based on the same structure presented in Figure 28-3. The assumptions in the various boxes may vary from one author to the other but the logic remains the same. The input parameters correspond to the operational conditions: bottom depth, bottom time, and gas protocol. They set the initial and boundary conditions for the various equations. The gas exchange model serves to evaluate the amount of available gas at the site. A second model is used to describe the gas exchanges between the bubble and its surrounding environment. Both models may interact depending on the assumptions. The safe ascent criterion is a decision on the critical phenomena to be controlled during the ascent.

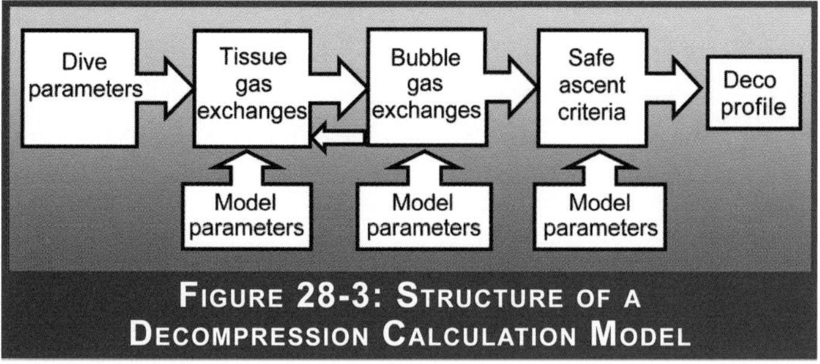

Figure 28-3: Structure of a Decompression Calculation Model

The Tissue Gas Exchange Model

Models require parameters to be defined. The number of parameters increases with the complexity of the model. It is currently admitted that models with a large number of parameters are purely descriptive and that models with a limited number parameters, corresponding to more pertinent assumptions, are more predictive. The consequence is that when the number of parameters increases, the domain of validity of the model shrinks.

Classic models used in table calculations are obviously over dimensioned in terms of parameters. Typically, the Bühlmann algorithm uses 16 compartments to calculate air tables. Considering the half-time and the two "a" and "b" coefficients for the safe ascent criteria of the various compartments, the model uses a total of 48 parameters to run. Although these tables are among of the best air tables available, it took Dr. Bühlmann a lifetime to adjust these parameters. The algorithm is fine as long it is used in its domain of validation that is mainly recreational diving. It could not be extrapolated for instance for very long bottom times as used in commercial diving.

The tissue gas exchange model is generally the main source of parameter proliferation because of the concept of tissue compartments. Tissue compartments are just an historical approach and their identification is not important. The use of a series of compartments avoids the difficulty of accurately defining the process of the gas exchanges, would it be perfusion, diffusion or combined perfusion and diffusion. Thus, in the ABM algorithms, the exponential compartments are considered as harmonics of a complex mathematical solution that are controlling the decompression one after the other. **For this reason, we used the general classic expression for compartment gas exchanges:**

(E 1) $$\frac{dPtis_{gas}}{dt} = \frac{0.693}{T}(Pa_{gas} - Ptis_{gas})$$

Where T is the compartment half-time as defined in the

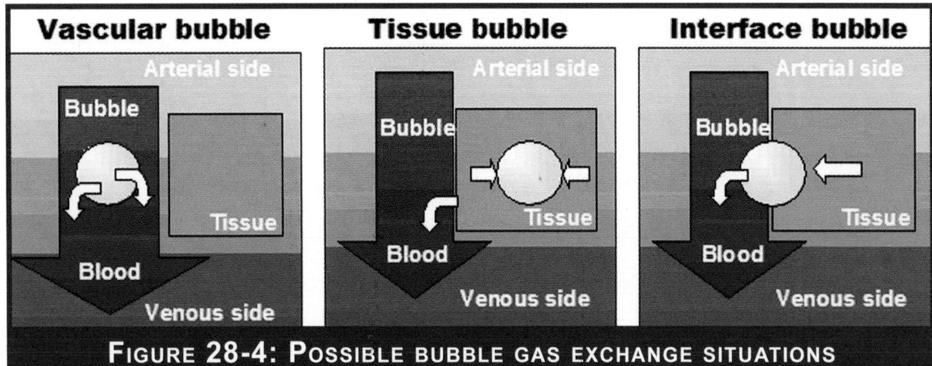

FIGURE 28-4: POSSIBLE BUBBLE GAS EXCHANGE SITUATIONS

perfusion equation, Pa and Ptis, the arterial and tissue inert gas tensions.

The ABM algorithms treat the half-time as a continuous variable. To remove any subjectivity in the selection of compartment half-times, we used a geometrical series. We selected the Renard's series, named after a French admiral who faced the standardization of ropes, sails, planks, etc. in navy arsenals, and elegantly solved the problem with a progression based on a square root of 10.

For instance, with 10 values per decade ($\sqrt[10]{10}$), the series gives the following values:

10 - 12.5 - 16 - 20 - 25 - 32 - 40 - 50 - 63 - 80 - 100 minutes

Experimentally, we found that the computation becomes stable when the number of compartments is set between 15 and 20 values per decade. This way, the description of the tissue gas exchange model only requires defining the boundaries. The fastest compartment obviously corresponds to instant equilibration and does need to be specified. The slowest compartment is defined as the one used in saturation decompressions. Based on Comex saturation experience, these values were set to 270 minutes for Heliox and 360 minutes for Nitrox saturation. This way the ABM gas exchange model only requires one parameter to be defined, corresponding to the half-time of the slowest compartment.

The Bubble Gas Exchanges Model

All gases surrounding of the bubble participate to the gas exchanges. Metabolic gases play an important role and especially CO_2. To cope with the complexity of the inert gas exchanges in the bubble, we decided to simplify the process by considering two extreme situations (Figure 28-4).

In the left box, the bubble is purely vascular and remains in place. The blood flows around it and exchanges gas by convection so efficiently that there is no laminar layer and no diffusion delay at the bubble interface. In these conditions, we adopted a formulation similar to the classic tissue perfusion equation for the bubble gas exchanges. We further assumed that the blood flow draining the bubble is a small fraction of the tissue perfusion and that the blood leaves the bubble equilibrated with its gas pressure. This permitted to arbitrary express the quantity of inert gas molecules transiting through the bubble interface into the blood as:

(E 2) $$\frac{dn,blood_{gas}}{dt} = C\frac{0.693}{T}(Pa_{gas} - Pb_{gas})$$

Where dn, $blood_{gas}$ is the number of molecules of inert gas passed from the bubble into the blood, Pa_{gas} the arterial inert gas tension, Pb_{gas} the bubble inert gas pressure, T the compartment half-time and C is a coefficient that accounts for the fraction of the tissue blood perfusion that governs these exchanges, the relative capacity of the bubble to the surrounding tissue, etc.

In the central box, the bubble is located in the tissue. The bubble exchanges gas with the surrounding tissue by diffusion. We used the classic assumption of a linear gradient in a surrounding shell and obtained a second general expression for the number of inert gas molecules diffusing through the bubble interface from the tissue.

(E 3) $$\frac{dn,tis_{gas}}{dt} = \frac{1}{K}(Ptis_{gas} - Pb_{gas})$$

Where dn,tis_{gas} is the number of molecules of inert gas diffusing from the tissue into the bubble, $Ptis_{gas}$ the tissue inert gas tension, Pb_{gas} the bubble inert gas pressure, K a coefficient that accounts the diffusibility of the gas, the thickness of the layer, the surface of the bubble, etc.

Finally, we imagined in the right box an intermediate situation where the bubble is at the interface between the blood and the tissue and exchanges gas through the two above mechanisms. The importance of the exchange varies with the relative area of the bubble exposed to each media. The ratio between the two exposed areas of the bubble is called a and varies from 0 to 1. **The inert gas mass balance of the bubble becomes:**

$$\text{(E4)}\ \frac{d(PbVb)}{dt} = R\tau\left(\alpha\frac{dn,tis_{gas}}{dt} + (1-\alpha)\frac{dn,blood_{gas}}{dt}\right)$$

Where R is the gas constant, τ is the absolute temperature and Vb the volume of the bubble.

The Safe Ascent Criteria

The ascent criteria of the ABM algorithm seeks the stability of an arterial bubble, with a critical size, stuck at the interface of the blood vessel and exchanging gas with both the blood and the tissue.

We translated this statement by specifying that the overall mass balance of the arterial bubble remains unchanged in these conditions:

$$\text{(E 5)}\quad \frac{d(PbVb)}{dt} = Pb\frac{dVb}{dt} + Vb\frac{dPb}{dt} = 0$$

At a constant ambient pressure, corresponding to the situation of a decompression stop, the stability of the bubble requires two conditions. **The first one is that the volume remains constant:**

$$\text{(E 6)}\quad \frac{dVb}{dt} = 0$$

...and the second one is that the various pressures are balanced on its' surface:

$$\text{(E 7)}\quad \frac{dPb}{dt} = 0$$

This last condition means that the sum of all the internal gas pressures equals the external ambient pressure plus the stabilization pressures (surface tension, skin elasticity, and tissue compliance). **This is written as:**

$$\text{(E 8)}\quad Pb_{gas} + Pb_{O_2} + Pb_{H_2O} + Pb_{CO_2} \leq Pamb + Pbstab$$

Where Pb_{gas}, Pb_{O2}, Pb_{H2O}, and Pb_{CO2} are respectively the pressures of the inert gas, oxygen, water vapor and CO_2 inside the bubble. Pamb is the ambient pressure and Pbstab is the sum of the various stabilization pressures.

Assuming Pb_{O2} is constant and equal to the tissue oxygen tension and introducing B, a coefficient of obvious definition, we obtained a simpler form of the criterion:

$$\text{(E 9)}\quad Pb_{gas} \leq Pamb + B$$

In these conditions, the gas transfers between the bubble and its surrounding are balanced. For each gas, the same amount of molecules enters and leaves the bubble during a unit of time. There is no gas accumulation inside the bubble. **Equations E 6 and E 5 give:**

$$\text{(E 10)}\quad (1-\alpha)\frac{dn,blood_{gas}}{dt} = -\alpha\frac{dn,tis_{gas}}{dt}$$

and yields:

$$\text{(E 11)}\quad \frac{\alpha}{K}(Ptis_{gas} - Pb_{gas}) = -(1-\alpha)C\frac{0.693}{T}(Pa_{gas} - Pb_{gas})$$

Finally, equation E 9 and E 11 are combined to eliminate Pb_{gas}. After defining a coefficient A for simplification, the final expression of the safe ascent criteria becomes:

$$\text{(E 12)}\quad Ptis_{gas} \leq (1+\frac{A}{T})(Pamb+B) - \frac{A}{T}Pa_{gas}$$

Equation (E 13) sets the condition for a safe ascent to the next stop according to the initial hypothesis: an arterial bubble, exchanging gas with blood and tissue that keeps a critical size during the ascent. It is a function similar to an M-value. With the tissue compartment tension evolution defined in E 3, it permits the classic computation of a decompression stop time. The rate of ascent to the first stop is not part of the model control and was set arbitrarily to 30 ft (9 m) per minute.

Properties of the ABM Model

The merit of the ABM-02 is to rely on an original bubble scenario, the Arterial Bubble assumption that was formulated into simple mathematical terms.

Jo Cribley diving on the *Hydro Atlantic,* South Forida

tables. The A/T coefficient works a little bit like the high gradient factor of the GAP algorithm.

The beauty of the ABM-02 algorithm mathematical expression is to provide a continuous variation from the tiny bubble scenario to the large bubble scenario as discussed in the arterial bubble assumption in Figure 28-2.

Another interesting feature of the AMB-02 expression is that it depends on the inert gas arterial tension and thus on the inspired PPO_2. With deeper dive, gas mixtures with lower oxygen percentages are selected. With deeper dives, the ABM-02 expression becomes more conservative and provides for deeper stops.

It is interesting to follow the evolution of the ABM algorithms. **This initial ABM-01 version reduced to a linear expression of Pamb presented below as E 13:**

(E 13) $$\mathbf{Ptis}_{\mathbf{gas}} \leq (1 + \frac{A}{T})(\mathbf{Pamb} + B)$$

The empirical coefficient A and B were adjusted by data fitting. With A = 8 and B = 0.4 for air diving they gave very similar tables to the Bühlmann's algorithm. This was expected from linear criteria.

The equation (E 12) of the ABM-02 is an evolution over equation (E 13) of the initial ABM-01 algorithm. The difference is comes from the A/T coefficient of the right hand side of the equation.

As the tissue compartment period increases, the A/T factor diminishes and can be neglected in the equation (E 13). Therefore, with slow tissue compartments, the ABM-02 has a similar behavior as the ABM-01. It means that for shallow stops closed to the surface, where slow tissues are directing the ascent, the ABM-02 is similar to a Bühlmann's model.

For rapid tissue compartment, with are involved in short bounce dive, and direct the initial part of the decompression, the A/T factor has a significant contribution in the equation (E 13) and the criteria very much differs from Bühlmann's tables. For short deep bounce dive, the ABM-02 algorithm provides deeper stops than for a Bühlmann decompression

As a conclusion, the advantages of the ABM algorithm are:

- It uses a realistic physiological model, the arterial bubble assumption
- It formulates the assumption is a simple mathematical way
- It uses a continuous expression of the tissue compartment time periods
- It requires a minimum of parameters
- It has been validated for air, Heliox and Trimix using a database
- Its' domain of validation ranges from surface to 600 ft (180 m)
- It produces deep stops for deep short bounce dives

The ABM-02 algorithm appears as an intermediate way between the Bühlmann and the VPM algorithms.

References

To obtain the French 1992 tables calculated with the ABM-01 algorithm, contact Imprimerie du Journal Officiel, 26 rue Desaix, 75732 Paris cedex 15, France and ask for an issue of « Mesures particulières de protection applicables aux scaphandriers. Fascicule Spécial no 74-48 bis. Bulletin Officiel du Ministère du Travail, Journal Officiel », ISBN 2-11-073322-5.

Chapter Twenty Nine ~ Modeling ~ Reduced Gradient Bubble Model

Gene Melton

Overview

Many decompression theories and algorithms have been developed over the last century. The classical Haldanian approach developed by Dr. Bühlmann was the first break though to permit the use of multi-gas mixes by recreational divers. Dr. Bühlmann's equations were a step in the right direction. Along the same time frame the Variable Permeability Model (***VPM***) was developed. VPM is discussed elsewhere. The Reduced Gradient Bubble Model (***RGBM***) roots started with VPM but swiftly evolved into a different method for the calculation of decompression requirements. At the time of this writing, all of the current decompression models use the same method to determine gas absorption and release. The method of determining where decompression must begin and the stop time requirements is the critical difference between the different algorithms. The number of tissues a model uses may vary but the general outcome of the model is essentially the same as long as there is some reasonable number of tissues considered. There is little to be gained using 32 tissues rather than 16 tissues for the decompression calculation other than a smoothing the transitions between the tissues. The fastest and slowest tissues along with an reasonable distribution in between are important for a reasonable stepped decompression profile.

Bubbles

Although not generally recognized as such, the decompression tables developed by Dr. Haldane, Dr. Bühlmann and the military permit bubble development with the goal of keeping the quantity of bubbles to a sub-clinical level where the diver remains asymptomatic. This approach allows the diver to develop bubbles during the decompression phase of the dive with the goal being no symptoms. The ***treatment*** phase of the dive is in the shallow ranges 30 fsw (9 msw) and less where the diver remains until sufficient time has passed so as to allow the bubbles to be eliminated before ascending to the next stop. The success of this approach has allowed millions of dives to be performed without clinical decompression symptoms. However, there were a number of cases where the dive developed symptoms for no apparent reason.

The RGBM was developed by Dr. Bruce Wienke. The

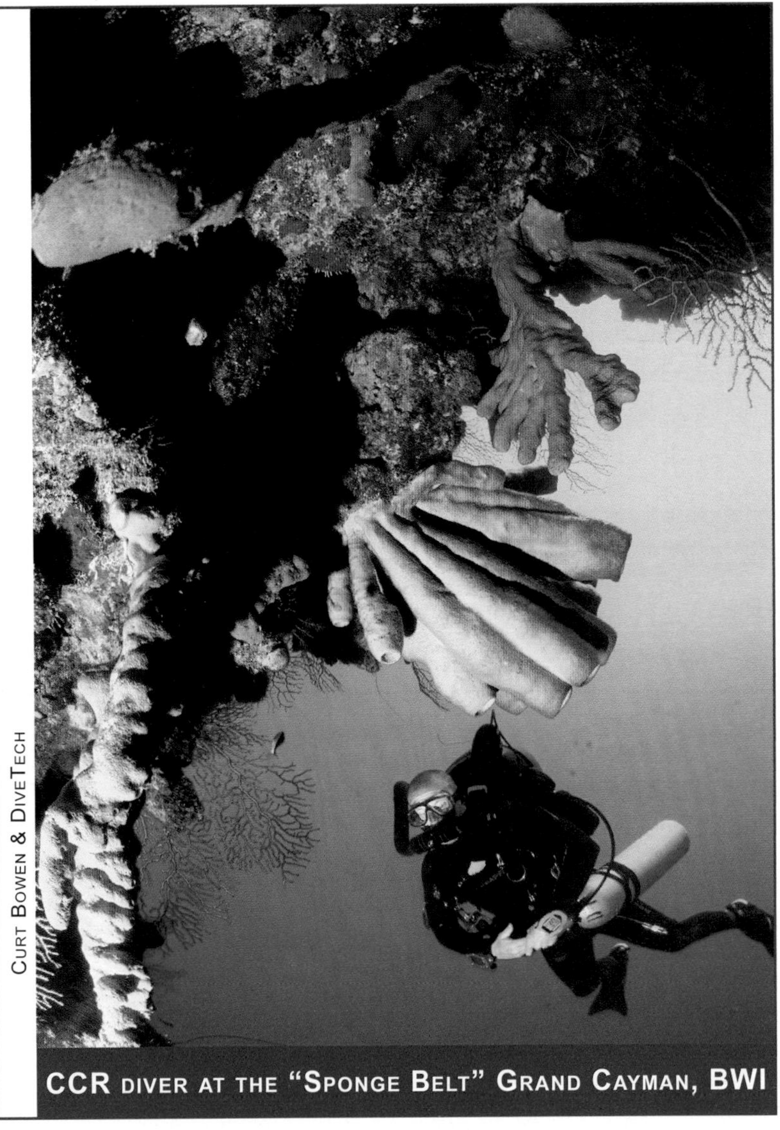

Curt Bowen & DiveTech

CCR diver at the "Sponge Belt" Grand Cayman, BWI

mathematics of RGBM is steeped in statistics and is best explained by Dr. Wienke in the books he has published on the subject. The website, www.rbgmdiving.com, has more detail and history about RGBM development as well as the titles of the books. The basic premise of RGBM is that the diver is much better off when the bubbles are never formed. With no bubbles produced, the need for the long shallow stops is reduced. Ideally the deep stops allow the elimination of sufficient dissolved gas to preclude bubble formation. This process is continued throughout the decompression process until the diver reaches the surface with no bubble production or growth.

RGBM takes into account many factors in the calculations: ascent rates 30 fsw per min (9 msw per min) or less, multi-day and multi-dive schedules, reverse profiles and bounce diving, helium-rich mixtures with recommended limited isobaric gas switches (the shallower the better) and the use of 100% in the shallow decompression stops.

RGBM Benefits & Considerations

The benefit of no bubble growth is seen in decompression profiles where the total decompression time of a RGBM profile is less than a Bühlmann profile. In any case the shorter shallow stops are important considerations in open ocean diving. The less time spent in the zone where the pressure changes caused by wave action the better. In the following example, 41 minutes at 10 fsw (3 msw) versus 61 minutes is significant. In a high sea conditions, the shorter time means less time trying to control depth and hang onto the decompression line.

The use of RGBM in cave diving can present decompression considerations. The nature of many caves may require the diver to ascend to depths requiring decompression in order to return to the surface. Gas planning in systems requiring deep in cave decompression is critical to the safe outcome of the dive. Failure to properly prepare can result in omitted decompression and the potential for DCS deep within the cave or a shortage of breathing mix at the end of the dive. Tables are not adequate for this type of diving. Real-time monitoring is mandatory for accurate decompression calculations. Tables will either be inaccurate or require (or not) decompression when the computational depth and times are guessed at beforehand.

RGBM Implementation

To date, pure RGBM schedules have been implemented in 3 ways: tables, software and a dive computer. There are approximately 500 schedules available for many depth and mix configurations including open and closed circuit.

Pure RGBM software packages available include ***GAP*** and the HydroSpace ***HS Explorer Simulator***. The GAP software is a graphical interface which displays both RGBM and Bühlmann schedules at the same time for the planned dive profile. The HydroSpace Explorer Simulator has limited RGBM output in the form of tables which may be used for planning and backup.

The only pure RGBM dive computer is HydroSpace Engineering's ***HS Explorer***. The HS Explorer provides real-time RGBM decompression calculations.

RGBM Testing

For any decompression algorithm to be useful it must be tested. The RGBM algorithm was tested by LANL with over 2000 uneventful dives. Additionally, thousands of dives have been performed using GAP software RGBM profiles. The HS Explorer adds thousands of real-time RGBM profiles to the list.

With potentially 25,000 technical dives, RGBM may be safer than any other decompression algorithm currently available.

Tom Mount

FRIENDS LIKE THESE AT DECO STOPS ALONG THE WALL IN GRAND CAYMAN CAUSE ONE TO KEEP A WATCHFUL EYE, ESPECIALLY WHEN DECO'ING IN MID-WATER.

```
*** Explorer Calculation Formula (CF) Comparison Table ***
*** HS Explorer Dive Computer Simulator - v5.0.0.4 - RGBM/Bühlmann ***
*** Copyright 2000-2008  HydroSpace Engineering Inc. ***
==========================================================================
Alt = 0, Mode = Open Circuit
Start Mix = 2, N2 = 0.26, He = 0.62, O2 = 0.12, PPO2 1.8 Depth = 461 fsw
Descent Mixes [(#) O2\He\N2, Switch Depth]:
              (2) 0.12\0.62\0.26,    0 fsw;  No descending mix changes
Bottom Mix = (2) 0.12\0.62\0.26, PPO2 1.8 Depth = 461 fsw, END = 98 fsw
Deco Mixes   [(#) O2\He\N2, Switch Depth]:
              (3) 0.32\0.40\0.28, 110 fsw;
              (4) 0.80\0.10\0.10,  30 fsw;
Decompression Stops in Feet Sea Water
```

D	BT	AT	230	220	210	200	190	180	170	160	150	140	130	120	110	100	90	80	70	60	50	40	30	20	10	TTS	(BT)	[D]	OTU
CF = 0, Algorithm: RGBM, F=100																													
300	30	3	1	0	1	1	2	1	3	3	3	4	6	5	4	3	6	6	7	12	12	19	13	20	31	172	(30)	[300]	197
CF = 5, Algorithm: ZH-L16C Bühlmann, Asymmetrical 100, F=100																													
300	30	5										1	1	2	2	4	3	4	8	6	15	13	17	24	47	156	(30)	[300]	205

```
D = Depth, BT = Bottom Time, AT = Ascent Time, TTS = Time To Surface
TTS includes Ascent Time, Decompression Time and Ascent Time between Stops
Equivalent Nitrogen Depth (END) is calculated on deepest depth
```

Figure 29-1: Comparison of decompression profiles for a 300 fsw dive

A note of caution: No decompression algorithm is a 100% guarantee against DCS. There are many variables and no two divers have the same physiology and physical makeup. The only 100% guarantee is to ***not*** dive.

RGBM Profile Data Bank

An extension of the aforementioned testing is the continuous gathering of RGBM dive data. Divers are encouraged to report their RGBM profiles so they may be forwarded to LANL. **The requested information includes:**

- Location
- Surface Interval
- Open/Closed Circuit
- Bottom mix
- Depth and time
- Descent/Ascent rate
- Decompression mixes and change depths
- Decompression stage depths and times
- Divers age, weight and gender
- Outcome

The more information that is gathered will provide more detailed data for RGBM statistical and risk analysis. Please send in your dive histories.

Figures 29-1 and 29-2, present a hypothetical open circuit dive to 300 fsw (90 msw) for 30 minutes. The bottom mix is 12% O_2, 62% He and 12% N_2. The down the (surface hypoxic) gas switch was ignored because it presents a trivial

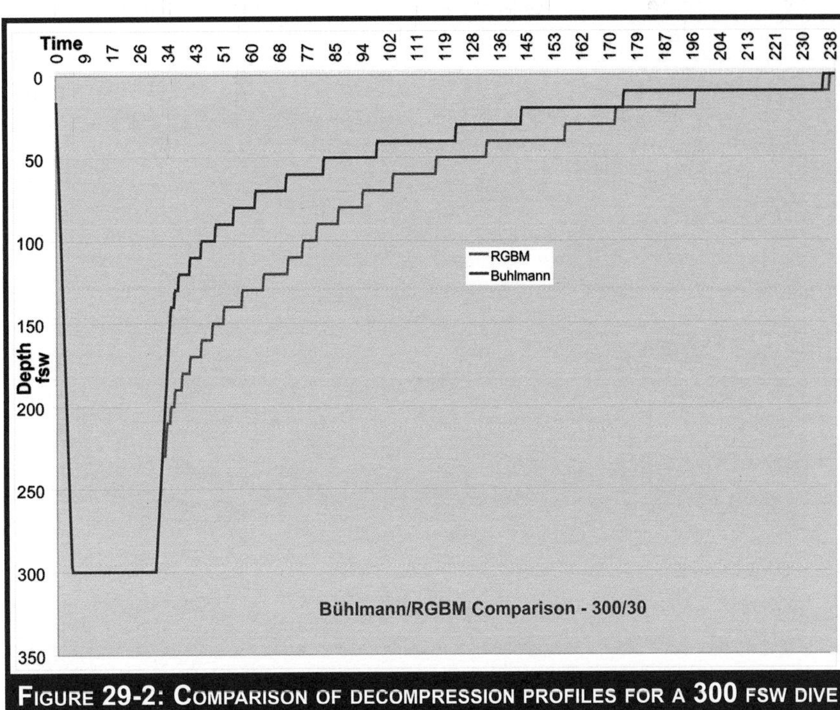

Figure 29-2: Comparison of decompression profiles for a 300 fsw dive

factor in the decompression calculation. In both RGBM and Bühlmann algorithm profiles the upward gas switches to 32/40/28 at 110 fsw (33 msw) and 80/0/20 at 30 fsw (9 msw). In the overall scheme of things the important information is the initiation of the decompression stops and the length of the shallow stops.

Note that the RGBM algorithm requires the initial stop at 230 fsw (34.5 msw) while the Bühlmann algorithm's first stop is at 140 fsw (42 msw). The difference being 90 ft (27 m) or 2.7 atmospheres. Inspection of the following graph of the two profiles reveals the ascent to the first stop in the Bühlmann algorithm. The RGBM profile is 15 minutes into the decompression schedule at the same depth the Bühlmann algorithm starts. The two schedules briefly touch at the 20 fsw (6 msw) stop then finally converge for the last 2/3's of the 10 fsw (3 msw) stop.

Observe also that RGBM has a much more gradual in the ascent profile. The Bühlmann schedule arrives at the 50 fsw (15 msw) stop in 43 minutes where as the RGBM takes 77 minutes to reach the same depth. It is easy to see that RGBM decompression schedules are more gradual and have lower tissue pressure gradients when compared to Bühlmann schedules.

Conclusion

RGBM presents an advanced decompression algorithm for technical diver. The deep stops prevent bubble generation and subsequent growth as is allowed by single phase mechanic algorithms. The methods for implementation are no different than other algorithms. Testing results and diver reports provide for the safety of RGBM profiles.

Mel Clark

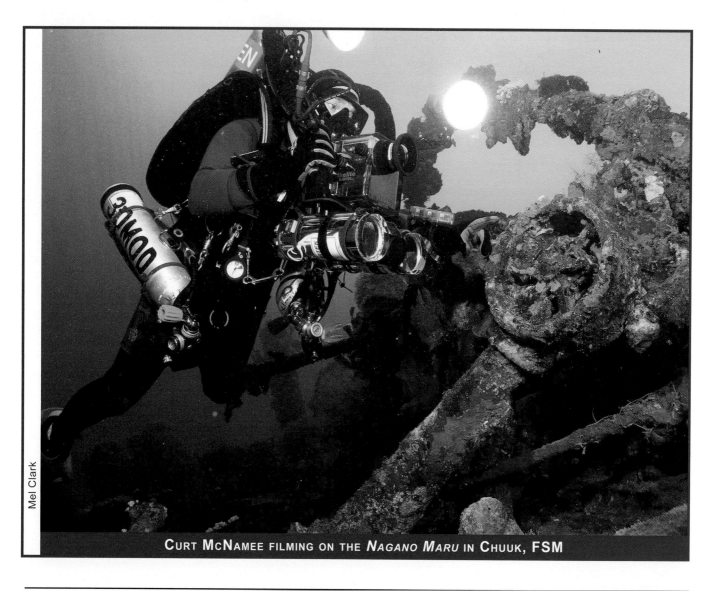

Curt McNamee filming on the *Nagano Maru* in Chuuk, FSM

Chapter Thirty ~ Modeling ~ Varying Permeability Model

Simon Pridmore and JP Imbert

Overview

The original study of Varying Permeability Models (***VPM***) was carried out during the 1970's and 1980's by a team of researchers at the University of Hawaii led by Dr. David Yount (see ***History of VPM*** sidebar on next page).

Their initial purpose was to observe and describe bubble formation and growth during depressurization of tubes of gelatin that were compressed in a small chamber. Through a plexi-glass viewing port in the chamber, using a microscope, the researchers could see, count and measure growing bubble populations.

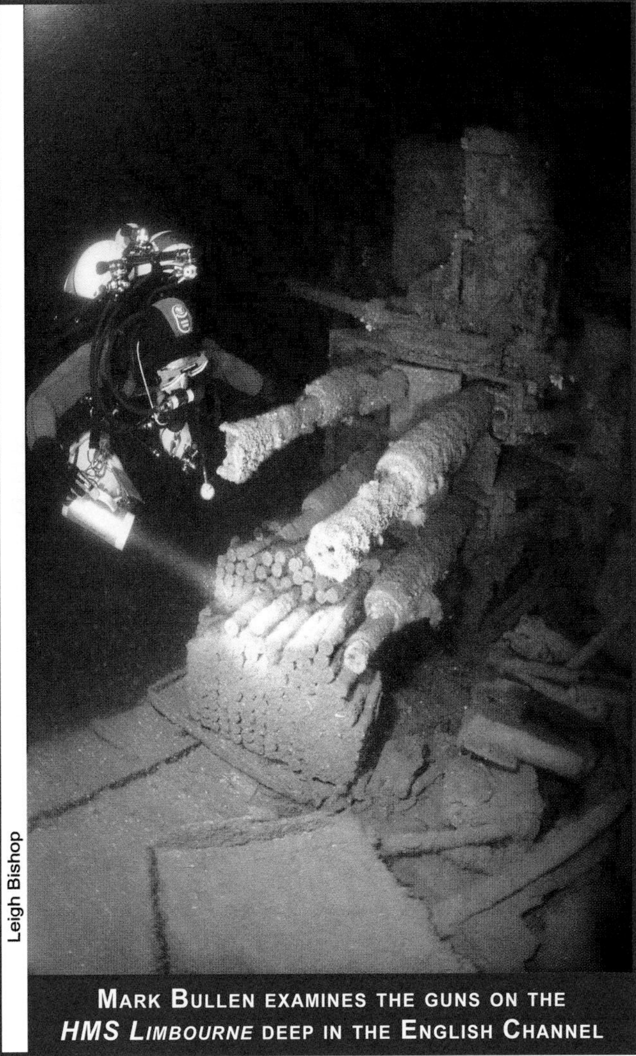
Leigh Bishop

Mark Bullen examines the guns on the *HMS Limbourne* deep in the English Channel

He established a relationship between the number of bubbles and the supersaturation gradient and this he defined as the difference between saturation pressure and decompression pressure, essentially Haldane's theory adapted to gelatine and quantified in terms of the number of bubbles. He expected to find a nice linear relationship but discovered a line that was far from straight.

So he reviewed his protocol. First he filtered the gelatin and used distilled water to remove all impurities. The bubbles almost disappeared. Then he added impurities and the number of bubbles dramatically increased. He concluded therefore that the bubbles were generated because of the impurities and that there were pre-existing seed-nuclei, ***93% of …*** (which were...) ***already present in the water in which the gelatin is prepared.***

The Yount Experiment

He speculated that if the nuclei were there from the start, it might be possible to eliminate them by compressing them. He therefore changed the experiment and subjected the gelatine tubes first to a ***crush*** pressure.

He found that the bubbles were more durable than he had thought. By increasing the pressure he managed to make the bubbles smaller but could not make them disappear. He tried a variety of methods.

Yount wanted to explain the bubbles' surprising stability during compression. He knew surface tension tended to

The History of the Varying Permeability Model

1974 – 1984: Series of Research Papers released by Yount, Hoffman and others on:

- **Bubble formation**
- **Bubble nucleation in supersaturated fluids**
- **Isobaric bubble growth**
- **Skins of varying permeability**
- **Determination of the radii of gas cavitation nuclei**
- **Application of a bubble formation model to decompression sickness**
- **Evolution, generation, and regeneration of gas cavitation nuclei**
- **Use of a cavitation model to calculate diving tables**
- **Microbubble fission in surfactant solutions**
- **Microscopic investigation of bubble formation nuclei**

1986: Varying Permeability Model (VPM) dive tables published by Yount and Hoffman

1994: Eric Maiken distributes his BASIC VPM program to divers and researchers

1995: The Yount and Hoffman (1986) VPM algorithm is made freely available to programmers and researchers at the teK95 Diving Technology Conference

1995: Eric Maiken releases his VPM program code reporting his experiences with non-Bühlmann based decompression.

1999: VPM development progresses with David Yount, Eric Maiken and Erik Baker working on repetitive diving and a paper for the Smithsonian conference on reverse dive profiles

2000: David Yount dies, aged 64

The core VPM algorithm is finalized. The algorithm has advanced beyond Yount/Hoffman's original 1986 paper to include, among other things, multiple inert gases and switches and the effects of multiple consecutive dives

Erik Baker's Fortan VPM program codes are finalized. This becomes the standard implementation of VPM

2001: Ross Hemingway adapts the VPM Fortan code by Erik Baker from DOS into a full Windows program. The new program is named V Planner

2002: VPM is adapted for use with CCR planning. As a result of diver feedback and documented experiences grow a revised model is released and named VPM-B

2004: IANTD includes VPM-B tables into all new training courses

2005 to Present:

- **V Planner program is further developed to include many of the current tech diving planning features and practices**
- **VPM-B/E model option introduced**
- **Delta P Technology announces an optional VPM/BE based alternative algorithm for its range of VR dive computers**

shrink bubbles and he introduced surfactants to prevent the bubbles from shrinking too much. Modern views on surfactants would challenge his findings but nevertheless he started using his model to trace the growth of an entire bubble population during a decompression. **Yount's conclusions were:**

- Seed nuclei exists in tissues
- Any gas bubble beyond a certain size, depending on the depth of a dive will increase in size during decompression
- During ascent the aim is to keep the volume of bubbles below a certain critical volume at the end of the decompression

With the help of Hoffman, in 1986 Yount computed decompression tables with extremely deep stops which were never tested and would have been forgotten by history if it had not been for Technical Diving.

Many years later in the mid-nineties technical divers were looking for decompression tables for deep Trimix dives and two key individuals picked up on the pioneeering work of Yount and Hoffman. The first, Bruce Wienke, developed an adaptation which he called the Reduced Gradient Bubble Model (***RGBM***). The second, Erik Baker, who had worked with Yount, was a cave diver who developed a number of versions of the VPM for his own use and generously announced these on the Internet, along with a number of excellent articles on the VPM (from which this article draws).

Then as part of the continuing quest of the technical diving community into deep stops, Ross Hemingway implemented the VPM into a well designed piece of software named ***V-Planner***. Via V-Planner the VPM algorithm became well-known and widely used by divers at the more extreme and exploratory end of the sport. This empirical testing led V-Planner to undergo a series of modifications to replace the original dramatically short shallow stops by stops of a more ***Bühlmann-like*** duration, more akin to what divers were used to.

What is the VPM?

The VPM presumes that microscopic voids and gas nuclei exist in water, and tissues that contain water, before the start of a dive. Any nuclei larger than a specific ***critical*** size, which is related to the maximum dive depth (***exposure pressure***), will grow upon decompression. The VPM aims to minimize the total volume of these growing bubbles by keeping the external pressure high, and the inspired inert gas partial pressures low, during decompression.

The term ***Varying Permeability*** refers to the different responses of bubble nuclei to pressurizations encountered on dives deeper than approximately 9 ATA, compared to shallower dives. On deep dives, nuclei are thought to become impermeable to the flow of gas, and the VPM generates more conservative tables for these deeper dives.

The first and last schedules produced for a short dive are often quite different. This results from the contribution of both the magnitude of the growth gradient and the time that the gradient acts to drive bubble growth. After a short dive, the tissues will off-gas rapidly to the circulation. Hence, because the time that the gradient acts is small, the magnitude of growth gradient can be increased by allowing shorter and shallower stops.

VPM tables handle the in- and out-gassing of dissolved gas in tissues the same way as conventional neo-Haldane calculations do. That is, parallel compartments with exponential half-times ranging from minutes to hours are used to model the uptake and elimination of inert gas by the body.

The VPM postulates that as a diver ascends, nuclei larger than a specific ***critical*** size, which is related to the maximum dive depth, descent rate, and breathing mix, will grow upon decompression.

The VPM aims to minimize the total volume of these

Michael Dudas

EVELYN DUDAS, MEMBER OF THE WOMEN DIVER'S HALL OF FAME, IS THE 1ST WOMAN TO DIVE THE *ANDRIA DORIA*, AND ONE OF THE 1ST FEMALE CAVE DIVERS CERTIFIED BY **IANTD.**

growing bubbles by keeping the external pressure large (through deep stops), and by keeping the inspired inert gas partial pressures low during decompression.

The VPM uses a step-by-step procedure to refine decompression schedules. In each step, a new ascent schedule is calculated. The total decompression time is fed back into the calculation to revise the critical gradients, and a more liberal schedule is produced at each step. This process is repeated until the decompression time converges to a length that corresponds to the formation of the maximal allowable amount of free gas bubbles. The total decompression time depends on the contributions of the magnitude of the growth gradient and the time that the gradient acts to drive bubble growth. After a short dive, the tissues will off-gas rapidly to circulation.

A divergence of the VPM from conventional calculations is in how a diver's ascent is controlled. Rather than setting pre-defined limits (like M-values) on the maximum pressure ratio between gas dissolved in tissues and ambient pressure, ascents are limited by gradients that depend on specific details of a particular dive, which include factors such as depth, gas mix, and descent rate. The objective is to control the volume of gas that evolves in the body due to the inevitable formation of bubbles. As long as this volume is kept smaller than a certain "***critical volume***," it is presumed that a diver's body has the ability to tolerate the bubbles. If the volume of bubbles exceeds the critical volume, then the diver is at risk of developing DCI.

VPM decompression computations handle the in- and out-gassing of dissolved gas in a set of compartments the

same way as standard dissolved gas algorithms. However, the VPM does not associate individual compartments with specific organs or tissues in the body. Parallel compartments with exponential half-times ranging from minutes to hours are used to model the body's range of time scales governing the uptake and elimination of dissolved inert gas.

The volume of the gas in bubbles is related to the product: (***Number of Bubbles***) ***x*** (***Gradient***) ***x*** (***Growth Time***). The number of growing bubbles is set by the maximum compression encountered on a dive. This crushing pressure is related to the deepest depth of the dive as well as the descent rate and gas mixture.

The gradients and bubble growth time are controlled by the ascent schedule, with the surface as the last decompression stop.

For the Neophyte: Questions Regarding VPM

What works, works. If you are a diver who engages in decompression diving and you have been using a decompression model for years that works for you and with which you are satisfied then why change it? If however you are dissatisfied in some way with the profiles your current computer or desktop decompression software is giving you or you have heard and read the many glowing reports on the benefits of the VPM model, then by all means see for yourself what the fuss is all about. Many divers around the world are using VPM and other bubble models in their diving, and feeling better post dive than they did on the models they were using before.

But bear in mind that VPM is a theory. There is a growing database of proven dives but this is still smaller than the database for competing models and there are few scientific results to review. Much reporting is subjective and anecdotal.

Note that VPM does require specific control of depth and time during decompression.

If you're getting started and unsure about VPM, try planning with conservatism of +4 and padding out the last two or three stops to look like any M-value deco model.

The VPM-B/E model variation introduced by Ross Hemingway is for exceptional, extreme, or extra long dives and exposures. It gives a more relaxed version of a plan for dives when extra safety is prudent. With bigger dives (typically more than 100 mins deco), a B/E model plan will diverge from the VPM-B, and produce something similar to a combined VPM-B and Haldane plan.

Divers who carry out very long deco dives often prefer this "best of both worlds," or combining theories approach to dive planning.

This is the sort of conservative approach applied in the IANTD VPM-B based waterproof decompression tables and to the new optional alternative VPM-based algorithm introduced for the Delta P VR range of decompression computers.

Then, if you are happy with the profiles generated and feel that you are being overly conservative, then over a series of dives work your way cautiously closer to a +3 or +2 setting, eliminating the additional padding, until you find a solution that best suits your needs.

Be aware that with the VPM:

1. Safe ascent criteria just boil down to a certain volume of gas not to exceed after surfacing;
2. There is no physiological analysis of possible different bubble sites and scenarios; and
3. There is no attempt to explain the fact that different profiles result in different symptoms.

Therefore it is not a universal panacea, nor is it a one-stop solution to the mysteries of decompression. It is only a theory that describes a part of the arterial bubble scenario. In the field of decompression science we have no answers as such, we still have only competing theories and, as JP Imbert describes so eloquently in his piece in Chapter 27 in this ***Encyclopedia***, combining theories is probably the best route available to today's divers. ~ ***Simon***

Further Reading

http://www.hhssoftware.com/v-planner/index.html
http://www.decompression.org/maiken/VPM/VPM_Algorithm.htm
http://www.gue.com/Research/Exercise/q3_1l.htm

Chapter Thirty One ~ Modeling ~ Gradient Factors

Matti Anttila Ph.D.

Remember your first diving classes and the lesson about a bubbling soda bottle as it relates to a too rapid ascent? No matter how deeply you study the decompression theory, this soda bubble analogy is still valid. However, it's time to introduce some more fundamentals of the issue. But let's start from the history.

History

Decompression theory is a relatively old science. Already in late 1800's, French physiologist Paul Bert (1833-1886) discovered decompression sickness and the need for decompression stops and slow ascend speed. Bert also studied the effects of oxygen to the humans, as he was more interested in the physiological effects of mountaineering and hot air ballooning. He also extended his studies to cover high pressure environments, and found out later about oxygen toxicity. Bert made a conclusion that high oxygen partial pressures affect humans chemically, not mechanically, as he described the causes of Central Nervous System (***CNS***) oxygen toxicity. When Bert studied air and nitrogen, he correctly determined the cause of the Decompression Sickness (***DCS***) to be caused by the nitrogen bubbles in the blood and other tissues (mechanical effects). Bert also did experiments on recompression therapy and oxygen administration in DCS cases. The most famous of Bert's books is "***La Pression barometrique***"[1], published in 1878, which dealt with the human physiology in low and high air-pressures.

While Bert laid the fundamentals to the decompression studies, it was John Scott Haldane (1860-1936), a Scottish physiologist who approached the problem of decompression theory with more scientific approach. In 1905, Haldane was appointed by the Royal Navy to perform research about Navy's diving operations. His focus was to study the decompression sickness and how it could be avoided. Haldane performed several tests and studied the effects of compressed air at depth, and in 1908 he published the results of his tests in the Journal of Medicine [2]. This article also contained his diving tables.

Haldane is considered to be the father of modern decompression theory. In his research, he made an important conclusion that a diver could surface from an indefinitely long 33 ft (10 m) dive without DCS. From this result, he determined that human body could tolerate pressure change with a factor of 2:1 (the pressure at 33 ft [10 m] is 2 ATA, while on the surface it is 1 ATA). Later this number was refined to be 1.58:1 by Robert Workman. Workman was an M.D. and decompression researcher in U.S. Navy during 1960's. He studied systematically the decompression model that was used in the U.S. Navy and which was then based on Haldane's research. In addition to refining the tissue pressure ratio, Workman found out that the ratio varied by tissue type (hence the term "tissue compartment" (***TC***), representing different half-times, e.g. speed of gas dissolving) and depth.

Dr. Albert A. Bühlmann (1923-1994) from Zürich developed decompression theory further. During his long research career, he extended the number of tissue compartments to 16, which was the basis of his ZH-L16 decompression model (***"ZH" as Zürich, "L" as Linear and "16" for the number of TCs***). The first set of ZH-L16 tables was published in 1990 (previous tables[3], published earlier, contained smaller amount of TCs).

Decompression Basics

Let's start from basics: A diver goes down and breathes compressed air from his/her cylinder. Air contains nitrogen, which, as an inert gas, dissolves into the diver's tissues. When the diver starts ascending, the ambient pressure decreases and dissolved nitrogen transfers from other tissues to the blood, from there to the lungs and finally leaves the body with each exhale cycle. Simple as that, is it?

James Rozzi

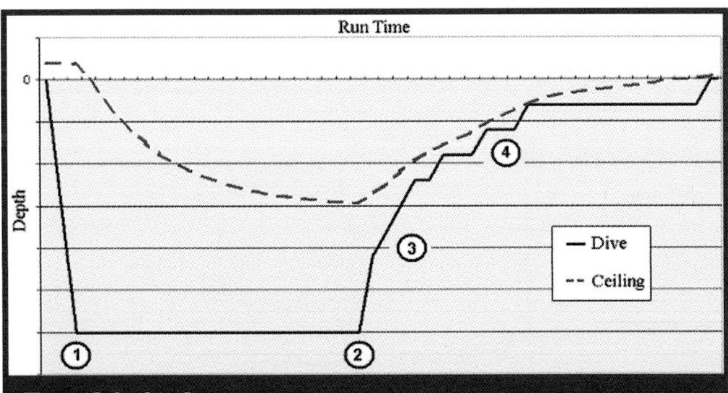

Fig. 31-1: A typical decompression dive profile with ceiling line visible. The numbers represent different phases (See Phases in Fig. 31-2)

In recreational diving, no decompression dives are being conducted. Divers are told to stay within their no-decompression limits (*NDL*) of bottom time. This NDL is shown in diving tables, and besides that, divers must stay within certain ascent speed. This information is generally enough for most divers, but what happens when we exceed the NDL and start accumulating decompression time?

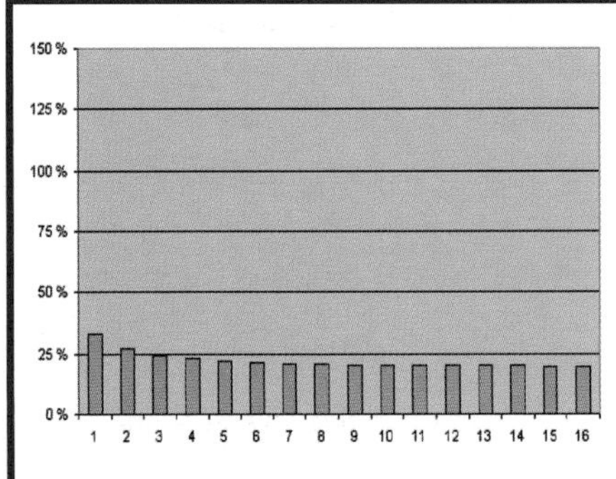

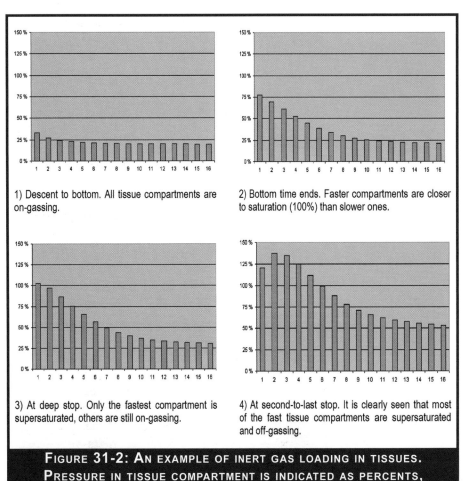

1) Descent to bottom. All tissue compartments are on-gassing.

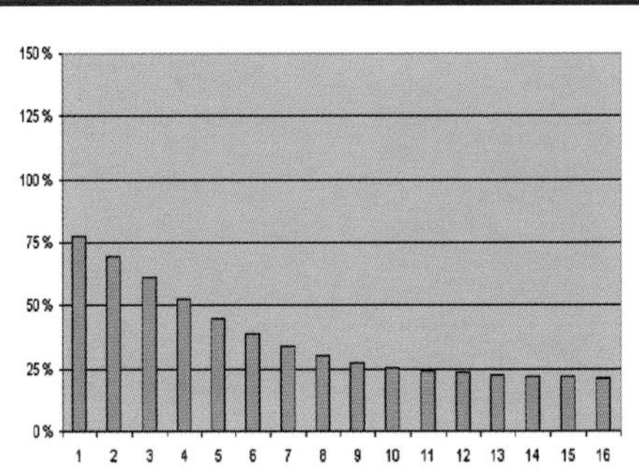

2) Bottom time ends. Faster compartments are closer to saturation (100%) than slower ones.

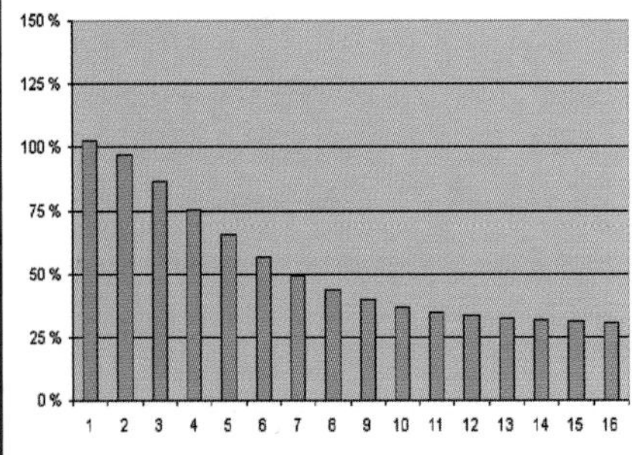

3) At deep stop. Only the fastest compartment is supersaturated, others are still on-gassing.

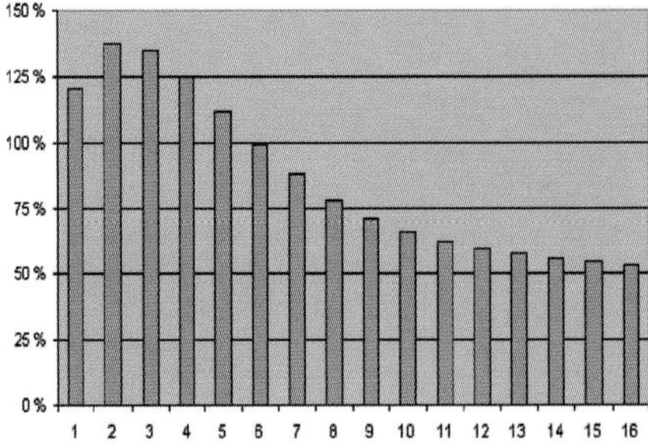

4) At second-to-last stop. It is clearly seen that most of the fast tissue compartments are supersaturated and off-gassing.

Figure 31-2: An example of inert gas loading in tissues. Pressure in tissue compartment is indicated as percents, 100% being ambient pressure.

Tissue Saturation & Ascent Ceiling

When we dive, we always have an invisible ceiling above us. This ceiling is a depth, which we can ascend to without getting DCS symptoms (generally speaking). The ceiling is based on the amount of dissolved inert gas in our tissues.

Figure 31-1 represents a typical decompression dive profile with multiple decompression stops. Before the dive, your "ceiling" is in fact ***negative*** depth (above surface), meaning that your tissues could tolerate certain overpressure gradient. As the run time increases and diver spends time at the bottom, the ceiling depth goes down and starts limiting the ascent possibilities, generating the need for decompression. In fact, some decompression software indicates the ceiling depth when user types in the desired dive levels. Diving computers indicate the ceiling as the deepest required decompression depth.

When the ascent starts, the diver can not ascend above the ceiling without risking the possibility of decompression sickness. The decompression stops are clearly visible in the dive profile in Figure 31-1. The closer one goes to the ceiling, the less margin of safety remains. The ceiling depth does not yet indicate on-gassing or off-gassing. Bühlmann used 16 tissue compartments to model inert gas dissolving in our body. These compartments either take more dissolved gas in (***on-gassing***) or expel dissolved gas out (***off-gassing***). The ceiling depth indicates the pressure change from current depth, in which the leading compartment off-gasses so fast, that further increased pressure drop would risk the possibility of DCS.

Figure 31-2 illustrates these 16 tissue compartments during the dive, presented in Figure 31-1. A tissue compartment (***TC***) has reached its saturation point when it is 100% full. During the ascent phase, a TC can go supersaturated (exceed 100%). The key of the decompression is to be supersaturated, but not so much that the dissolved gas would form excess bubbles to our tissues and blood.

As shown, the amount of dissolved gas, or specifically the partial pressure of the dissolved inert gas in our tissues, tends to follow the ambient pressure in which we are during the dive. The bigger the pressure difference (i.e. ***pressure gradient***), the faster the gas dissolves, in both directions. This leads to an obvious question: Why not just come up? What are the limits of supersaturation, and how are they defined?

DIVERS TOURING CARGO DECK OF *KT12* OFF THE EAST COAST OF SARDINIA

M-Values

Back to the history: Robert Workman introduced the term ***M-value***, which means ***Maximum*** inert gas pressure in a hypothetical tissue compartment which it can tolerate without DCS. As mentioned, Haldane found out in his research that M-value is 2, and Workman refined it to be 1.58. (This number comes from pressure change from 2 ATA to 1 ATA, and taking into account that air has 79% inert gases, mainly nitrogen.)

Workman determined the M-values using depths (pressure values) instead of ratios of pressure, which he then used to form a linear projection as a function of depth. The slope of the M-value line is called ΔM (***delta-M***) and it represents the change of M-value with a change in depth (***depth pressure)***.

Bühlmann used the same method than Workman to express the M-values, but instead of using the depth pressure (relative pressure), he used absolute pressure, which is 1 ATA higher at depth. This difference is shown in Figure 31-3, where Workman's M-value line goes above Bühlmann's M-value line.

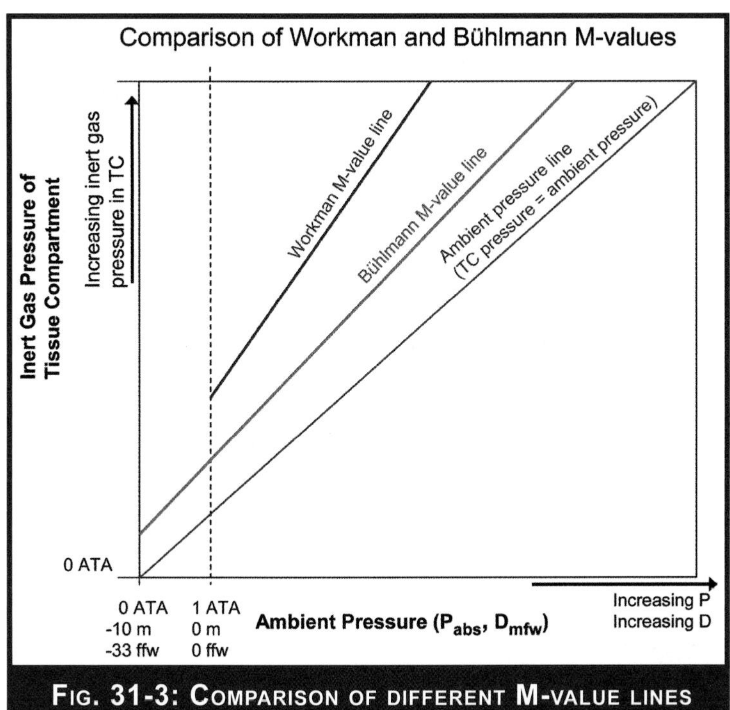

FIG. 31-3: COMPARISON OF DIFFERENT M-VALUE LINES

Figure 31-3 shows a comparison between Workman and Bühlmann M-value lines. A more detailed explanation can be found in literature[4], but it is easy to spot the greatest differences: while Workman M-value line is steeper than Bühlmann M-value line, there is also less margin for safety. Workman M-values also allow higher supersaturation than Bühlmann's.

To make things a bit more complex, it should be noted that while the M-values vary by tissue compartment, also two sets of M-values are used for each TC; M_0-values (of ***depth pressure, indicating surfacing pressure. M_0 is pronounced "M naught"***) and M-values of pressure ratio (*ΔM, "**delta-M**"* values). Workman defined the relationship of these different M-values as:

$$M = M_0 \times \Delta M \cdot d$$

where:

M = partial pressure limit for each TC (in ATA units)
M_0 = partial pressure limit at sea level for each TC (ATA)
ΔM = increase of M per depth, defined for each TC (ATA/m)
d = depth (m)

These sets of values are listed in literature [4]. However, they concern the same thing: maximum allowed overpressure of the tissue compartments. It is also important to know, that decompression illness does not exactly follow the M-values. More sickness occurs at and above the pressures represented by the M-values, and less sickness occurs when divers stay well below the M-values.

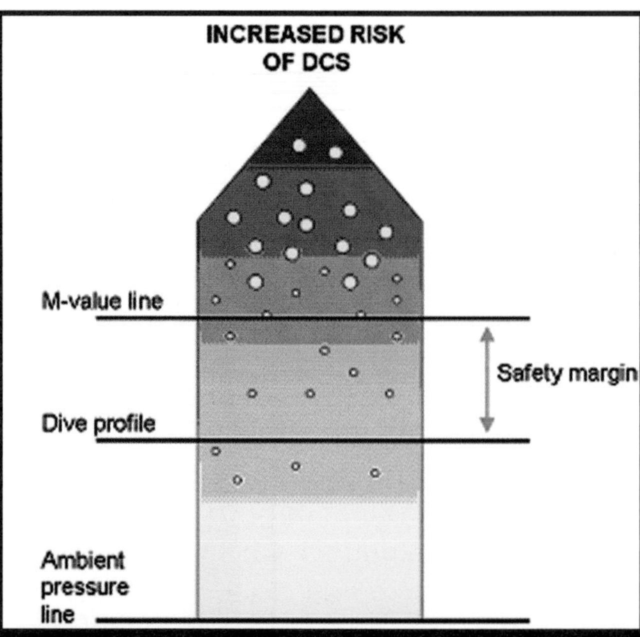

Figure 31-5: Silent bubbles are present in our tissues even when no DCS symptoms are present. It is important to know one's personal safety margin and individual susceptability to DCS.

Gradient Factors

Gradient Factors (*GF*) are meant to offer conservatism settings for Bühlmann's decompression model. As mentioned in the previous chapter, M-value line sets a limit which is not supposed to be exceeded during ascent and decompression. However, as no decompression model can positively prevent all DCS cases, and because both dives and divers are individual, additional safety margin should be applied.

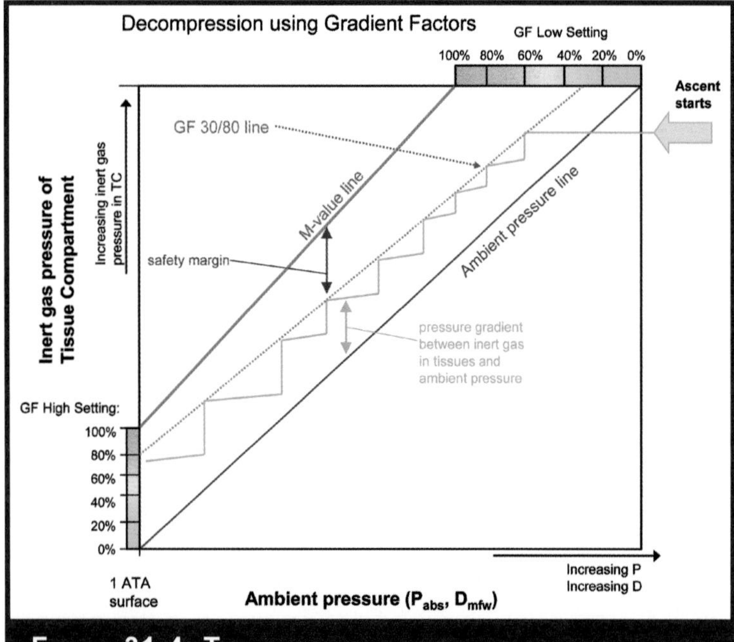

Figure 31-4: The one-tissue model of decompression graph starts from top right and slants down to the left, between the ambient pressure and gradient factor (GF) lines. The GF line stays below the M-value line and forms the safety margin for decompression. Pure Bühlmann decompression follows the M-value line (GF 100/100).

As shown in Figure 31-3, ascent and decompression occurs between the M-value line and Ambient Pressure line. Inert gas pressure in tissue compartments must exceed the ambient pressure to enable off-gassing. On the other hand, we do not want to go too close to the M-value line for safety reasons. Gradient Factors define the conservatism here.

The GF defines the amount of inert gas supersaturation in leading tissue compartment. Thus, GF 0% means that there is no supersaturation occurring and inert gas partial pressure equals ambient pressure in leading compartment (***Note: The leading TC is not necessarily the fastest TC!***) GF 100% means that decompression is being done in a situation where the leading TC is at its Bühlmann's M-value line and risk for DCS is far greater than using lower GF. (***Note: Sometimes, especially in equations and calculations, GF's may be numbered as 0.00 ... 1.00 instead of percentage. However, these are effectively the same thing as 100% = 1.***)

Some diver's did not like the idea of using the same conservatism factor throughout the ascent. Instead of having one GF, there was need to change the safety margin during the ascent. This led to two GF values;

"*GF Low*" and "*GF High.*" Low Gradient Factor defines the first decompression stop, while High Gradient Factor defines the surfacing value. Using this method, the GF actually changes throughout the ascent. This is illustrated in Figure 31-4, where GF Low and GF High form start and end points to a ***Gradient Factor Line***. In this line graph, decompression starts when the inert gas partial pressure in diver's TC's reaches 30% of the of the way between the Ambient Pressure line and the M-value line. Then the diver spends time at that stop until partial pressure drops low enough in the TC's for enabling ascent to the next stop, which again has a bit higher GF. These two GF values are often written as "*GF Low-% / High-%,*" e.g. GF 30/80, where 30% is GF Low value and 80% is GF High value.

Practical Applications & Safe Diving Habits

No decompression model can positively prevent divers getting hit. M-values do not represent any hard line between ***no DCS symptoms*** and ***getting hit***. In fact, modern decompression science has proven that there might be bubbles present in our tissues even when there are no DCS symptoms after a dive. Therefore, M-values neither represent a bubble-free situation, but ***tolerable*** amount of "***silent***" bubbles in tissues.

It is important to understand that certain dives and different people may need different safety margins. Therefore it is good to know the practical differences between dive plans where different Gradient Factors are used. **Let's take another example:**

A diver goes to 165 ft (50 m) for 20 minutes bottom time, using Trimix 18 45 (18% oxygen, 45% helium) as back gas, and oxygen for decompression from 20 ft (6 m) on. Descent rate is 50 ft/min (15 m/min) and ascent rate is 33 ft/min (10 m/min). Decompression algorithm is based on Bühlmann ZH-L16B and the different decompression tables, based on five different GFs, are shown in Figure 31-6.

These GF parameters are commonly used for different types of dives (e.g. rebreather, deep/cold dives, default values in some decompression SW) and GF 100/100 is shown here as a reference, since it is pure Bühlmann table (containing no margin, so it is also not very safe!) As clearly shown in Figure 31-6, low GF Low numbers generate deeper stops. In fact, some divers use GF Low value of 10% to generate "deep stops"[5]. Deep stops, also called "***Pyle Stops,***" are a means to reduce micro-bubbles during deeper phase of ascent. However, during deep stops, many slower tissues are still on-gassing and thus total decompression time will increase. (But again, safety is worth some added hang-time!) Small ***GF High*** values generate longer shallow stops, as also seen in Figure 31-6.

It is easy to modify the dive plan even drastically by using different gradient factors. Most modern decompression software provides either conservatism settings (in verbal terms or numbers) or gradient factors. A diver can modify the total dive time easily by even tens of minutes with these settings, not to mention also the decompression gas needed. But this is also a pitfall; consider a situation where decompression software indicates that you need an

BÜHLMANN ZH-L16

Depth: 165 ft (50 m)
BT: 20 min
Back gas: Trimix 18 45
Deco gas: O2

Depth ft (m):	Time At Depth With Different Gradient Factors:					Gas:	Note:
	GF 10/90	GF 20/70	GF 30/85	GF 36/95	GF 100/100		
165 ft (50 m)	20	20	20	20	20	Trimix 18 45	Run time: 3...20min
100 ft (30 m)	1					Trimix 18 45	
90 ft (27 m)	1	1				Trimix 18 45	
80 ft (24 m)	1	1	1			Trimix 18 45	
70 ft (21 m)	1	2	1	1		Trimix 18 45	
60 ft (18 m)	1	3	2	2		Trimix 18 45	
50 ft (15 m)	3	3	3	2		Trimix 18 45	
40 ft (12 m)	3	5	3	3	2	Trimix 18 45	
30 ft (9 m)	7	10	7	5	3	Trimix 18 45	
20 ft (6 m)	5	6	5	4	4	O2	PPO2 1.6 ATA
10 ft (3 m)	8	13	9	7	7	O2	PPO2 1.3 ATA
Total Dive Time:	**54**	**67**	**54**	**48**	**40**		

Figure 31-6: Decompression tables for 165 ft (50 m) / 20 minutes BT using various Gradient Factors

FUNDAMENTAL KNOWLEDGE ABOUT THE GRADIENT FACTORS IS ESSENTIAL FOR YOUR SAFE DIVING. ON LONG DECOMPRESSION DIVES, SAFETY MARGINS NOT ONLY CONTRIBUTE TO PREVENT DCS, BUT ALSO TO GAS PLANNING, LOGISTICS AND EQUIPMENT CONSIDERATIONS. A GOOD DIVER ADAPTS HIS/HER PERSONAL GRADIENT FACTORS ACCODING TO PERSONAL FITNESS, ENVIRONMENT AND DIVE TYPE. NO MATTER WHICH DIVING GEAR YOU USE, DECOMPRESSION AND THE NEED FOR CONSERVATISM ALWAYS FOLLOWS YOUR PLAN!

intermediate decompression mix fill pressure which is just above your cylinder capacity (including margins). Now, an easy but dangerous choice would be altering the gradient factors so that the decompression time decreases, leading to lower decompression gas need.

Divers using computers, which have user-configurable gradient factors, should understand how modifying their GF's will affect to their decompression profiles. Too many divers simply use the default settings or copy their GF parameters from other divers or even from the Internet, no matter what kind of a dive they are doing. Some divers have higher susceptibility to DCS and some dives are physically more demanding than others. Although the gradient factor method provides substantial flexibility in controlling the decompression profiles and thus the dive plan and gas logistics, it just might be worth to hang there a bit longer sometimes.

As always in diving, it remains ***YOUR*** responsibility to choose the gradient factors and conservatism appropriate for you!

References

1. Bert, Paul: *La Pression barométrique, recherches de physiologie expérimentale*, 1878
2. Boycott, A.E., Damant, G.C.C., and Haldane, J.S: *The Prevention of Compressed Air Illness*, The Journal of Medicine (Journal of Hygiene, Volume 8, 1908, pp. 342-443)
3. Bühlmann, Albert A.: *Decompression - Decompression Sickness.* Berlin: Springer-Verlag, 1984
4. Baker, Erik C.: *Understanding M-values*
5. Baker, Erik C.: *Clearing Up The Confusion About "Deep Stops"*

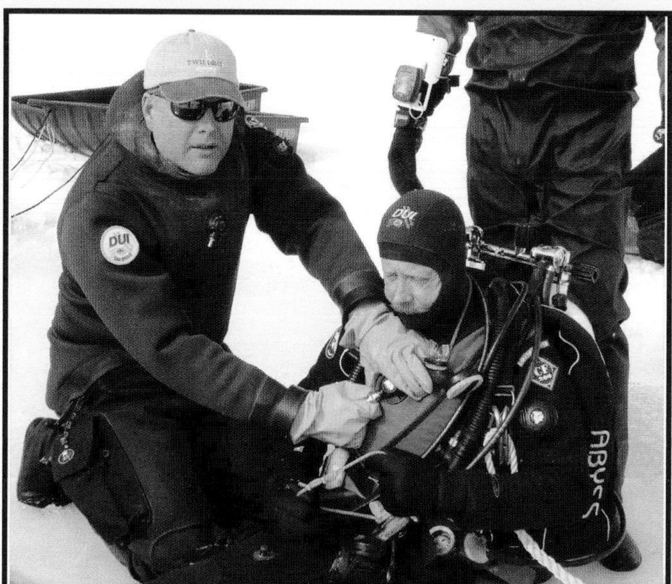

PHOTOS COURTESY R. TODD SMITH

... AND WE ARE STILL WORKING THE ICE FROM ALL ANGLES

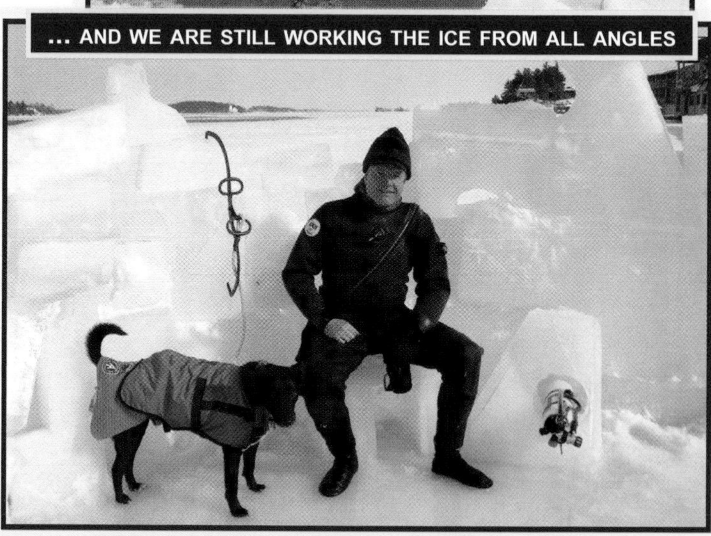

Section Six

Authors & Contributors

Photo Courtesy DiveTech, Grand Cayman

Photo courtesy Mel Clark

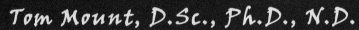

Tom Mount has a master's degree in Health Sciences, a D.Sc. in Martial Sciences, a Ph.D. in Natural Health Science and a N.D. as a Naturopathic Doctor and is currently studying Integral Energy medicine at the famed Holus Graduate School and Seminary. Tom is a certified Master Past Lives Therapist in Clinical Hypnotherapy, practices and teaches Qi Gong and is certified in numerous energy healing modalities. He is on the Board of Directors of the Society for Vitalistic Health (SFVH).

At age 9 Tom made two major decisions about his life; the first was after reading a book about a sponge diver creating a desire to become a diver. The second was to become a martial arts devotee and at age nine he commenced boxing and later began studying Asian martial arts. After honorable discharge from the US Navy, Tom became a true diving pioneer in cave diving, deep diving, mixed gas diving, and was instrumental in formulation of original concepts accepted in CCR diving.

Tom Mount, D.Sc., Ph.D., N.D.

Tom received the NOGI for Sports Education, Beneath the Sea's Diver of the Year award, Rebreather Worlds Lifetime Achievement Award and multiple certificates of recognition. He is a three-time inductee to the United States Martial Arts Association Hall of Fame. A Grand Master in martial arts he was appointed to the USMA Grand Masters Council.

Tom is a saturation diver and was the Saturation Diver Supervisor on the NOAA FLARE program. He was a founding member of NACD and for many years was the Diving Officer at the University of Miami Rosensteil School of Marine and Atmospheric Sciences and then Tom became the YMCA SCUBA program Training Director in Key West, Florida. Tom is the Founder of Ki Survival Systems, and is currently Chairperson of the IANTD Board of Directors.

Continued on page 338

Tom Mount, D.Sc., Ph.D., N.D. continued from page 337

Tom's experiences in survival led to studying the process of survival and then sharing his experiences and knowledge with others. He feels our primary strengths lie in the ability to use intuition and our use of Chi.

He is married to Reverend Patti Mount, M.A., current CEO of IANTD; Patti is a CCR Trimix and technical cave/wreck diver, Women Divers Hall of Fame inaugural member, PlatinumPro 5000 inaugural member, homeopathic practitioner and she is in Who's Who in Business and Who's Who in Diving.

Tom considers his Three Elements of Survival and Existence to be the key to life. These are:

> "Knowledge is Essential, Survival is Practical."
> "Always remain in life itself, and not on the problems that exist in the path."
> "We all die thus, it is the Quality of Life, not quantity that defines having lived."

Tom has written numerous books plus published papers on diving, photography, martial arts, etc. As well, he has worked on film productions with Bruno Valletti, John Stoneman, Jacques and Phillippe Cousteau.

A partial list of diving text authored by Tom Mount includes:

- The Cave Diving Manual (NACD 1971)
- UM RSMAS Diving Manual (UM RSMAS 1972)
- Practical Diving (University of Miami Press 1975)
- Safe Cave Diving (NACD 1974)
- Army Corps of Engineers Training Manual (YMCA 1979)
- Greatest Adventure Photography (SeaMount Publishing 1985)
- New Practical Diving (University of Miami Press 1978)
- Mixed Gas Diving (Watersports Publishing 1993)
- Technical Diver / Normoxic Trimix Manual & Workbook (IANTD 1991)
- Trimix Manual & Workbook (IANTD 1991)
- Advanced Deep Diving Manual & Workbook (IANTD 1991)
- Cave Diving Manual & Workbook (IANTD 1993)
- Technical Diver Encyclopedia (IANTD 1998 & 2nd Ed. 2000)
- Revised Technical Diver Encyclopedia (IANTD 2003)
- Tek CCR Manual (IANTD 2004)
- Tek Lite Manual (IANTD 2005)
- Open Water Diver Manual (IANTD 2000)
- Revised Open Water Diver Manual (IANTD 2007)

Joseph Dituri, M.S.

LCDR Joseph Dituri enlisted in the U.S. Navy due to his desire to be a Navy diver and later was commissioned into the Special Operations Officer pipeline. Currently he is a U. S. Navy Saturation Diving Officer with 23 years of service and holds a commercial saturation diving supervisor rating from the Association of Diving Contractors.

Joseph earned a Bachelor's Degree in Computer Science from the University of South Carolina and a Master's Degree in Astronautical Engineering from Naval Postgraduate School. His current assignment for the Navy is Officer-in-Charge of Deep Submergence Unit's Diving Systems Detachment in San Diego, where he is responsible for all tethered submarine rescue. He is one of only 23 qualified 2000 fsw (600 msw) "Hardsuit" pilots and has worked in every facet of diving within the U.S. Navy. A few of his former duties in the USN include: Diving Officer at Mobile Diving and Salvage Unit One and the Operations / Salvage Officer onboard *USS Salvor*. Following a change of designator to Engineering Duty Officer (Diving Officer), he served at Pearl Harbor Naval Shipyard as a Nuclear Project Superintendent, SUPSHIP Project Manager, and Business Operations Officer. LCDR Dituri is a member of the Acquisition Professional community and is a Level III Program Manager capable of managing programs of $4 Billion. His personal awards include three Navy Achievement Medals, an Army Commendation Medal, and two Navy Commendation Medals.

Joseph is an avid technical / rebreather diver who owns part of the International Association of Nitrox and Technical Divers while serving as their Training Director. He is also an Instructor Trainer for Diver's Alert Network and a Hyperbaric Physician Instructor for the International Board of Undersea Medicine (IBUM). In a civilian capacity Joseph has trained hundreds of technical divers to dive and physicians in the use of hyperbaric

Continued on page 340

Joseph Dituri, M.S. continued from page 339

medicine. He is a contributing author to the Navy Diving Manual and has been published in several journals and magazines including those produced by the American Society of Naval Engineers and American Institute of Aeronautics and Astronautics. Joe is a veteran of numerous deep diving expeditions and has an affinity to explore the undersea environment.

A sample listing of training materials Joseph has developed include IANTD Rescue Diver, IANTD Dolphin and Ray Training manuals, IBUM & IANTD Diving Medical Technician Manual as well as the revolutionary series of IANTD "FUNdamentals" DVDs for Rescue Diver, Divemaster and Rebreather Diver. He has assisted in production of IANTD Standards and Procedures, numerous training slides used in IANTD programs as well as the IANTD Nitrox Diver Manual, IANTD Public Safety Diver Manual, IANTD Azimuth Rebreather Diver Manual and IANTD Overhead Diving Manual.

Joseph is married to the former Amy M. Entress. Together they have three children. He enjoys skydiving, martial arts and has a long-term goal of being an astronaut upon retirement from military service.

The opinions expressed herein are possessed solely by the author and do not necessarily reflect those of any organization with which the author may be affiliated. Joe's commitment to this publication is completely separate from his military duties.

Matti Anttila has an M.Sc. in Technical Physics and a Ph.D. in Space Flight Instrumentation, so diving science is close to his heart. He was trained as a minehunter diver in the Finnish Navy in 1995 using semi-closed rebreathers, and later Matti pursued them for recreational and then technical diving. In the late 1990's he began teaching IANTD technical diving in Finland. Currently he is on the IANTD International Board of Advisors and is an IANTD Trimix Instructor Trainer. Matti is interested in diving technology, experimental diving and cave diving, but still finds it equally nice to teach open water diving class for beginners or Trimix diving for more advanced divers.

Matti Anttila, Ph.D.

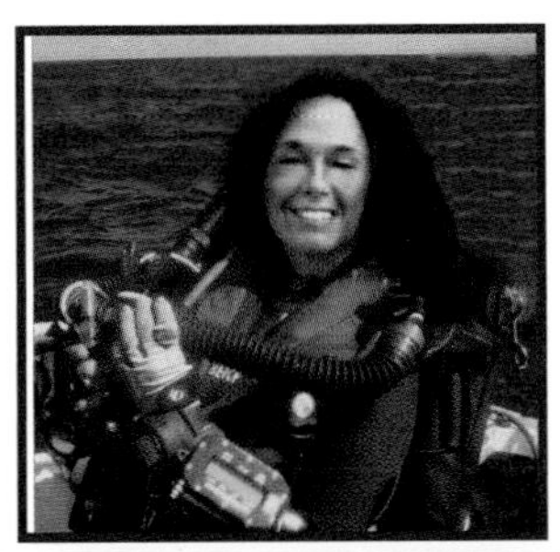

Dr. Peri M. Blum offers training and certification through IANTD in open circuit (OC) and closed circuit rebreather (CCR) SCUBA diving. Thanks to this unique combination of skills, students are trained by a professional who understands and works with divers in building on strengths and overcoming weaknesses, while recognizing individual needs, goals, and lifestyles.

Peri Blum, Psy.D.

Dr. Blum, who is in independent private practice, specializes in a number of areas, including medical and sports psychology. Dr. Blum also works extensively with children, adolescents, and at-risk youth and their families.

Dr. Blum has over 30 years diving experience and more than 15 years studying and practicing psychology. Dr. Blum's technical and instructor training is under the IANTD programs. Dr. Blum's dive career includes assisting in training divers from all over the world, working on the Looe Key Artificial Reef Project, preparing for toxic oil spills, and field-testing dive equipment. Dr. Blum is also involved in writing and editing across numerous topics and fields.

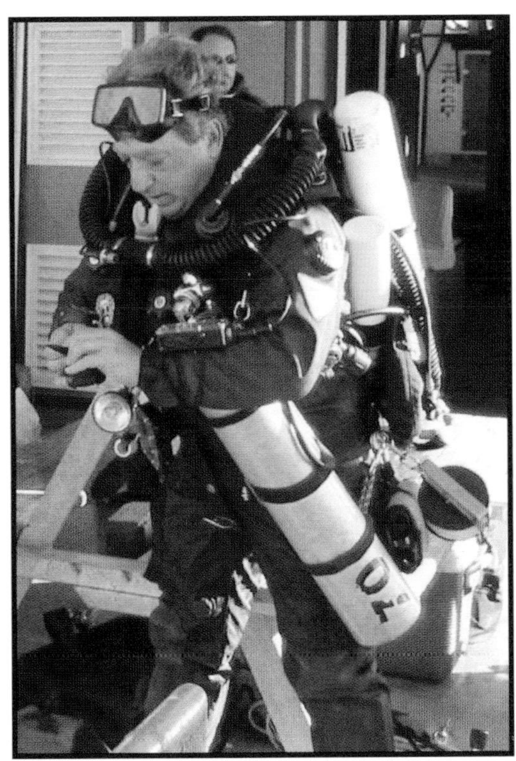

Joe Citelli did his first free dives as a teenager in the waters off City Island, NYC and became an avid diver when he moved to Florida. During the 1980's Joe used the Navy Dive Manual to learn decompression diving and cobbled together a set of doubles to pursue diving deeper wrecks. Recognizing the need for formal training he became Cave certified and later participated in the first IANTD Trimix course ever offered. With no books or texts, this class was the one in which students and teacher collaborated to derive and perfect some of the formulas and methods in use today. Joe can usually be found diving deep wrecks all over the Southeastern US, the Gulf Coast of Florida and occasionally in the Northeastern US.

Joe Citelli

David Doolette, Ph.D.

David Doolette is currently working at the USN EDU in Panama City specializing in projects involved with Diving Physiology. Formerly he was a research fellow in the department of Anesthesia and Intensive Care in the University of Adelaide Royal Hospital, Australia. He has been trained in neurophysiology and neuropharmacology. This background and his diving pursuits led to his interest in diving physiology. David's current works involve decompression illness, decompression modeling, and health management for divers. David has been diving since 1979 and is devoted to cave exploration.

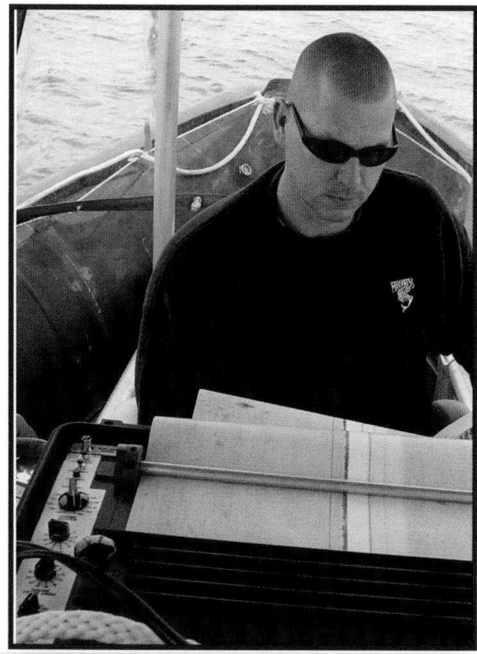

Jeff Gourley

Jeff Gourley was born in Arizona in 1967. At the age of six he designed and built an underwater habitat in his pool and consequently discovered the dangers of hypercapnia, and as they say, the rest is history. Jeff learned to SCUBA dive in 1985 and has achieved practically every rating or certification related to Underwater Exploration: CCR Trimix Instructor Trainer-IANTD ITT #403, CCR Cave, Instructor and user ratings on the Optima, Inspiration, Megalodon, Evolution, KISS, Azimuth, Dolphin, LarV, Mark 15, Cis-Lunar...to name a few. He is a certified Chamber Operator, Gas Blender, Side Scan Sonar Tec, and ROV Operator. He also holds the following medical ratings: Military Medic, IEMT - State of Arizona, DMT - Undersea and Hyperbaric Medical Society, Chamber Operator - International Board of Undersea Medicine. Jeff's work experiences include the design of various CCR's and components, marketing, publishing, diving safety/stunt work, underwater film and photography. His other interests include surfing, mixed martial arts, repelling, and he is a gourmet chef.

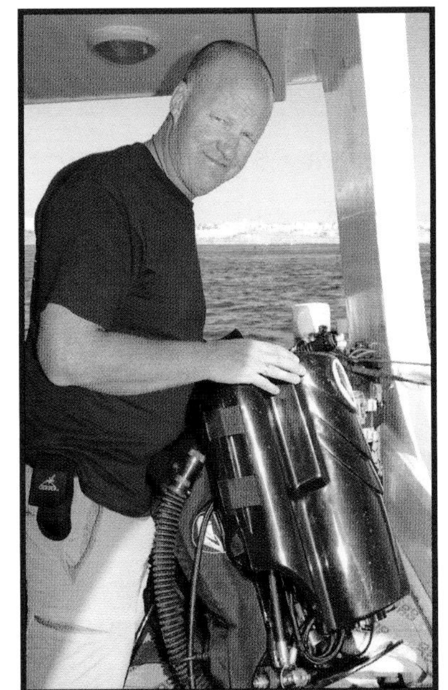

Kevin Gurr

Kevin Gurr was the first certified Technical Diving Instructor outside of the USA and is an IANTD IT at all levels and has been instrumental in expanding Technical and mixed gas CCR diving globally. A Marine engineer and professional diver, Kevin developed an EANx dive computer in the late 1980's, he is the co-author of Proplanner Decompression software, the designer of the VR3 mixed gas dive computer, the Ouroboros and Sentinel Rebreathers.

He led the first sport diving expedition to the *HMHS Britannic*, has dived the *Lusitania*, the *USS Monitor*, and made a MIR submersible dive on the *Titanic* plus several archaeological and filming expeditions.

Kevin is an active Caver/Cave diver and Instructor and given the choice between fast women and fast motorcycles would probably choose the motorcycle.

Jean-Pierre "JP" Imbert

Jean-Pierre (JP) IMBERT spent 20 year in the offshore industry as Diving and Safety Manager of Comex, a major offshore diving contractor in the North Sea. He was involved in research programs such as hydrogen diving and deep projects in Norway.

As an engineer, JP developed a special skill for decompression modeling and he is the producer of a long list of tables and procedures for the diving industry. He has published widely on decompression modeling including a chapter in the IANTD Technical Diver Encyclopedia (1998, 2000 & Revised 2003).

He is presently deeply involved with work on solving the tiny bubbles equations in an attempt to design the ultimate bubble growth decompression tables. JP is highly respected worldwide as one of most knowledgeable decompression modeling researchers.

Jean-Pierre is proud to be a Technical Diving Instructor and Instructor Trainer in IANTD. He is the former IANTD Licensee for France, and currently is on the IANTD Board of Advisors.

Gene Melton

Gene Melton is a graduate of the University of Florida. He developed repetitive group designations and surface interval credit tables for the USN Exceptional Exposure tables. This work was published in "Practical Diving" by Tom Mount. Later he wrote the "Nitrox Blender's Handbook" which is published by IANTD. Gene was in the initial group of cave instructors certified by the NSS-CDS and is a Life Member and Fellow of the NSS and a Life Member of NSS-CDS. As a submersible pilot/electronics engineer/diver, Gene performed submersible lockout dives to 600'. After 15 years in the Space Shuttle Solid Rocket Booster Retrieval program he left the Kennedy Space Center to work on the Super-Conducting Super Collider project. When the SSCL project was closed, Gene moved back to Florida and started development of the HS Explorer dive computer. To date, the HS Explorer is the only dive computer to fully implement the RGBM deep stop algorithm. Further developments include the Explorer PPO_2 monitors and the Neptune Closed Circuit Rebreather. Gene's instructor credentials include IANTD, NSS-CDS CCR Cave and FAA Airplane, Single and Multi-engine.

Simon Mitchell, M.B. ChB., Ph.D.

Dr. Simon Mitchell's 30 year diving career has included more than 6000 dives spanning many disciplines including sport, scientific, commercial, and military diving. In recent years his diving interests have focused on photography and technical diving. He is an avid deep mixed gas diver and uses an Mk15.5 closed circuit rebreather. Simon is a diving physician and anaesthesiologist and has more than 40 papers in international medical literature. He recently co-authored the second edition of "Deeper into Diving" with John Lippmann, and authored 2 chapters on decompression sickness in the most recent edition of Bennett and Elliott. He is currently Vice President of the Undersea and Hyperbaric Medicine Society, and Chairman of the Society's Diving Committee.

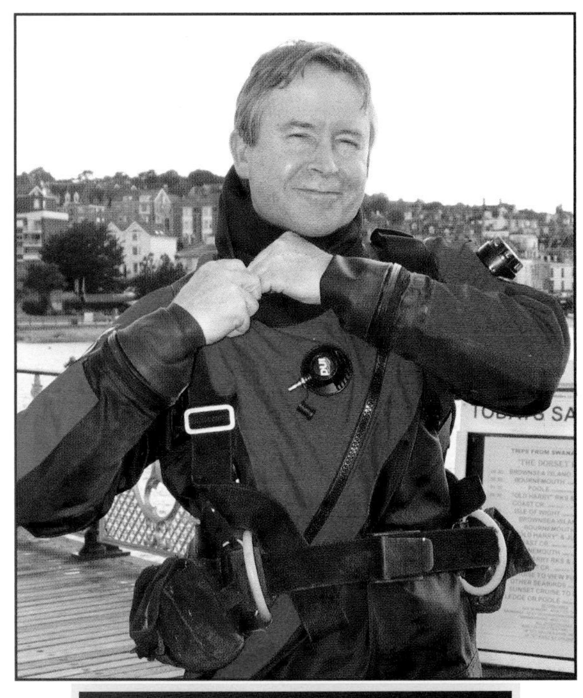

Simon Pridmore

Simon Pridmore - Simon Pridmore is a former Hong Kong Police Officer and Assistant Political Adviser to the Governor of Hong Kong. He was one of the pioneers who introduced technical diving to Asia in the mid-1990s, has been a member of the IANTD Board of Advisors since 1995 and ran a dive centre in Guam for 7 years while holding the IANTD License for Micronesia. Since 2003 Simon has been the IANTD Licensee in the United Kingdom, is an IANTD Instructor Trainer Trainer and works with VR Technology, developers of the VR3, the Ouroboros and Sentinel Closed Circuit Rebreathers.

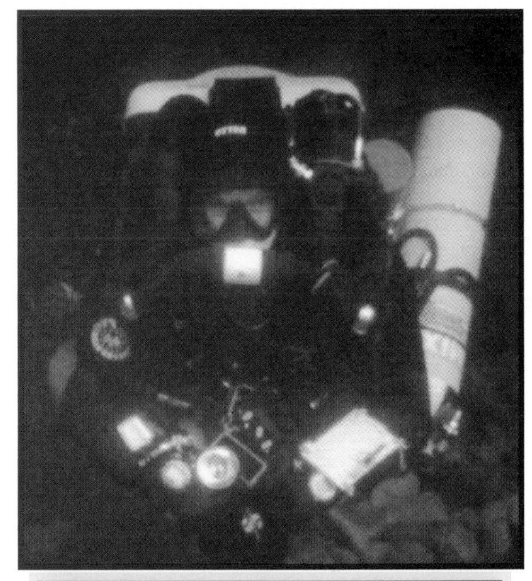

Martin Robson

Martin Robson is an IANTD Open Circuit and CCR Trimix Cave Instructor Trainer Trainer. He specializes in overhead environment and closed circuit rebreather training and was the first ever IANTD CCR Cave Instructor Trainer. Martin regularly contributes to training manuals on all aspects of technical diving and has been published in magazines in the UK, USA, Scandinavia and Russia. He is an experienced cave explorer having conducted substantial expeditions with major penetration to depths over 600 ft (180 m) in the caves of Europe. Martin enjoys diving in extreme environments and has taught and dived in caves, wrecks, flooded mines and under ice from the arctic circle to the equator.

David Sawatzky, M.D.

David Sawatzky is currently a physician with the Canadian Armed Forces in Halifax, Nova Scotia, Canada. He was a Diving Medical Specialist on contract at Defence Research and Development Toronto (formerly DCIEM) from 1998 to 2005. Previously he was the Canadian Forces Staff Officer in Hyperbaric Medicine at DCIEM (1986-1993) and later the Senior Medical Officer at Garrison Support Unit Toronto (1993-1998). He writes a diving medicine column for Canada's Diver Magazine and Australia's Sport Diver Magazine, is on the Board of Advisors for IANTD, and is an active Cave, Trimix and Closed Circuit Rebreather Diver / Instructor / Instructor Trainer. David has done over 600 cave dives, most of them original exploration/survey dives in Canada's cold, remote and challenging caves.

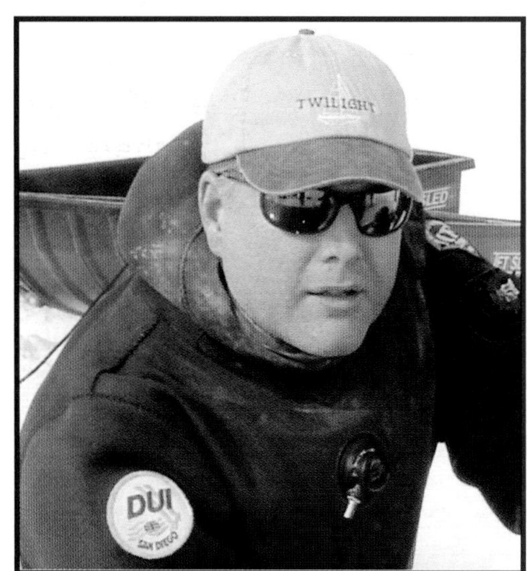

R. Todd Smith

R. Todd Smith began diving in 1981 in Lake Superior and ice diving there in 1983. Combining extensive experience in cold weather back country travel, mountaineering and ice and technical diving he authored the PADI Ice Diving course in 1989, followed by "Beneath A Crystal Ceiling, the Complete Guide to Ice Diving" (available through IANTD). He has trained hundreds of ice divers and police, military and public safety divers across the U.S. and more people learn ice diving through his materials and procedures that any other. His ice diving pursuits extend throughout New England, the Great Lakes and both polar regions, in addition to extensive deep wreck and cave diving world wide. Todd is an IANTD Instructor Trainer Trainer and PADI Course Director. He and his wife Anita, a USCG licensed Captain and technical diver, plan their next adventures from their base camp on Cape Cod.

Roberto Trindade, M.S.

Roberto Trindade, M.S. - Roberto holds a MS in Psychology and is specialized in pscicomotricity, psicopedagogy and marine archeology. Roberto holds Instructor Trainer credentials with IANTD, DAN and PDIC. He has also earned instructor certifications with PADI, NAUI, CMAS, SSI, TDI and HSA. He is also certified to teach First Aid / CPR / AED with many agencies, including the National Safety Council and the International Federation of Red Cross and Crescent Societies. He is also a certified Water Rescue Instructor with the National Pool and Waterpark Lifeguard. Roberto is a member of the Historical Diving Society, the Brazilian Speleological Society, the Undersea and Hyperbaric Medical Society, among other societies.

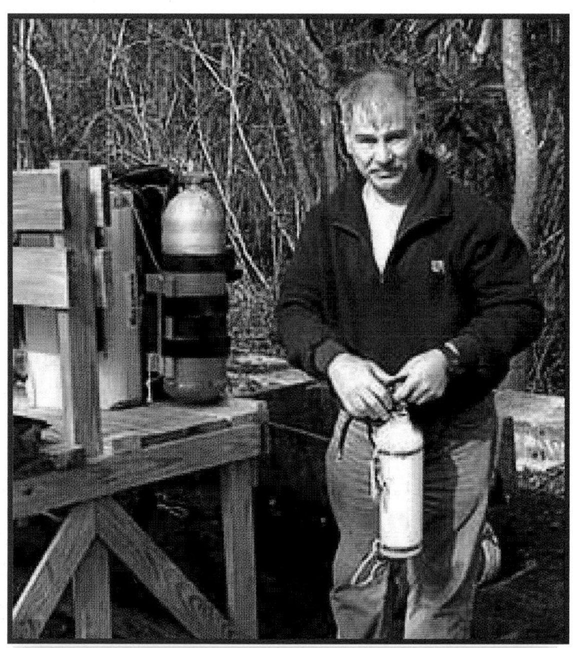

John Zumrick, M.D.

John Zumrick, M.D., Capt., MC USN (Ret.), is a former Medical Research officer and Senior Medical officer at the US Navy Experiential Diving Unit. While there, he was responsible for major investigations on CCR diving apparatus, thermal protection, and deep saturation diving experiments. He has been the subject of numerous diving physiological experiments and was a dive subject on many saturations, one lasting 37 days which reached 1,500 fsw (458.7 msw). In his off-duty time John, an IANTD Trimix Diver, can be found cave diving in Florida, the Bahamas, and Mexico. John started cave diving in 1971 and has been responsible for original exploration of numerous springs and caves. He is a fellow of the National Speleological Society and of the New York Explorers Club.

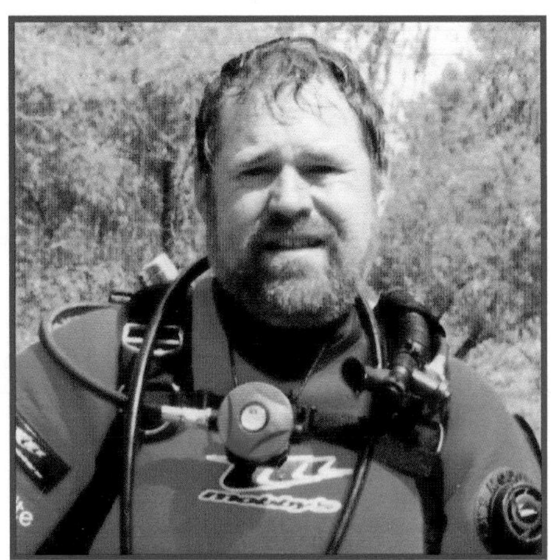

Lamar Hires

Lamar Hires is a modern day explorer and dive pioneer. A legend among cave divers, Lamar is known for his expertise in sidemount diving. He developed the very first training guidelines for sidemounting and has taught many well-known sidemount divers.

Underwater exploration, education and conservation are a passion that has led Lamar all over the world. He has mapped and explored cave systems from the rugged mountains of Japan to the remote jungles of the Dominican Republic. Not a stranger to the ocean, Lamar's curiosity for exploration has taken him to the rarely dived icy waters of the Antarctic as well as countless wreck dives off the coasts of Florida and the eastern United States.

When Lamar began diving in 1979, exploration-quality dive equipment was not commercially available. In 1984, Lamar joined a start-up dive equipment company called "Dive Rite" and there he helped bring to market the first buoyancy compensator for double tanks known as the "Classic Wing." Dive Rite also mass produced the first metal backplate and invented the "Bridge," which was the industry's first Nitrox-compatible dive computer. In 1997, Lamar purchased Dive Rite and has grown the company into a worldwide dive manufacturer with distribution in over sixty countries.

Affiliations & Awards

IANTD Board of Advisors (current)

National Speleological Society, Chairman (1992-1994)

National Speleological Society, Training Chairman (1987-1992)

International Underwater Cave Rescue and Recovery (IUCRR) Training Coordinator (current)

National Speleological Society, Lifetime Fellow Award

Florida Springs Exploration Award, 2000

Contributing writer for *Advanced Diver Magazine, Divers Magazine, Scuba Times and Sport Diver Magazine*

Contributing author NSS-CDS Cave Diving Manual

Contributing author IANTD Technical Diver Encyclopedia (1998, 2000 & 2003)

IANTD Instructor Trainer: NSS-CDS instructor and former Training Director

Appendix

Photo Mel Clark of Leon Scamahorn

Photo Karen Flynn of Jeff Johnson in Dos Ojos Air Dome

Appendix A

Glossary of Terms

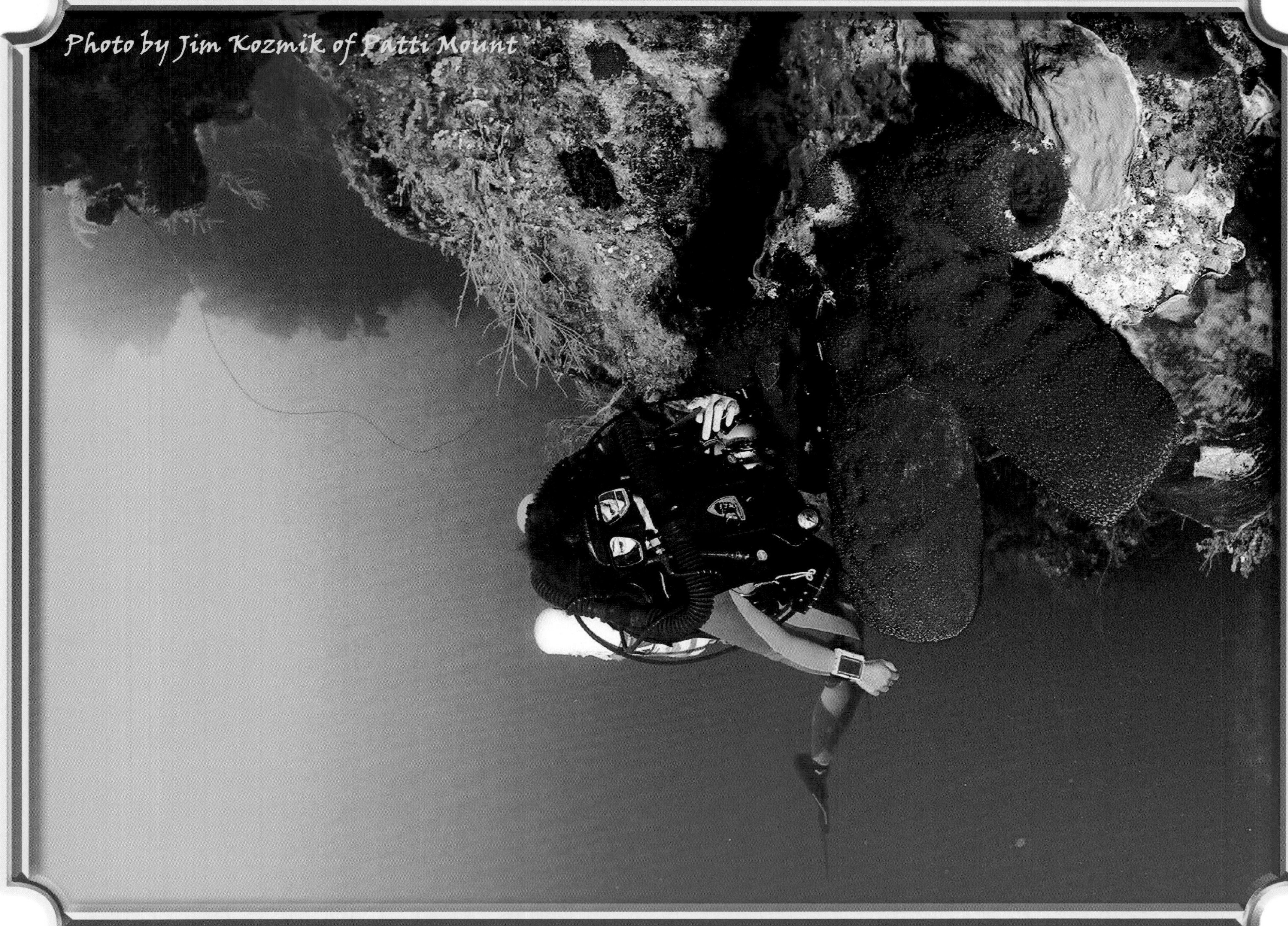

Photo by Jim Kozmik of Patti Mount

A

Air Cell: A type of buoyancy compensator (**BC**). See **BC**.

AB Model: Arterial Bubble Model. Developed to describe and explain **Type II DCS** symptoms.

ACE: Angiotension Converting Enzyme.

ADS: Atmospheric Diving Suits; one atmosphere suits. These suits are pressure vessels where the pilot is completely isolated from sea pressure, and therefore is not affected by the increase of pressure at depth.

Aerobic: Requiring oxygen, such as 'aerobic exercise.'

ADP: Adenosine Diphosphate. **ADP** has two phosphate molecules attached to it**. S**ee **Adenosine Triphosphate** above.

ADV: Automatic Diluent Addition Valve; found on most CCR units.

AED: Automated External Defibrillator.

Alveoli: Miniature sacks of tissue connected to the lung's surface. Gas exchange takes place in the **alveoli.**

Ambient Pressure: The pressure that is characteristic of the surrounding atmosphere.

AMP: Adenosine Monophophate. See **Adenosine Triphosphate** above.

AMTE/PL: Admiralty Marine Technology Establishment, Physiological Laboratory.

Anabolism: A set of metabolic pathways that construct molecules from smaller units using energy provided by **catabolism**.

Antioxidants: Essential chemicals (vitamins) that inhibit **free radical** formation or repair **free radical** damage.

Arteriosclerosis: A disease of the blood vessels caused by plaque accumulating on the walls of the blood vessels or at a junction between blood vessels.

ATA, ata: Atmospheres Absolute.

ATP: Adenosine Triphosphate. ATP is the biomolecule in which cells store energy. **ATP** is composed of an Adenosine molecule with three high-energy phosphate molecules attached, one after the other. The more phosphate molecules attached to the adenosine molecule, the greater the amount of energy the molecule is capable of storing.

ATM, atm: An imperial measurement equaling 14.7 psig. **ATM** is also used to define ambient pressure, including the air column over water. One **ATM** is equal to 33 feet of sea water, or 34 feet of fresh water. **ATM**, etcetera, may be used interchangeably with the metric term 'Bar' when referring to partial pressures.

AUE: Association of Underwater Explorers. "A coalition of divers dedicated to the research, exploration, documentation, and preservation of submerged cultural resources." Quote courtesy of AUE, http://www.uwex.us

B

Back-gas; backgas: The gas literally carried on the diver's back.

Bar: Measure of pressure; metric. It is the equivalent to 14.50 pounds of force per square inch

(psi) Imperial. Therefore, one metric **Bar** is approximately equal to one atmosphere of pressure (14.7 psi). The terms **Bar** and **ATA** may be used interchangeably when referring to partial pressures.

Bailout bottle: A slang term for a type of cylinder used for bailout purposes while diving on CCR units.

BC or BCD: Buoyancy Compensating Device. A device used to either adjust a diver's buoyancy or provide surface floatation. **BCs** are not considered Personal Floatation Devices (**PFDs**). Unlike **BCs, PFDs** are required equipment by certain state and federal agencies under certain circumstances.

Best Mix: The most appropriate percentage of oxygen, nitrogen, and other breathing gases in a specific breathing medium at a pre-defined depth.

BOA: Board of Advisors.

BOD: Board of Directors.

BOV: Bailout Valve. A valve connected to the **CCR** mouthpiece that allows the diver to bailout to Open Circuit equipment without going off the **CCR** loop.

BT: 'Bottom Time' or the amount of time spent at depth during a dive.

Buddy cylinder: An additional stage or bailout cylinder carried if solo diving or if there is a high likelihood of team separation during the course of the dive.

C

C: Centigrade, see Centigrade/Celsius.

Capillaries: The smallest of all blood vessels.

Carbon Dioxide: See CO_2.

Carbon Monoxide: See CO.

Cardiac: Having to do with the heart.

Catabolism: A set of **metabolic** pathways which break **molecules** into smaller units in order to release **energy**.

cc: Cubic Centimeters.

CCR: Closed Circuit Rebreather.

CCR loop: The breathing loop on a **CCR** unit.

Centigrade/Celsius: Metric measurement of temperature. To convert **Centigrade/Celsius** to **Fahrenheit**: Multiply the degrees **Centigrade/Celsius** by 9/5 (1.80) and add 32.

CF; cu. ft; cu ft; cft: Cubic Feet. Imperial measure of volume used to determine the amount of gas in a diving cylinder.

CFM: Cubic Feet per Minute, Imperial-US measurement of volume flow.

Cis: A term meaning the subject chemical groups are on the same side of a carbon-to-carbon double bond. In this text, **cis** refers to certain configurations of fat molecules. **'Cis-fats'** are considered 'good' fats. See also **Trans**.

cm: Centimeter, metric length measure. 1 inch equals 2.54 centimeters.

CNS: Central Nervous System.

CNS% or %CNS: The percent of central nervous system oxygen exposure.

CO: Carbon Monoxide, a highly toxic, colorless, odorless, and tasteless gas produced by the combustion of hydrocarbons (petroleum fuels used in engines, and smoking tobacco or cannabis).

CO_2: Carbon Dioxide, which is a normal by-product of respiration. Carbon dioxide can be harmful if allowed to accumulate. See Hypercapnia.

CO_2 Retention: The build-up of carbon dioxide in body tissue. Individuals that tend to accumulate carbon dioxide more than average are termed CO_2 retainers.

CON-VENTID: Mnemonic for the symptoms of oxygen poisoning.

Counterlungs (CL): **Counterlungs,** or "breathing bags," are part of a rebreather unit's **breathing loop.**

CP: Creatine Phosphate; a small amount of the body's energy is stored as CP.

CPR: Cardio-pulmonary Respiration.

Cubic Feet: Imperial-US measurement of volume. Another way of expressing this volume is feet cubed, cu ft, or Ft^3.

Cubes; cubes: Cubic feet (see above).

CV Model: The Critical Volume Model for **Type I DCS** symptoms.

D

DAN: Divers Alert Network.

D-ring: A 'D' shaped ring used for attaching equipment.

DCI: Decompression Illness/Injury. The direct result of not allowing for the safe elimination of excess or accumulated gas in body tissue. **DCI** is also referred to as **DCS**, or decompression sickness. Although there are subtle differences in medical terminology for decompression illness, decompression injury, and decompression sickness, the end result is the same; treatment in a recompression chamber.

DCCR: Diver-Controlled CCR Unit; a type of **MCCR**. See also **MCCR, CCR**.

DCS: Decompression Sickness. See DCI.

Deco: Slang for the term 'decompression,' as in 'deco bottle' or 'deco stop.'

Deco Bottle: Slang term for a dive cylinder filled with an **oxygen**-rich gas used for **decompression** purposes.

Deco Stop: Staged **decompression** stops. See **Decompression.**

Decompression: A period of time a diver must spend at a constant depth at the end of a dive to safely eliminate absorbed inert gases from the diver's body to avoid decompression sickness. The amount of time a diver requires to decompress is often called a "**decompression obligation**."

Diatomic: Diatomic stands for molecules made from two atoms of either the same or different chemical elements.

DIN: Deutsches Institut für Normung, a European regulatory association. DIN also refers to a certain type of tank and regulator valve. Technical divers prefer 'DIN' valves over the yoke-type valves found on most recreational cylinders and regulators.

Doppler: An acoustic measuring device or method used by scientists to measure the passage of bubbles in the arteries or veins of divers. **Doppler** devices are used on divers to track nitrogen microseed or bubble placement in the arterial system.

Doppler Effect: The findings produced by **Doppler** use on divers. Such tests are also known as '**Doppler Studies**.'

Doubles: Two SCUBA cylinders joined together by a manifold to create a single gas supply, which effectively doubles the available gas supply. Although some use the terms 'twins' and 'doubles' interchangeably, there is a very critical difference between the two concepts. See '**Twins**' for more information.

DPV: Diver Propulsion Vehicle, alias scooter, sled, torpedo, etc. Any motorized device used for transporting submerged divers.

DSV: Diver Supply Valve. The mouthpiece plus an on/off switch found on CCR loops.

Drysuit: A suit that insulates via a pocket of air between the diver and the water with the ability to use undergarments.

E

EAD: Equivalent Air Depth, or the depth at which the partial pressure of nitrogen in air (.79) is equivalent to the partial pressure of nitrogen in the gas mix.

EAN: Enriched Air Nitrox, or gas mixtures with percentages of oxygen greater than 21%.

EANx: Nitrox gas mix, oxygen level not determined ("x" variable).

ECM: European term for **CPR (see CPR).**

EAR: European term for Rescue Breathing.

ECCR: Electronic CCR unit; the electronics add oxygen if the level of oxygen set by the diver and entered into the CCR unit's electronic memory (usually in one or two handsets) falls below a certain point, or if the oxygen level drops below .20.

EDU: United States Navy Experimental Diving Unit.

EEG: Electroencephalograph. An instrument used to measure brain wave activity.

Enzyme: A highly specialized, biologically active protein. Enzymes are the tools with which the body controls metabolism.

EPIRB: Emergency position indicating radio beacon; devices used to signal maritime distress.

F

Fahrenheit: Imperial-US measurement of temperature. To convert **Fahrenheit** to **Centigrade/Celsius:** Subtract 32 from the degrees **Fahrenheit** and multiply by 5/9 (.556).

Feet: Imperial-US measurement of length or depth. 1 foot equals .305 meters.

Feet cubed: Imperial-US measurement of volume. 1 cubic foot equals 28.32 free liters.

FFW: An Imperial-US measurement of depth in feet of fresh water.

Fg: Fraction (percentage) of a gas in a mix.

FHe: Percentage of helium in the gas mix.

FLPM: Free Liters Per Minute.

Flying; Flown: Diving or dived a CCR unit.

FMEA: Failure Mode Effect Analysis.

FN_2: Fraction of Nitrogen in a gas mix.

FO_2: Fraction of Oxygen in a gas mix.

Free Radical: A highly destructive, oxygen-compound molecule. Free radicals are short-lived because they are so energetically active (looking for something to bind to or combine with). They can and will bind to just about any other molecule, which results in either destroying or disrupting the molecule's function.

FSW, fsw: Feet Salt Water. Imperial-US measurement of depth in feet of salt water.

Ft, ft: See **feet**.

Ft^3: Cubic Feet, see **feet cubed**.

G

GABA: Gamma-aminobutyric Acid. GABA is a neurotransmitter responsible for brain functioning.

GI: Gastro-intestinal tract.

g/l: Grams per liter.

H

Hb: An abbreviation for Hemoglobin. See **Hgb.**

HBO: Hyperbaric Oxygen or Hyperbaric Oxygenation.

HDL: High-density lipids.

He: An abbreviation for Helium.

Heliair: Any gas mixture of Air and Helium.

Heliox: Any gas mixture of Oxygen and Helium.

Helium: An inert biologically unreactive gas.

Hemoglobin: A complex protein and iron molecule found in red blood cells (**RBC**) that transports **oxygen** and **carbon dioxide**. **Hemoglobin**, which means "iron bearing," is the iron atom embedded in the protein that binds the **oxygen** and **carbon dioxide** molecules.

Hg: An abbreviation for Mercury.

Hgb: Abbreviation for Hemoglobin.

Hogarthian Style: A particular gear configuration, some say gear configuration philosophy, named in honor of William Hogarth Main.

HPG: High Pressure Gauge.

HPNS: High Pressure Nervous Syndrome.

HSE: Health and Safety Executive, United Kingdom.

Hydrox: Any gas mixture of hydrogen and oxygen, or hydrogen, helium and oxygen.

Hypercapnia: A potentially fatal condition for divers caused by an excessive build-up of carbon dioxide in either body tissue or inspired air.

Hyperoxia: A potentially fatal excess of oxygen in the blood. Beyond a certain depth, hyperoxia can lead to oxygen toxicity (*OxTox*), which causes seizures and possible death.

HUD: Head Up Display or Heads Up Display or Heads-up Display.

I

IAND, Inc.: The International Association of Nitrox Divers, Incorporated dba IANTD.

IANTD: The International Association of Nitrox and Technical Divers; *The Leader in Diver Education.*

J

No J entries

K

K: Chemical symbol for potassium

Kit: European term for the dive gear ensemble.

Kitting; De-Kitting: Terms for assembling and breaking down the dive **kit.**

kPa: Kilo-pascals, which is a metric measurement of pressure.

L

L; l; ltr: Liter of gas; metric measurement of the amount of unpressurized gas a cylinder may hold. 1 **liter** equals 0.035 cubic feet. One of the finer points of the metric system is that a **liter of gas** is referred to differently from a **liter of a liquid**. **Liters of gas** are formally referred to as **free liters.** Many of our international colleagues, especially British colleagues, request that IANTD refer to a **liter of gas** as a **free liter of gas**.

LDL: Low Density Lipid.

LED: Light Emitting Diode.

Lipid: A compound that is oily to the touch, insoluble in water, and together with proteins and carbohydrates constitute the principle structure of cells

LP: Low Pressure.

LPI: Low Pressure Inflator.

M

M; m; m.: Meter. A metric measure of length; singular or plural.

mbar: Millibar. A metric measure of pressure.

MCCR: Mechanical CCR unit. The diver adds oxygen to the breathing mix manually.

Meds: Slang term for medications.

Mercury: Known also as "quicksilver," **mercury** is a chemical element with the symbol **Hg.**

Metabolism: A set of chemical reactions that occur in living organisms in order to maintain life. **Metabolic** processes allow organisms to grow and reproduce, maintain their structures, and respond to their environments. **Metabolism** is usually divided into two categories; **catabolism** breaks down large molecules to harvest energy, whereas **anabolism** uses energy to construct cellular components.

Meter: Metric measurement of length or depth. 1 meter equals 3.28 feet.

Metre; metres: See **Meter.**

MFW: Metric measurement of depth in Meters of Fresh Water.

ml: Milliliter. A metric measurement of volume equaling one-thousandth of a liter.

mm: Millimeter. A metric measurement of length equaling one-thousandth of a meter.

mmHg: Millimeters of Mercury. An Imperial-US measure of pressure.

MOD: Maximum Operational Depth. MOD refers to the maximum depth a specific gas mix can be dived to without increasing the risk of oxygen toxicity or other negative effects of pressure.

"Mr. Murphy": American slang term. See **Murphy's Law**.

MSW; msw: Meters Salt Water. **MSW** is a metric measurement of depth in meters of salt water.

Murphy's Law: Anything that can go wrong will go wrong.

Myoglobin: A type of protein that binds with oxygen; A small amount is stored within muscles, thereby increasing their energy resources.

N

Na: The chemical symbol for Sodium.

N_2: Nitrogen.

Narcosis: A detrimental physiological and mental state produced by high levels of absorbed nitrogen (nitrogen narcosis) or inert gases (inert gas narcosis) such as Hydrogen or Neon.

Ne: Neon, an inert biologically unreactive gas.

Nitrogen: An inert diatomic (2 atom) gas. Air consists of approximately 78% diatomic **nitrogen**. **Diatomic** nitrogen is chemically unreactive in higher life forms as the two atoms are so tightly bound. Lower life forms, such as nitrogen-fixing bacterial, can use (metabolize) **diatomic nitrogen**.

Nitrogen narcosis: See Narcosis.

Nitrox: Any gas mixture of oxygen and nitrogen other than air (with air being approximately 21% oxygen).

NREM: Non-Rapid Eye Movement. See REM.

NSAIDS: Non-Steroidal Anti-Inflammatory Drugs.

NSS: National Speleological Society (USA).

NSS-CDS: National Speleological Society, Cave Diving Section: The NSS Cave Diving Section

is the largest cave diving organization in the United States... they also dive sea caves in the Northeast, survey Bahamas Blue Holes, and conduct studies of various caves and springs in Mexico, and the Caribbean... The section is also active in the development of underwater rescue equipment, and sponsors a comprehensive cave diver and instructor training program. It also publishes *Underwater Speleology*. Courtesy of NSS-CDS, http://www.nsscds.com/whatis.html.

NOAA: The National Oceanic and Atmospheric Administration (USA).

O

O_2: Oxygen.

OC: Open Circuit or open-circuit.

Off-board: Used when referring to CCR diving; the gas mixes carried in the diver's bailout bottles.

On-Board: Fully integrated CCR gas cylinders.

OTC: Over The Counter.

OTU: Oxygen Toxicity Unit. See "**oxygen toxicity**."

Oxygen: Required to sustain life (i.e., run metabolism), **oxygen** is nature's most common oxidant and is a necessary ingredient required for combustion/respiration.

Oxygen Toxicity: Oxygen toxicity, or the "Paul Bert effect" or the "Lorrain Smith effect" is severe **hyperoxia** caused by breathing oxygen at elevated partial pressures. The above-normal concentration of oxygen within the body caused by elevated **PO_2** levels can cause cell damage in two principal regions: the central nervous system (**CNS**); and the lungs (**pulmonary**). Over time, it can also cause damage to th e retina and may be implicated in some retinopathic conditions.

Oxidizer: A substance or molecular formation that adds oxygen to another substance or molecular formation. Oxidizers help in fuel combustion.

P

P: The ambient pressure of a gas mix.

Partial pressure: Refers to the percentage of a specific gas in a breathing mix. In air, oxygen has a partial pressure of approximately 21% and nitrogen has a partial pressure of approximately 79%.

PCO_2: Partial pressure of Carbon Dioxide.

Pg: Partial pressure of any gas within a gas mix.

pH; ph; PH: A measure of acidity or alkalinity of a given solution.

PO_2; PPO2; PpO_2; ppO_2; pO2: Partial pressure of oxygen in a gas mix.

Psi: Pounds per Square Inch of pressure acting on a given area (includes atmospheric pressure in the calculation).

Psig: Pounds of force, gauge, or psi without including the effect of atmospheric pressure (a 3500 psig tank has 3500 psig at surface or at depth). However most use the terms 'psi' and 'psig' as interchangeable; in such situations, 'psi' refers to 'psig.'

Pulmonary: Having to do with the lungs.

Q

No Q entries

R

RBC: Red Blood Cells.

Rebreathers: A generic term for Closed Circuit or Semi-closed Circuit Rebreathers.

Recompression: Recompression therapy; using a chamber, known as a hyperbaric chamber, to aid in removing **nitrogen** from a diver suspected of suffering from **decompression illness**. The diver is placed under increased pressure for a certain length of time. Divers may need a number of treatments, known as **recompression** series, in order to treat the effects of **decompression illnesses**.

REM: Rapid Eye Movement; a natural part of the sleep cycle. **REM** sleep in adult humans typically occupies 20-25% of total sleep, about 90-120 minutes of a night's sleep.

Renal: Having to do with the kidneys.

Respiration: A **metabolic** process that involves the exchange of gases. In air breathing mammals, inhaled oxygen is exchanged with exhaled **Carbon Dioxide**.

RMV: Respiratory Minute Volume; the amount of gas exhaled in one minute.

RNPL: Royal Naval Physiologic Laboratory.

RNT: Residual nitrogen time; a calculation used in multi-dive planning that is based on the amount of nitrogen remaining in the body following a dive.

RQ: Respiratory Quotient; the ratio of carbon dioxide produced to the amount of oxygen consumed during cellular processes. RQ values are used to determine scrubber duration.

Runtime: Total in-water dive time from the start of the descent through the ascent.

S

SAC: Surface air consumption rate.

Schrader valve: See LPI.

SCR: Semi-Closed Rebreather.

Scrubber; CO_2 scrubber: A chemical compound used in CCRs to remove carbon dioxide from the breathing loop.

SCUBA: Self-Contained Underwater Breathing Apparatus.

Setpoint: The amount of oxygen an ECCR diver enters into the unit's electronic memory (changeable before, during, or after a dive) that defines the least percentage of oxygen required before the unit injects oxygen into the breathing mix; the lowest percentage of oxygen allowed by the ECCR manufacturer before oxygen is automatically injected into the breathing mix.

SI; S.I.T; SIT: Surface Interval; the time spent out of the water between dives.

SMB: Surface marker buoy.

Spike; Spiking: A sudden increase in PO_2 that can occur, for a number of reasons, when diving a CCR unit.

SRF: Surface Ratio Factor.

Stage bottle: A cylinder used to stage decompression or to hold a 'travel gas' while performing dives.

Sur-D: Surface Decompression which is usually performed as a pre-planned event in a Hyperbaric Chamber as a decompression procedure.

T

Tank: A cylinder, usually carried on the back, used to hold pressurized gas mixes for diving.

Travel gas: Gas contained in a cylinder that is carried by a deep diver in order to exit a depth dive in case of an out-of gas emergency. Travel gas usually has a lower amount of oxygen than decompression gas, and is worn under the diver's arms open-circuit decompression dives. This type of cylinder is also worn most frequently under the diver's arms.

TOD: Target Operating Depth or the depth a diver plans to descend to.

Trimix: Any breathable mixture of Nitrogen, Oxygen, and Helium.

Twins: Term used in the United States to describe a configuration where two independent SCUBA cylinders are worn on the back creating **twin** independent air supplies. Such back-mounted, dual independent gas supplies have been shown to be a major cause of diving fatalities. **Note**: British sources, such as author Kevin Gurr, often refer to "doubles" (see **Doubles**) as "**twins.**"

U

UPTD: 'Unit Pulmonary Toxic Dose;' a way of calculating and measuring oxygen toxicity.

UHMS: The Undersea and Hyperbaric Medicine Society

V

VCO_2: Volume of Carbon Dioxide production.

V_E: Pronounced "V dot E" and refers to Expired Total Ventilation.

VO_2: Volume of Oxygen production.

VO_2max: The Maximum amount of Oxygen the body can transport and utilize during incremental exercise, or exercise that increases over time. It is also known as 'aerobic capacity,' 'maximal oxygen consumption' and 'maximal oxygen uptake.'

W

WBC: White Blood Cells.

X

No X entries

Y

No Y entries

Z

No Z entries

Appendix B Tables & Charts

ITEM #	DESCRIPTION
C-3200	IANTD EAD/MOD
C-3204	IANTD EAD/MOD Metric
C-3201	IANTD OTU/CNS
C-3202	IANTD Gas Management/SRF
C-3502	IANTD 26% w/75% Deco
C-3602	IANTD 25% w/78% Deco
C-3104	IANTD 1.3 – 1.4 PO_2 14/44 Diluent
C-3105	IANTD 1.2 – 1.4 PO_2 8/60 Diluent
C-3700	IANTD Helium Mix Guide/Tech PO_2
C-3706	IANTD Trimix END
C-3717	IANTD Runtime Trimix 19/40
C-3718	IANTD Runtime Trimix 14/50
C-3719	IANTD Runtime Trimix 12/60

Please Note: All of the IANTD Tables referred to in this text, as well as numerous others, are available in a Soft, Foldable, Waterproof Version intended to be placed in the BC or wetsuit/drysuit pocket for your training and back-up use. Thay are all available for sale at your local IANTD Dive Shop located worldwide at www.iantd.com

IANTD EAD / MOD TABLES

24 % O2

ACTUAL DEPTH FSW	40	50	60	70	80	90	100	110	120	130	140	150	160	170	180
EAD	37	47	56	66	76	85	95	105	114	124	133	143	153	162	172
PO2	0.53	0.60	0.68	0.75	0.82	0.89	0.97	1.04	1.11	1.19	1.26	1.33	1.40	1.48	1.55
OTU PER MIN	0.10	0.27	0.42	0.56	0.69	0.82	0.95	1.07	1.18	1.30	1.41	1.52	1.63	1.74	1.85
% CNS	0.00	0.14	0.16	0.19	0.23	0.27	0.31	0.36	0.42	0.46	0.51	0.58	0.67	0.78	1.04

PO2	MOD FSW
1.30	146
1.35	153
1.40	160
1.45	166
1.50	173
1.55	180
1.60	187

26 % O2

ACTUAL DEPTH FSW	40	50	60	70	80	90	100	110	120	130	140	150	160	170
EAD	35	45	54	63	73	82	92	101	110	120	129	138	148	157
PO2	0.58	0.65	0.73	0.81	0.89	0.97	1.05	1.13	1.21	1.28	1.36	1.44	1.52	1.60
OTU PER MIN	0.21	0.38	0.53	0.68	0.81	0.95	1.08	1.21	1.33	1.45	1.57	1.69	1.81	1.92
% CNS	0.00	0.16	0.19	0.23	0.27	0.31	0.36	0.43	0.48	0.54	0.62	0.72	0.93	1.72

PO2	MOD FSW
1.30	132
1.35	138
1.40	145
1.45	151
1.50	157
1.55	164
1.60	170

28 % O2

ACTUAL DEPTH FSW	40	50	60	70	80	90	100	110	120	130	140	150
EAD	34	43	52	61	70	79	88	97	106	116	125	134
PO2	0.62	0.70	0.79	0.87	0.96	1.04	1.13	1.21	1.30	1.38	1.47	1.55
OTU PER MIN	0.30	0.48	0.63	0.79	0.93	1.07	1.21	1.34	1.47	1.60	1.73	1.86
% CNS	0.14	0.18	0.21	0.26	0.30	0.36	0.43	0.48	0.55	0.64	0.76	1.11

PO2	MOD FSW
1.30	120
1.35	126
1.40	132
1.45	138
1.50	144
1.55	150
1.60	156

30 % O2

ACTUAL DEPTH FSW	40	50	60	70	80	90	100	110	120	130	140
EAD	32	41	49	58	67	76	85	94	103	111	120
PO2	0.66	0.75	0.85	0.94	1.03	1.12	1.21	1.30	1.39	1.48	1.57
OTU PER MIN	0.40	0.57	0.74	0.89	1.05	1.19	1.34	1.48	1.62	1.75	1.88
% CNS	0.16	0.20	0.24	0.29	0.35	0.42	0.48	0.56	0.65	0.79	1.30

PO2	MOD FSW
1.30	110
1.35	116
1.40	121
1.45	127
1.50	132
1.55	138
1.60	143

38 % O2

ACTUAL DEPTH FSW	40	50	60	70	80	90	100
EAD	24	32	40	48	56	64	71
PO2	0.84	0.96	1.07	1.19	1.30	1.42	1.53
OTU PER MIN	0.73	0.93	1.12	1.30	1.48	1.65	1.82
% CNS	0.24	0.30	0.39	0.46	0.56	0.68	0.98

PO2	MOD FSW
1.30	80
1.35	84
1.40	89
1.45	93
1.50	97
1.55	102
1.60	106

36 % O2

ACTUAL DEPTH FSW	40	50	60	70	80	90	100	110
EAD	26	34	42	50	59	67	75	83
PO2	0.80	0.91	1.01	1.12	1.23	1.34	1.45	1.56
OTU PER MIN	0.65	0.84	1.02	1.20	1.37	1.54	1.70	1.87
% CNS	0.22	0.28	0.34	0.43	0.50	0.60	0.74	1.19

PO2	MOD FSW
1.30	86
1.35	91
1.40	95
1.45	100
1.50	105
1.55	109
1.60	114

34 % O2

ACTUAL DEPTH FSW	40	50	60	70	80	90	100	110	120
EAD	28	36	45	53	61	70	78	86	95
PO2	0.75	0.86	0.96	1.06	1.16	1.27	1.37	1.47	1.58
OTU PER MIN	0.57	0.75	0.93	1.10	1.27	1.43	1.58	1.74	1.89
% CNS	0.20	0.25	0.30	0.38	0.45	0.52	0.63	0.78	1.30

PO2	MOD FSW
1.30	93
1.35	98
1.40	103
1.45	108
1.50	113
1.55	117
1.60	122

32 % O2

ACTUAL DEPTH FSW	40	50	60	70	80	90	100	110	120	130
EAD	30	38	47	56	64	73	81	90	99	107
PO2	0.71	0.80	0.90	1.00	1.10	1.19	1.29	1.39	1.48	1.58
OTU PER MIN	0.48	0.66	0.83	1.00	1.16	1.31	1.46	1.61	1.75	1.90
% CNS	0.18	0.22	0.28	0.33	0.41	0.47	0.54	0.64	0.79	1.47

PO2	MOD FSW
1.30	101
1.35	106
1.40	111
1.45	117
1.50	122
1.55	127
1.60	132

Warning: DO NOT attempt to use these tables unless you are fully trained & certified in the use of Gas Mixtures Other Than Air, or are under the supervision of a Gas Mixtures Other Than Air Instructor. Proper use of these tables will reduce the risk of decompression sickness & oxygen toxicity, but no table or computer can eliminate those risks.

WWW.IANTD.COM

C-3200

IANTD EAD / MOD TABLES

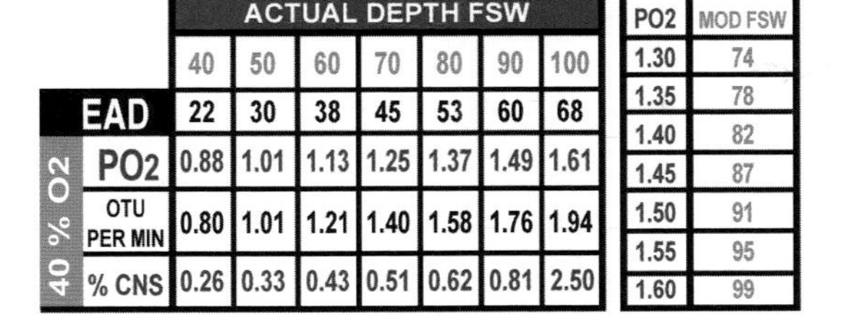

40 % O2

ACTUAL DEPTH FSW	40	50	60	70	80	90	100
EAD	22	30	38	45	53	60	68
PO2	0.88	1.01	1.13	1.25	1.37	1.49	1.61
OTU PER MIN	0.80	1.01	1.21	1.40	1.58	1.76	1.94
% CNS	0.26	0.33	0.43	0.51	0.62	0.81	2.50

PO2	MOD FSW
1.30	74
1.35	78
1.40	82
1.45	87
1.50	91
1.55	95
1.60	99

60 % O2

DEPTH FSW	10	15	20	30	40	50
EAD	0	0	0	0	4	9
PO2	0.78	0.87	0.96	1.15	1.33	1.51
OTU PER MIN	0.62	0.79	0.94	1.24	1.52	1.79
% CNS	0.21	0.26	0.31	0.44	0.57	0.83

PO2	MOD FSW
1.30	39
1.35	41
1.40	44
1.45	47
1.50	50
1.55	52
1.60	55

80 % O2

FSW	10	15	20	30
EAD	0	0	0	0
PO2	1.04	1.16	1.28	1.53
OTU PER MIN	1.07	1.26	1.45	1.82
% CNS	0.36	0.44	0.54	0.93

PO2	MOD FSW
1.30	21
1.35	23
1.40	25
1.45	27
1.50	29
1.55	31
1.60	33

45 % O2

ACTUAL DEPTH FSW	10	15	20	30	40	50	60	70	80
EAD	0	0	4	11	18	25	32	38	46
PO2	0.59	0.65	0.72	0.86	1.00	1.13	1.27	1.40	1.54
OTU PER MIN	0.23	0.37	0.51	0.76	0.99	1.21	1.43	1.63	1.84
% CNS	0.00	0.16	0.18	0.25	0.33	0.43	0.52	0.65	1.04

PO2	MOD FSW
1.30	62
1.35	66
1.40	70
1.45	73
1.50	77
1.55	81
1.60	84

65 % O2

DEPTH FSW	10	15	20	30	40
EAD	0	0	0	0	0
PO2	0.85	0.95	1.04	1.24	1.44
OTU PER MIN	0.74	0.92	1.07	1.39	1.69
% CNS	0.24	0.30	0.36	0.51	0.71

PO2	MOD FSW
1.30	33
1.35	36
1.40	38
1.45	41
1.50	43
1.55	46
1.60	48

85 % O2

FSW	10	15	20
EAD	0	0	0
PO2	1.11	1.24	1.37
OTU PER MIN	1.18	1.39	1.58
% CNS	0.42	0.51	0.62

PO2	MOD FSW
1.30	17
1.35	19
1.40	21
1.45	23
1.50	25
1.55	27
1.60	29

50 % O2

ACTUAL DEPTH FSW	10	15	20	30	40	50	60	70
EAD	0	0	1	7	13	20	26	32
PO2	0.65	0.73	0.80	0.95	1.11	1.26	1.41	1.56
OTU PER MIN	0.37	0.51	0.66	0.92	1.17	1.41	1.64	1.85
% CNS	0.16	0.19	0.22	0.30	0.42	0.51	0.67	1.19

PO2	MOD FSW
1.30	53
1.35	56
1.40	59
1.45	63
1.50	66
1.55	69
1.60	73

70 % O2

DEPTH FSW	10	15	20	30	40
EAD	0	0	0	0	0
PO2	0.91	1.02	1.12	1.34	1.55
OTU PER MIN	0.85	1.04	1.20	1.53	1.85
% CNS	0.28	0.35	0.43	0.58	1.04

PO2	MOD FSW
1.30	28
1.35	31
1.40	33
1.45	35
1.50	38
1.55	40
1.60	42

90 % O2

FSW	10	15	20
EAD	0	0	0
PO2	1.17	1.30	1.45
OTU PER MIN	1.28	1.48	1.70
% CNS	0.46	0.56	0.72

PO2	MOD FSW
1.30	15
1.35	17
1.40	18
1.45	20
1.50	22
1.55	24
1.60	26

55 % O2

ACTUAL DEPTH FSW	10	15	20	30	40	50	60
EAD	0	0	0	3	9	14	20
PO2	0.72	0.8	0.88	1.05	1.22	1.38	1.55
OTU PER MIN	0.50	0.65	0.80	1.08	1.35	1.60	1.85
% CNS	0.18	0.22	0.26	0.37	0.48	0.64	1.11

PO2	MOD FSW
1.30	45
1.35	48
1.40	51
1.45	54
1.50	57
1.55	60
1.60	63

75 % O2

FSW	10	15	20	30
EAD	0	0	0	0
PO2	0.98	1.09	1.20	1.43
OTU PER MIN	0.96	1.15	1.33	1.68
% CNS	0.31	0.41	0.48	0.71

PO2	MOD FSW
1.30	24
1.35	26
1.40	29
1.45	31
1.50	33
1.55	35
1.60	37

95 % O2

FSW	10	15	20
EAD	0	0	0
PO2	1.24	1.38	1.53
OTU PER MIN	1.38	1.61	1.82
% CNS	0.50	0.63	0.93

PO2	MOD FSW
1.30	12
1.35	14
1.40	16
1.45	17
1.50	19
1.55	21
1.60	23

100 % O2

FSW	10	15	20
EAD	0	0	0
PO2	1.30	1.45	1.61
OTU PER MIN	1.48	1.70	1.93
% CNS	0.56	0.72	2.22

PO2	MOD FSW
1.30	10
1.35	12
1.40	13
1.45	15
1.50	17
1.55	18
1.60	20

C-3200B

WWW.IANTD.COM

IANTD METRIC EAD / MOD TABLES

24 % O2

Actual Depth MSW	12	15	18	21	24	27	30	33	36	39	42	45	48	51	54
EAD	11.2	14.1	16.9	19.8	22.7	25.6	28.5	31.4	34.3	37.1	40.0	42.9	45.8	48.7	51.6
PO2	0.53	0.60	0.67	0.74	0.82	0.89	0.96	1.03	1.10	1.18	1.25	1.32	1.39	1.46	1.54
OTU PER MIN	0.09	0.26	0.41	0.55	0.68	0.81	0.93	1.05	1.17	1.28	1.40	1.51	1.62	1.72	1.83
% CNS	0.00	0.14	0.16	0.20	0.23	0.27	0.30	0.35	0.42	0.46	0.51	0.57	0.65	0.75	1.04

PO2	MOD Mtr
1.30	44.2
1.35	46.3
1.40	48.3
1.45	50.4
1.50	52.5
1.55	54.6
1.60	56.7

26 % O2

Actual Depth MSW	12	15	18	21	24	27	30	33	36	39	42	45	48	51
EAD	10.6	13.4	16.2	19.0	21.8	24.7	27.5	30.3	33.1	35.9	38.7	41.5	44.3	47.1
PO2	0.57	0.65	0.73	0.81	0.88	0.96	1.04	1.12	1.20	1.27	1.35	1.43	1.51	1.59
OTU PER MIN	0.20	0.37	0.52	0.67	0.80	0.94	1.07	1.19	1.32	1.44	1.56	1.67	1.79	1.90
% CNS	0.00	0.16	0.19	0.23	0.26	0.30	0.36	0.42	0.48	0.52	0.60	0.71	0.92	2.00

PO2	MOD Mtr
1.30	40.0
1.35	41.9
1.40	43.8
1.45	45.8
1.50	47.7
1.55	49.6
1.60	51.5

28 % O2

Actual Depth MSW	12	15	18	21	24	27	30	33	36	39	42	45
EAD	10.1	12.8	15.5	18.3	21.0	23.7	26.5	29.2	31.9	34.7	37.4	40.1
PO2	0.62	0.70	0.78	0.87	0.95	1.04	1.12	1.20	1.29	1.37	1.46	1.54
OTU PER MIN	0.30	0.47	0.63	0.78	0.92	1.06	1.20	1.33	1.46	1.59	1.71	1.84
% CNS	0.14	0.18	0.21	0.26	0.30	0.36	0.42	0.48	0.55	0.62	0.75	1.04

PO2	MOD Mtr
1.30	36.4
1.35	38.2
1.40	40.0
1.45	41.8
1.50	43.6
1.55	45.4
1.60	47.1

30 % O2

Actual Depth MSW	12	15	18	21	24	27	30	33	36	39	42
EAD	9.5	12.2	14.8	17.5	20.1	22.8	25.4	28.1	30.8	33.4	36.1
PO2	0.66	0.75	0.84	0.93	1.02	1.11	1.20	1.29	1.38	1.47	1.56
OTU PER MIN	0.39	0.56	0.73	0.88	1.03	1.18	1.32	1.46	1.60	1.73	1.87
% CNS	0.16	0.20	0.24	0.29	0.34	0.42	0.48	0.55	0.64	0.76	1.2

PO2	MOD Mtr
1.30	33.3
1.35	35.0
1.40	36.7
1.45	38.3
1.50	40.0
1.55	41.7
1.60	43.3

32 % O2

Actual Depth MSW	12	15	18	21	24	27	30	33	36	39
EAD	8.9	11.5	14.1	16.7	19.3	21.8	24.4	27.0	29.6	32.2
PO2	0.70	0.80	0.90	0.99	1.09	1.18	1.28	1.38	1.47	1.57
OTU PER MIN	0.48	0.65	0.82	0.99	1.14	1.30	1.45	1.59	1.74	1.88
% CNS	0.18	0.22	0.28	0.32	0.41	0.46	0.54	0.64	0.76	1.30

PO2	MOD Mtr
1.30	30.6
1.35	32.2
1.40	33.8
1.45	35.3
1.50	36.9
1.55	38.4
1.60	40.0

34 % O2

Actual Depth MSW	12	15	18	21	24	27	30	33	36
EAD	8.4	10.9	13.4	15.9	18.4	20.9	23.4	25.9	28.4
PO2	0.75	0.85	0.95	1.05	1.16	1.26	1.36	1.46	1.56
OTU PER MIN	0.56	0.74	0.92	1.09	1.25	1.41	1.57	1.72	1.87
% CNS	0.20	0.24	0.30	0.36	0.44	0.51	0.62	0.75	1.20

PO2	MOD Mtr
1.30	28.2
1.35	29.7
1.40	31.2
1.45	32.6
1.50	34.1
1.55	35.6
1.60	37.1

36 % O2

Actual Depth MSW	12	15	18	21	24	27	30	33
EAD	7.8	10.3	12.7	15.1	17.5	20.0	22.4	24.8
PO2	0.79	0.90	1.01	1.12	1.22	1.33	1.44	1.55
OTU PER MIN	0.64	0.83	1.01	1.19	1.36	1.53	1.69	1.85
% CNS	0.21	0.28	0.33	0.42	0.48	0.58	0.72	1.11

PO2	MOD Mtr
1.30	26.1
1.35	27.5
1.40	28.9
1.45	30.3
1.50	31.7
1.55	33.1
1.60	34.4

38 % O2

Actual Depth MSW	12	15	18	21	24	27	30
EAD	7.3	9.6	12.0	14.3	16.7	19.0	21.4
PO2	0.84	0.95	1.06	1.18	1.29	1.41	1.52
OTU PER MIN	0.72	0.92	1.11	1.29	1.46	1.64	1.81
% CNS	0.24	0.30	0.37	0.46	0.55	0.67	0.93

PO2	MOD Mtr
1.30	24.2
1.35	25.5
1.40	26.8
1.45	28.2
1.50	29.5
1.55	30.8
1.60	32.1

PRODUCED BY TOM MOUNT, MARK OWENS & CLAYTON BOHM

C-3204

IANTD METRIC EAD / MOD TABLES

40 % O2

ACTUAL DEPTH MSW	12	15	18	21	24	27	30
EAD	6.7	9.0	11.3	13.5	15.8	18.1	20.4
PO2	0.88	1.00	1.12	1.24	1.36	1.48	1.60
OTU PER MIN	0.80	1.00	1.20	1.38	1.57	1.75	1.92
% CNS	0.26	0.33	0.42	0.50	0.62	0.79	2.22

PO2	MOD Mtr
1.30	22.5
1.35	23.8
1.40	25.0
1.45	26.3
1.50	27.5
1.55	28.8
1.60	30.0

60 % O2

DEPTH MSW	3	6	9	12	15
EAD	0	0	0	1.1	2.7
PO2	0.78	0.96	1.14	1.32	1.50
OTU PER MIN	0.62	0.93	1.23	1.51	1.78
% CNS	0.21	0.30	0.43	0.57	0.83

PO2	MOD Mtr
1.30	11.7
1.35	12.5
1.40	13.3
1.45	14.2
1.50	15.0
1.55	15.8
1.60	16.7

80 % O2

MSW	3	6	9
EAD	0	0	0
PO2	1.04	1.28	1.52
OTU PER MIN	1.07	1.45	1.81
% CNS	0.36	0.54	0.93

PO2	MOD Mtr
1.30	6.3
1.35	6.9
1.40	7.5
1.45	8.1
1.50	8.8
1.55	9.4
1.60	10.0

45 % O2

ACTUAL DEPTH MSW	3	6	9	12	15	18	21	24
EAD	0	1.1	3.2	5.3	7.4	9.5	11.6	13.7
PO2	0.59	0.72	0.86	0.99	1.13	1.26	1.40	1.53
OTU PER MIN	0.23	0.51	0.75	0.98	1.20	1.42	1.62	1.82
% CNS	0.00	0.18	0.25	0.32	0.43	0.51	0.67	0.99

PO2	MOD Mtr
1.30	18.9
1.35	20.0
1.40	21.1
1.45	22.2
1.50	23.3
1.55	24.4
1.60	25.6

65 % O2

DEPTH MSW	3	6	9	12
EAD	0	0	0	0
PO2	0.85	1.04	1.24	1.43
OTU PER MIN	0.73	1.07	1.38	1.67
% CNS	0.24	0.36	0.50	0.71

PO2	MOD Mtr
1.30	10.0
1.35	10.8
1.40	11.5
1.45	12.3
1.50	13.1
1.55	13.8
1.60	14.6

85 % O2

MSW	3	6
EAD	0	0
PO2	1.11	1.36
OTU PER MIN	1.17	1.57
% CNS	0.42	0.62

PO2	MOD Mtr
1.30	5.3
1.35	5.9
1.40	6.5
1.45	7.1
1.50	7.6
1.55	8.2
1.60	8.8

50 % O2

ACTUAL DEPTH MSW	3	6	9	12	15	18	21
EAD	0	0.1	2.0	3.9	5.8	7.7	9.6
PO2	0.65	0.80	0.95	1.10	1.25	1.40	1.55
OTU PER MIN	0.37	0.65	0.92	1.16	1.40	1.63	1.85
% CNS	0.16	0.22	0.30	0.42	0.51	0.67	1.11

PO2	MOD Mtr
1.30	16.0
1.35	17.0
1.40	18.0
1.45	19.0
1.50	20.0
1.55	21.0
1.60	22.0

70 % O2

DEPTH MSW	3	6	9	12
EAD	0	0	0	0
PO2	0.91	1.12	1.33	1.54
OTU PER MIN	0.85	1.20	1.52	1.84
% CNS	0.28	0.42	0.58	1.04

PO2	MOD Mtr
1.30	8.6
1.35	9.3
1.40	10.0
1.45	10.7
1.50	11.4
1.55	12.1
1.60	12.9

90 % O2

MSW	3	6
EAD	0	0
PO2	1.17	1.44
OTU PER MIN	1.27	1.69
% CNS	0.45	0.72

PO2	MOD Mtr
1.30	4.4
1.35	5.0
1.40	5.6
1.45	6.1
1.50	6.7
1.55	7.2
1.60	7.8

55 % O2

ACTUAL DEPTH MSW	3	6	9	12	15	18
EAD	0	0	0.8	2.5	4.2	5.9
PO2	0.72	0.88	1.05	1.21	1.38	1.54
OTU PER MIN	0.50	0.80	1.07	1.34	1.59	1.84
% CNS	0.18	0.26	0.36	0.48	0.64	1.04

PO2	MOD Mtr
1.30	13.6
1.35	14.5
1.40	15.5
1.45	16.4
1.50	17.3
1.55	18.2
1.60	19.1

75 % O2

MSW	3	6	9
EAD	0	0	0
PO2	0.98	1.20	1.43
OTU PER MIN	0.96	1.32	1.67
% CNS	0.31	0.48	0.71

PO2	MOD Mtr
1.30	7.3
1.35	8.0
1.40	8.7
1.45	9.3
1.50	10.0
1.55	10.7
1.60	11.3

95 % O2

MSW	3	6
EAD	0	0
PO2	1.24	1.52
OTU PER MIN	1.38	1.81
% CNS	0.50	0.93

PO2	MOD Mtr
1.30	3.7
1.35	4.2
1.40	4.7
1.45	5.3
1.50	5.8
1.55	6.3
1.60	6.8

100% O2

MSW	3	6
EAD	0	0
PO2	1.30	1.60
OTU PER MIN	1.48	1.92
% CNS	0.56	2.22

PO2	MOD Mtr
1.30	3.0
1.35	3.5
1.40	4.0
1.45	4.5
1.50	5.0
1.55	5.5
1.60	6.0

PRODUCED BY TOM MOUNT, MARK OWENS & CLAYTON BOHM C-3204B

IANTD OTU / CNS O2 TRACKING TABLE

PO2	1 Min	5 Min	10 Min	20 Min	30 Min	40 Min	50 Min	60 Min
	OTU - CNS	OTU - CNS	OTU - CNS	OTU - CNS	OTU - CNS	OTU - CNS	OTU - CNS	OTU - CNS
0.60	0.26 - 0.14	1.31 - 0.69	2.63 - 1.39	5.26 - 2.78	7.89 - 4.17	10.52 - 5.56	13.15 - 6.94	15.78 - 8.33
0.65	0.37 - 0.16	1.84 - 0.78	3.68 - 1.55	7.36 - 3.10	11.04 - 4.65	14.73 - 6.20	18.41 - 7.75	22.09 - 9.30
0.70	0.47 - 0.18	2.34 - 0.88	4.67 - 1.75	9.35 - 3.51	14.02 - 5.26	18.70 - 7.02	23.37 - 8.77	28.05 - 10.53
0.75	0.56 - 0.20	2.81 - 0.98	5.63 - 1.96	11.25 - 3.92	16.88 - 5.88	22.50 - 7.84	28.13 - 9.80	33.75 - 11.76
0.80	0.65 - 0.22	3.27 - 1.11	6.54 - 2.22	13.09 - 4.44	19.63 - 6.67	26.18 - 8.89	32.72 - 11.11	39.27 - 13.33
0.85	0.74 - 0.25	3.72 - 1.23	7.44 - 2.47	14.88 - 4.94	22.31 - 7.41	29.75 - 9.88	37.19 - 12.35	44.63 - 14.81
0.90	0.83 - 0.28	4.15 - 1.39	8.31 - 2.78	16.62 - 5.56	24.93 - 8.33	33.24 - 11.11	41.55 - 13.89	49.86 - 16.67
0.95	0.92 - 0.30	4.58 - 1.52	9.16 - 3.03	18.33 - 6.06	27.49 - 9.09	36.65 - 12.12	45.81 - 15.15	54.98 - 18.18
1.00	1.00 - 0.33	5.00 - 1.67	10.00 - 3.33	20.00 - 6.67	30.00 - 10.00	40.00 - 13.33	50.00 - 16.67	60.00 - 20.00
1.05	1.08 - 0.37	5.41 - 1.85	10.82 - 3.70	21.65 - 7.41	32.47 - 11.11	43.29 - 14.81	54.12 - 18.52	64.94 - 22.22
1.10	1.16 - 0.42	5.82 - 2.08	11.63 - 4.17	23.27 - 8.33	34.90 - 12.50	46.54 - 16.67	58.17 - 20.83	69.80 - 25.00
1.15	1.24 - 0.44	6.22 - 2.19	12.43 - 4.39	24.87 - 8.77	37.30 - 13.16	49.73 - 17.54	62.16 - 21.93	74.60 - 26.32
1.20	1.32 - 0.48	6.61 - 2.38	13.22 - 4.76	26.44 - 9.52	39.67 - 14.29	52.89 - 19.05	66.11 - 23.81	79.33 - 28.57
1.25	1.40 - 0.51	7.00 - 2.56	14.00 - 5.13	28.00 - 10.26	42.00 - 15.38	56.00 - 20.51	70.00 - 25.64	84.01 - 30.77
1.30	1.48 - 0.56	7.39 - 2.78	14.77 - 5.56	29.54 - 11.11	44.31 - 16.67	59.09 - 22.22	73.86 - 27.78	88.63 - 33.33
1.35	1.55 - 0.61	7.77 - 3.03	15.53 - 6.06	31.07 - 12.12	46.60 - 18.18	62.13 - 24.24	77.67 - 30.30	93.20 - 36.36
1.40	1.63 - 0.67	8.14 - 3.33	16.29 - 6.67	32.58 - 13.33	48.86 - 20.00	65.15 - 26.67	81.44 - 33.33	97.73 - 40.00
1.45	1.70 - 0.72	8.52 - 3.62	17.04 - 7.25	34.07 - 14.49	51.11 - 21.74	68.14 - 28.99	85.18 - 36.23	102.2 - 43.48
1.50	1.78 - 0.83	8.89 - 4.17	17.78 - 8.33	35.55 - 16.67	53.33 - 25.00	71.11 - 33.33	88.88 - 41.67	106.6 - 50.00
1.55	1.85 - 1.11	9.26 - 5.56	18.51 - 11.11	37.02 - 22.22	55.53 - 33.33	74.05 - 44.44	92.56 - 55.56	111.1 - 66.67
1.60	1.92 - 2.22	9.62 - 11.11	19.24 - 22.22	38.48 - 44.44	57.72 - 66.67	76.96 - 88.89	96.20 - 111.1	115.4 - 133.3

OTU's ARE TRACKED IN UNITS. CNS O2 IS TRACKED IN PERCENT OF CLOCK. IF DIVE EXCEEDS 60 MINUTES, SUBTRACT 60 FROM TOTAL DIVE TIME, RE-ENTER CHART FOR TIME IN EXCESS OF 60 MINUTES AND ADD THAT VALUE TO 60 MINUTE VALUE.

 WWW.IANTD.COM

C-3201

DEPTH		EANx (%O2)															
FSW	MSW	21%	24%	26%	28%	30%	32%	34%	36%	38%	40%	50%	60%	70%	80%	90%	100%
10	3.0	0.27	0.31	0.34	0.36	0.39	0.42	0.44	0.47	0.50	0.52	0.65	0.78	0.91	1.04	1.17	1.30
20	6.1	0.34	0.39	0.42	0.45	0.48	0.51	0.55	0.58	0.61	0.64	0.80	0.96	1.12	1.28	1.45	1.61
30	9.1	0.40	0.46	0.50	0.53	0.57	0.61	0.65	0.69	0.73	0.76	0.95	1.15	1.34	1.53		
40	12.2	0.46	0.53	0.58	0.62	0.66	0.71	0.75	0.80	0.84	0.88	1.11	1.33	1.55			
50	15.2	0.53	0.60	0.65	0.70	0.75	0.80	0.86	0.91	0.96	1.01	1.26	1.51				
60	18.3	0.59	0.68	0.73	0.79	0.85	0.90	0.96	1.01	1.07	1.13	1.41					
70	21.3	0.66	0.75	0.81	0.87	0.94	1.00	1.06	1.12	1.19	1.25	1.56					
80	24.4	0.72	0.82	0.89	0.96	1.03	1.10	1.16	1.23	1.30	1.37						
90	27.4	0.78	0.89	0.97	1.04	1.12	1.19	1.27	1.34	1.42	1.49						
100	30.5	0.85	0.97	1.05	1.13	1.21	1.29	1.37	1.45	1.53	1.61						
110	33.5	0.91	1.04	1.13	1.21	1.30	1.39	1.47	1.56								
120	36.6	0.97	1.11	1.21	1.30	1.39	1.47	1.58									
130	39.6	1.04	1.19	1.28	1.38	1.48	1.58										
140	42.7	1.10	1.26	1.36	1.47	1.57											
150	45.7	1.16	1.33	1.44	1.55												
160	48.8	1.23	1.40	1.52													
170	51.8	1.29	1.48	1.60													
180	54.9	1.36	1.55														
190	57.9	1.42															
200	61.0	1.48															
210	64.0	1.55															
220	67.1	1.61															

1. FIND THE DEPTH OF YOUR DIVE ON THE LEFT HAND SIDE OF TABLE.

2. FIND EANx MIX IN TOP ROW.

3. READ PO2 AT INTERSECTION OF DEPTH ROW, AND EANx COLUMN.

start	SURFACE INTERVAL							
%	30	60	90	2hrs	3hrs	4hrs	5hrs	6hrs
100	83	66	49	41	24	16	11	7
95	79	63	46	38	22	15	10	7
90	75	59	44	37	22	15	10	7
85	71	56	42	35	21	14	9	6
80	66	53	39	32	19	13	9	6
75	62	49	37	31	18	12	8	5
70	58	46	34	28	17	11	7	5
65	54	43	32	27	16	11	7	5
60	50	40	29	24	14	9	6	4
55	46	36	27	22	13	9	6	4
50	41	33	24	20	12	8	5	3
45	37	30	22	18	11	7	5	3
40	33	26	20	17	10	7	5	3
35	29	23	17	14	8	5	3	2
30	25	20	15	12	7	5	3	2
25	21	16	12	10	6	4	3	2
20	17	13	10	8	5	3	2	1
15	12	10	7	6	3	2	1	1
10	8	7	5	4	2	1	1	1

RESIDUAL PERCENT CNS O2 CLOCK

Warning: DO NOT attempt to use these tables unless you are fully trained & certified in the use of Gas Mixtures Other Than Air, or are under the supervision of a Gas Mixtures Other Than Air Instructor. Proper use of these tables will reduce the risk of decompression sickness & oxygen toxicity, but no table or computer can

C-3201B

IANTD GAS MANAGEMENT / TURN PRESSURE

Starting PSIG	Surface Air Consumption Rate Factor														
PSIG	0.67	0.68	0.69	0.70	0.71	0.72	0.73	0.74	0.75	0.76	0.77	0.78	0.79	0.80	0.81
2000	1340	1360	1380	1400	1420	1440	1460	1480	1500	1520	1540	1560	1580	1600	1620
2100	1407	1428	1449	1470	1491	1512	1533	1554	1575	1596	1617	1638	1659	1680	1701
2200	1474	1496	1518	1540	1562	1584	1606	1628	1650	1672	1694	1716	1738	1760	1782
2300	1541	1564	1587	1610	1633	1656	1679	1702	1725	1748	1771	1794	1817	1840	1863
2400	1608	1632	1656	1680	1704	1728	1752	1776	1800	1824	1848	1872	1896	1920	1944
2500	1675	1700	1725	1750	1775	1800	1825	1850	1875	1900	1925	1950	1975	2000	2025
2600	1742	1768	1794	1820	1846	1872	1898	1924	1950	1976	2002	2028	2054	2080	2106
2700	1809	1836	1863	1890	1917	1944	1971	1998	2025	2052	2079	2106	2133	2160	2187
2800	1876	1904	1932	1960	1988	2016	2044	2072	2100	2128	2156	2184	2212	2240	2268
2900	1943	1972	2001	2030	2059	2088	2117	2146	2175	2204	2233	2262	2291	2320	2349
3000	2010	2040	2070	2100	2130	2160	2190	2220	2250	2280	2310	2340	2370	2400	2430
3100	2077	2108	2139	2170	2201	2232	2263	2294	2325	2356	2387	2418	2449	2480	2511
3200	2144	2176	2208	2240	2272	2304	2336	2368	2400	2432	2464	2496	2528	2560	2592
3300	2211	2244	2277	2310	2343	2376	2409	2442	2475	2508	2541	2574	2607	2640	2673
3400	2278	2312	2346	2380	2414	2448	2482	2516	2550	2584	2618	2652	2686	2720	2754
3500	2345	2380	2415	2450	2485	2520	2555	2590	2625	2660	2695	2730	2765	2800	2835
3600	2412	2448	2484	2520	2556	2592	2628	2664	2700	2736	2772	2808	2844	2880	2916
3700	2479	2516	2553	2590	2627	2664	2701	2738	2775	2812	2849	2886	2923	2960	2997
3800	2546	2584	2622	2660	2698	2736	2774	2812	2850	2888	2926	2964	3002	3040	3078
3900	2613	2652	2691	2730	2769	2808	2847	2886	2925	2964	3003	3042	3081	3120	3159
4000	2680	2720	2760	2800	2840	2880	2920	2960	3000	3040	3060	3120	3160	3200	3240

 C-3202

IANTD GAS MANAGEMENT
PSIG / CUBIC FOOT CONVERSION TABLE

CYLINDER SIZE	PSIG	100	500	1000	1500	2000	2500	3000	3500	4000
	2475/70	2.80	14.10	28.30	42.40	56.60	70.70	84.80	99.00	113.10
	2640/45	1.70	8.50	17.00	25.60	34.10	42.60	51.10	59.70	68.20
	2640/66	2.50	12.50	25.00	37.50	50.00	62.50	75.00	87.50	100.00
	2640/85	3.22	16.10	32.20	48.30	64.40	80.50	96.60	112.70	128.80
	2640/95	3.60	18.00	36.00	54.00	72.00	90.00	108.00	125.90	143.90
	2640/104	3.90	19.70	39.40	59.10	78.80	98.50	118.20	137.90	157.60
	2640/108	4.10	20.50	40.90	61.40	81.80	102.30	122.70	143.20	163.60
	2640/121	4.60	22.90	45.80	68.80	91.70	114.60	137.50	160.40	183.30
	3000/70	2.30	11.70	23.30	35.00	46.70	58.30	70.00	81.70	93.30
	3000/80	2.70	13.30	26.70	40.00	53.30	66.70	80.00	93.30	106.70
	3190/95	3.00	14.90	29.80	44.70	59.60	74.50	89.30	104.20	119.10
	3190/120	3.80	18.80	37.60	56.40	75.20	94.00	112.90	131.70	150.50
	3190/140	4.40	21.90	43.90	65.80	87.80	109.70	131.70	153.60	175.50
	3500/65	1.90	9.30	18.60	27.90	37.10	46.40	55.70	65.00	74.30
	3500/80	2.30	11.40	22.90	34.30	45.70	57.10	68.60	80.00	91.40
	3500/100	2.90	14.30	28.60	42.90	57.10	71.40	85.70	100.00	114.30
	3500/120	3.40	17.10	34.30	51.40	68.60	85.70	102.90	120.00	137.10

Warning: DO NOT attempt to use these tables unless you are fully trained & certified in the use of Gas Mixtures Other Than Air, or are under the supervision of a Gas Mixtures Other Than Air Instructor. Proper use of these tables will reduce the risk of decompression sickness & oxygen toxicity, but no table or computer can eliminate those risks.

SAC RATION FACTOR (SRF)

LOWEST SAC \ HIGHEST SAC	1.15	1.10	1.05	1.00	0.95	0.90	0.85	0.80	0.75	0.70	0.65	0.60	0.55	0.50	0.45	0.40	0.35
1.15	0.67																
1.10	0.67	0.67															
1.05	0.68	0.67	0.67														
1.00	0.68	0.68	0.67	0.67													
0.95	0.69	0.68	0.68	0.67	0.67												
0.90	0.69	0.69	0.68	0.68	0.67	0.67											
0.85	0.70	0.70	0.69	0.69	0.68	0.67	0.67										
0.80	0.71	0.70	0.70	0.69	0.69	0.68	0.67	0.67									
0.75	0.72	0.71	0.71	0.70	0.69	0.69	0.68	0.67	0.67								
0.70	0.73	0.72	0.71	0.71	0.70	0.70	0.69	0.68	0.67	0.67							
0.65	0.73	0.73	0.72	0.72	0.71	0.70	0.70	0.69	0.68	0.68	0.67						
0.60	0.74	0.74	0.73	0.73	0.72	0.71	0.71	0.70	0.69	0.68	0.68	0.67					
0.55	0.76	0.75	0.74	0.74	0.73	0.73	0.72	0.71	0.70	0.69	0.69	0.68	0.67				
0.50	0.77	0.76	0.76	0.75	0.74	0.74	0.73	0.72	0.71	0.71	0.70	0.69	0.68	0.67			
0.45	0.78	0.78	0.77	0.76	0.76	0.75	0.74	0.74	0.73	0.72	0.71	0.70	0.69	0.68	0.67		
0.40	0.79	0.79	0.78	0.78	0.77	0.76	0.76	0.75	0.74	0.73	0.72	0.71	0.70	0.69	0.68	0.67	
0.35	0.81	0.81	0.80	0.79	0.79	0.78	0.77	0.77	0.76	0.75	0.74	0.73	0.72	0.71	0.70	0.68	0.67

WWW.IANTD.COM

C-3202B

IANTD EAN 26% DIVING & DECOMPRESSION TABLES

(A)

Depth (Feet)	40	50	60	70	80	90	100	110	120	130	140
Depth (Meters)	12	15	18	21	24	27	30	33	36	39	42
No Decompression Limits (Minutes)	125	75	51	35	25	20	17	14	14	12	10

(B) BOTTOM TIMES

Repetitive Group	40	50	60	70	80	90	100	110	120	130	140
A	19	16	14	12	11	10	9	8	8	7	7
B	25	20	17	15	13	12	11	10	10	9	8
C	37	29	25	22	20	18	16	11	11	10	9
D	57	41	33	28	24	19	17	14	14	12	10
E	82	59	44	35	25	20					
F	111	65	51								
G	125	75									
H											
K											
L											

(C) SURFACE INTERVALS

Repetitive Group	G	F	E	D	C	B	A	
A							00:00 01:59	02:00
B						00:00 00:19	00:20 01:59	02:00
C					00:00 00:09	00:10 00:24	00:25 02:59	03:00
D				00:00 00:09	00:10 00:14	00:15 00:29	00:30 02:59	03:00
E			00:00 00:09	00:10 00:14	00:15 00:24	00:25 00:44	00:45 03:59	04:00
F		00:00 00:19	00:20 00:29	00:30 00:44	00:45 01:14	01:15 01:29	01:30 07:59	08:00
G	00:00 00:24	00:25 00:44	00:45 00:59	01:00 01:14	01:15 01:39	01:40 02:09	02:10 11:59	12:00
H	00:50 01:04	01:05 01:34	01:35 02:09	02:10 02:59	03:00 03:59	04:00 05:39	05:40 23:59	24:00
K	03:00 03:59	04:00 04:59	05:00 05:59	06:00 06:59	07:00 07:59	08:00 09:19	09:20 38:59	39:00
L	06:00 06:59	07:00 08:29	08:30 09:59	10:00 11:59	12:00 13:59	14:00 16:29	16:30 47:59	48:00

(D) REPETITIVE GROUP AT END OF S.I.

(E) REPETITIVE DIVE TABLES

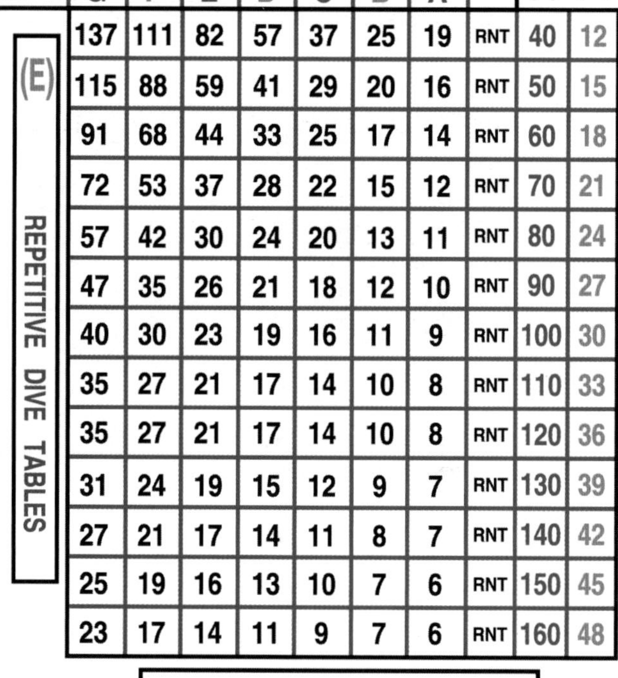

G	F	E	D	C	B	A		DEPTH (ft)	(m)
137	111	82	57	37	25	19	RNT	40	12
115	88	59	41	29	20	16	RNT	50	15
91	68	44	33	25	17	14	RNT	60	18
72	53	37	28	22	15	12	RNT	70	21
57	42	30	24	20	13	11	RNT	80	24
47	35	26	21	18	12	10	RNT	90	27
40	30	23	19	16	11	9	RNT	100	30
35	27	21	17	14	10	8	RNT	110	33
35	27	21	17	14	10	8	RNT	120	36
31	24	19	15	12	9	7	RNT	130	39
27	21	17	14	11	8	7	RNT	140	42
25	19	16	13	10	7	6	RNT	150	45
23	17	14	11	9	7	6	RNT	160	48

RESIDUAL NITROGEN TIME

Warning: DO NOT attempt to use these tables unless you are fully trained & certified in the use of Gas Mixtures Other Than Air, or are under the supervision of a Gas Mixtures Other Than Air Instructor. Proper use of these tables will reduce the risk of decompression sickness & oxygen toxicity, but no table or computer can eliminate those risks.

These Tables Are For EAN 26% with EAN 26% As Deco Gas Or Accelerated Deco Using EAN 75% Oxygen Or Greater At 20 And 15 Foot (6 & 4.5 m) Stops. The 15 Foot (4.5 m) Stops MUST Be Taken At 15 Feet (4.5 m). These Tables Are Based On Bühlmann's ZHL-16 Algorithm For 0-1000 Feet (0-300m) Above Sea Level. They Were Produced Using Cybortronix DPA Software. The Repetitive Dive Groups Are Not Transferable To ANY Other Tables. A Three Minute Safety Stop Is Required For All Dives. These Tables Do Not Account For Physical Condition Of Diver, Difficulty Of Dive, Water Temperature, Etc.

(A) Planned Depth
(B) Bottom Time In Depth Column
(C) Read Across To Find Surface Interval
(D) Locate RNT After S. I.
(E) Read Down To Planned Repetitive Dive Depth. Read RNT

C-3502

WWW.IANTD.COM

IANTD EAN 26% DECOMPRESSION TABLES WITH EAN 75% DECOMPRESSION

Depth m	Depth ft	Min	9 m / 30 ft	6 m / 20 ft	4.5 m / 15 ft	75% O2 6 m / 20 ft	75% O2 4.5 m / 15 ft	RG
15	50	100			1		1	H
		120			7		4	H
		150			18		9	H
18	60	60			2		1	F
		70			5		3	G
		80			9		5	G
		90			13		7	H
		100			19		10	H
		110			25		13	K
		120			29		16	K
21	70	40			2		1	E
		50			6		4	F
		60			10		6	G
		70			16		9	H
		80			23		12	H
		90			31		17	H
		100			37		20	K
		110			44		23	K
		120			60		27	K
24	80	30			2		2	E
		40			7		5	F
		50			13		8	G
		60			20		12	G
		70			29		16	H
		80		1	38	1	20	K
		90		3	43	2	24	K
		100		5	58	3	27	K
		110		7	74	5	32	L
		120	1	9	87	6	38	L
27	90	20			1		1	E
		30			6		4	F
		40			13		8	G
		50		1	20	1	11	G
		60		3	29	2	16	H

Depth m	Depth ft	Min	15 m / 50 ft	12 m / 40 ft	9 m / 30 ft	6 m / 20 ft	4.5 m / 15 ft	75% O2 6 m / 20 ft	75% O2 4.5 m / 15 ft	RG
27	90	70				5	38	4	20	H
		80			2	6	45	4	25	K
		90			4	8	65	5	27	K
		100			7	8	83	6	36	K
		110			10	10	96	6	43	L
		120			12	13	109	8	48	L
30	100	20					3		2	E
		30					10		7	F
		40				1	17	1	11	G
		50			1	4	25	3	14	H
		60			3	5	37	4	19	H
		70			6	6	45	4	25	K
		80			9	8	67	5	28	K
		90			12	9	86	6	38	K
		100		1	15	12	100	8	45	L
		110		3	18	13	119	8	52	L
		120		5	21	13	139	8	59	L
33	110	15					2		2	D
		20					5		4	E
		30				1	13	1	8	G
		40			1	4	21	3	12	G
		50			5	4	33	3	17	H
		60			8	6	43	4	24	K
		70		2	10	8	64	5	28	K
		80		4	13	9	87	6	38	L
		90		6	16	12	102	8	46	L
		100		8	20	13	125	8	54	L
		110		12	23	13	150	8	63	L
36	120	15					3		3	D
		20					7		5	E
		30			1	2	16	2	9	G
		40			5	4	25	3	14	G
		50		1	8	5	40	4	21	H

Depth m	Depth ft	Min	18 m / 60 ft	15 m / 50 ft	12 m / 40 ft	9 m / 30 ft	6 m / 20 ft	4.5 m / 15 ft	75% O2 6 m / 20 ft	75% O2 4.5 m / 15 ft	RG
36	120	60			4	10	7	56	5	26	K
		70			7	13	9	83	6	36	K
		80			9	16	13	100	8	45	L
		90		2	11	21	13	126	8	54	L
		100		3	14	24	13	155	8	64	L
39	130	15						5		4	D
		20					1	9	1	6	E
		30				3	3	18	2	11	G
		40			2	6	4	32	3	17	G
		50			5	9	6	45	4	24	H
		60		1	7	12	9	73	6	31	K
		70		3	9	16	11	97	7	44	L
		80		5	12	20	13	123	8	53	L
		90		7	14	24	14	153	9	63	L
		100		10	17	26	18	184	10	74	L
42	140	15					1	6	1	4	E
		20				1	2	10	1	7	F
		30			1	5	3	22	2	12	G
		40			4	7	6	37	4	20	H
		50		2	6	11	7	57	5	26	K
		60		4	9	14	10	88	6	39	L
		70		7	11	19	13	113	8	50	L
		80	1	9	14	24	13	146	8	61	L
		90	3	11	16	27	17	182	10	73	L
45	150	10						3		2	D
		20				2	2	12	2	7	F
		30			3	5	4	25	3	14	G
		40		2	5	9	6	42	4	23	H
		50		5	7	12	9	72	6	30	L
		60	2	6	10	17	12	100	8	45	L
		70	3	9	13	22	14	133	9	56	L
51	160	10						4		3	E
		20			1	3	2	14	2	8	F
		30		1	4	6	4	29	3	16	H
		40		4	6	10	7	46	4	26	L
		50	2	6	9	14	9	86	6	38	L
		60	5	8	11	20	13	117	8	51	L

ACCELERATED DECOMPRESSION
MUST BE COMPLETED
ON 75% OR GREATER OXYGEN

WWW.IANTD.COM

C-3502B

IANTD *RUNTIME* TABLES FOR EAN 25% WITH EAN 78% ACCELERATED DECO

DEPTH m ft	MIN	METERS/FEET ≥78% O2 12 / 40	9 / 30	6 / 20	4.5 / 15	% CNS
27 90	70			76	95	30
	80		83	88	111	37
	90		94	100	125	41
	100		105	112	144	49
	110		117	124	162	57
	120		128	136	180	62
	130		140	149	197	69
	140		152	161	214	76
	150		164	173	232	84
	160		175	184	249	89
	165		181	190	258	92
	170	172	187	196	267	95
	175	178	193	204	277	98
	180	184	199	212	287	102
30 100	60		65	68	86	34
	70		76	80	103	39
	80		88	93	118	46
	90		100	105	138	55
	100	103	112	119	159	61
	110	114	125	132	178	70
	120	126	138	146	198	77
	130	138	152	160	218	84
	135	144	158	166	228	88
	140	149	164	172	238	93
	145	155	171	179	248	96
	150	162	178	187	259	100

DEPTH m ft	MIN	METERS/FEET ≥78% O2 15 / 50	12 / 40	9 / 30	6 / 20	4.5 / 15	% CNS
33 110	50			56	58	74	34
	60			68	71	93	42
	70		74	81	85	110	47
	80		86	94	99	131	57
	90		98	107	114	155	68
	100		110	121	129	176	77
	110		123	136	144	197	86
	115		130	143	151	209	90
	120		136	150	158	220	95
	125		142	157	162	231	100
	130		149	164	172	243	105
36 120	40			46	48	63	31
	50		54	59	62	82	39
	60		66	72	76	102	47
	70		79	87	92	123	57
	80		92	101	108	149	69
	85		98	108	117	161	74
	90	94	105	116	124	173	79
	95	100	112	124	133	185	85
	100	106	119	132	140	196	90
	105	111	126	140	149	209	95
	110	117	132	147	155	221	100

DEPTH m ft	MIN	METERS/FEET ≥78% O2 18 / 60	15 / 50	12 / 40	9 / 30	6 / 20	4.5 / 15	% CNS
39 130	30				36	38	48	23
	40			44	49	52	67	32
	50			57	64	67	89	41
	60			70	78	83	110	50
	70		75	84	94	100	138	63
	80		87	98	110	118	165	75
	85		94	106	119	127	178	79
	90		100	113	127	135	190	85
	95		105	120	135	143	203	90
	100		112	128	144	152	218	98
	105		118	136	152	161	231	102
	110		125	144	160	172	246	108
42 140	20				25	26	32	19
	30			35	38	40	51	27
	40			48	53	56	73	36
	50		54	62	68	72	97	47
	60		67	76	85	90	123	60
	65		73	84	93	100	139	66
	70		79	91	101	109	153	74
	75		86	99	111	119	167	81
	80	84	92	107	120	128	181	86
	85	89	99	115	129	137	195	92
	90	96	106	123	138	146	211	99

(see other side)

C-3602

IANTD *RUNTIME* TABLES FOR EAN 25% WITH EAN 78% ACCELERATED DECO

(continued)

DEPTH m ft	MIN	21 m / 70 ft	18 m / 60 ft	15 m / 50 ft	12 m / 40 ft	9 m / 30 ft	6 m / 20 ft	4.5 m / 15 ft	% CNS
45 150	20					26	28	35	22
	30				37	40	44	56	31
	40			44	51	56	61	81	43
	50			58	66	73	79	106	55
	55			65	74	82	89	121	64
	60		64	71	81	91	98	137	72
	65		70	78	89	100	109	153	79
	70		76	85	98	110	119	169	87
	75		82	92	106	120	129	183	94
	80		88	99	114	129	138	199	100
48 160	15					21	22	27	20
	20				25	28	30	37	24
	25				31	35	37	48	31
	30				38	43	46	60	38
	35			41	46	52	55	74	45
	40			47	54	61	65	88	52
	45			55	62	70	75	101	60
	50		58	61	70	79	85	116	69
	55		62	68	78	89	95	134	78
	60		68	76	87	98	106	151	87
	65		74	83	96	109	117	168	94
	70	74	81	90	105	120	128	184	103

Meters/Feet stops: ≥ 78% O2

DEPTH m ft	MIN	21 m / 70 ft	18 m / 60 ft	15 m / 50 ft	12 m / 40 ft	9 m / 30 ft	6 m / 20 ft	4.5 m / 15 ft	% CNS
51 170	15					22	23	28	22
	20				27	29	31	39	24
	25			30	34	37	40	52	32
	30			36	41	46	49	65	40
	35			43	50	55	59	80	46
	40		45	50	58	65	69	94	54
	45		52	58	67	75	80	109	63
	50		58	64	75	84	90	128	73
	55	60	65	73	85	95	103	148	84
	60	66	71	80	94	106	114	165	91
	65	72	78	88	104	118	126	182	99

Run Times are computed as the departure time from each stop, using Cybortronics DPA Software.

Decompression Run Times in Green Columns must be completed using EAN 78%.

Increase FiO2 will increase CNS O2 figures.

To obtain repetitive group, Please see IANTD Accelerated Decompression Tables for EAN 26%, or convert to EAD and use repetitive group from IANTD Accelerated Decompression Tables for Air.

Warning: DO NOT attempt to use these tables unless you are fully trained & certified in the use of Gas Mixtures Other Than Air, or are under the supervision of a Gas Mixtures Other Than Air Instructor. Proper use of these tables will reduce the risk of decompression sickness & oxygen toxicity, but no table or computer can eliminate those risks.

These Tables Are For EAN 25% with EAN 25% As Deco Gas Or Accelerated Deco Using EAN 78% Oxygen Or Greater At 20 And 15 Foot (6 & 4.5 m) Stops. The 15 Foot (4.5 m) Stops MUST Be Taken At 15 Feet (4.5 m). These Tables Are Based On Bühlmann's ZHL-16 Algorithm For 0-1000 Feet (0-300m) Above Sea Level. They Were Produced Using Cybortronix DPA Software. The Repetitive Dive Groups Are Not Transferable To ANY Other Tables. A Three Minute Safety Stop Is Required For All Dives. These Tables Do Not Account For Physical Condition Of Diver, Difficulty Of Dive, Water Temperature, Etc.

(A) Planned Depth
(B) Bottom Time In Depth Column
(C) Read Across To Find Surface Interval
(D) Locate RNT After S. I.
(E) Read Down To Planned Repetitive Dive Depth. Read RNT

C-3602B

IANTD CONSTANT 1.3 - 1.4 PO_2 14 / 44 DILUENT DECO TABLES

WARNING!
DO NOT
attempt to use these tables unless you are fully trained & certified in the use of trimix & CCR systems or are under the direct supervision of an instructor. Proper use of tables will reduce the risk of DCS & oxygen toxicity, but no table or computer can eliminate those risks.

These tables are based on VPM-B and are derived from V-Planner Software.

Descent Rate 60 fpm
Ascent Rate 30 fpm
Last Stop Depth 15 Ft.
Bottom Time Includes Descent Time
Stop Times Include Travel Time Between Stops
Sea Level to 1000 Ft
Nominal Conservatism Level

		1.3 PO2 14 / 44												1.40 PO2 14/44				
		160 ft	150 ft	140 ft	130 ft	120 ft	110 ft	100 ft	90 ft	80 ft	70 ft	60 ft	50 ft	40 ft	30 ft	20 ft	15 ft	CNS
		48m	45m	42m	39m	36m	33m	30m	27m	24m	21m	18m	15m	12m	9m	6m	4.5m	%
170 ft 51m	10											14	15	16	17	18	20	11
	15										19	20	21	22	24	25	31	17
	20								23	24	25	26	27	29	32	34	42	24
	25								28	29	30	31	33	36	39	41	52	30
	30								33	34	35	37	39	43	47	50	62	36
	35							38	39	40	41	43	46	50	55	59	74	43
	40							43	44	45	47	49	53	58	64	67	85	50
	45							48	49	50	52	55	59	64	71	75	96	56
	50							53	54	55	58	61	66	72	79	84	106	62
	55							58	59	61	64	67	72	79	87	92	117	69
	60							63	64	66	69	73	79	86	95	100	128	75
180 ft 54m	10										14	15	16	17	18	19	22	12
	15									19	20	21	22	23	26	27	33	19
	20							23	24	25	26	27	29	31	34	36	45	26
	25							28	29	30	31	33	35	38	42	45	56	32
	30							33	34	35	36	39	42	45	50	53	67	39
	35						38	39	40	41	43	46	49	54	60	63	80	47
	40						43	44	45	46	49	52	56	61	68	72	92	54
	45						48	49	50	52	55	58	63	69	76	81	103	60
	50						53	54	55	58	61	65	70	77	85	90	115	68
	55						58	59	61	63	67	71	77	84	93	99	127	75
190 ft 57m	10									14	15	16	17	18	19	20	24	13
	15								19	20	21	22	23	25	27	29	36	20
	20						23	24	25	26	27	28	30	33	36	38	49	28
	25						28	29	30	31	32	34	37	41	45	48	60	35
	30					33	34	35	36	37	39	42	45	49	55	58	74	43
	35					38	39	40	41	43	45	48	52	57	64	68	87	51
	40					43	44	45	46	49	51	55	60	65	73	77	99	58
200 ft 60m	10								14	15	16	17	18	19	20	21	26	14
	15							19	20	21	22	23	24	26	29	31	39	22
	20					23	24	25	26	27	28	30	32	35	39	41	52	30
	25					28	29	30	31	32	34	36	39	43	48	51	65	38
	30				33	34	35	36	37	39	41	44	48	53	59	62	80	47
	35				38	39	40	41	42	45	47	51	55	61	68	72	93	54
	40				43	44	45	46	48	51	54	58	63	69	77	82	106	62
210 ft 63m	10							14	15	16	17	18	19	20	22	23	28	15
	15						19	20	21	22	23	24	26	28	31	33	42	24
	20				23	24	25	26	27	28	29	31	34	37	42	44	56	32
	25				28	29	30	31	32	34	36	38	42	46	51	55	70	41
	30			33	34	35	36	37	38	41	43	47	51	56	63	66	86	50
	35			38	39	40	41	42	44	47	50	54	59	65	72	77	99	58
	40			43	44	45	46	48	50	53	57	61	66	74	82	88	113	66
220 ft 66m	10						14	15	16	17	18	19	20	21	23	24	30	17
	15					19	20	21	22	23	24	25	27	30	33	35	45	26
	20			23	24	25	26	27	28	29	31	33	36	40	44	47	60	35
	25			28	29	30	31	32	34	35	38	41	44	49	55	58	74	43
	30		33	34	35	36	37	38	40	43	45	49	54	59	66	70	92	54
	35		38	39	40	41	42	44	46	49	53	57	62	69	77	82	106	62
	40		43	44	45	46	48	50	53	56	60	65	71	78	88	93	122	72
230 ft 69m	10					14	15	16	17	18	19	20	21	22	25	26	33	18
	15				19	20	21	22	23	24	25	27	29	32	36	38	48	27
	20		23	24	25	26	27	28	29	30	32	35	38	42	47	50	64	37
	25		28	29	30	31	32	33	35	37	40	43	47	52	58	62	80	47
	30	33	34	35	36	37	38	40	42	45	48	52	57	63	71	76	98	57
	35	38	39	40	41	42	44	46	49	52	55	60	66	73	82	87	114	67
	40	43	44	45	46	47	50	52	55	59	63	68	75	82	93	99	129	76
240 ft 72m	10						15	16	17	18	19	20	21	23	25	27	34	19
	15			19	20	21	22	23	24	25	26	28	31	34	38	40	51	29
	20	23	24	25	26	27	28	29	30	32	34	37	41	45	50	54	69	40
	25	28	29	30	31	32	33	35	37	39	42	45	50	55	62	66	85	49

 C-3104

IANTD CONSTANT 1.3 - 1.4 PO_2 14 / 44 DILUENT DECOMPRESSION TABLES

!!! REPETITIVE DIVE TABLE 120 MIN SURFACE INTERVAL !!!

!!! REPETITIVE DIVE TABLE 120 MIN SURFACE INTERVAL !!!

		PO_2 1.3 14/44												PO_2 1.4 14/44				
		160 ft 48m	150 ft 45m	140 ft 42m	130 ft 39m	120 ft 36m	110 ft 33m	100 ft 30m	90 ft 27m	80 ft 24m	70 ft 21m	60 ft 18m	50 ft 15m	40 ft 12m	30 ft 9m	20 ft 6m	15 ft 3m	CNS
REP 170 ft 51m	10											14	15	16	17	18	20	16
	15										19	20	21	22	24	25	31	26
	20								23	24	25	26	27	29	32	34	43	37
	25								28	29	30	31	33	36	39	42	54	46
	30							33	34	35	36	38	40	44	48	51	68	58
	35							38	39	40	41	44	47	51	56	60	80	68
	40							43	44	45	47	49	53	58	64	68	93	80
	45							48	49	50	53	56	60	65	72	78	106	91
	50							53	54	56	58	62	66	72	81	86	120	102
REP 180 ft 54m	10										14	15	16	17	18	19	22	18
	15									19	20	21	22	23	26	27	34	28
	20							23	24	25	26	27	28	31	34	36	46	39
	25							28	29	30	31	32	35	38	42	45	59	50
	30							33	34	35	37	39	42	45	51	54	72	62
	35						38	39	40	41	43	46	49	54	60	64	88	75
	40						43	44	45	47	49	52	56	61	69	74	102	87
	45						48	49	50	52	55	58	63	69	78	83	116	99
	50						53	54	55	58	61	65	70	77	87	93	131	112
REP 190 ft 57m	10									14	15	16	17	18	19	20	24	20
	15								19	20	21	22	23	25	27	29	37	31
	20						23	24	25	26	27	28	30	33	37	39	51	44
	25						28	29	30	31	33	35	37	41	46	48	65	55
	30					33	34	35	36	37	39	42	45	50	56	59	81	69
	35					38	39	40	41	43	45	48	52	57	64	69	95	82
	40					43	44	45	46	49	51	55	59	65	74	79	111	95
REP 200 ft 60m	10								14	15	16	17	18	19	20	21	26	21
	15							19	20	21	22	23	24	26	29	31	40	34
	20					23	24	25	26	27	28	30	32	35	39	42	55	47
	25					28	29	30	31	32	34	36	39	43	48	52	70	60
	30				33	34	35	36	37	39	41	44	48	53	59	63	88	75
	35				38	39	40	41	43	45	48	51	56	61	69	74	104	89
	40				43	44	45	46	48	51	54	58	63	70	79	85	120	102
REP 210 ft 63m	10							14	15	16	17	18	19	20	22	23	29	24
	15						19	20	21	22	23	24	26	28	31	33	43	36
	20				23	24	25	26	27	28	29	31	34	37	42	45	59	50
	25				28	29	30	31	32	34	36	38	42	46	52	55	75	64
	30			33	34	35	36	37	39	41	43	47	51	56	63	68	95	81
	35			38	39	40	41	42	45	47	50	54	59	65	74	79	113	96
REP 220 ft 66m	10						14	15	16	17	18	19	20	21	23	24	31	25
	15					19	20	21	22	23	24	25	27	30	34	36	47	40
	20			23	24	25	26	27	28	29	31	33	36	40	45	48	65	55
	25			28	29	30	31	32	34	36	38	41	45	49	56	60	83	70
	30		33	34	35	36	37	38	40	43	46	49	54	60	68	73	103	88
	35		38	39	40	41	42	44	47	49	53	57	62	69	79	85	122	104
REP 230 ft 69m	10					14	15	16	17	18	19	20	21	22	25	26	33	27
	15				19	20	21	22	23	24	25	27	29	32	36	38	51	43
	20		23	24	25	26	27	28	29	31	33	35	39	43	48	52	70	59
	25		28	29	30	31	32	33	35	37	40	43	47	52	59	63	88	75
	30	33	34	35	36	37	38	40	42	45	48	52	57	63	72	78	111	94
	35	38	39	40	41	42	44	46	49	52	56	60	66	73	84	91	131	111
REP 240 ft 72m	10						15	16	17	18	19	20	21	23	25	27	34	28
	15			19	20	21	22	23	24	25	26	28	31	34	38	41	54	46
	20	23	24	25	26	27	28	29	30	32	34	37	41	45	51	55	75	64
	25	28	29	30	31	32	33	35	37	39	42	46	50	55	63	68	95	81

!!! REPETITIVE DIVE TABLE 120 MIN SURFACE INTERVAL !!!

IANTD CONSTANT 1.2 - 1.4 PO_2 8 / 60 DILUENT DECOMPRESSION TABLES

Depth	Bottom Time	PO2 1.3 8/60																				PO2 1.4 8/60					CNS
		250 ft 75m	240 ft 72m	230 ft 69m	220 ft 66m	210 ft 63m	200 ft 60m	190 ft 57m	180 ft 54m	170 ft 51m	160 ft 48m	150 ft 45m	140 ft 42m	130 ft 39m	120 ft 36m	110 ft 33m	100 ft 30m	90 ft 27m	80 ft 24m	70 ft 21m	60 ft 18m	50 ft 15m	40 ft 12m	30 ft 9m	20 ft 6m	15 ft 4.5m	%
250 ft 75m	10											14	15	16	17	18	19	20	21	22	23	25	27	31	33	42	22
	15									18	19	20	21	22	23	24	25	26	28	30	33	36	40	44	48	62	33
	20									23	24	25	26	27	28	29	31	33	35	38	41	45	50	57	60	79	43
	25								28	29	30	31	32	33	34	36	38	41	44	47	52	57	64	72	77	101	55
	30								33	34	35	36	37	38	40	42	45	48	51	56	61	67	75	85	91	119	65
	35								38	39	40	41	42	44	46	49	52	55	60	65	71	78	87	99	106	139	77
260 ft 78m	10											14	15	16	17	18	19	20	21	22	23	25	28	31	33	42	22
	15								18	19	20	21	22	23	24	25	26	27	29	32	35	38	42	47	51	65	35
	20								23	24	25	26	27	28	29	30	32	34	37	40	44	48	53	60	64	84	46
	25							28	29	30	31	32	33	34	36	38	40	43	46	50	55	61	67	76	81	107	59
	30							33	34	35	36	37	38	40	42	44	47	51	55	59	65	72	80	90	97	128	70
	35							38	39	40	41	42	44	46	48	51	54	58	63	68	75	83	92	105	112	147	81
270 ft 81m	10										14	15	16	17	18	19	20	21	22	23	25	27	30	33	36	45	24
	15							18	19	20	21	22	23	24	25	26	27	29	31	33	37	40	45	50	54	70	38
	20							23	24	25	26	27	28	29	30	32	34	36	39	42	46	51	57	64	69	89	48
	25						28	29	30	31	32	33	34	35	37	40	42	45	48	53	58	64	71	81	86	114	63
	30						33	34	35	36	37	38	40	42	44	47	50	53	58	63	69	76	85	96	103	136	75
	35						38	39	40	41	42	44	46	48	51	54	57	62	66	73	79	88	98	111	119	158	87
280 ft 84m	10									14	15	16	17	18	19	20	21	22	23	24	26	29	32	36	38	49	26
	15								19	20	21	22	23	24	25	26	27	29	31	34	37	41	45	51	55	71	38
	20						23	24	25	26	27	28	29	30	32	34	36	38	41	45	49	54	60	68	73	96	52
	25					28	29	30	31	32	33	34	35	37	39	41	44	47	51	56	61	68	75	85	92	121	67
	30					33	34	35	36	37	38	39	41	43	46	49	52	56	61	66	73	80	89	102	109	144	79
	35					38	39	40	41	42	43	45	47	50	53	56	60	64	69	76	83	92	103	117	126	166	92
290 ft 87m	10								14	15	16	17	18	19	20	21	22	23	24	26	28	31	34	38	41	52	28
	15							19	20	21	22	23	24	25	26	27	29	31	33	36	39	43	48	54	58	76	41
	20					23	24	25	26	27	28	29	30	31	33	35	37	40	43	47	52	57	63	72	77	101	55
	25				28	29	30	31	32	33	34	35	37	39	41	44	47	50	54	59	65	72	80	91	98	129	71
	30				33	34	35	36	37	38	39	41	43	45	48	51	54	59	63	69	76	84	94	107	115	152	84
	35				38	39	40	41	42	43	45	47	49	52	55	59	63	68	73	80	88	97	109	124	133	176	97
300 ft 90m	10							14	15	16	17	18	19	20	21	22	23	24	25	27	30	33	36	41	43	56	30
	15						19	20	21	22	23	24	25	26	27	28	30	32	35	38	41	46	51	57	61	80	43
	20				23	24	25	26	27	28	29	30	31	33	35	37	39	42	46	50	55	61	67	77	82	108	59
	25			28	29	30	31	32	33	34	35	36	38	40	43	46	49	52	57	62	69	75	85	96	103	136	75
	30			33	34	35	36	37	38	39	41	43	45	47	50	53	57	62	67	73	80	89	99	113	122	161	89
	35			38	39	40	41	42	43	45	47	49	52	55	58	62	66	71	78	84	94	103	116	132	141	187	103
310 ft 93m	10								15	16	17	18	19	20	21	22	23	24	26	28	30	33	36	41	44	57	30
	15					19	20	21	22	23	24	25	26	27	28	30	32	34	37	40	44	49	54	61	66	86	47
	20			23	24	25	26	27	28	29	30	31	32	34	36	38	41	44	48	52	57	63	71	80	86	113	62
	25		28	29	30	31	32	33	34	35	36	38	40	42	45	48	51	55	60	65	72	80	89	102	109	144	79
	30		33	34	35	36	37	38	39	40	42	44	46	49	52	56	60	64	70	77	85	94	105	119	128	170	94
320 ft 96m	10							15	16	17	18	19	20	21	22	23	24	25	27	29	32	35	39	43	47	60	32
	15				19	20	21	22	23	24	25	26	27	28	30	32	34	36	39	42	47	51	57	65	70	91	49
	20		23	24	25	26	27	28	29	30	31	32	34	36	38	40	43	47	51	55	61	67	75	85	92	121	66
	25	28	29	30	31	32	33	34	35	36	38	40	42	44	47	50	54	58	63	69	76	84	94	107	115	152	84
	30	33	34	35	36	37	38	39	40	42	44	46	49	52	55	59	63	68	74	81	90	99	111	127	136	180	99
330 ft 99m	10						15	16	17	18	19	20	21	22	23	24	25	27	29	31	34	37	41	46	50	64	34
	15			19	20	21	22	23	24	25	26	27	28	29	31	33	35	38	41	44	49	54	60	68	73	96	52
	20	23	24	25	26	27	28	29	30	31	32	34	36	38	40	43	46	49	54	58	65	71	80	91	97	129	71

WARNING! DO NOT attempt to use these tables unless you are fully trained & certified in the use of trimix & CCR systems or are under the direct supervision of an instructor. Proper use of tables will reduce the risk of DCS & oxygen toxicity, but no table or computer can eliminate those risks.

These tables are based on VPM-B and are derived from V-Planner Software.

Descent Rate 60 fpm
Ascent Rate 30 fpm
Last Stop Depth 15 Ft.
Bottom Time Includes Descent Time
Stop Times Include Travel Time Between Stops
Sea Level to 1000 Ft
Nominal Conservatism Level

C-3105

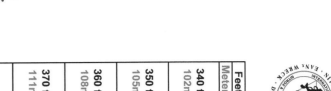

IANTD CONSTANT 1.2 - 1.4 PO_2 8 / 60 DILUENT DECOMPRESSION TABLES

		1.2 PO2 8/60																		1.3 PO2 8/60									1.4 PO2 8/60				
Feet		320	310	300	290	280	270	260	250	240	230	220	210	200	190	180	170	160	150	140	130	120	110	100	90	80	70	60	50	40	30	20	CNS
Meters		96	93	90	87	84	81	78	75	72	69	66	63	60	57	54	51	48	45	42	39	36	33	30	27	24	21	18	15	12	9	6	%
340 ft 102m	10												15	16	17	18	19	20	21	22	23	24	25	26	28	30	33	36	40	44	50	72	40
	15									19	20	21	22	23	24	25	26	27	28	29	31	33	35	37	40	43	47	52	58	64	74	108	62
	20							23	24	25	26	27	28	29	30	31	32	34	36	38	40	42	45	48	52	57	62	68	76	85	98	143	82
	25						28	29	30	31	32	33	34	35	36	38	40	42	44	46	49	52	56	60	65	71	77	85	95	107	122	181	105
350 ft 105m	10											15	16	17	18	19	20	21	22	23	24	25	26	28	30	32	35	38	42	47	53	76	43
	15								19	20	21	22	23	24	25	26	27	28	29	31	32	34	37	39	42	45	50	55	61	68	78	114	65
	20						23	24	25	26	27	28	29	30	31	32	34	35	37	39	41	44	47	50	55	59	65	71	79	89	102	150	86
	25					28	29	30	31	32	33	34	35	36	37	39	41	43	45	48	51	54	58	62	67	73	80	89	98	111	128	189	109
360 ft 108m	10										15	16	17	18	19	20	21	22	23	24	25	26	27	29	31	33	36	40	44	49	56	80	45
	15							19	20	21	22	23	24	25	26	27	28	29	30	32	34	36	38	41	44	48	52	58	64	72	82	120	69
	20					23	24	25	26	27	28	29	30	31	32	33	35	37	39	41	43	46	49	53	57	62	68	75	84	94	108	159	92
	25				28	29	30	31	32	33	34	35	36	37	39	41	43	45	48	51	54	57	61	66	71	78	85	94	105	118	136	201	116
370 ft 111m	10									15	16	17	18	19	20	21	22	23	24	25	26	27	29	31	33	35	39	42	47	52	59	85	48
	15						19	20	21	22	23	24	25	26	27	28	29	30	32	34	36	38	40	43	46	51	55	61	67	76	86	127	73
	20				23	24	25	26	27	28	29	30	31	32	33	35	36	38	40	42	45	48	51	55	60	65	71	78	87	98	112	166	96
	25			28	29	30	31	32	33	34	35	36	37	39	40	42	44	47	50	53	56	60	64	68	75	81	89	98	110	123	142	211	122
380 ft 114m	10									15	16	17	18	19	20	21	22	23	24	25	26	27	29	31	33	36	39	43	47	53	59	85	48
	15					19	20	21	22	23	24	25	26	27	28	29	30	32	33	35	37	39	42	45	49	53	58	64	71	80	91	134	77
	20			23	24	25	26	27	28	29	30	31	32	33	34	36	38	40	42	45	47	50	54	58	63	68	75	83	92	104	119	176	102
	25		28	29	30	31	32	33	34	35	36	37	38	40	42	44	46	49	52	55	58	62	67	72	78	84	93	103	115	129	148	221	128
390 ft 117m	10								15	16	17	18	19	20	21	22	23	24	25	26	27	29	30	32	35	38	41	45	49	55	62	89	50
	15				19	20	21	22	23	24	25	26	27	28	29	30	31	33	35	37	39	41	44	47	51	56	61	67	74	84	96	141	81
	20		23	24	25	26	27	28	29	30	31	32	33	34	36	37	39	41	44	46	49	52	56	61	65	71	78	87	96	109	124	183	106
	25	28	29	30	31	32	33	34	35	36	37	38	40	42	44	46	48	51	54	57	61	65	69	75	81	88	97	107	120	136	156	231	134
400 ft 120m	10							15	16	17	18	19	20	21	22	23	24	25	26	27	28	30	32	34	36	39	43	47	52	58	66	95	54
	15			19	20	21	22	23	24	25	26	27	28	29	30	31	32	34	36	38	40	43	46	49	53	58	63	70	78	87	100	146	84
	20	23	24	25	26	27	28	29	30	31	32	33	34	35	37	39	41	43	46	49	52	55	59	64	69	75	82	91	101	114	131	193	111

WARNING! DO NOT attempt to use these tables unless you are fully trained & certified in the use of Trimix & CCR systems or are under the direct supervision of an instructor. Proper use of tables will reduce the risk of DCS & oxygen toxicity, but no table or computer can eliminate those risks.

These tables are based on VPM-B and are derived from V-Planner Software.

Descent Rate 60 fpm
Ascent Rate 30 fpm
Last Stop Depth 15 Ft.
Bottom Time Includes Descent Time
Stop Times Include Travel Time Between Stops
Sea Level to 1000 Ft
Nominal Conservatism Level

 C-3105B

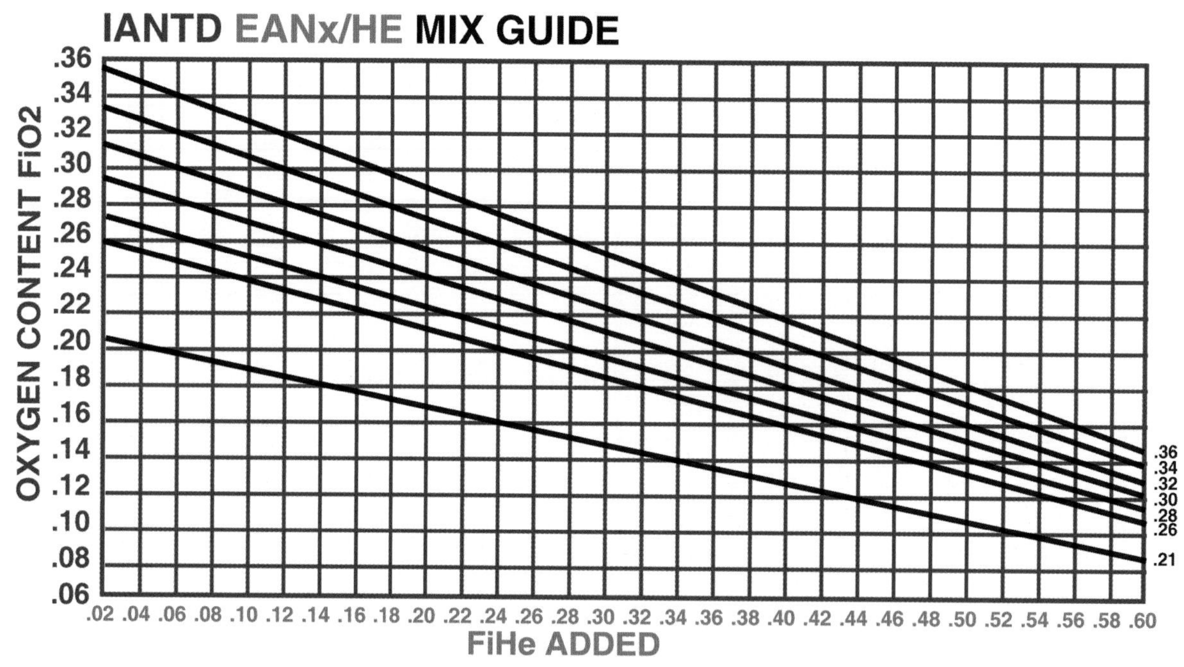

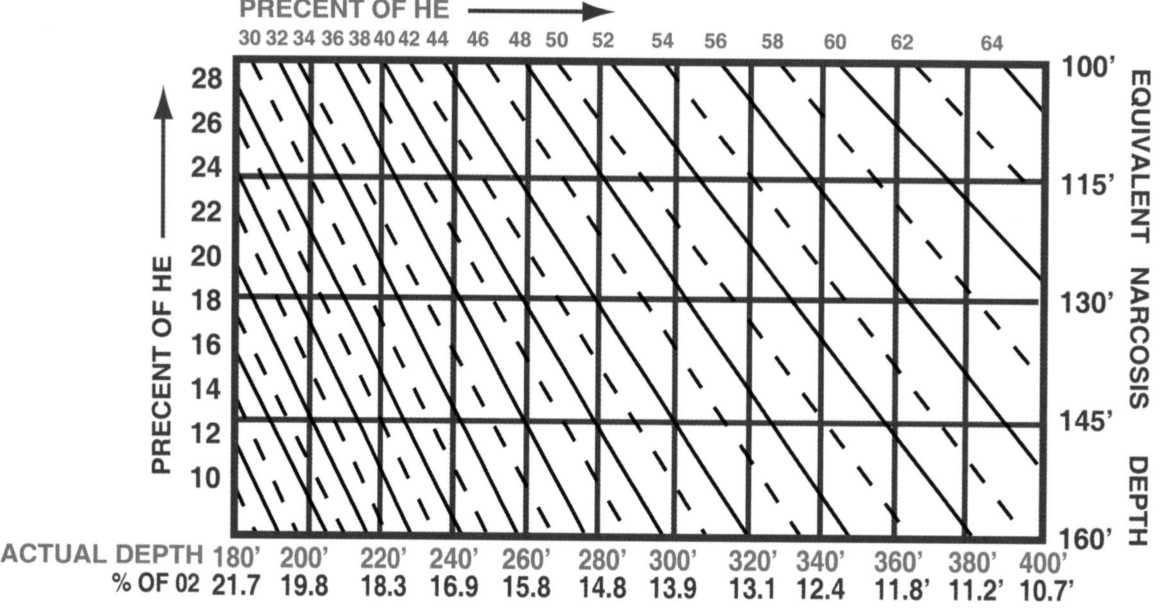

Produced by: Tom Mount & Mark Owens

C-3700

www.iantd.com

IANTD Hypoxic PO2 Table

FSW	0.20	0.19	0.18	0.17	0.16	0.15	0.14	0.13	0.12	0.11	0.10	0.09	0.08
10	0.26	0.25	0.23	0.22	0.21	0.20	0.18	0.17	0.16	0.14	0.13	0.12	0.10
15.0	0.29	0.28	0.26	0.25	0.23	0.22	0.20	0.19	0.17	0.16	0.15	0.13	0.12
20	0.32	0.31	0.29	0.27	0.26	0.24	0.22	0.21	0.19	0.18	0.16	0.14	0.13
30	0.38	0.36	0.34	0.32	0.31	0.29	0.27	0.25	0.23	0.21	0.19	0.17	0.15
40	0.44	0.42	0.40	0.38	0.35	0.33	0.31	0.29	0.27	0.24	0.22	0.20	0.18
50	0.50	0.48	0.45	0.43	0.40	0.38	0.35	0.33	0.30	0.28	0.25	0.23	0.20
60	0.56	0.54	0.51	0.48	0.45	0.42	0.39	0.37	0.34	0.31	0.28	0.25	0.23
70	0.62	0.59	0.56	0.53	0.50	0.47	0.44	0.41	0.37	0.34	0.31	0.28	0.25
80	0.68	0.65	0.62	0.58	0.55	0.51	0.48	0.45	0.41	0.38	0.34	0.31	0.27
90	0.75	0.71	0.67	0.63	0.60	0.56	0.52	0.48	0.45	0.41	0.37	0.34	0.30
100	0.81	0.77	0.73	0.69	0.64	0.60	0.56	0.52	0.48	0.44	0.40	0.36	0.32
110	0.87	0.82	0.78	0.74	0.69	0.65	0.61	0.56	0.52	0.48	0.43	0.39	0.35
120	0.93	0.88	0.83	0.79	0.74	0.70	0.65	0.60	0.56	0.51	0.46	0.42	0.37
130	0.99	0.94	0.89	0.84	0.79	0.74	0.69	0.64	0.59	0.54	0.49	0.44	0.40
140	1.05	1.00	0.94	0.89	0.84	0.79	0.73	0.68	0.63	0.58	0.52	0.47	0.42
150	1.11	1.05	1.00	0.94	0.89	0.83	0.78	0.72	0.67	0.61	0.55	0.50	0.44
160	1.17	1.11	1.05	0.99	0.94	0.88	0.82	0.76	0.70	0.64	0.58	0.53	0.47
170	1.23	1.17	1.11	1.05	0.98	0.92	0.86	0.80	0.74	0.68	0.62	0.55	0.49
180	1.29	1.23	1.16	1.10	1.03	0.97	0.90	0.84	0.77	0.71	0.65	0.58	0.52
190	1.35	1.28	1.22	1.15	1.08	1.01	0.95	0.88	0.81	0.74	0.68	0.61	0.54
200	1.41	1.34	1.27	1.20	1.13	1.06	0.99	0.92	0.85	0.78	0.71	0.64	0.56
210	1.47	1.40	1.33	1.25	1.18	1.10	1.03	0.96	0.88	0.81	0.74	0.66	0.59
220	1.53	1.46	1.38	1.30	1.23	1.15	1.07	1.00	0.92	0.84	0.77	0.69	0.61
230	1.59	1.51	1.43	1.35	1.28	1.20	1.12	1.04	0.96	0.88	0.80	0.72	0.64
240	1.65	1.57	1.49	1.41	1.32	1.24	1.16	1.08	0.99	0.91	0.83	0.74	0.66
250		1.63	1.54	1.46	1.37	1.29	1.20	1.11	1.03	0.94	0.86	0.77	0.69
260			1.60	1.51	1.42	1.33	1.24	1.15	1.07	0.98	0.89	0.80	0.71
270			1.65	1.56	1.47	1.38	1.29	1.19	1.10	1.01	0.92	0.83	0.73
280				1.61	1.52	1.42	1.33	1.23	1.14	1.04	0.95	0.85	0.76
290					1.57	1.47	1.37	1.27	1.17	1.08	0.98	0.88	0.78
300					1.61	1.51	1.41	1.31	1.21	1.11	1.01	0.91	0.81
310						1.56	1.46	1.35	1.25	1.14	1.04	0.94	0.83
320						1.60	1.50	1.39	1.28	1.18	1.07	0.96	0.86
330							1.54	1.43	1.32	1.21	1.10	0.99	0.88
340							1.58	1.47	1.36	1.24	1.13	1.02	0.90
350							1.62	1.51	1.39	1.28	1.16	1.04	0.93
360								1.55	1.43	1.31	1.19	1.07	0.95
370								1.59	1.47	1.34	1.22	1.10	0.98
380								1.63	1.50	1.38	1.25	1.13	1.00
390									1.54	1.41	1.28	1.15	1.03
400									1.57	1.44	1.31	1.18	1.05
410									1.61	1.48	1.34	1.21	1.07
420										1.51	1.37	1.24	1.10
430										1.54	1.40	1.26	1.12
440										1.58	1.43	1.29	1.15
450										1.61	1.46	1.32	1.17
460											1.49	1.34	1.20
470											1.52	1.37	1.22
480											1.55	1.40	1.24
490											1.58	1.43	1.27
500											1.62	1.45	1.29

Produced by: Tom Mount & Mark Owens C-3700B

IANTD
TABLE OF EQUIVALENT NARCOSIS DEPTHS
FOR TRIMIX DIVING

ACTUAL DEPTH		EQUIVALENT NARCOSIS DEPTHS FOR 1.4 PO_2											
		END 70 FSW 21 MSW		END 80 FSW 24 MSW		END 90 FSW 27 MSW		END 100 FSW 30 MSW		END 110 FSW 33 MSW		END 120 FSW 36 MSW	
FSW/MSW	Fi O_2	Fi HE	Fi N_2	Fi HE	Fi N_2	Fi HE	Fi N_2	Fi HE	Fi N_2	Fi HE	Fi N_2	Fi HE	Fi N_2
150 / 45	0.25	0.30	0.44	0.26	0.49	0.22	0.53	0.17	0.57	0.13	0.62	0.09	0.66
160 / 48	0.24	0.34	0.42	0.30	0.46	0.26	0.50	0.22	0.54	0.18	0.59	0.13	0.63
170 / 51	0.23	0.37	0.40	0.33	0.44	0.29	0.48	0.25	0.52	0.22	0.56	0.18	0.60
180 / 54	0.22	0.40	0.38	0.36	0.42	0.33	0.46	0.29	0.49	0.25	0.53	0.22	0.57
190 / 57	0.21	0.43	0.36	0.39	0.40	0.36	0.44	0.32	0.47	0.29	0.51	0.25	0.54
200 / 60	0.20	0.45	0.35	0.42	0.38	0.38	0.42	0.35	0.45	0.32	0.48	0.28	0.52
210 / 63	0.19	0.48	0.33	0.44	0.37	0.41	0.40	0.38	0.43	0.34	0.46	0.31	0.50

ACTUAL DEPTH		EQUIVALENT NARCOSIS DEPTHS FOR 1.3 PO_2											
		END 70 FSW 21 MSW		END 80 FSW 24 MSW		END 90 FSW 27 MSW		END 100 FSW 30 MSW		END 110 FSW 33 MSW		END 120 FSW 36 MSW	
FSW/MSW	Fi O_2	Fi HE	Fi N_2	Fi HE	Fi N_2	Fi HE	Fi N_2	Fi HE	Fi N_2	Fi HE	Fi N_2	Fi HE	Fi N_2
150 / 45	0.23	0.32	0.44	0.28	0.49	0.23	0.53	0.19	0.57	0.15	0.62	0.11	0.66
160 / 48	0.22	0.36	0.42	0.32	0.46	0.27	0.50	0.23	0.54	0.19	0.59	0.15	0.63
170 / 51	0.21	0.39	0.40	0.35	0.44	0.31	0.48	0.27	0.52	0.23	0.56	0.19	0.60
180 / 54	0.20	0.42	0.38	0.38	0.42	0.34	0.46	0.31	0.49	0.27	0.53	0.23	0.57
190 / 57	0.19	0.44	0.36	0.41	0.40	0.37	0.44	0.34	0.47	0.30	0.51	0.27	0.54
200 / 60	0.18	0.47	0.35	0.43	0.38	0.40	0.42	0.36	0.45	0.33	0.48	0.30	0.52
210 / 63	0.18	0.49	0.33	0.46	0.37	0.42	0.40	0.39	0.43	0.36	0.46	0.33	0.50

Produced By Tom Mount, Mark Owens, and Clayton Bohm

C-3706

www.iantd.com

IANTD

TABLE OF EQUIVALENT NARCOSIS DEPTHS FOR TRIMIX DIVING

ACTUAL DEPTH		EQUIVALENT NARCOSIS DEPTHS FOR 1.3 PO_2																	
		END 80 FSW 24 MSW		END 90 FSW 27 MSW		END 100 FSW 30 MSW		END 110 FSW 33 MSW		END 120 FSW 36 MSW		END 130 FSW 39 MSW		END 140 FSW 42 MSW		END 150 FSW 45 MSW		END 160 FSW 48 MSW	
FSW/MSW	Fi O2	Fi HE	Fi N2	Fi HE	Fi N2	Fi HE	Fi N2	Fi HE	Fi N2	Fi HE	Fi N2	Fi HE	Fi N2	Fi HE	Fi N2	Fi HE	Fi N2	Fi HE	Fi N2
210 / 63	0.18	0.46	0.37	0.42	0.40	0.39	0.43	0.36	0.46	0.33	0.50	0.29	0.53	0.26	0.56	0.23	0.59	0.20	0.63
220 / 66	0.17	0.48	0.35	0.45	0.38	0.42	0.42	0.38	0.45	0.35	0.48	0.32	0.51	0.29	0.54	0.26	0.57	0.23	0.60
230 / 69	0.16	0.50	0.34	0.47	0.37	0.44	0.40	0.41	0.43	0.38	0.46	0.35	0.49	0.32	0.52	0.29	0.55	0.26	0.58
240 / 72	0.16	0.52	0.33	0.49	0.36	0.46	0.38	0.43	0.41	0.40	0.44	0.37	0.47	0.34	0.50	0.31	0.53	0.28	0.56
250 / 75	0.15	0.53	0.32	0.51	0.34	0.48	0.37	0.45	0.40	0.42	0.43	0.39	0.46	0.37	0.48	0.34	0.51	0.31	0.54
260 / 78	0.15	0.55	0.30	0.52	0.33	0.49	0.36	0.47	0.39	0.44	0.41	0.41	0.44	0.39	0.47	0.36	0.49	0.33	0.52
270 / 81	0.14	0.56	0.29	0.54	0.32	0.51	0.35	0.49	0.37	0.46	0.40	0.43	0.42	0.41	0.45	0.38	0.48	0.36	0.50
280 / 84	0.14	0.58	0.29	0.55	0.31	0.53	0.34	0.50	0.36	0.48	0.39	0.45	0.41	0.43	0.44	0.40	0.46	0.38	0.49
290 / 87	0.13	0.59	0.28	0.57	0.30	0.54	0.33	0.52	0.35	0.49	0.37	0.47	0.40	0.44	0.42	0.42	0.45	0.40	0.47
300 / 91	0.13	0.60	0.27	0.58	0.29	0.56	0.32	0.53	0.34	0.51	0.36	0.48	0.39	0.46	0.41	0.44	0.43	0.41	0.46

Warning: DO NOT attempt to use these tables unless you are fully trained & certified in the use of Gas Mixtures Other Than Air, or are under the supervision of a Gas Mixtures Other Than Air Instructor. Proper use of these tables will reduce the risk of decompression sickness & oxygen toxicity, but no table or computer can eliminate those risks.

Produced By Tom Mount, Mark Owens, and Clayton Bohm

C-3706B

www.iantd.com

IANTD TRIMIX 19 / 40 DIVING & DECOMPRESSION TABLES

		Trimix 19 / 40									EAN 70				
		130 ft	120 ft	110 ft	100 ft	90 ft	80 ft	70 ft	60 ft	50 ft	40 ft	30 ft	20 ft	15 ft	CNS
	MIN	39m	36m	33m	30m	27m	24m	21m	18m	15m	12m	9m	6m	4.5m	%
130 ft 39m	10											14	15	16	5
	15									18	19	20	21	25	8
	20									23	24	26	27	33	11
	25								28	29	31	33	35	43	15
	30								33	35	37	40	42	53	18
	35								38	41	43	47	49	62	20
	40								44	48	51	55	58	74	25
	45								50	54	57	62	65	83	27
	50								55	60	64	69	73	93	31
	55								60	66	70	76	80	103	34
	60							63	66	72	77	83	87	112	38
140 ft 42m	10										14	15	16	18	6
	15								18	19	20	22	23	28	9
	20							23	24	25	27	29	30	38	13
	25							28	29	31	33	36	38	48	17
	30							33	35	38	40	44	46	58	20
	35							38	40	44	47	51	53	68	23
	40							43	47	51	54	59	62	80	27
	45							49	53	58	62	67	71	91	31
	50							54	58	64	68	74	78	102	35
	55							59	64	70	75	82	86	112	39
150 ft 45m	10									14	15	16	17	19	7
	15							18	19	20	21	23	24	30	11
	20						23	24	25	27	29	31	33	42	15
	25						28	29	31	33	36	39	41	52	19
	30						33	34	37	40	43	47	49	63	23
	35						38	39	43	47	50	55	58	75	27
	40						43	45	49	55	59	64	68	88	31
	45						48	51	55	62	66	72	76	100	35
	50						54	57	62	69	74	80	85	111	40
160 ft 48m	10								14	15	16	17	18	21	8
	15								19	21	22	24	25	32	12
	20						23	24	26	28	30	33	35	44	17
	25					28	29	30	33	36	39	42	44	57	22
	30					33	34	36	39	43	46	50	53	69	26
	35					38	39	42	46	51	54	59	63	82	30
	40					43	45	48	52	58	62	68	72	94	35
	45					48	50	54	59	66	71	78	82	108	41
	50					53	56	60	66	74	79	86	92	121	45
170 ft 51m	10							14	15	16	17	18	19	23	8
	15					18	19	20	21	23	25	27	28	36	14
	20					23	24	25	27	30	32	35	37	48	18
	25				28	29	30	32	35	39	42	46	48	63	24
	30				33	34	35	38	42	46	50	54	57	75	29
	35				38	39	41	44	48	54	58	63	67	88	33
	40				43	44	47	50	55	62	67	73	77	102	39
	45				48	50	53	56	62	70	75	82	88	115	43
	50				53	55	58	63	69	78	84	92	97	128	48
180 ft 54m	10						14	15	16	17	18	20	21	26	10
	15						19	20	22	24	26	28	30	38	15
	20				23	24	25	27	29	33	35	39	41	53	20
	25			28	29	30	31	33	37	41	44	49	52	68	26
	30			33	34	35	37	40	44	50	54	59	63	82	32
	35			38	39	40	43	46	51	58	62	68	73	96	37
	40			43	44	46	49	53	59	66	71	78	83	109	42
	45			48	49	51	55	59	65	74	80	87	93	123	48
190 ft 57m	10						14	15	16	17	19	20	21	26	11
	15					19	20	21	23	26	28	30	32	41	16
	20			23	24	25	26	28	31	35	38	41	44	57	23
	25			28	29	30	32	35	38	43	46	51	54	71	28
	30		33	34	35	36	39	42	47	53	57	63	67	88	35
	35		38	39	40	42	45	49	54	61	66	73	77	103	41
	40		43	44	45	48	51	56	62	70	76	83	89	117	47
200 ft 60m	10					14	15	16	17	18	20	21	22	28	12
	15				19	20	21	22	25	27	29	32	34	44	18
	20		23	24	25	26	27	30	33	37	40	44	47	61	25
	25		28	29	30	32	34	37	41	47	50	55	59	77	31
	30	33	34	35	36	38	41	44	50	56	61	67	71	95	39
	35	38	39	40	42	44	47	52	58	66	71	78	84	111	45
	40	43	44	45	47	50	54	59	66	75	81	89	95	127	52
210 ft 63m	10						15	16	17	19	20	22	23	29	12
	15			19	20	21	22	24	26	29	32	35	37	48	21
	20	23	24	25	26	27	29	31	35	39	43	47	50	65	28
	25	28	29	30	31	33	35	39	43	49	53	58	62	82	34
	30	33	34	35	37	39	42	46	52	58	63	70	74	98	42
	35	38	39	41	43	45	49	54	60	69	74	82	87	116	48

C-3717

 Nominal Conservatism

WARNING!
DO NOT
attempt to use these tables unless you are fully trained & certified in the use of trimix or are under the direct supervison of an Instructor.

Proper use of decompression tables will reduce the risk of DCS & oxygen toxicity, but no table or computer can eliminate those risks.

These tables are based on VPM-B and are derived from V-Planner Software.

Descent Rate 60 fpm
Ascent Rate 30 fpm
Bottom Time Includes Descent Time.
Stop Time includes Travel Time between stops.
Sea Level to 1000 ft.

IANTD TRIMIX 19 / 40 DIVING & DECOMPRESSION TABLES

!!! REPETITIVE DIVE TABLE 120 MIN SURFACE INTERVAL !!!

!!! REPETITIVE DIVE TABLE 120 MIN SURFACE INTERVAL !!!

		Trimix 19 / 40									EAN 70				
		130 ft	120 ft	110 ft	100 ft	90 ft	80 ft	70 ft	60 ft	50 ft	40 ft	30 ft	20 ft	15 ft	CNS
	MIN	39m	36m	33m	30m	27m	24m	21m	18m	15m	12m	9m	6m	4.5m	%
130 ft 39m	15									18	19	20	21	25	13
	20								23	24	26	27	28	36	19
	25								28	30	32	34	36	47	25
	30								33	36	39	42	44	60	32
	35								39	43	46	50	52	73	37
	40								44	48	51	56	59	83	43
	45								50	55	59	64	68	97	50
140 ft 42m	10										14	15	16	17	10
	15								18	19	20	21	22	28	15
	20								23	25	27	29	30	39	22
	25							28	29	32	34	37	39	53	28
	30							33	35	39	42	45	48	67	35
	35							39	42	45	49	53	57	80	43
	40							44	47	52	56	61	65	94	50
	45							49	53	58	62	69	74	107	57
150 ft 45m	10									14	15	16	17	19	11
	15							18	19	20	22	23	25	32	19
	20							23	24	27	29	31	33	44	25
	25						28	29	31	34	37	40	42	58	33
	30						33	34	37	41	44	48	51	73	41
	35						38	41	44	49	53	58	62	90	49
	40						43	46	50	56	60	66	71	104	57
	45						49	52	56	62	67	74	80	118	65
160 ft 48m	10								14	15	16	17	18	22	13
	15						18	19	20	22	24	26	27	35	21
	20						23	24	26	29	31	34	36	48	28
	25					28	29	30	33	37	40	44	46	65	38
	30					33	34	36	39	44	47	52	56	80	46
	35					38	40	42	46	51	55	61	65	96	55
	40					43	45	48	52	59	64	71	77	114	65
170 ft 51m	10							14	15	16	17	18	19	24	14
	15							19	20	22	24	26	27	36	23
	20				23	24	25	26	28	32	34	38	40	56	32
	25				28	29	30	32	35	39	42	47	50	71	42
	30				33	34	36	38	42	47	51	57	61	89	52
	35				38	39	41	44	48	55	59	66	71	105	60
	40				43	45	47	51	55	63	68	76	82	122	70
180 ft 54m	10						14	15	16	17	18	20	21	26	16
	15						19	20	22	24	26	28	30	41	25
	20				23	24	25	27	29	33	36	39	42	58	35
	25			28	29	30	31	34	37	42	45	50	54	78	46
	30			33	34	35	37	40	44	50	54	61	65	96	57
	35			38	39	41	43	47	51	59	64	71	77	115	67
	40			43	44	46	49	53	59	67	73	82	89	133	78
190 ft 57m	10						14	15	16	17	18	20	21	27	18
	15					19	20	21	23	26	28	31	33	45	28
	20			23	24	25	26	28	31	35	38	42	45	64	40
	25		28	29	30	31	33	36	39	45	49	54	59	86	52
	30		33	34	35	37	39	43	47	54	59	66	71	106	64
	35		38	39	40	42	45	49	54	63	68	77	83	125	75
200 ft 60m	10					14	15	16	17	19	20	22	23	30	19
	15				19	20	21	22	25	28	30	33	35	49	31
	20		23	24	25	26	28	30	33	38	41	46	49	71	44
	25		28	29	30	32	34	37	41	47	51	57	61	91	56
	30	33	34	35	36	38	41	45	50	57	62	70	76	114	71
	35	38	39	40	42	44	48	52	58	67	73	82	90	136	83
210 ft 63m	10						15	16	17	19	21	22	24	31	21
	15			19	20	21	22	24	26	30	32	36	38	54	35
	20	23	24	25	26	27	29	32	35	40	44	49	52	76	49
	25	28	29	30	31	33	36	39	43	50	54	61	66	98	62
	30	33	34	35	37	39	42	46	52	60	65	74	79	120	76

!!! REPETITIVE DIVE TABLE 120 MIN SURFACE INTERVAL !!!

!!! REPETITIVE DIVE TABLE 120 MIN SURFACE INTERVAL !!!

 C-3717B

IANTD TRIMIX 14 / 50 DIVING & DECOMPRESSION TABLES

		14/50 Trimix															50 EAN					Oxygen		
	ft	220	210	200	190	180	170	160	150	140	130	120	110	100	90	80	70	60	50	40	30	20	15	CNS
	m	66	63	60	57	54	51	48	45	42	39	36	33	30	27	24	21	18	15	12	9	6	4.5	%
200 ft 60m	10													14	15	16	17	18	19	20	22	24	29	15
	15											18	19	20	21	22	24	25	27	29	32	34	44	22
	20										23	24	25	26	28	30	32	34	36	39	44	47	61	31
	25										28	29	30	32	34	38	40	42	45	50	56	60	78	39
	30										33	34	36	38	41	45	47	50	54	59	67	71	93	46
	35										38	40	42	45	48	53	56	59	63	70	79	84	110	55
	40										43	45	47	50	54	60	63	67	72	79	90	95	125	62
210 ft 63m	10												14	15	16	17	18	19	20	21	24	25	32	15
	15										18	19	20	21	22	24	25	27	29	31	35	37	48	23
	20									23	24	25	26	27	29	32	34	36	39	42	48	51	66	33
	25									28	29	30	31	34	36	40	42	45	48	53	60	63	83	41
	30									33	34	35	37	40	43	47	50	53	57	63	71	76	99	52
	35									38	39	41	43	47	50	55	58	62	67	73	83	89	117	61
	40									43	45	47	50	53	58	63	67	71	76	84	95	102	134	71
220 ft 66m	10											14	15	16	17	18	19	20	21	23	26	27	35	16
	15									18	19	20	21	22	24	26	27	29	31	34	38	41	52	27
	20								23	24	25	26	27	29	31	34	36	38	41	45	51	54	70	35
	25								28	29	30	31	33	35	38	42	44	47	51	56	63	67	88	45
	30								33	34	35	37	39	42	46	50	53	56	60	67	76	81	106	55
	35								38	39	41	43	46	49	53	59	62	66	71	78	90	95	126	64
	40								43	44	46	49	52	56	61	67	71	75	81	90	102	109	144	76
230 ft 69m	10										14	15	16	17	18	19	20	21	23	25	28	30	37	19
	15								18	19	20	21	22	23	25	27	29	31	33	36	41	43	56	28
	20							23	24	25	26	27	28	30	33	36	38	41	44	48	55	58	76	39
	25							28	29	30	31	33	35	37	41	44	47	50	54	59	67	72	94	51
	30							33	34	35	36	38	41	44	48	53	56	60	64	71	81	86	113	59
	35							38	39	40	42	44	47	51	56	61	65	69	74	82	93	100	131	71
	40							43	44	46	48	51	54	59	64	71	75	80	86	95	109	116	153	81
240 ft 72m	10										14	15	16	17	18	19	20	21	23	25	28	30	38	20
	15							18	19	20	21	22	23	24	26	29	31	33	35	38	44	46	60	30
	20							23	24	25	26	27	29	31	34	37	39	42	45	50	56	60	78	42
	25						28	29	30	31	32	34	36	39	43	47	50	53	57	63	72	77	100	53
	30						33	34	35	36	38	40	43	46	51	56	59	63	68	75	86	91	120	62
	35						38	39	40	42	44	47	50	54	59	65	69	73	79	88	100	107	141	76
	40						43	44	45	47	50	53	56	61	67	74	78	83	90	100	114	121	160	84
250 ft 75m	10									14	15	16	17	18	19	20	22	23	24	27	30	32	40	21
	15								19	20	21	22	23	25	27	29	31	33	36	39	44	47	61	33
	20						23	24	25	26	27	28	31	33	36	40	42	45	49	53	61	64	85	43
	25					28	29	30	31	32	34	36	38	42	45	50	53	57	61	68	77	82	108	58
	30					33	34	35	36	38	40	42	45	49	54	59	63	67	72	80	91	97	128	69
	35					38	39	40	41	43	46	49	52	57	62	69	73	78	84	93	106	113	150	80
	40					43	44	45	47	49	52	55	59	64	71	78	83	88	95	105	121	129	170	91
260 ft 78m	10								14	15	16	17	18	19	20	22	23	25	27	29	32	34	44	23
	15							19	20	21	22	23	24	26	28	31	33	35	38	42	47	50	65	35
	20					23	24	25	26	27	28	30	32	35	38	42	45	47	51	56	64	68	90	48
	25				28	29	30	31	32	33	35	37	40	43	47	53	56	60	65	71	82	87	115	61
	30				33	34	35	36	37	39	41	44	47	51	56	62	66	70	76	84	96	103	135	74
	35				38	39	40	41	43	45	48	51	55	60	65	73	77	82	89	99	113	120	159	85
	40				43	44	45	46	48	51	54	57	62	67	74	82	87	92	101	111	127	136	180	99
270 ft 81m	10									15	16	17	18	19	20	22	24	25	27	29	33	35	45	24
	15						19	20	21	22	23	24	26	28	30	33	35	38	40	45	50	54	70	39
	20				23	24	25	26	27	28	29	31	34	37	40	44	47	50	54	60	68	73	95	52
	25				28	29	30	31	32	34	36	38	41	45	49	54	58	61	66	73	84	89	117	63
	30			33	34	35	36	37	39	41	43	46	50	54	59	66	70	75	81	90	102	109	144	79
	35			38	39	40	41	42	44	47	50	53	57	62	69	76	81	86	93	103	118	126	167	92
280 ft 84m	10								15	16	17	18	19	20	21	23	25	26	28	31	35	37	47	25
	15					19	20	21	22	23	24	25	27	29	32	35	37	40	43	47	54	57	74	39
	20			23	24	25	26	27	28	29	31	33	35	39	42	47	50	53	57	64	72	77	101	55
	25			28	29	30	31	32	33	35	37	40	43	47	52	57	61	64	70	77	88	94	124	69
	30		33	34	35	36	37	38	40	42	45	48	52	57	62	70	74	79	86	95	109	116	153	83
	35		38	39	40	41	42	44	46	49	52	56	60	65	72	80	85	90	99	109	125	134	177	99
290 ft 87m	10							15	16	17	18	19	20	21	23	25	27	28	30	33	37	40	51	28
	15				19	20	21	22	23	24	25	26	28	31	34	37	39	42	45	50	57	60	79	42
	20		23	24	25	26	27	28	29	30	32	34	37	40	44	49	52	56	60	67	76	81	107	59
	25		28	29	30	31	32	33	35	37	39	42	45	49	54	60	64	68	74	82	93	100	131	74
	30		33	34	35	36	37	39	41	43	46	49	53	58	64	72	76	81	88	97	112	119	157	86
300 ft 90m	10						15	16	17	18	19	20	21	22	24	26	28	30	32	35	39	42	53	30
	15			19	20	21	22	23	24	25	26	28	30	32	36	39	42	44	48	53	60	64	84	47
	20			24	25	26	27	28	29	31	33	35	38	41	45	51	54	57	62	69	79	84	110	60
	25	28	29	30	31	32	33	34	36	38	41	44	47	52	57	64	68	72	78	87	99	106	140	79
	30	33	34	35	36	37	38	40	42	45	48	51	56	61	67	75	80	85	92	102	117	125	165	93

WARNING!

DO NOT

attempt to use these tables unless you are fully trained & certified in the use of trimix or are under the direct supervison of an Instructor.

Proper use of decompression tables will reduce the risk of DCS & oxygen toxicity, but no table or computer can eliminate those risks.

These tables are based on VPM-B and are derived from V-Planner Software.

Descent Rate 60 fpm
Ascent Rate 30 fpm
Bottom Time Includes Descent Time.
Stop Time includes Travel Time between stops.
Sea Level to 1000 ft.

 C-3718 Nominal Conservatism

IANTD TRIMIX 14 / 50 DIVING & DECOMPRESSION TABLES

!!! REPETITIVE DIVE TABLE 120 MIN SURFACE INTERVAL !!!

!!! REPETITIVE DIVE TABLE 120 MIN SURFACE INTERVAL !!!

		14 / 50 Trimix														50 EAN					Oxygen		CNS
	ft	210	200	190	180	170	160	150	140	130	120	110	100	90	80	70	60	50	40	30	20	15	CNS
	m	63	60	57	54	51	48	45	42	39	36	33	30	27	24	21	18	15	12	9	6	4.5	%
200 ft 60m REP	10												14	15	16	17	18	19	20	23	24	31	23
	15										18	19	20	21	23	24	25	27	30	33	36	49	40
	20									23	24	25	26	28	30	32	34	36	40	45	49	69	57
	25									28	29	30	32	35	38	40	42	46	50	58	63	91	75
	30									33	34	36	38	41	45	48	50	54	60	70	76	111	90
	35									38	40	42	45	48	53	56	59	64	71	83	90	133	108
210 ft 63m REP	10											14	15	16	17	18	19	20	21	24	25	33	24
	15									18	19	20	21	22	24	26	27	29	32	36	39	53	43
	20								23	24	25	26	28	30	33	35	37	39	44	50	54	77	63
	25								28	29	30	32	34	37	40	42	45	48	54	62	67	97	79
	30								33	34	36	38	40	44	48	51	54	58	65	75	82	121	101
220 ft 66m REP	10										14	15	16	17	18	19	20	21	23	26	28	36	28
	15								18	19	20	21	22	24	26	27	29	31	34	39	42	58	48
	20							23	24	25	26	27	29	32	35	37	39	42	47	54	58	84	68
	25							28	29	30	31	33	36	39	42	45	47	51	57	66	71	105	87
	30							33	34	35	37	39	42	46	51	54	57	62	69	81	88	131	109
230 ft 69m REP	10									14	15	16	17	18	19	20	21	23	25	28	30	39	32
	15							18	19	20	21	22	23	25	28	29	31	34	37	42	45	64	52
	20						23	24	25	26	27	29	31	33	37	39	41	45	50	57	62	90	75
	25						28	29	30	31	33	35	38	41	45	48	51	55	61	71	77	114	97
	30						33	34	35	37	39	41	45	48	54	57	60	66	74	86	94	139	118
240 ft 72m REP	10									14	15	16	17	18	19	20	21	23	25	28	30	40	33
	15						18	19	20	21	22	23	24	27	29	31	33	35	39	45	48	68	56
	20					23	24	25	26	27	28	30	32	35	39	41	44	47	53	61	66	97	81
	25					28	29	30	31	32	34	37	40	43	48	51	54	59	65	76	83	123	105
250 ft 75m REP	10								14	15	16	17	18	19	21	22	23	25	27	31	33	45	36
	15							19	20	21	22	23	25	27	30	32	34	36	40	46	50	70	60
	20					23	24	25	26	27	29	31	33	36	40	42	45	49	55	63	68	100	84
	25				28	29	30	31	32	34	36	38	42	45	50	53	57	62	69	81	88	131	112
260 ft 78m REP	10							14	15	16	17	18	19	20	22	23	25	27	29	33	35	48	39
	15						19	20	21	22	23	25	27	29	32	34	36	39	43	50	54	77	65
	20				23	24	25	26	27	28	30	32	35	38	42	45	47	51	58	67	73	107	93
	25			28	29	30	31	32	33	35	37	40	44	48	53	56	60	65	73	86	94	140	121
270 ft 81m REP	10								15	16	17	18	19	21	22	24	25	27	30	33	36	49	43
	15					19	20	21	22	23	24	26	28	30	34	36	38	41	46	53	57	82	70
	20			23	24	25	26	27	28	30	32	34	37	41	45	48	51	55	62	72	79	115	101
280 ft 84m REP	10							15	16	17	18	19	20	22	24	26	27	29	32	36	39	53	45
	15				19	20	21	22	23	24	25	27	30	32	36	38	41	44	49	57	62	89	76
	20		23	24	25	26	27	28	29	31	33	35	39	42	47	50	53	58	65	76	83	123	108
290 ft 87m REP	10						15	16	17	18	19	20	21	23	25	27	28	31	34	38	41	57	50
	15			19	20	21	22	23	24	25	27	29	31	34	38	40	43	47	52	60	65	95	82
	20	23	24	25	26	27	28	29	30	32	35	37	41	44	50	53	56	62	69	81	88	131	114
300 ft 90m REP	10					15	16	17	18	19	20	21	22	24	27	28	30	33	36	41	44	61	52
	15		19	20	21	22	23	24	25	26	28	30	32	36	39	42	44	48	54	63	68	99	87
	20	23	24	25	26	27	28	29	31	33	35	38	41	45	51	54	58	63	71	83	90	134	117

!!! REPETITIVE DIVE TABLE 120 MIN SURFACE INTERVAL !!!

!!! REPETITIVE DIVE TABLE 120 MIN SURFACE INTERVAL !!!

IANTD TRIMIX 12/60 RUNTIME DECOMPRESSION TABLES

		Trimix 12/60									Trimix 21/30										EAN 40							EAN 80			
Feet		290	280	270	260	250	240	230	220	210	200	190	180	170	160	150	140	130	120	110	100	90	80	70	60	50	40	30	20	15	CNS
Meters		87	84	81	78	75	72	69	66	63	60	57	54	51	48	45	42	39	36	33	30	27	24	21	18	15	12	9	6	4.5	%
300 ft 90m	10											14	15	16	17	18	19	20	21	22	23	24	25	26	27	29	33	37	39	52	25
	15										19	20	21	22	23	24	25	26	27	28	29	30	32	34	36	40	45	51	55	74	37
	20								23	24	25	26	27	28	29	30	31	32	33	34	36	38	40	43	47	51	58	65	71	96	49
	25							28	29	30	31	32	33	34	35	36	37	38	40	42	44	46	50	53	58	64	72	82	88	122	61
	30							33	34	35	36	37	38	39	40	41	42	44	47	50	52	55	58	62	68	75	85	97	104	144	72
310 ft 93m	10											15	16	17	18	19	20	21	22	23	24	25	26	27	28	31	34	38	41	55	27
	15									19	20	21	22	23	24	25	26	27	28	29	30	31	33	35	38	42	47	53	57	78	39
	20							23	24	25	26	27	28	29	30	31	32	33	34	36	38	40	42	45	49	54	61	69	75	102	52
	25						28	29	30	31	32	33	34	35	36	37	38	40	42	44	46	49	52	55	61	67	76	86	93	128	65
	30						33	34	35	36	37	38	39	40	41	42	44	46	49	52	54	57	60	65	71	79	89	101	109	151	76
320 ft 96m	10											15	16	17	18	19	20	21	22	23	24	25	26	27	29	31	35	39	42	56	28
	15								19	20	21	22	23	24	25	26	27	28	29	30	31	33	35	37	40	44	49	56	60	82	41
	20						23	24	25	26	27	28	29	30	31	32	33	34	35	37	39	41	44	47	51	56	64	72	78	107	55
	25						28	29	30	31	32	33	34	35	36	37	38	40	42	45	47	50	53	56	62	68	77	87	95	130	66
	30					33	34	35	36	37	38	39	40	41	42	44	46	48	51	54	57	60	63	68	74	82	93	106	114	158	82
330 ft 99m	10										15	16	17	18	19	20	21	22	23	24	25	26	27	28	30	33	36	41	44	58	30
	15							19	20	21	22	23	24	25	26	27	28	29	30	31	32	34	36	39	42	46	52	59	63	87	44
	20					23	24	25	26	27	28	29	30	31	32	33	34	35	37	39	41	43	46	49	53	59	67	76	82	113	58
	25					28	29	30	31	32	33	34	35	36	37	38	40	42	44	47	49	52	55	59	65	71	81	92	99	137	70
	30					33	34	35	36	37	38	39	40	41	43	44	46	49	51	55	58	60	64	69	75	84	94	108	116	160	84
340 ft 102m	10									15	16	17	18	19	20	21	22	23	24	25	26	27	28	29	31	34	38	43	46	62	31
	15						19	20	21	22	23	24	25	26	27	28	29	30	31	32	34	35	38	40	44	48	54	61	66	90	47
	20				23	24	25	26	27	28	29	30	31	32	33	34	35	36	38	41	43	45	48	52	56	62	70	80	86	119	62
	25				28	29	30	31	32	33	34	35	36	37	38	39	41	43	46	49	51	54	57	62	67	74	85	96	104	144	74
	30				33	34	35	36	37	38	39	40	41	43	44	46	48	50	53	57	60	63	67	72	78	87	99	113	122	168	88

WARNING! DO NOT attempt to use these tables unless you are fully trained & certified in the use of Helium/Trimix, or are under the supervision of a Helium/Trimix Instructor. Proper use of these tables will reduce the risk of decompression sickness & oxygen toxicity, but no table or computer can eliminate those risks. These tables are based on VPM-B and are derived from V-Planner Software.

C-3719

IANTD TRIMIX 12 / 60 RUNTIME DECOMPRESSION TABLES

		Trimix 12/60									Trimix 21/30										EAN 40							EAN 80			
Feet		290	280	270	260	250	240	230	220	210	200	190	180	170	160	150	140	130	120	110	100	90	80	70	60	50	40	30	20	15	CNS
Meters		87	84	81	78	75	72	69	66	63	60	57	54	51	48	45	42	39	36	33	30	27	24	21	18	15	12	9	6	4.5	%
350 ft 105m	10								15	16	17	18	19	20	21	22	23	24	25	26	27	28	29	31	33	36	41	46	49	66	33
	15					19	20	21	22	23	24	25	26	27	28	29	30	31	32	34	35	37	40	42	46	51	57	65	70	95	49
	20					24	25	26	27	28	29	30	31	32	33	34	35	37	39	41	43	45	49	52	57	63	71	81	87	120	63
	25			28	29	30	31	32	33	34	35	36	37	38	39	41	43	45	48	50	53	56	59	64	70	77	88	100	108	149	79
	30			33	34	35	36	37	38	39	40	41	43	44	45	47	50	52	55	59	62	65	70	75	82	91	103	117	127	176	93
360 ft 108m	10								15	16	17	18	19	20	21	22	23	24	25	26	27	28	29	31	33	36	41	46	49	66	33
	15				19	20	21	22	23	24	25	26	27	28	29	30	31	32	33	35	37	39	41	44	48	53	60	68	73	99	52
	20				24	25	26	27	28	29	30	31	32	33	34	35	36	38	40	43	45	48	51	54	59	66	74	84	91	125	66
	25		28	29	30	31	32	33	34	35	36	37	38	39	41	42	44	47	49	53	56	58	62	67	73	81	92	105	113	156	83
	30		33	34	35	36	37	38	39	41	42	43	44	46	48	50	52	54	58	62	65	69	73	78	86	95	109	124	134	186	98
370 ft 111m	10							15	16	17	18	19	20	21	22	23	24	25	26	27	28	29	30	32	35	38	43	48	52	69	35
	15			19	20	21	22	23	24	25	26	27	28	29	30	31	32	33	34	36	38	40	43	46	50	55	62	71	76	104	56
	20			24	25	26	27	28	29	30	31	32	33	34	35	36	38	40	42	45	47	50	53	57	62	69	78	88	96	132	70
	25	28	29	30	31	32	33	34	35	36	37	38	39	41	42	44	46	48	51	55	58	61	65	70	76	85	96	110	118	164	89
	30	33	34	35	36	37	38	39	40	42	43	44	46	47	49	51	54	56	60	64	67	71	76	82	89	99	113	129	139	193	104
380 ft 114m	10								16	17	18	19	20	21	22	23	24	25	26	27	28	29	30	32	35	38	43	48	52	69	36
	15		19	20	21	22	23	24	25	26	27	28	29	30	31	32	33	34	36	38	40	42	45	48	52	58	65	74	80	110	59
	20		24	25	26	27	28	29	30	31	32	33	34	35	36	38	39	41	44	47	49	52	55	59	65	71	82	93	100	138	73
	25		29	30	31	32	33	34	35	36	37	38	40	41	42	44	46	49	52	55	58	61	65	70	77	86	97	111	119	165	90
390 ft 117m	10							16	17	18	19	20	21	22	23	24	25	26	27	28	29	30	32	34	37	40	45	51	55	73	39
	15		19	20	21	22	23	24	25	26	27	28	29	30	31	32	33	34	36	38	40	42	45	48	52	58	66	75	80	110	60
	20	24	25	26	27	28	29	30	31	32	33	34	35	36	37	39	41	43	45	48	51	54	57	62	67	74	85	96	104	144	81
	25	29	30	31	32	33	34	35	36	38	39	40	41	43	44	46	49	51	54	58	61	64	69	74	81	90	102	116	126	174	98
400 ft 120m	10						16	17	18	19	20	21	22	23	24	25	26	27	28	29	30	31	33	36	38	42	47	53	57	77	42
	15	19	20	21	22	23	24	25	26	27	28	29	30	31	32	33	34	36	37	40	42	44	47	51	55	61	69	78	84	116	66
	20	25	26	27	28	29	30	31	32	33	34	35	36	37	39	40	42	45	47	50	53	56	59	64	70	78	88	101	108	150	89

Descent rate	60 fpm
Ascent rate	30 fpm
Last stop depth	15 ft

Bottom time includes descent time
Stop times include travel time between stops
Nominal conservatism level
Sea level to 1000 ft

VPM-B Decompression Tables
Tables produced with V-Planner

C-3719B

What decompression theory is all about; getting there and back!
Jean Marc Blache photographs a diver on the P38 in the Bay of La Ciotat, South of France

Notes: